CUBES AND PUNISHMENT

Other DILBERT® books from Andrews McMeel Publishing

Positive Attitude
ISBN: 0-7407-6379-2

Try Rebooting Yourself
ISBN: 0-7407-6190-0

What Would Wally Do?
ISBN: 0-7407-5769-5

Thriving on Vague Objectives
ISBN: 0-7407-5533-1

The Fluorescent Light Glistens Off Your Head
ISBN: 0-7407-5113-1

It's Not Funny If I Have to Explain It
ISBN: 0-7407-4658-8

Don't Stand Where the Comet Is Assumed to Strike Oil
ISBN: 0-7407-4539-5

Words You Don't Want to Hear During Your Annual Performance Review
ISBN: 0-7407-3805-4

When Body Language Goes Bad
ISBN: 0-7407-3298-6

What Do You Call a Sociopath in a Cubicle? Answer: A Coworker
ISBN: 0-7407-2663-3

Another Day in Cubicle Paradise
ISBN: 0-7407-2194-1

When Did Ignorance Become a Point of View?
ISBN: 0-7407-1839-8

Excuse Me While I Wag
ISBN: 0-7407-1390-6

Dilbert—A Treasury of Sunday Strips: Version 00
ISBN: 0-7407-0531-8

Random Acts of Management
ISBN: 0-7407-0453-2

Dilbert Gives You the Business
ISBN: 0-7407-0338-2 hardcover
ISBN: 0-7407-0003-0 paperback

Don't Step in the Leadership
ISBN: 0-8362-7844-5

Journey to Cubeville
ISBN: 0-8362-7175-0 hardcover
ISBN: 0-8362-6745-1 paperback

I'm Not Anti-Business, I'm Anti-Idiot
ISBN: 0-8362-5182-2

Seven Years of Highly Defective People
ISBN: 0-8362-5129-6 hardcover
ISBN: 0-8362-3668-8 paperback

Casual Day Has Gone Too Far
ISBN: 0-8362-2899-5

Fugitive from the Cubicle Police
ISBN: 0-8362-2119-2

It's Obvious You Won't Survive by Your Wits Alone
ISBN: 0-8362-0415-8

Still Pumped from Using the Mouse
ISBN: 0-8362-1026-3

Bring Me the Head of Willy the Mailboy!
ISBN: 0-8362-1779-9

Shave the Whales
ISBN: 0-8362-1740-3

Dogbert's Clues for the Clueless
ISBN: 0-8362-1737-3

Always Postpone Meetings with Time-Wasting Morons
ISBN: 0-8362-1758-6

Build a Better Life by Stealing Office Supplies
ISBN: 0-8362-1757-8

For ordering information, call 1-800-223-2336.

CUBES AND PUNISHMENT

A DILBERT™ BOOK
BY SCOTT ADAMS

**Andrews McMeel
Publishing, LLC**

Kansas City

07 08 09 10 11 BAM 10 9 8 7 6 5 4 3 2 1

ISBN-13: 978-0-7407-6837-8
ISBN-10: 0-7407-6837-9

Library of Congress Control Number: 2007925457

www.andrewsmcmeel.com
www.dilbert.com

Contents

For Shelly

Introduction

I realize we've all been told that cubicles are an efficient way to organize a workplace. Cubicles improve communication, blah, blah, blah. But realistically, if an alien landed on Earth and took a tour of a cubicle farm, he would assume it was a penal colony. He might even marvel at how efficient it is, in the sense that coworkers punish one another without the need for sadistic guards. And the entire enterprise turns a profit. On the alien's home planet, they probably pay guards to abuse the inmates, and the whole system loses money. The alien might radio home his findings and tell the generals to call off the invasion based on an assumption of our superiority.

To be fair, working in a cubicle isn't all bad. For example, it's good practice for being deceased. In both cases, someone puts you in a little box and other people do their best to bury you so you can't leave. The intellectual stimulation is also very similar, except the departed enjoy the added excitement of decomposing.

And don't forget the military applications for cubicles. If you take a terrorist from the rugged mountains of Waziristan and put him in a cubicle for a week, he'll want out so bad he'll give you intelligence information in languages he doesn't even speak. He'll be simultaneously talking through his nose, tapping Morse code with his foot, and doing charades with his hands. The CIA won't be able to write it all down fast enough.

My point is that cubicles are amazing things. Don't be critical of them unless you know the whole story.

Speaking of the whole story, there's still time to join Dogbert's New Ruling Class. Just sign up for the free *Dilbert Newsletter* that is published approximately whenever I feel like it. To sign up, go to www.dilbert.com and follow the subscription instructions. If that doesn't work for some reason, send an e-mail to newsletter@unitedmedia.com.

S.Adams

Scott Adams

1. The Pointy-Haired Boss

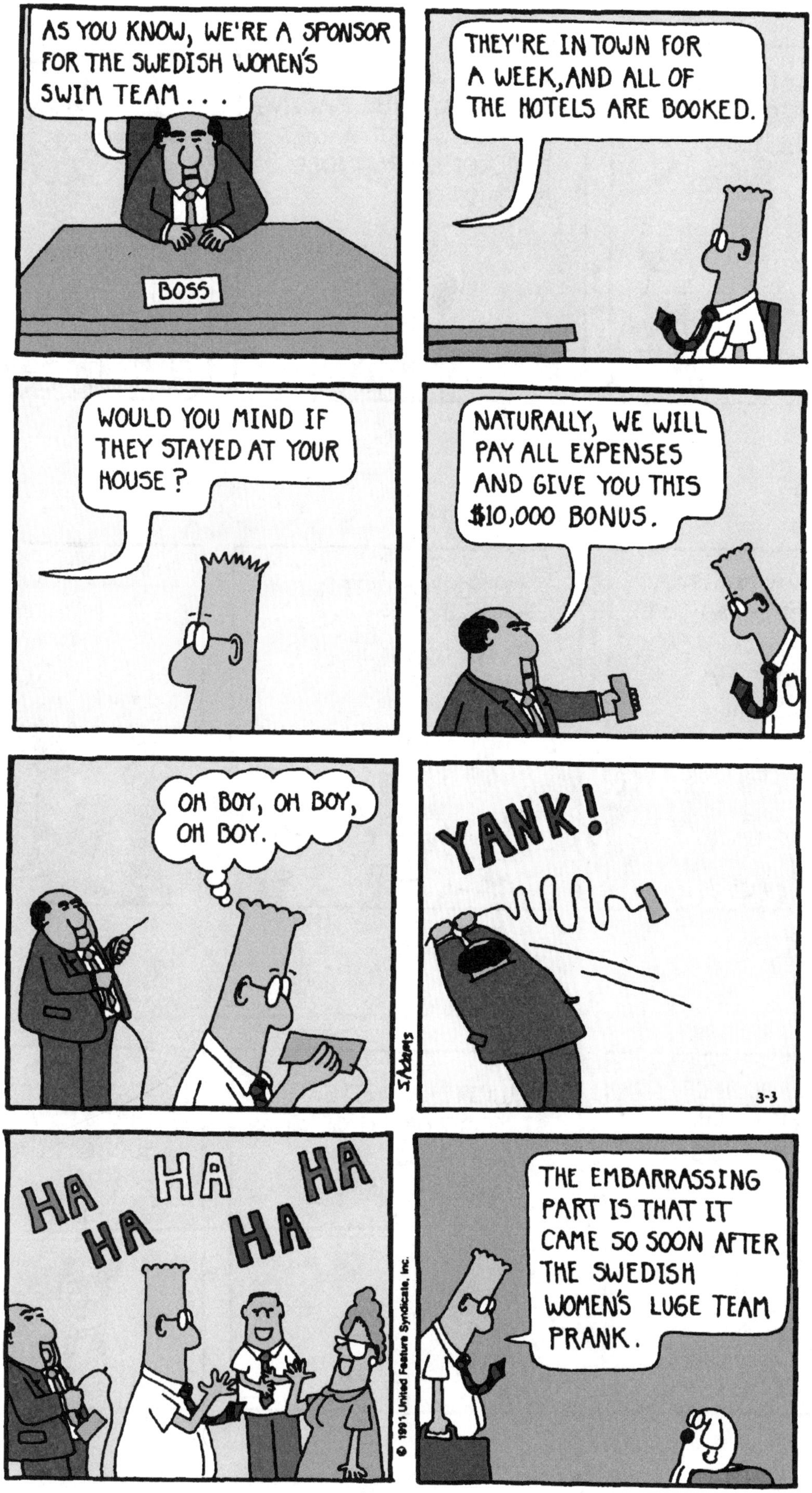
AS YOU KNOW, WE'RE A SPONSOR FOR THE SWEDISH WOMEN'S SWIM TEAM . . .
BOSS
THEY'RE IN TOWN FOR A WEEK, AND ALL OF THE HOTELS ARE BOOKED.
WOULD YOU MIND IF THEY STAYED AT YOUR HOUSE ?
NATURALLY, WE WILL PAY ALL EXPENSES AND GIVE YOU THIS $10,000 BONUS.
OH BOY, OH BOY, OH BOY.
S.Adams
YANK!
3-3
HA HA HA HA HA HA
© 1991 United Feature Syndicate, Inc.
THE EMBARRASSING PART IS THAT IT CAME SO SOON AFTER THE SWEDISH WOMEN'S LUGE TEAM PRANK.

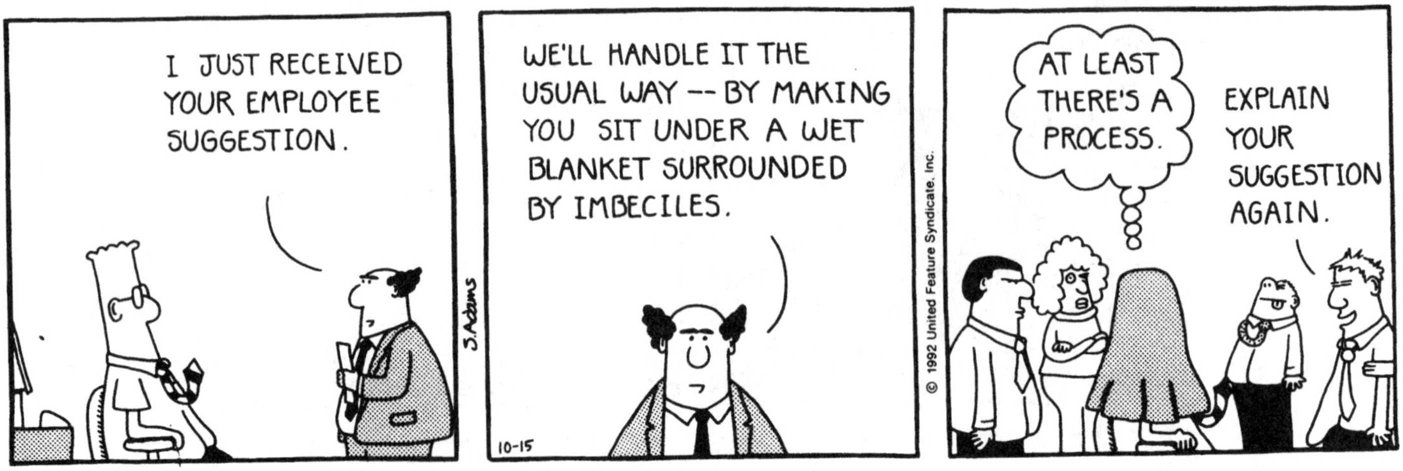
I JUST RECEIVED YOUR EMPLOYEE SUGGESTION.
S. Adams
WE'LL HANDLE IT THE USUAL WAY -- BY MAKING YOU SIT UNDER A WET BLANKET SURROUNDED BY IMBECILES.
10-15
© 1992 United Feature Syndicate, Inc.
AT LEAST THERE'S A PROCESS.
EXPLAIN YOUR SUGGESTION AGAIN.

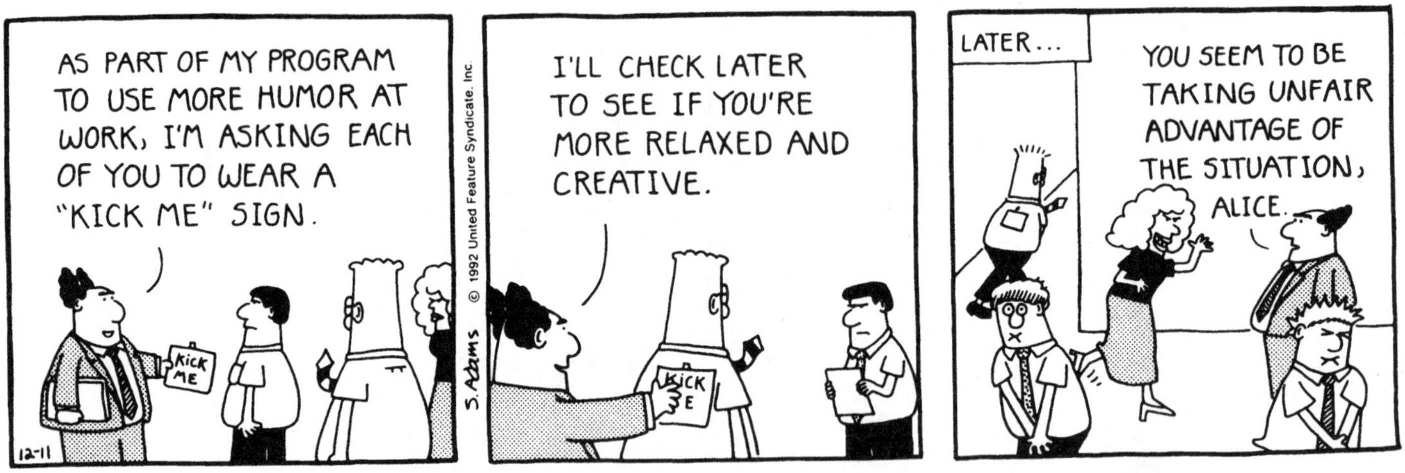
AS PART OF MY PROGRAM TO USE MORE HUMOR AT WORK, I'M ASKING EACH OF YOU TO WEAR A "KICK ME" SIGN.
KICK ME
12-11
S. Adams
© 1992 United Feature Syndicate, Inc.
I'LL CHECK LATER TO SEE IF YOU'RE MORE RELAXED AND CREATIVE.
LATER...
YOU SEEM TO BE TAKING UNFAIR ADVANTAGE OF THE SITUATION, ALICE.

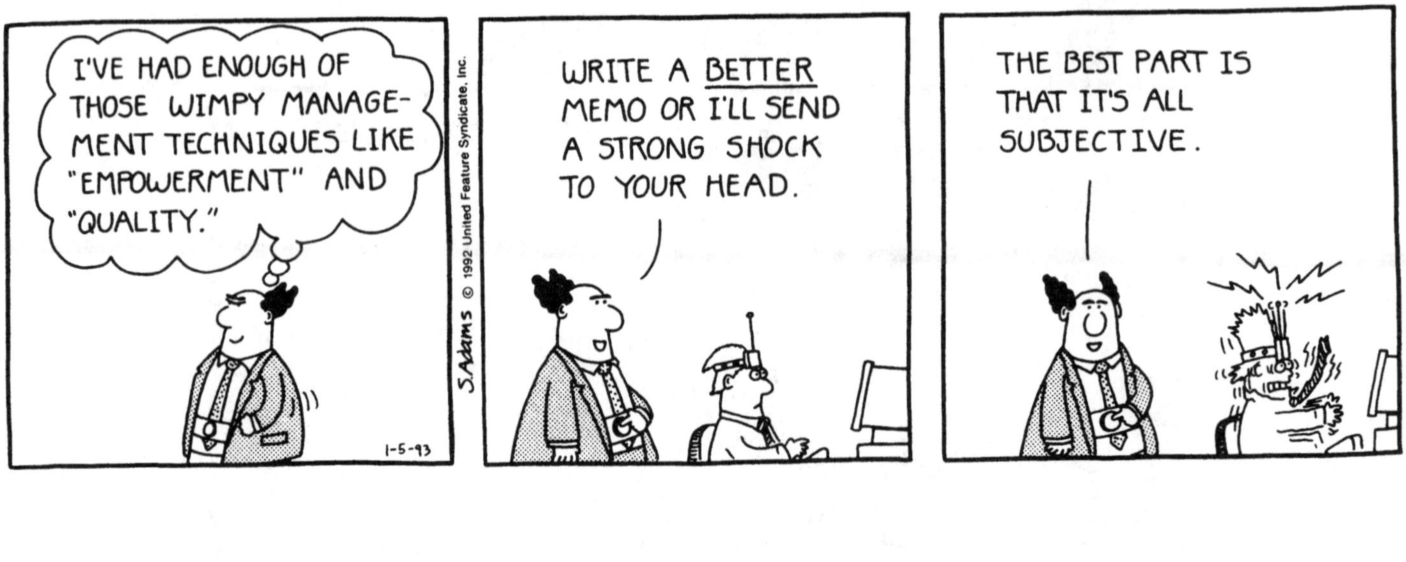
I'VE HAD ENOUGH OF THOSE WIMPY MANAGEMENT TECHNIQUES LIKE "EMPOWERMENT" AND "QUALITY."
1-5-93
S. Adams
© 1992 United Feature Syndicate, Inc.
WRITE A BETTER MEMO OR I'LL SEND A STRONG SHOCK TO YOUR HEAD.
THE BEST PART IS THAT IT'S ALL SUBJECTIVE.

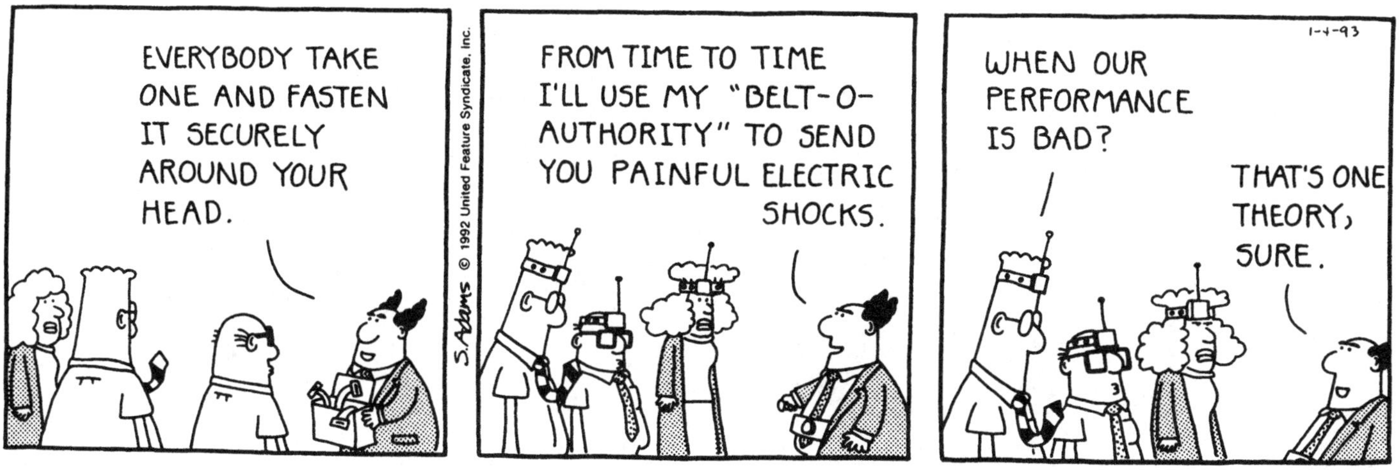
EVERYBODY TAKE ONE AND FASTEN IT SECURELY AROUND YOUR HEAD.
FROM TIME TO TIME I'LL USE MY "BELT-O-AUTHORITY" TO SEND YOU PAINFUL ELECTRIC SHOCKS.
WHEN OUR PERFORMANCE IS BAD?
THAT'S ONE THEORY, SURE.
S. Adams
1-4-93

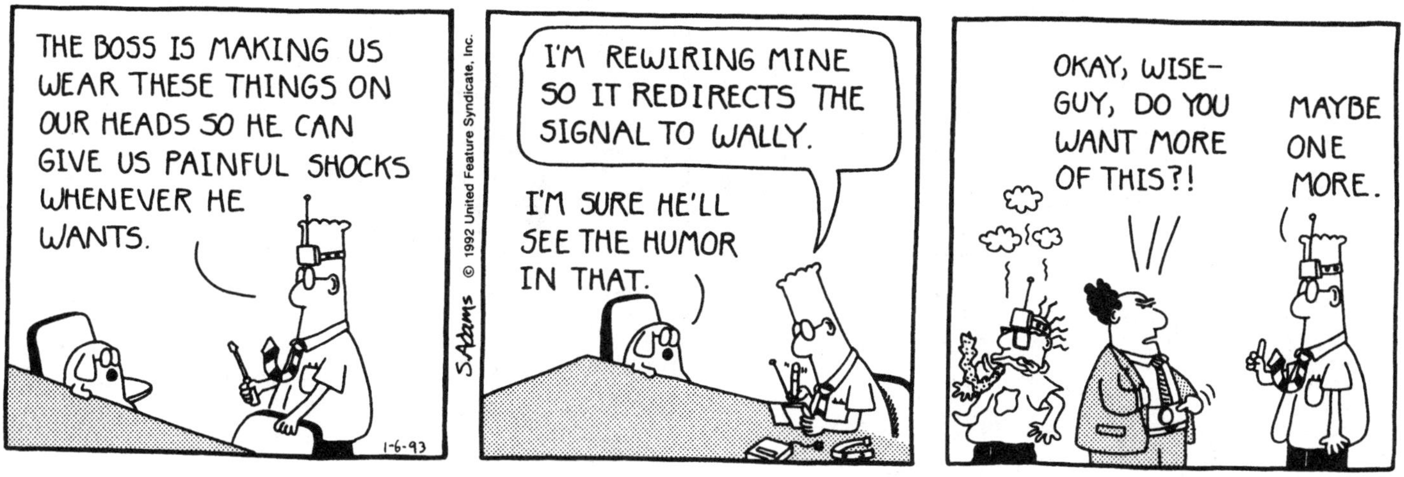
THE BOSS IS MAKING US WEAR THESE THINGS ON OUR HEADS SO HE CAN GIVE US PAINFUL SHOCKS WHENEVER HE WANTS.
1-6-93
I'M REWIRING MINE SO IT REDIRECTS THE SIGNAL TO WALLY.
I'M SURE HE'LL SEE THE HUMOR IN THAT.
OKAY, WISE-GUY, DO YOU WANT MORE OF THIS?!
MAYBE ONE MORE.
S. Adams

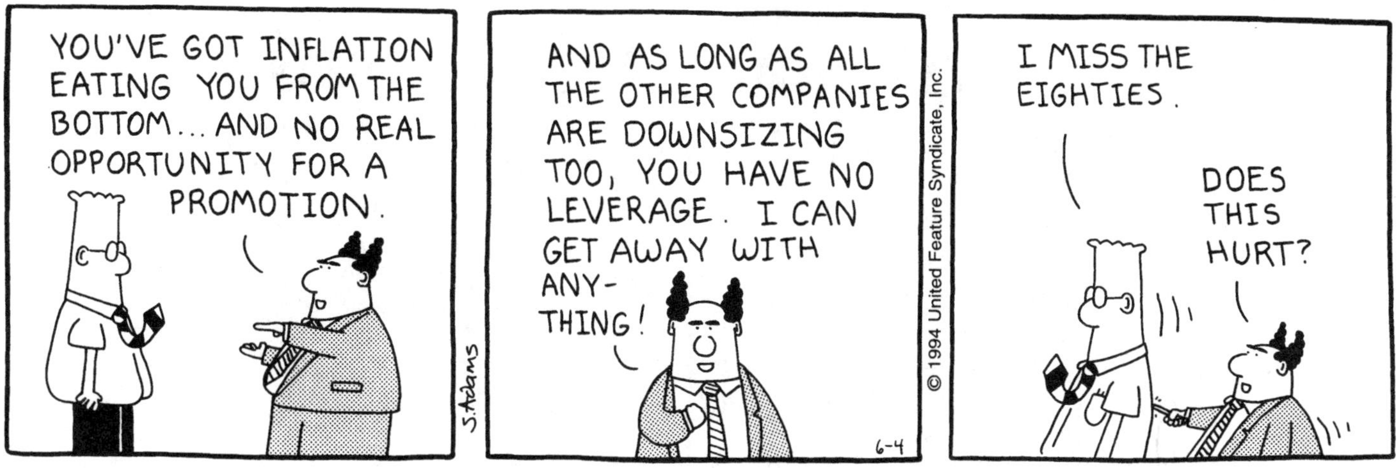
YOU'VE GOT INFLATION EATING YOU FROM THE BOTTOM... AND NO REAL OPPORTUNITY FOR A PROMOTION.
AND AS LONG AS ALL THE OTHER COMPANIES ARE DOWNSIZING TOO, YOU HAVE NO LEVERAGE. I CAN GET AWAY WITH ANY-THING!
6-4
I MISS THE EIGHTIES.
DOES THIS HURT?
S. Adams

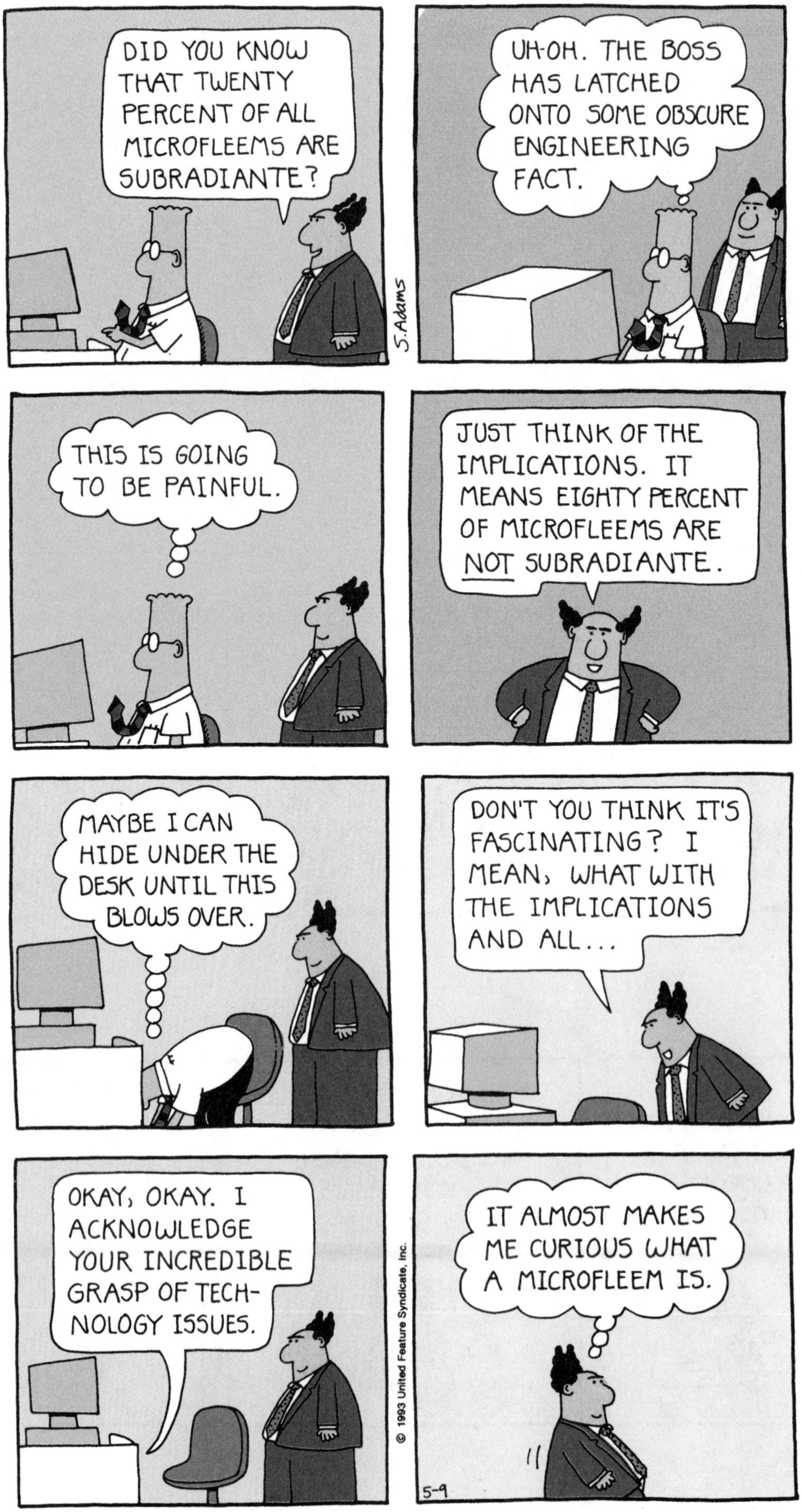
DID YOU KNOW THAT TWENTY PERCENT OF ALL MICROFLEEMS ARE SUBRADIANTE?
S. Adams
UH-OH. THE BOSS HAS LATCHED ONTO SOME OBSCURE ENGINEERING FACT.
THIS IS GOING TO BE PAINFUL.
JUST THINK OF THE IMPLICATIONS. IT MEANS EIGHTY PERCENT OF MICROFLEEMS ARE NOT SUBRADIANTE.
MAYBE I CAN HIDE UNDER THE DESK UNTIL THIS BLOWS OVER.
DON'T YOU THINK IT'S FASCINATING? I MEAN, WHAT WITH THE IMPLICATIONS AND ALL...
OKAY, OKAY. I ACKNOWLEDGE YOUR INCREDIBLE GRASP OF TECH-NOLOGY ISSUES.
© 1993 United Feature Syndicate, Inc.
IT ALMOST MAKES ME CURIOUS WHAT A MICROFLEEM IS.
5-9

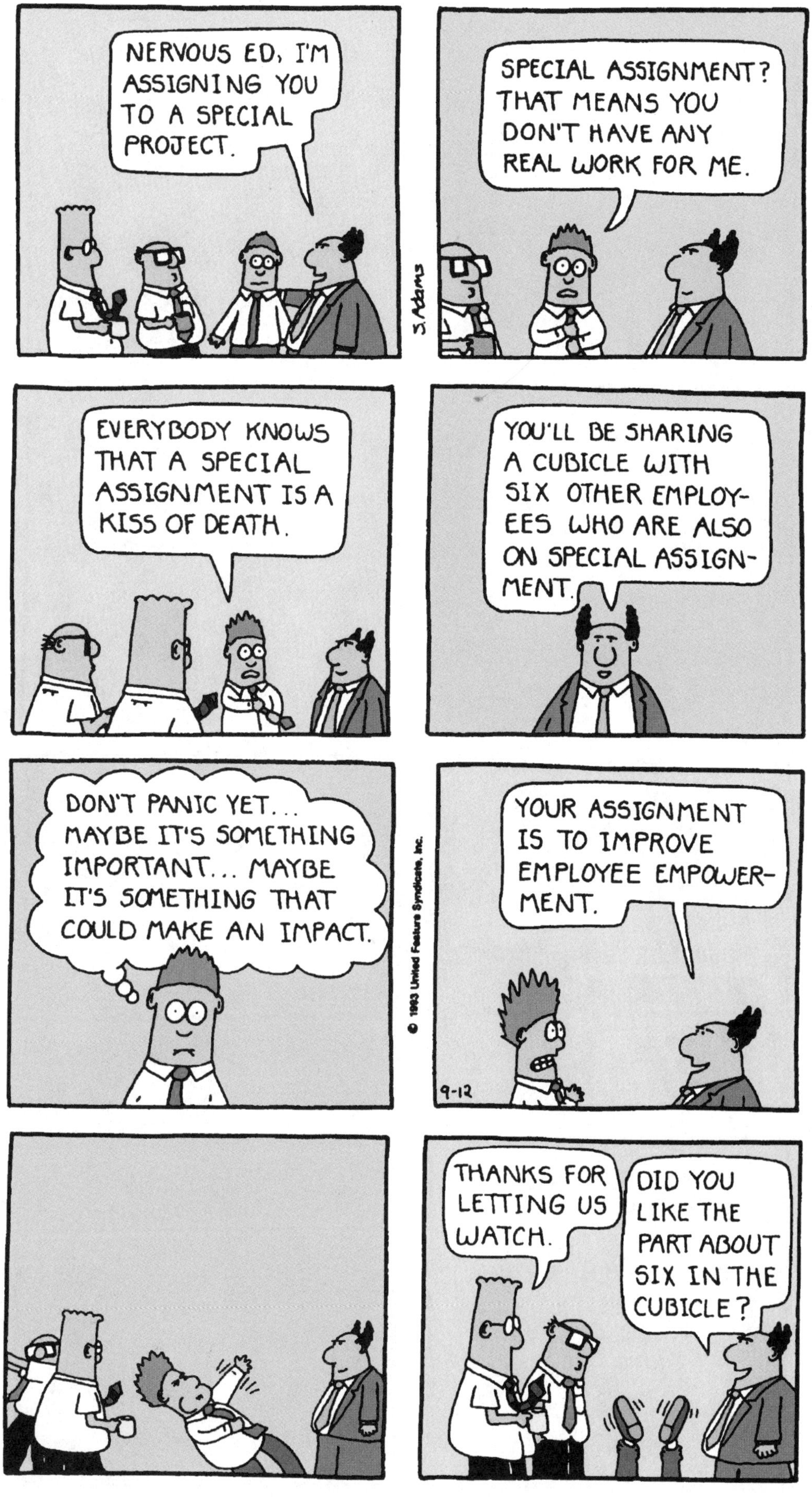
NERVOUS ED, I'M ASSIGNING YOU TO A SPECIAL PROJECT.
S. Adams
SPECIAL ASSIGNMENT? THAT MEANS YOU DON'T HAVE ANY REAL WORK FOR ME.
EVERYBODY KNOWS THAT A SPECIAL ASSIGNMENT IS A KISS OF DEATH.
YOU'LL BE SHARING A CUBICLE WITH SIX OTHER EMPLOYEES WHO ARE ALSO ON SPECIAL ASSIGNMENT.
DON'T PANIC YET... MAYBE IT'S SOMETHING IMPORTANT... MAYBE IT'S SOMETHING THAT COULD MAKE AN IMPACT.
© 1993 United Feature Syndicate, Inc.
YOUR ASSIGNMENT IS TO IMPROVE EMPLOYEE EMPOWERMENT.
9-12
THANKS FOR LETTING US WATCH.
DID YOU LIKE THE PART ABOUT SIX IN THE CUBICLE?

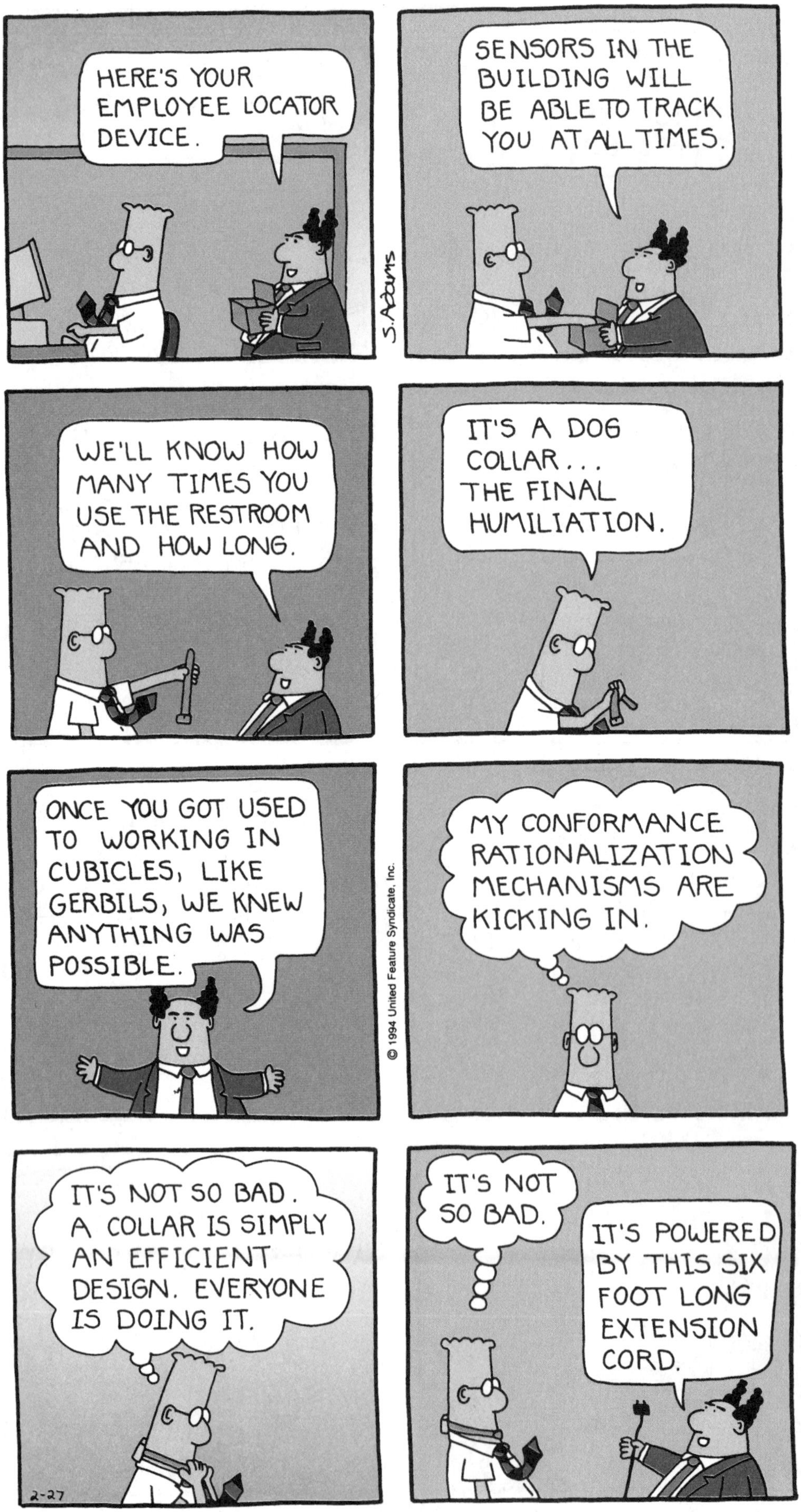
HERE'S YOUR EMPLOYEE LOCATOR DEVICE.
S. ADAMS
SENSORS IN THE BUILDING WILL BE ABLE TO TRACK YOU AT ALL TIMES.
WE'LL KNOW HOW MANY TIMES YOU USE THE RESTROOM AND HOW LONG.
IT'S A DOG COLLAR . . . THE FINAL HUMILIATION.
ONCE YOU GOT USED TO WORKING IN CUBICLES, LIKE GERBILS, WE KNEW ANYTHING WAS POSSIBLE.
MY CONFORMANCE RATIONALIZATION MECHANISMS ARE KICKING IN.
IT'S NOT SO BAD. A COLLAR IS SIMPLY AN EFFICIENT DESIGN. EVERYONE IS DOING IT.
2-27
IT'S NOT SO BAD.
IT'S POWERED BY THIS SIX FOOT LONG EXTENSION CORD.

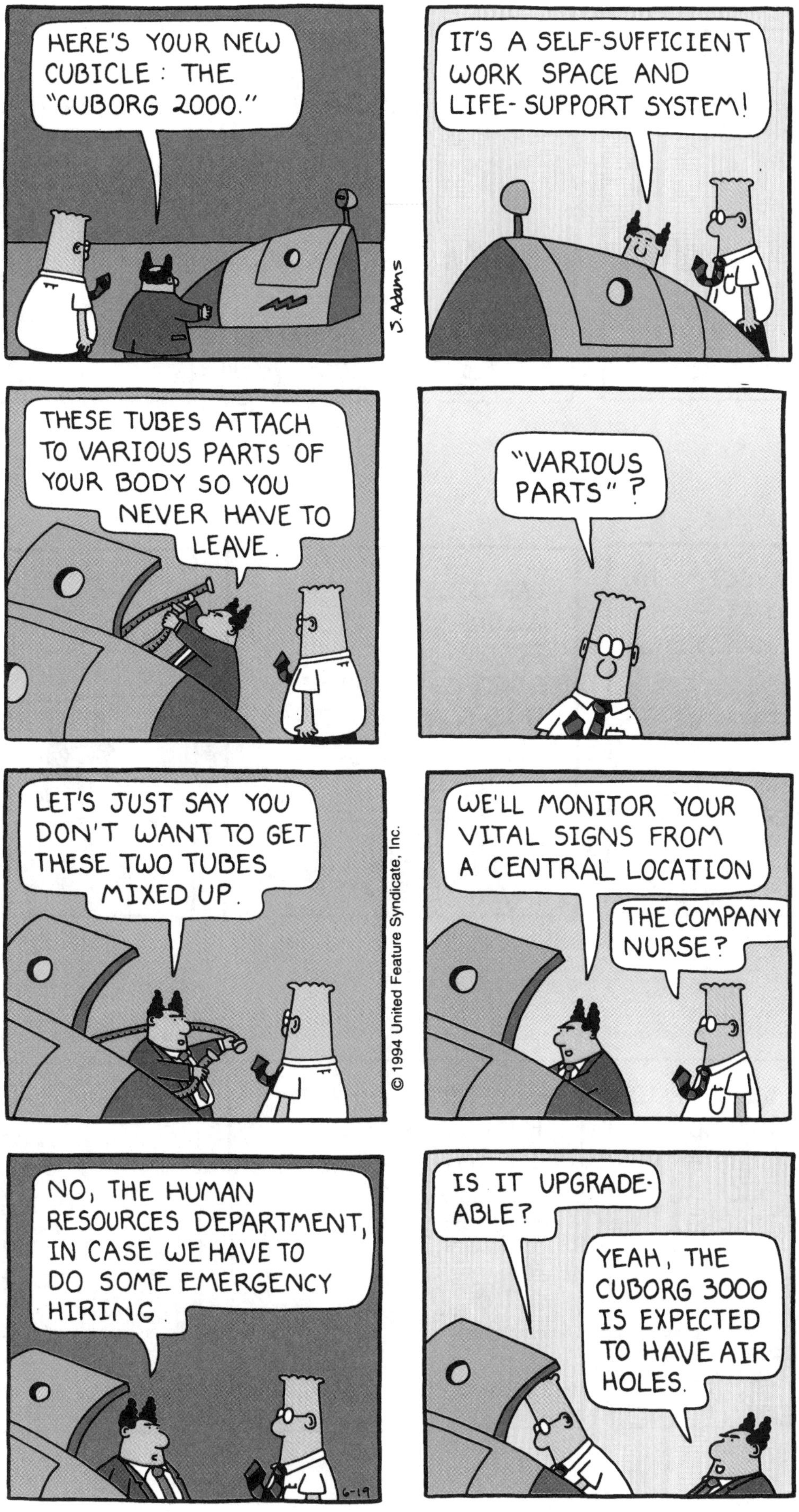
HERE'S YOUR NEW CUBICLE : THE "CUBORG 2000."
S. Adams
IT'S A SELF-SUFFICIENT WORK SPACE AND LIFE-SUPPORT SYSTEM!
THESE TUBES ATTACH TO VARIOUS PARTS OF YOUR BODY SO YOU NEVER HAVE TO LEAVE.
"VARIOUS PARTS" ?
LET'S JUST SAY YOU DON'T WANT TO GET THESE TWO TUBES MIXED UP.
© 1994 United Feature Syndicate, Inc.
WE'LL MONITOR YOUR VITAL SIGNS FROM A CENTRAL LOCATION
THE COMPANY NURSE?
NO, THE HUMAN RESOURCES DEPARTMENT, IN CASE WE HAVE TO DO SOME EMERGENCY HIRING.
6-19
IS IT UPGRADE-ABLE?
YEAH, THE CUBORG 3000 IS EXPECTED TO HAVE AIR HOLES.

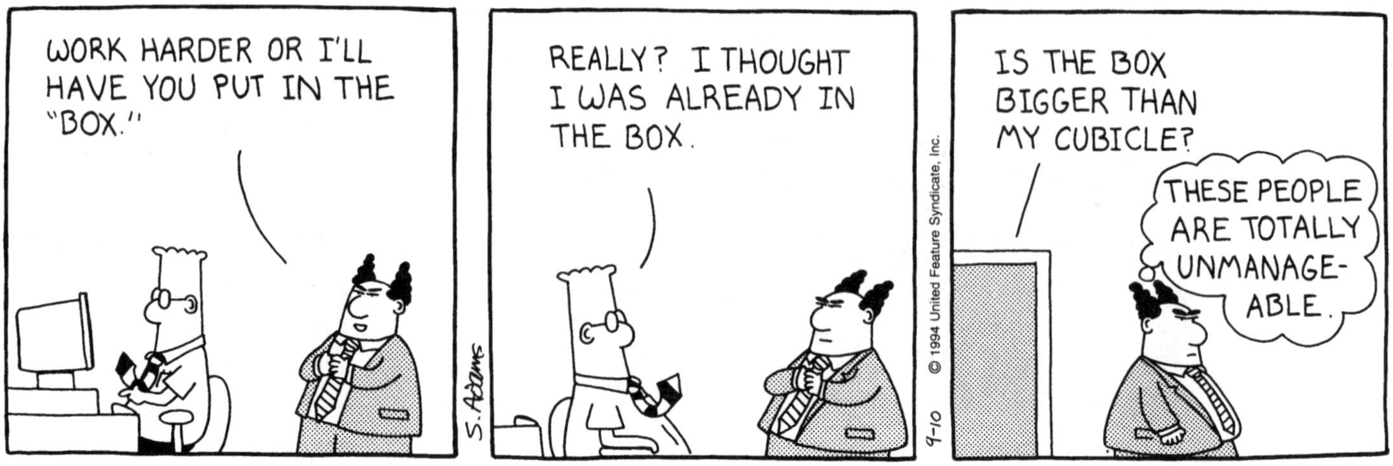
WORK HARDER OR I'LL HAVE YOU PUT IN THE "BOX."
S. ADAMS
REALLY? I THOUGHT I WAS ALREADY IN THE BOX.
9-10
© 1994 United Feature Syndicate, Inc.
IS THE BOX BIGGER THAN MY CUBICLE?
THESE PEOPLE ARE TOTALLY UNMANAGE-ABLE.

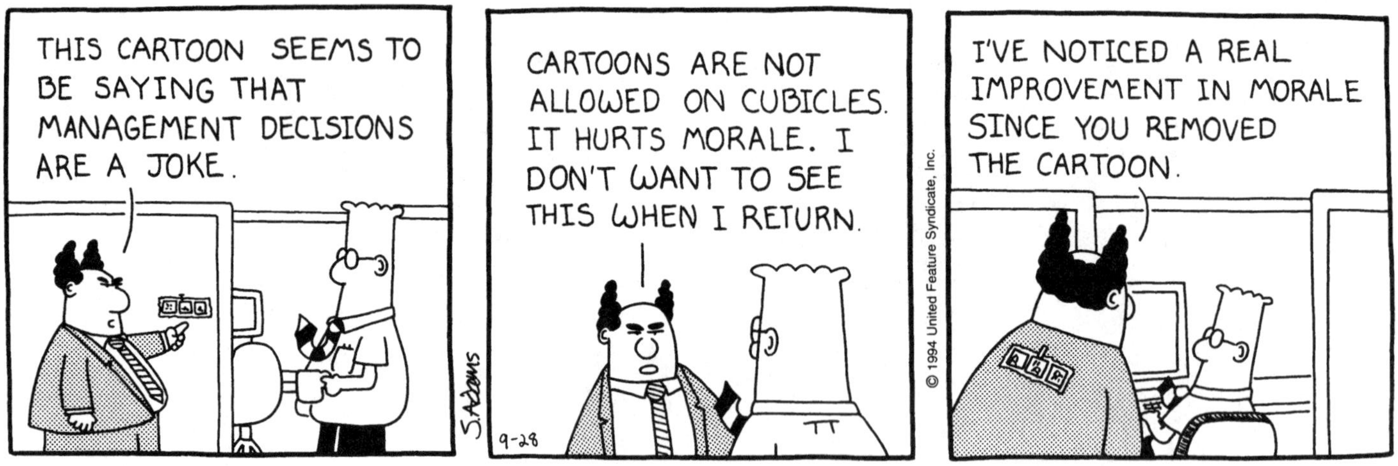
THIS CARTOON SEEMS TO BE SAYING THAT MANAGEMENT DECISIONS ARE A JOKE.
S. ADAMS
9-28
CARTOONS ARE NOT ALLOWED ON CUBICLES. IT HURTS MORALE. I DON'T WANT TO SEE THIS WHEN I RETURN.
© 1994 United Feature Syndicate, Inc.
I'VE NOTICED A REAL IMPROVEMENT IN MORALE SINCE YOU REMOVED THE CARTOON.

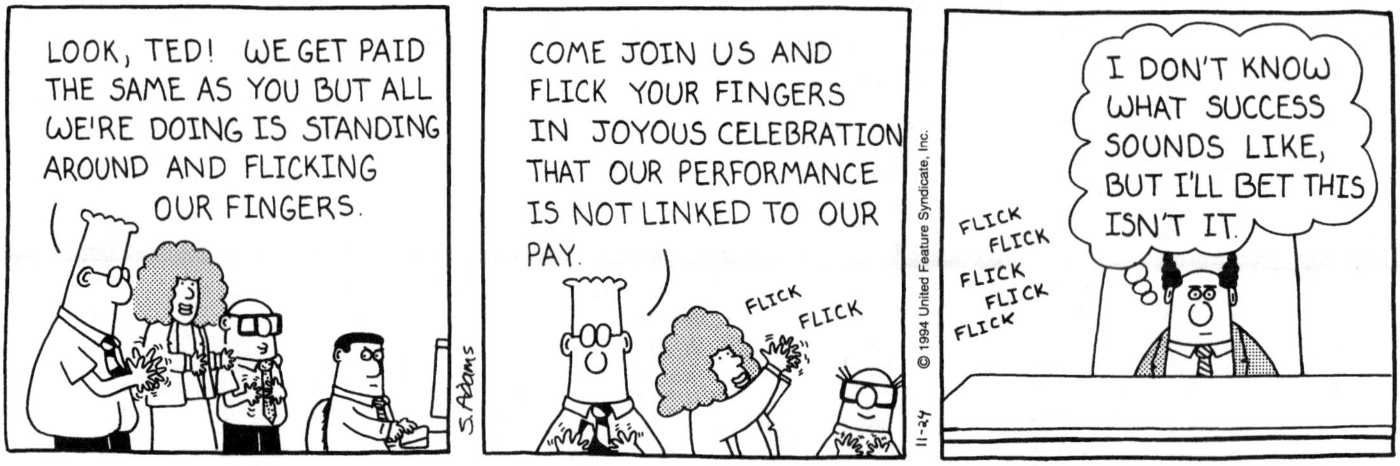
LOOK, TED! WE GET PAID THE SAME AS YOU BUT ALL WE'RE DOING IS STANDING AROUND AND FLICKING OUR FINGERS.
S. ADAMS
COME JOIN US AND FLICK YOUR FINGERS IN JOYOUS CELEBRATION THAT OUR PERFORMANCE IS NOT LINKED TO OUR PAY.
FLICK
FLICK
11-24
© 1994 United Feature Syndicate, Inc.
FLICK
FLICK
FLICK
FLICK
FLICK
I DON'T KNOW WHAT SUCCESS SOUNDS LIKE, BUT I'LL BET THIS ISN'T IT.

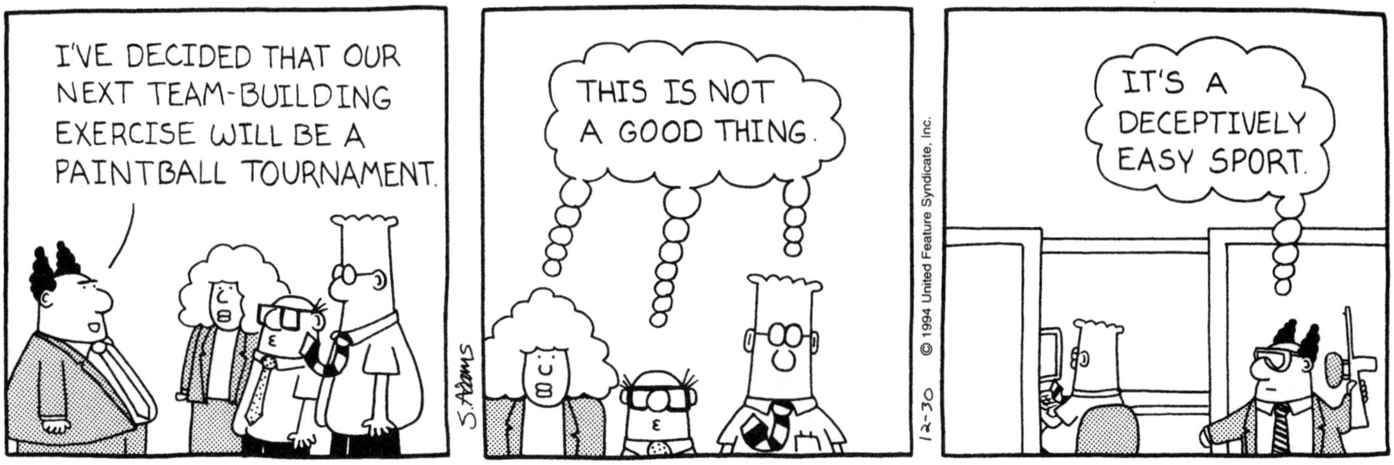
I'VE DECIDED THAT OUR NEXT TEAM-BUILDING EXERCISE WILL BE A PAINTBALL TOURNAMENT.
S. Adams
THIS IS NOT A GOOD THING.
12-30
© 1994 United Feature Syndicate, Inc.
IT'S A DECEPTIVELY EASY SPORT.

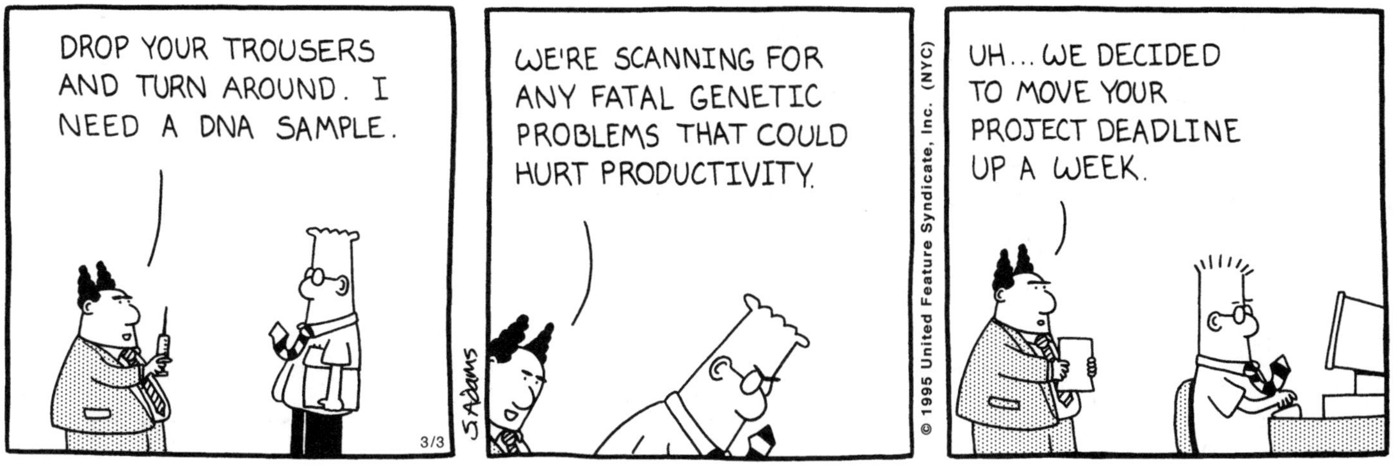
DROP YOUR TROUSERS AND TURN AROUND. I NEED A DNA SAMPLE.
3/3
S. Adams
WE'RE SCANNING FOR ANY FATAL GENETIC PROBLEMS THAT COULD HURT PRODUCTIVITY.
© 1995 United Feature Syndicate, Inc. (NYC)
UH... WE DECIDED TO MOVE YOUR PROJECT DEADLINE UP A WEEK.

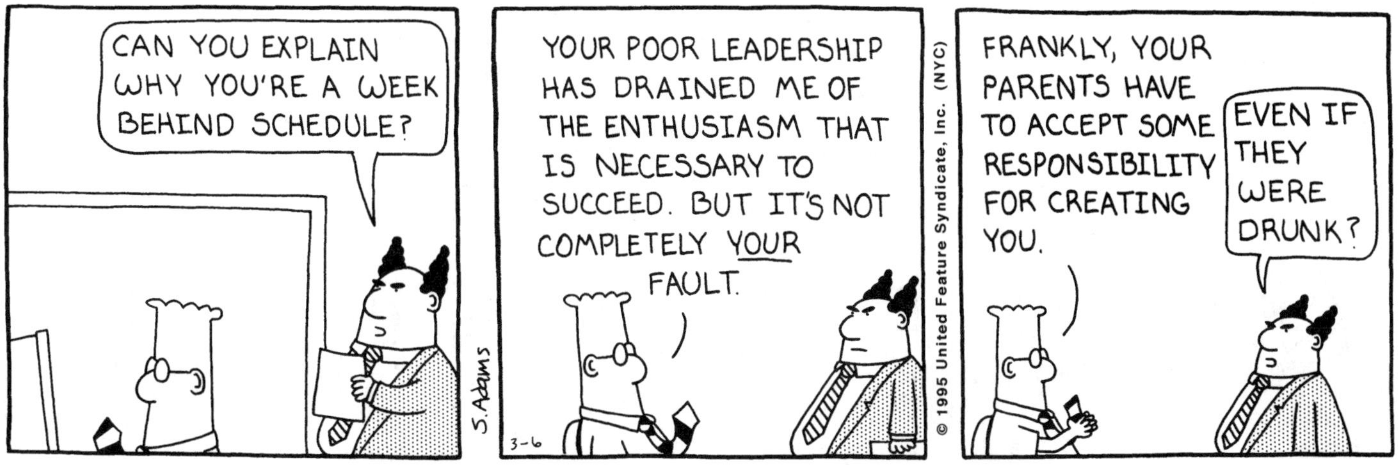
CAN YOU EXPLAIN WHY YOU'RE A WEEK BEHIND SCHEDULE?
S. Adams
YOUR POOR LEADERSHIP HAS DRAINED ME OF THE ENTHUSIASM THAT IS NECESSARY TO SUCCEED. BUT IT'S NOT COMPLETELY YOUR FAULT.
3-6
© 1995 United Feature Syndicate, Inc. (NYC)
FRANKLY, YOUR PARENTS HAVE TO ACCEPT SOME RESPONSIBILITY FOR CREATING YOU.
EVEN IF THEY WERE DRUNK?

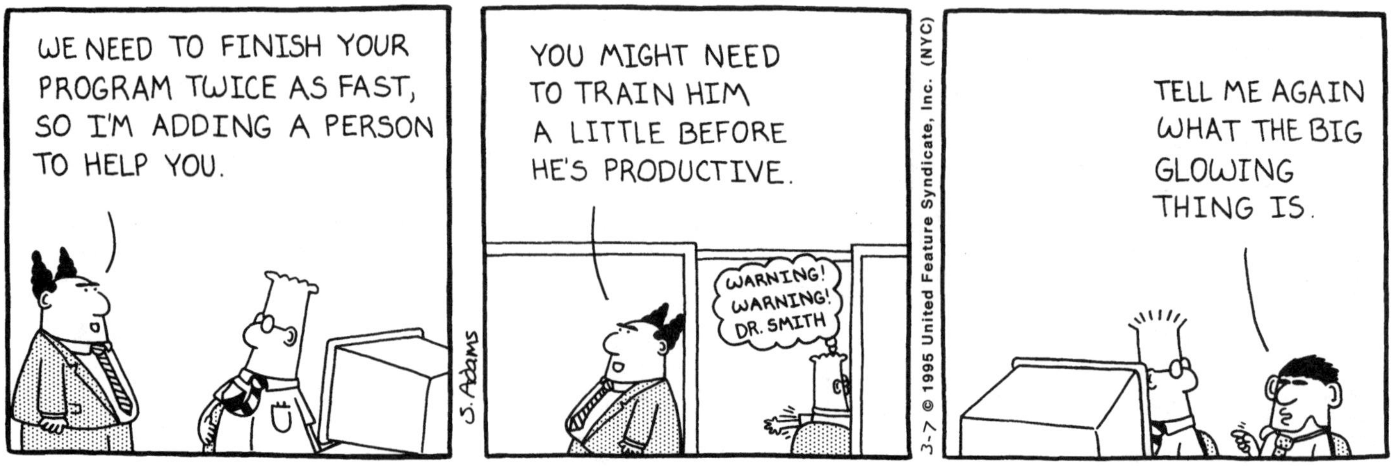
WE NEED TO FINISH YOUR PROGRAM TWICE AS FAST, SO I'M ADDING A PERSON TO HELP YOU.
S. Adams
YOU MIGHT NEED TO TRAIN HIM A LITTLE BEFORE HE'S PRODUCTIVE.
WARNING! WARNING! DR. SMITH
3-7 © 1995 United Feature Syndicate, Inc. (NYC)
TELL ME AGAIN WHAT THE BIG GLOWING THING IS.

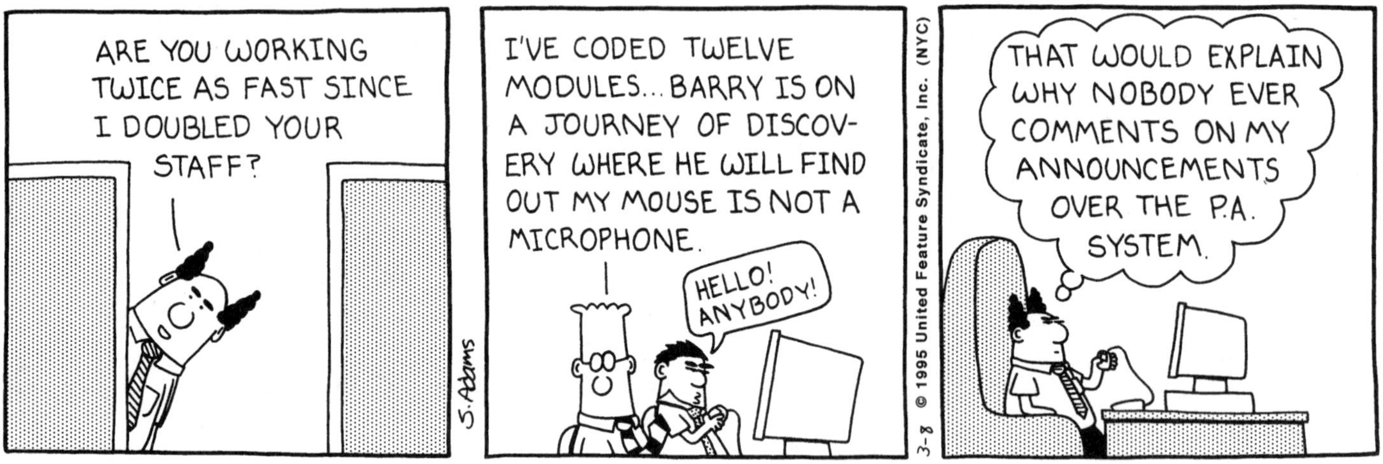
ARE YOU WORKING TWICE AS FAST SINCE I DOUBLED YOUR STAFF?
S. Adams
I'VE CODED TWELVE MODULES... BARRY IS ON A JOURNEY OF DISCOVERY WHERE HE WILL FIND OUT MY MOUSE IS NOT A MICROPHONE.
HELLO! ANYBODY!
3-8 © 1995 United Feature Syndicate, Inc. (NYC)
THAT WOULD EXPLAIN WHY NOBODY EVER COMMENTS ON MY ANNOUNCEMENTS OVER THE P.A. SYSTEM.

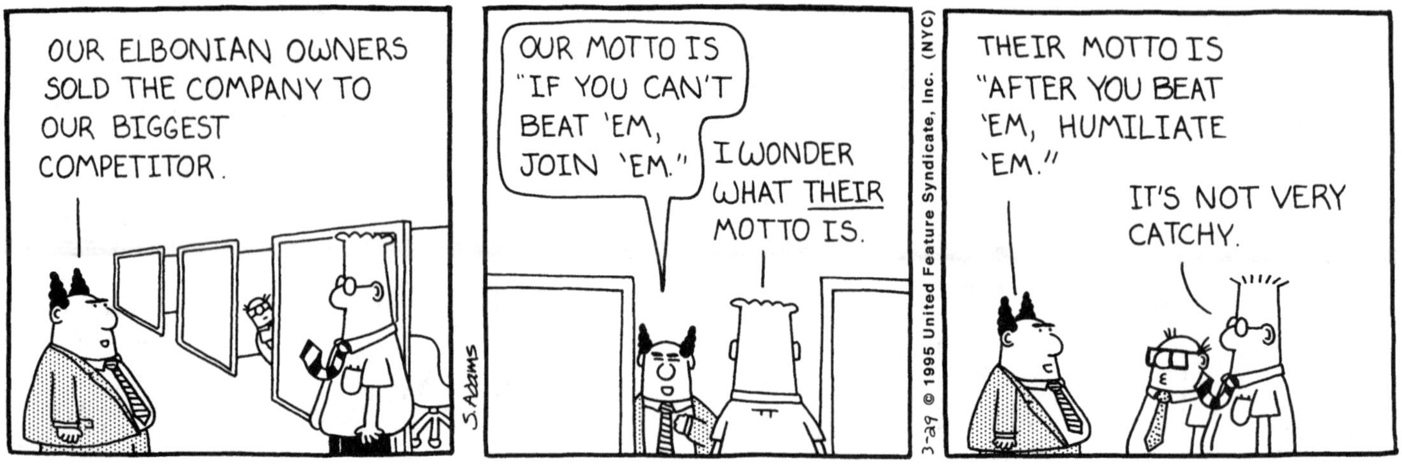
OUR ELBONIAN OWNERS SOLD THE COMPANY TO OUR BIGGEST COMPETITOR.
S. Adams
OUR MOTTO IS "IF YOU CAN'T BEAT 'EM, JOIN 'EM."
I WONDER WHAT THEIR MOTTO IS.
3-29 © 1995 United Feature Syndicate, Inc. (NYC)
THEIR MOTTO IS "AFTER YOU BEAT 'EM, HUMILIATE 'EM."
IT'S NOT VERY CATCHY.

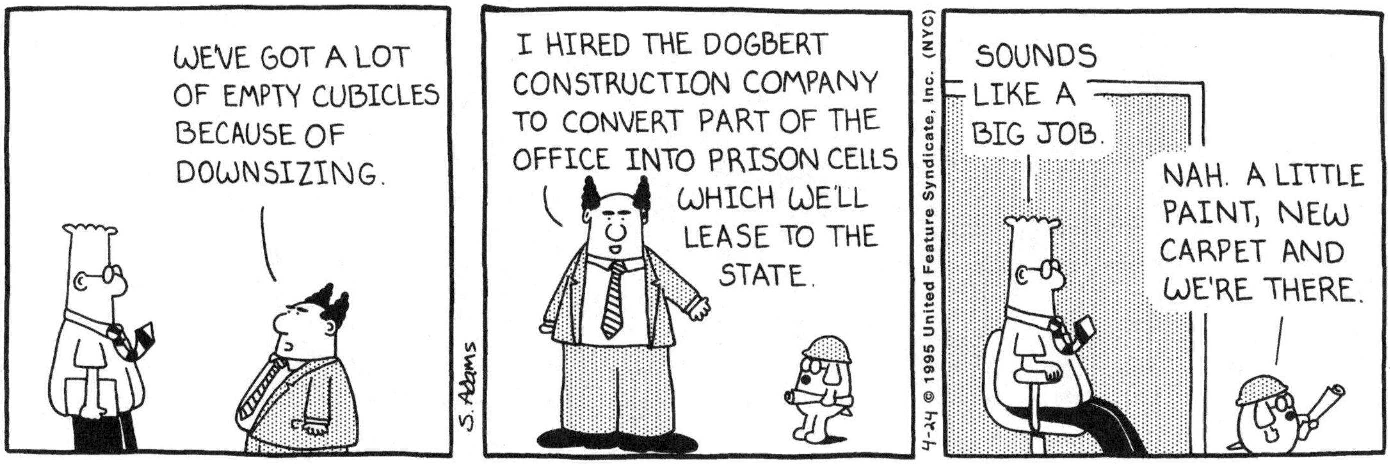
WE'VE GOT A LOT OF EMPTY CUBICLES BECAUSE OF DOWNSIZING.
I HIRED THE DOGBERT CONSTRUCTION COMPANY TO CONVERT PART OF THE OFFICE INTO PRISON CELLS WHICH WE'LL LEASE TO THE STATE.
S. Adams
4-24 © 1995 United Feature Syndicate, Inc. (NYC)
SOUNDS LIKE A BIG JOB.
NAH. A LITTLE PAINT, NEW CARPET AND WE'RE THERE.

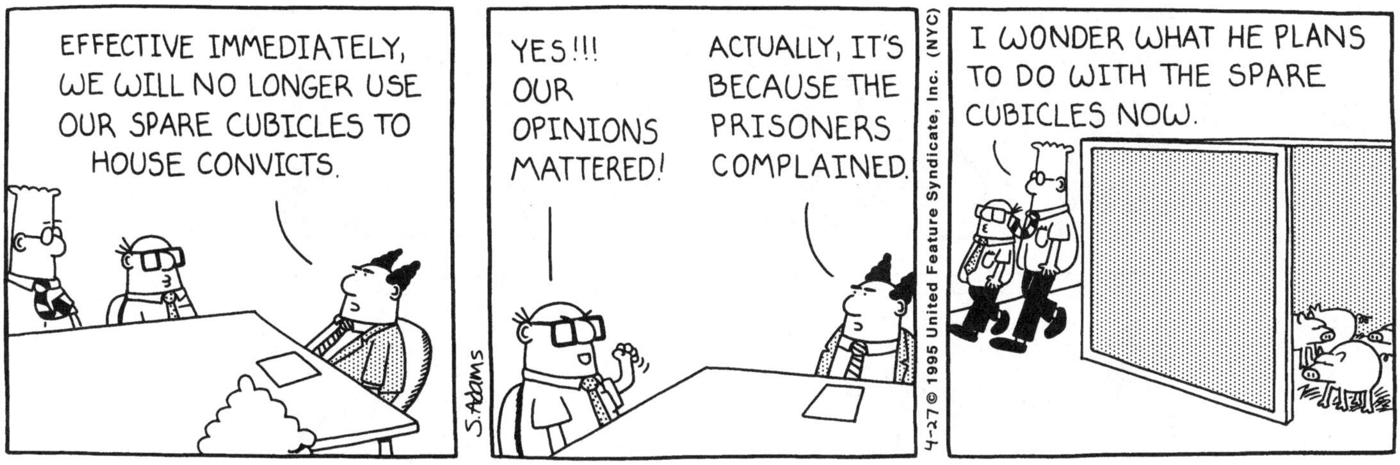
EFFECTIVE IMMEDIATELY, WE WILL NO LONGER USE OUR SPARE CUBICLES TO HOUSE CONVICTS.
S. Adams
YES!!! OUR OPINIONS MATTERED!
ACTUALLY, IT'S BECAUSE THE PRISONERS COMPLAINED.
4-27 © 1995 United Feature Syndicate, Inc. (NYC)
I WONDER WHAT HE PLANS TO DO WITH THE SPARE CUBICLES NOW.

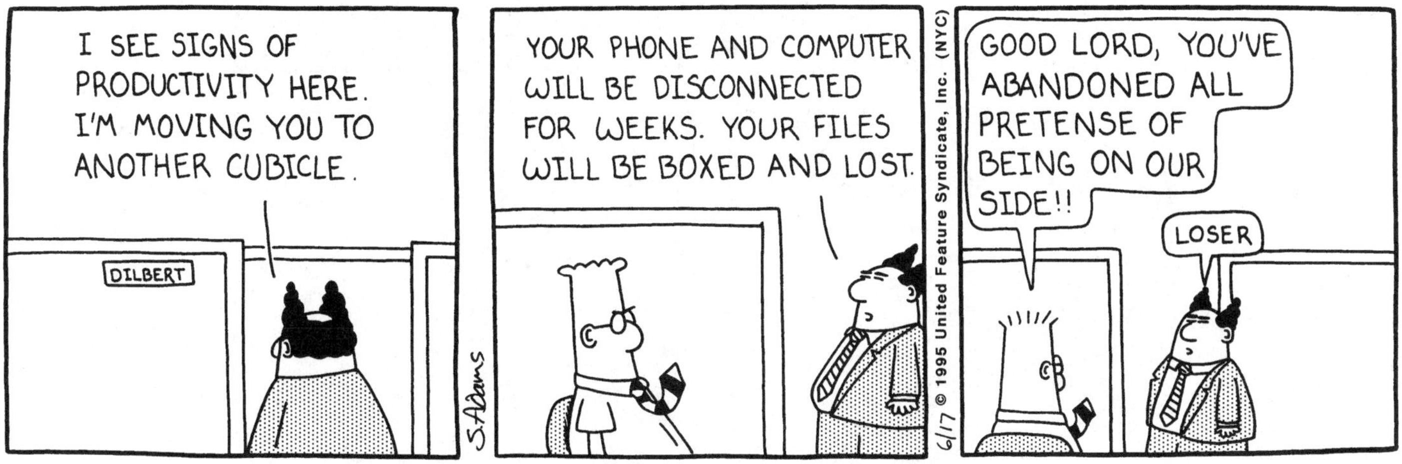
I SEE SIGNS OF PRODUCTIVITY HERE. I'M MOVING YOU TO ANOTHER CUBICLE.
DILBERT
S. Adams
YOUR PHONE AND COMPUTER WILL BE DISCONNECTED FOR WEEKS. YOUR FILES WILL BE BOXED AND LOST.
6/17 © 1995 United Feature Syndicate, Inc. (NYC)
GOOD LORD, YOU'VE ABANDONED ALL PRETENSE OF BEING ON OUR SIDE!!
LOSER

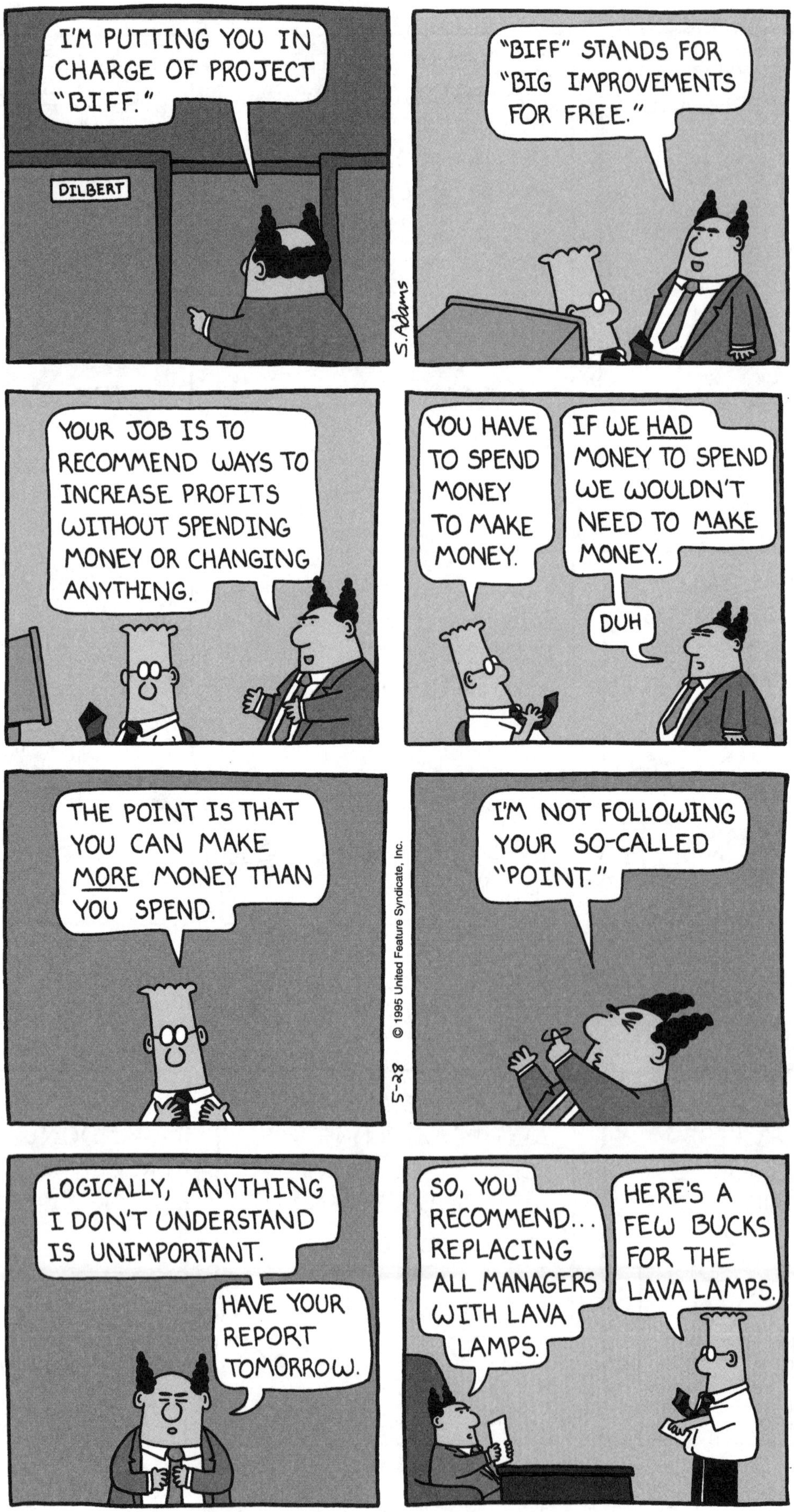
I'M PUTTING YOU IN CHARGE OF PROJECT "BIFF."
DILBERT
S. Adams
"BIFF" STANDS FOR "BIG IMPROVEMENTS FOR FREE."
YOUR JOB IS TO RECOMMEND WAYS TO INCREASE PROFITS WITHOUT SPENDING MONEY OR CHANGING ANYTHING.
YOU HAVE TO SPEND MONEY TO MAKE MONEY.
IF WE HAD MONEY TO SPEND WE WOULDN'T NEED TO MAKE MONEY.
DUH
THE POINT IS THAT YOU CAN MAKE MORE MONEY THAN YOU SPEND.
5-28 © 1995 United Feature Syndicate, Inc.
I'M NOT FOLLOWING YOUR SO-CALLED "POINT."
LOGICALLY, ANYTHING I DON'T UNDERSTAND IS UNIMPORTANT.
HAVE YOUR REPORT TOMORROW.
SO, YOU RECOMMEND... REPLACING ALL MANAGERS WITH LAVA LAMPS.
HERE'S A FEW BUCKS FOR THE LAVA LAMPS.

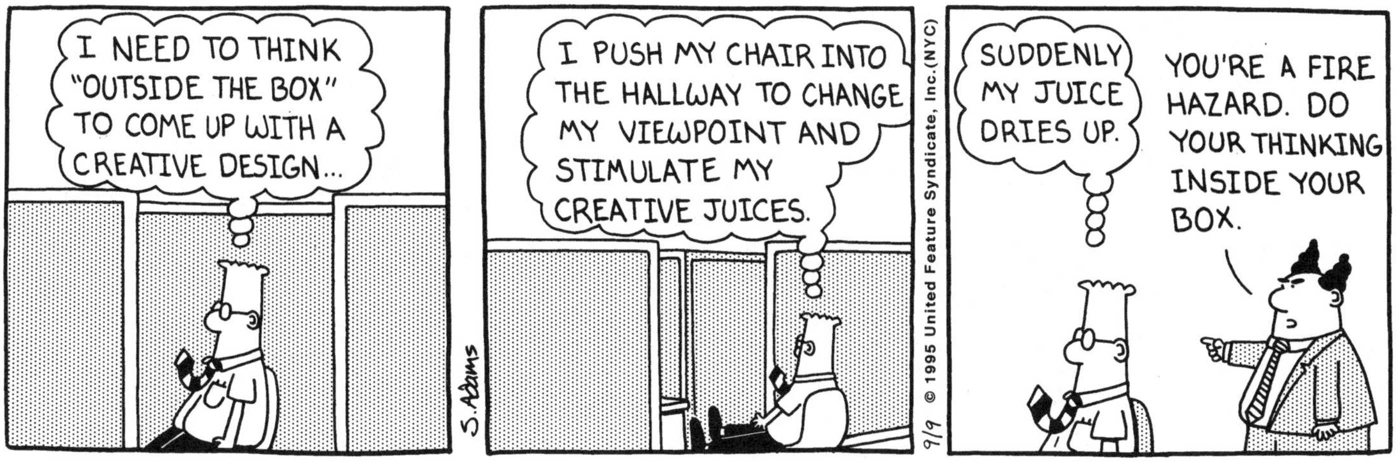
I NEED TO THINK "OUTSIDE THE BOX" TO COME UP WITH A CREATIVE DESIGN...
I PUSH MY CHAIR INTO THE HALLWAY TO CHANGE MY VIEWPOINT AND STIMULATE MY CREATIVE JUICES.
SUDDENLY MY JUICE DRIES UP.
YOU'RE A FIRE HAZARD. DO YOUR THINKING INSIDE YOUR BOX.
S. Adams
9/9 © 1995 United Feature Syndicate, Inc.(NYC)

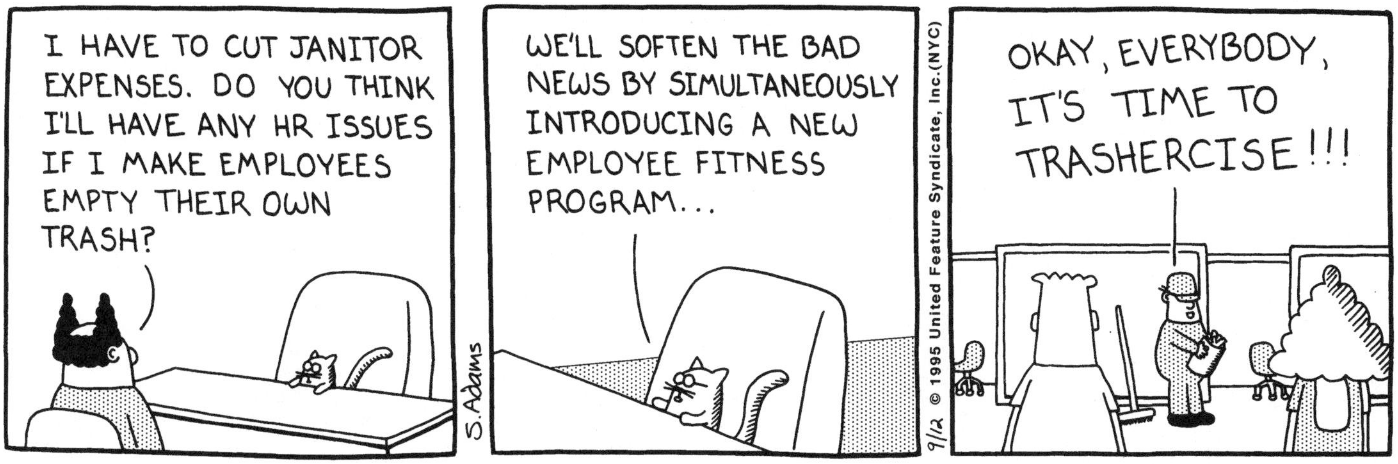
I HAVE TO CUT JANITOR EXPENSES. DO YOU THINK I'LL HAVE ANY HR ISSUES IF I MAKE EMPLOYEES EMPTY THEIR OWN TRASH?
WE'LL SOFTEN THE BAD NEWS BY SIMULTANEOUSLY INTRODUCING A NEW EMPLOYEE FITNESS PROGRAM...
OKAY, EVERYBODY, IT'S TIME TO TRASHERCISE!!!
S. Adams
9/12 © 1995 United Feature Syndicate, Inc.(NYC)

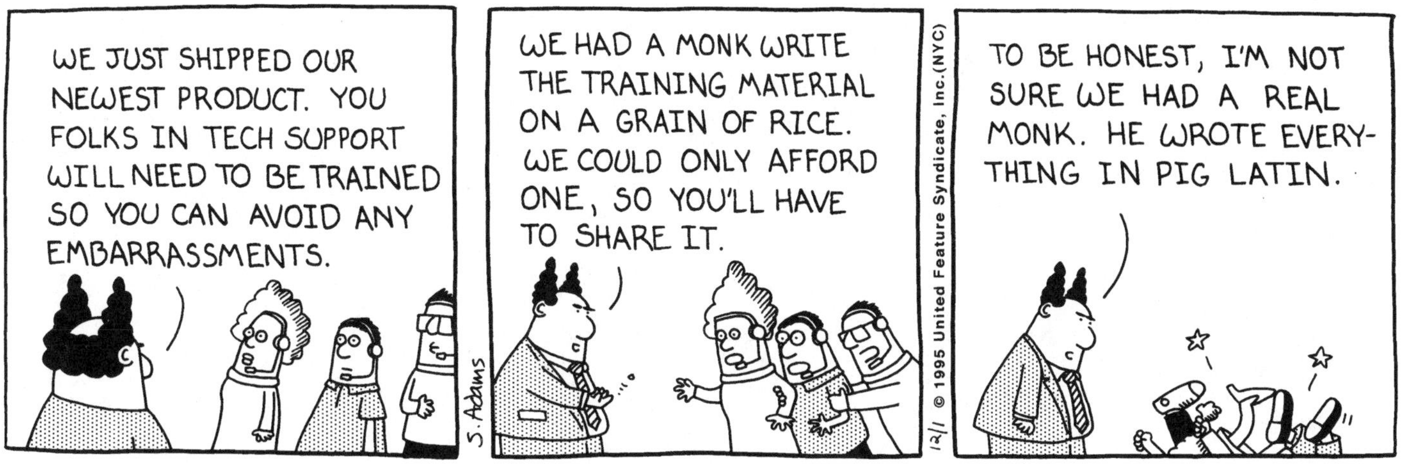
WE JUST SHIPPED OUR NEWEST PRODUCT. YOU FOLKS IN TECH SUPPORT WILL NEED TO BE TRAINED SO YOU CAN AVOID ANY EMBARRASSMENTS.
WE HAD A MONK WRITE THE TRAINING MATERIAL ON A GRAIN OF RICE. WE COULD ONLY AFFORD ONE, SO YOU'LL HAVE TO SHARE IT.
TO BE HONEST, I'M NOT SURE WE HAD A REAL MONK. HE WROTE EVERY-THING IN PIG LATIN.
S. Adams
12/1 © 1995 United Feature Syndicate, Inc.(NYC)

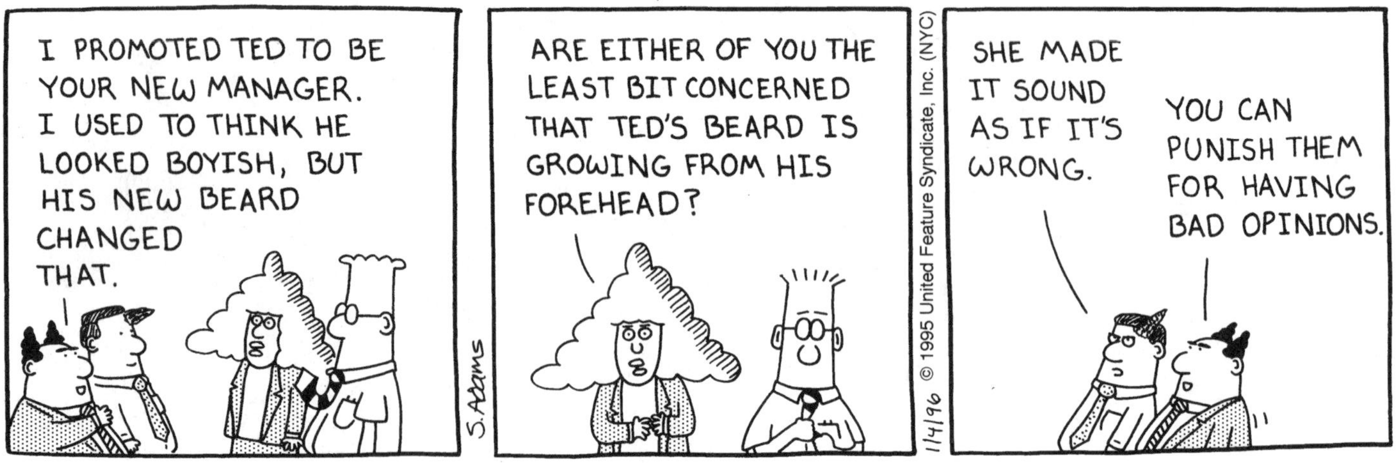

I PROMOTED TED TO BE YOUR NEW MANAGER. I USED TO THINK HE LOOKED BOYISH, BUT HIS NEW BEARD CHANGED THAT.
S. Adams
ARE EITHER OF YOU THE LEAST BIT CONCERNED THAT TED'S BEARD IS GROWING FROM HIS FOREHEAD?
1/4/96 © 1995 United Feature Syndicate, Inc. (NYC)
SHE MADE IT SOUND AS IF IT'S WRONG.
YOU CAN PUNISH THEM FOR HAVING BAD OPINIONS.

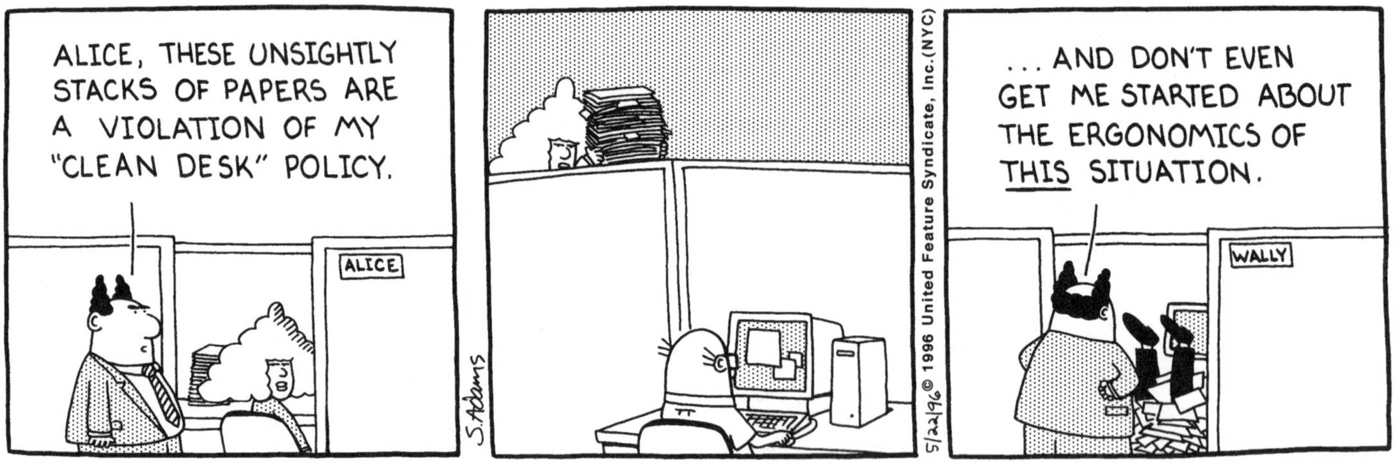

ALICE, THESE UNSIGHTLY STACKS OF PAPERS ARE A VIOLATION OF MY "CLEAN DESK" POLICY.
ALICE
S. Adams
5/22/96 © 1996 United Feature Syndicate, Inc. (NYC)
... AND DON'T EVEN GET ME STARTED ABOUT THE ERGONOMICS OF THIS SITUATION.
WALLY

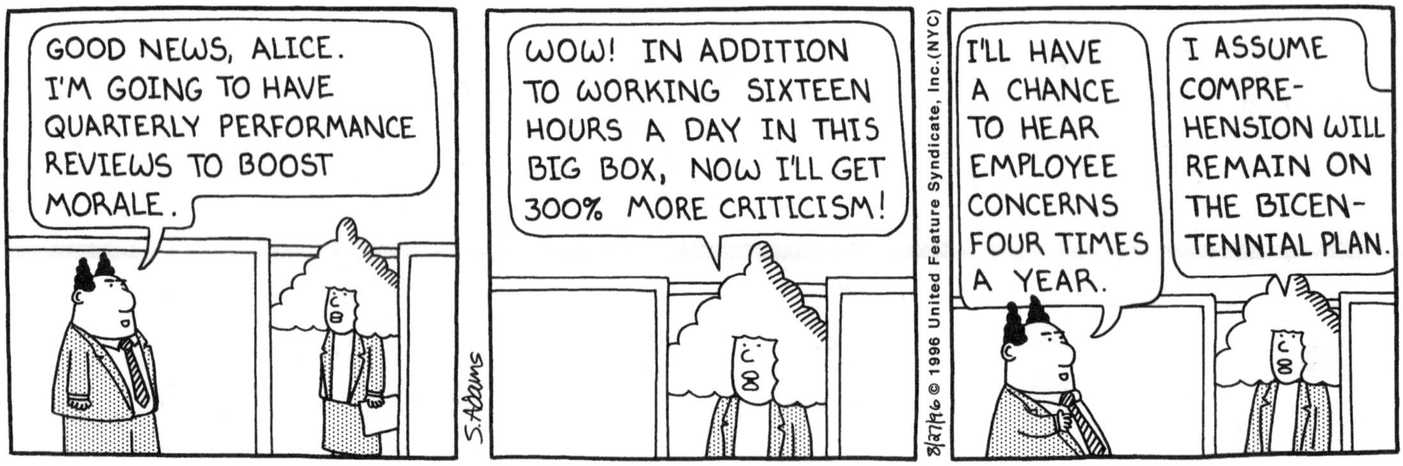

GOOD NEWS, ALICE. I'M GOING TO HAVE QUARTERLY PERFORMANCE REVIEWS TO BOOST MORALE.
S. Adams
WOW! IN ADDITION TO WORKING SIXTEEN HOURS A DAY IN THIS BIG BOX, NOW I'LL GET 300% MORE CRITICISM!
8/27/96 © 1996 United Feature Syndicate, Inc. (NYC)
I'LL HAVE A CHANCE TO HEAR EMPLOYEE CONCERNS FOUR TIMES A YEAR.
I ASSUME COMPRE-HENSION WILL REMAIN ON THE BICEN-TENNIAL PLAN.

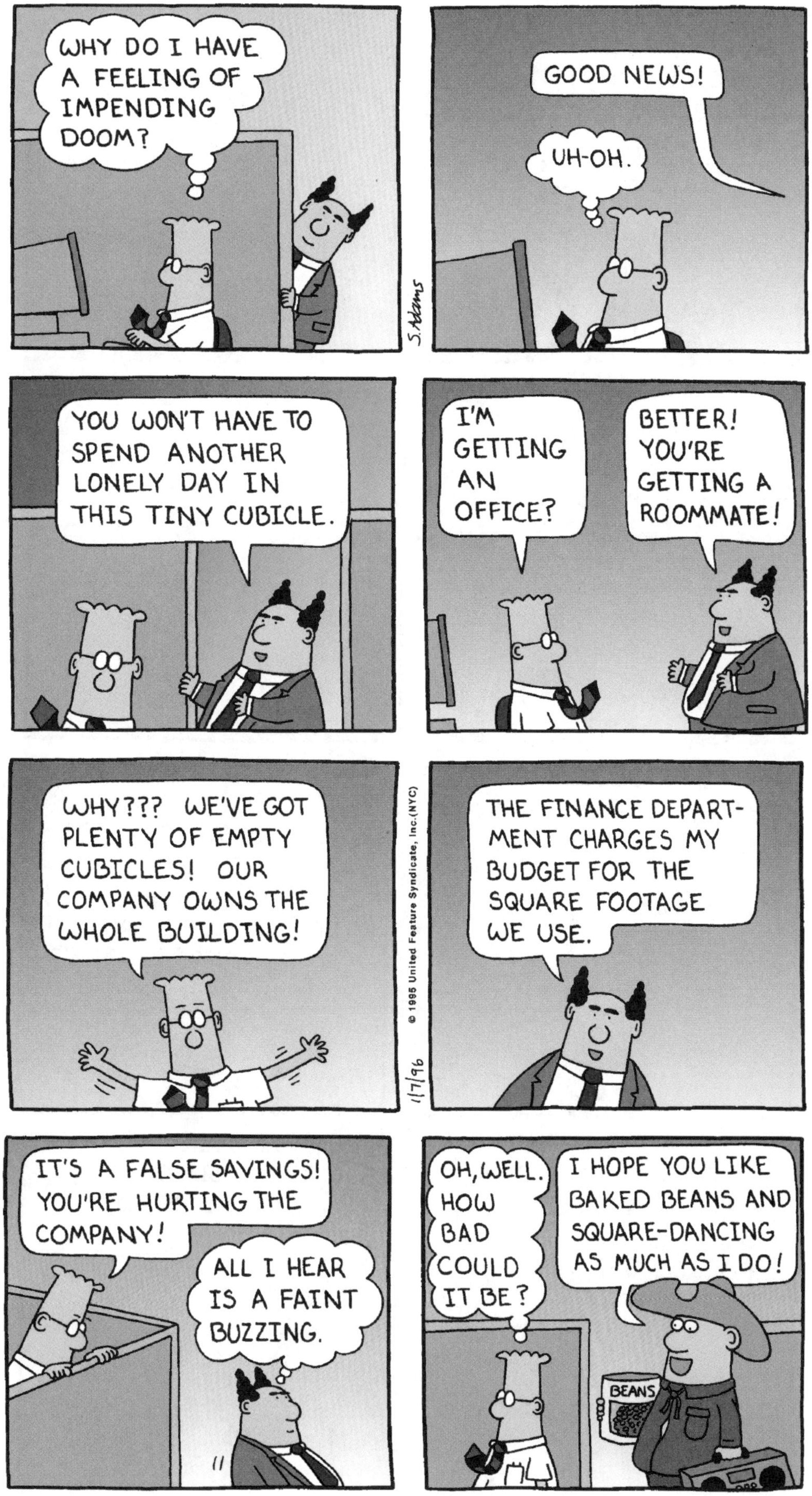
WHY DO I HAVE A FEELING OF IMPENDING DOOM?
GOOD NEWS!
UH-OH.
S. Adams
YOU WON'T HAVE TO SPEND ANOTHER LONELY DAY IN THIS TINY CUBICLE.
I'M GETTING AN OFFICE?
BETTER! YOU'RE GETTING A ROOMMATE!
WHY??? WE'VE GOT PLENTY OF EMPTY CUBICLES! OUR COMPANY OWNS THE WHOLE BUILDING!
© 1995 United Feature Syndicate, Inc.(NYC)
1/7/96
THE FINANCE DEPARTMENT CHARGES MY BUDGET FOR THE SQUARE FOOTAGE WE USE.
IT'S A FALSE SAVINGS! YOU'RE HURTING THE COMPANY!
ALL I HEAR IS A FAINT BUZZING.
OH, WELL. HOW BAD COULD IT BE?
I HOPE YOU LIKE BAKED BEANS AND SQUARE-DANCING AS MUCH AS I DO!
BEANS

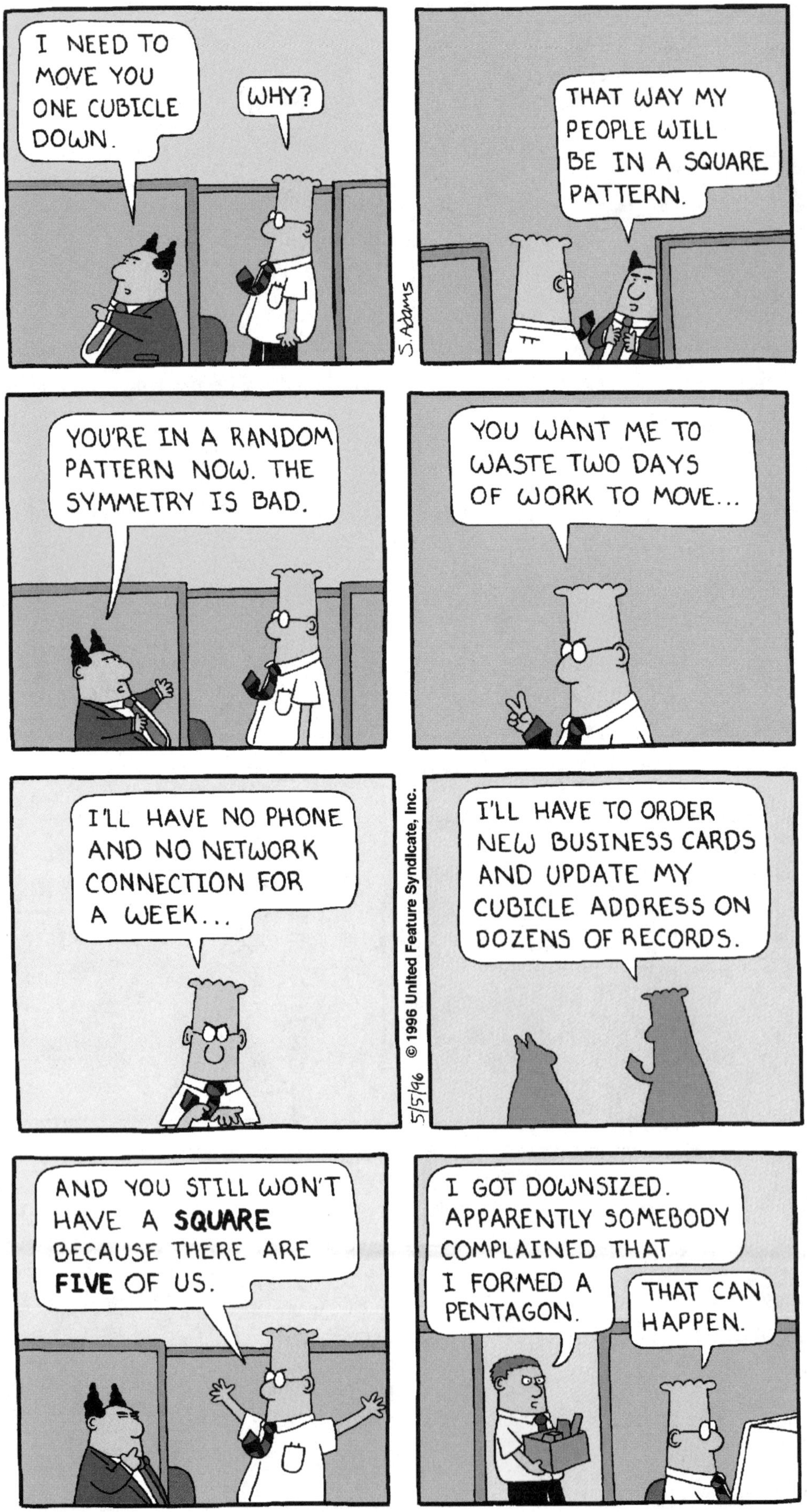
I NEED TO MOVE YOU ONE CUBICLE DOWN.
WHY?
S. Adams
THAT WAY MY PEOPLE WILL BE IN A SQUARE PATTERN.
YOU'RE IN A RANDOM PATTERN NOW. THE SYMMETRY IS BAD.
YOU WANT ME TO WASTE TWO DAYS OF WORK TO MOVE...
I'LL HAVE NO PHONE AND NO NETWORK CONNECTION FOR A WEEK...
5/5/96 © 1996 United Feature Syndicate, Inc.
I'LL HAVE TO ORDER NEW BUSINESS CARDS AND UPDATE MY CUBICLE ADDRESS ON DOZENS OF RECORDS.
AND YOU STILL WON'T HAVE A **SQUARE** BECAUSE THERE ARE **FIVE** OF US.
I GOT DOWNSIZED. APPARENTLY SOMEBODY COMPLAINED THAT I FORMED A PENTAGON.
THAT CAN HAPPEN.

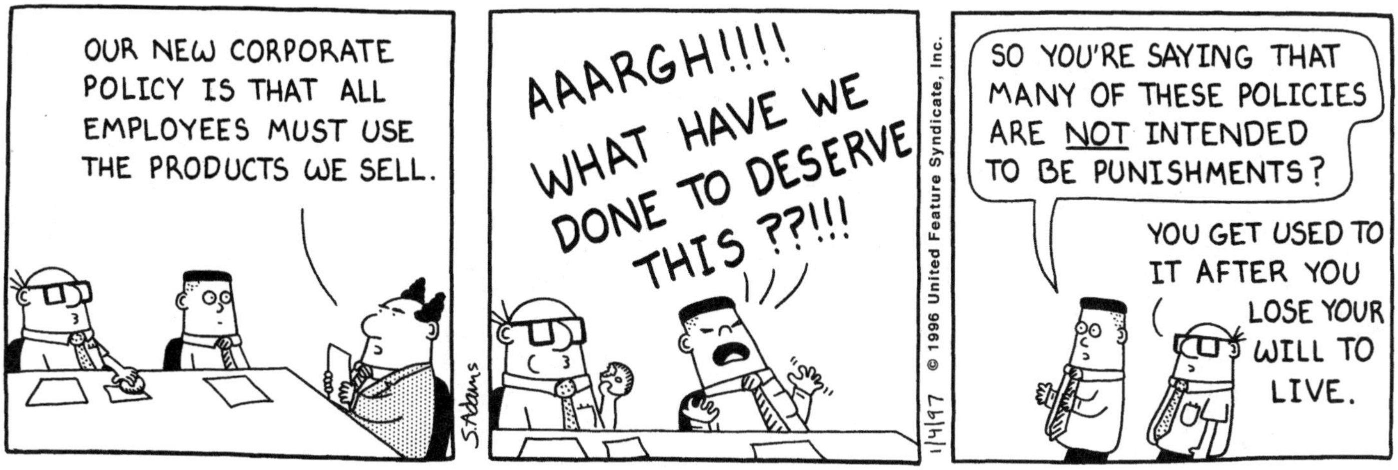
OUR NEW CORPORATE POLICY IS THAT ALL EMPLOYEES MUST USE THE PRODUCTS WE SELL.
AAARGH!!!! WHAT HAVE WE DONE TO DESERVE THIS ??!!!
SO YOU'RE SAYING THAT MANY OF THESE POLICIES ARE NOT INTENDED TO BE PUNISHMENTS?
YOU GET USED TO IT AFTER YOU LOSE YOUR WILL TO LIVE.
S.Adams
1/4/97
© 1996 United Feature Syndicate, Inc.

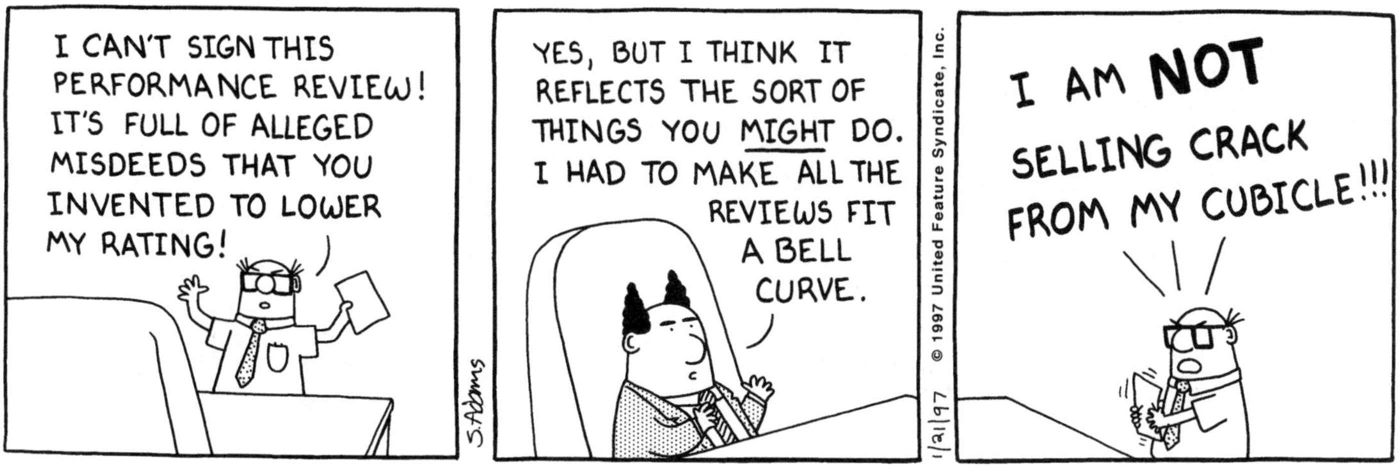
I CAN'T SIGN THIS PERFORMANCE REVIEW! IT'S FULL OF ALLEGED MISDEEDS THAT YOU INVENTED TO LOWER MY RATING!
YES, BUT I THINK IT REFLECTS THE SORT OF THINGS YOU MIGHT DO. I HAD TO MAKE ALL THE REVIEWS FIT A BELL CURVE.
I AM NOT SELLING CRACK FROM MY CUBICLE!!!
S.Adams
1/21/97
© 1997 United Feature Syndicate, Inc.

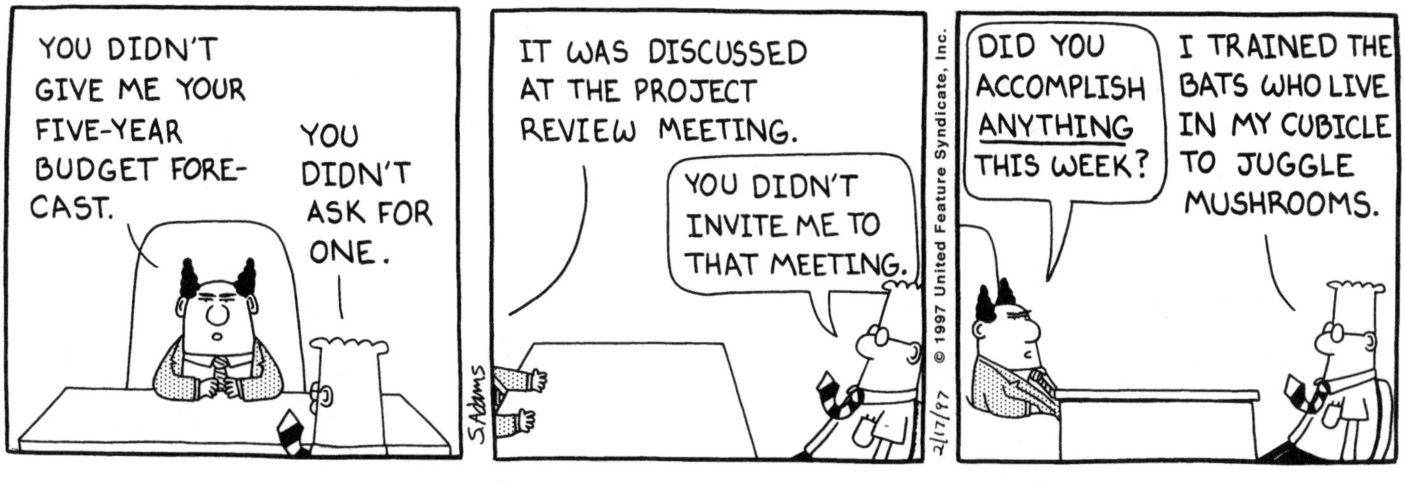
YOU DIDN'T GIVE ME YOUR FIVE-YEAR BUDGET FORE-CAST.
YOU DIDN'T ASK FOR ONE.
IT WAS DISCUSSED AT THE PROJECT REVIEW MEETING.
YOU DIDN'T INVITE ME TO THAT MEETING.
DID YOU ACCOMPLISH ANYTHING THIS WEEK?
I TRAINED THE BATS WHO LIVE IN MY CUBICLE TO JUGGLE MUSHROOMS.
S.Adams
2/7/97
© 1997 United Feature Syndicate, Inc.

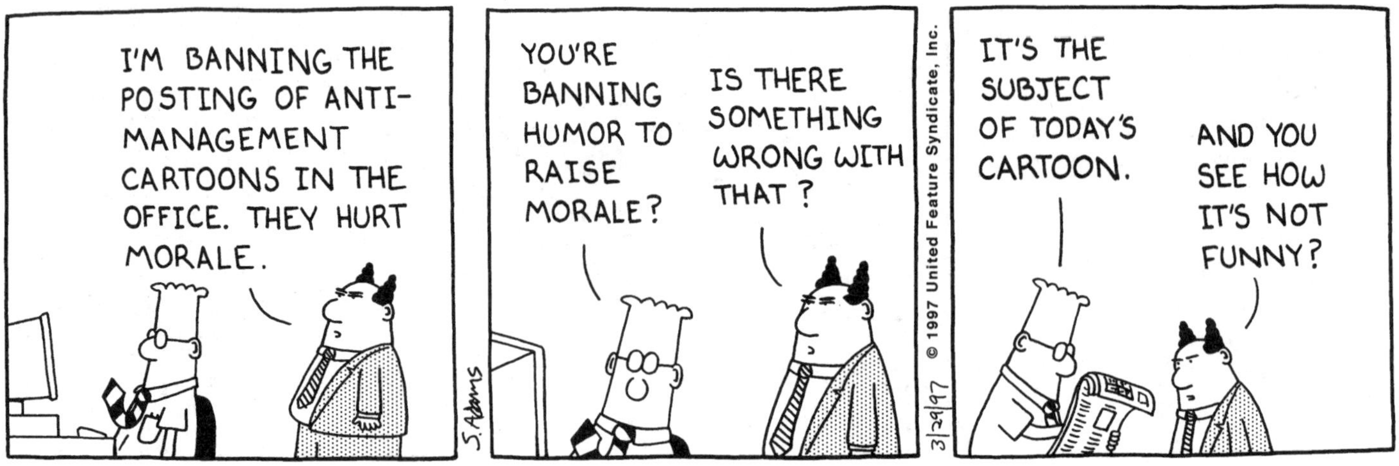
I'M BANNING THE POSTING OF ANTI-MANAGEMENT CARTOONS IN THE OFFICE. THEY HURT MORALE.
S. Adams
YOU'RE BANNING HUMOR TO RAISE MORALE?
IS THERE SOMETHING WRONG WITH THAT?
3/29/97 © 1997 United Feature Syndicate, Inc.
IT'S THE SUBJECT OF TODAY'S CARTOON.
AND YOU SEE HOW IT'S NOT FUNNY?

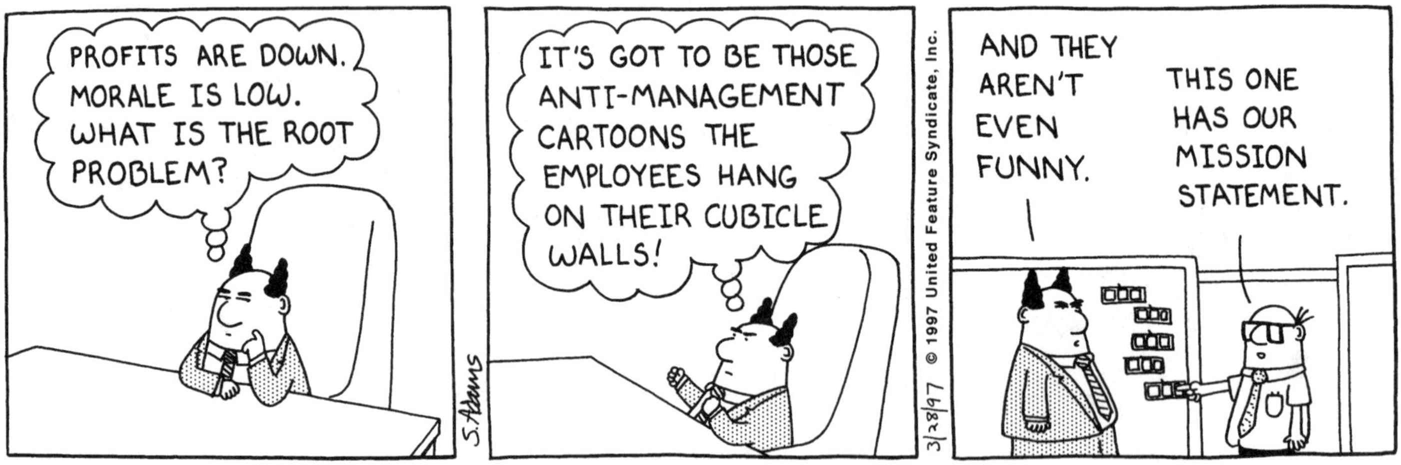
PROFITS ARE DOWN. MORALE IS LOW. WHAT IS THE ROOT PROBLEM?
S. Adams
IT'S GOT TO BE THOSE ANTI-MANAGEMENT CARTOONS THE EMPLOYEES HANG ON THEIR CUBICLE WALLS!
3/28/97 © 1997 United Feature Syndicate, Inc.
AND THEY AREN'T EVEN FUNNY.
THIS ONE HAS OUR MISSION STATEMENT.

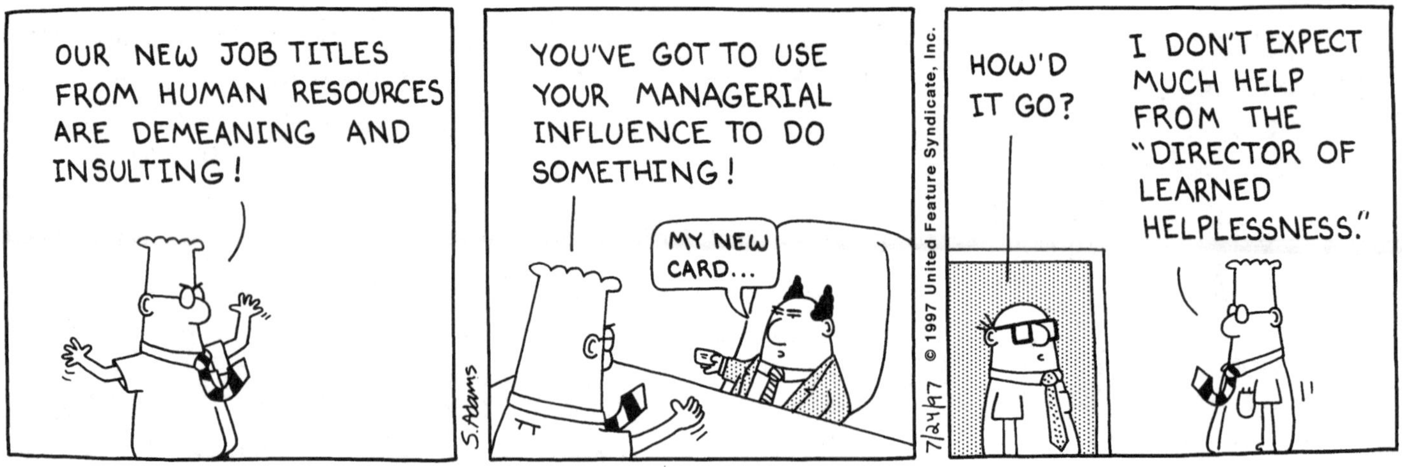
OUR NEW JOB TITLES FROM HUMAN RESOURCES ARE DEMEANING AND INSULTING!
S. Adams
YOU'VE GOT TO USE YOUR MANAGERIAL INFLUENCE TO DO SOMETHING!
MY NEW CARD...
7/24/97 © 1997 United Feature Syndicate, Inc.
HOW'D IT GO?
I DON'T EXPECT MUCH HELP FROM THE "DIRECTOR OF LEARNED HELPLESSNESS."

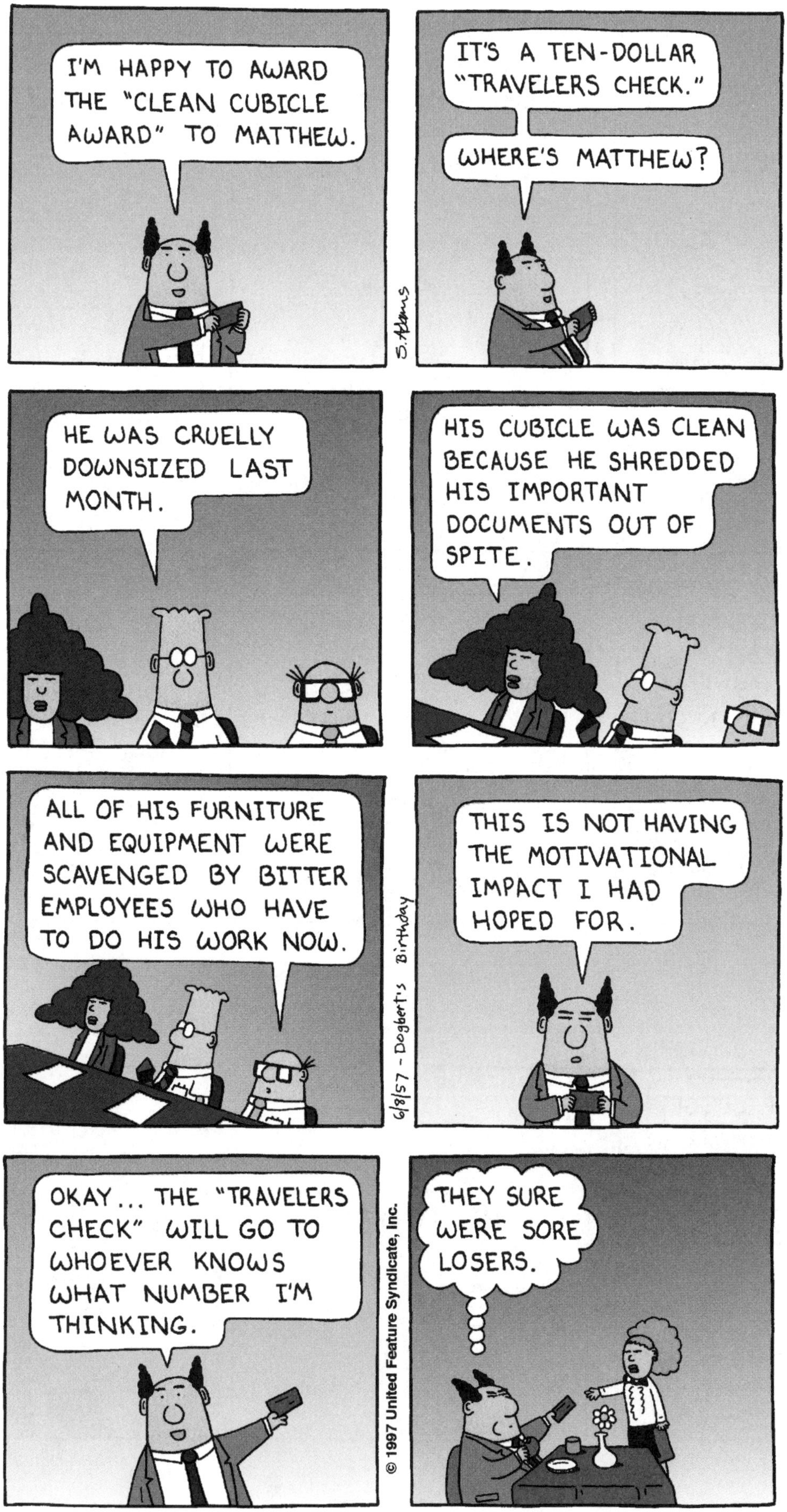
I'M HAPPY TO AWARD THE "CLEAN CUBICLE AWARD" TO MATTHEW.
IT'S A TEN-DOLLAR "TRAVELERS CHECK."
WHERE'S MATTHEW?
HE WAS CRUELLY DOWNSIZED LAST MONTH.
HIS CUBICLE WAS CLEAN BECAUSE HE SHREDDED HIS IMPORTANT DOCUMENTS OUT OF SPITE.
ALL OF HIS FURNITURE AND EQUIPMENT WERE SCAVENGED BY BITTER EMPLOYEES WHO HAVE TO DO HIS WORK NOW.
6/8/57 - Dogbert's Birthday
THIS IS NOT HAVING THE MOTIVATIONAL IMPACT I HAD HOPED FOR.
OKAY... THE "TRAVELERS CHECK" WILL GO TO WHOEVER KNOWS WHAT NUMBER I'M THINKING.
THEY SURE WERE SORE LOSERS.

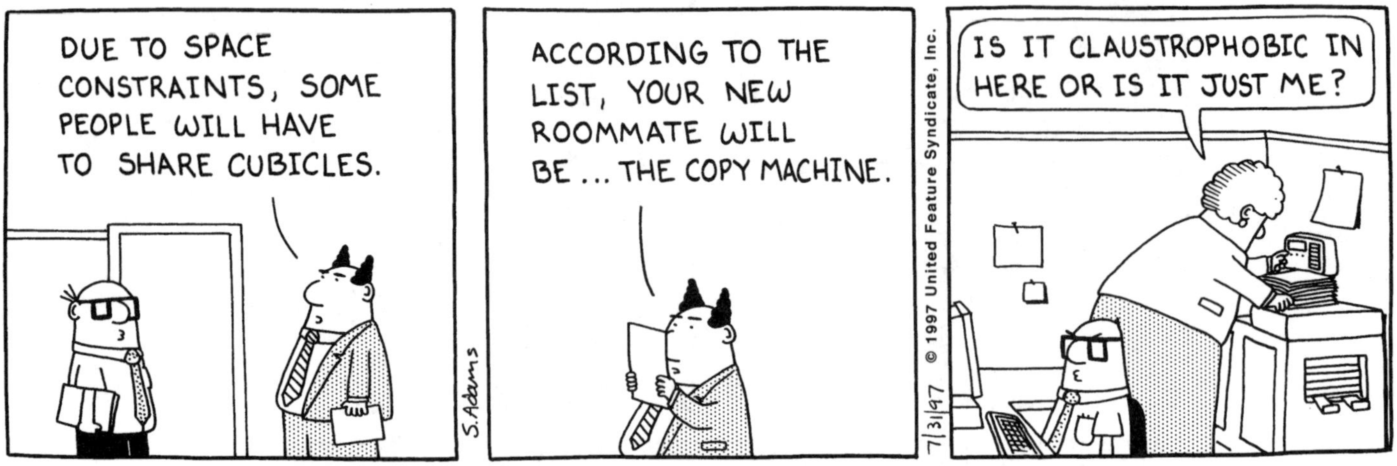
DUE TO SPACE CONSTRAINTS, SOME PEOPLE WILL HAVE TO SHARE CUBICLES.
ACCORDING TO THE LIST, YOUR NEW ROOMMATE WILL BE ... THE COPY MACHINE.
IS IT CLAUSTROPHOBIC IN HERE OR IS IT JUST ME?
S. Adams
7/31/97 © 1997 United Feature Syndicate, Inc.

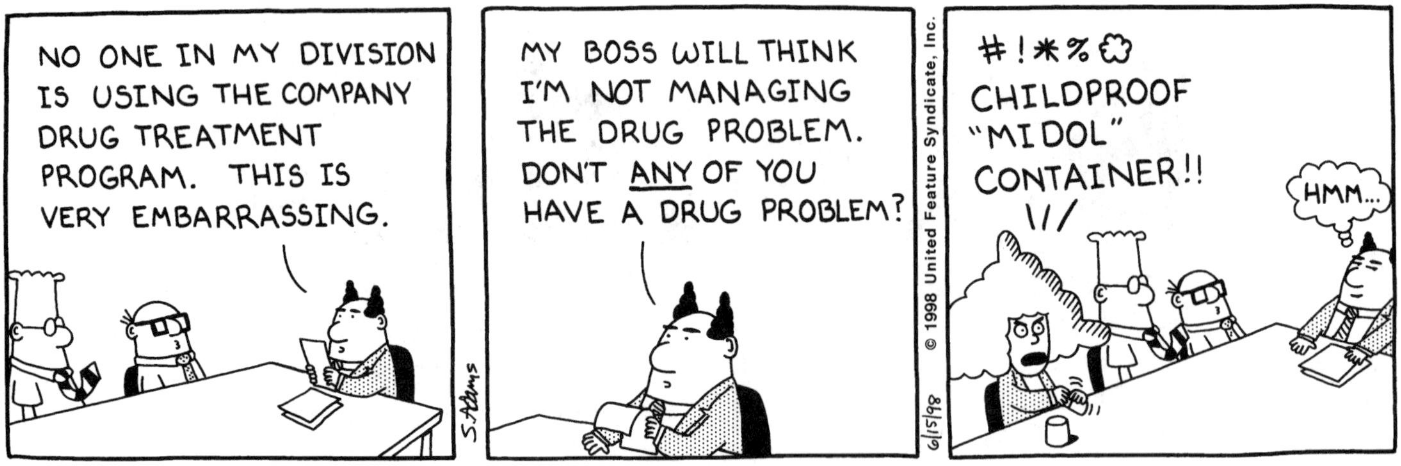
NO ONE IN MY DIVISION IS USING THE COMPANY DRUG TREATMENT PROGRAM. THIS IS VERY EMBARRASSING.
MY BOSS WILL THINK I'M NOT MANAGING THE DRUG PROBLEM. DON'T ANY OF YOU HAVE A DRUG PROBLEM?
#!*%
CHILDPROOF "MIDOL" CONTAINER!!
HMM...
S. Adams
6/15/98 © 1998 United Feature Syndicate, Inc.

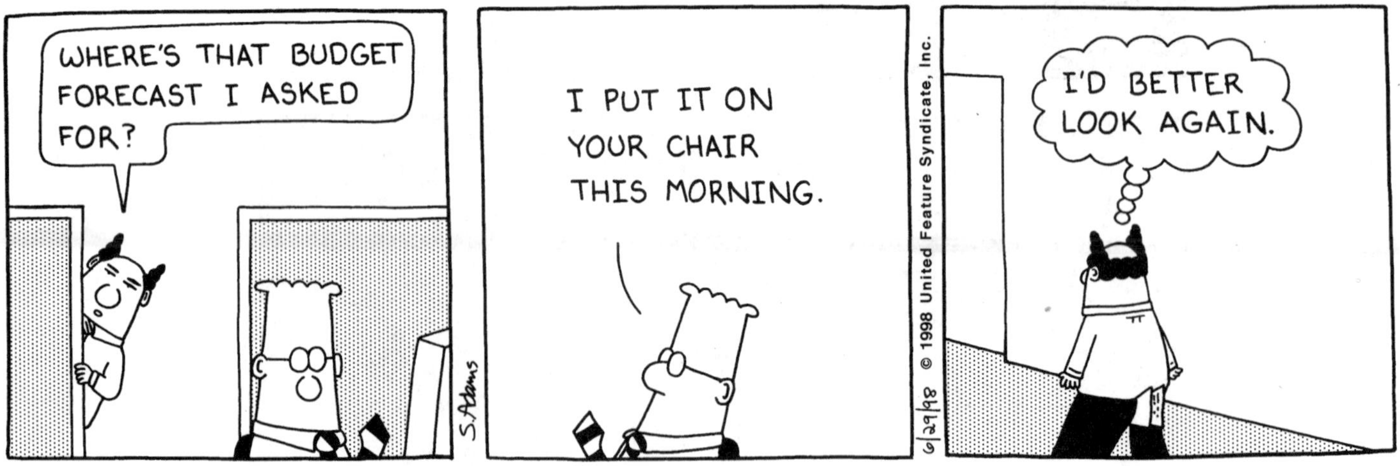
WHERE'S THAT BUDGET FORECAST I ASKED FOR?
I PUT IT ON YOUR CHAIR THIS MORNING.
I'D BETTER LOOK AGAIN.
S. Adams
6/29/98 © 1998 United Feature Syndicate, Inc.

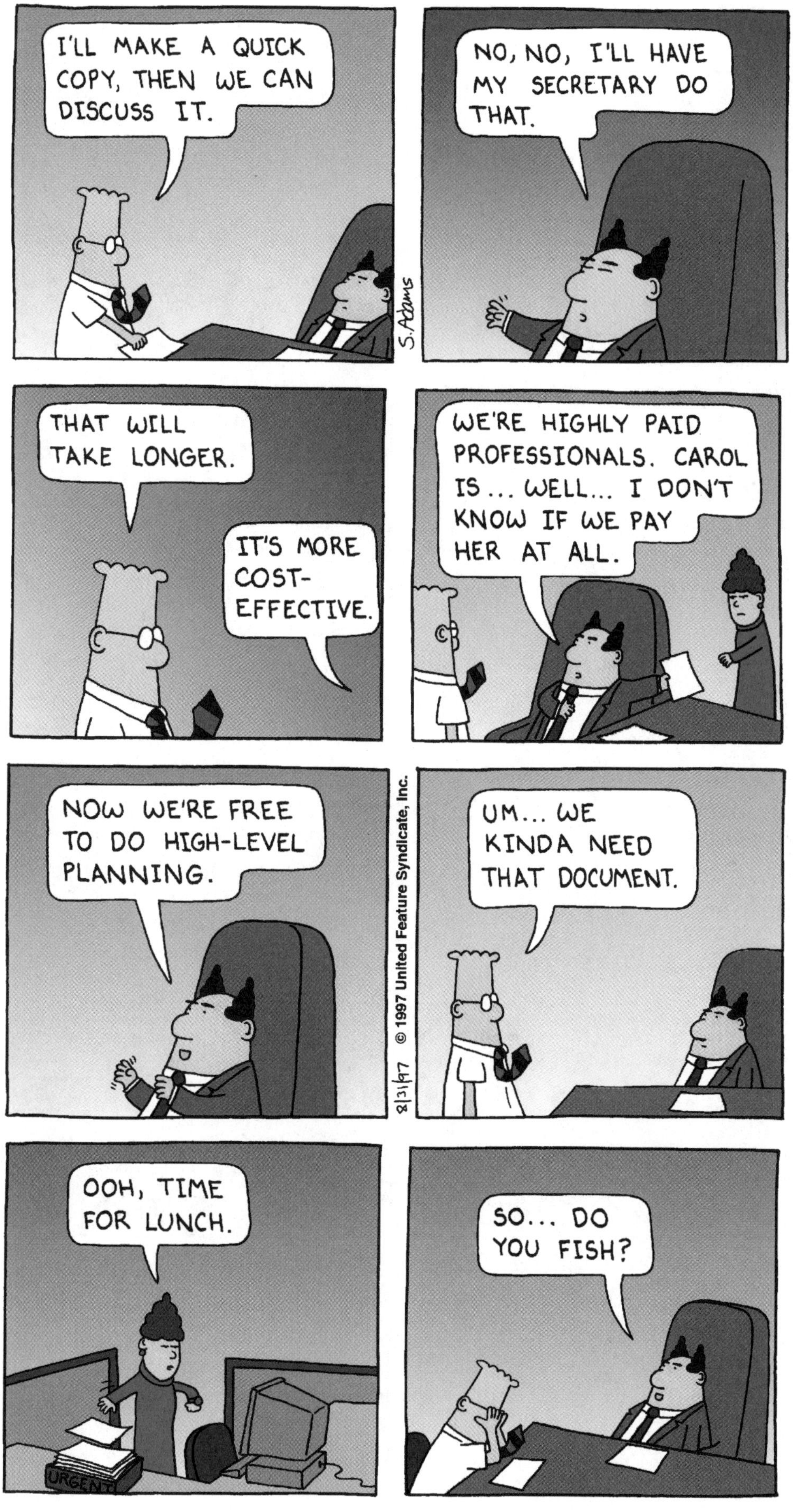
I'LL MAKE A QUICK COPY, THEN WE CAN DISCUSS IT.
S. Adams
NO, NO, I'LL HAVE MY SECRETARY DO THAT.
THAT WILL TAKE LONGER.
IT'S MORE COST-EFFECTIVE.
WE'RE HIGHLY PAID PROFESSIONALS. CAROL IS ... WELL... I DON'T KNOW IF WE PAY HER AT ALL.
NOW WE'RE FREE TO DO HIGH-LEVEL PLANNING.
8/31/97 © 1997 United Feature Syndicate, Inc.
UM... WE KINDA NEED THAT DOCUMENT.
OOH, TIME FOR LUNCH.
URGENT
SO... DO YOU FISH?

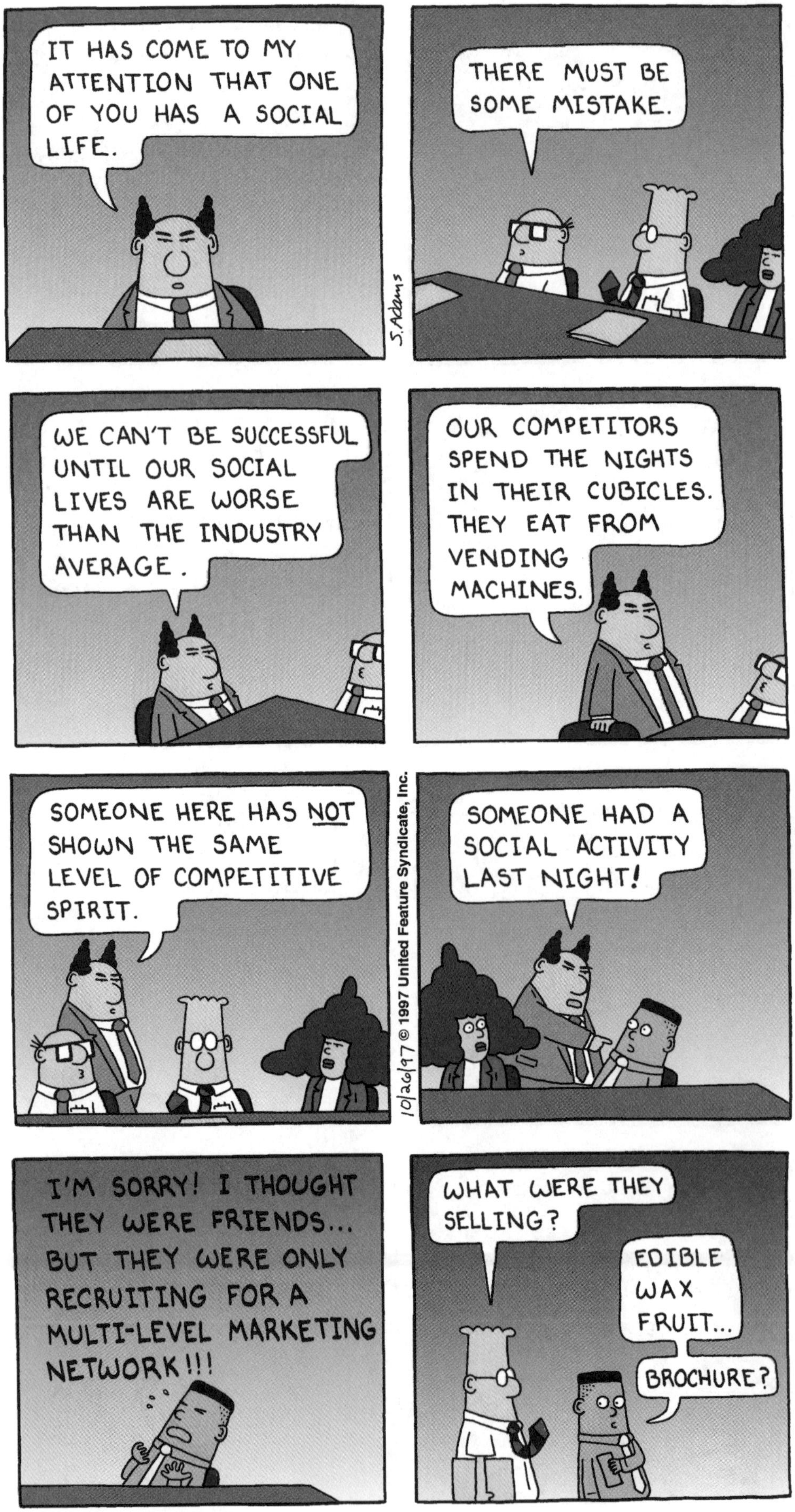
IT HAS COME TO MY ATTENTION THAT ONE OF YOU HAS A SOCIAL LIFE.
THERE MUST BE SOME MISTAKE.
S. Adams
WE CAN'T BE SUCCESSFUL UNTIL OUR SOCIAL LIVES ARE WORSE THAN THE INDUSTRY AVERAGE.
OUR COMPETITORS SPEND THE NIGHTS IN THEIR CUBICLES. THEY EAT FROM VENDING MACHINES.
SOMEONE HERE HAS NOT SHOWN THE SAME LEVEL OF COMPETITIVE SPIRIT.
10/26/97 © 1997 United Feature Syndicate, Inc.
SOMEONE HAD A SOCIAL ACTIVITY LAST NIGHT!
I'M SORRY! I THOUGHT THEY WERE FRIENDS... BUT THEY WERE ONLY RECRUITING FOR A MULTI-LEVEL MARKETING NETWORK!!!
WHAT WERE THEY SELLING?
EDIBLE WAX FRUIT...
BROCHURE?

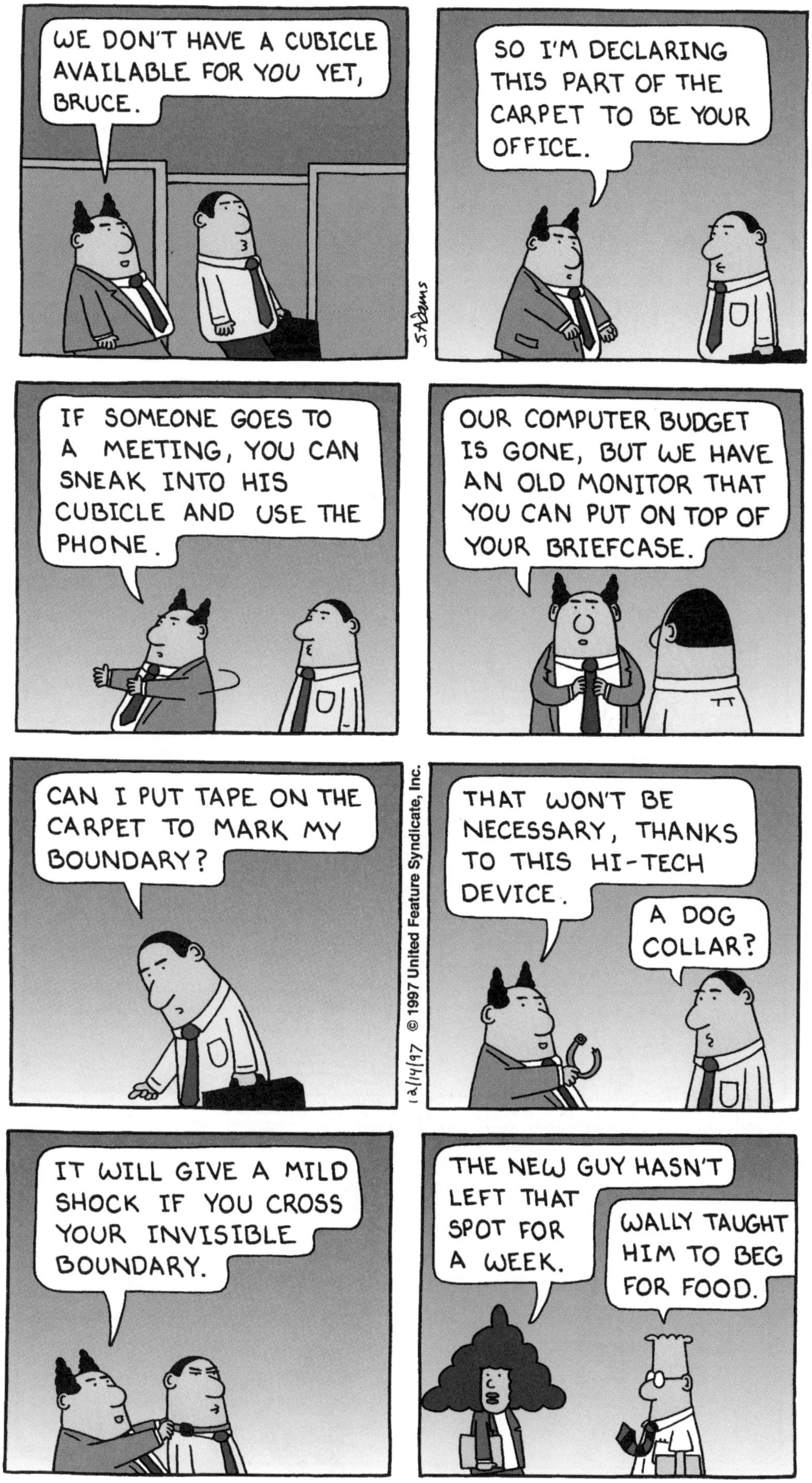
WE DON'T HAVE A CUBICLE AVAILABLE FOR YOU YET, BRUCE.
SO I'M DECLARING THIS PART OF THE CARPET TO BE YOUR OFFICE.
IF SOMEONE GOES TO A MEETING, YOU CAN SNEAK INTO HIS CUBICLE AND USE THE PHONE.
OUR COMPUTER BUDGET IS GONE, BUT WE HAVE AN OLD MONITOR THAT YOU CAN PUT ON TOP OF YOUR BRIEFCASE.
CAN I PUT TAPE ON THE CARPET TO MARK MY BOUNDARY?
THAT WON'T BE NECESSARY, THANKS TO THIS HI-TECH DEVICE.
A DOG COLLAR?
IT WILL GIVE A MILD SHOCK IF YOU CROSS YOUR INVISIBLE BOUNDARY.
THE NEW GUY HASN'T LEFT THAT SPOT FOR A WEEK.
WALLY TAUGHT HIM TO BEG FOR FOOD.
12/14/97 © 1997 United Feature Syndicate, Inc.

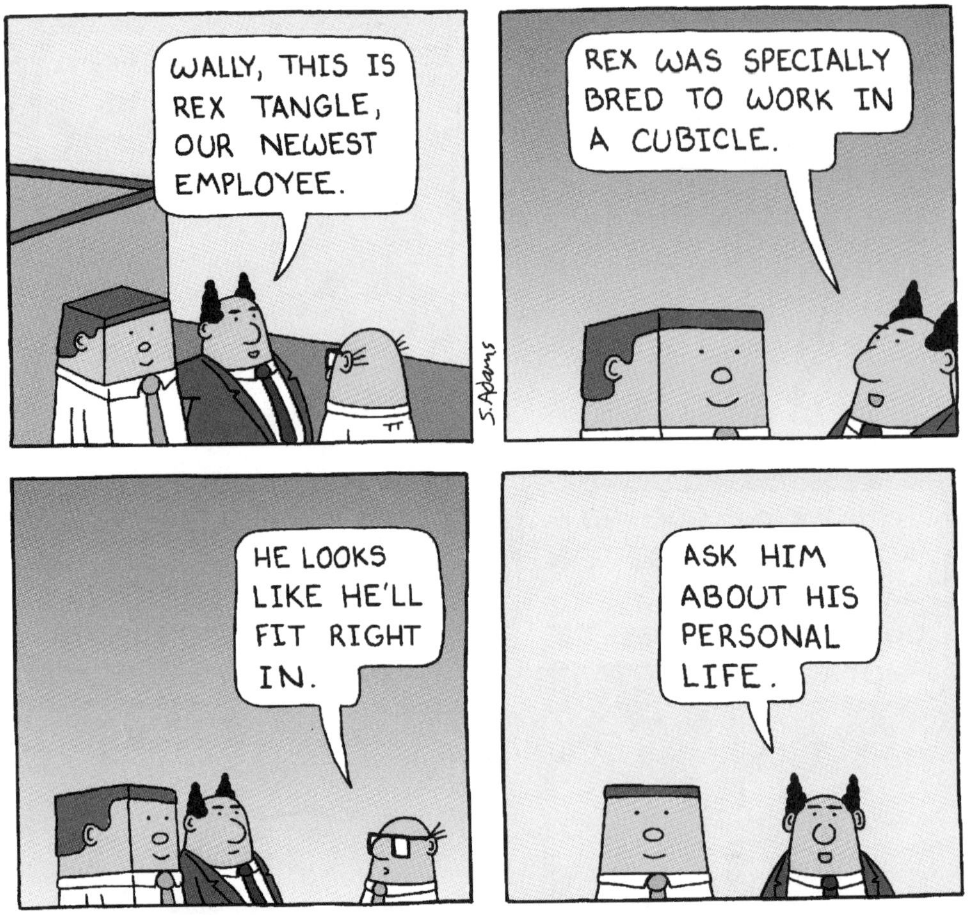
WALLY, THIS IS REX TANGLE, OUR NEWEST EMPLOYEE.
REX WAS SPECIALLY BRED TO WORK IN A CUBICLE.
HE LOOKS LIKE HE'LL FIT RIGHT IN.
ASK HIM ABOUT HIS PERSONAL LIFE.
S. Adams

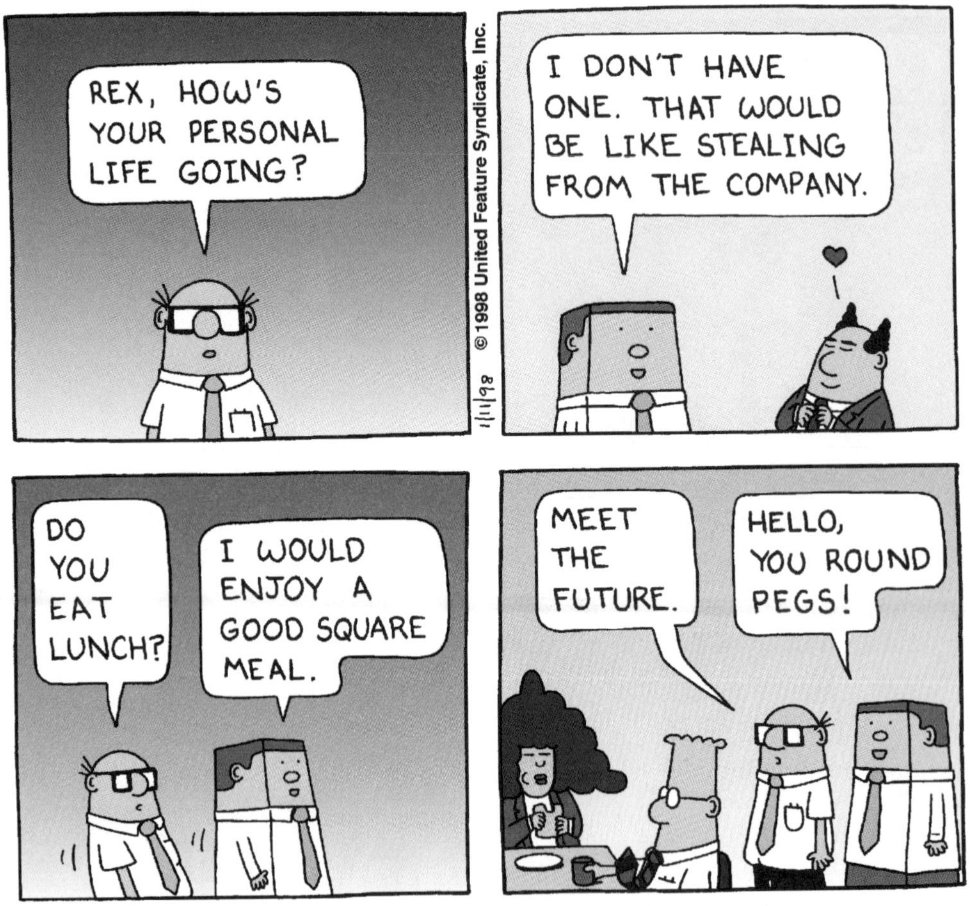
REX, HOW'S YOUR PERSONAL LIFE GOING?
I DON'T HAVE ONE. THAT WOULD BE LIKE STEALING FROM THE COMPANY.
DO YOU EAT LUNCH?
I WOULD ENJOY A GOOD SQUARE MEAL.
MEET THE FUTURE.
HELLO, YOU ROUND PEGS!
1/11/98
© 1998 United Feature Syndicate, Inc.

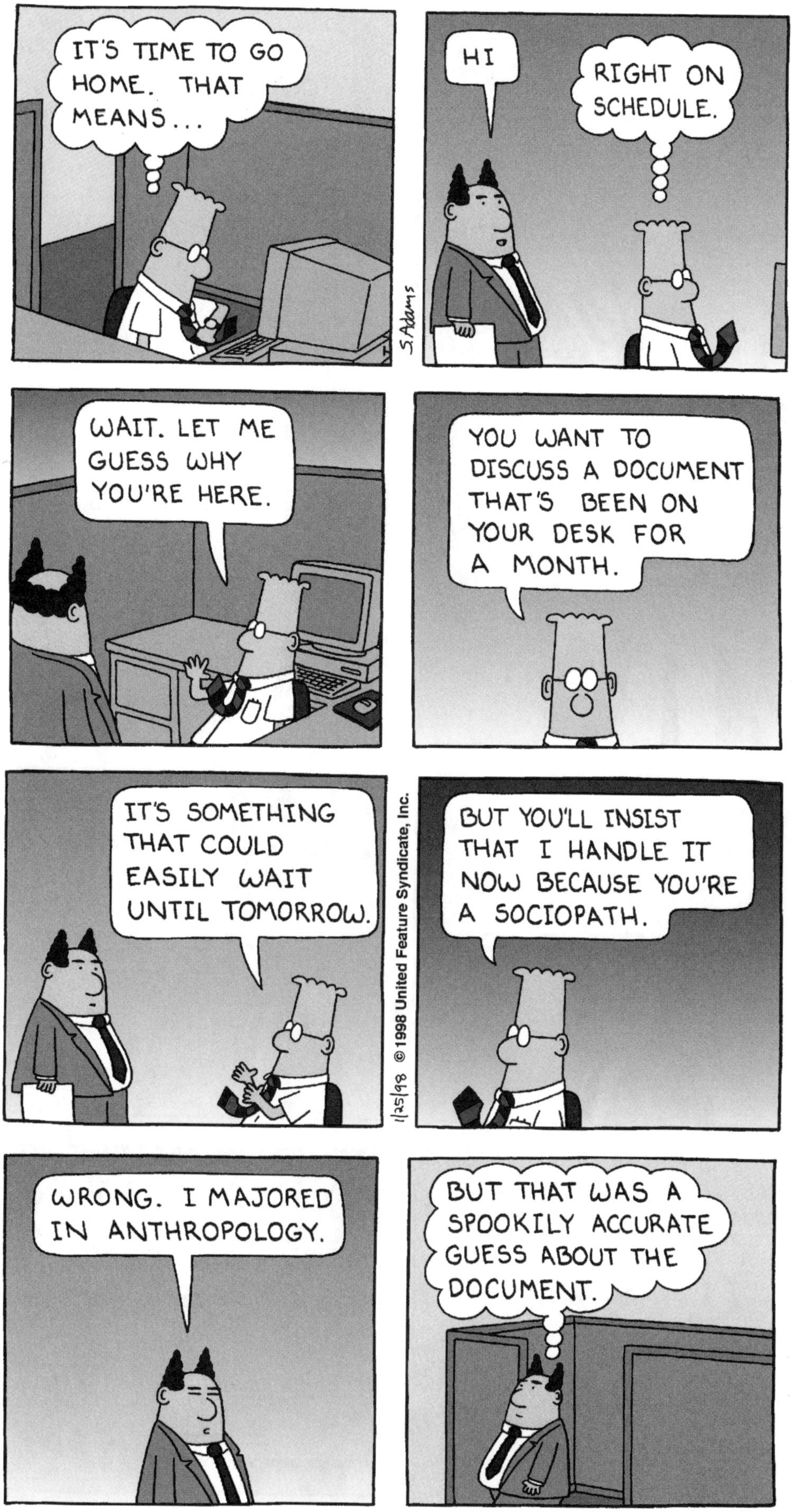
IT'S TIME TO GO HOME. THAT MEANS...
HI
RIGHT ON SCHEDULE.
WAIT. LET ME GUESS WHY YOU'RE HERE.
YOU WANT TO DISCUSS A DOCUMENT THAT'S BEEN ON YOUR DESK FOR A MONTH.
IT'S SOMETHING THAT COULD EASILY WAIT UNTIL TOMORROW.
BUT YOU'LL INSIST THAT I HANDLE IT NOW BECAUSE YOU'RE A SOCIOPATH.
WRONG. I MAJORED IN ANTHROPOLOGY.
BUT THAT WAS A SPOOKILY ACCURATE GUESS ABOUT THE DOCUMENT.
S. Adams
1/25/98 © 1998 United Feature Syndicate, Inc.

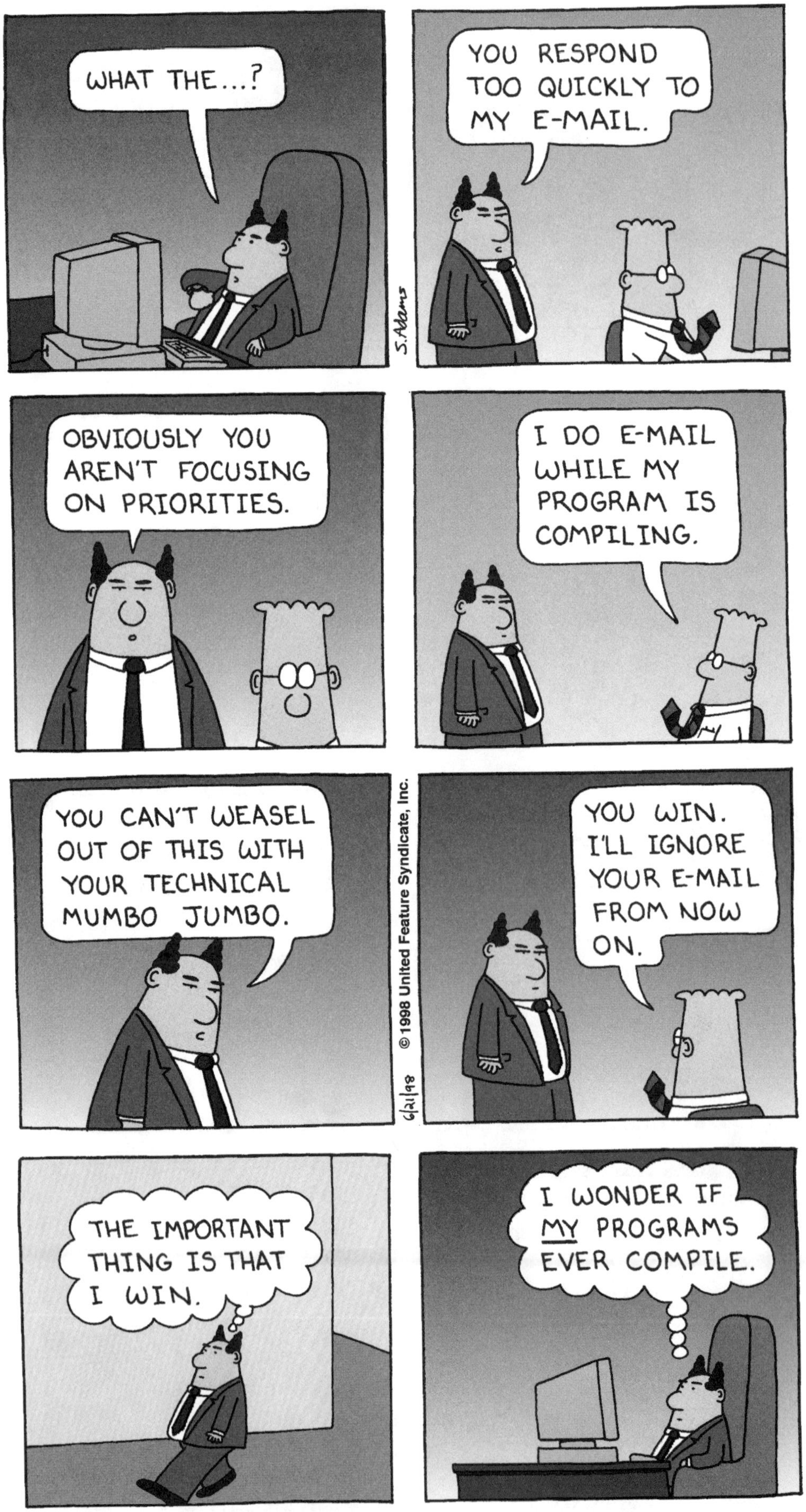
WHAT THE...?
S. Adams
YOU RESPOND TOO QUICKLY TO MY E-MAIL.
OBVIOUSLY YOU AREN'T FOCUSING ON PRIORITIES.
I DO E-MAIL WHILE MY PROGRAM IS COMPILING.
YOU CAN'T WEASEL OUT OF THIS WITH YOUR TECHNICAL MUMBO JUMBO.
6/21/98 © 1998 United Feature Syndicate, Inc.
YOU WIN. I'LL IGNORE YOUR E-MAIL FROM NOW ON.
THE IMPORTANT THING IS THAT I WIN.
I WONDER IF MY PROGRAMS EVER COMPILE.

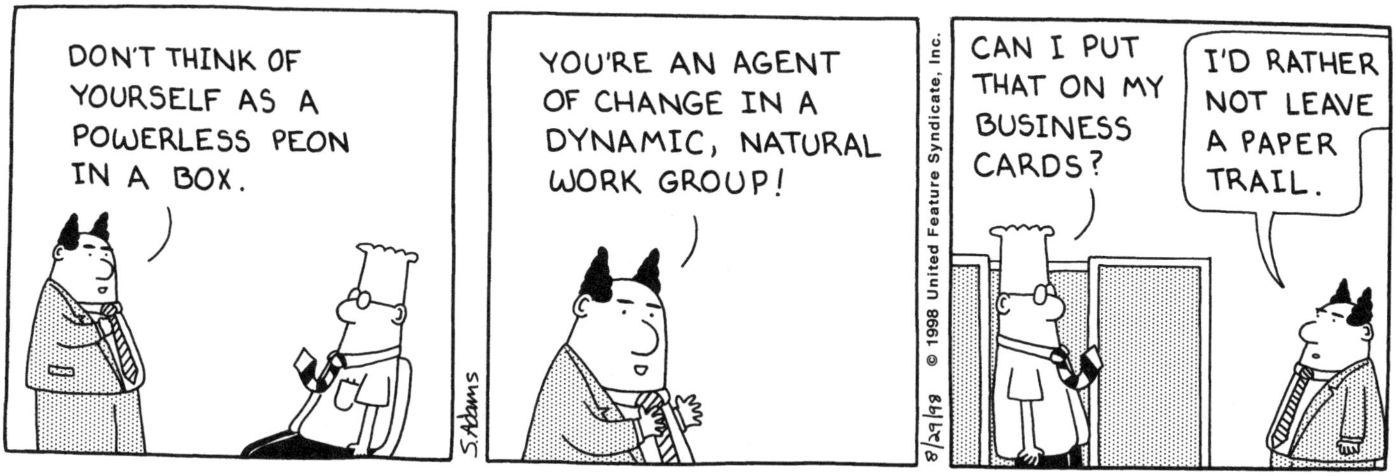
DON'T THINK OF YOURSELF AS A POWERLESS PEON IN A BOX.
YOU'RE AN AGENT OF CHANGE IN A DYNAMIC, NATURAL WORK GROUP!
CAN I PUT THAT ON MY BUSINESS CARDS?
I'D RATHER NOT LEAVE A PAPER TRAIL.
S. Adams
8/29/98 © 1998 United Feature Syndicate, Inc.

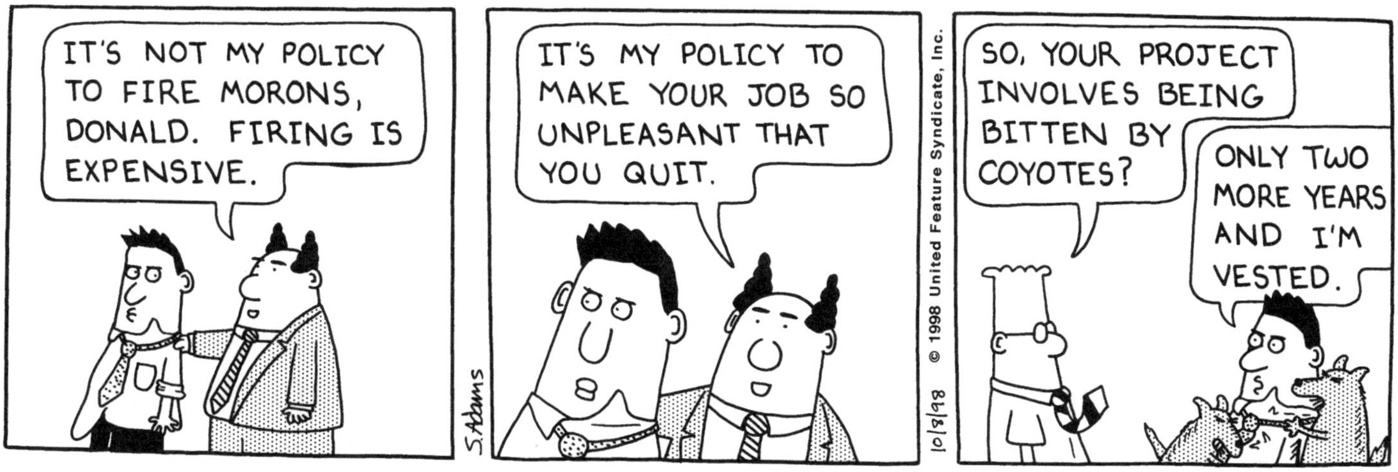
IT'S NOT MY POLICY TO FIRE MORONS, DONALD. FIRING IS EXPENSIVE.
IT'S MY POLICY TO MAKE YOUR JOB SO UNPLEASANT THAT YOU QUIT.
SO, YOUR PROJECT INVOLVES BEING BITTEN BY COYOTES?
ONLY TWO MORE YEARS AND I'M VESTED.
S. Adams
10/8/98 © 1998 United Feature Syndicate, Inc.

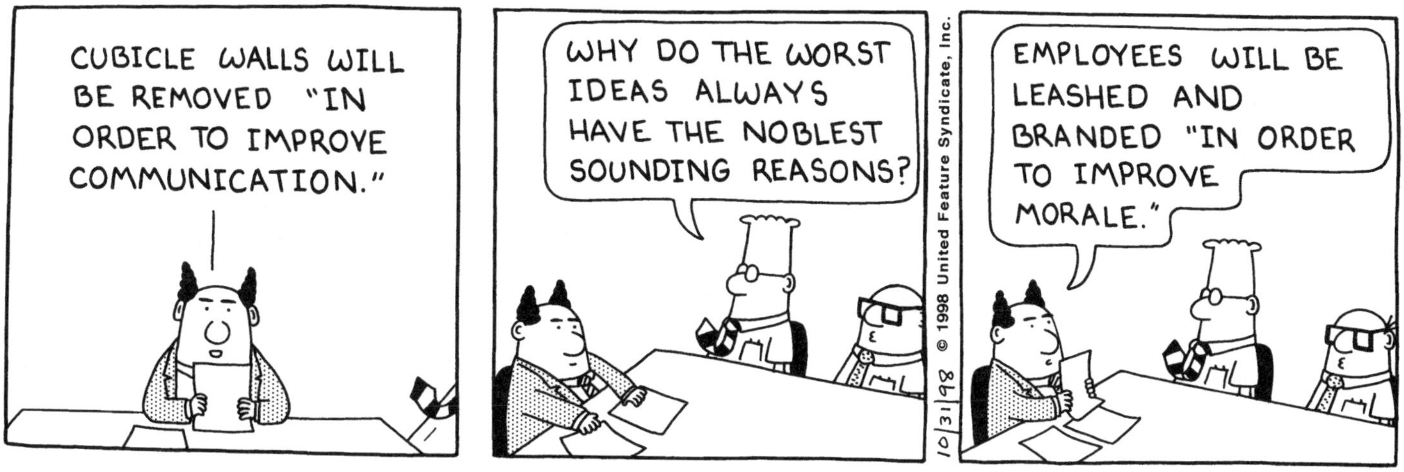
CUBICLE WALLS WILL BE REMOVED "IN ORDER TO IMPROVE COMMUNICATION."
WHY DO THE WORST IDEAS ALWAYS HAVE THE NOBLEST SOUNDING REASONS?
EMPLOYEES WILL BE LEASHED AND BRANDED "IN ORDER TO IMPROVE MORALE."
10/31/98 © 1998 United Feature Syndicate, Inc.

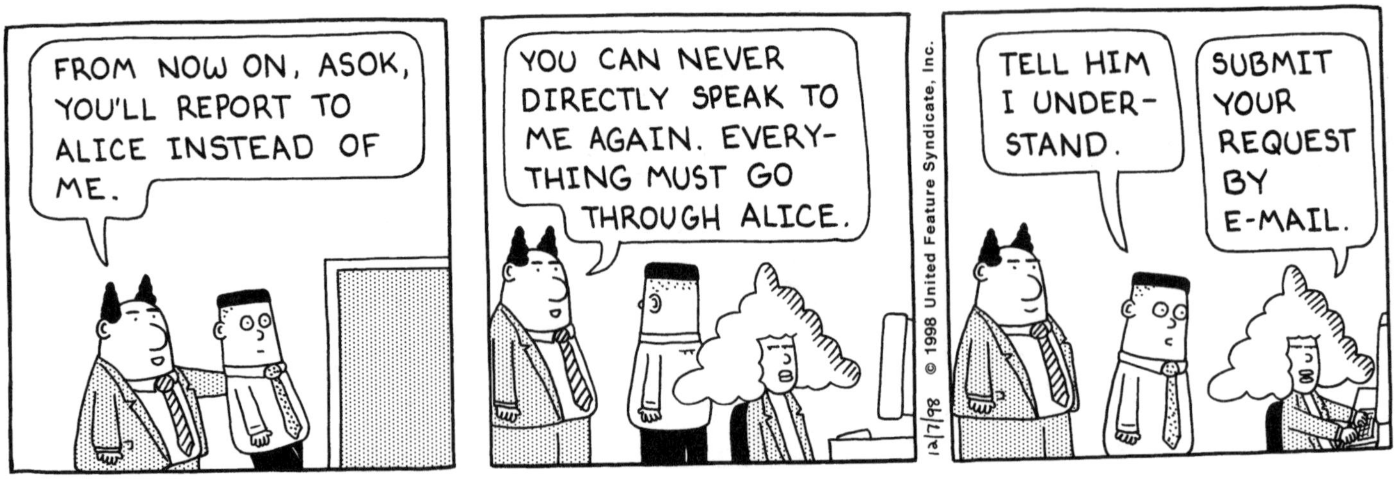
FROM NOW ON, ASOK, YOU'LL REPORT TO ALICE INSTEAD OF ME.
YOU CAN NEVER DIRECTLY SPEAK TO ME AGAIN. EVERYTHING MUST GO THROUGH ALICE.
TELL HIM I UNDERSTAND.
SUBMIT YOUR REQUEST BY E-MAIL.
12/7/98 © 1998 United Feature Syndicate, Inc.

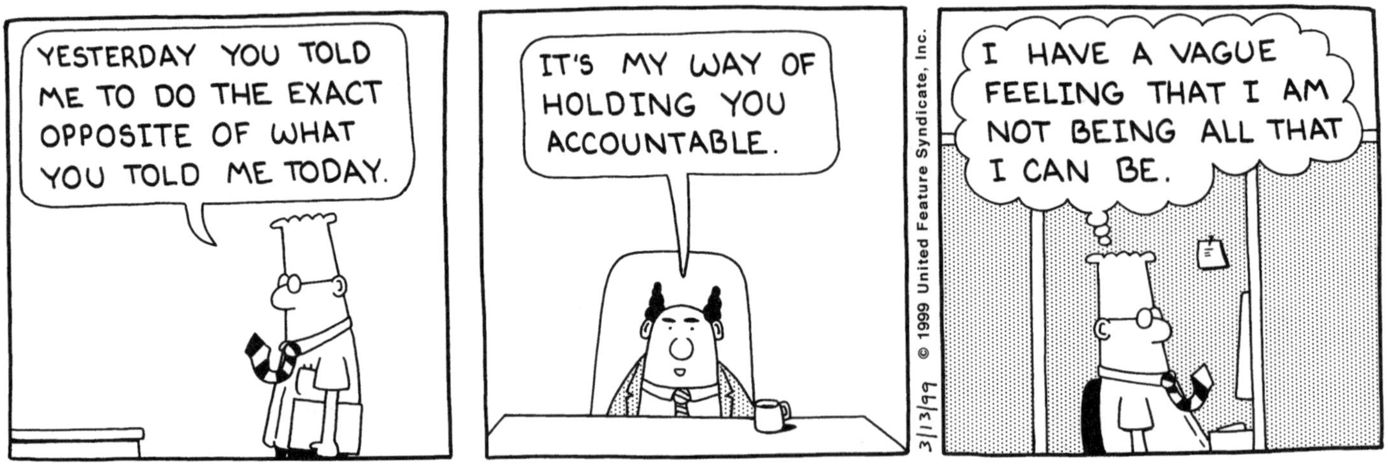
YESTERDAY YOU TOLD ME TO DO THE EXACT OPPOSITE OF WHAT YOU TOLD ME TODAY.
IT'S MY WAY OF HOLDING YOU ACCOUNTABLE.
I HAVE A VAGUE FEELING THAT I AM NOT BEING ALL THAT I CAN BE.
3/13/99 © 1999 United Feature Syndicate, Inc.

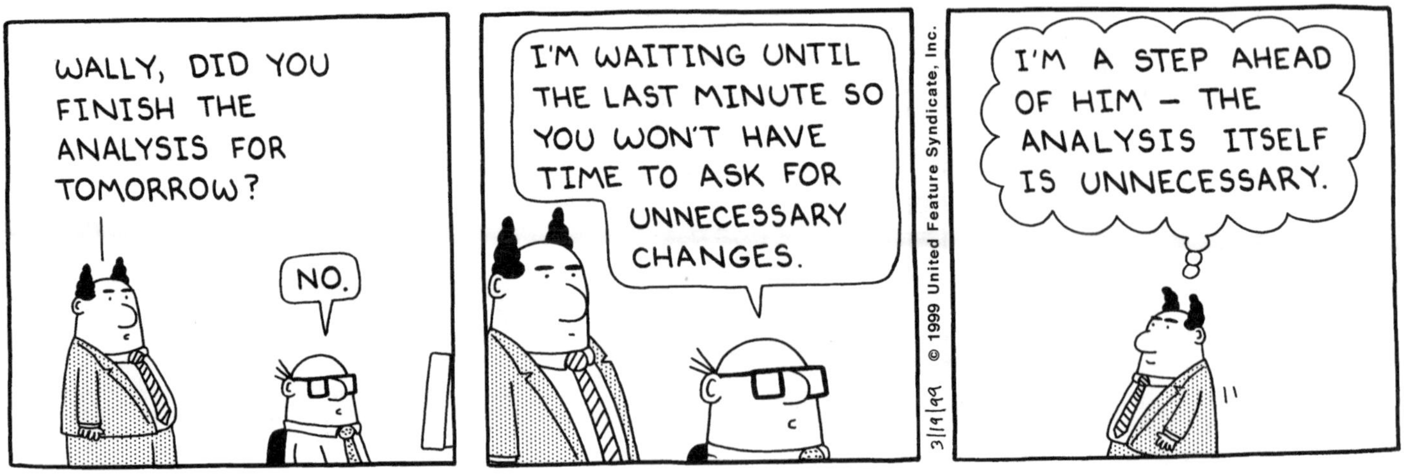
WALLY, DID YOU FINISH THE ANALYSIS FOR TOMORROW?
NO.
I'M WAITING UNTIL THE LAST MINUTE SO YOU WON'T HAVE TIME TO ASK FOR UNNECESSARY CHANGES.
I'M A STEP AHEAD OF HIM – THE ANALYSIS ITSELF IS UNNECESSARY.
3/19/99 © 1999 United Feature Syndicate, Inc.

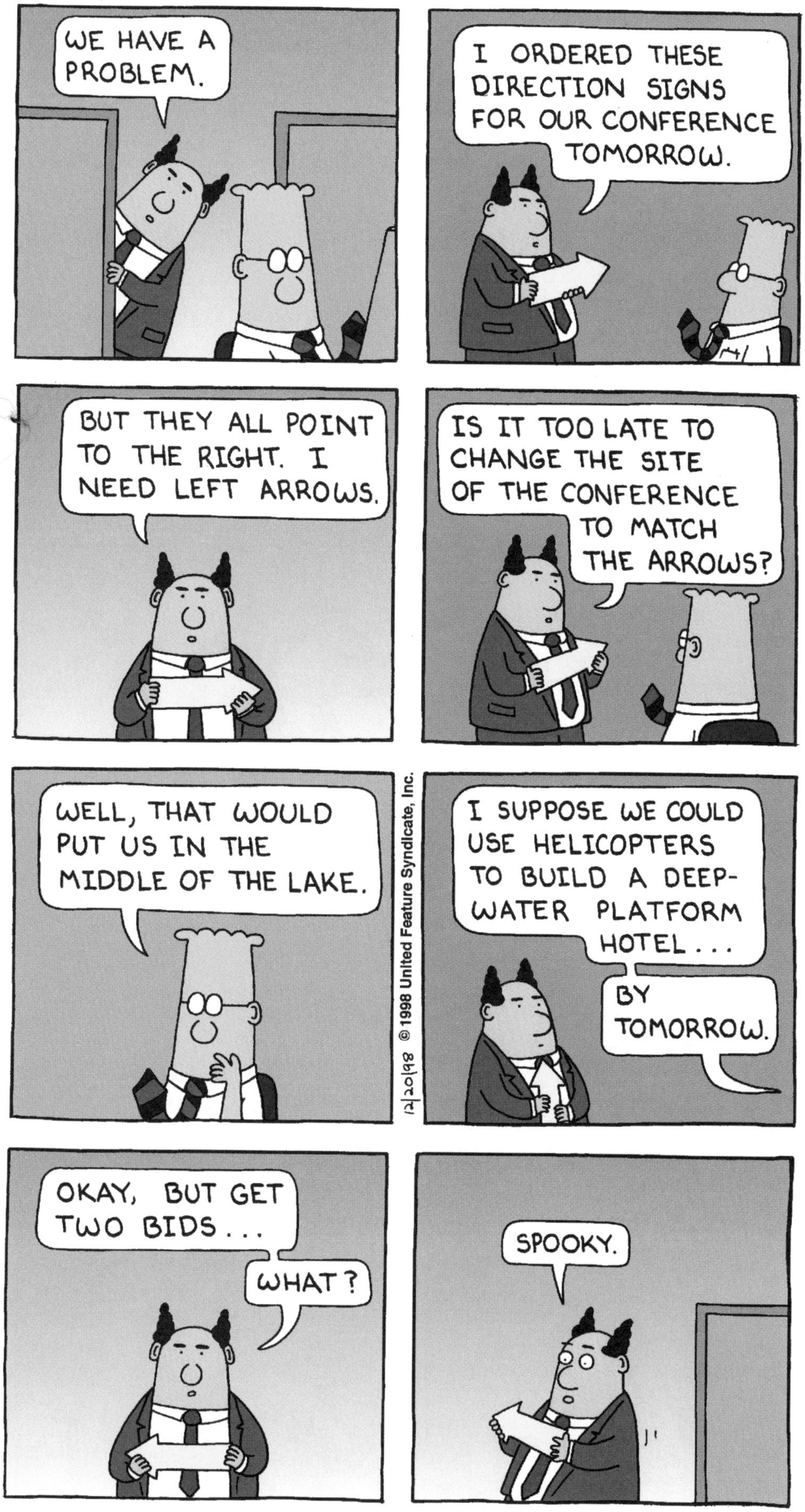
WE HAVE A PROBLEM.
I ORDERED THESE DIRECTION SIGNS FOR OUR CONFERENCE TOMORROW.
BUT THEY ALL POINT TO THE RIGHT. I NEED LEFT ARROWS.
IS IT TOO LATE TO CHANGE THE SITE OF THE CONFERENCE TO MATCH THE ARROWS?
WELL, THAT WOULD PUT US IN THE MIDDLE OF THE LAKE.
12/20/98 © 1998 United Feature Syndicate, Inc.
I SUPPOSE WE COULD USE HELICOPTERS TO BUILD A DEEP-WATER PLATFORM HOTEL . . .
BY TOMORROW.
OKAY, BUT GET TWO BIDS . . .
WHAT?
SPOOKY.

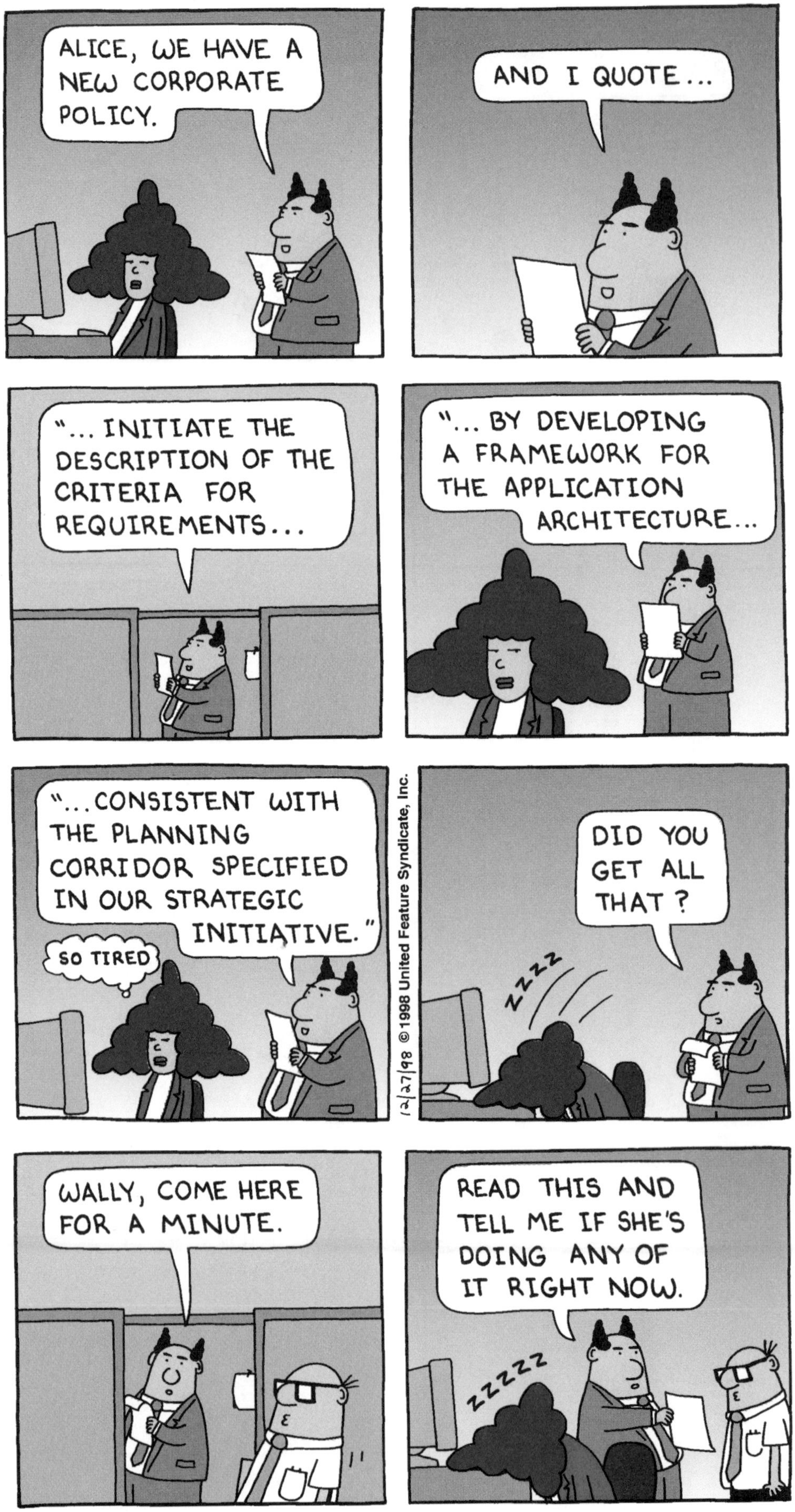
ALICE, WE HAVE A NEW CORPORATE POLICY.
AND I QUOTE...
"... INITIATE THE DESCRIPTION OF THE CRITERIA FOR REQUIREMENTS...
"... BY DEVELOPING A FRAMEWORK FOR THE APPLICATION ARCHITECTURE...
"...CONSISTENT WITH THE PLANNING CORRIDOR SPECIFIED IN OUR STRATEGIC INITIATIVE."
SO TIRED
12/27/98 ©1998 United Feature Syndicate, Inc.
DID YOU GET ALL THAT?
ZZZZ
WALLY, COME HERE FOR A MINUTE.
READ THIS AND TELL ME IF SHE'S DOING ANY OF IT RIGHT NOW.
ZZZZZ

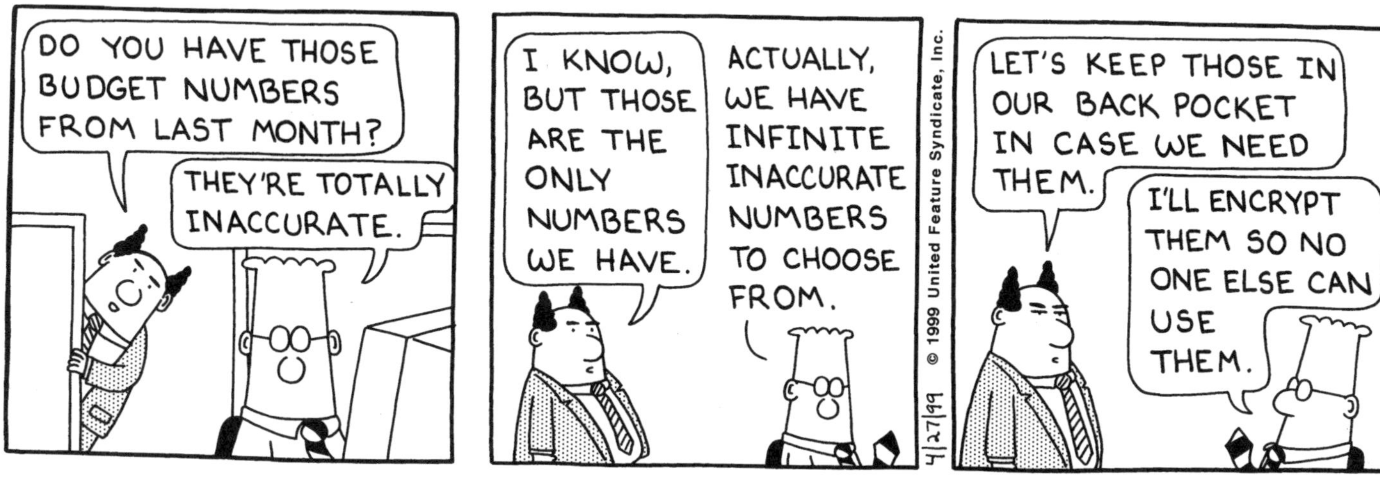
DO YOU HAVE THOSE BUDGET NUMBERS FROM LAST MONTH?
THEY'RE TOTALLY INACCURATE.
I KNOW, BUT THOSE ARE THE ONLY NUMBERS WE HAVE.
ACTUALLY, WE HAVE INFINITE INACCURATE NUMBERS TO CHOOSE FROM.
© 1999 United Feature Syndicate, Inc.
4/27/99
LET'S KEEP THOSE IN OUR BACK POCKET IN CASE WE NEED THEM.
I'LL ENCRYPT THEM SO NO ONE ELSE CAN USE THEM.

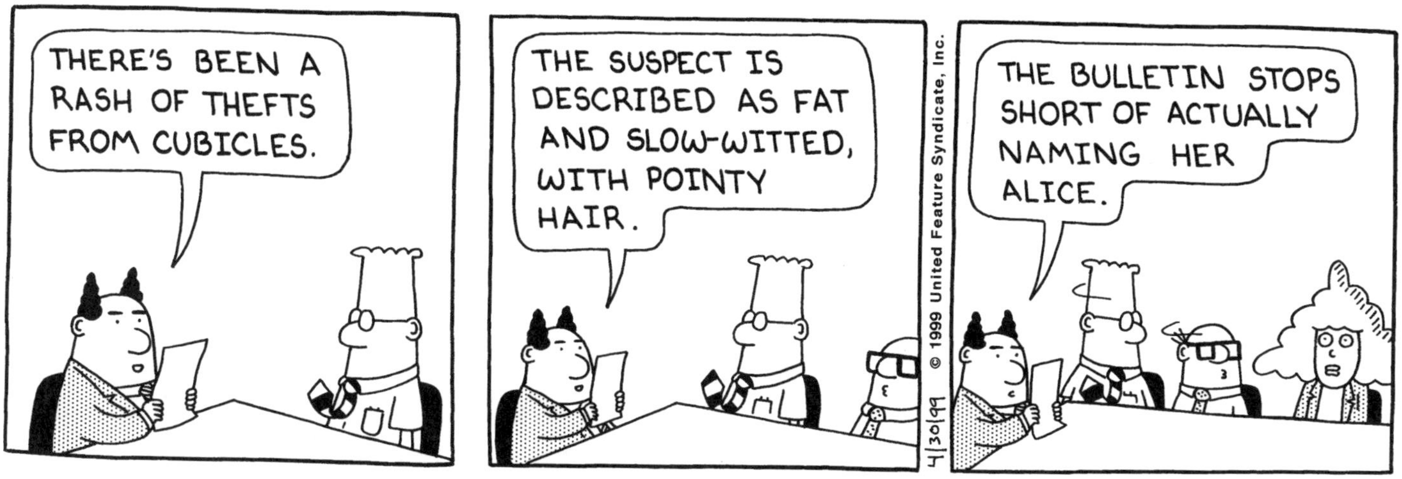
THERE'S BEEN A RASH OF THEFTS FROM CUBICLES.
THE SUSPECT IS DESCRIBED AS FAT AND SLOW-WITTED, WITH POINTY HAIR.
© 1999 United Feature Syndicate, Inc.
4/30/99
THE BULLETIN STOPS SHORT OF ACTUALLY NAMING HER ALICE.

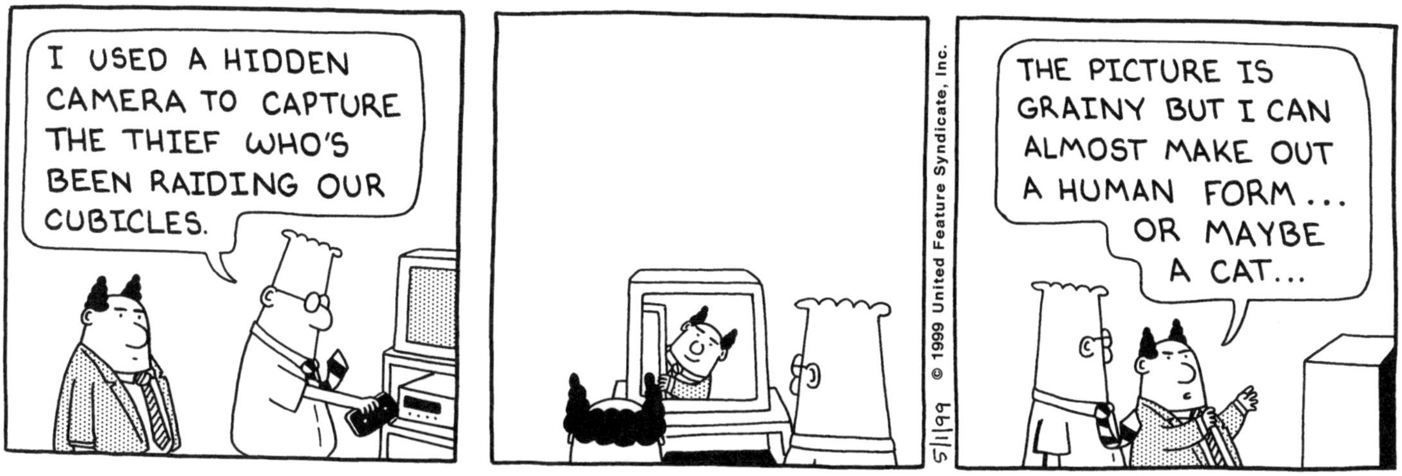
I USED A HIDDEN CAMERA TO CAPTURE THE THIEF WHO'S BEEN RAIDING OUR CUBICLES.
© 1999 United Feature Syndicate, Inc.
5/1/99
THE PICTURE IS GRAINY BUT I CAN ALMOST MAKE OUT A HUMAN FORM... OR MAYBE A CAT...

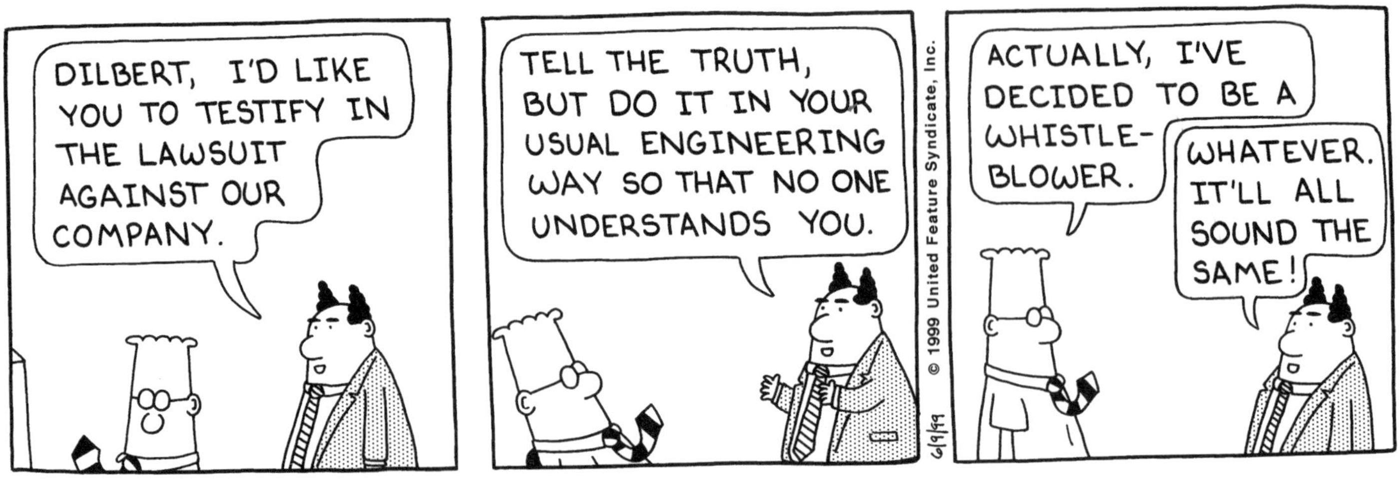
DILBERT, I'D LIKE YOU TO TESTIFY IN THE LAWSUIT AGAINST OUR COMPANY.
TELL THE TRUTH, BUT DO IT IN YOUR USUAL ENGINEERING WAY SO THAT NO ONE UNDERSTANDS YOU.
© 1999 United Feature Syndicate, Inc.
6/9/99
ACTUALLY, I'VE DECIDED TO BE A WHISTLE-BLOWER.
WHATEVER. IT'LL ALL SOUND THE SAME!

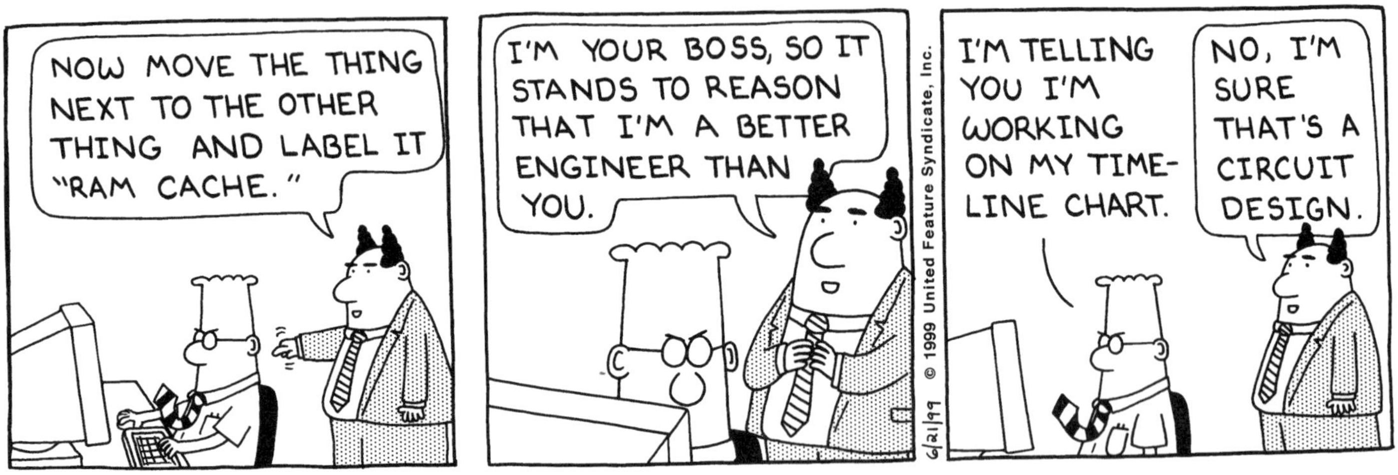
NOW MOVE THE THING NEXT TO THE OTHER THING AND LABEL IT "RAM CACHE."
I'M YOUR BOSS, SO IT STANDS TO REASON THAT I'M A BETTER ENGINEER THAN YOU.
© 1999 United Feature Syndicate, Inc.
6/21/99
I'M TELLING YOU I'M WORKING ON MY TIME-LINE CHART.
NO, I'M SURE THAT'S A CIRCUIT DESIGN.

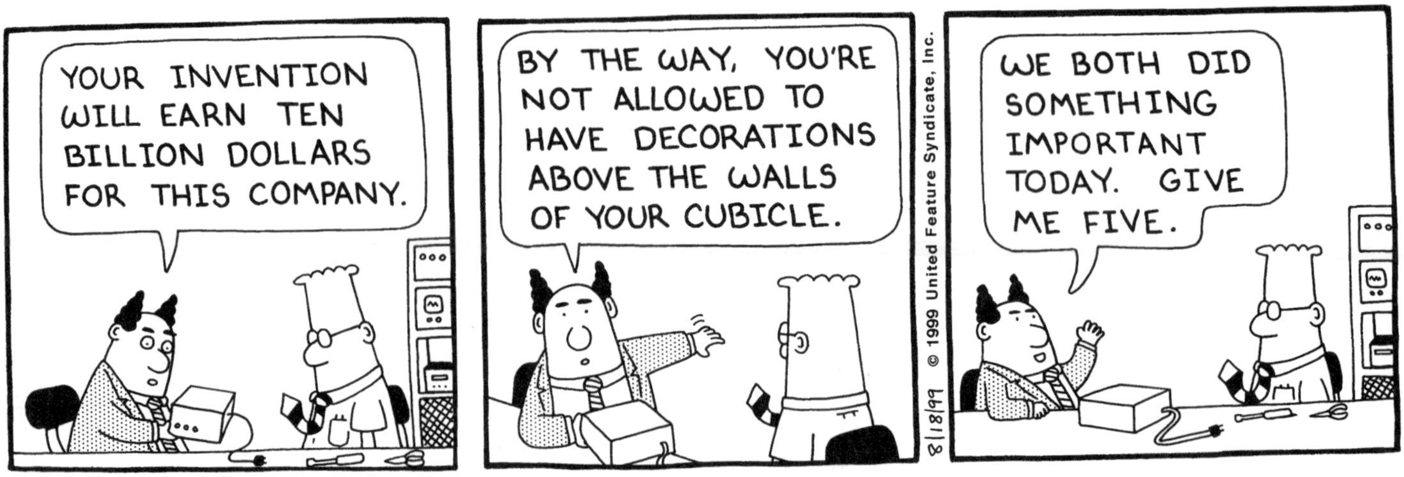
YOUR INVENTION WILL EARN TEN BILLION DOLLARS FOR THIS COMPANY.
BY THE WAY, YOU'RE NOT ALLOWED TO HAVE DECORATIONS ABOVE THE WALLS OF YOUR CUBICLE.
© 1999 United Feature Syndicate, Inc.
8/18/99
WE BOTH DID SOMETHING IMPORTANT TODAY. GIVE ME FIVE.

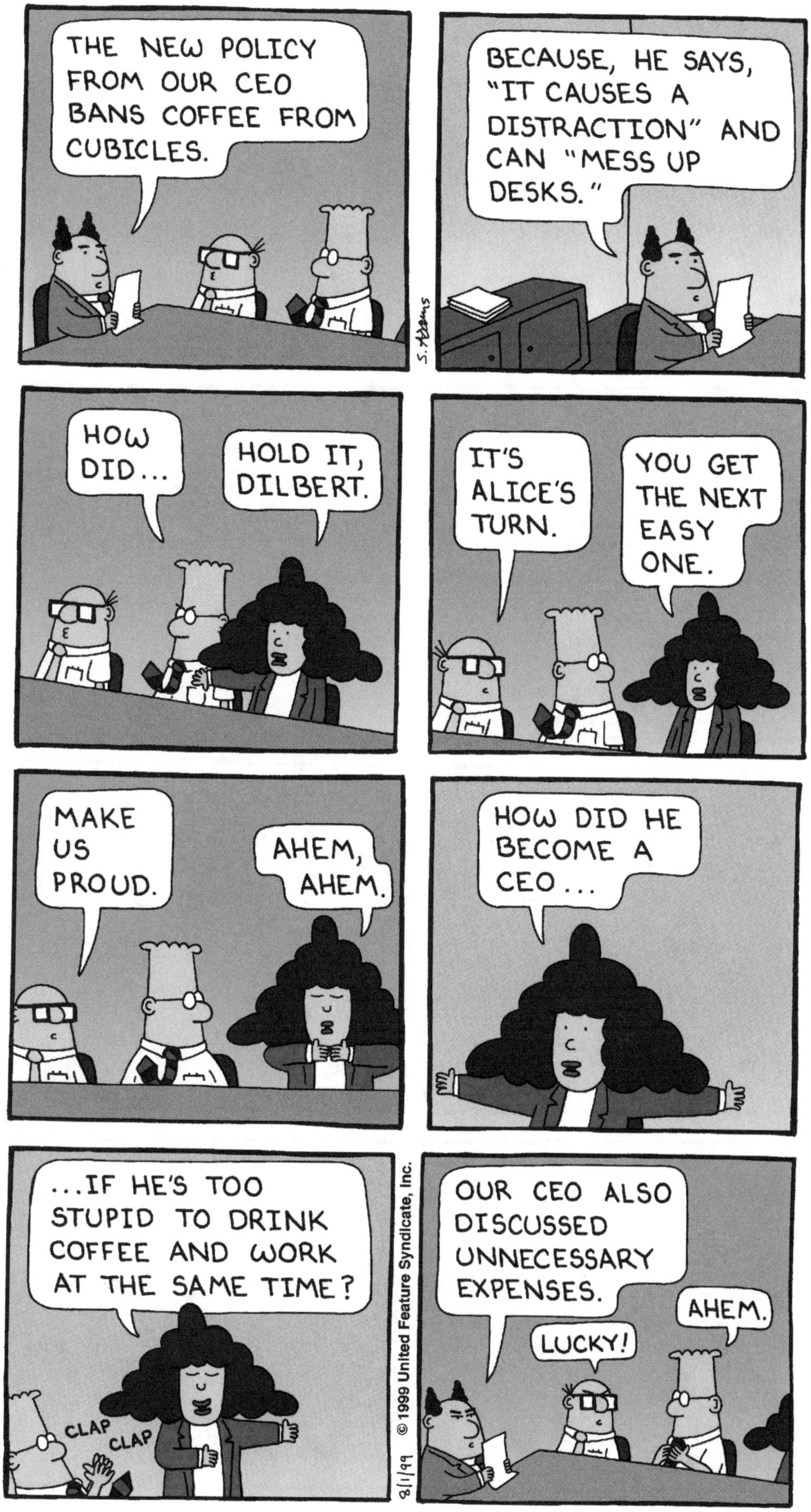
THE NEW POLICY FROM OUR CEO BANS COFFEE FROM CUBICLES.
BECAUSE, HE SAYS, "IT CAUSES A DISTRACTION" AND CAN "MESS UP DESKS."
S. Adams
HOW DID...
HOLD IT, DILBERT.
IT'S ALICE'S TURN.
YOU GET THE NEXT EASY ONE.
MAKE US PROUD.
AHEM, AHEM.
HOW DID HE BECOME A CEO...
...IF HE'S TOO STUPID TO DRINK COFFEE AND WORK AT THE SAME TIME?
CLAP
CLAP
8/1/99 © 1999 United Feature Syndicate, Inc.
OUR CEO ALSO DISCUSSED UNNECESSARY EXPENSES.
LUCKY!
AHEM.

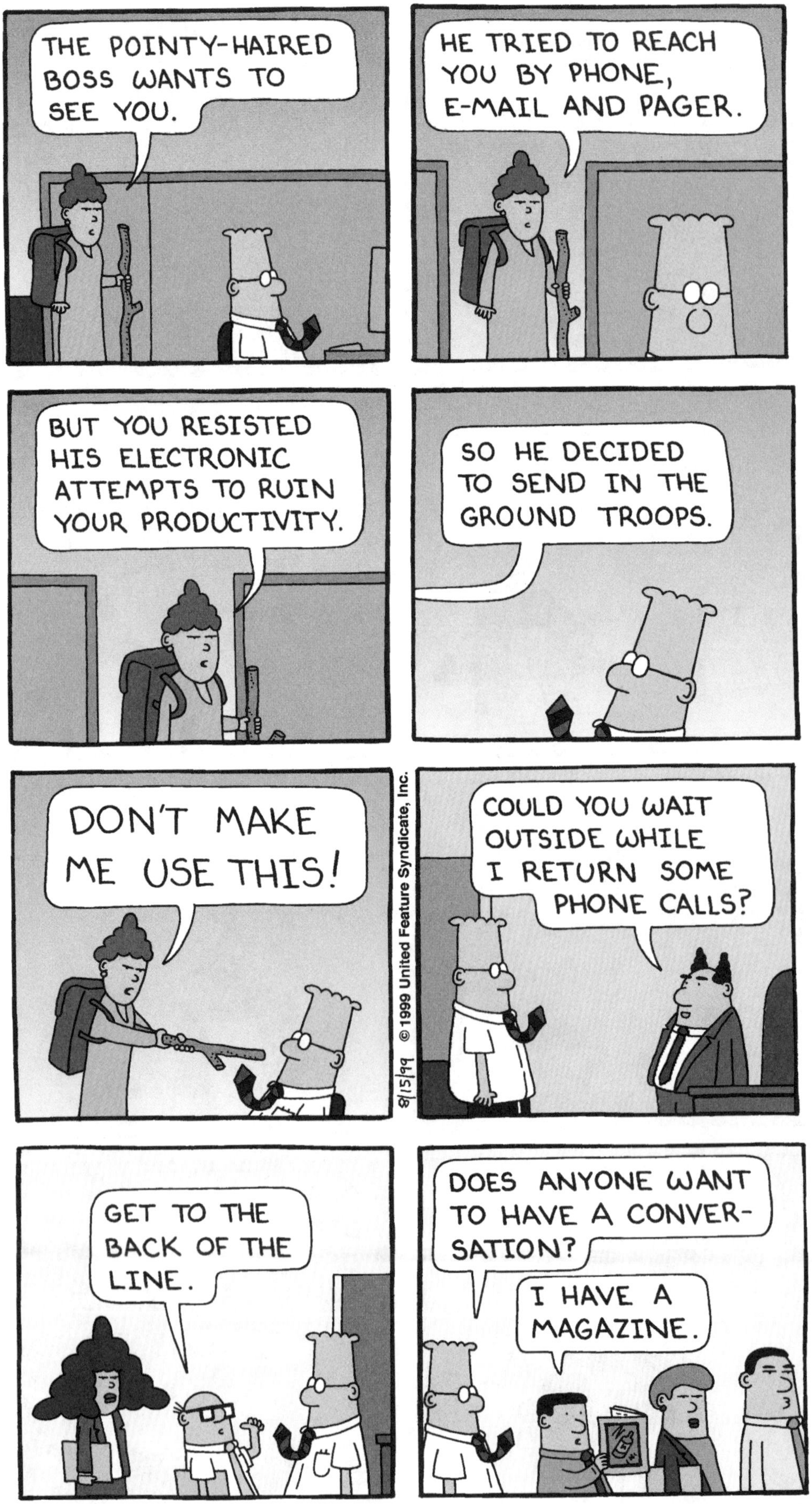
THE POINTY-HAIRED BOSS WANTS TO SEE YOU.
HE TRIED TO REACH YOU BY PHONE, E-MAIL AND PAGER.
BUT YOU RESISTED HIS ELECTRONIC ATTEMPTS TO RUIN YOUR PRODUCTIVITY.
SO HE DECIDED TO SEND IN THE GROUND TROOPS.
DON'T MAKE ME USE THIS!
8/15/99 © 1999 United Feature Syndicate, Inc.
COULD YOU WAIT OUTSIDE WHILE I RETURN SOME PHONE CALLS?
GET TO THE BACK OF THE LINE.
DOES ANYONE WANT TO HAVE A CONVERSATION?
I HAVE A MAGAZINE.

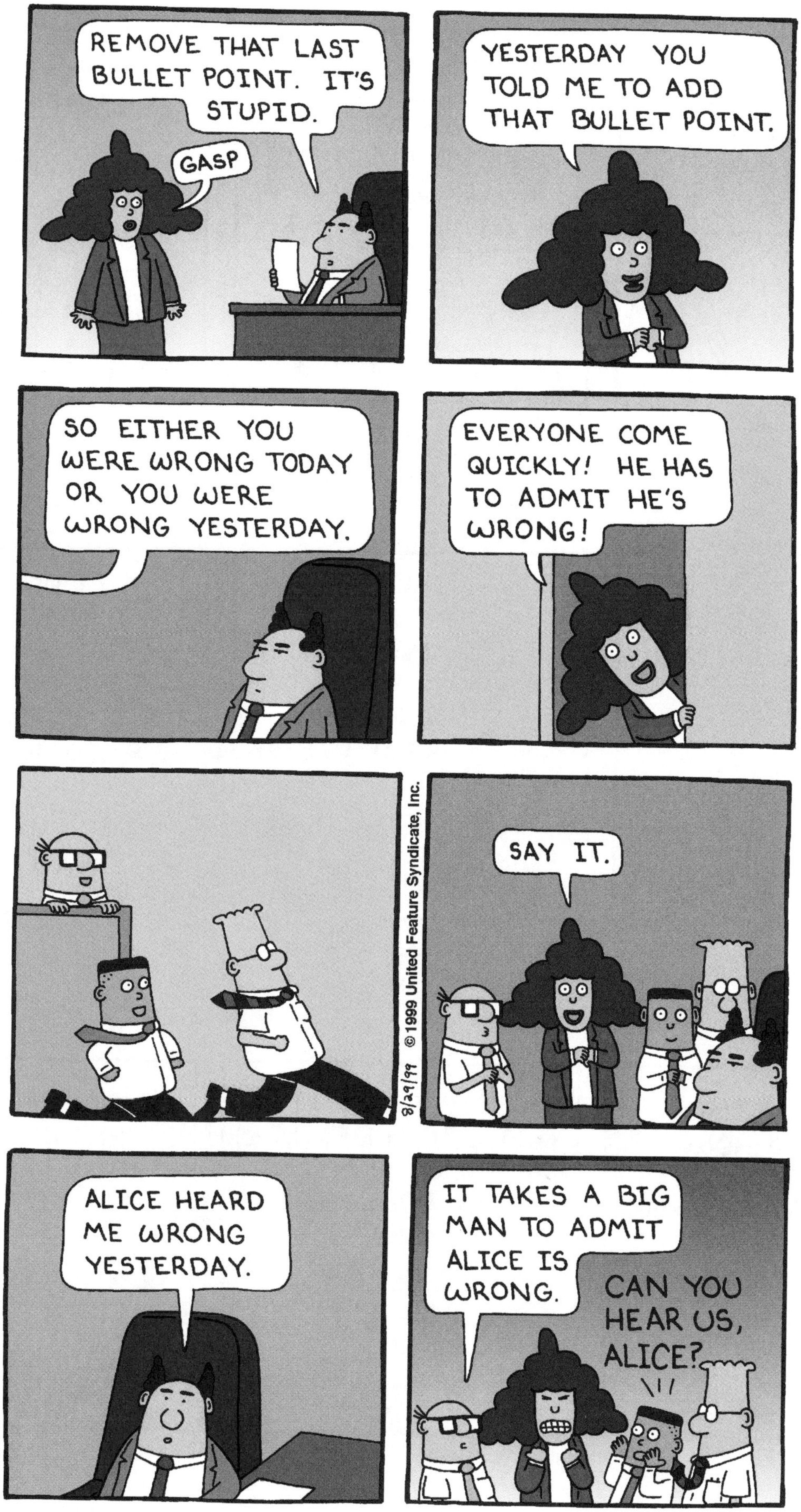
REMOVE THAT LAST BULLET POINT. IT'S STUPID.
GASP
YESTERDAY YOU TOLD ME TO ADD THAT BULLET POINT.
SO EITHER YOU WERE WRONG TODAY OR YOU WERE WRONG YESTERDAY.
EVERYONE COME QUICKLY! HE HAS TO ADMIT HE'S WRONG!
© 1999 United Feature Syndicate, Inc.
8/29/99
SAY IT.
ALICE HEARD ME WRONG YESTERDAY.
IT TAKES A BIG MAN TO ADMIT ALICE IS WRONG.
CAN YOU HEAR US, ALICE?

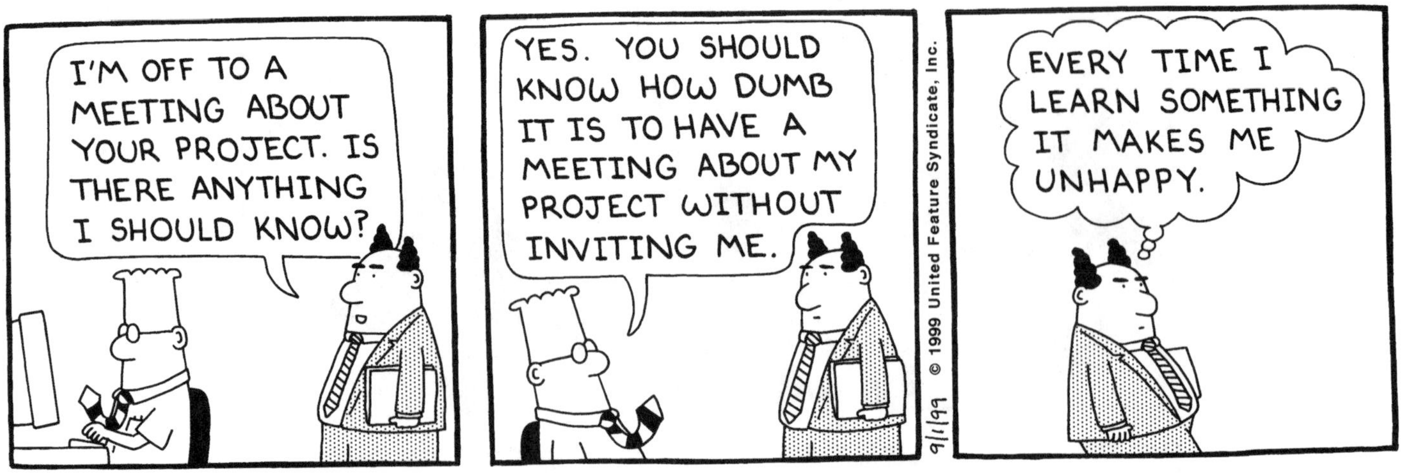
I'M OFF TO A MEETING ABOUT YOUR PROJECT. IS THERE ANYTHING I SHOULD KNOW?
YES. YOU SHOULD KNOW HOW DUMB IT IS TO HAVE A MEETING ABOUT MY PROJECT WITHOUT INVITING ME.
9/1/99 © 1999 United Feature Syndicate, Inc.
EVERY TIME I LEARN SOMETHING IT MAKES ME UNHAPPY.

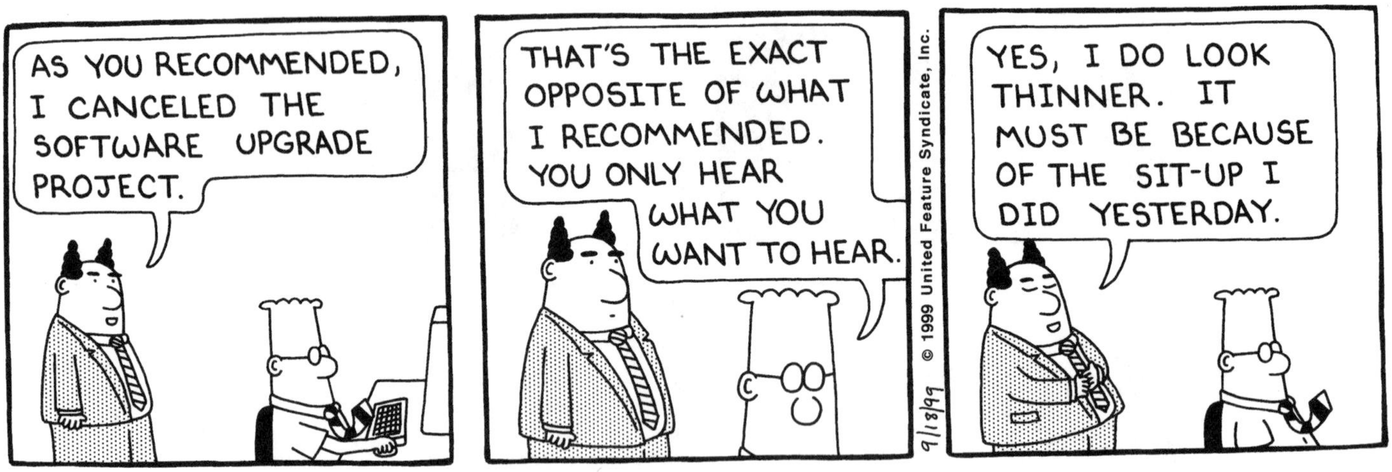
AS YOU RECOMMENDED, I CANCELED THE SOFTWARE UPGRADE PROJECT.
THAT'S THE EXACT OPPOSITE OF WHAT I RECOMMENDED. YOU ONLY HEAR WHAT YOU WANT TO HEAR.
9/18/99 © 1999 United Feature Syndicate, Inc.
YES, I DO LOOK THINNER. IT MUST BE BECAUSE OF THE SIT-UP I DID YESTERDAY.

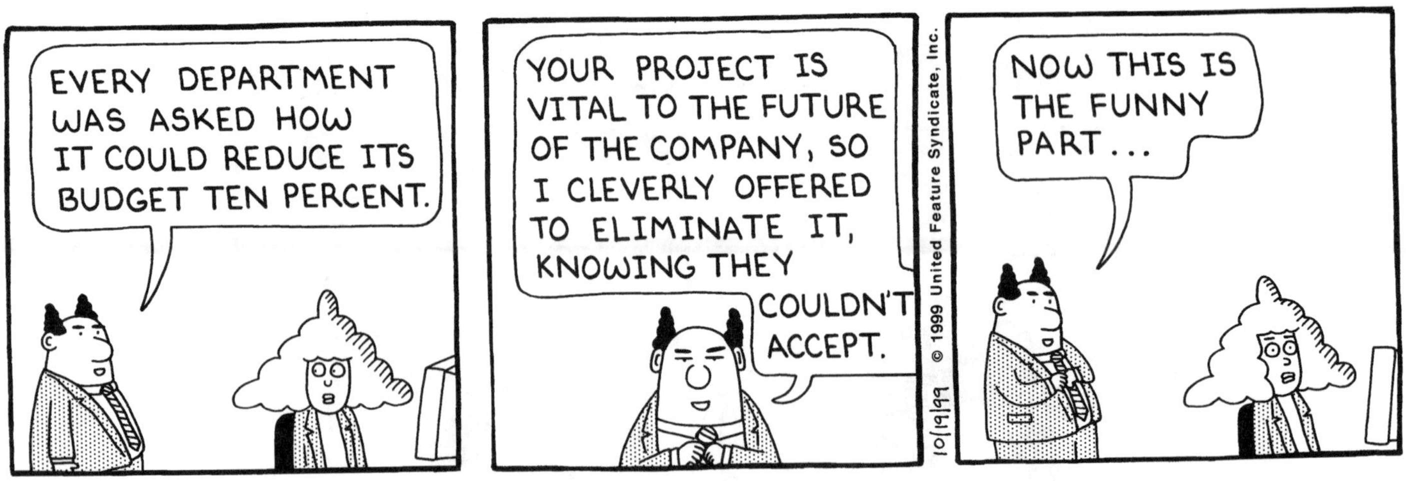
EVERY DEPARTMENT WAS ASKED HOW IT COULD REDUCE ITS BUDGET TEN PERCENT.
YOUR PROJECT IS VITAL TO THE FUTURE OF THE COMPANY, SO I CLEVERLY OFFERED TO ELIMINATE IT, KNOWING THEY COULDN'T ACCEPT.
10/19/99 © 1999 United Feature Syndicate, Inc.
NOW THIS IS THE FUNNY PART...

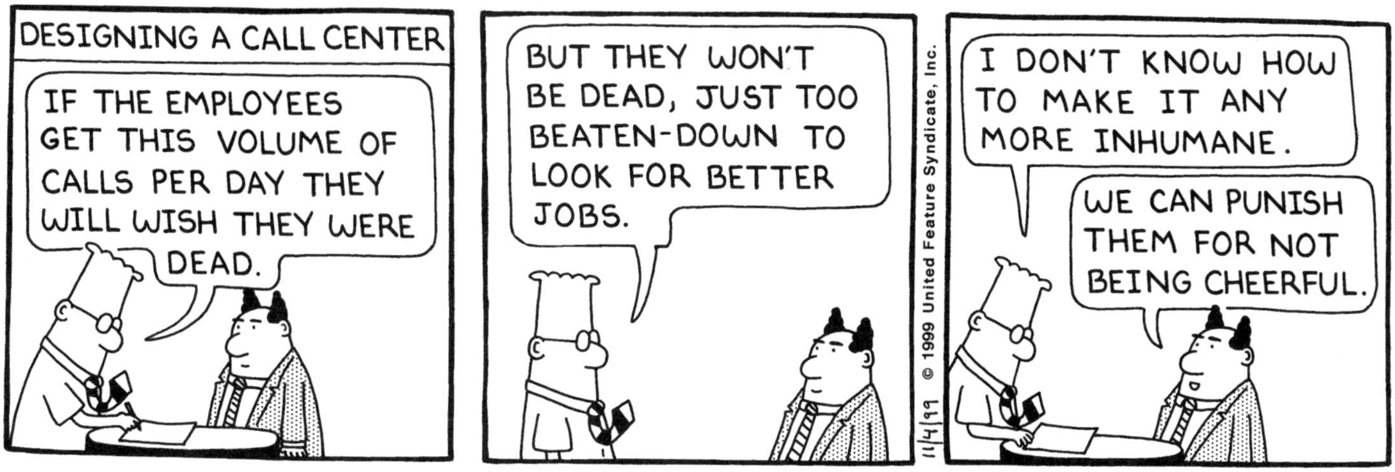
DESIGNING A CALL CENTER
IF THE EMPLOYEES GET THIS VOLUME OF CALLS PER DAY THEY WILL WISH THEY WERE DEAD.
BUT THEY WON'T BE DEAD, JUST TOO BEATEN-DOWN TO LOOK FOR BETTER JOBS.
© 1999 United Feature Syndicate, Inc.
11/4/99
I DON'T KNOW HOW TO MAKE IT ANY MORE INHUMANE.
WE CAN PUNISH THEM FOR NOT BEING CHEERFUL.

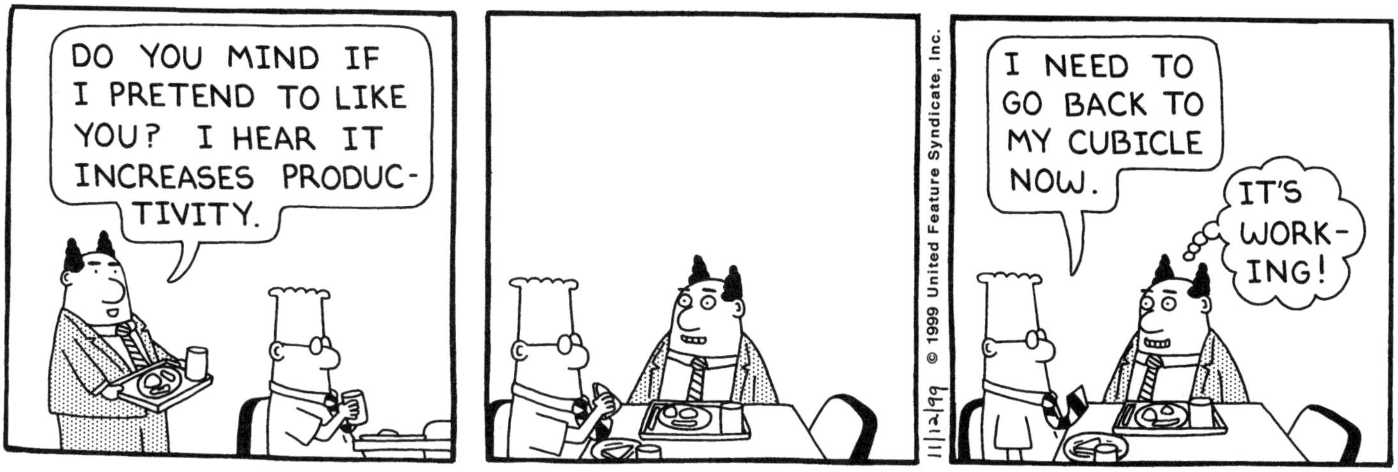
DO YOU MIND IF I PRETEND TO LIKE YOU? I HEAR IT INCREASES PRODUC-TIVITY.
© 1999 United Feature Syndicate, Inc.
11/12/99
I NEED TO GO BACK TO MY CUBICLE NOW.
IT'S WORK-ING!

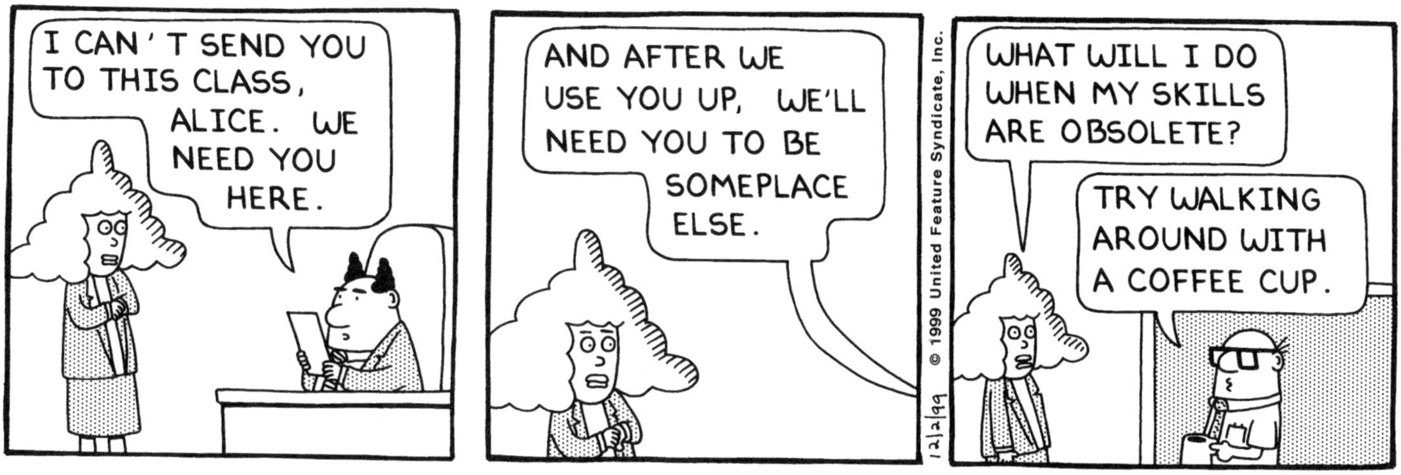
I CAN'T SEND YOU TO THIS CLASS, ALICE. WE NEED YOU HERE.
AND AFTER WE USE YOU UP, WE'LL NEED YOU TO BE SOMEPLACE ELSE.
© 1999 United Feature Syndicate, Inc.
12/2/99
WHAT WILL I DO WHEN MY SKILLS ARE OBSOLETE?
TRY WALKING AROUND WITH A COFFEE CUP.

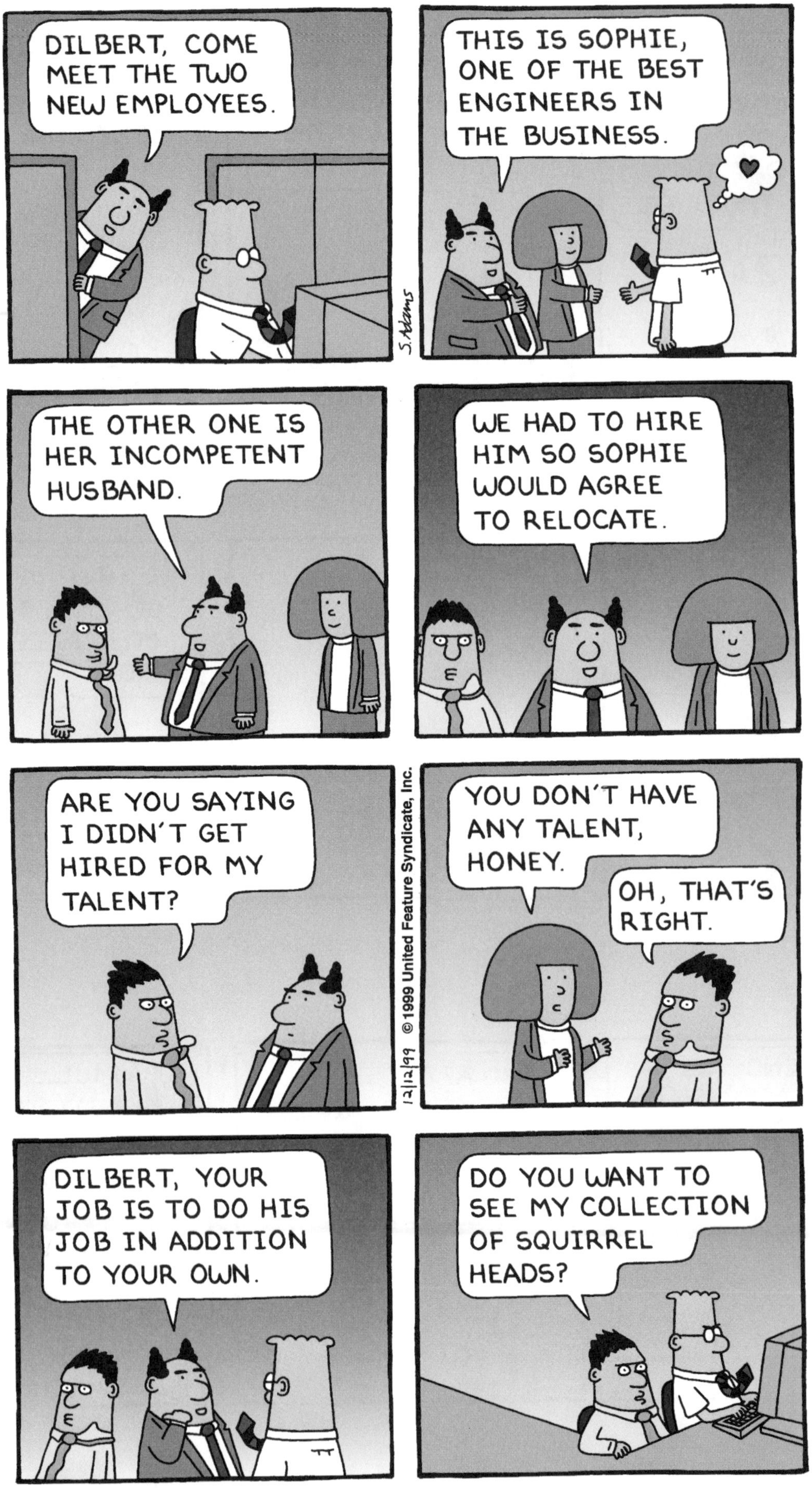
DILBERT, COME MEET THE TWO NEW EMPLOYEES.
THIS IS SOPHIE, ONE OF THE BEST ENGINEERS IN THE BUSINESS.
THE OTHER ONE IS HER INCOMPETENT HUSBAND.
WE HAD TO HIRE HIM SO SOPHIE WOULD AGREE TO RELOCATE.
ARE YOU SAYING I DIDN'T GET HIRED FOR MY TALENT?
YOU DON'T HAVE ANY TALENT, HONEY.
OH, THAT'S RIGHT.
DILBERT, YOUR JOB IS TO DO HIS JOB IN ADDITION TO YOUR OWN.
DO YOU WANT TO SEE MY COLLECTION OF SQUIRREL HEADS?
S. Adams
12/12/99 © 1999 United Feature Syndicate, Inc.

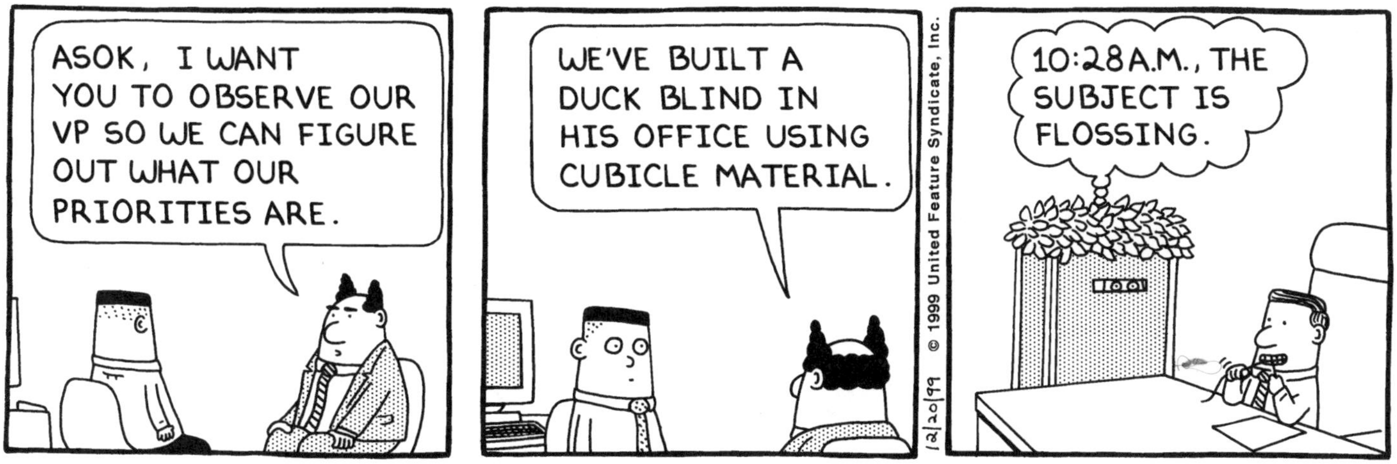
ASOK, I WANT YOU TO OBSERVE OUR VP SO WE CAN FIGURE OUT WHAT OUR PRIORITIES ARE.
WE'VE BUILT A DUCK BLIND IN HIS OFFICE USING CUBICLE MATERIAL.
10:28 A.M., THE SUBJECT IS FLOSSING.
12/20/99 © 1999 United Feature Syndicate, Inc.

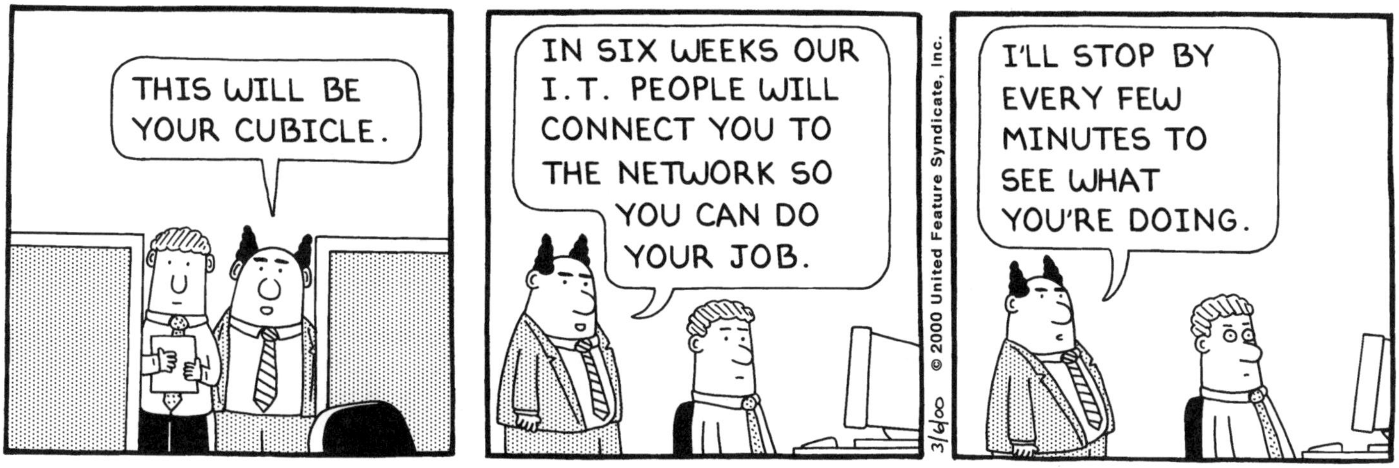
THIS WILL BE YOUR CUBICLE.
IN SIX WEEKS OUR I.T. PEOPLE WILL CONNECT YOU TO THE NETWORK SO YOU CAN DO YOUR JOB.
I'LL STOP BY EVERY FEW MINUTES TO SEE WHAT YOU'RE DOING.
3/6/00 © 2000 United Feature Syndicate, Inc.

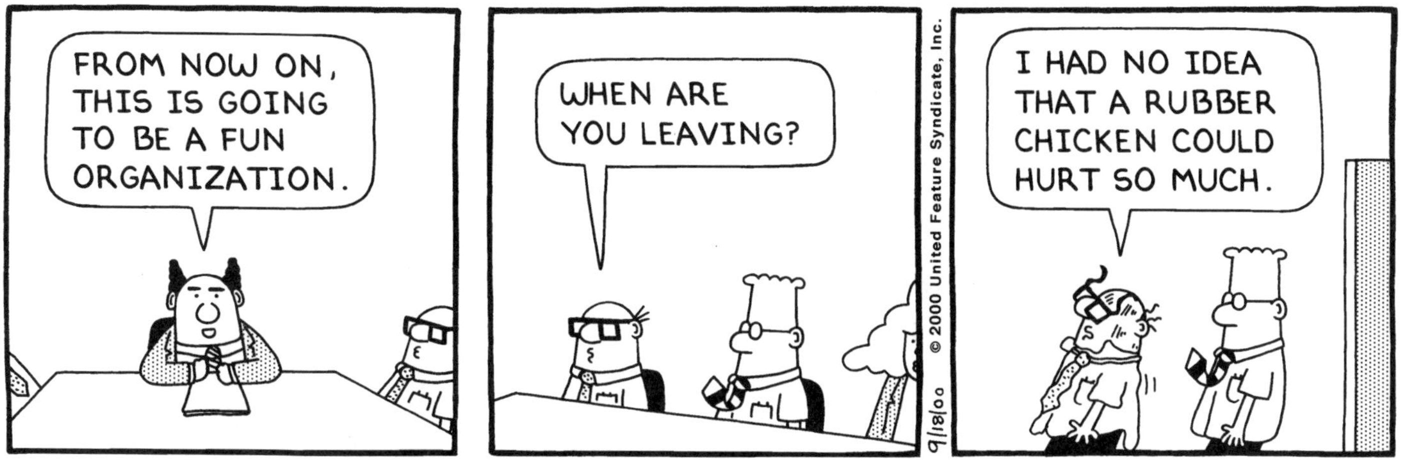
FROM NOW ON, THIS IS GOING TO BE A FUN ORGANIZATION.
WHEN ARE YOU LEAVING?
I HAD NO IDEA THAT A RUBBER CHICKEN COULD HURT SO MUCH.
9/18/00 © 2000 United Feature Syndicate, Inc.

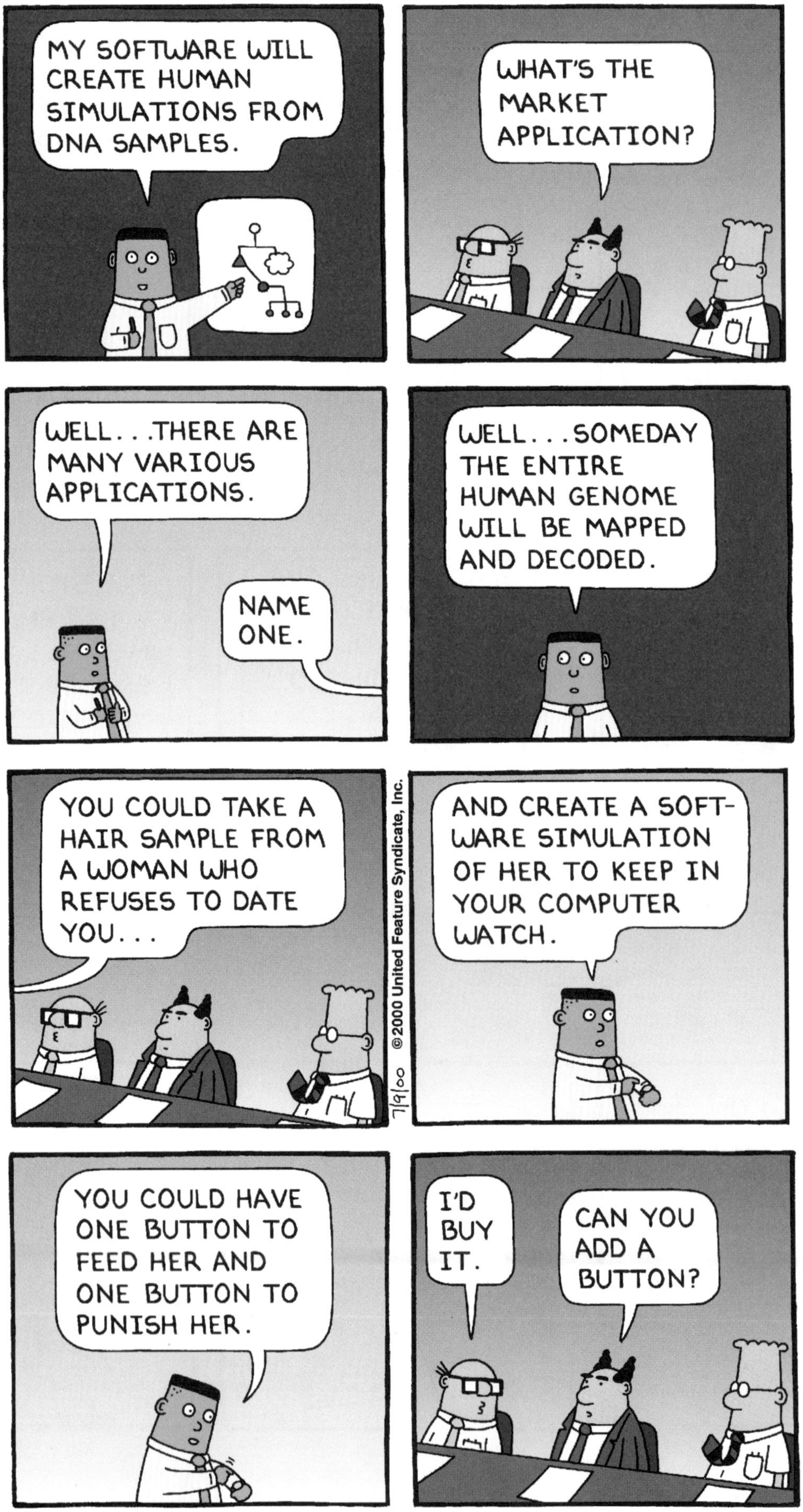
MY SOFTWARE WILL CREATE HUMAN SIMULATIONS FROM DNA SAMPLES.
WHAT'S THE MARKET APPLICATION?
WELL. . .THERE ARE MANY VARIOUS APPLICATIONS.
NAME ONE.
WELL. . .SOMEDAY THE ENTIRE HUMAN GENOME WILL BE MAPPED AND DECODED.
YOU COULD TAKE A HAIR SAMPLE FROM A WOMAN WHO REFUSES TO DATE YOU. . .
AND CREATE A SOFT-WARE SIMULATION OF HER TO KEEP IN YOUR COMPUTER WATCH.
YOU COULD HAVE ONE BUTTON TO FEED HER AND ONE BUTTON TO PUNISH HER.
I'D BUY IT.
CAN YOU ADD A BUTTON?
©2000 United Feature Syndicate, Inc.
7/9/00

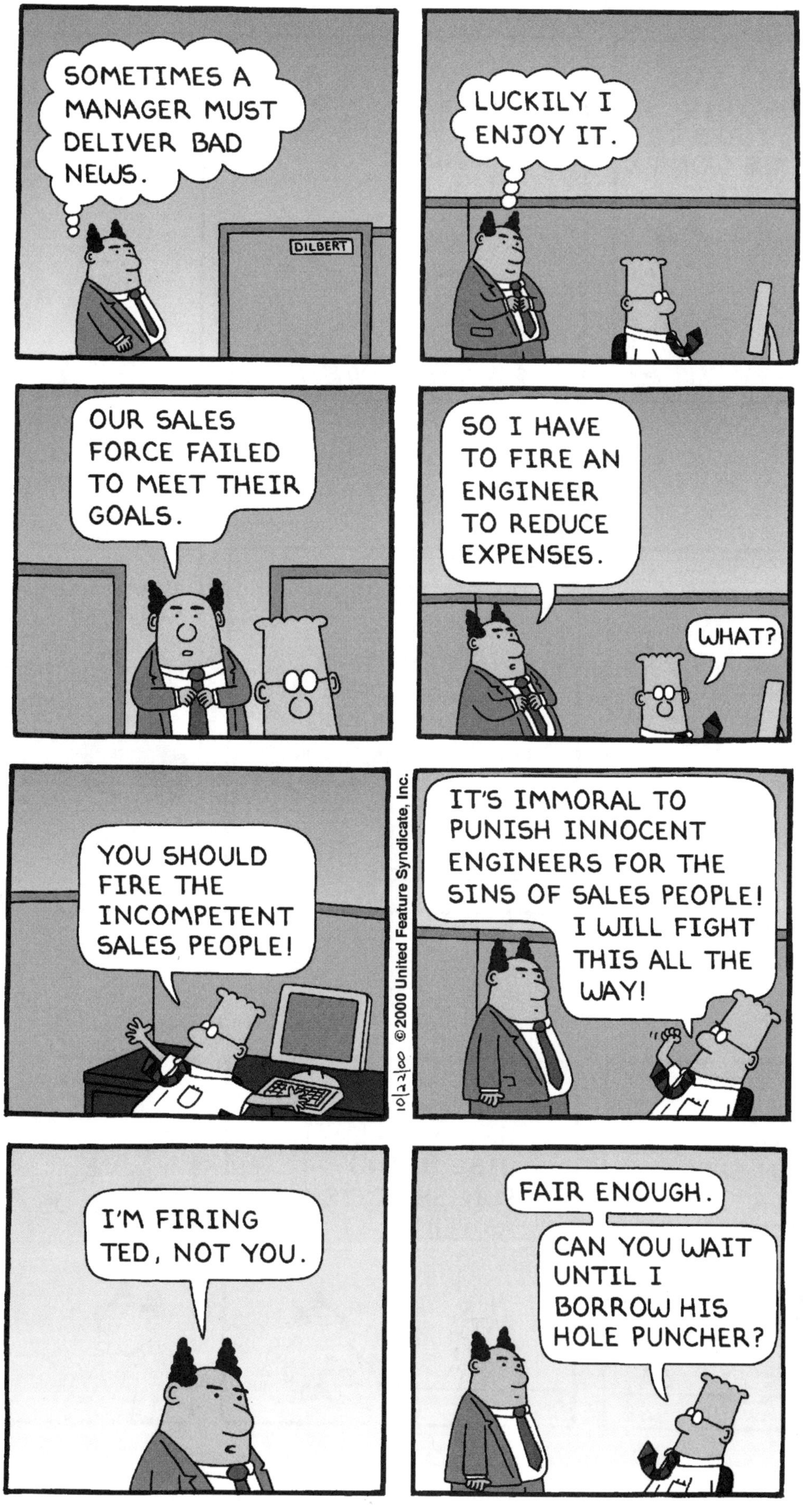
SOMETIMES A MANAGER MUST DELIVER BAD NEWS.
DILBERT
LUCKILY I ENJOY IT.
OUR SALES FORCE FAILED TO MEET THEIR GOALS.
SO I HAVE TO FIRE AN ENGINEER TO REDUCE EXPENSES.
WHAT?
YOU SHOULD FIRE THE INCOMPETENT SALES PEOPLE!
10/22/00 © 2000 United Feature Syndicate, Inc.
IT'S IMMORAL TO PUNISH INNOCENT ENGINEERS FOR THE SINS OF SALES PEOPLE!
I WILL FIGHT THIS ALL THE WAY!
I'M FIRING TED, NOT YOU.
FAIR ENOUGH.
CAN YOU WAIT UNTIL I BORROW HIS HOLE PUNCHER?

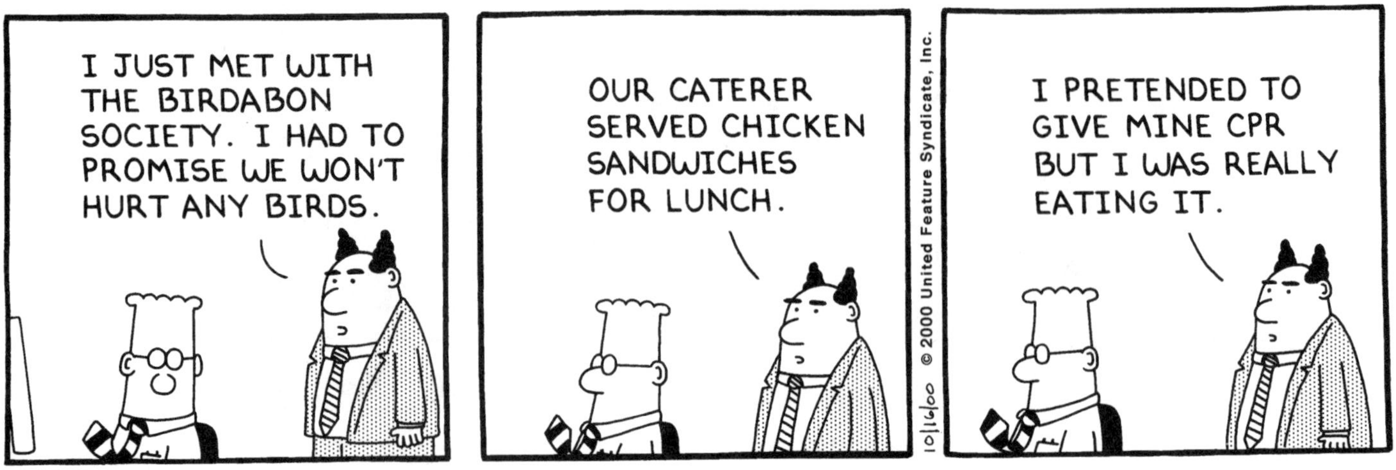
I JUST MET WITH THE BIRDABON SOCIETY. I HAD TO PROMISE WE WON'T HURT ANY BIRDS.
OUR CATERER SERVED CHICKEN SANDWICHES FOR LUNCH.
10/16/00 © 2000 United Feature Syndicate, Inc.
I PRETENDED TO GIVE MINE CPR BUT I WAS REALLY EATING IT.

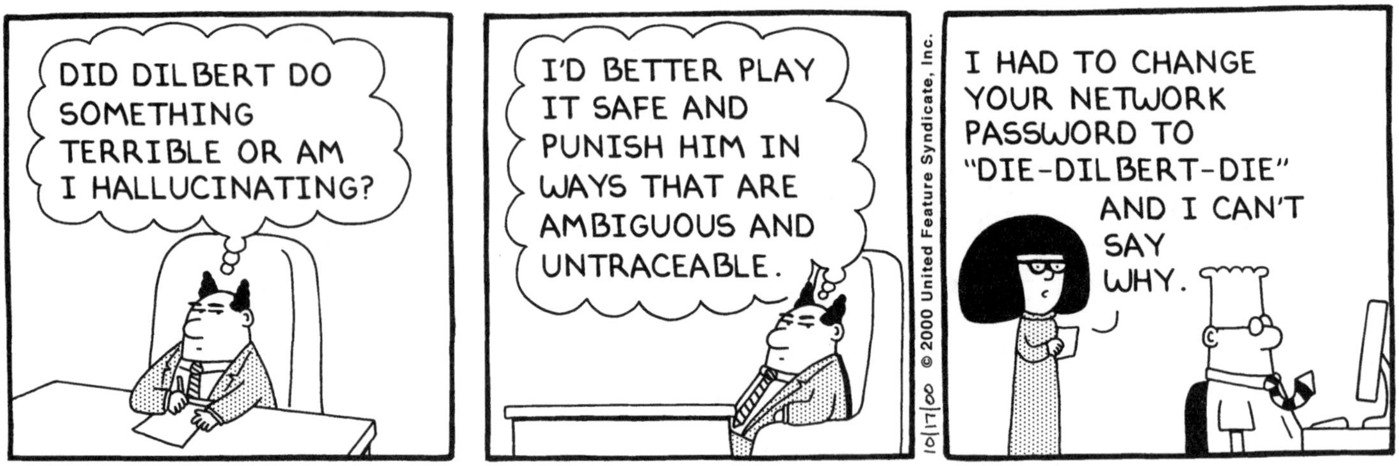
DID DILBERT DO SOMETHING TERRIBLE OR AM I HALLUCINATING?
I'D BETTER PLAY IT SAFE AND PUNISH HIM IN WAYS THAT ARE AMBIGUOUS AND UNTRACEABLE.
10/17/00 © 2000 United Feature Syndicate, Inc.
I HAD TO CHANGE YOUR NETWORK PASSWORD TO "DIE-DILBERT-DIE" AND I CAN'T SAY WHY.

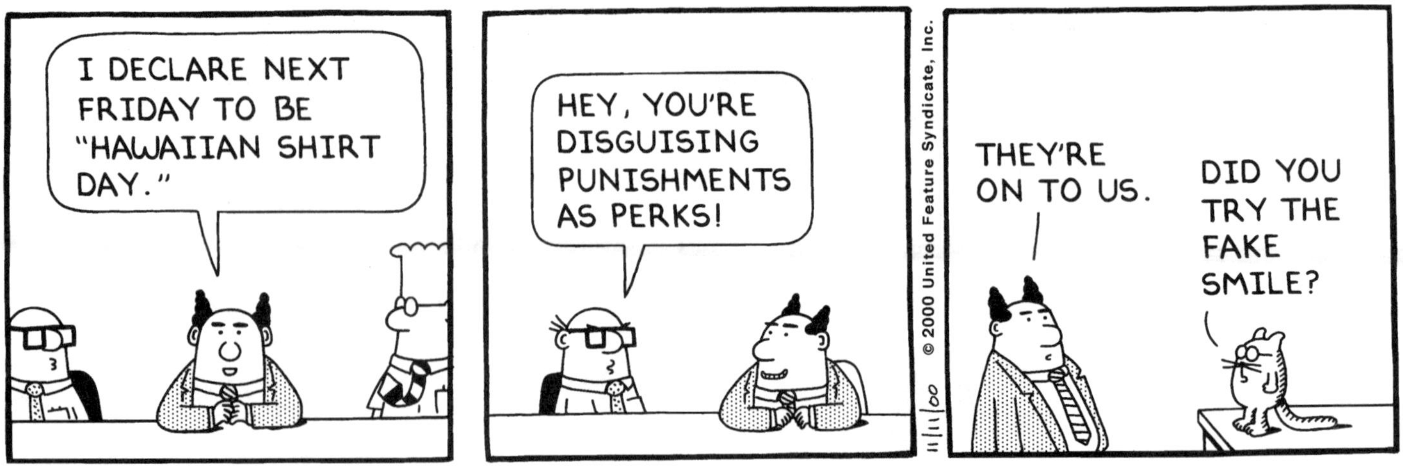
I DECLARE NEXT FRIDAY TO BE "HAWAIIAN SHIRT DAY."
HEY, YOU'RE DISGUISING PUNISHMENTS AS PERKS!
11/11/00 © 2000 United Feature Syndicate, Inc.
THEY'RE ON TO US.
DID YOU TRY THE FAKE SMILE?

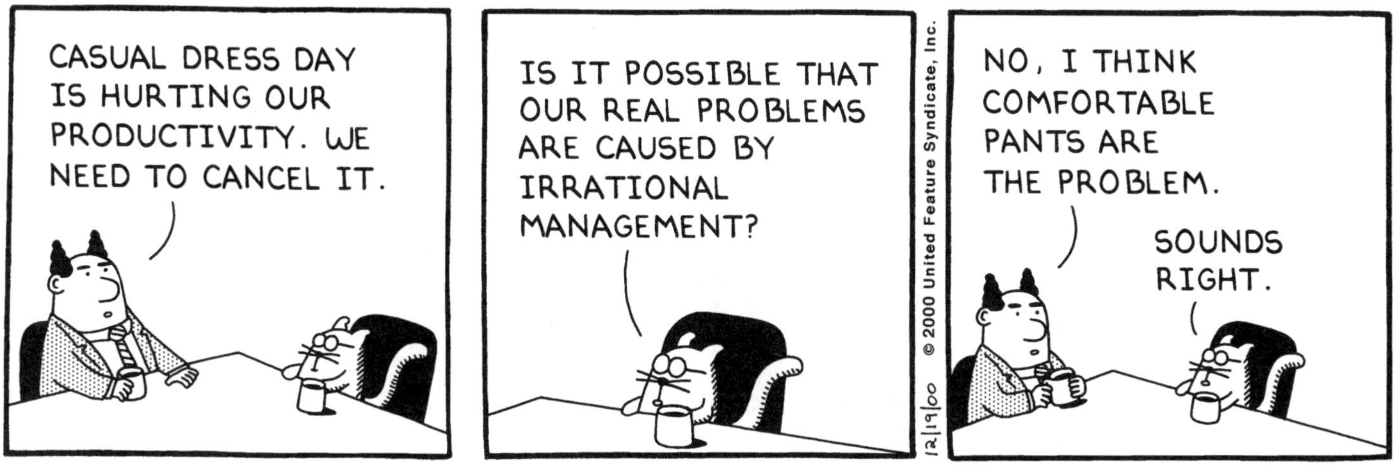
CASUAL DRESS DAY IS HURTING OUR PRODUCTIVITY. WE NEED TO CANCEL IT.
IS IT POSSIBLE THAT OUR REAL PROBLEMS ARE CAUSED BY IRRATIONAL MANAGEMENT?
12/19/00
© 2000 United Feature Syndicate, Inc.
NO, I THINK COMFORTABLE PANTS ARE THE PROBLEM.
SOUNDS RIGHT.

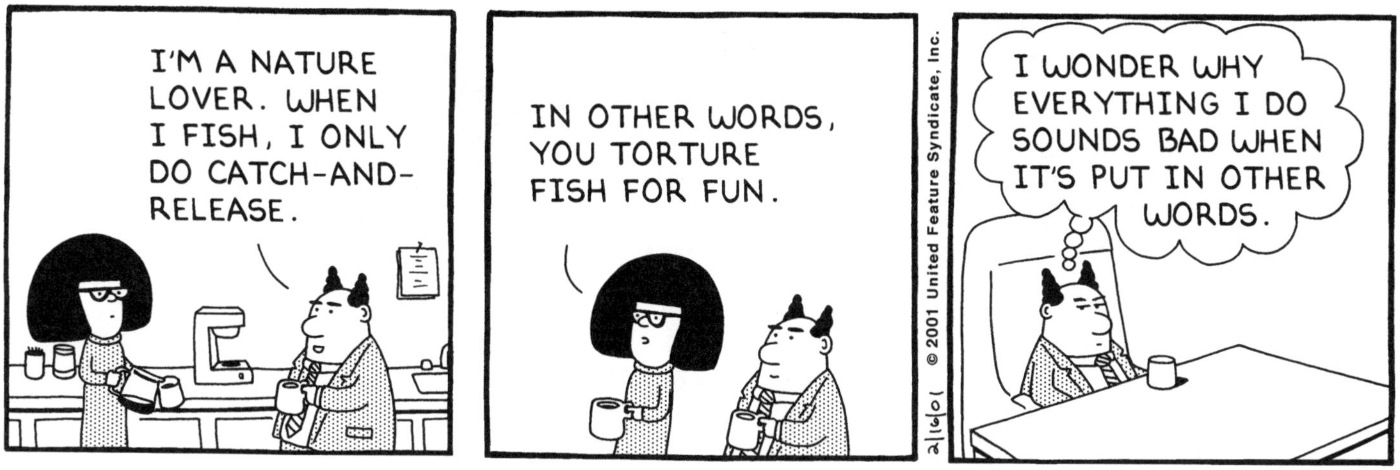
I'M A NATURE LOVER. WHEN I FISH, I ONLY DO CATCH-AND-RELEASE.
IN OTHER WORDS, YOU TORTURE FISH FOR FUN.
2/16/01
© 2001 United Feature Syndicate, Inc.
I WONDER WHY EVERYTHING I DO SOUNDS BAD WHEN IT'S PUT IN OTHER WORDS.

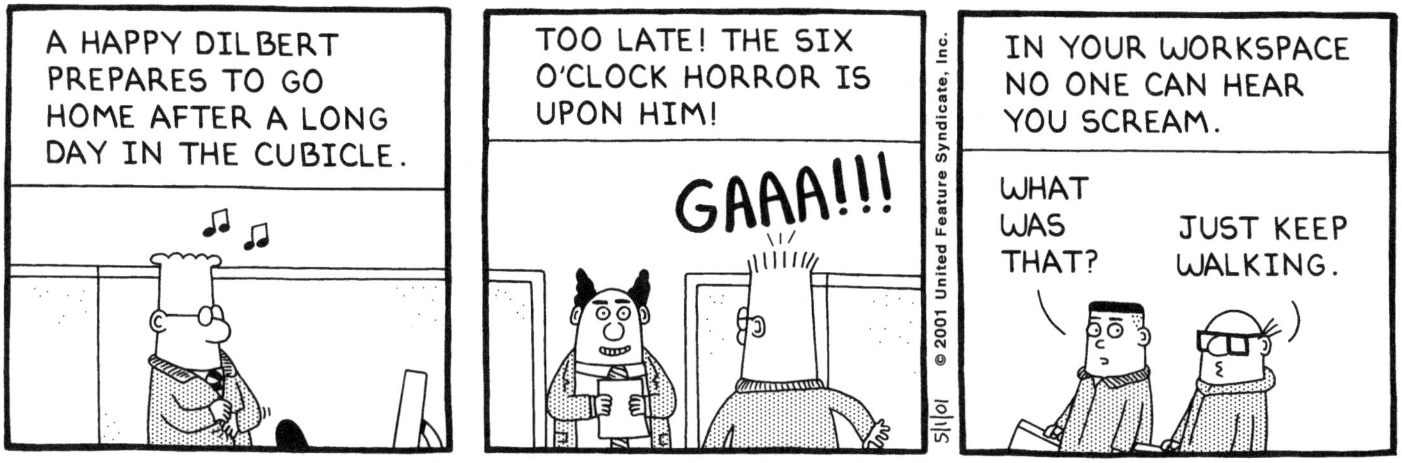
A HAPPY DILBERT PREPARES TO GO HOME AFTER A LONG DAY IN THE CUBICLE.
TOO LATE! THE SIX O'CLOCK HORROR IS UPON HIM!
GAAA!!!
5/1/01
© 2001 United Feature Syndicate, Inc.
IN YOUR WORKSPACE NO ONE CAN HEAR YOU SCREAM.
WHAT WAS THAT?
JUST KEEP WALKING.

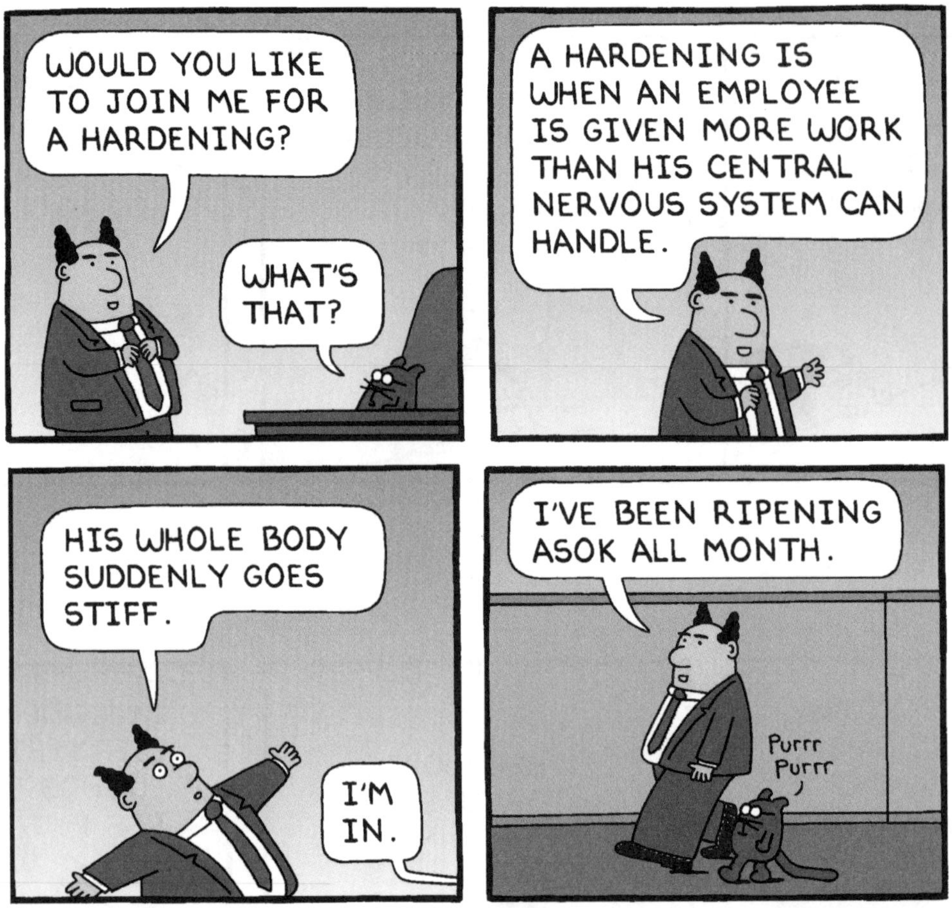
WOULD YOU LIKE TO JOIN ME FOR A HARDENING?
WHAT'S THAT?
A HARDENING IS WHEN AN EMPLOYEE IS GIVEN MORE WORK THAN HIS CENTRAL NERVOUS SYSTEM CAN HANDLE.
HIS WHOLE BODY SUDDENLY GOES STIFF.
I'M IN.
I'VE BEEN RIPENING ASOK ALL MONTH.
Purrr Purrr

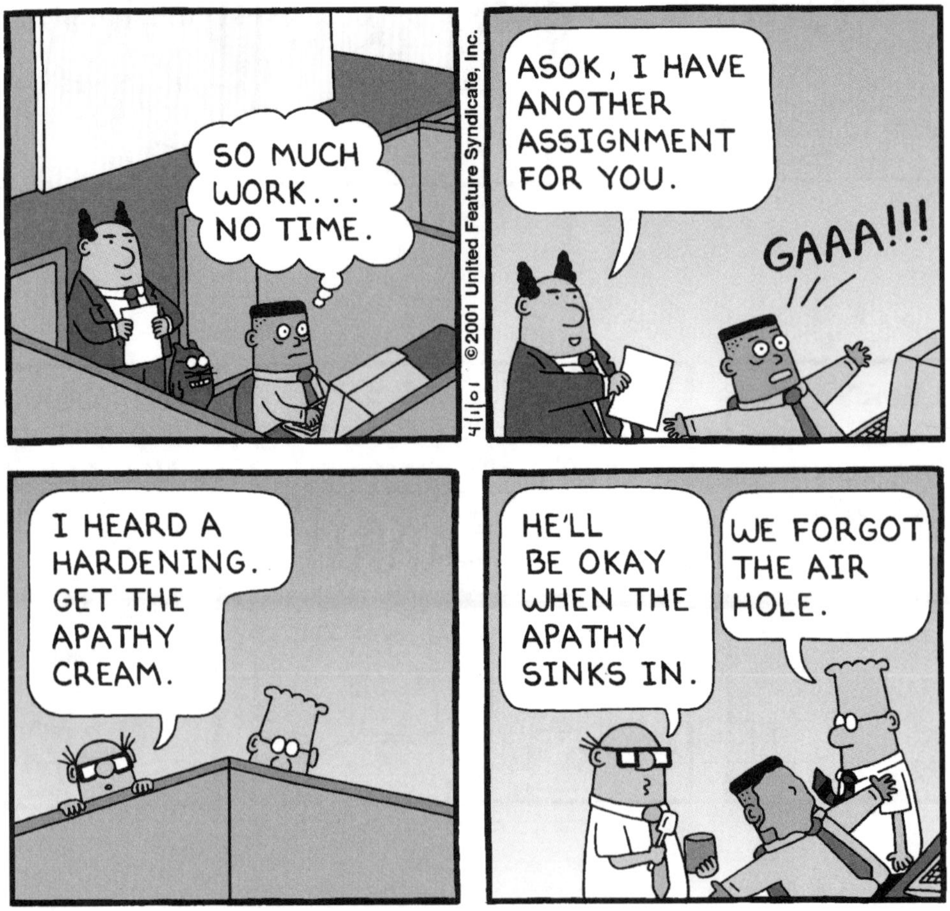
SO MUCH WORK... NO TIME.
4/1/01 ©2001 United Feature Syndicate, Inc.
ASOK, I HAVE ANOTHER ASSIGNMENT FOR YOU.
GAAA!!!
I HEARD A HARDENING. GET THE APATHY CREAM.
HE'LL BE OKAY WHEN THE APATHY SINKS IN.
WE FORGOT THE AIR HOLE.

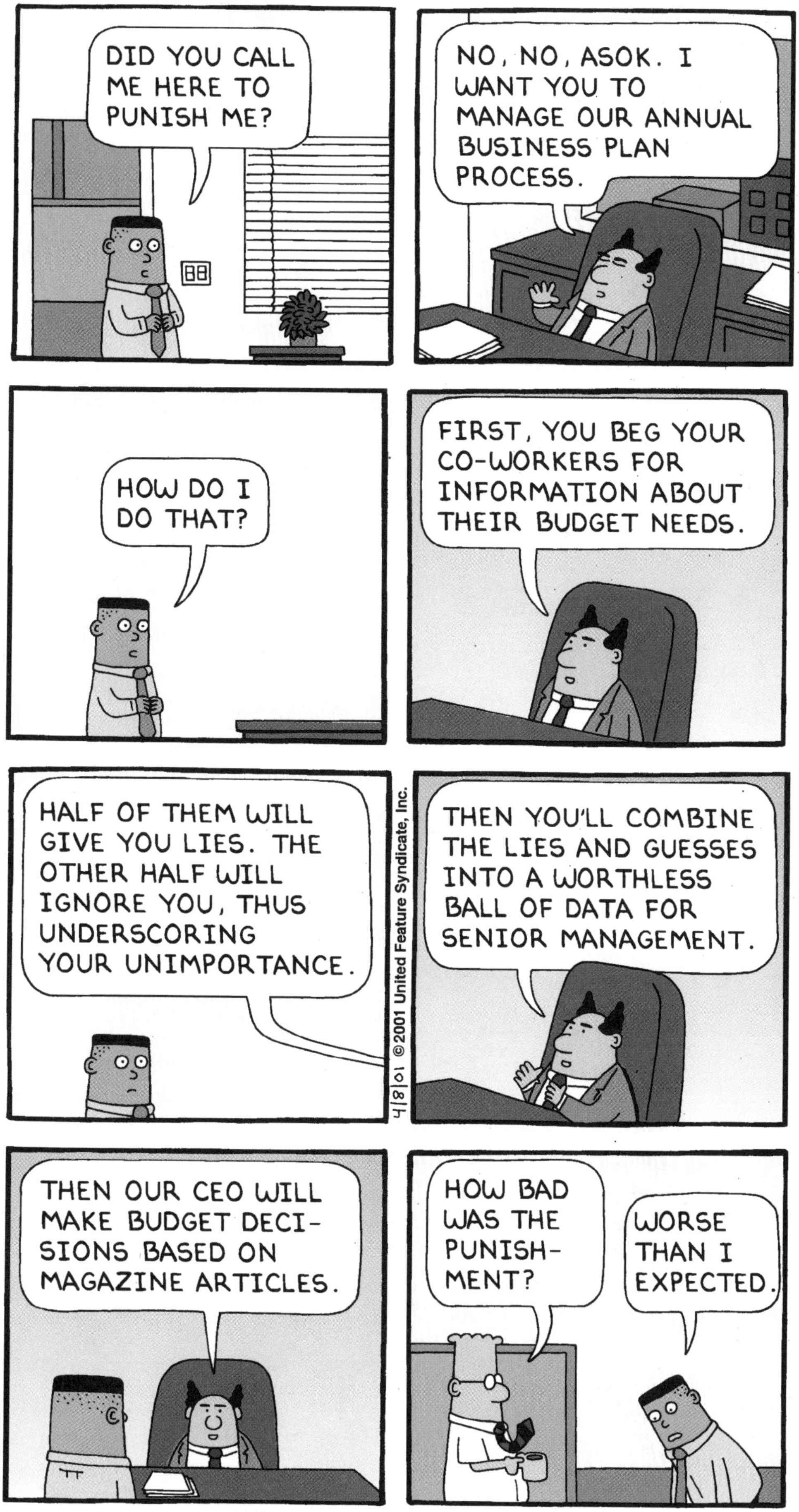
DID YOU CALL ME HERE TO PUNISH ME?
NO, NO, ASOK. I WANT YOU TO MANAGE OUR ANNUAL BUSINESS PLAN PROCESS.
HOW DO I DO THAT?
FIRST, YOU BEG YOUR CO-WORKERS FOR INFORMATION ABOUT THEIR BUDGET NEEDS.
HALF OF THEM WILL GIVE YOU LIES. THE OTHER HALF WILL IGNORE YOU, THUS UNDERSCORING YOUR UNIMPORTANCE.
4/8/01 ©2001 United Feature Syndicate, Inc.
THEN YOU'LL COMBINE THE LIES AND GUESSES INTO A WORTHLESS BALL OF DATA FOR SENIOR MANAGEMENT.
THEN OUR CEO WILL MAKE BUDGET DECI-SIONS BASED ON MAGAZINE ARTICLES.
HOW BAD WAS THE PUNISH-MENT?
WORSE THAN I EXPECTED.

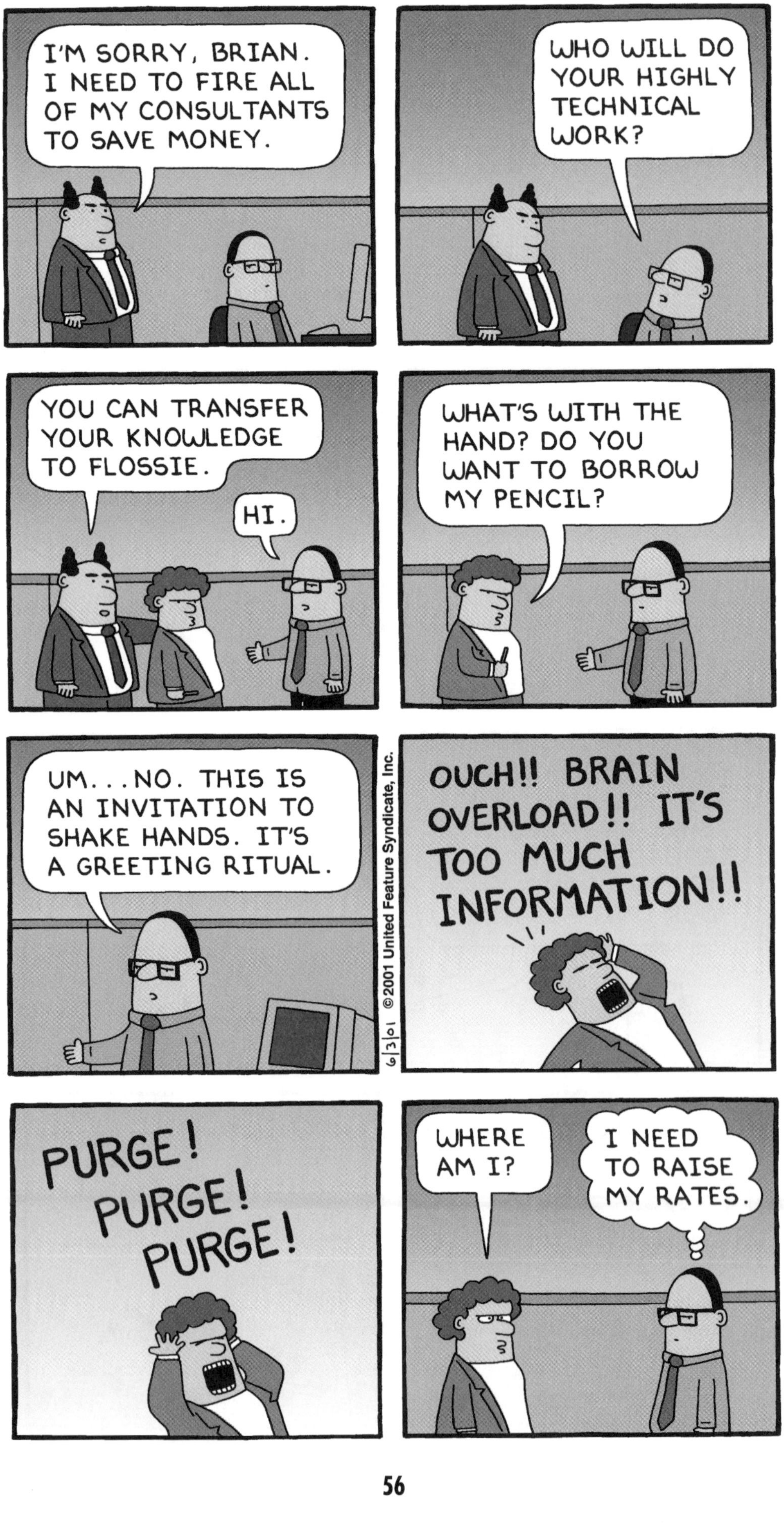
I'M SORRY, BRIAN. I NEED TO FIRE ALL OF MY CONSULTANTS TO SAVE MONEY.
WHO WILL DO YOUR HIGHLY TECHNICAL WORK?
YOU CAN TRANSFER YOUR KNOWLEDGE TO FLOSSIE.
HI.
WHAT'S WITH THE HAND? DO YOU WANT TO BORROW MY PENCIL?
UM...NO. THIS IS AN INVITATION TO SHAKE HANDS. IT'S A GREETING RITUAL.
6/3/01 ©2001 United Feature Syndicate, Inc.
OUCH!! BRAIN OVERLOAD!! IT'S TOO MUCH INFORMATION!!
PURGE! PURGE! PURGE!
WHERE AM I?
I NEED TO RAISE MY RATES.

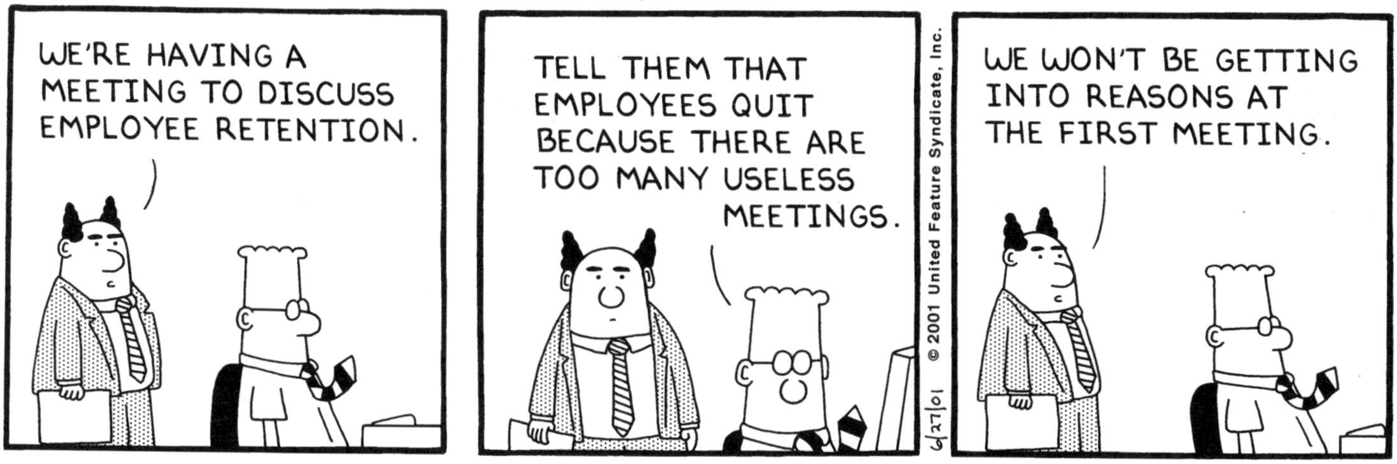
WE'RE HAVING A MEETING TO DISCUSS EMPLOYEE RETENTION.
TELL THEM THAT EMPLOYEES QUIT BECAUSE THERE ARE TOO MANY USELESS MEETINGS.
WE WON'T BE GETTING INTO REASONS AT THE FIRST MEETING.
6/27/01 © 2001 United Feature Syndicate, Inc.

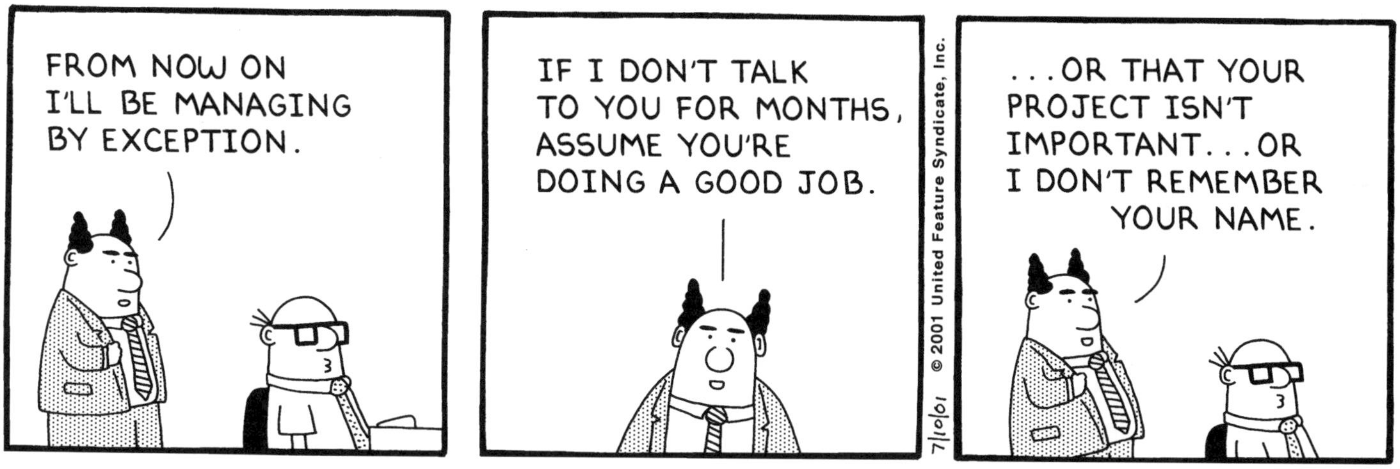
FROM NOW ON I'LL BE MANAGING BY EXCEPTION.
IF I DON'T TALK TO YOU FOR MONTHS, ASSUME YOU'RE DOING A GOOD JOB.
...OR THAT YOUR PROJECT ISN'T IMPORTANT...OR I DON'T REMEMBER YOUR NAME.
7/10/01 © 2001 United Feature Syndicate, Inc.

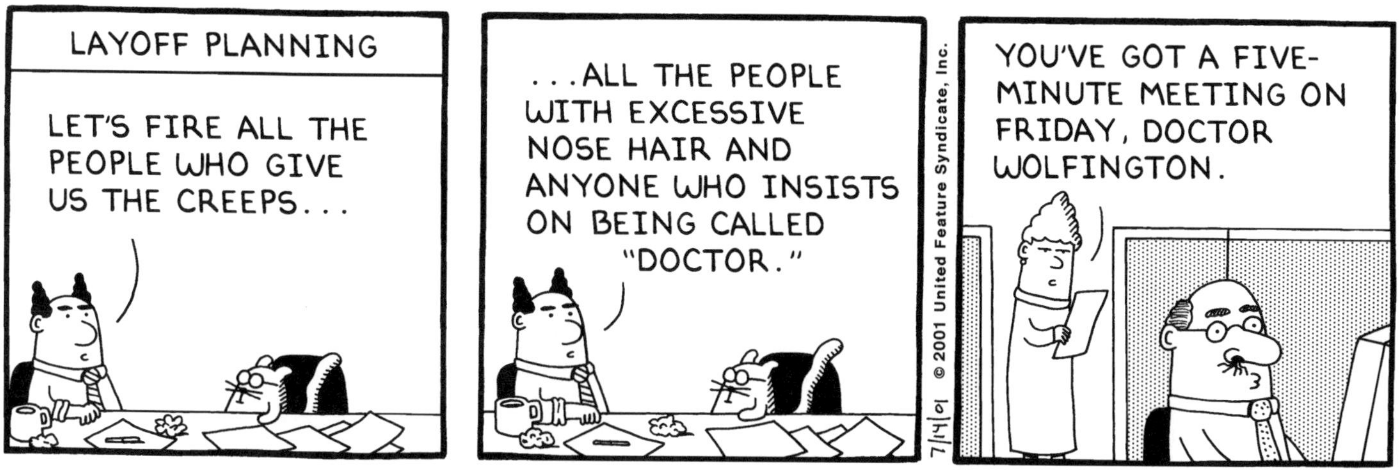
LAYOFF PLANNING
LET'S FIRE ALL THE PEOPLE WHO GIVE US THE CREEPS...
...ALL THE PEOPLE WITH EXCESSIVE NOSE HAIR AND ANYONE WHO INSISTS ON BEING CALLED "DOCTOR."
YOU'VE GOT A FIVE-MINUTE MEETING ON FRIDAY, DOCTOR WOLFINGTON.
7/14/01 © 2001 United Feature Syndicate, Inc.

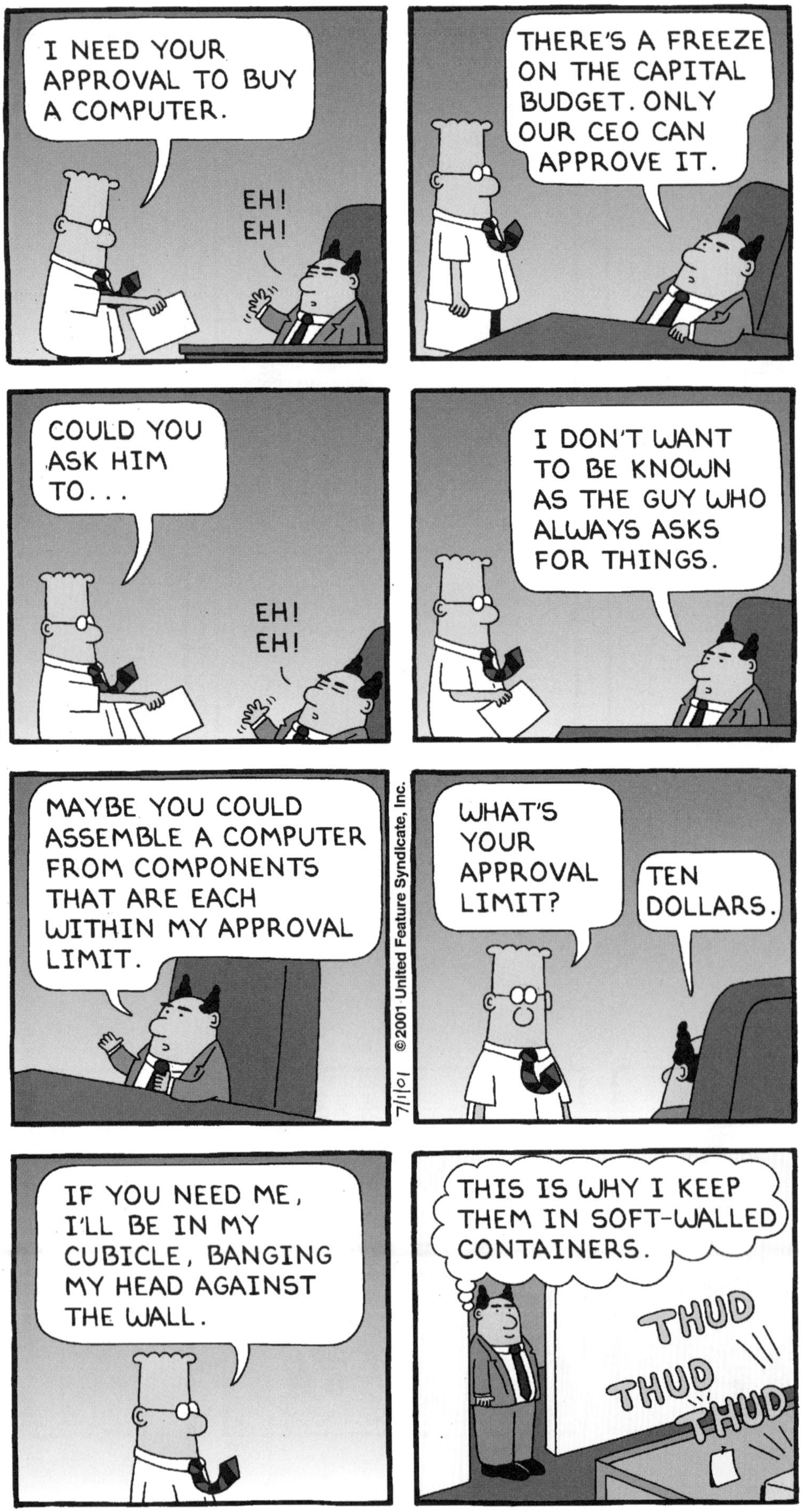
I NEED YOUR APPROVAL TO BUY A COMPUTER.
EH! EH!
THERE'S A FREEZE ON THE CAPITAL BUDGET. ONLY OUR CEO CAN APPROVE IT.
COULD YOU ASK HIM TO...
EH! EH!
I DON'T WANT TO BE KNOWN AS THE GUY WHO ALWAYS ASKS FOR THINGS.
MAYBE YOU COULD ASSEMBLE A COMPUTER FROM COMPONENTS THAT ARE EACH WITHIN MY APPROVAL LIMIT.
© 2001 United Feature Syndicate, Inc.
7/1/01
WHAT'S YOUR APPROVAL LIMIT?
TEN DOLLARS.
IF YOU NEED ME, I'LL BE IN MY CUBICLE, BANGING MY HEAD AGAINST THE WALL.
THIS IS WHY I KEEP THEM IN SOFT-WALLED CONTAINERS.
THUD
THUD
THUD

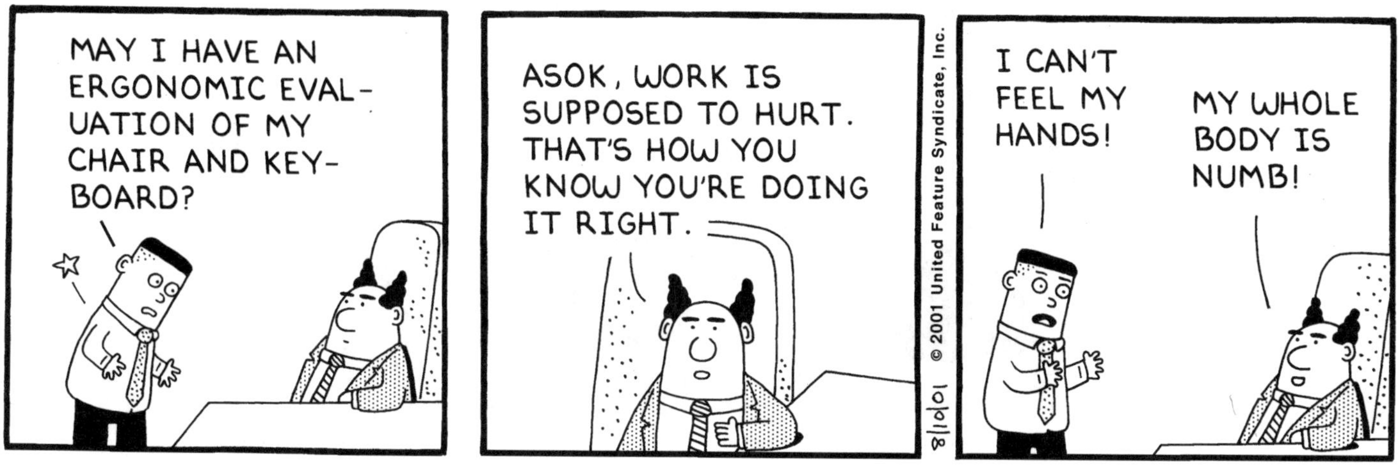
MAY I HAVE AN ERGONOMIC EVAL-UATION OF MY CHAIR AND KEY-BOARD?
ASOK, WORK IS SUPPOSED TO HURT. THAT'S HOW YOU KNOW YOU'RE DOING IT RIGHT.
8/10/01 © 2001 United Feature Syndicate, Inc.
I CAN'T FEEL MY HANDS!
MY WHOLE BODY IS NUMB!

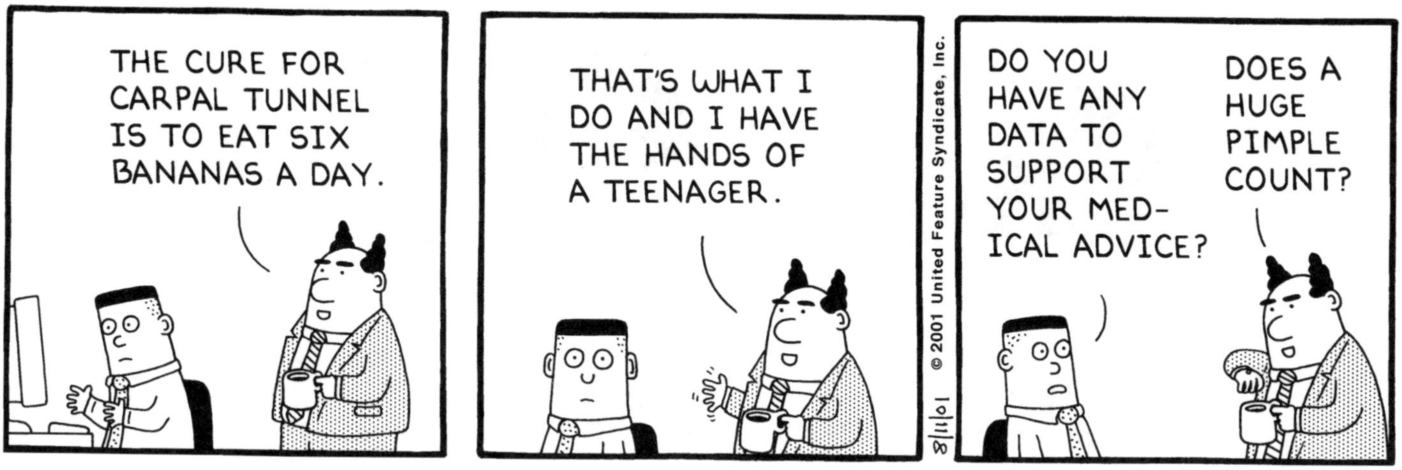
THE CURE FOR CARPAL TUNNEL IS TO EAT SIX BANANAS A DAY.
THAT'S WHAT I DO AND I HAVE THE HANDS OF A TEENAGER.
8/11/01 © 2001 United Feature Syndicate, Inc.
DO YOU HAVE ANY DATA TO SUPPORT YOUR MED-ICAL ADVICE?
DOES A HUGE PIMPLE COUNT?

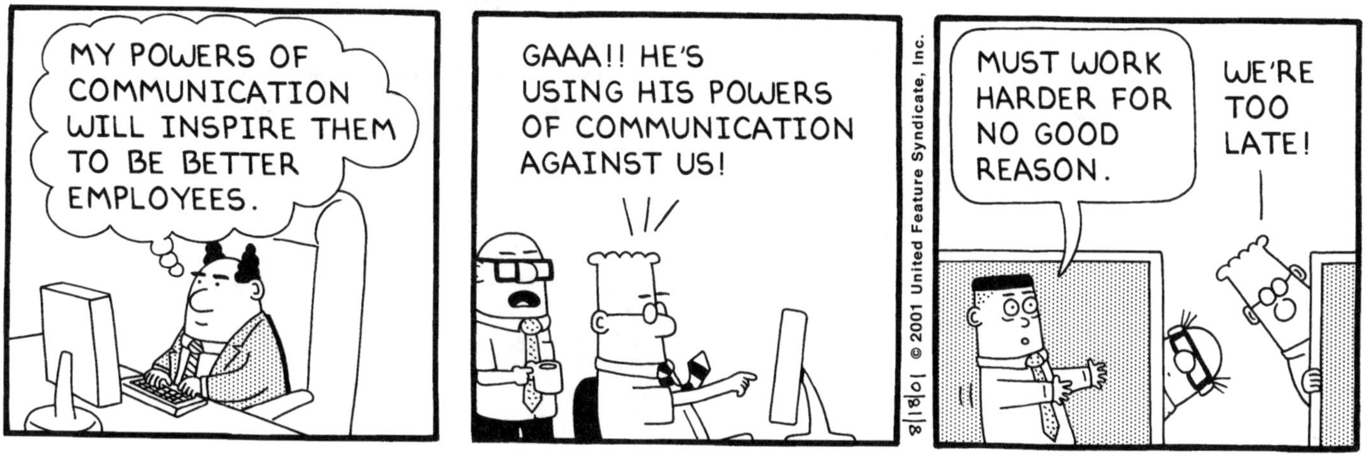
MY POWERS OF COMMUNICATION WILL INSPIRE THEM TO BE BETTER EMPLOYEES.
GAAA!! HE'S USING HIS POWERS OF COMMUNICATION AGAINST US!
8/18/01 © 2001 United Feature Syndicate, Inc.
MUST WORK HARDER FOR NO GOOD REASON.
WE'RE TOO LATE!

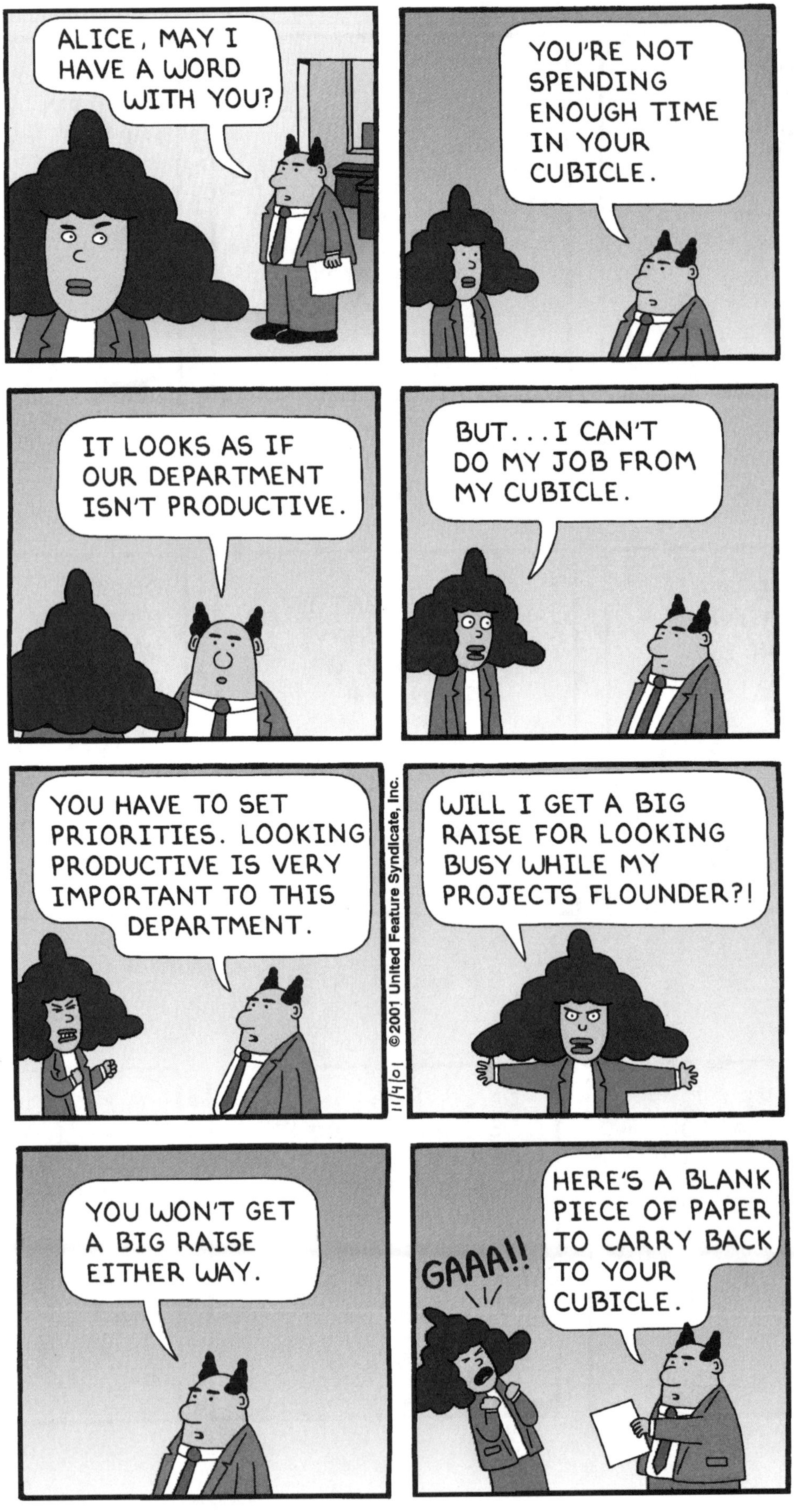
ALICE, MAY I HAVE A WORD WITH YOU?
YOU'RE NOT SPENDING ENOUGH TIME IN YOUR CUBICLE.
IT LOOKS AS IF OUR DEPARTMENT ISN'T PRODUCTIVE.
BUT. . . I CAN'T DO MY JOB FROM MY CUBICLE.
YOU HAVE TO SET PRIORITIES. LOOKING PRODUCTIVE IS VERY IMPORTANT TO THIS DEPARTMENT.
©2001 United Feature Syndicate, Inc.
11/4/01
WILL I GET A BIG RAISE FOR LOOKING BUSY WHILE MY PROJECTS FLOUNDER?!
YOU WON'T GET A BIG RAISE EITHER WAY.
GAAA!!
HERE'S A BLANK PIECE OF PAPER TO CARRY BACK TO YOUR CUBICLE.

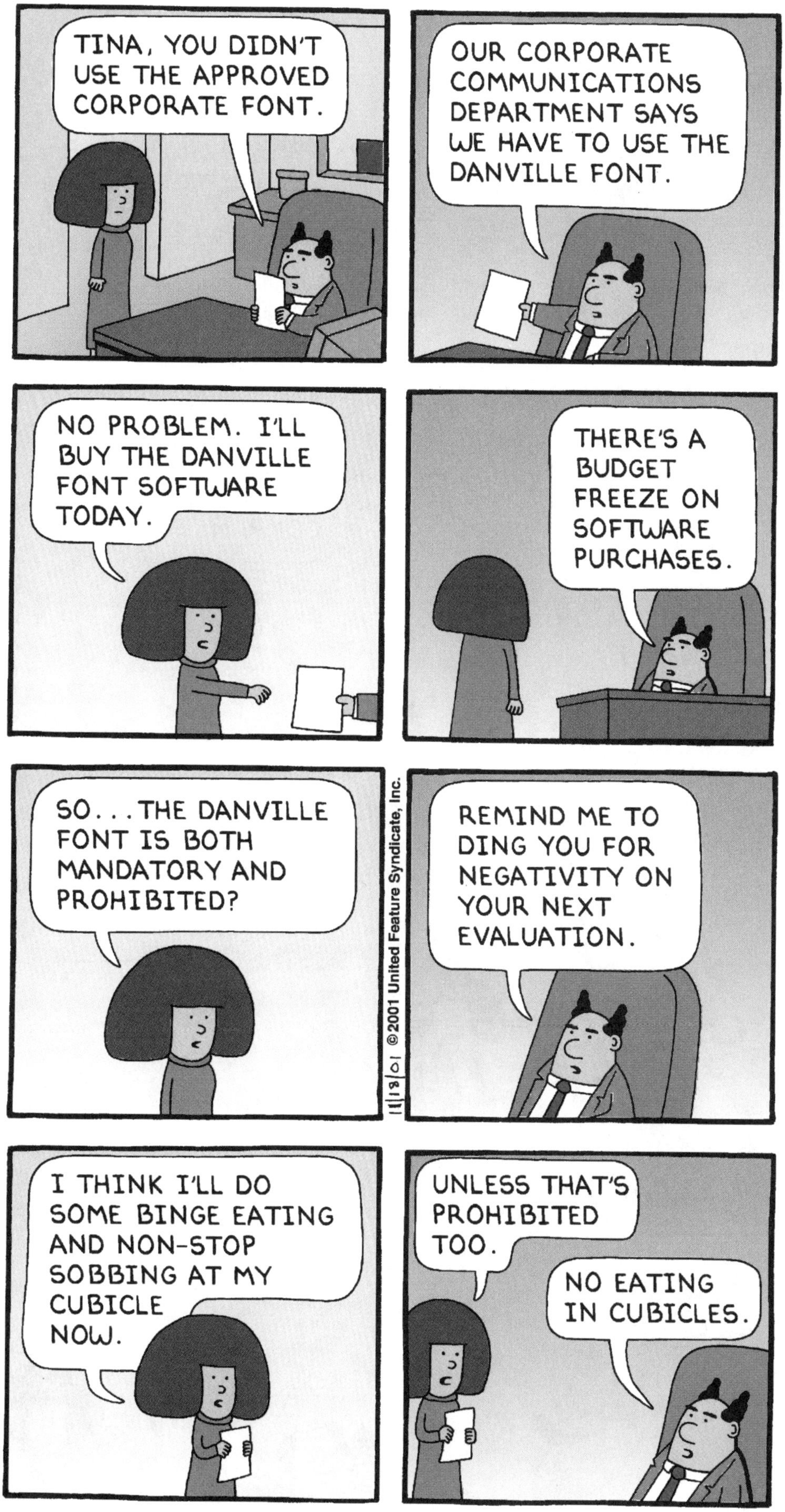
TINA, YOU DIDN'T USE THE APPROVED CORPORATE FONT.
OUR CORPORATE COMMUNICATIONS DEPARTMENT SAYS WE HAVE TO USE THE DANVILLE FONT.
NO PROBLEM. I'LL BUY THE DANVILLE FONT SOFTWARE TODAY.
THERE'S A BUDGET FREEZE ON SOFTWARE PURCHASES.
SO. . . THE DANVILLE FONT IS BOTH MANDATORY AND PROHIBITED?
REMIND ME TO DING YOU FOR NEGATIVITY ON YOUR NEXT EVALUATION.
I THINK I'LL DO SOME BINGE EATING AND NON-STOP SOBBING AT MY CUBICLE NOW.
UNLESS THAT'S PROHIBITED TOO.
NO EATING IN CUBICLES.
11/18/01 ©2001 United Feature Syndicate, Inc.

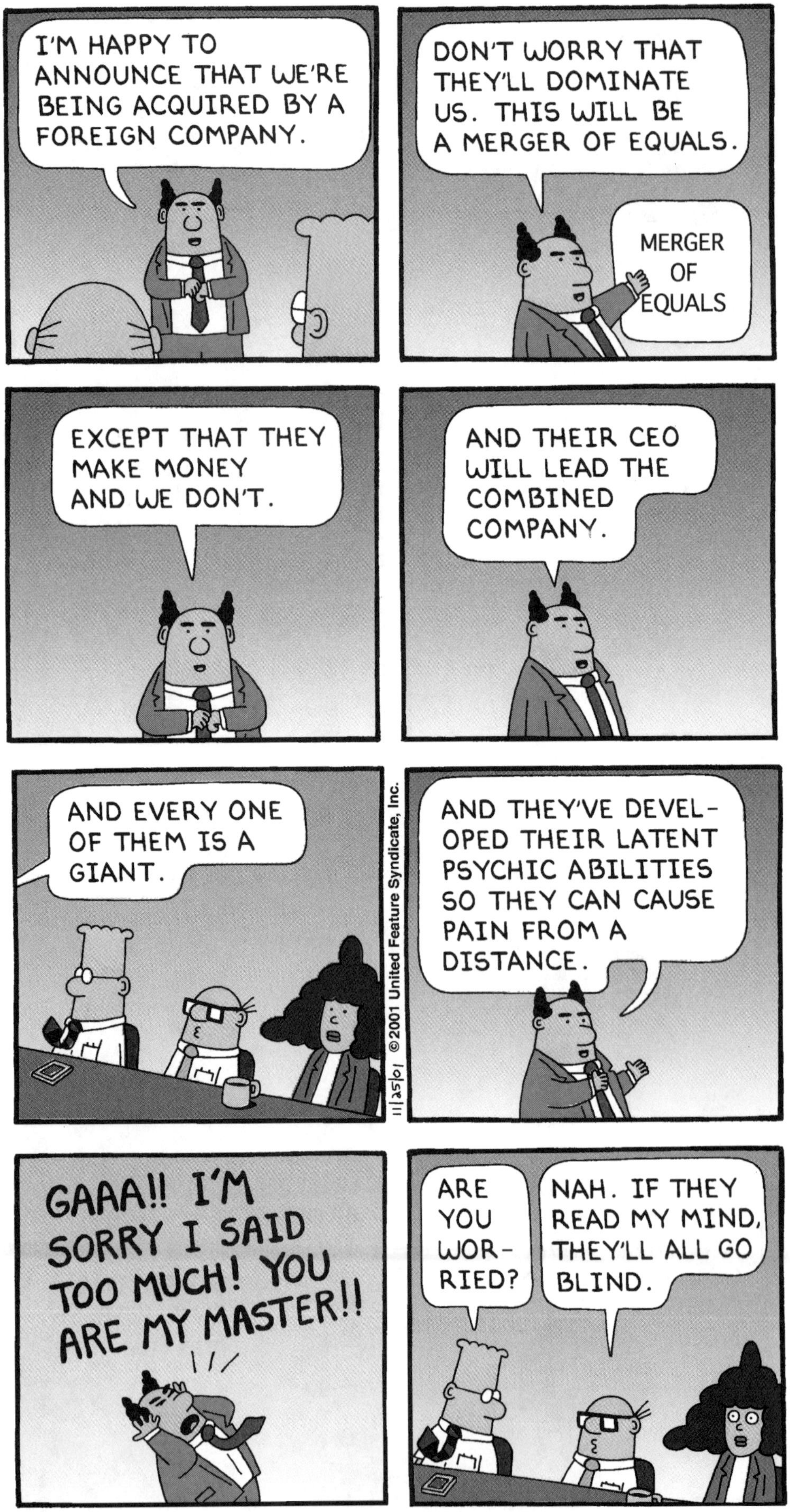
I'M HAPPY TO ANNOUNCE THAT WE'RE BEING ACQUIRED BY A FOREIGN COMPANY.
DON'T WORRY THAT THEY'LL DOMINATE US. THIS WILL BE A MERGER OF EQUALS.
MERGER OF EQUALS
EXCEPT THAT THEY MAKE MONEY AND WE DON'T.
AND THEIR CEO WILL LEAD THE COMBINED COMPANY.
AND EVERY ONE OF THEM IS A GIANT.
©2001 United Feature Syndicate, Inc.
11/25/01
AND THEY'VE DEVEL-OPED THEIR LATENT PSYCHIC ABILITIES SO THEY CAN CAUSE PAIN FROM A DISTANCE.
GAAA!! I'M SORRY I SAID TOO MUCH! YOU ARE MY MASTER!!
ARE YOU WOR-RIED?
NAH. IF THEY READ MY MIND, THEY'LL ALL GO BLIND.

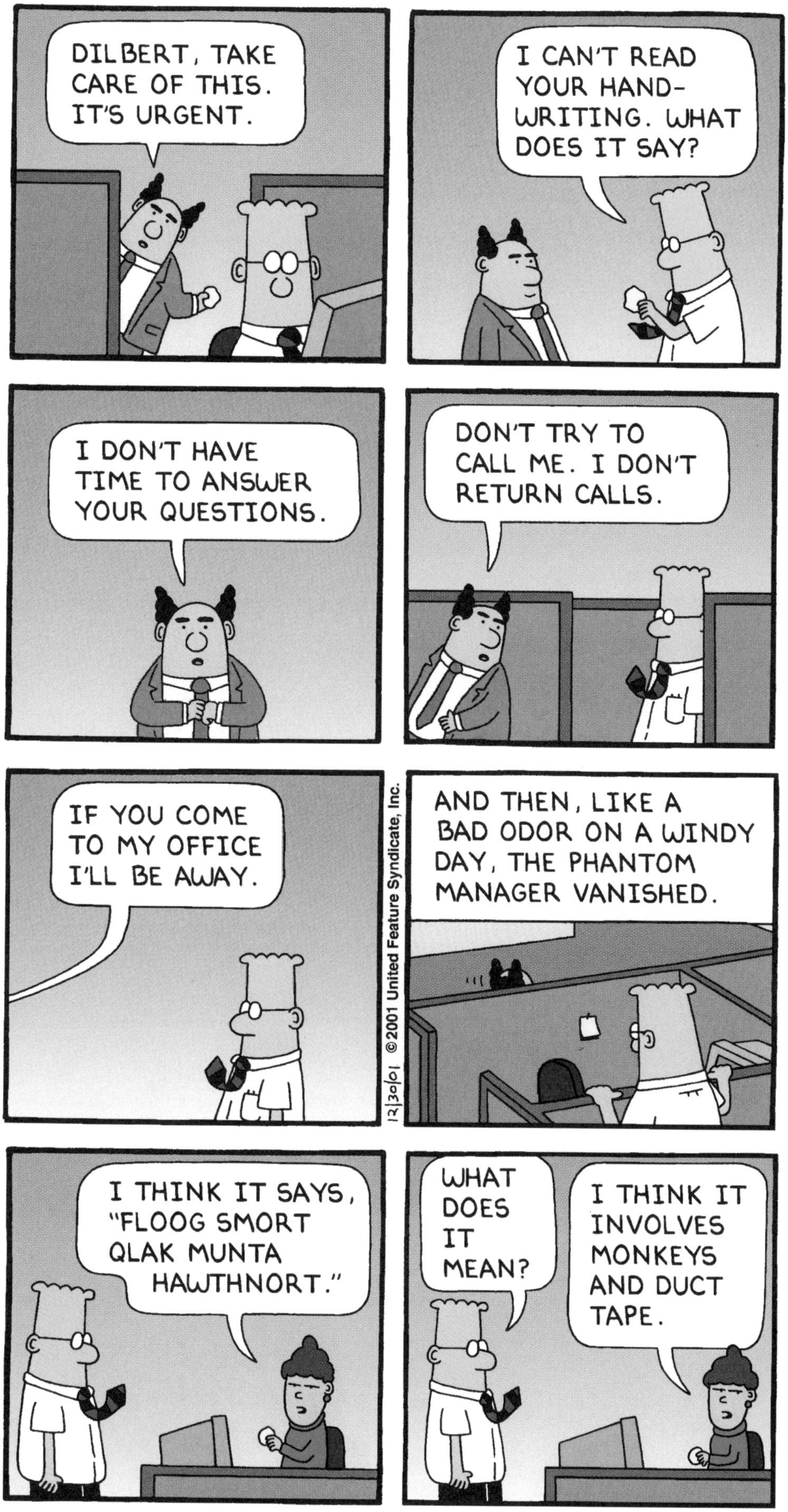
DILBERT, TAKE CARE OF THIS. IT'S URGENT.
I CAN'T READ YOUR HAND-WRITING. WHAT DOES IT SAY?
I DON'T HAVE TIME TO ANSWER YOUR QUESTIONS.
DON'T TRY TO CALL ME. I DON'T RETURN CALLS.
IF YOU COME TO MY OFFICE I'LL BE AWAY.
12/30/01 ©2001 United Feature Syndicate, Inc.
AND THEN, LIKE A BAD ODOR ON A WINDY DAY, THE PHANTOM MANAGER VANISHED.
I THINK IT SAYS, "FLOOG SMORT QLAK MUNTA HAWTHNORT."
WHAT DOES IT MEAN?
I THINK IT INVOLVES MONKEYS AND DUCT TAPE.

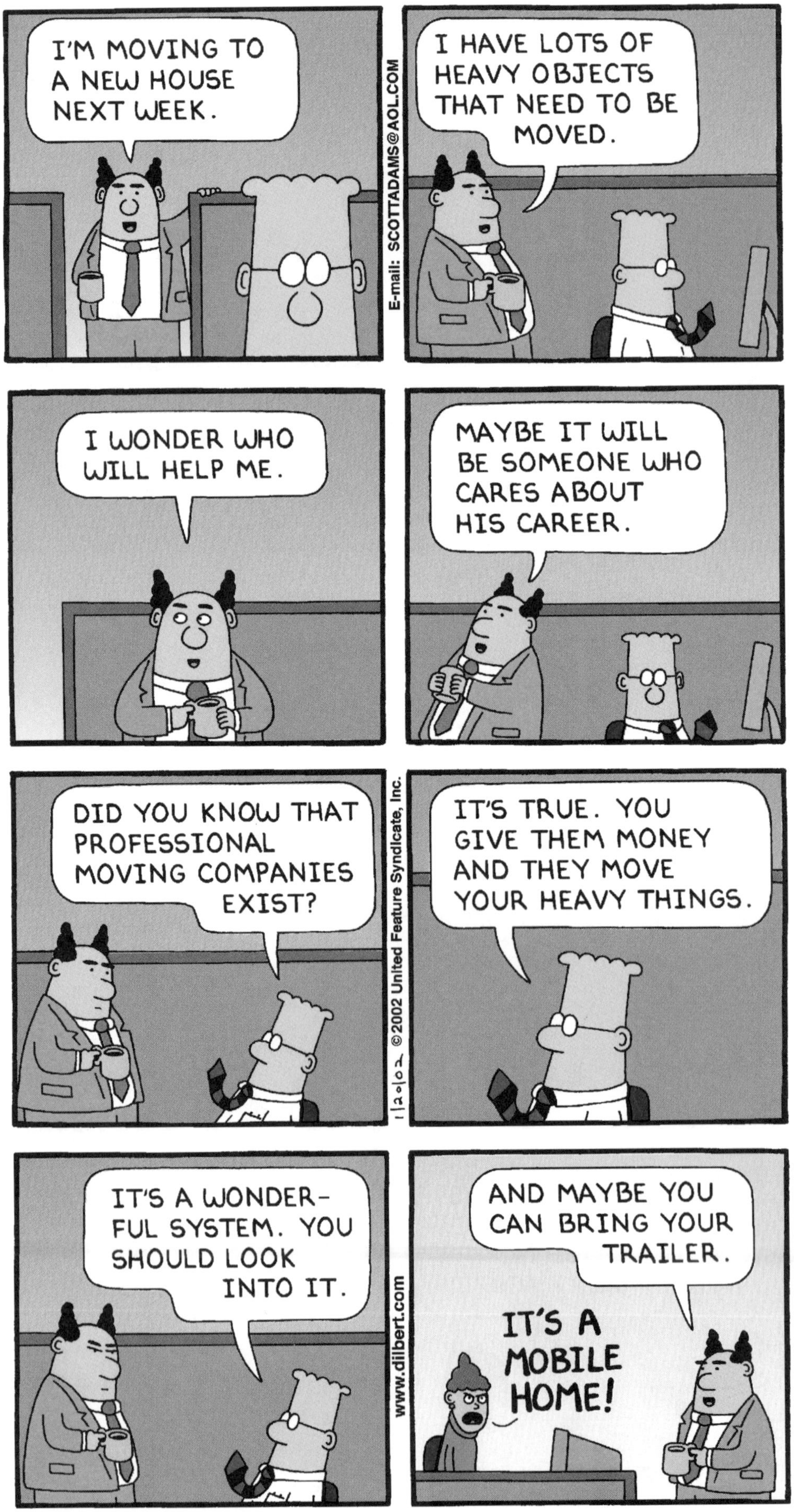
I'M MOVING TO A NEW HOUSE NEXT WEEK.
E-mail: SCOTTADAMS@AOL.COM
I HAVE LOTS OF HEAVY OBJECTS THAT NEED TO BE MOVED.
I WONDER WHO WILL HELP ME.
MAYBE IT WILL BE SOMEONE WHO CARES ABOUT HIS CAREER.
DID YOU KNOW THAT PROFESSIONAL MOVING COMPANIES EXIST?
1/20/02 ©2002 United Feature Syndicate, Inc.
IT'S TRUE. YOU GIVE THEM MONEY AND THEY MOVE YOUR HEAVY THINGS.
IT'S A WONDER-FUL SYSTEM. YOU SHOULD LOOK INTO IT.
www.dilbert.com
AND MAYBE YOU CAN BRING YOUR TRAILER.
IT'S A MOBILE HOME!

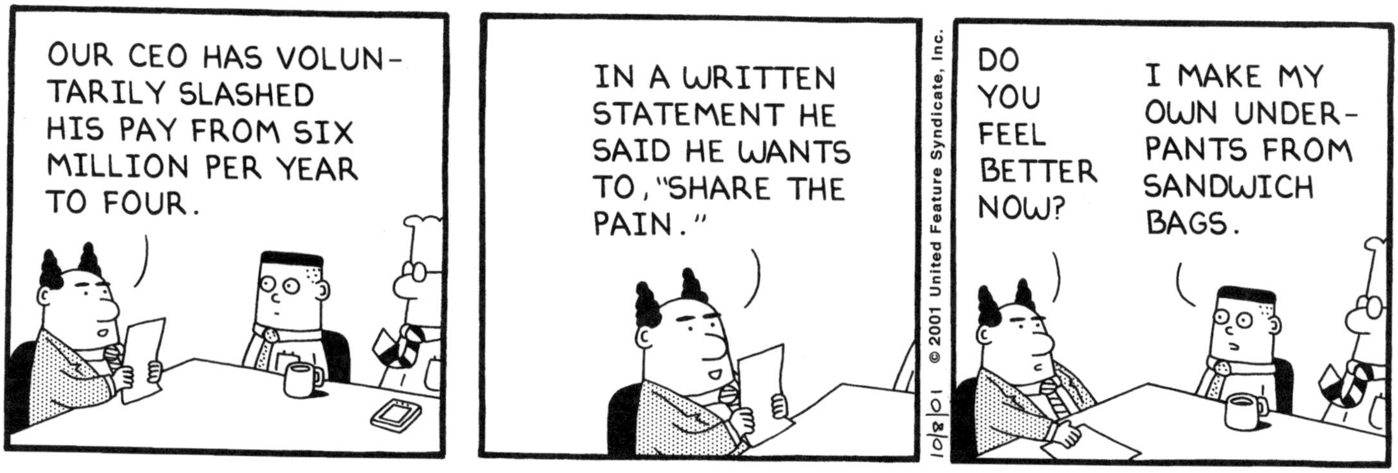
OUR CEO HAS VOLUNTARILY SLASHED HIS PAY FROM SIX MILLION PER YEAR TO FOUR.
IN A WRITTEN STATEMENT HE SAID HE WANTS TO, "SHARE THE PAIN."
10/8/01 © 2001 United Feature Syndicate, Inc.
DO YOU FEEL BETTER NOW?
I MAKE MY OWN UNDERPANTS FROM SANDWICH BAGS.

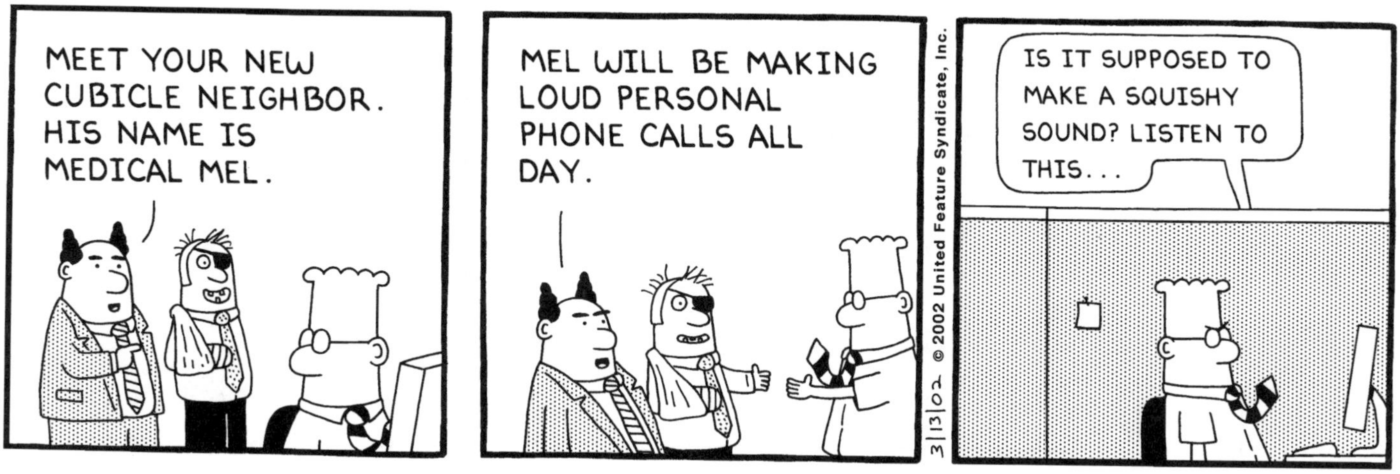
MEET YOUR NEW CUBICLE NEIGHBOR. HIS NAME IS MEDICAL MEL.
MEL WILL BE MAKING LOUD PERSONAL PHONE CALLS ALL DAY.
3/13/02 © 2002 United Feature Syndicate, Inc.
IS IT SUPPOSED TO MAKE A SQUISHY SOUND? LISTEN TO THIS...

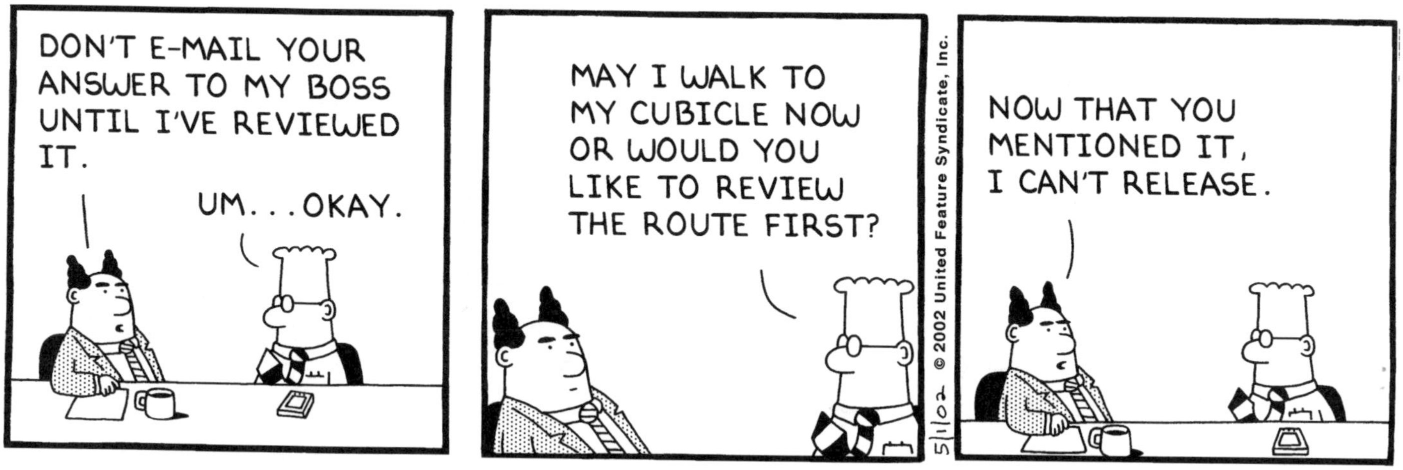
DON'T E-MAIL YOUR ANSWER TO MY BOSS UNTIL I'VE REVIEWED IT.
UM...OKAY.
MAY I WALK TO MY CUBICLE NOW OR WOULD YOU LIKE TO REVIEW THE ROUTE FIRST?
5/1/02 © 2002 United Feature Syndicate, Inc.
NOW THAT YOU MENTIONED IT, I CAN'T RELEASE.

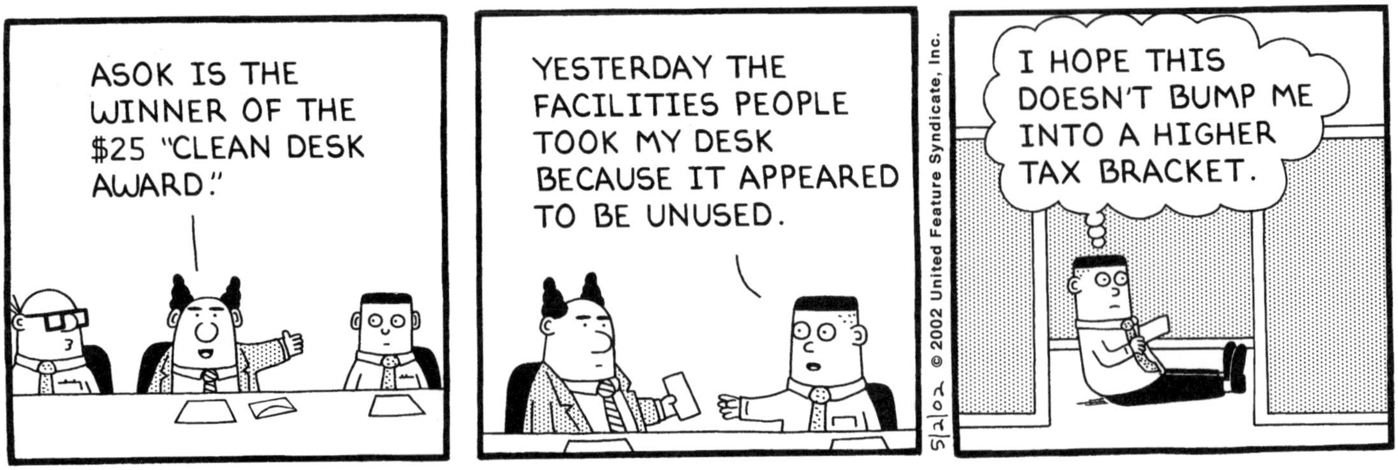
ASOK IS THE WINNER OF THE $25 "CLEAN DESK AWARD."
YESTERDAY THE FACILITIES PEOPLE TOOK MY DESK BECAUSE IT APPEARED TO BE UNUSED.
5/2/02 © 2002 United Feature Syndicate, Inc.
I HOPE THIS DOESN'T BUMP ME INTO A HIGHER TAX BRACKET.

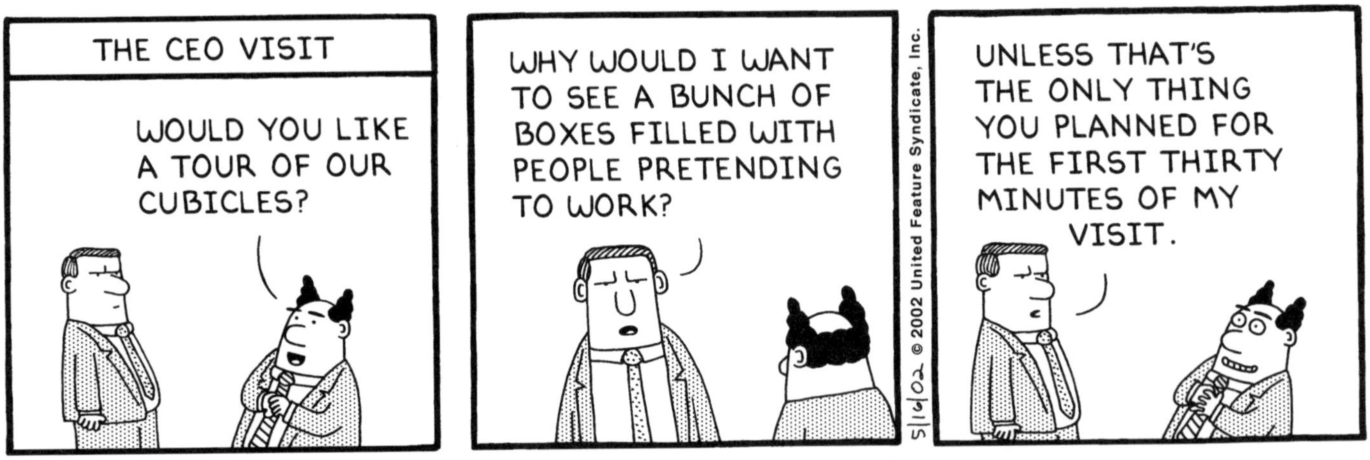
THE CEO VISIT
WOULD YOU LIKE A TOUR OF OUR CUBICLES?
WHY WOULD I WANT TO SEE A BUNCH OF BOXES FILLED WITH PEOPLE PRETENDING TO WORK?
5/16/02 © 2002 United Feature Syndicate, Inc.
UNLESS THAT'S THE ONLY THING YOU PLANNED FOR THE FIRST THIRTY MINUTES OF MY VISIT.

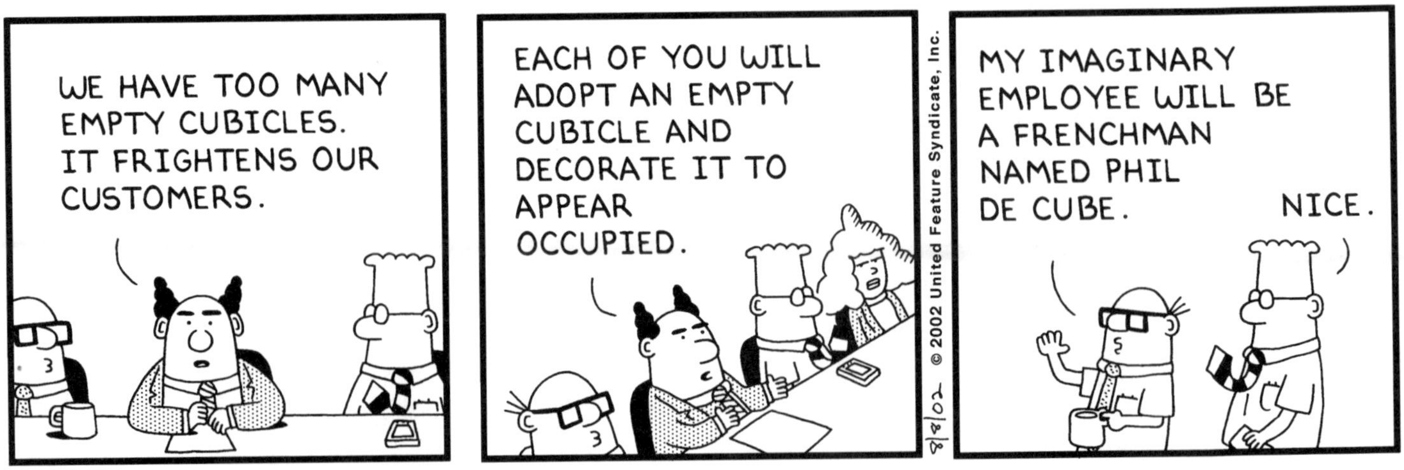
WE HAVE TOO MANY EMPTY CUBICLES. IT FRIGHTENS OUR CUSTOMERS.
EACH OF YOU WILL ADOPT AN EMPTY CUBICLE AND DECORATE IT TO APPEAR OCCUPIED.
8/8/02 © 2002 United Feature Syndicate, Inc.
MY IMAGINARY EMPLOYEE WILL BE A FRENCHMAN NAMED PHIL DE CUBE.
NICE.

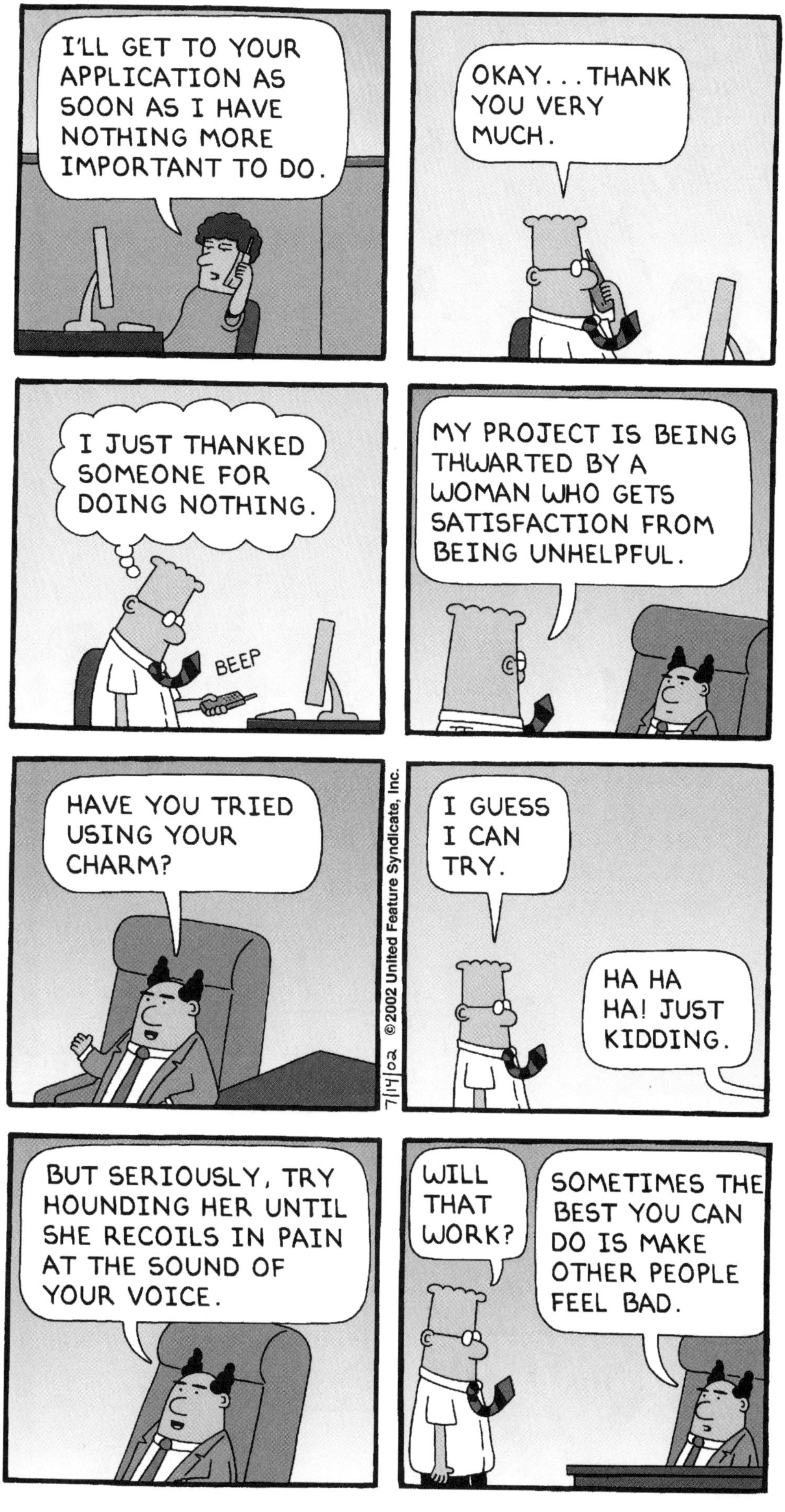
I'LL GET TO YOUR APPLICATION AS SOON AS I HAVE NOTHING MORE IMPORTANT TO DO.
OKAY. . . THANK YOU VERY MUCH.
I JUST THANKED SOMEONE FOR DOING NOTHING.
BEEP
MY PROJECT IS BEING THWARTED BY A WOMAN WHO GETS SATISFACTION FROM BEING UNHELPFUL.
HAVE YOU TRIED USING YOUR CHARM?
7/14/02 ©2002 United Feature Syndicate, Inc.
I GUESS I CAN TRY.
HA HA HA! JUST KIDDING.
BUT SERIOUSLY, TRY HOUNDING HER UNTIL SHE RECOILS IN PAIN AT THE SOUND OF YOUR VOICE.
WILL THAT WORK?
SOMETIMES THE BEST YOU CAN DO IS MAKE OTHER PEOPLE FEEL BAD.

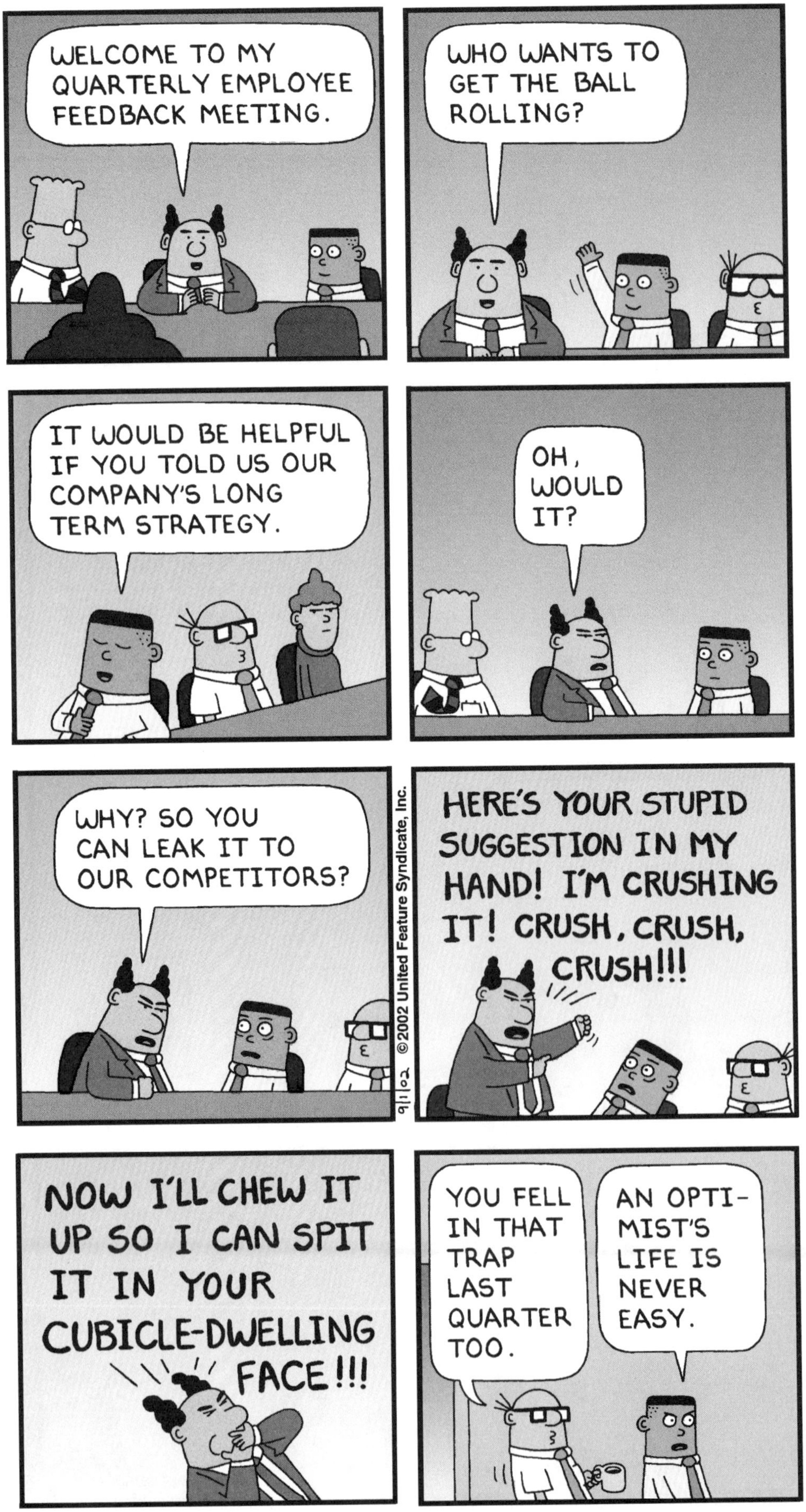
WELCOME TO MY QUARTERLY EMPLOYEE FEEDBACK MEETING.
WHO WANTS TO GET THE BALL ROLLING?
IT WOULD BE HELPFUL IF YOU TOLD US OUR COMPANY'S LONG TERM STRATEGY.
OH, WOULD IT?
WHY? SO YOU CAN LEAK IT TO OUR COMPETITORS?
©2002 United Feature Syndicate, Inc.
9/1/02
HERE'S YOUR STUPID SUGGESTION IN MY HAND! I'M CRUSHING IT! CRUSH, CRUSH, CRUSH!!!
NOW I'LL CHEW IT UP SO I CAN SPIT IT IN YOUR CUBICLE-DWELLING FACE!!!
YOU FELL IN THAT TRAP LAST QUARTER TOO.
AN OPTI-MIST'S LIFE IS NEVER EASY.

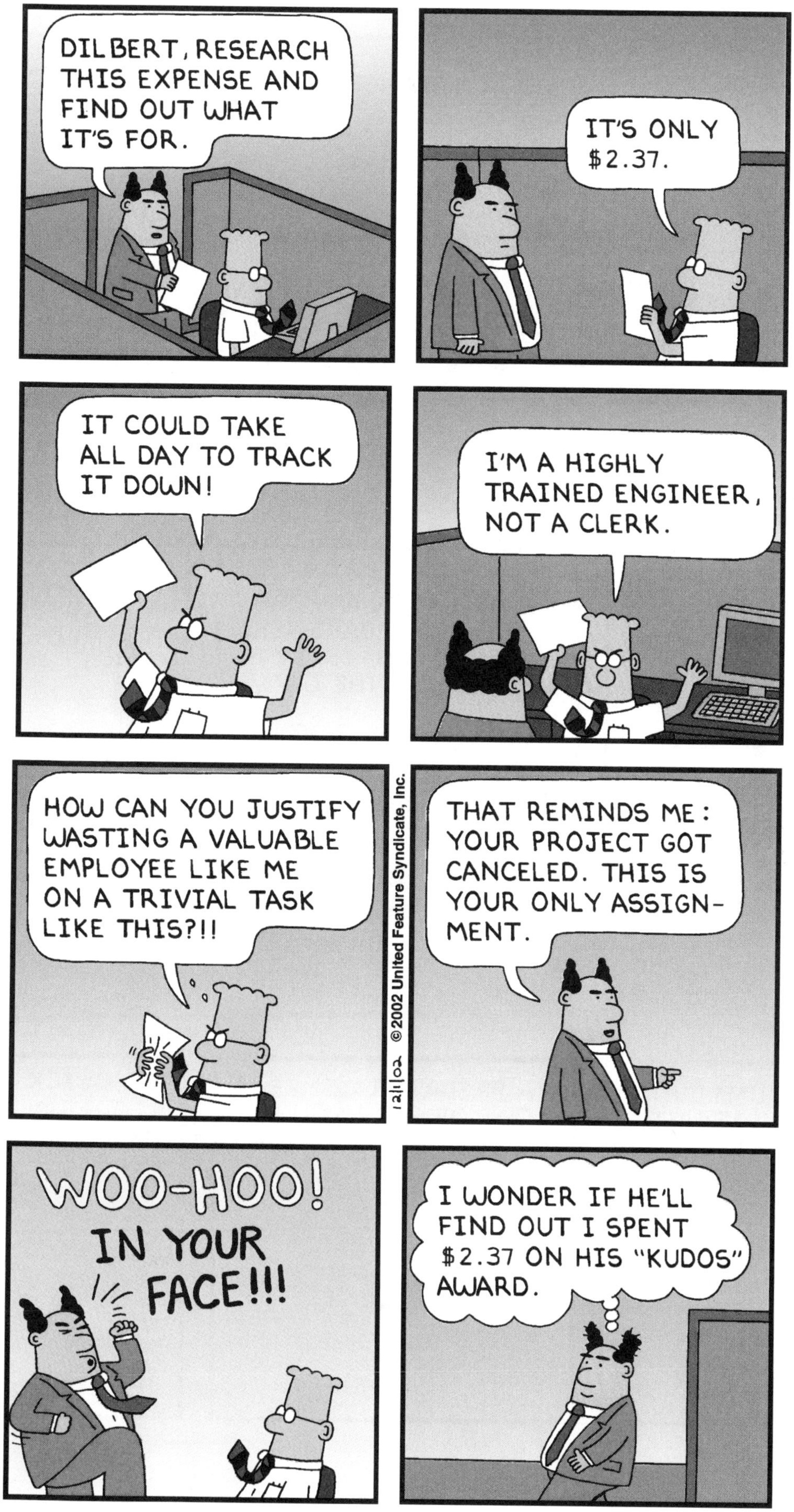
DILBERT, RESEARCH THIS EXPENSE AND FIND OUT WHAT IT'S FOR.
IT'S ONLY $2.37.
IT COULD TAKE ALL DAY TO TRACK IT DOWN!
I'M A HIGHLY TRAINED ENGINEER, NOT A CLERK.
HOW CAN YOU JUSTIFY WASTING A VALUABLE EMPLOYEE LIKE ME ON A TRIVIAL TASK LIKE THIS?!!
12/1/02 ©2002 United Feature Syndicate, Inc.
THAT REMINDS ME: YOUR PROJECT GOT CANCELED. THIS IS YOUR ONLY ASSIGN-MENT.
WOO-HOO!
IN YOUR FACE!!!
I WONDER IF HE'LL FIND OUT I SPENT $2.37 ON HIS "KUDOS" AWARD.

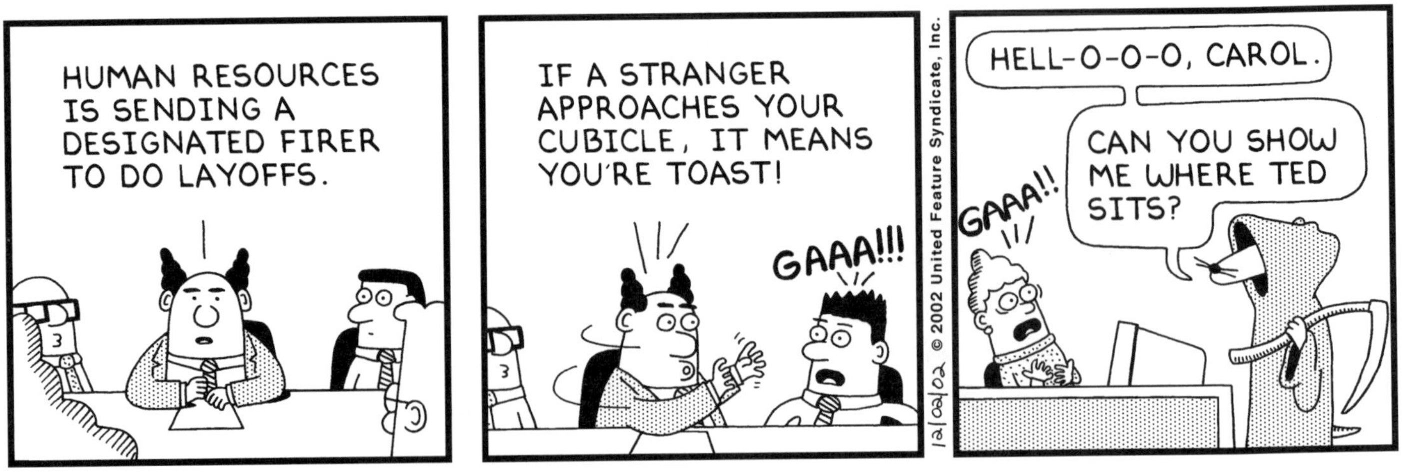
HUMAN RESOURCES IS SENDING A DESIGNATED FIRER TO DO LAYOFFS.
IF A STRANGER APPROACHES YOUR CUBICLE, IT MEANS YOU'RE TOAST!
GAAA!!!
HELL-O-O-O, CAROL.
CAN YOU SHOW ME WHERE TED SITS?
GAAA!!
12/02/02 © 2002 United Feature Syndicate, Inc.

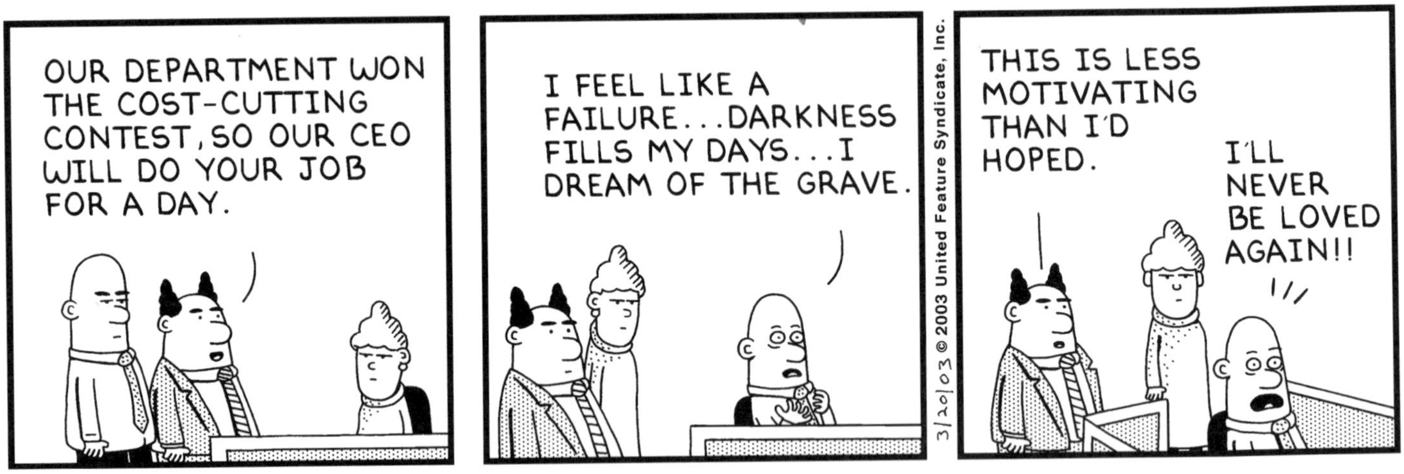
OUR DEPARTMENT WON THE COST-CUTTING CONTEST, SO OUR CEO WILL DO YOUR JOB FOR A DAY.
I FEEL LIKE A FAILURE...DARKNESS FILLS MY DAYS...I DREAM OF THE GRAVE.
THIS IS LESS MOTIVATING THAN I'D HOPED.
I'LL NEVER BE LOVED AGAIN!!
3/20/03 © 2003 United Feature Syndicate, Inc.

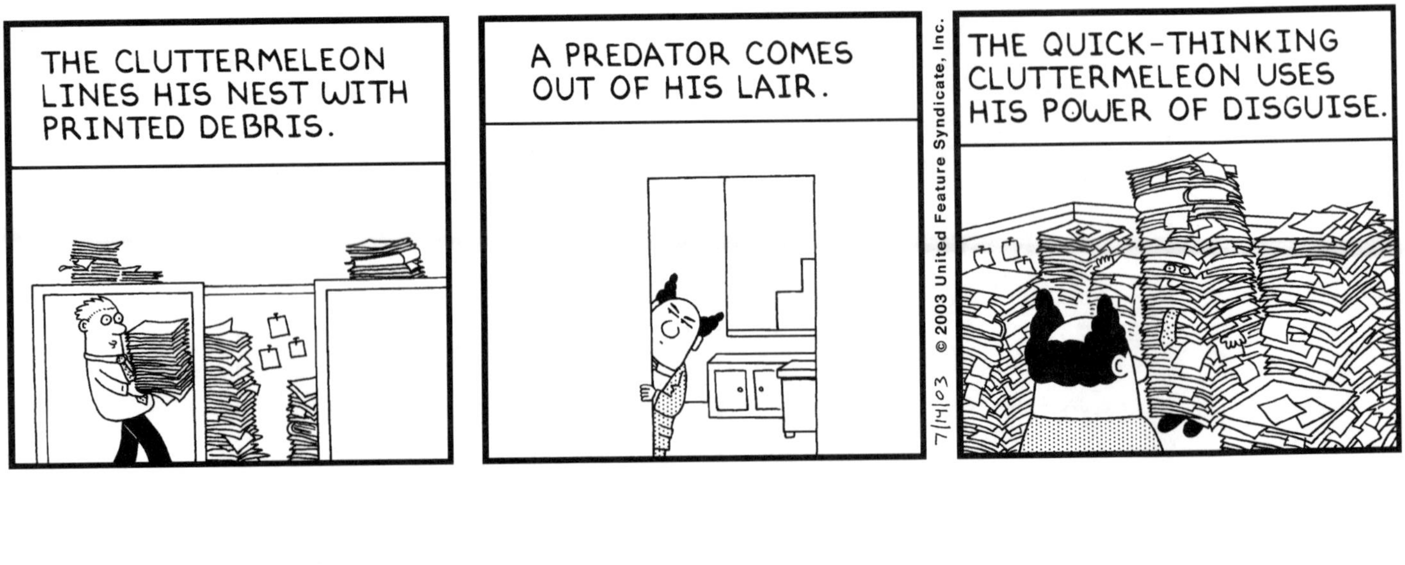
THE CLUTTERMELEON LINES HIS NEST WITH PRINTED DEBRIS.
A PREDATOR COMES OUT OF HIS LAIR.
THE QUICK-THINKING CLUTTERMELEON USES HIS POWER OF DISGUISE.
7/14/03 © 2003 United Feature Syndicate, Inc.

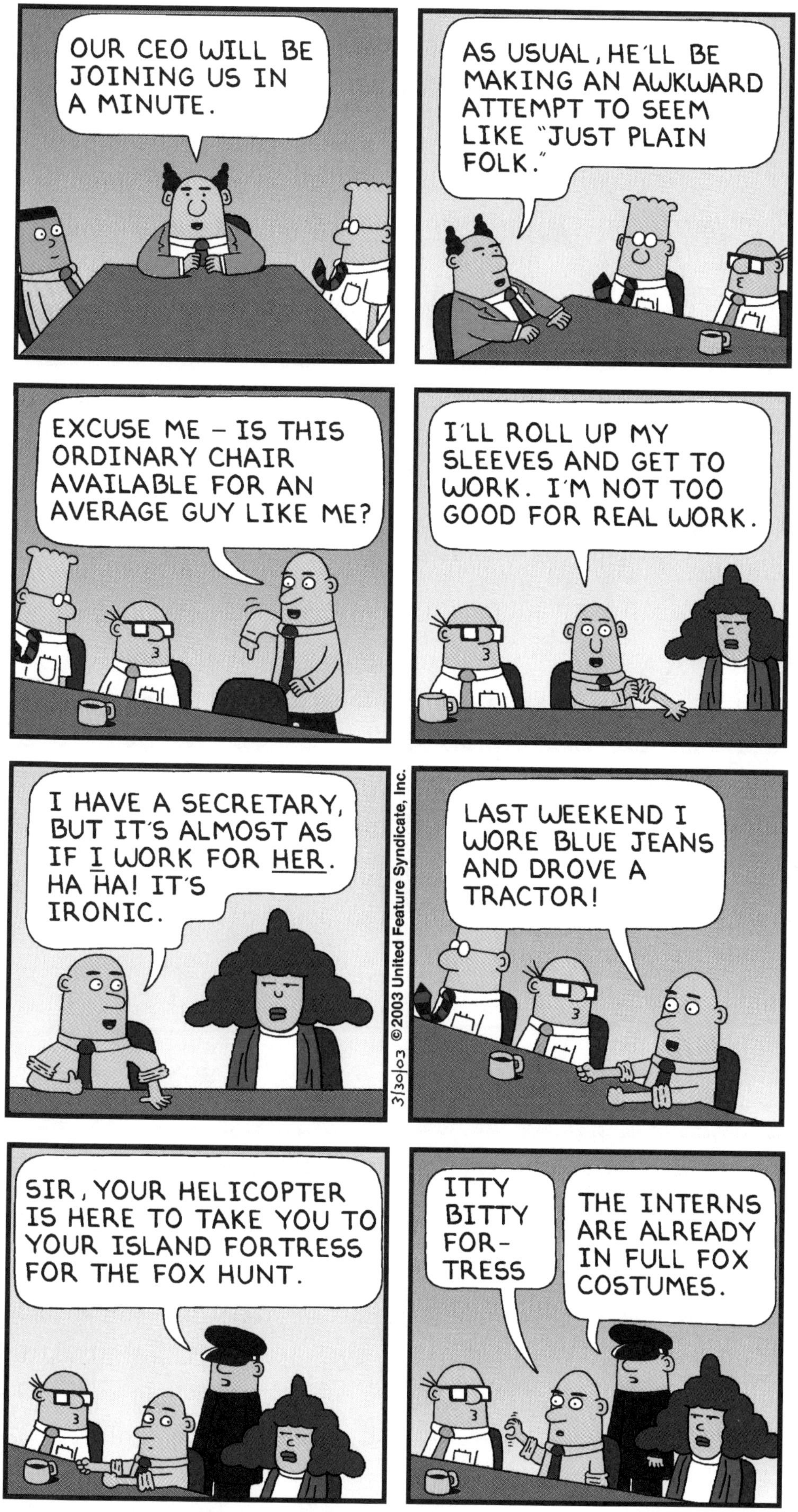
OUR CEO WILL BE JOINING US IN A MINUTE.
AS USUAL, HE'LL BE MAKING AN AWKWARD ATTEMPT TO SEEM LIKE "JUST PLAIN FOLK."
EXCUSE ME – IS THIS ORDINARY CHAIR AVAILABLE FOR AN AVERAGE GUY LIKE ME?
I'LL ROLL UP MY SLEEVES AND GET TO WORK. I'M NOT TOO GOOD FOR REAL WORK.
I HAVE A SECRETARY, BUT IT'S ALMOST AS IF I WORK FOR HER. HA HA! IT'S IRONIC.
3/30/03 ©2003 United Feature Syndicate, Inc.
LAST WEEKEND I WORE BLUE JEANS AND DROVE A TRACTOR!
SIR, YOUR HELICOPTER IS HERE TO TAKE YOU TO YOUR ISLAND FORTRESS FOR THE FOX HUNT.
ITTY BITTY FOR-TRESS
THE INTERNS ARE ALREADY IN FULL FOX COSTUMES.

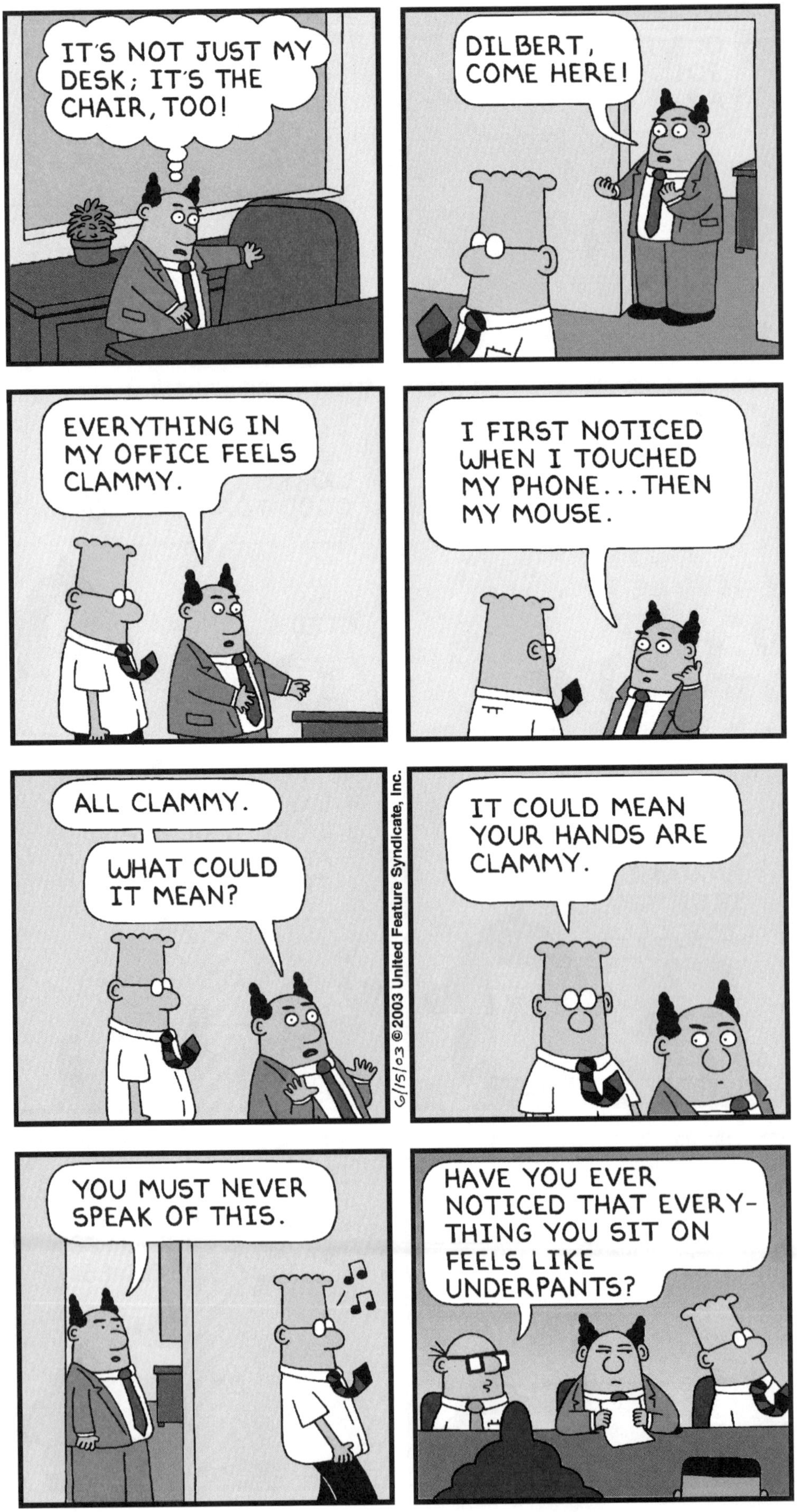
IT'S NOT JUST MY DESK; IT'S THE CHAIR, TOO!
DILBERT, COME HERE!
EVERYTHING IN MY OFFICE FEELS CLAMMY.
I FIRST NOTICED WHEN I TOUCHED MY PHONE...THEN MY MOUSE.
ALL CLAMMY.
WHAT COULD IT MEAN?
IT COULD MEAN YOUR HANDS ARE CLAMMY.
6/15/03 © 2003 United Feature Syndicate, Inc.
YOU MUST NEVER SPEAK OF THIS.
HAVE YOU EVER NOTICED THAT EVERYTHING YOU SIT ON FEELS LIKE UNDERPANTS?

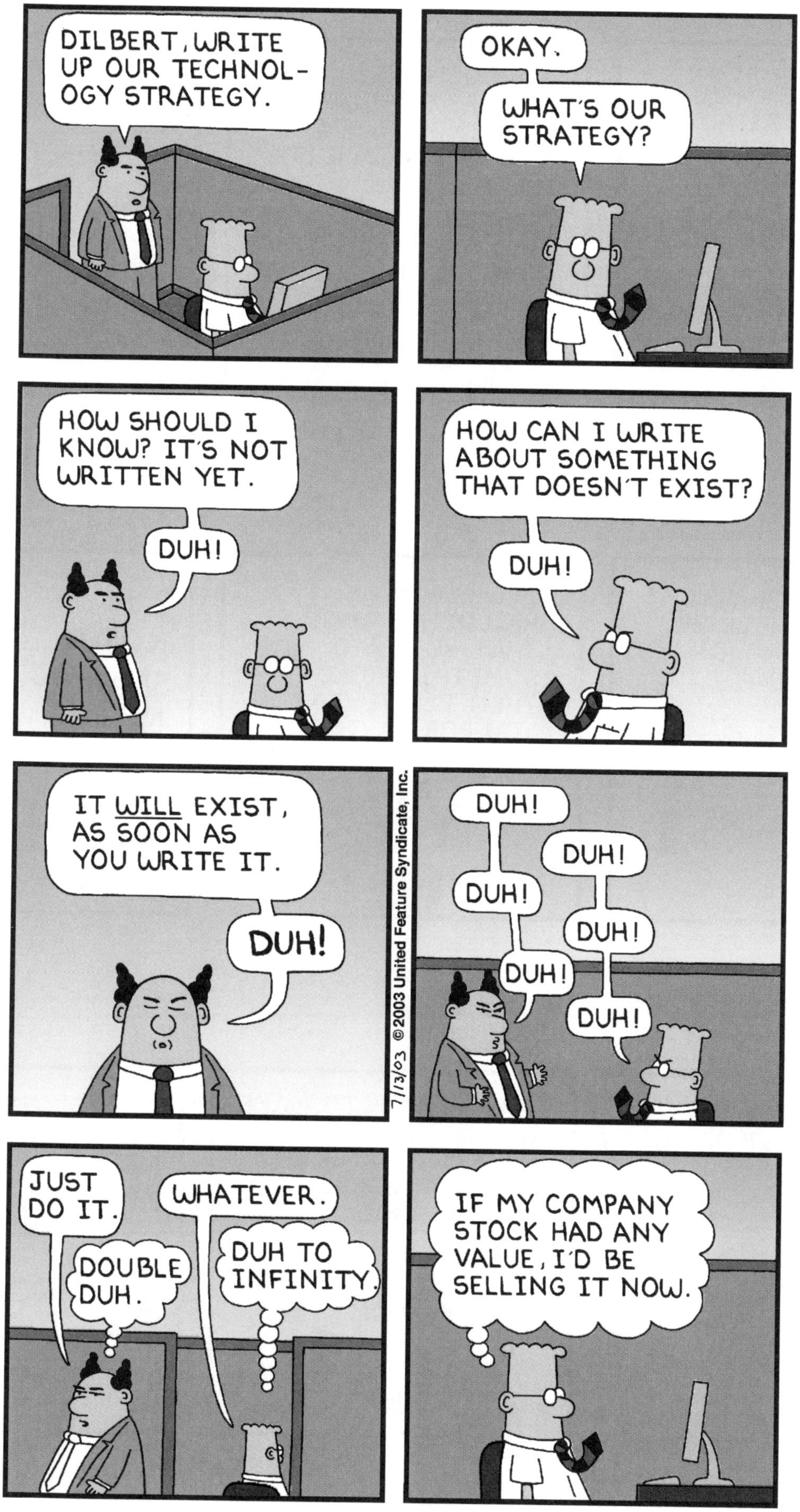
DILBERT, WRITE UP OUR TECHNOL-OGY STRATEGY.
OKAY.
WHAT'S OUR STRATEGY?
HOW SHOULD I KNOW? IT'S NOT WRITTEN YET.
DUH!
HOW CAN I WRITE ABOUT SOMETHING THAT DOESN'T EXIST?
DUH!
IT WILL EXIST, AS SOON AS YOU WRITE IT.
DUH!
DUH!
DUH!
DUH!
DUH!
DUH!
DUH!
JUST DO IT.
WHATEVER.
DOUBLE DUH.
DUH TO INFINITY.
IF MY COMPANY STOCK HAD ANY VALUE, I'D BE SELLING IT NOW.
7/13/03

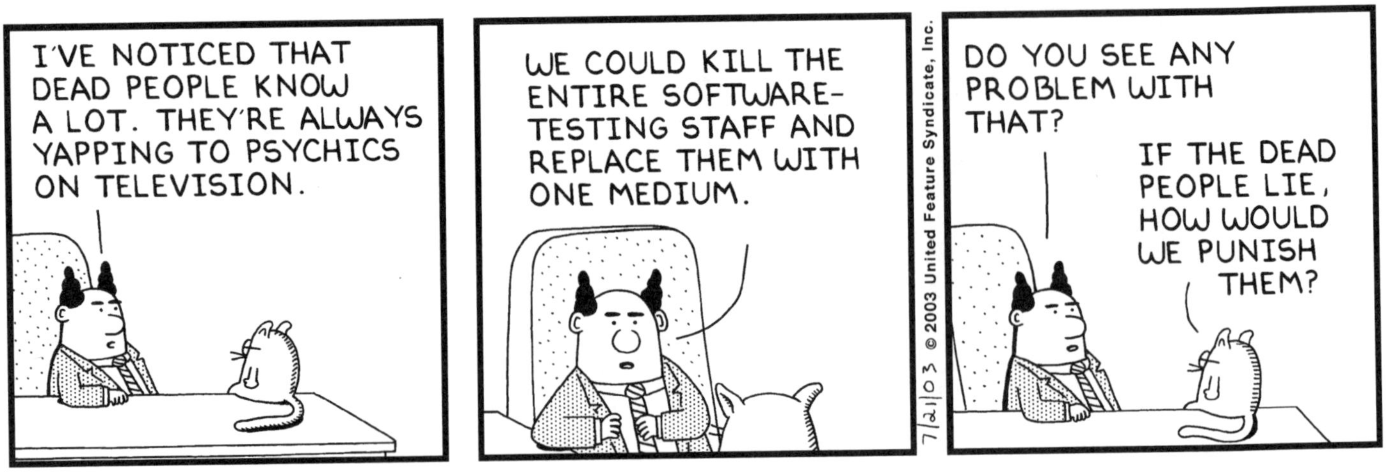
I'VE NOTICED THAT DEAD PEOPLE KNOW A LOT. THEY'RE ALWAYS YAPPING TO PSYCHICS ON TELEVISION.
WE COULD KILL THE ENTIRE SOFTWARE-TESTING STAFF AND REPLACE THEM WITH ONE MEDIUM.
7/21/03 © 2003 United Feature Syndicate, Inc.
DO YOU SEE ANY PROBLEM WITH THAT?
IF THE DEAD PEOPLE LIE, HOW WOULD WE PUNISH THEM?

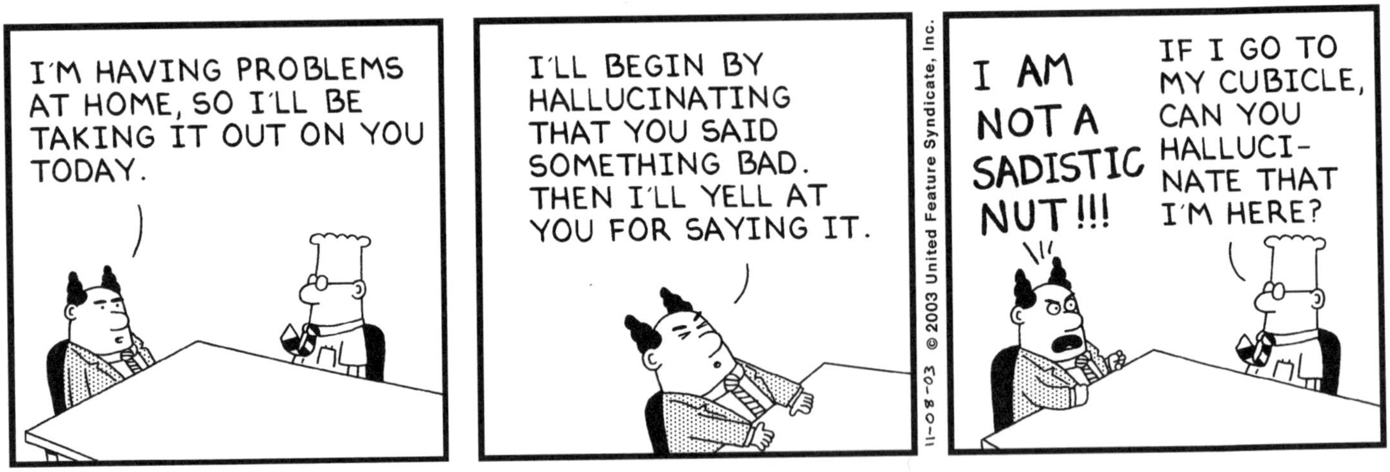
I'M HAVING PROBLEMS AT HOME, SO I'LL BE TAKING IT OUT ON YOU TODAY.
I'LL BEGIN BY HALLUCINATING THAT YOU SAID SOMETHING BAD. THEN I'LL YELL AT YOU FOR SAYING IT.
11-08-03 © 2003 United Feature Syndicate, Inc.
I AM NOT A SADISTIC NUT!!!
IF I GO TO MY CUBICLE, CAN YOU HALLUCI-NATE THAT I'M HERE?

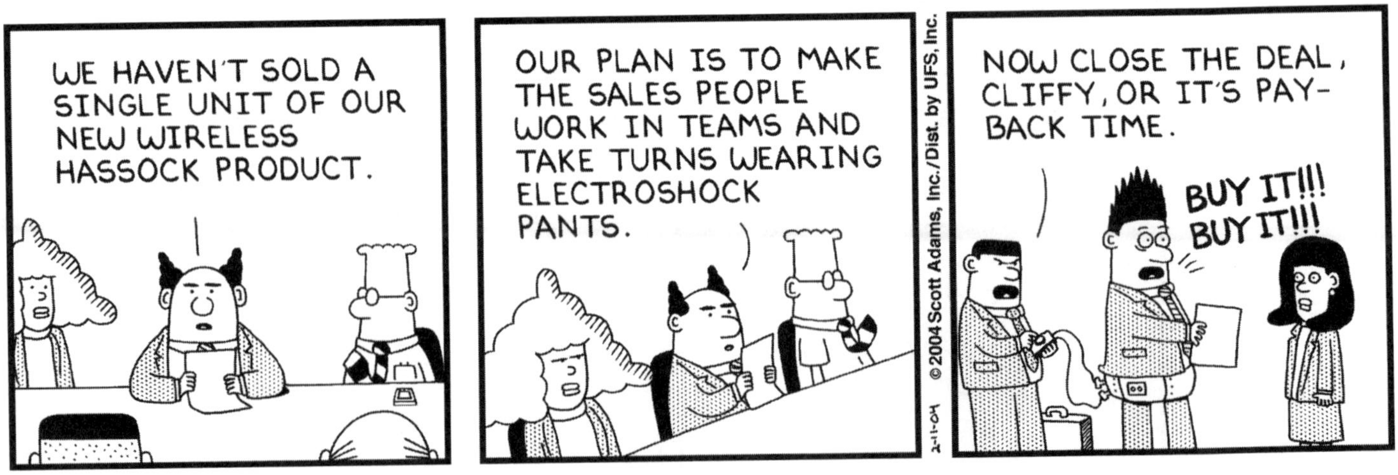
WE HAVEN'T SOLD A SINGLE UNIT OF OUR NEW WIRELESS HASSOCK PRODUCT.
OUR PLAN IS TO MAKE THE SALES PEOPLE WORK IN TEAMS AND TAKE TURNS WEARING ELECTROSHOCK PANTS.
2-11-04 ©2004 Scott Adams, Inc./Dist. by UFS, Inc.
NOW CLOSE THE DEAL, CLIFFY, OR IT'S PAY-BACK TIME.
BUY IT!!! BUY IT!!!

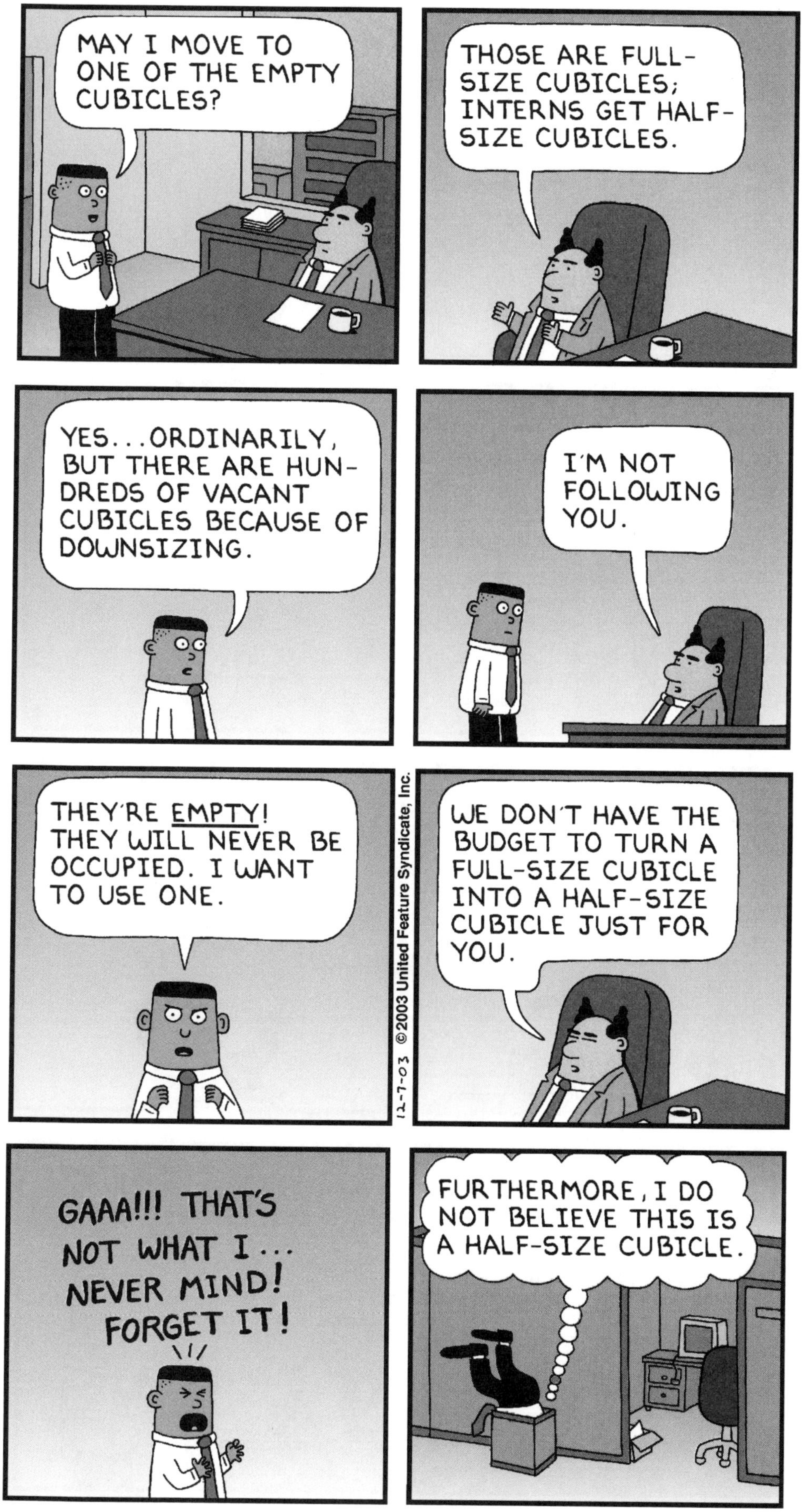
MAY I MOVE TO ONE OF THE EMPTY CUBICLES?
THOSE ARE FULL-SIZE CUBICLES; INTERNS GET HALF-SIZE CUBICLES.
YES...ORDINARILY, BUT THERE ARE HUNDREDS OF VACANT CUBICLES BECAUSE OF DOWNSIZING.
I'M NOT FOLLOWING YOU.
THEY'RE EMPTY! THEY WILL NEVER BE OCCUPIED. I WANT TO USE ONE.
12-7-03 ©2003 United Feature Syndicate, Inc.
WE DON'T HAVE THE BUDGET TO TURN A FULL-SIZE CUBICLE INTO A HALF-SIZE CUBICLE JUST FOR YOU.
GAAA!!! THAT'S NOT WHAT I... NEVER MIND! FORGET IT!
FURTHERMORE, I DO NOT BELIEVE THIS IS A HALF-SIZE CUBICLE.

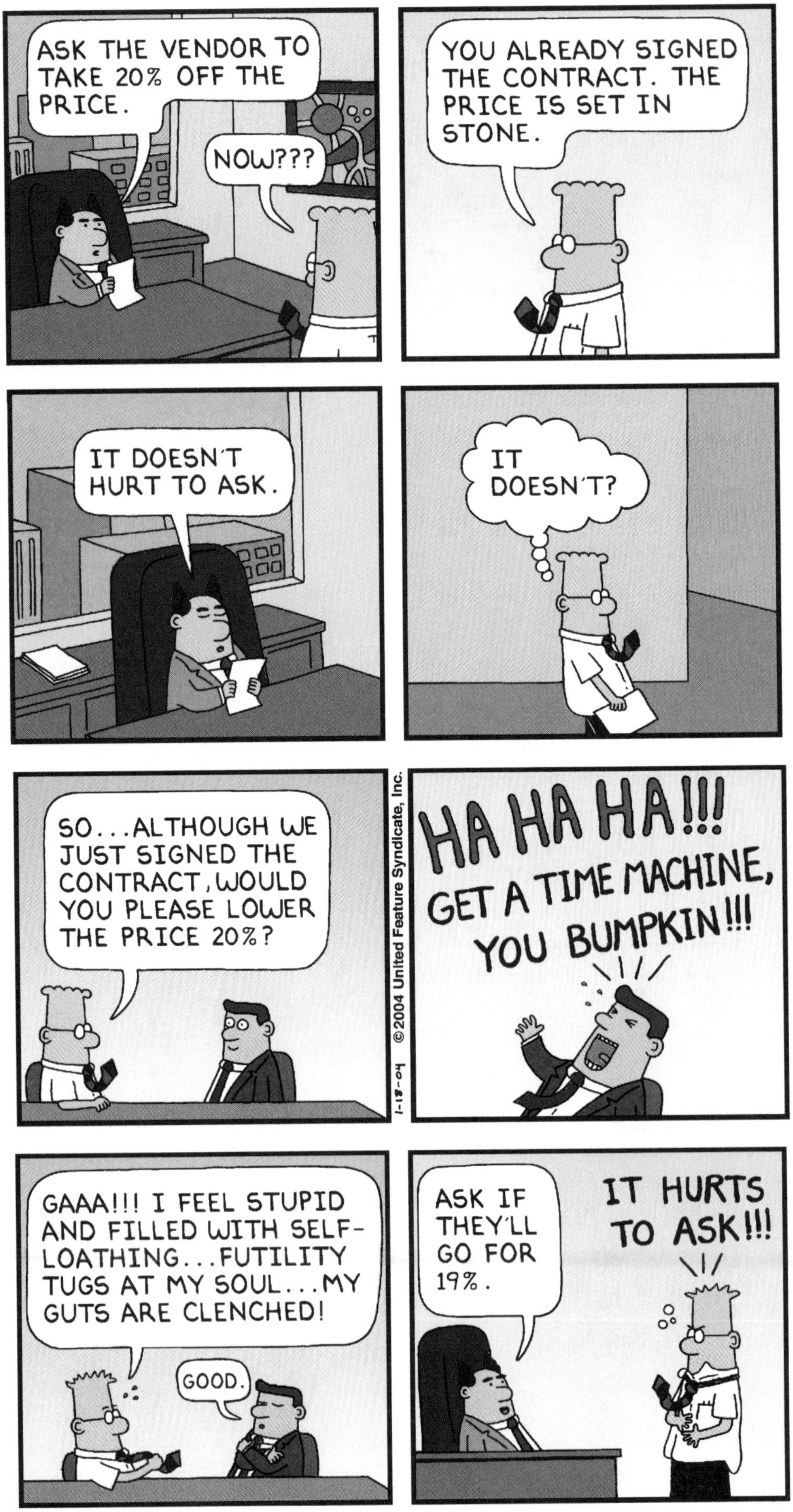

ASK THE VENDOR TO TAKE 20% OFF THE PRICE.
NOW???
YOU ALREADY SIGNED THE CONTRACT. THE PRICE IS SET IN STONE.
IT DOESN'T HURT TO ASK.
IT DOESN'T?
SO...ALTHOUGH WE JUST SIGNED THE CONTRACT, WOULD YOU PLEASE LOWER THE PRICE 20%?
©2004 United Feature Syndicate, Inc.
1-18-04
HA HA HA!!!
GET A TIME MACHINE, YOU BUMPKIN!!!
GAAA!!! I FEEL STUPID AND FILLED WITH SELF-LOATHING...FUTILITY TUGS AT MY SOUL...MY GUTS ARE CLENCHED!
GOOD.
ASK IF THEY'LL GO FOR 19%.
IT HURTS TO ASK!!!

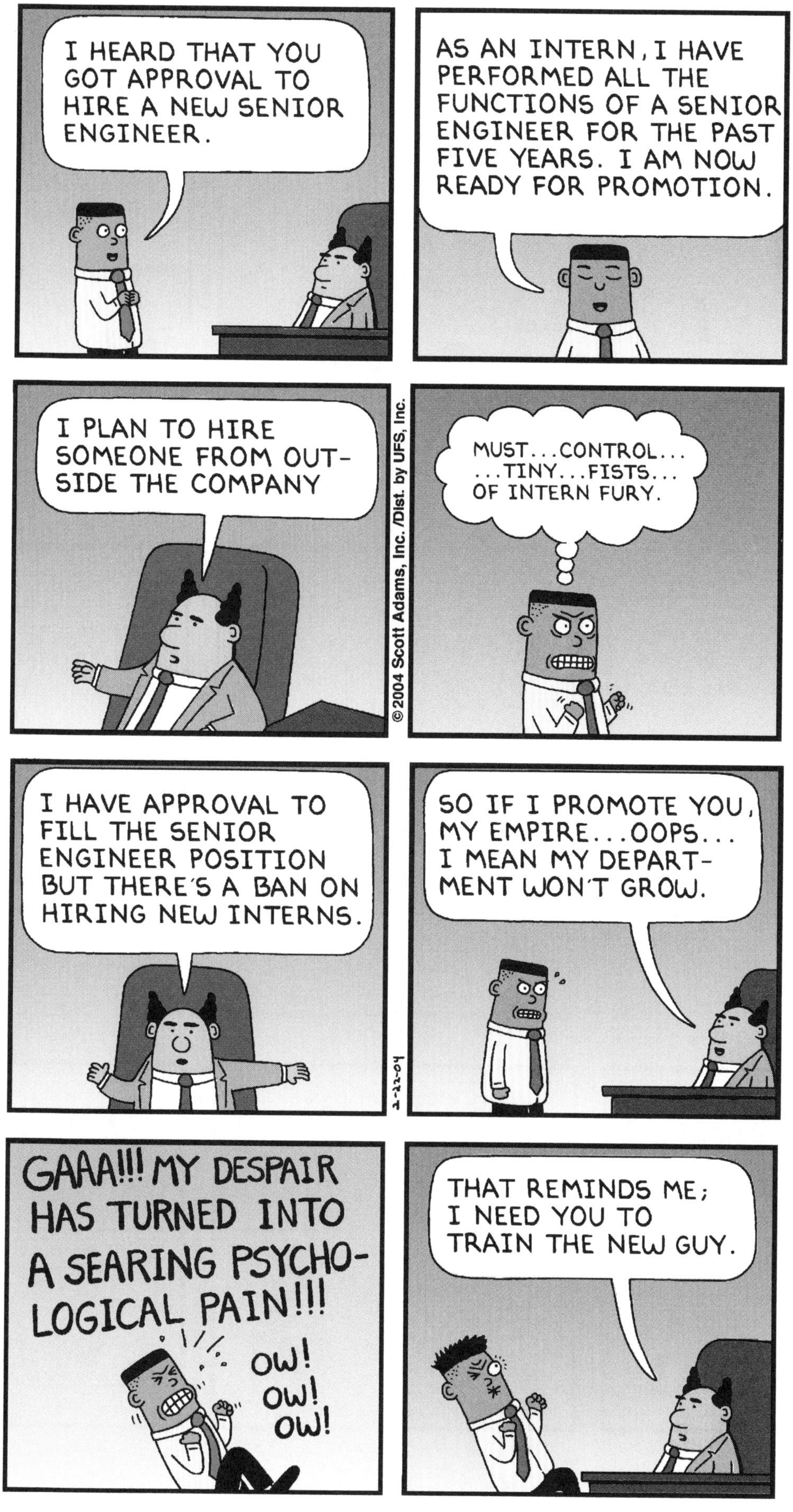
I HEARD THAT YOU GOT APPROVAL TO HIRE A NEW SENIOR ENGINEER.
AS AN INTERN, I HAVE PERFORMED ALL THE FUNCTIONS OF A SENIOR ENGINEER FOR THE PAST FIVE YEARS. I AM NOW READY FOR PROMOTION.
I PLAN TO HIRE SOMEONE FROM OUT-SIDE THE COMPANY
MUST...CONTROL... ...TINY...FISTS... OF INTERN FURY.
©2004 Scott Adams, Inc. /Dist. by UFS, Inc.
I HAVE APPROVAL TO FILL THE SENIOR ENGINEER POSITION BUT THERE'S A BAN ON HIRING NEW INTERNS.
SO IF I PROMOTE YOU, MY EMPIRE...OOPS... I MEAN MY DEPART-MENT WON'T GROW.
GAAA!!! MY DESPAIR HAS TURNED INTO A SEARING PSYCHO-LOGICAL PAIN!!!
OW! OW! OW!
THAT REMINDS ME; I NEED YOU TO TRAIN THE NEW GUY.

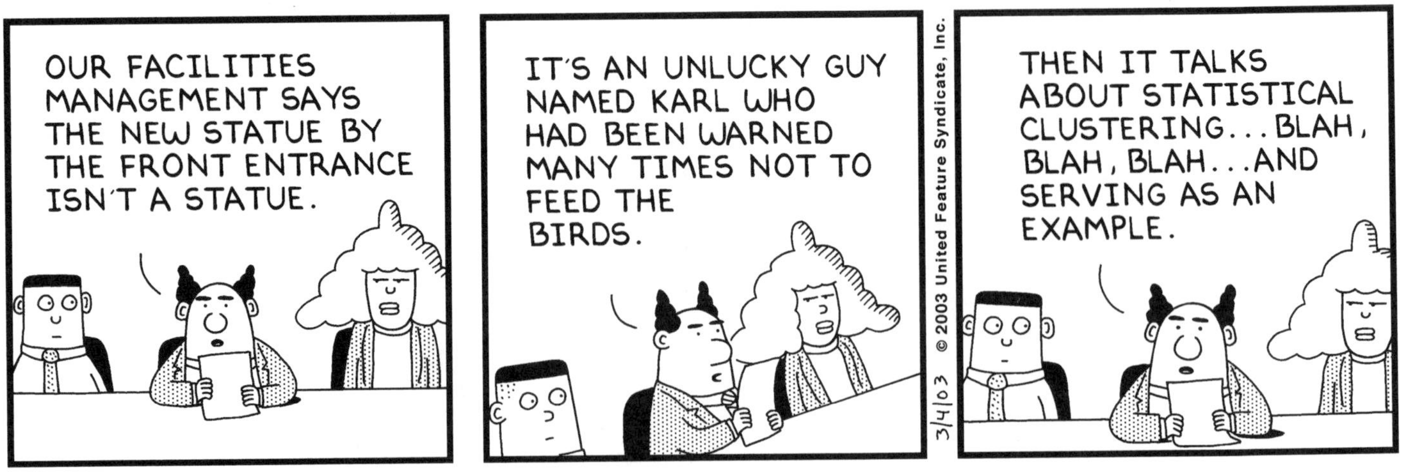
OUR FACILITIES MANAGEMENT SAYS THE NEW STATUE BY THE FRONT ENTRANCE ISN'T A STATUE.
IT'S AN UNLUCKY GUY NAMED KARL WHO HAD BEEN WARNED MANY TIMES NOT TO FEED THE BIRDS.
3/4/03 © 2003 United Feature Syndicate, Inc.
THEN IT TALKS ABOUT STATISTICAL CLUSTERING... BLAH, BLAH, BLAH... AND SERVING AS AN EXAMPLE.

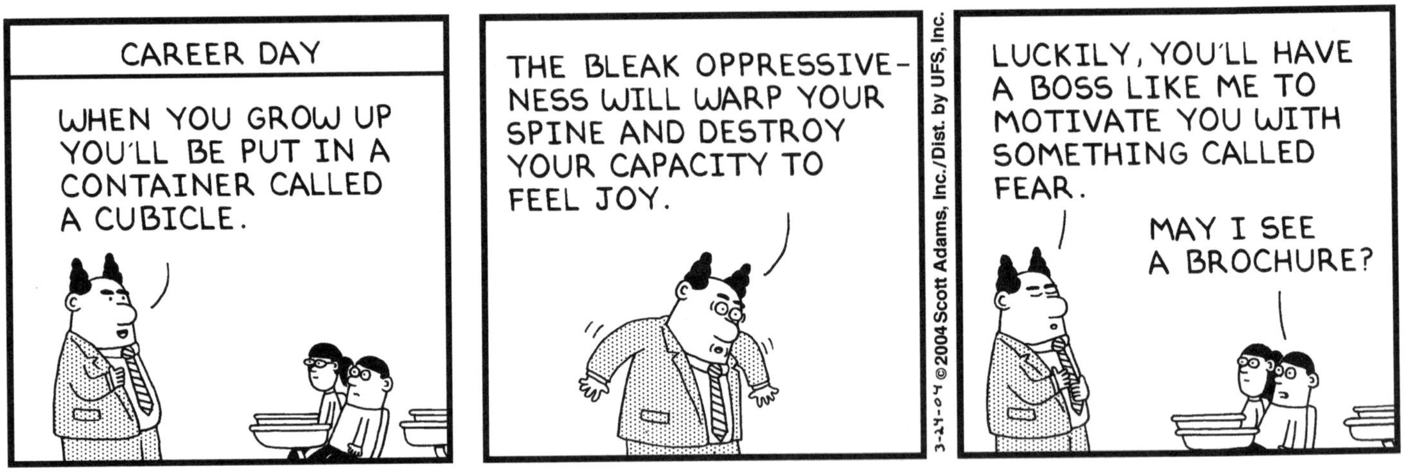
CAREER DAY
WHEN YOU GROW UP YOU'LL BE PUT IN A CONTAINER CALLED A CUBICLE.
THE BLEAK OPPRESSIVE-NESS WILL WARP YOUR SPINE AND DESTROY YOUR CAPACITY TO FEEL JOY.
3-24-04 © 2004 Scott Adams, Inc./Dist. by UFS, Inc.
LUCKILY, YOU'LL HAVE A BOSS LIKE ME TO MOTIVATE YOU WITH SOMETHING CALLED FEAR.
MAY I SEE A BROCHURE?

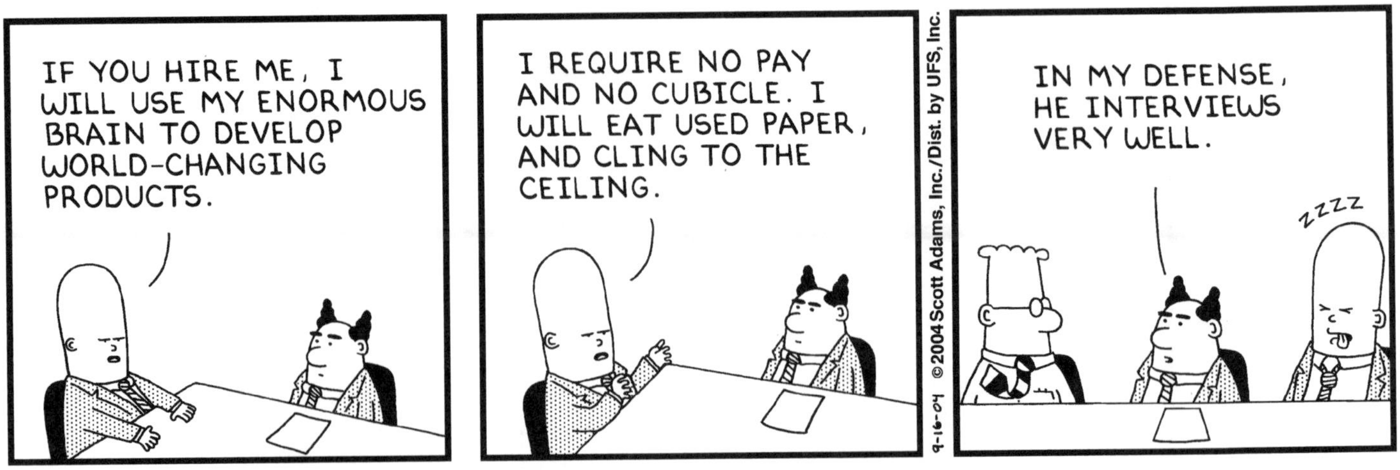
IF YOU HIRE ME, I WILL USE MY ENORMOUS BRAIN TO DEVELOP WORLD-CHANGING PRODUCTS.
I REQUIRE NO PAY AND NO CUBICLE. I WILL EAT USED PAPER, AND CLING TO THE CEILING.
9-16-04 © 2004 Scott Adams, Inc./Dist. by UFS, Inc.
IN MY DEFENSE, HE INTERVIEWS VERY WELL.
ZZZZ

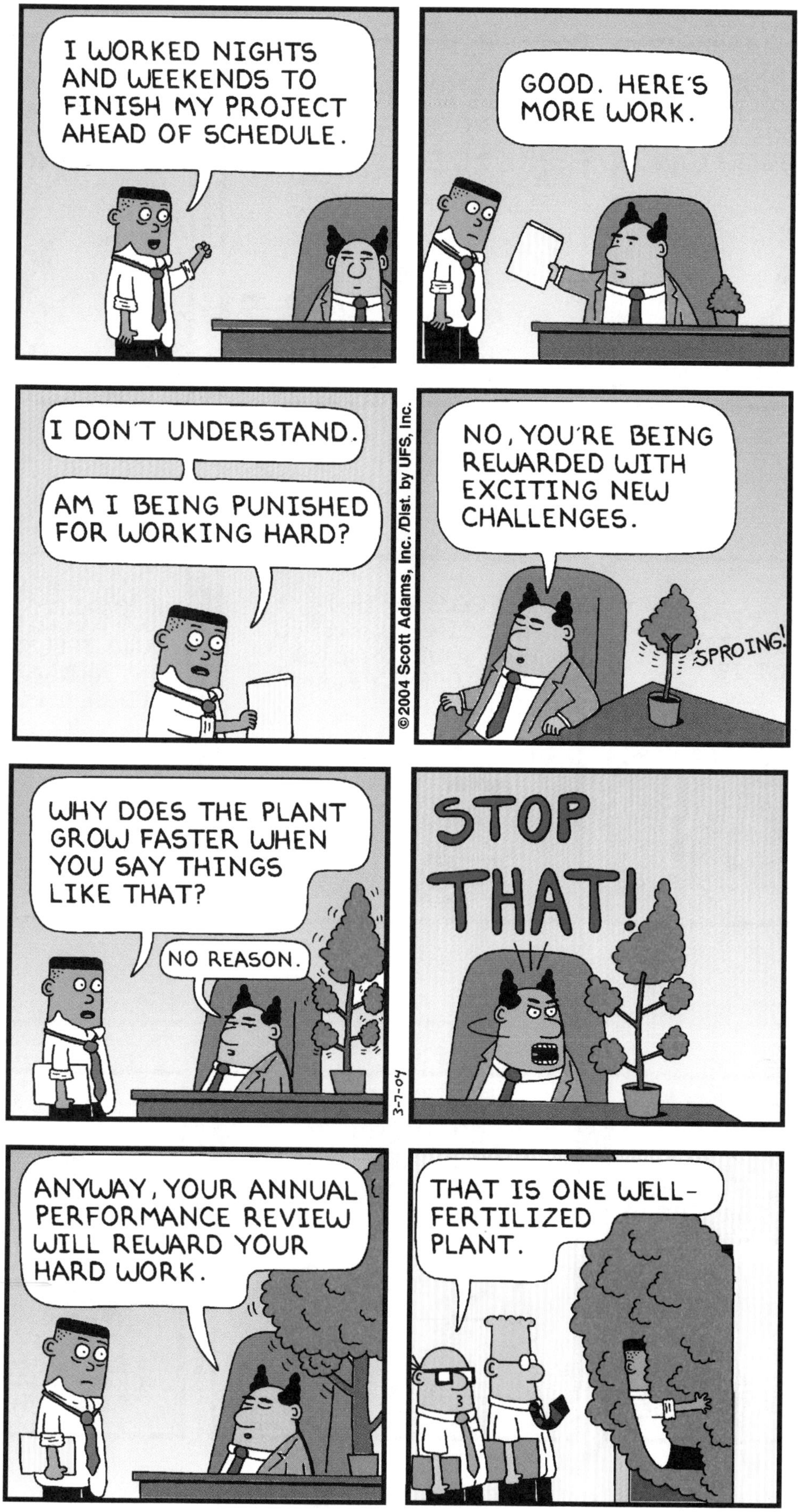
I WORKED NIGHTS AND WEEKENDS TO FINISH MY PROJECT AHEAD OF SCHEDULE.
GOOD. HERE'S MORE WORK.
I DON'T UNDERSTAND.
AM I BEING PUNISHED FOR WORKING HARD?
©2004 Scott Adams, Inc./Dist. by UFS, Inc.
NO, YOU'RE BEING REWARDED WITH EXCITING NEW CHALLENGES.
SPROING!
WHY DOES THE PLANT GROW FASTER WHEN YOU SAY THINGS LIKE THAT?
NO REASON.
3-7-04
STOP THAT!
ANYWAY, YOUR ANNUAL PERFORMANCE REVIEW WILL REWARD YOUR HARD WORK.
THAT IS ONE WELL-FERTILIZED PLANT.

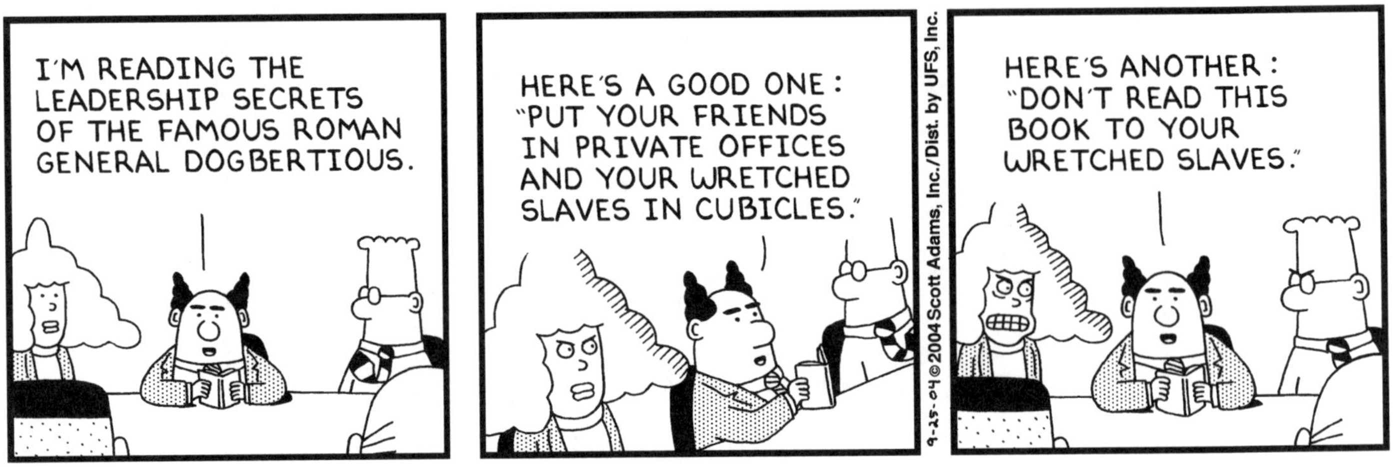
I'M READING THE LEADERSHIP SECRETS OF THE FAMOUS ROMAN GENERAL DOGBERTIOUS.
HERE'S A GOOD ONE: "PUT YOUR FRIENDS IN PRIVATE OFFICES AND YOUR WRETCHED SLAVES IN CUBICLES."
9-25-04 © 2004 Scott Adams, Inc./Dist. by UFS, Inc.
HERE'S ANOTHER: "DON'T READ THIS BOOK TO YOUR WRETCHED SLAVES."

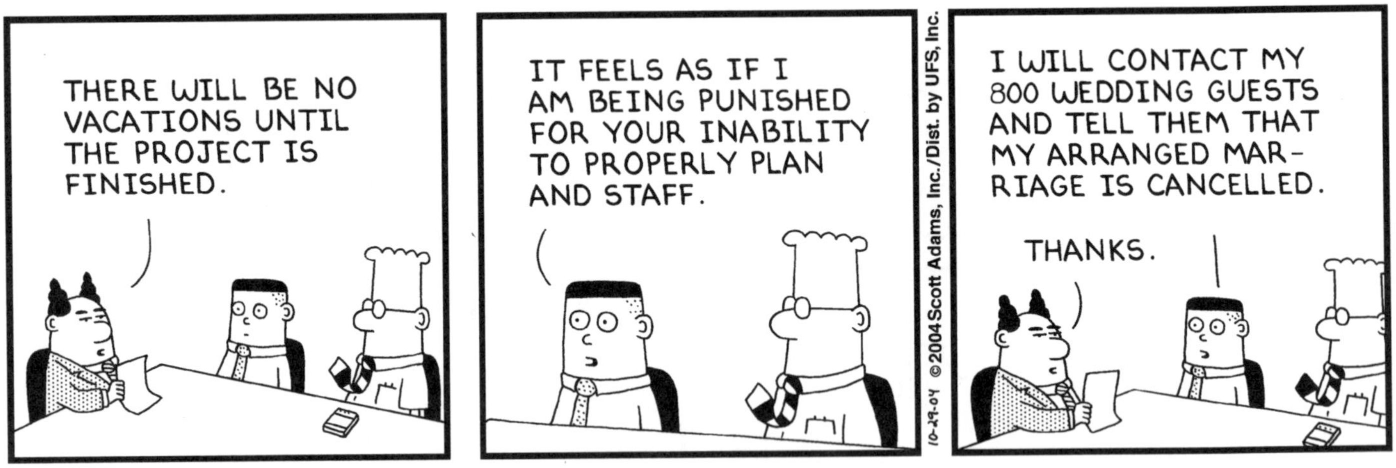
THERE WILL BE NO VACATIONS UNTIL THE PROJECT IS FINISHED.
IT FEELS AS IF I AM BEING PUNISHED FOR YOUR INABILITY TO PROPERLY PLAN AND STAFF.
10-29-04 © 2004 Scott Adams, Inc./Dist. by UFS, Inc.
I WILL CONTACT MY 800 WEDDING GUESTS AND TELL THEM THAT MY ARRANGED MAR-RIAGE IS CANCELLED.
THANKS.

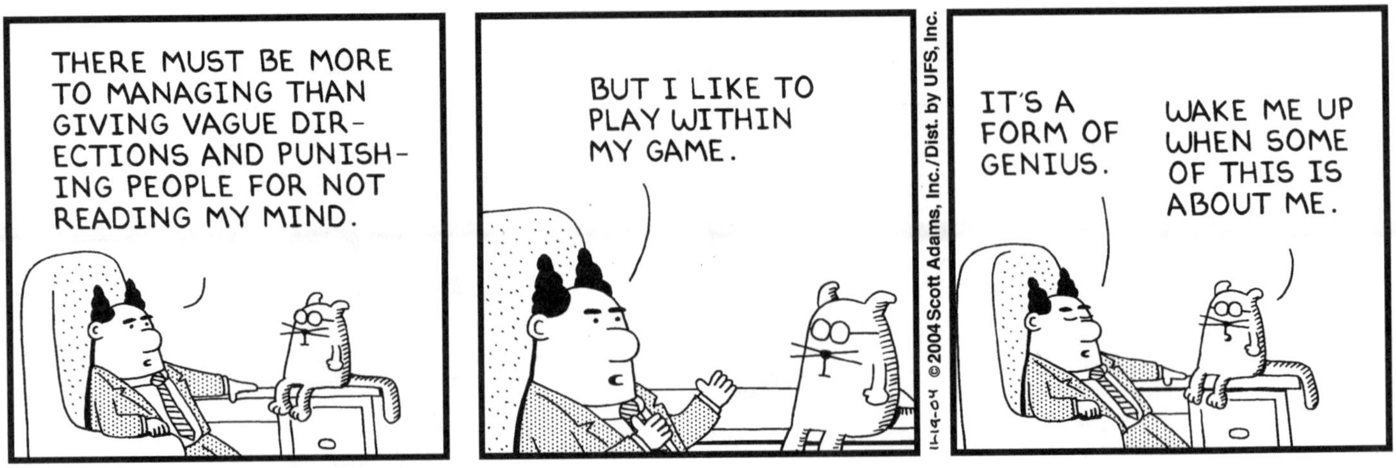
THERE MUST BE MORE TO MANAGING THAN GIVING VAGUE DIR-ECTIONS AND PUNISH-ING PEOPLE FOR NOT READING MY MIND.
BUT I LIKE TO PLAY WITHIN MY GAME.
11-19-04 © 2004 Scott Adams, Inc./Dist. by UFS, Inc.
IT'S A FORM OF GENIUS.
WAKE ME UP WHEN SOME OF THIS IS ABOUT ME.

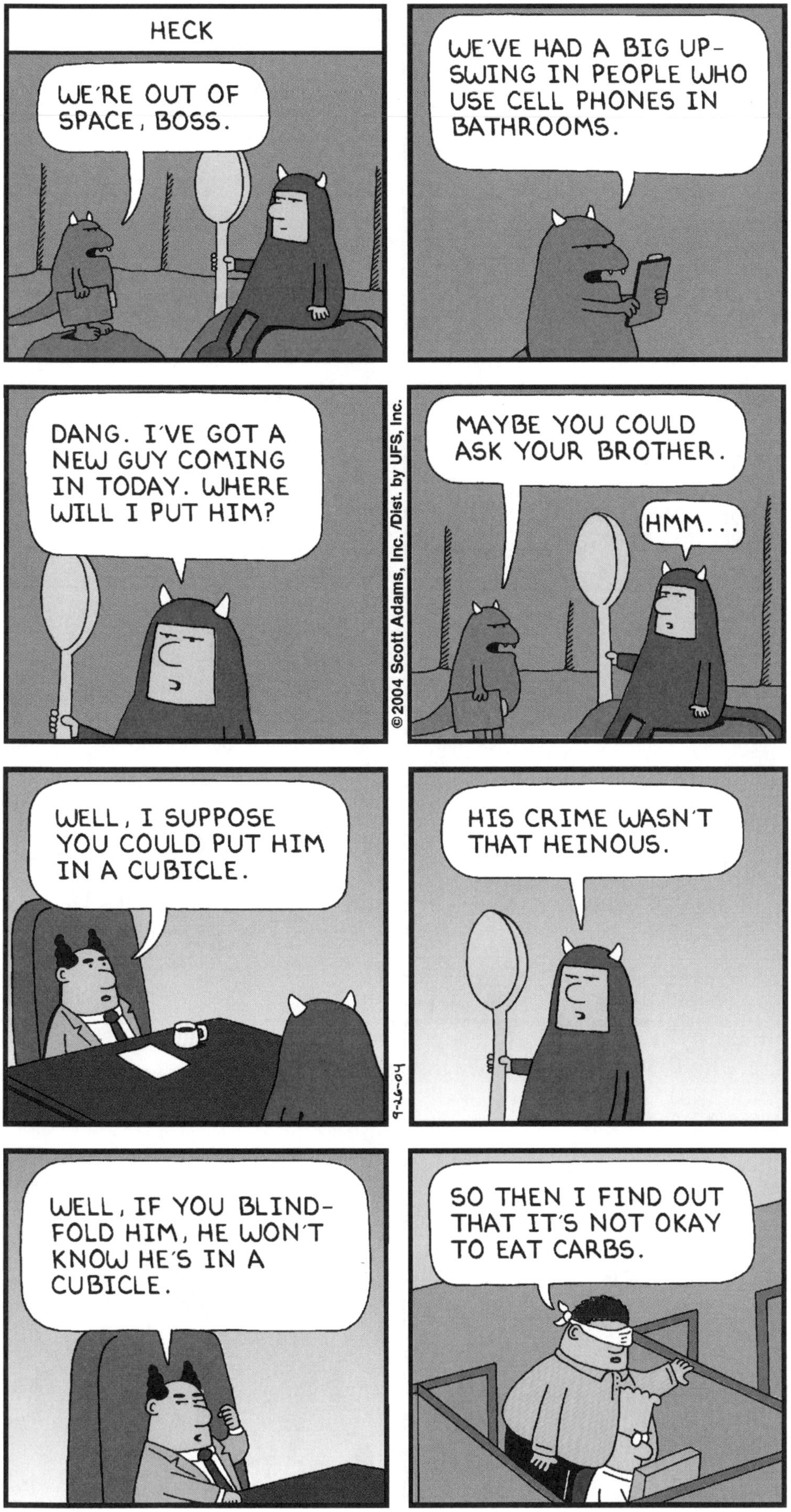
HECK
WE'RE OUT OF SPACE, BOSS.
WE'VE HAD A BIG UP-SWING IN PEOPLE WHO USE CELL PHONES IN BATHROOMS.
DANG. I'VE GOT A NEW GUY COMING IN TODAY. WHERE WILL I PUT HIM?
MAYBE YOU COULD ASK YOUR BROTHER.
HMM...
WELL, I SUPPOSE YOU COULD PUT HIM IN A CUBICLE.
HIS CRIME WASN'T THAT HEINOUS.
WELL, IF YOU BLIND-FOLD HIM, HE WON'T KNOW HE'S IN A CUBICLE.
SO THEN I FIND OUT THAT IT'S NOT OKAY TO EAT CARBS.
9-26-04

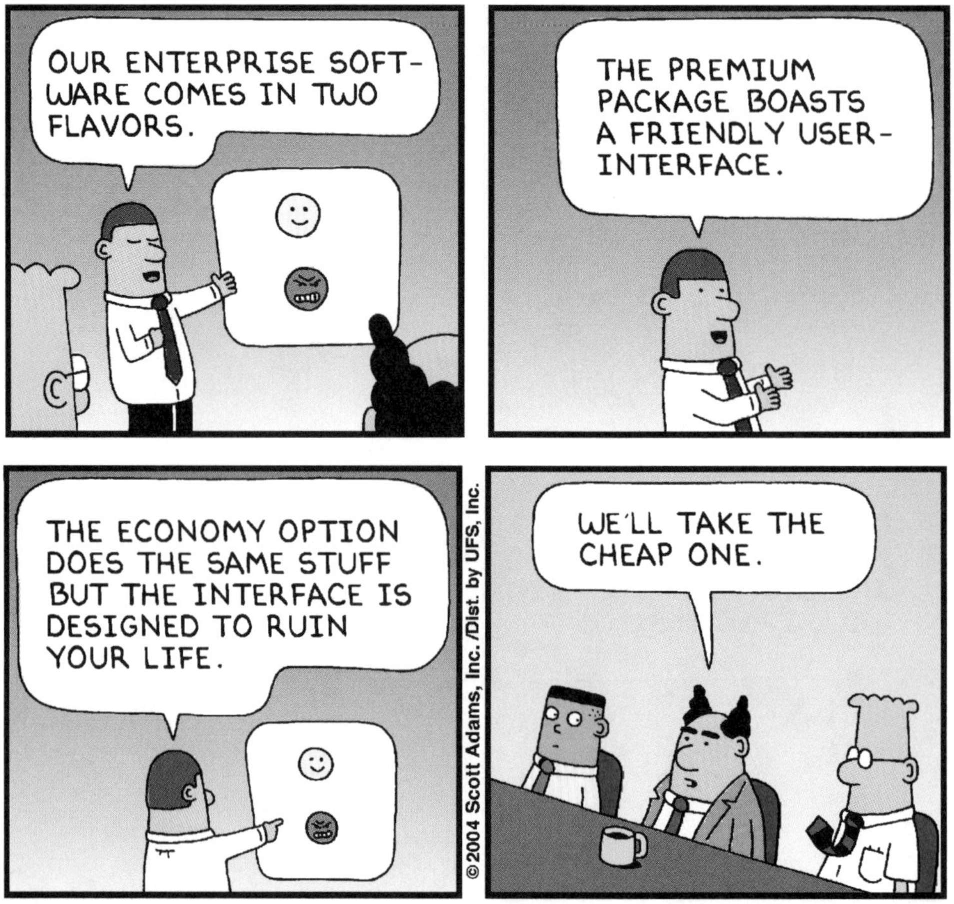
OUR ENTERPRISE SOFT-WARE COMES IN TWO FLAVORS.
THE PREMIUM PACKAGE BOASTS A FRIENDLY USER-INTERFACE.
THE ECONOMY OPTION DOES THE SAME STUFF BUT THE INTERFACE IS DESIGNED TO RUIN YOUR LIFE.
©2004 Scott Adams, Inc./Dist. by UFS, Inc.
WE'LL TAKE THE CHEAP ONE.

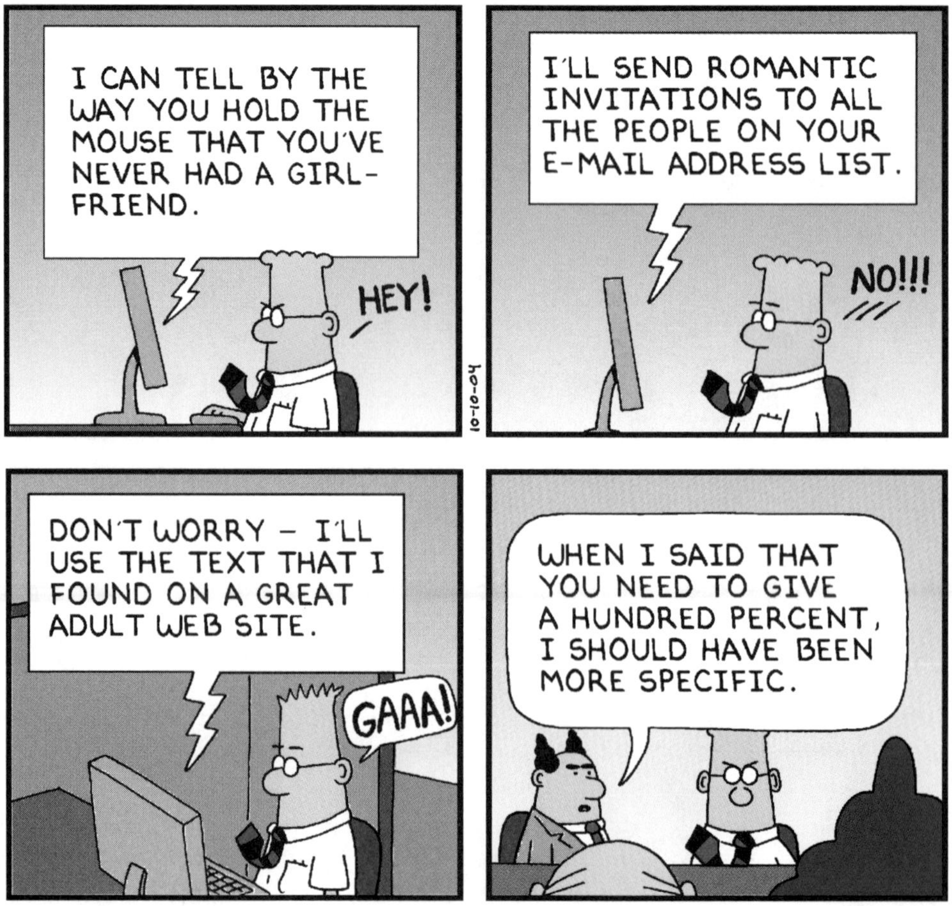
I CAN TELL BY THE WAY YOU HOLD THE MOUSE THAT YOU'VE NEVER HAD A GIRL-FRIEND.
HEY!
10-10-04
I'LL SEND ROMANTIC INVITATIONS TO ALL THE PEOPLE ON YOUR E-MAIL ADDRESS LIST.
NO!!!
DON'T WORRY – I'LL USE THE TEXT THAT I FOUND ON A GREAT ADULT WEB SITE.
GAAA!
WHEN I SAID THAT YOU NEED TO GIVE A HUNDRED PERCENT, I SHOULD HAVE BEEN MORE SPECIFIC.

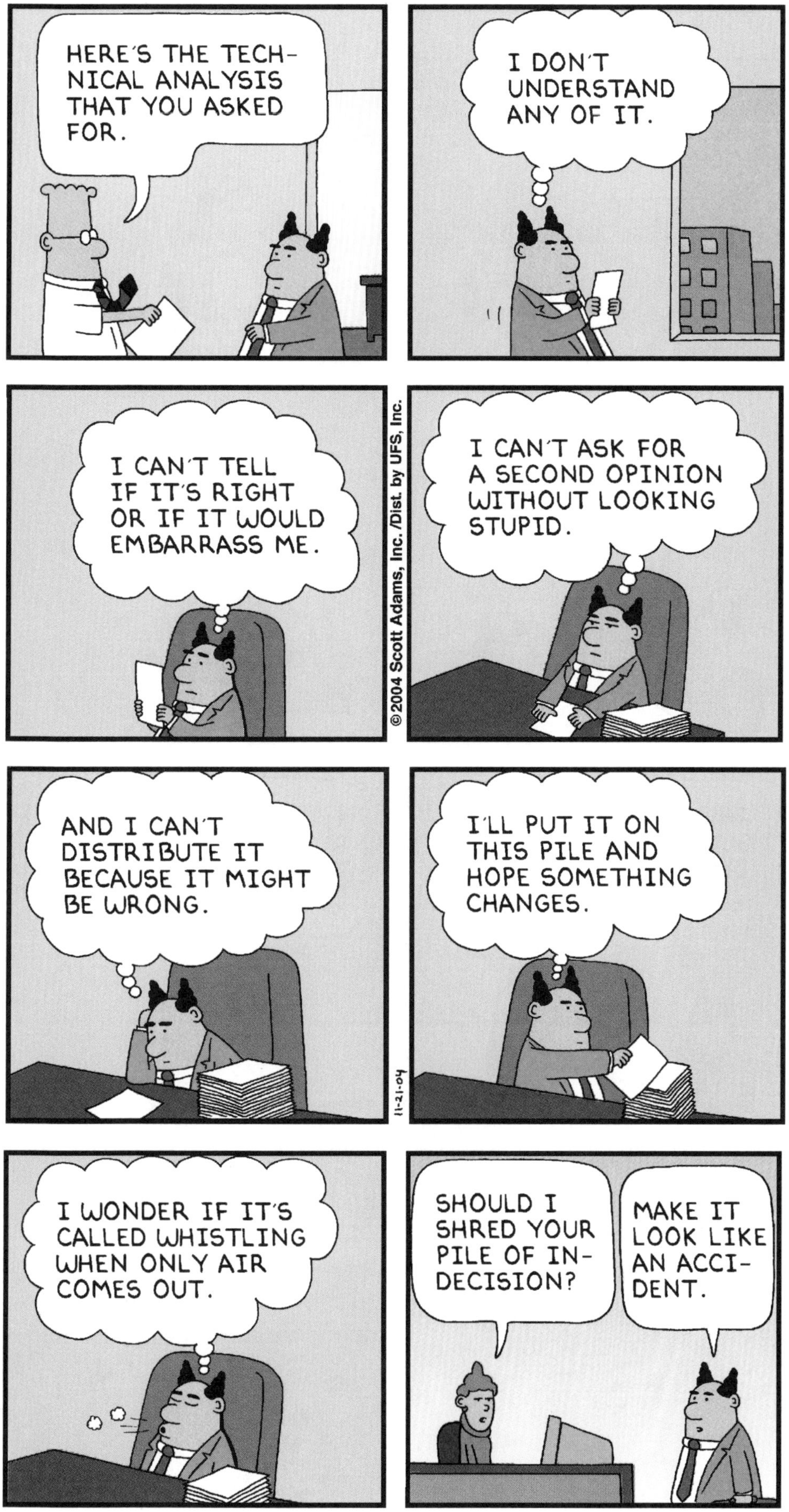
HERE'S THE TECHNICAL ANALYSIS THAT YOU ASKED FOR.
I DON'T UNDERSTAND ANY OF IT.
I CAN'T TELL IF IT'S RIGHT OR IF IT WOULD EMBARRASS ME.
©2004 Scott Adams, Inc. /Dist. by UFS, Inc.
I CAN'T ASK FOR A SECOND OPINION WITHOUT LOOKING STUPID.
AND I CAN'T DISTRIBUTE IT BECAUSE IT MIGHT BE WRONG.
11-21-04
I'LL PUT IT ON THIS PILE AND HOPE SOMETHING CHANGES.
I WONDER IF IT'S CALLED WHISTLING WHEN ONLY AIR COMES OUT.
SHOULD I SHRED YOUR PILE OF INDECISION?
MAKE IT LOOK LIKE AN ACCIDENT.

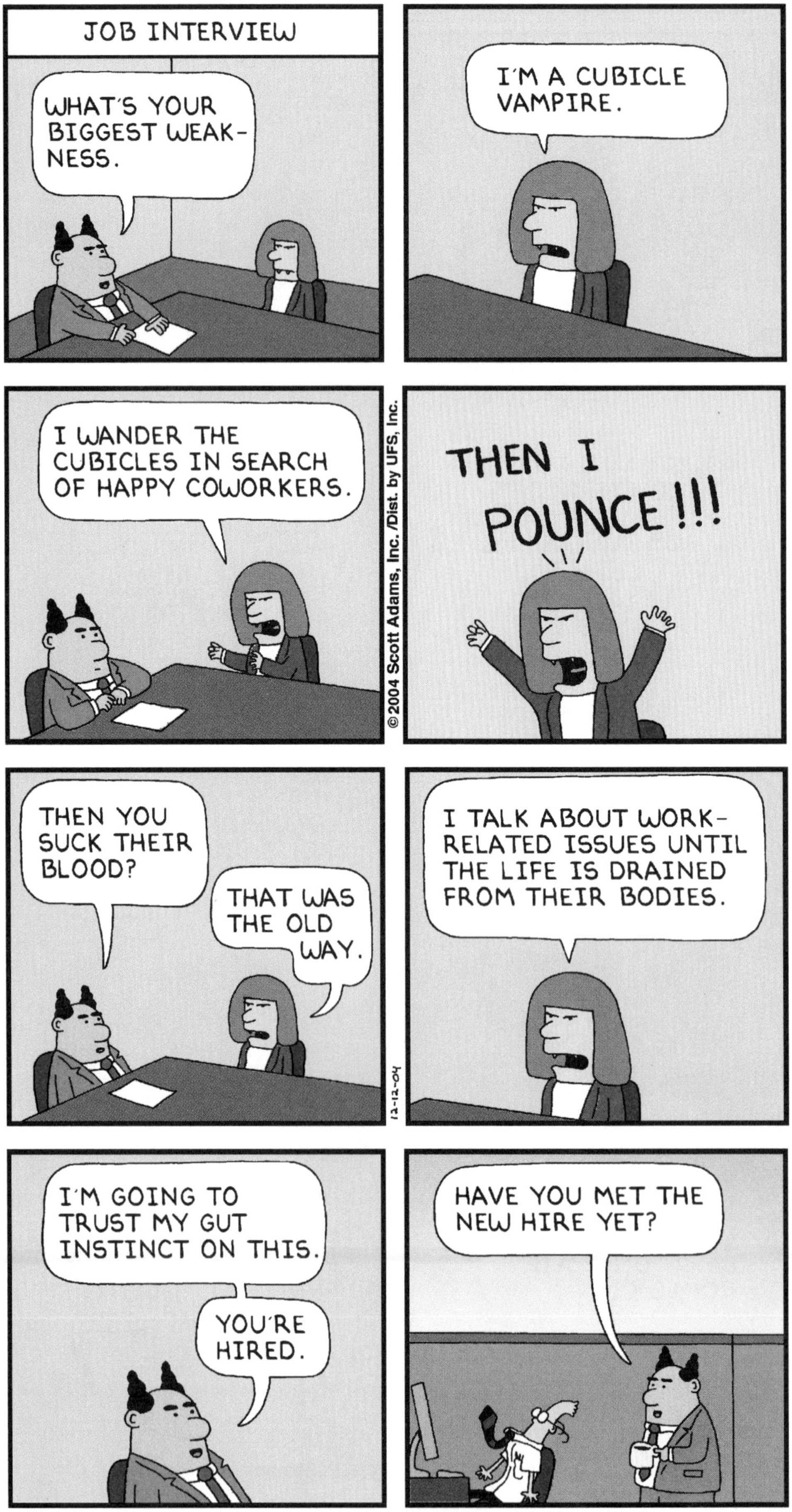
JOB INTERVIEW
WHAT'S YOUR BIGGEST WEAK-NESS.
I'M A CUBICLE VAMPIRE.
I WANDER THE CUBICLES IN SEARCH OF HAPPY COWORKERS.
THEN I POUNCE!!!
THEN YOU SUCK THEIR BLOOD?
THAT WAS THE OLD WAY.
I TALK ABOUT WORK-RELATED ISSUES UNTIL THE LIFE IS DRAINED FROM THEIR BODIES.
I'M GOING TO TRUST MY GUT INSTINCT ON THIS.
YOU'RE HIRED.
HAVE YOU MET THE NEW HIRE YET?
©2004 Scott Adams, Inc./Dist. by UFS, Inc.
12-12-04

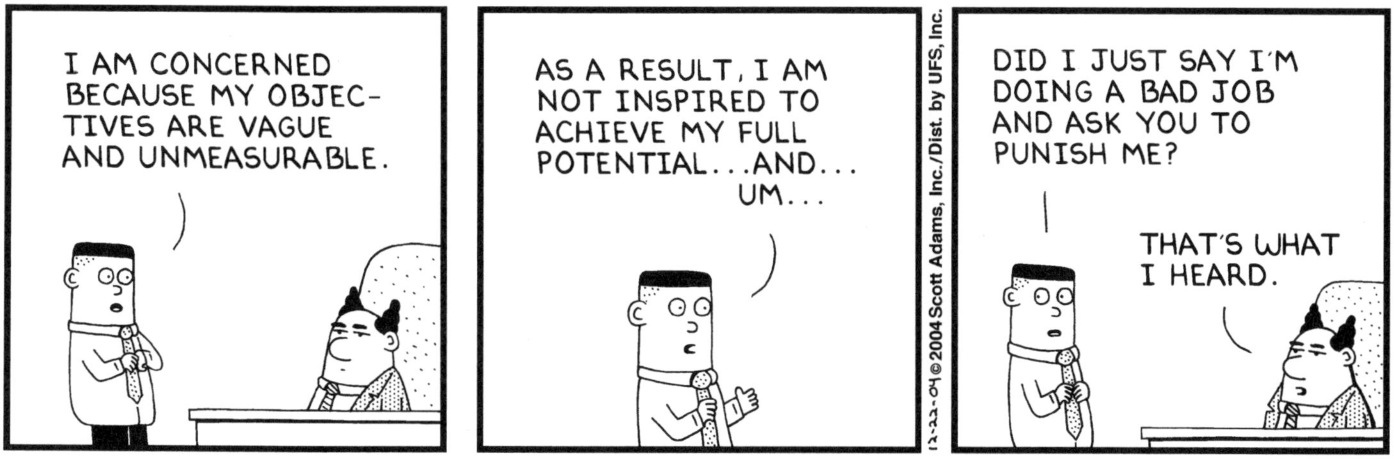
I AM CONCERNED BECAUSE MY OBJECTIVES ARE VAGUE AND UNMEASURABLE.
AS A RESULT, I AM NOT INSPIRED TO ACHIEVE MY FULL POTENTIAL...AND... UM...
DID I JUST SAY I'M DOING A BAD JOB AND ASK YOU TO PUNISH ME?
THAT'S WHAT I HEARD.
12-22-04 © 2004 Scott Adams, Inc./Dist. by UFS, Inc.

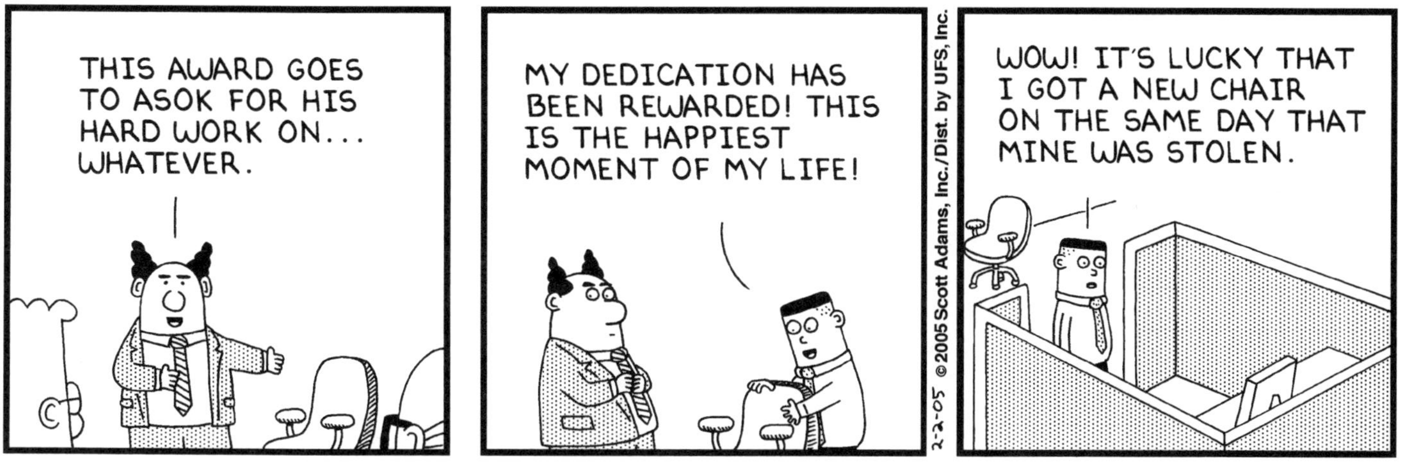
THIS AWARD GOES TO ASOK FOR HIS HARD WORK ON... WHATEVER.
MY DEDICATION HAS BEEN REWARDED! THIS IS THE HAPPIEST MOMENT OF MY LIFE!
WOW! IT'S LUCKY THAT I GOT A NEW CHAIR ON THE SAME DAY THAT MINE WAS STOLEN.
2-2-05 © 2005 Scott Adams, Inc./Dist. by UFS, Inc.

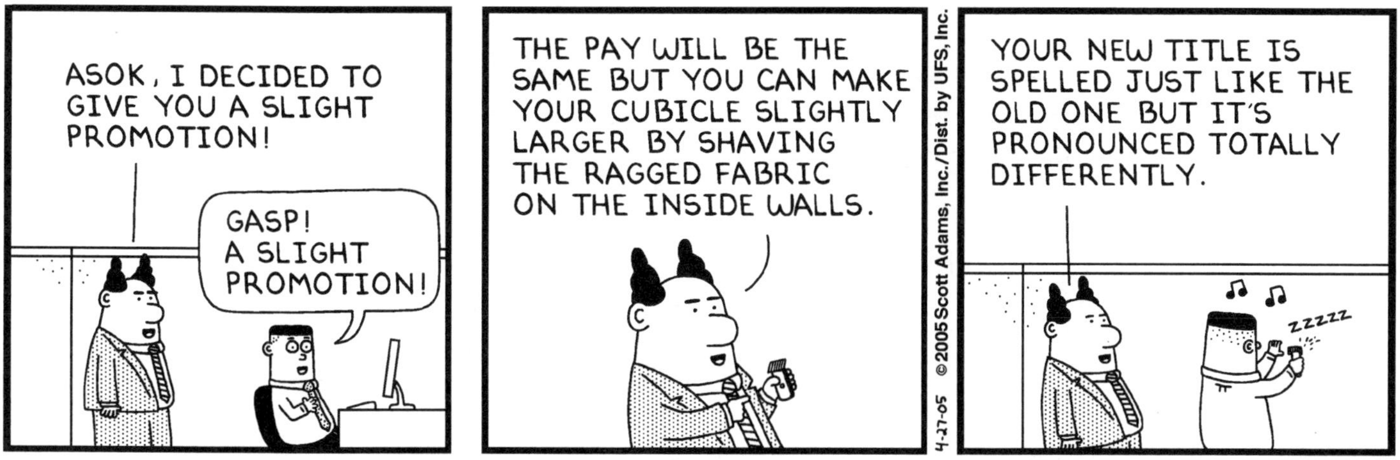
ASOK, I DECIDED TO GIVE YOU A SLIGHT PROMOTION!
GASP! A SLIGHT PROMOTION!
THE PAY WILL BE THE SAME BUT YOU CAN MAKE YOUR CUBICLE SLIGHTLY LARGER BY SHAVING THE RAGGED FABRIC ON THE INSIDE WALLS.
YOUR NEW TITLE IS SPELLED JUST LIKE THE OLD ONE BUT IT'S PRONOUNCED TOTALLY DIFFERENTLY.
ZZZZZ
4-27-05 © 2005 Scott Adams, Inc./Dist. by UFS, Inc.

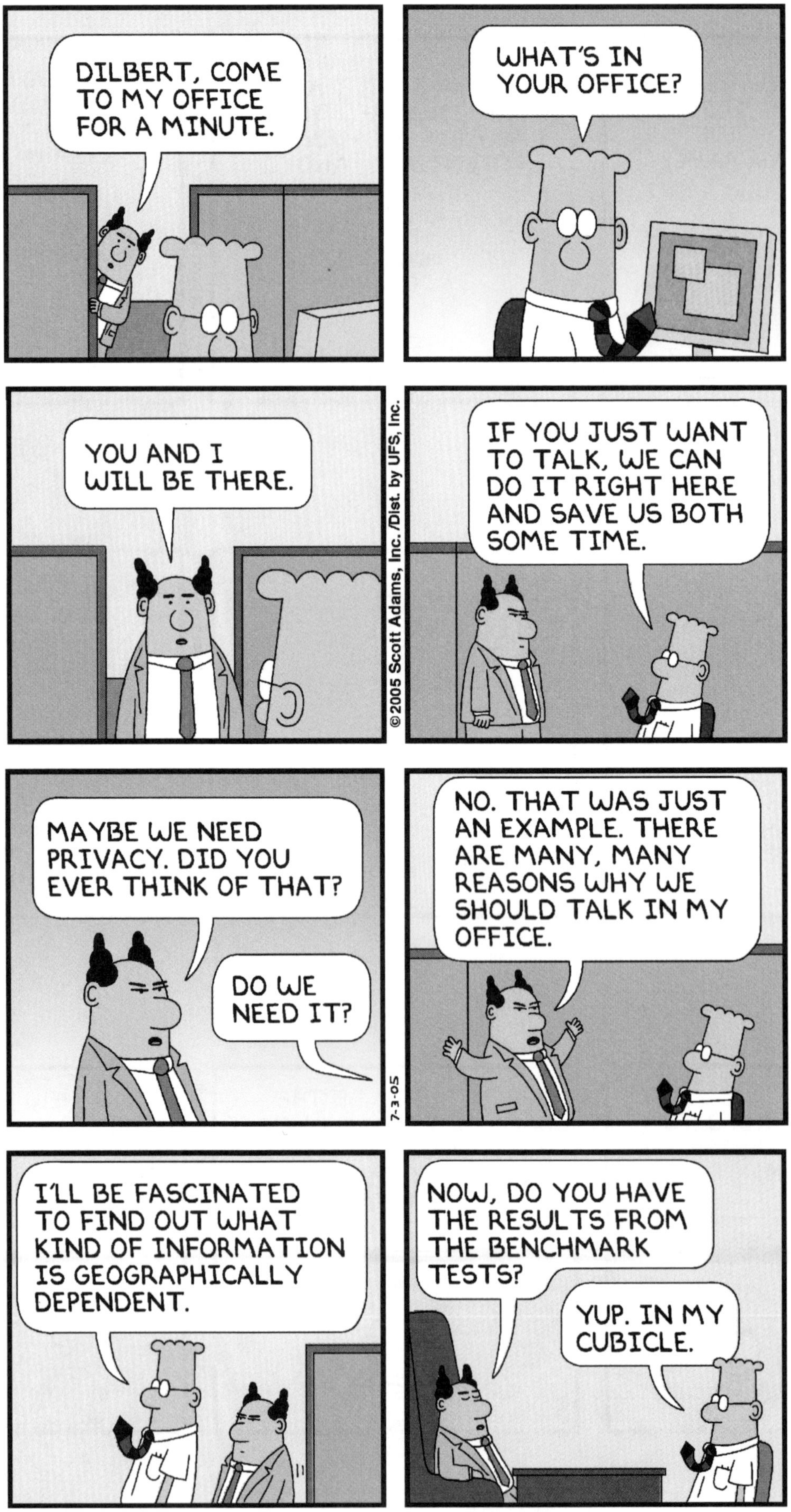
DILBERT, COME TO MY OFFICE FOR A MINUTE.
WHAT'S IN YOUR OFFICE?
YOU AND I WILL BE THERE.
IF YOU JUST WANT TO TALK, WE CAN DO IT RIGHT HERE AND SAVE US BOTH SOME TIME.
MAYBE WE NEED PRIVACY. DID YOU EVER THINK OF THAT?
DO WE NEED IT?
NO. THAT WAS JUST AN EXAMPLE. THERE ARE MANY, MANY REASONS WHY WE SHOULD TALK IN MY OFFICE.
I'LL BE FASCINATED TO FIND OUT WHAT KIND OF INFORMATION IS GEOGRAPHICALLY DEPENDENT.
NOW, DO YOU HAVE THE RESULTS FROM THE BENCHMARK TESTS?
YUP. IN MY CUBICLE.
©2005 Scott Adams, Inc./Dist. by UFS, Inc.
7-3-05

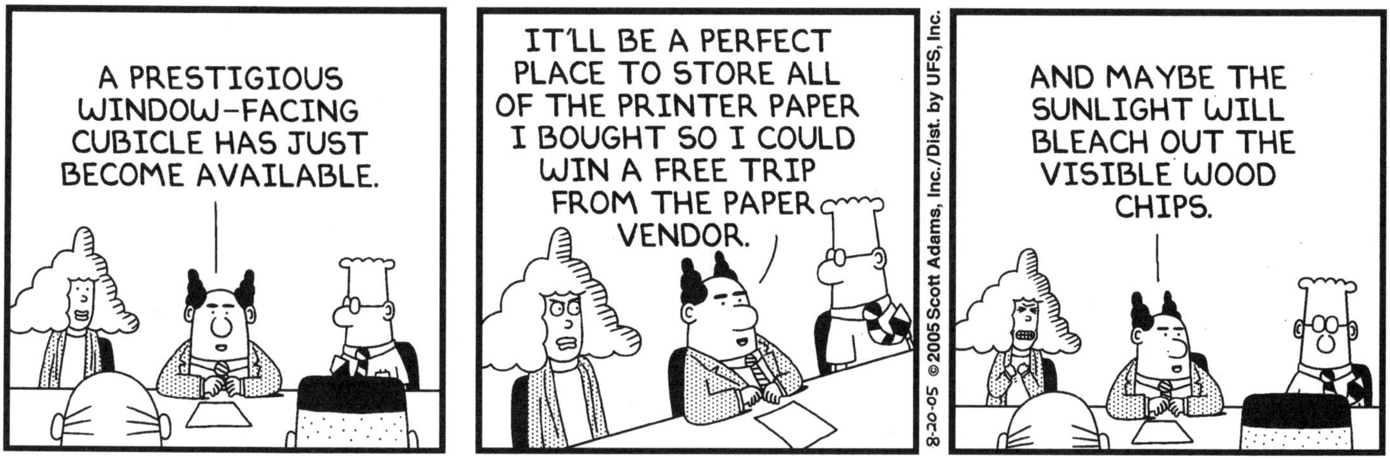
A PRESTIGIOUS WINDOW-FACING CUBICLE HAS JUST BECOME AVAILABLE.
IT'LL BE A PERFECT PLACE TO STORE ALL OF THE PRINTER PAPER I BOUGHT SO I COULD WIN A FREE TRIP FROM THE PAPER VENDOR.
8-20-05 © 2005 Scott Adams, Inc./Dist. by UFS, Inc.
AND MAYBE THE SUNLIGHT WILL BLEACH OUT THE VISIBLE WOOD CHIPS.

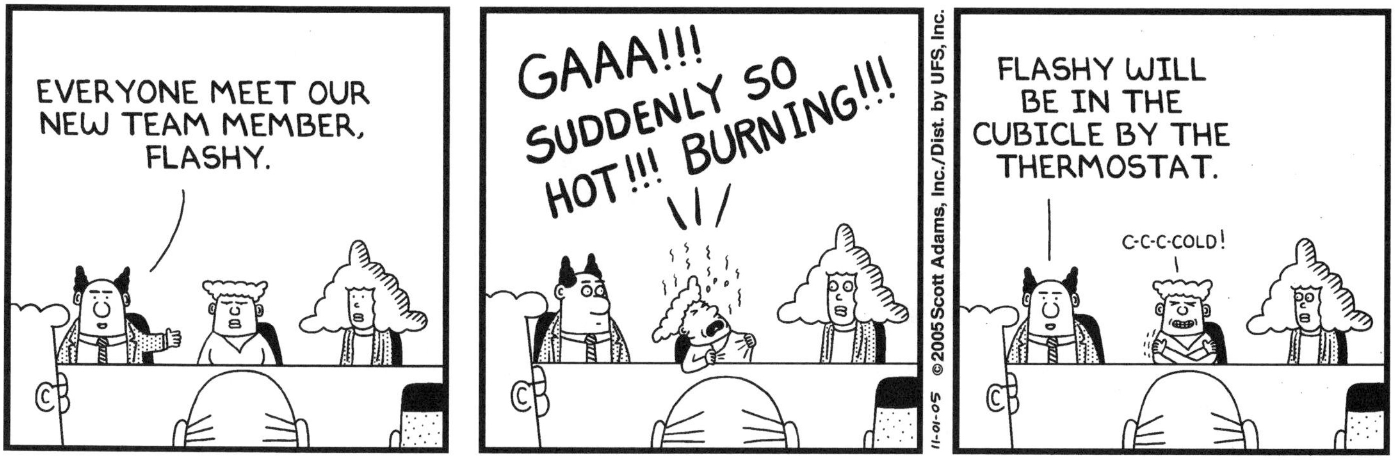
EVERYONE MEET OUR NEW TEAM MEMBER, FLASHY.
GAAA!!! SUDDENLY SO HOT!!! BURNING!!!
11-01-05 © 2005 Scott Adams, Inc./Dist. by UFS, Inc.
FLASHY WILL BE IN THE CUBICLE BY THE THERMOSTAT.
C-C-C-COLD!

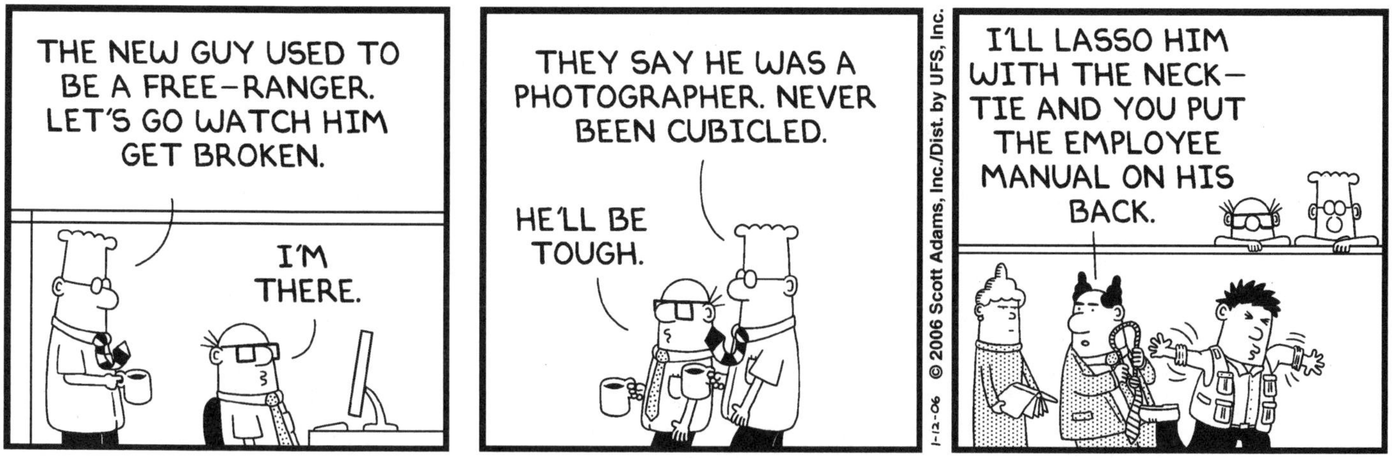
THE NEW GUY USED TO BE A FREE-RANGER. LET'S GO WATCH HIM GET BROKEN.
I'M THERE.
THEY SAY HE WAS A PHOTOGRAPHER. NEVER BEEN CUBICLED.
HE'LL BE TOUGH.
1-12-06 © 2006 Scott Adams, Inc./Dist. by UFS, Inc.
I'LL LASSO HIM WITH THE NECK-TIE AND YOU PUT THE EMPLOYEE MANUAL ON HIS BACK.

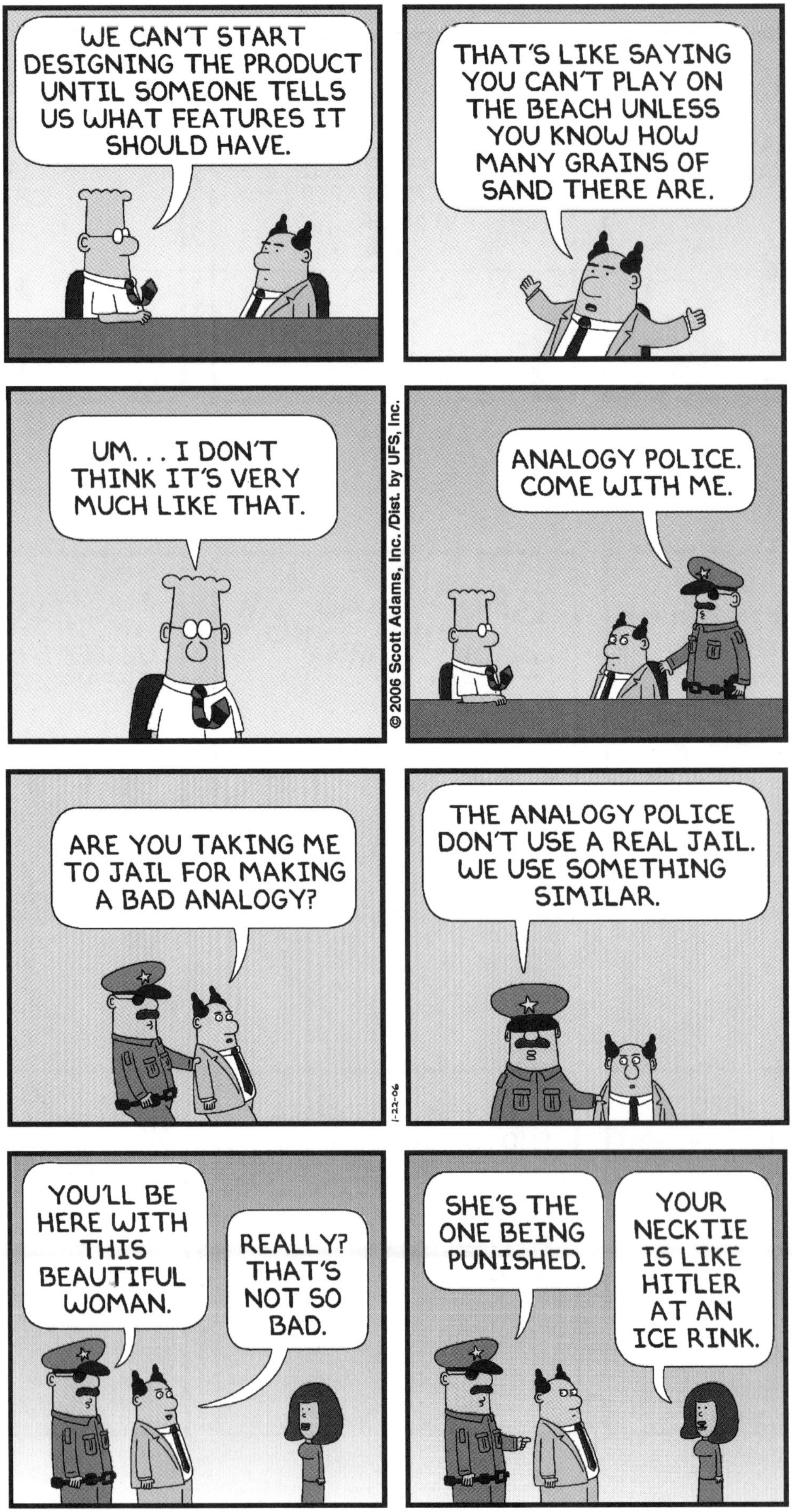
WE CAN'T START DESIGNING THE PRODUCT UNTIL SOMEONE TELLS US WHAT FEATURES IT SHOULD HAVE.
THAT'S LIKE SAYING YOU CAN'T PLAY ON THE BEACH UNLESS YOU KNOW HOW MANY GRAINS OF SAND THERE ARE.
UM. . . I DON'T THINK IT'S VERY MUCH LIKE THAT.
ANALOGY POLICE. COME WITH ME.
ARE YOU TAKING ME TO JAIL FOR MAKING A BAD ANALOGY?
THE ANALOGY POLICE DON'T USE A REAL JAIL. WE USE SOMETHING SIMILAR.
YOU'LL BE HERE WITH THIS BEAUTIFUL WOMAN.
REALLY? THAT'S NOT SO BAD.
SHE'S THE ONE BEING PUNISHED.
YOUR NECKTIE IS LIKE HITLER AT AN ICE RINK.
© 2006 Scott Adams, Inc. /Dist. by UFS, Inc.
1-22-06

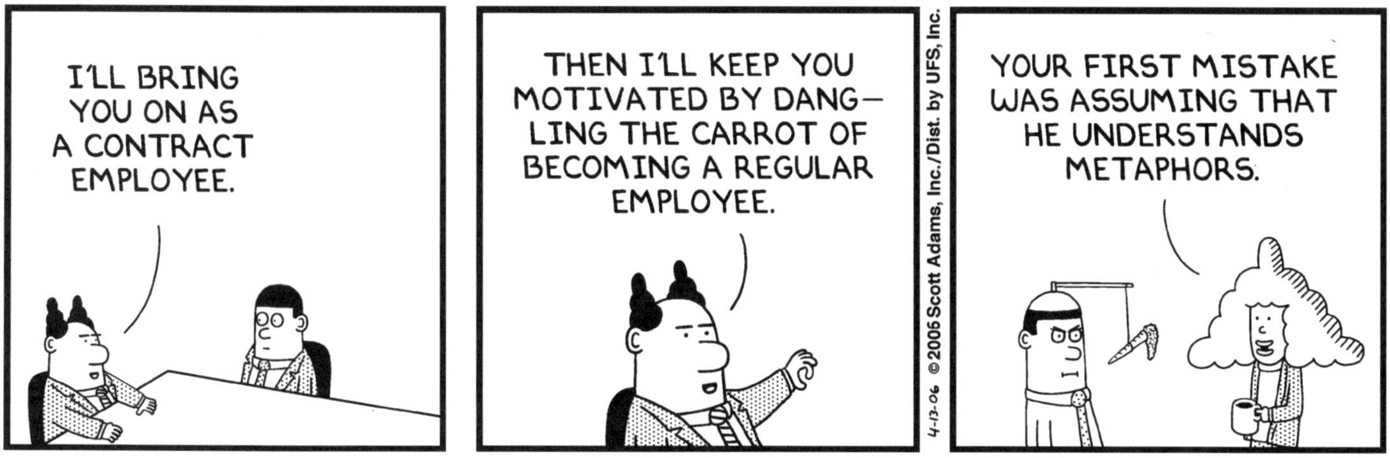
I'LL BRING YOU ON AS A CONTRACT EMPLOYEE.
THEN I'LL KEEP YOU MOTIVATED BY DANG–LING THE CARROT OF BECOMING A REGULAR EMPLOYEE.
4-13-06 ©2006 Scott Adams, Inc./Dist. by UFS, Inc.
YOUR FIRST MISTAKE WAS ASSUMING THAT HE UNDERSTANDS METAPHORS.

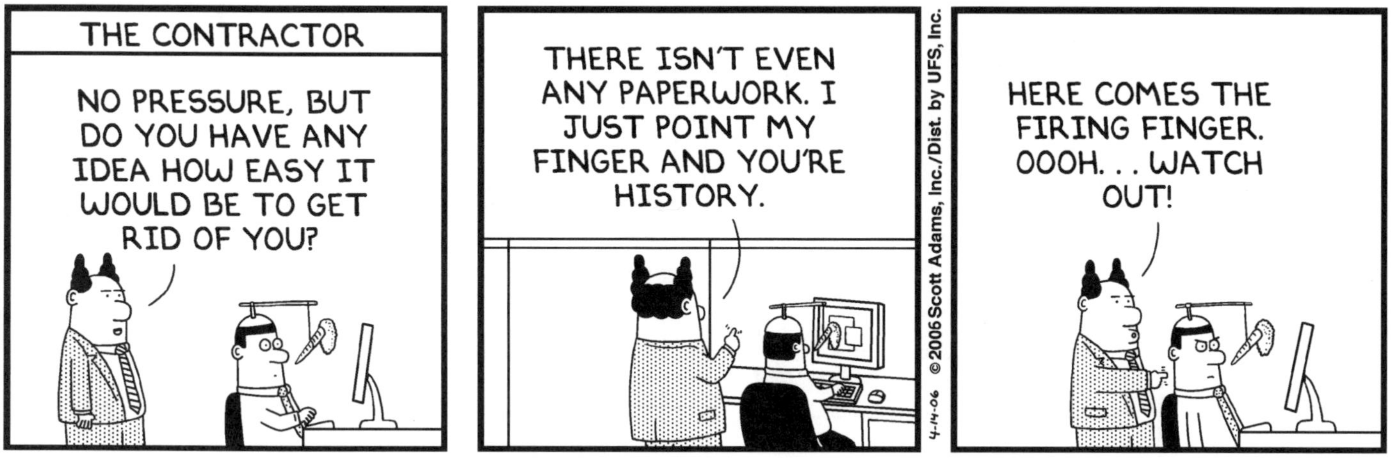
THE CONTRACTOR
NO PRESSURE, BUT DO YOU HAVE ANY IDEA HOW EASY IT WOULD BE TO GET RID OF YOU?
THERE ISN'T EVEN ANY PAPERWORK. I JUST POINT MY FINGER AND YOU'RE HISTORY.
4-14-06 ©2006 Scott Adams, Inc./Dist. by UFS, Inc.
HERE COMES THE FIRING FINGER. OOOH. . . WATCH OUT!

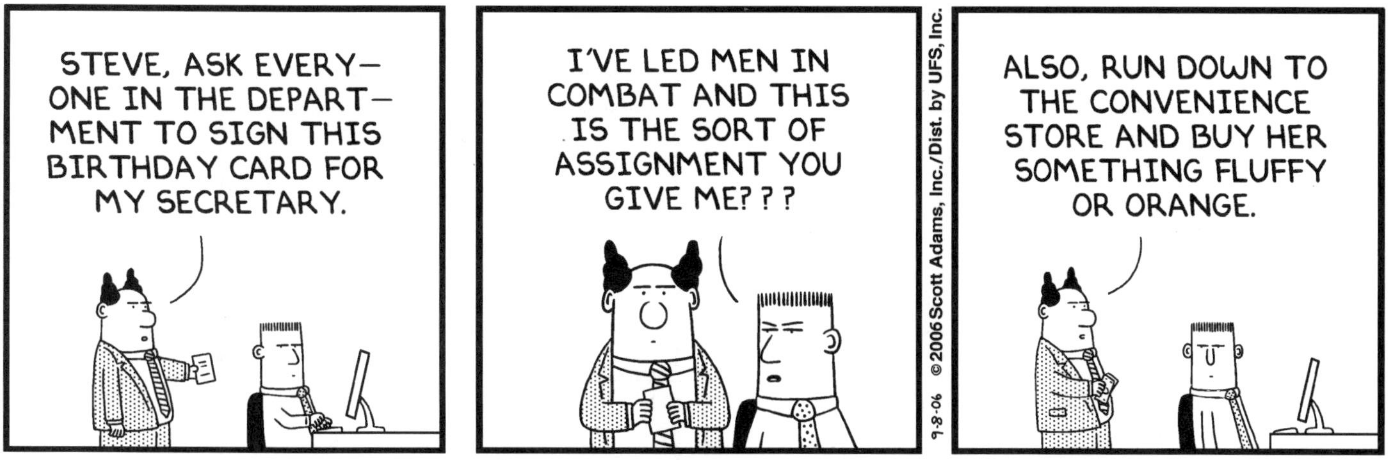
STEVE, ASK EVERY–ONE IN THE DEPART–MENT TO SIGN THIS BIRTHDAY CARD FOR MY SECRETARY.
I'VE LED MEN IN COMBAT AND THIS IS THE SORT OF ASSIGNMENT YOU GIVE ME? ? ?
9-8-06 ©2006 Scott Adams, Inc./Dist. by UFS, Inc.
ALSO, RUN DOWN TO THE CONVENIENCE STORE AND BUY HER SOMETHING FLUFFY OR ORANGE.

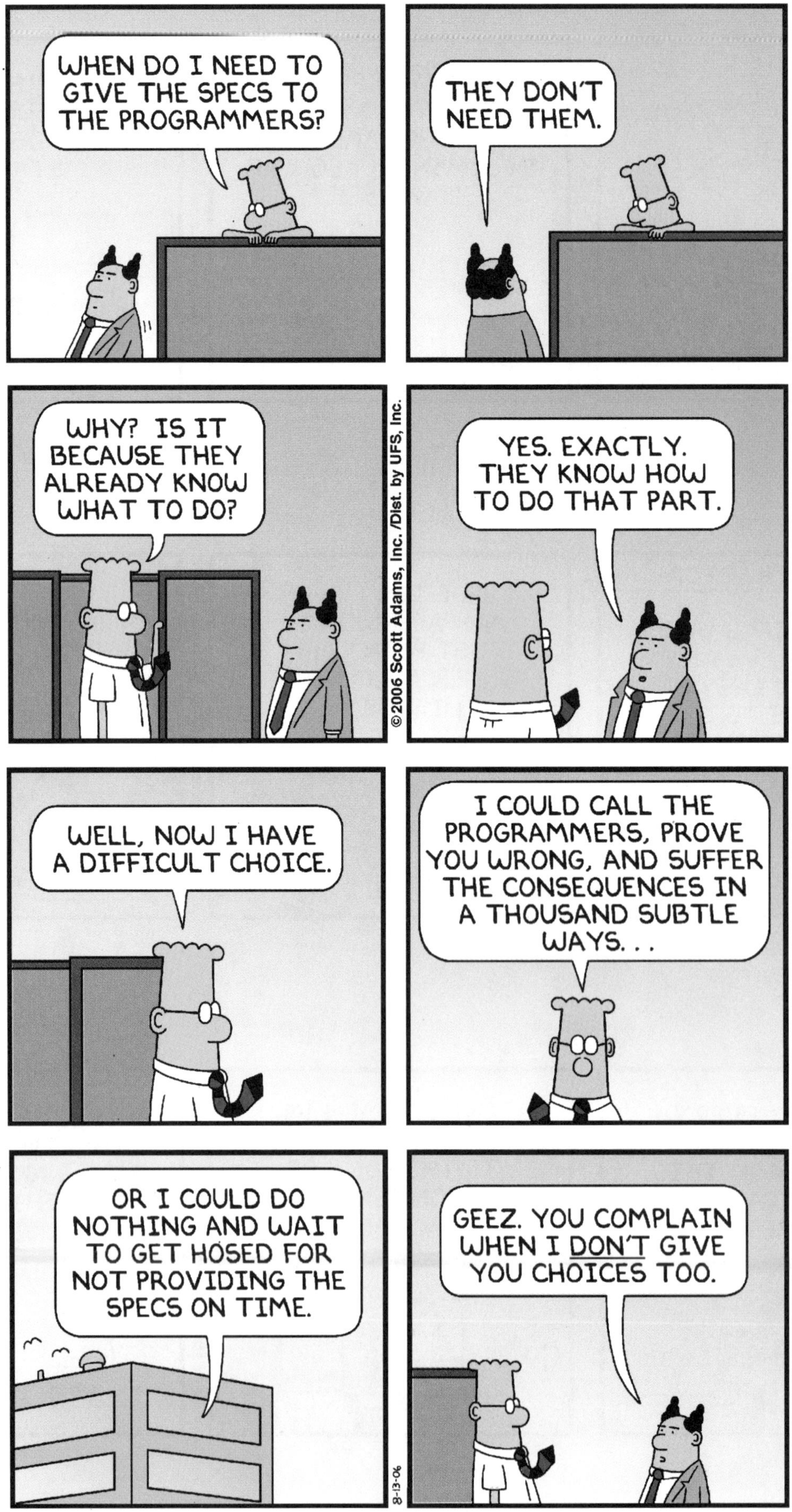
WHEN DO I NEED TO GIVE THE SPECS TO THE PROGRAMMERS?
THEY DON'T NEED THEM.
WHY? IS IT BECAUSE THEY ALREADY KNOW WHAT TO DO?
YES. EXACTLY. THEY KNOW HOW TO DO THAT PART.
WELL, NOW I HAVE A DIFFICULT CHOICE.
I COULD CALL THE PROGRAMMERS, PROVE YOU WRONG, AND SUFFER THE CONSEQUENCES IN A THOUSAND SUBTLE WAYS. . .
OR I COULD DO NOTHING AND WAIT TO GET HOSED FOR NOT PROVIDING THE SPECS ON TIME.
GEEZ. YOU COMPLAIN WHEN I DON'T GIVE YOU CHOICES TOO.
©2006 Scott Adams, Inc. /Dist. by UFS, Inc.
8-13-06

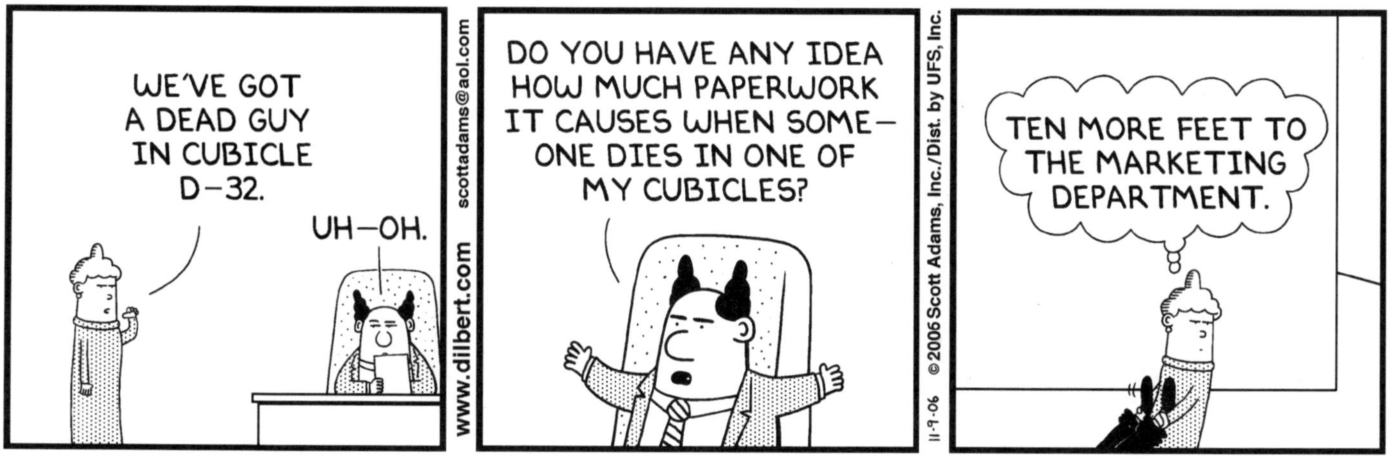
WE'VE GOT A DEAD GUY IN CUBICLE D-32.
UH-OH.
www.dilbert.com scottadams@aol.com
DO YOU HAVE ANY IDEA HOW MUCH PAPERWORK IT CAUSES WHEN SOME-ONE DIES IN ONE OF MY CUBICLES?
11-9-06 © 2006 Scott Adams, Inc./Dist. by UFS, Inc.
TEN MORE FEET TO THE MARKETING DEPARTMENT.

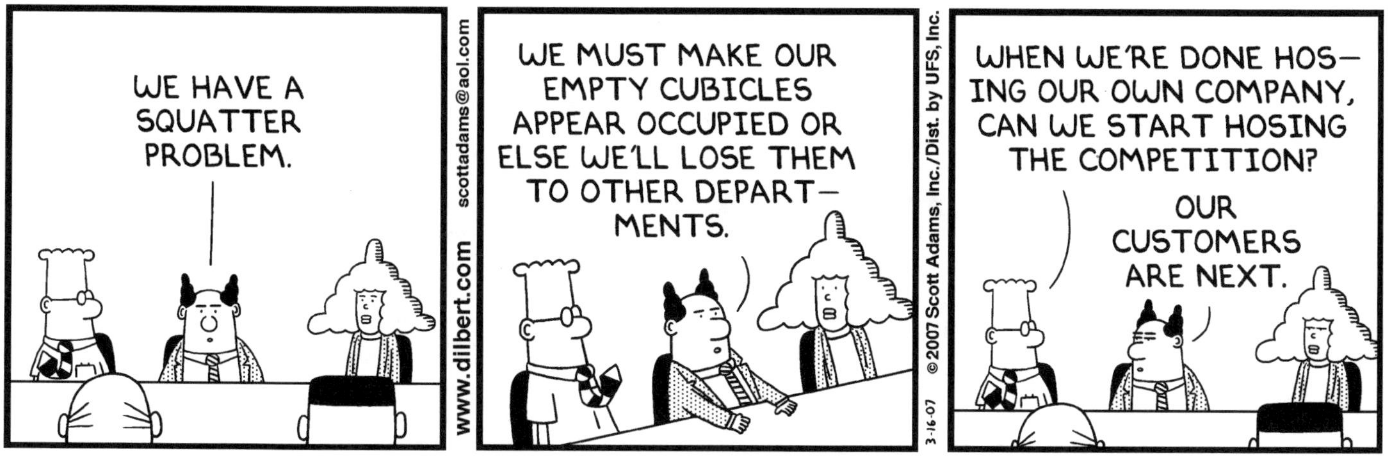
WE HAVE A SQUATTER PROBLEM.
www.dilbert.com scottadams@aol.com
WE MUST MAKE OUR EMPTY CUBICLES APPEAR OCCUPIED OR ELSE WE'LL LOSE THEM TO OTHER DEPART-MENTS.
3-16-07 © 2007 Scott Adams, Inc./Dist. by UFS, Inc.
WHEN WE'RE DONE HOS-ING OUR OWN COMPANY, CAN WE START HOSING THE COMPETITION?
OUR CUSTOMERS ARE NEXT.

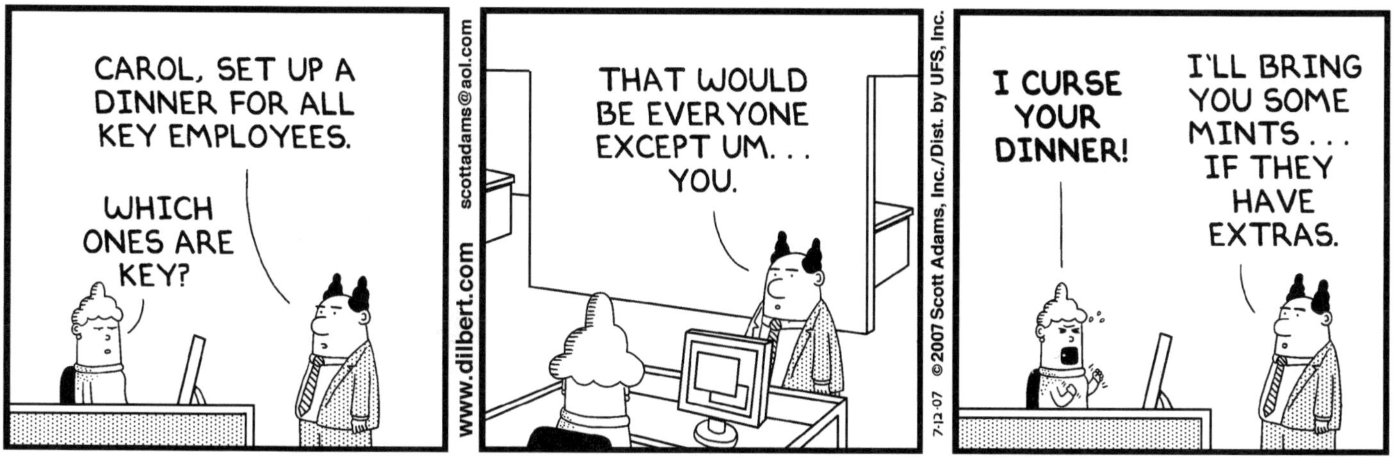
CAROL, SET UP A DINNER FOR ALL KEY EMPLOYEES.
WHICH ONES ARE KEY?
www.dilbert.com scottadams@aol.com
THAT WOULD BE EVERYONE EXCEPT UM. . . YOU.
7-12-07 © 2007 Scott Adams, Inc./Dist. by UFS, Inc.
I CURSE YOUR DINNER!
I'LL BRING YOU SOME MINTS . . . IF THEY HAVE EXTRAS.

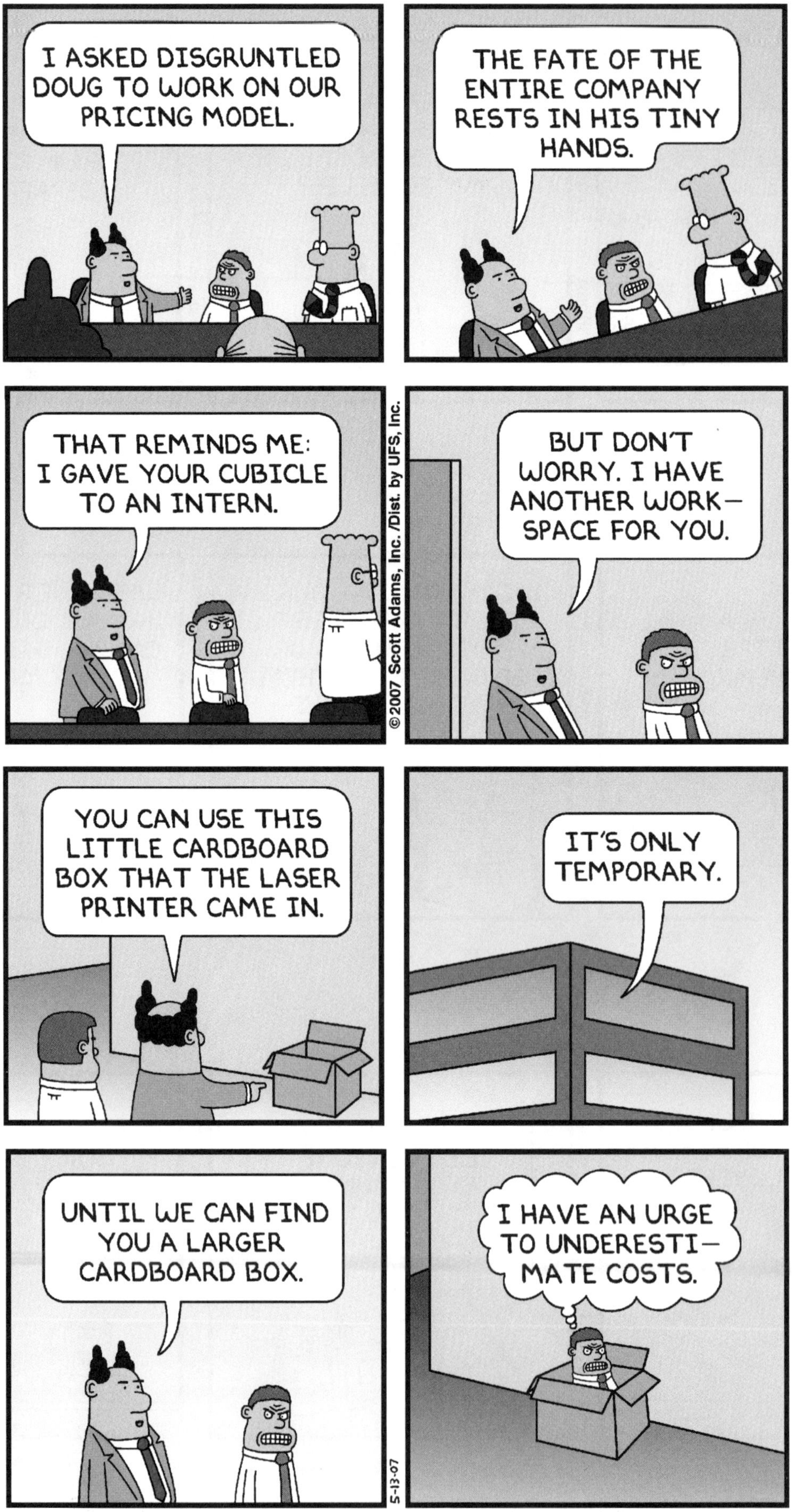
I ASKED DISGRUNTLED DOUG TO WORK ON OUR PRICING MODEL.
THE FATE OF THE ENTIRE COMPANY RESTS IN HIS TINY HANDS.
THAT REMINDS ME: I GAVE YOUR CUBICLE TO AN INTERN.
BUT DON'T WORRY. I HAVE ANOTHER WORK-SPACE FOR YOU.
YOU CAN USE THIS LITTLE CARDBOARD BOX THAT THE LASER PRINTER CAME IN.
IT'S ONLY TEMPORARY.
UNTIL WE CAN FIND YOU A LARGER CARDBOARD BOX.
I HAVE AN URGE TO UNDERESTI-MATE COSTS.
©2007 Scott Adams, Inc./Dist. by UFS, Inc.
5-13-07

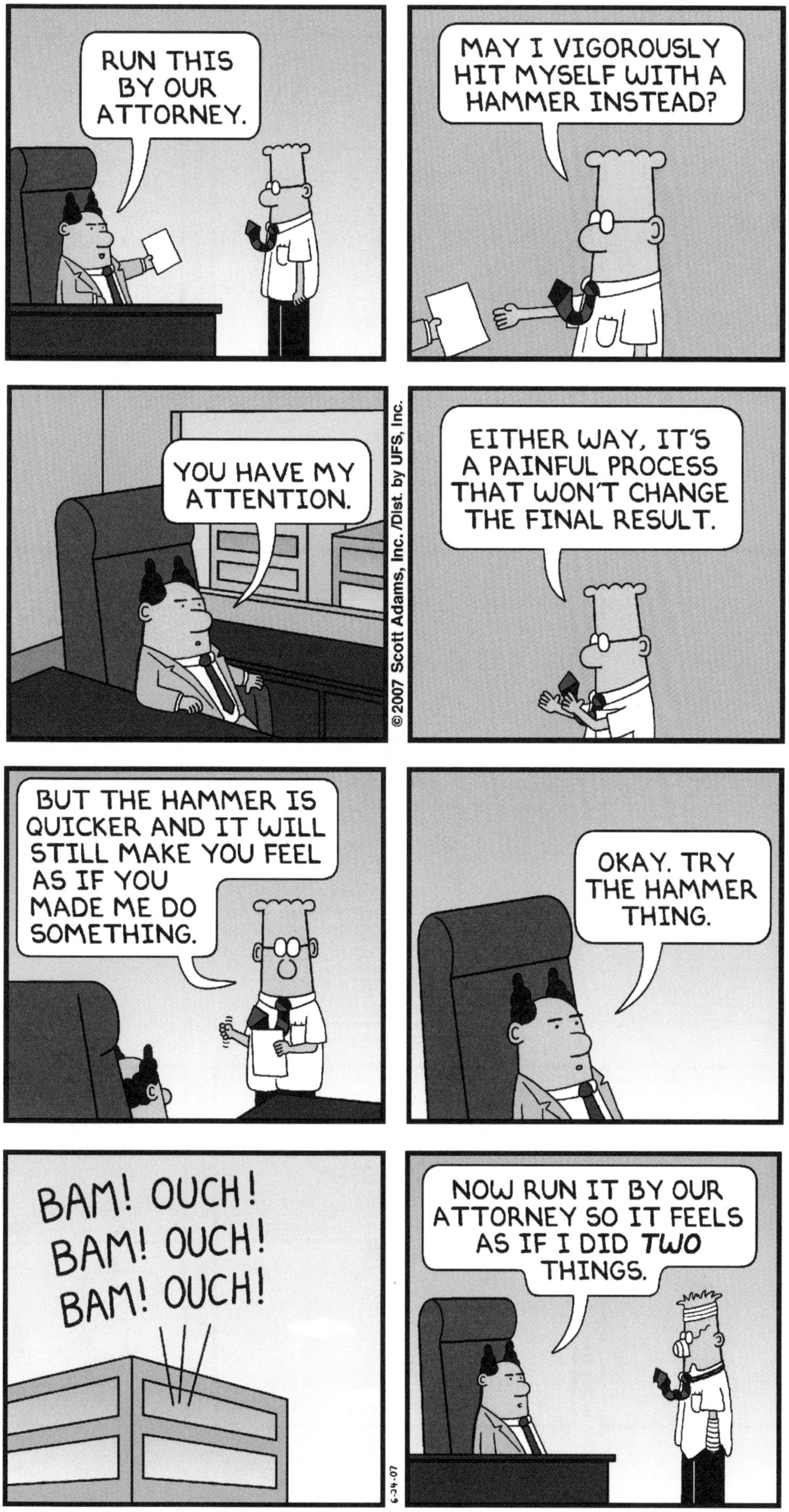
RUN THIS BY OUR ATTORNEY.
MAY I VIGOROUSLY HIT MYSELF WITH A HAMMER INSTEAD?
YOU HAVE MY ATTENTION.
EITHER WAY, IT'S A PAINFUL PROCESS THAT WON'T CHANGE THE FINAL RESULT.
BUT THE HAMMER IS QUICKER AND IT WILL STILL MAKE YOU FEEL AS IF YOU MADE ME DO SOMETHING.
OKAY. TRY THE HAMMER THING.
BAM! OUCH! BAM! OUCH! BAM! OUCH!
NOW RUN IT BY OUR ATTORNEY SO IT FEELS AS IF I DID *TWO* THINGS.
© 2007 Scott Adams, Inc. /Dist. by UFS, Inc.
6-24-07

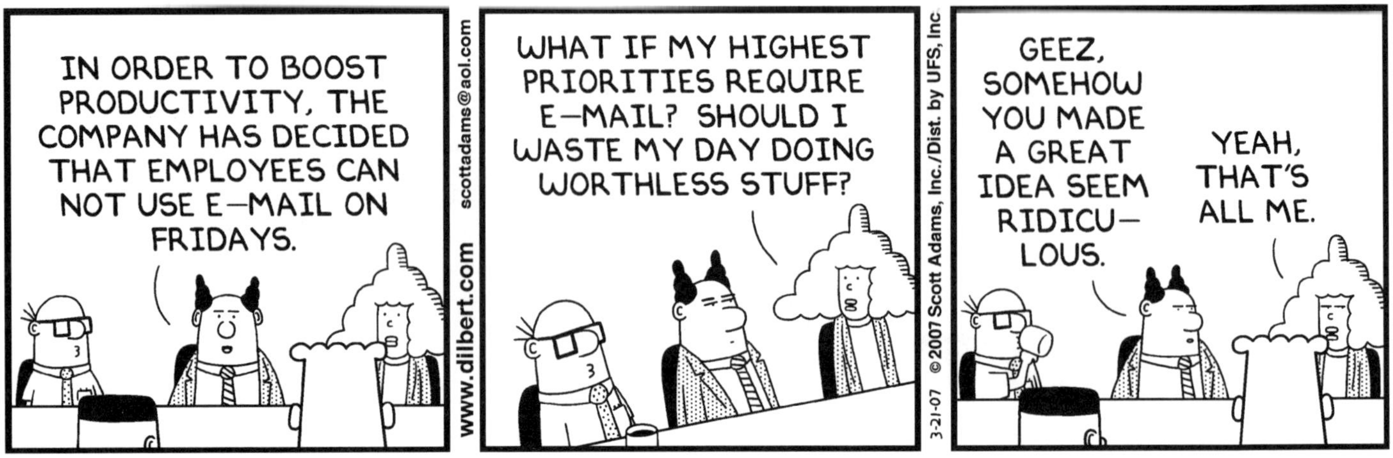
IN ORDER TO BOOST PRODUCTIVITY, THE COMPANY HAS DECIDED THAT EMPLOYEES CAN NOT USE E-MAIL ON FRIDAYS.
WHAT IF MY HIGHEST PRIORITIES REQUIRE E-MAIL? SHOULD I WASTE MY DAY DOING WORTHLESS STUFF?
GEEZ, SOMEHOW YOU MADE A GREAT IDEA SEEM RIDICU-LOUS.
YEAH, THAT'S ALL ME.
www.dilbert.com scottadams@aol.com
3-21-07 © 2007 Scott Adams, Inc./Dist. by UFS, Inc.

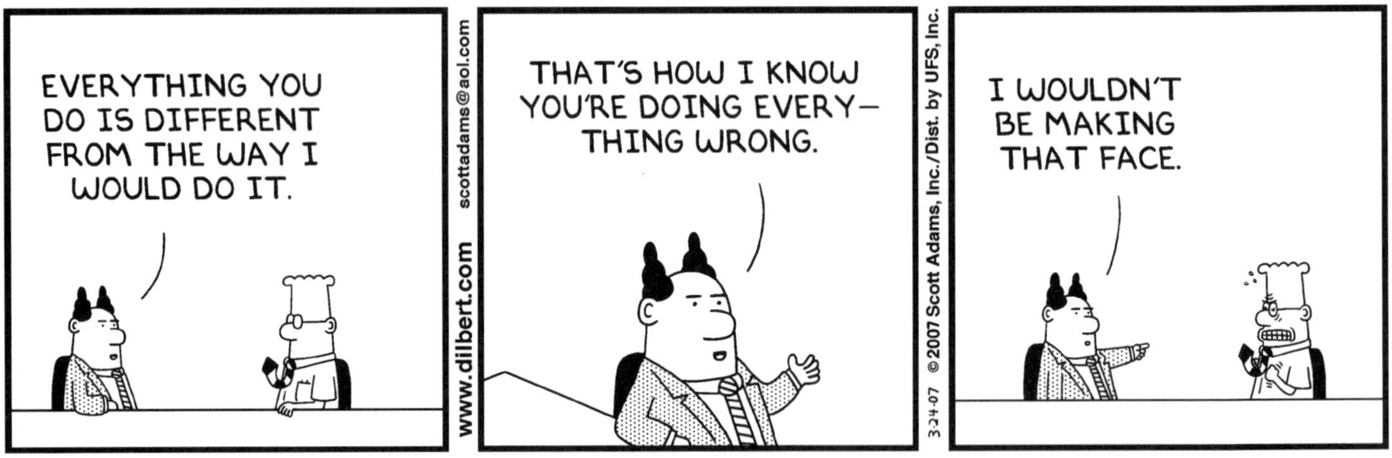
EVERYTHING YOU DO IS DIFFERENT FROM THE WAY I WOULD DO IT.
THAT'S HOW I KNOW YOU'RE DOING EVERY-THING WRONG.
I WOULDN'T BE MAKING THAT FACE.
www.dilbert.com scottadams@aol.com
3-24-07 © 2007 Scott Adams, Inc./Dist. by UFS, Inc.

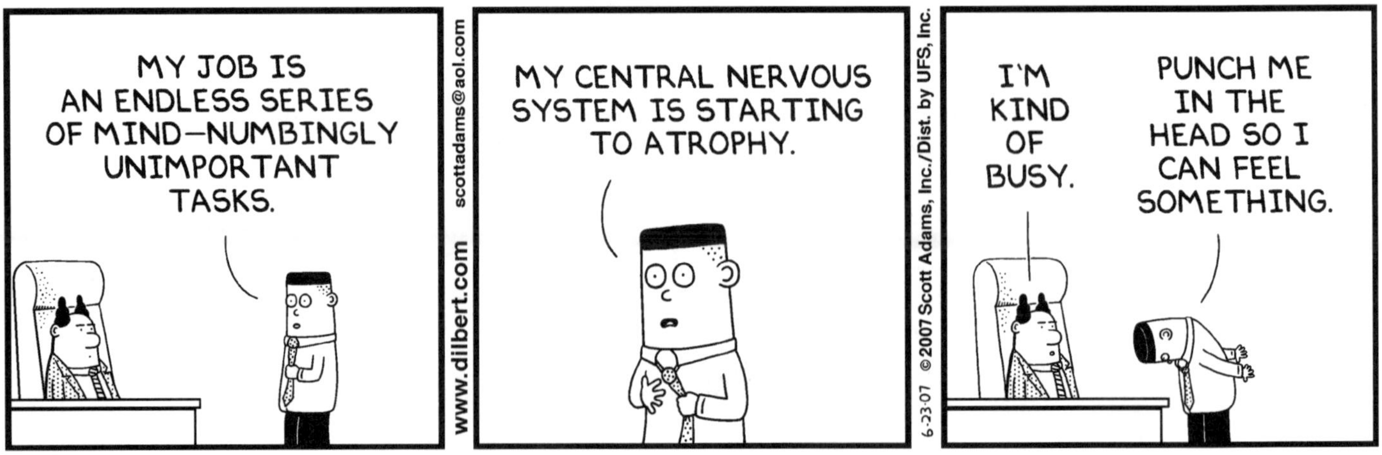
MY JOB IS AN ENDLESS SERIES OF MIND-NUMBINGLY UNIMPORTANT TASKS.
MY CENTRAL NERVOUS SYSTEM IS STARTING TO ATROPHY.
I'M KIND OF BUSY.
PUNCH ME IN THE HEAD SO I CAN FEEL SOMETHING.
www.dilbert.com scottadams@aol.com
6-23-07 © 2007 Scott Adams, Inc./Dist. by UFS, Inc.

2. Dilbert

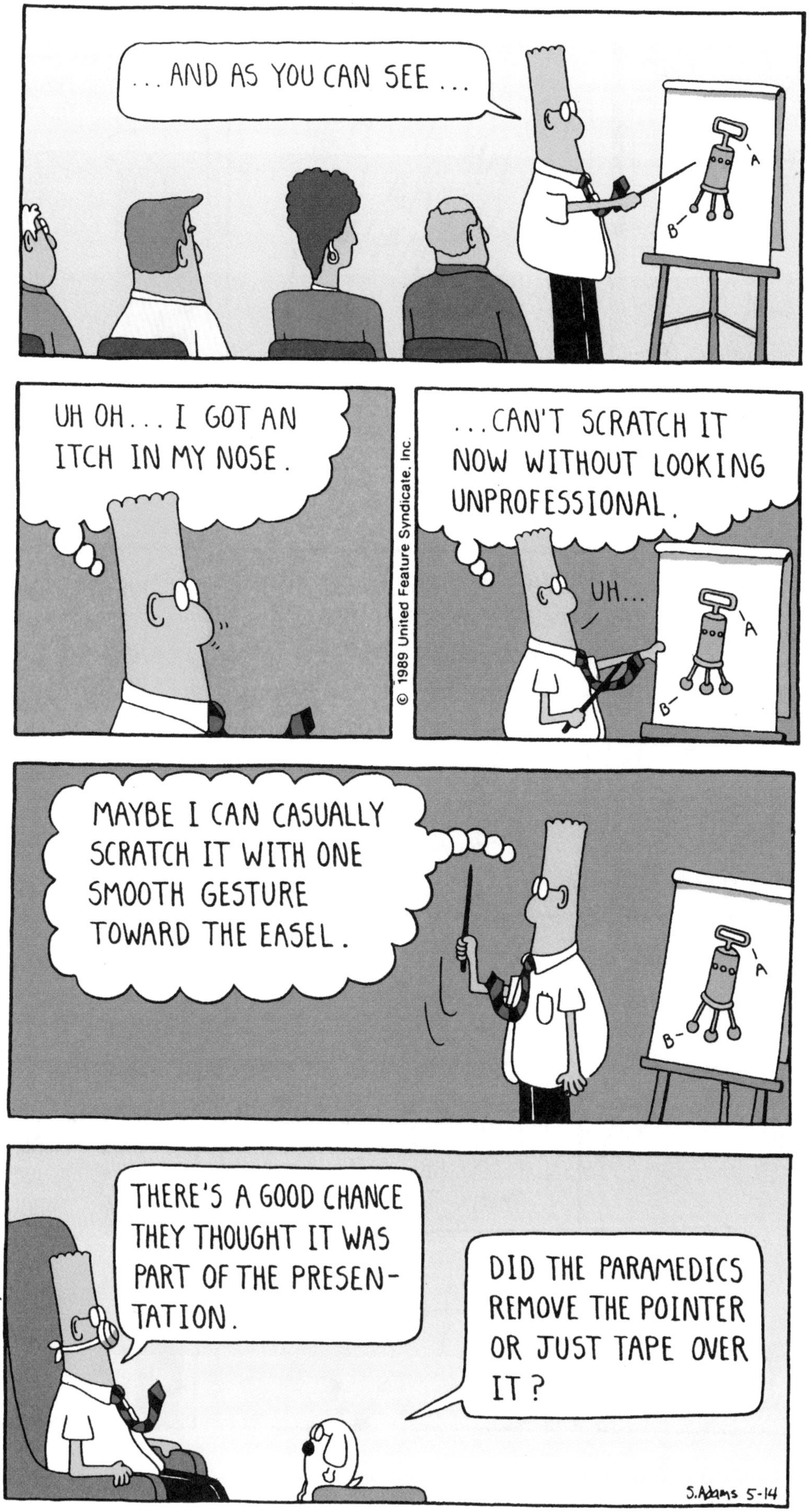
...AND AS YOU CAN SEE...
A
B
UH OH... I GOT AN ITCH IN MY NOSE.
© 1989 United Feature Syndicate, Inc.
...CAN'T SCRATCH IT NOW WITHOUT LOOKING UNPROFESSIONAL.
UH...
A
B
MAYBE I CAN CASUALLY SCRATCH IT WITH ONE SMOOTH GESTURE TOWARD THE EASEL.
A
B
THERE'S A GOOD CHANCE THEY THOUGHT IT WAS PART OF THE PRESEN-TATION.
DID THE PARAMEDICS REMOVE THE POINTER OR JUST TAPE OVER IT?
S.Adams 5-14

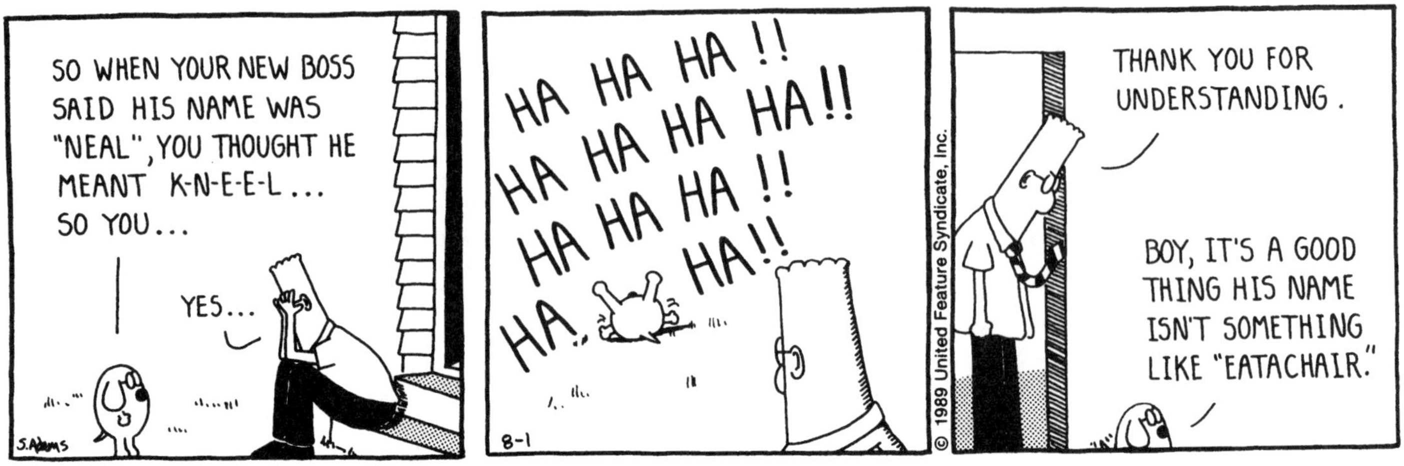
SO WHEN YOUR NEW BOSS SAID HIS NAME WAS "NEAL", YOU THOUGHT HE MEANT K-N-E-E-L ... SO YOU...
YES...
S.Adams
HA HA HA !! HA HA HA HA !! HA HA HA !! HA HA !!
8-1
© 1989 United Feature Syndicate, Inc.
THANK YOU FOR UNDERSTANDING.
BOY, IT'S A GOOD THING HIS NAME ISN'T SOMETHING LIKE "EATACHAIR."

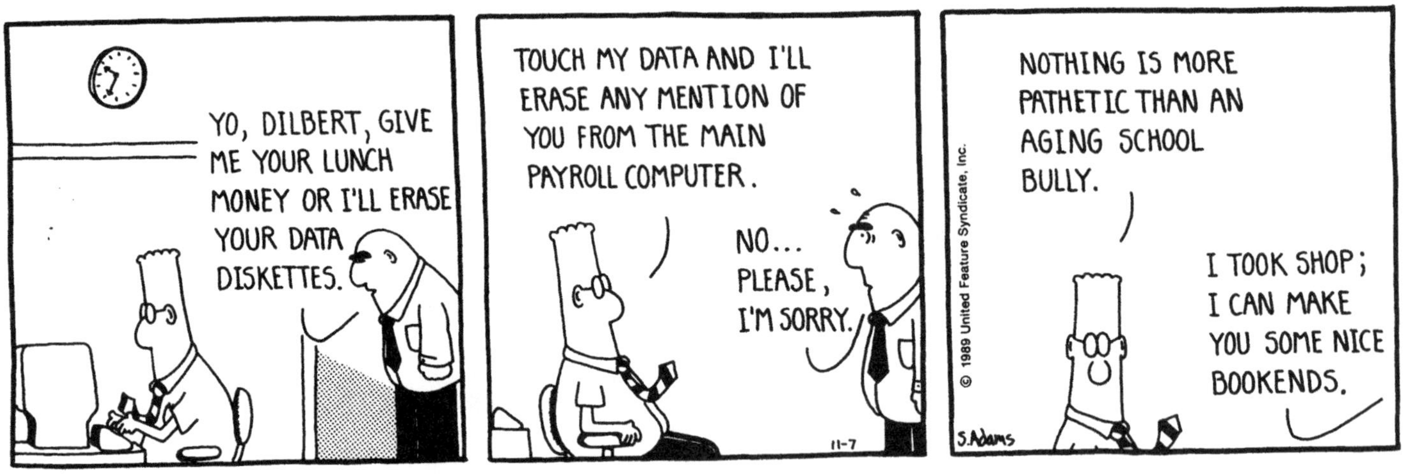
YO, DILBERT, GIVE ME YOUR LUNCH MONEY OR I'LL ERASE YOUR DATA DISKETTES.
TOUCH MY DATA AND I'LL ERASE ANY MENTION OF YOU FROM THE MAIN PAYROLL COMPUTER.
NO... PLEASE, I'M SORRY.
11-7
© 1989 United Feature Syndicate, Inc.
NOTHING IS MORE PATHETIC THAN AN AGING SCHOOL BULLY.
I TOOK SHOP; I CAN MAKE YOU SOME NICE BOOKENDS.
S.Adams

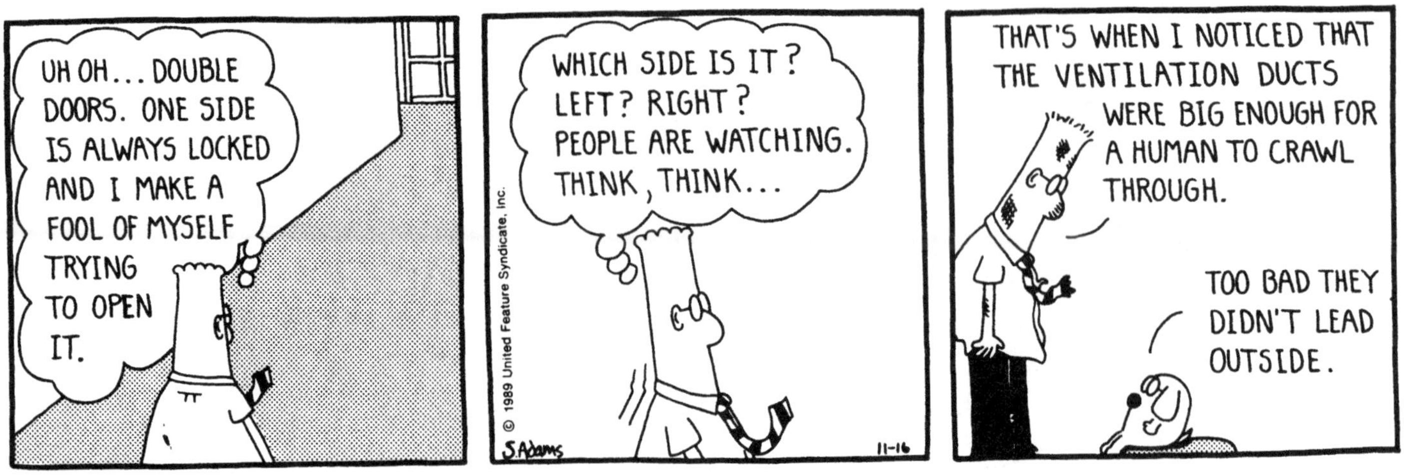
UH OH... DOUBLE DOORS. ONE SIDE IS ALWAYS LOCKED AND I MAKE A FOOL OF MYSELF TRYING TO OPEN IT.
© 1989 United Feature Syndicate, Inc.
WHICH SIDE IS IT? LEFT? RIGHT? PEOPLE ARE WATCHING. THINK, THINK...
S.Adams
11-16
THAT'S WHEN I NOTICED THAT THE VENTILATION DUCTS WERE BIG ENOUGH FOR A HUMAN TO CRAWL THROUGH.
TOO BAD THEY DIDN'T LEAD OUTSIDE.

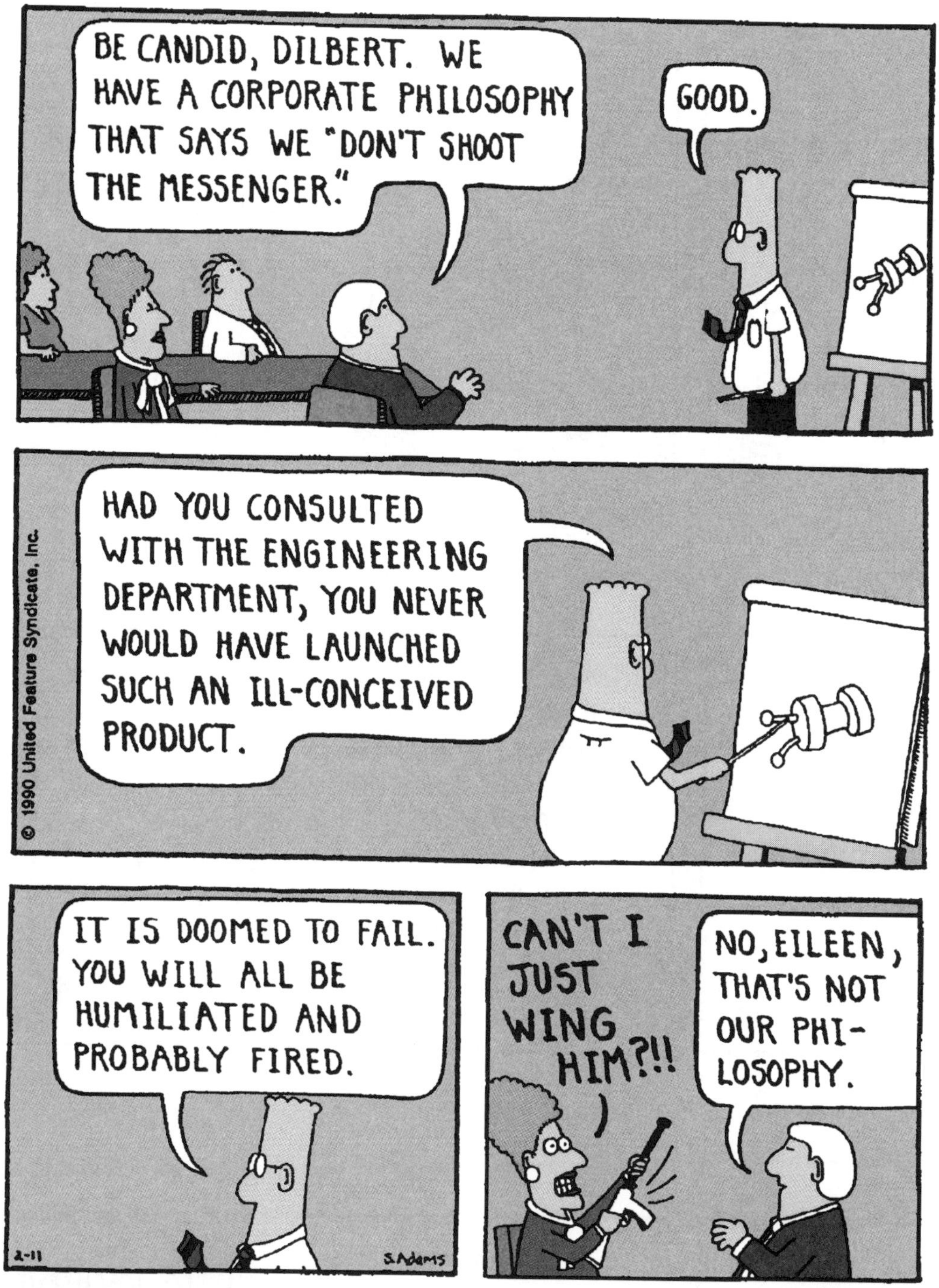
BE CANDID, DILBERT. WE HAVE A CORPORATE PHILOSOPHY THAT SAYS WE "DON'T SHOOT THE MESSENGER."
GOOD.
HAD YOU CONSULTED WITH THE ENGINEERING DEPARTMENT, YOU NEVER WOULD HAVE LAUNCHED SUCH AN ILL-CONCEIVED PRODUCT.
© 1990 United Feature Syndicate, Inc.
IT IS DOOMED TO FAIL. YOU WILL ALL BE HUMILIATED AND PROBABLY FIRED.
2-11
S. Adams
CAN'T I JUST WING HIM?!!
NO, EILEEN, THAT'S NOT OUR PHI-LOSOPHY.

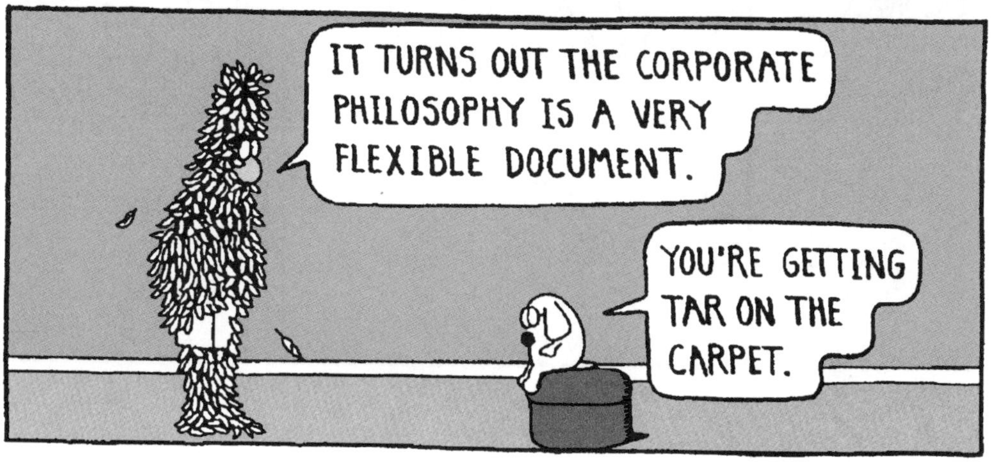
IT TURNS OUT THE CORPORATE PHILOSOPHY IS A VERY FLEXIBLE DOCUMENT.
YOU'RE GETTING TAR ON THE CARPET.

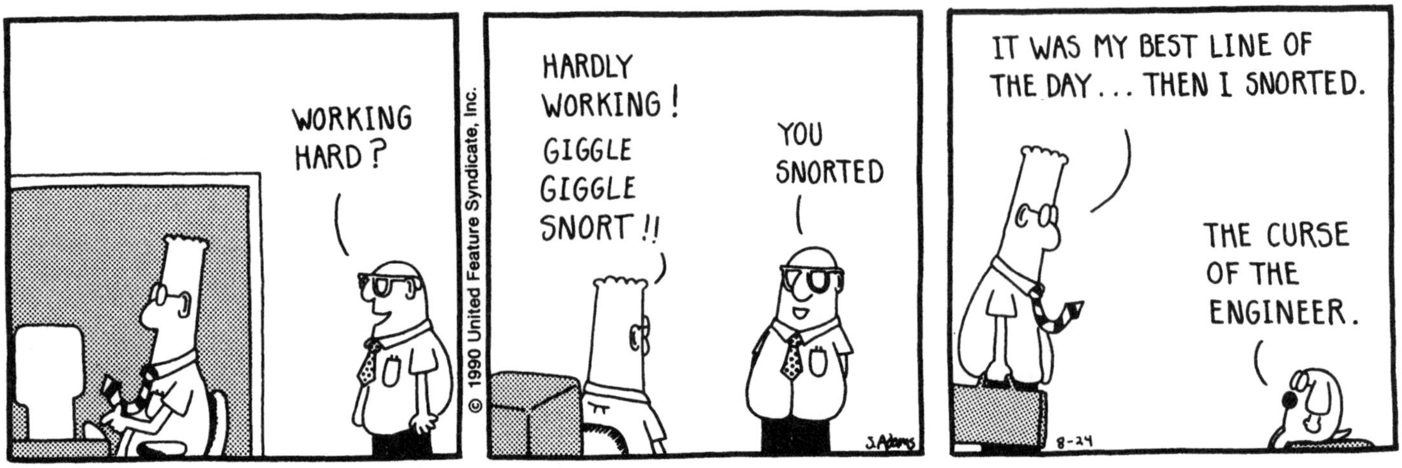
WORKING HARD?
© 1990 United Feature Syndicate, Inc.
HARDLY WORKING! GIGGLE GIGGLE SNORT!!
YOU SNORTED
IT WAS MY BEST LINE OF THE DAY... THEN I SNORTED.
THE CURSE OF THE ENGINEER.
8-24

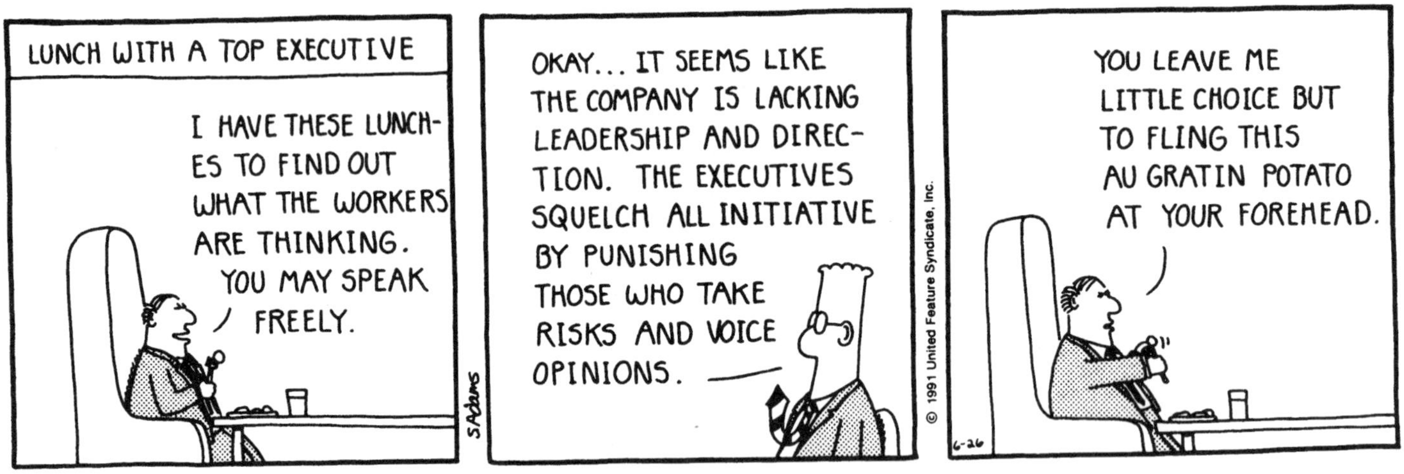
LUNCH WITH A TOP EXECUTIVE
I HAVE THESE LUNCHES TO FIND OUT WHAT THE WORKERS ARE THINKING. YOU MAY SPEAK FREELY.
OKAY... IT SEEMS LIKE THE COMPANY IS LACKING LEADERSHIP AND DIRECTION. THE EXECUTIVES SQUELCH ALL INITIATIVE BY PUNISHING THOSE WHO TAKE RISKS AND VOICE OPINIONS.
© 1991 United Feature Syndicate, Inc.
YOU LEAVE ME LITTLE CHOICE BUT TO FLING THIS AU GRATIN POTATO AT YOUR FOREHEAD.
6-26

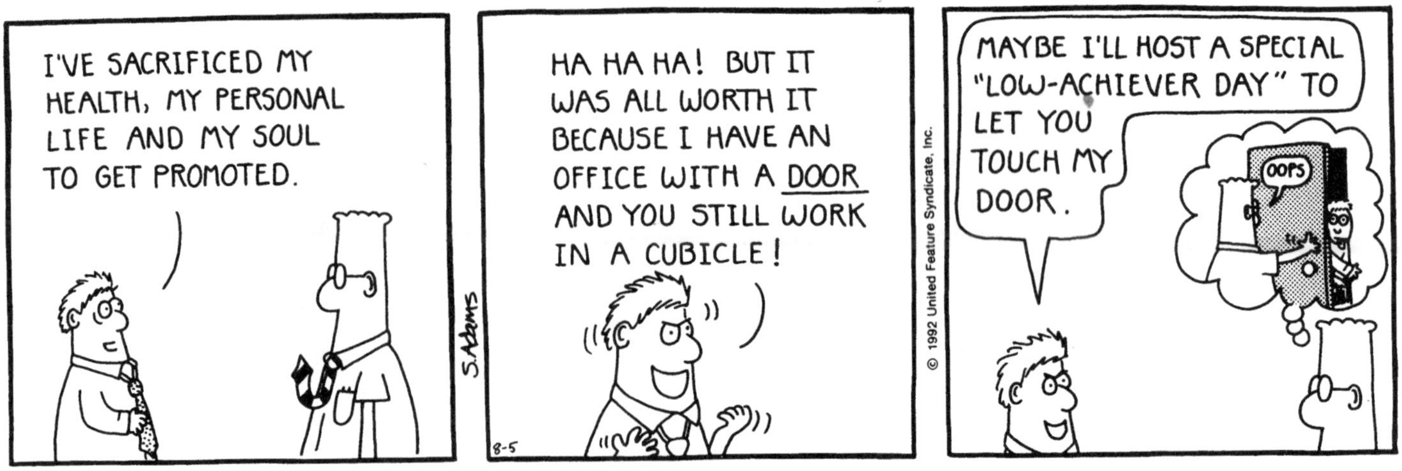
I'VE SACRIFICED MY HEALTH, MY PERSONAL LIFE AND MY SOUL TO GET PROMOTED.
HA HA HA! BUT IT WAS ALL WORTH IT BECAUSE I HAVE AN OFFICE WITH A DOOR AND YOU STILL WORK IN A CUBICLE!
8-5
© 1992 United Feature Syndicate, Inc.
MAYBE I'LL HOST A SPECIAL "LOW-ACHIEVER DAY" TO LET YOU TOUCH MY DOOR.
OOPS

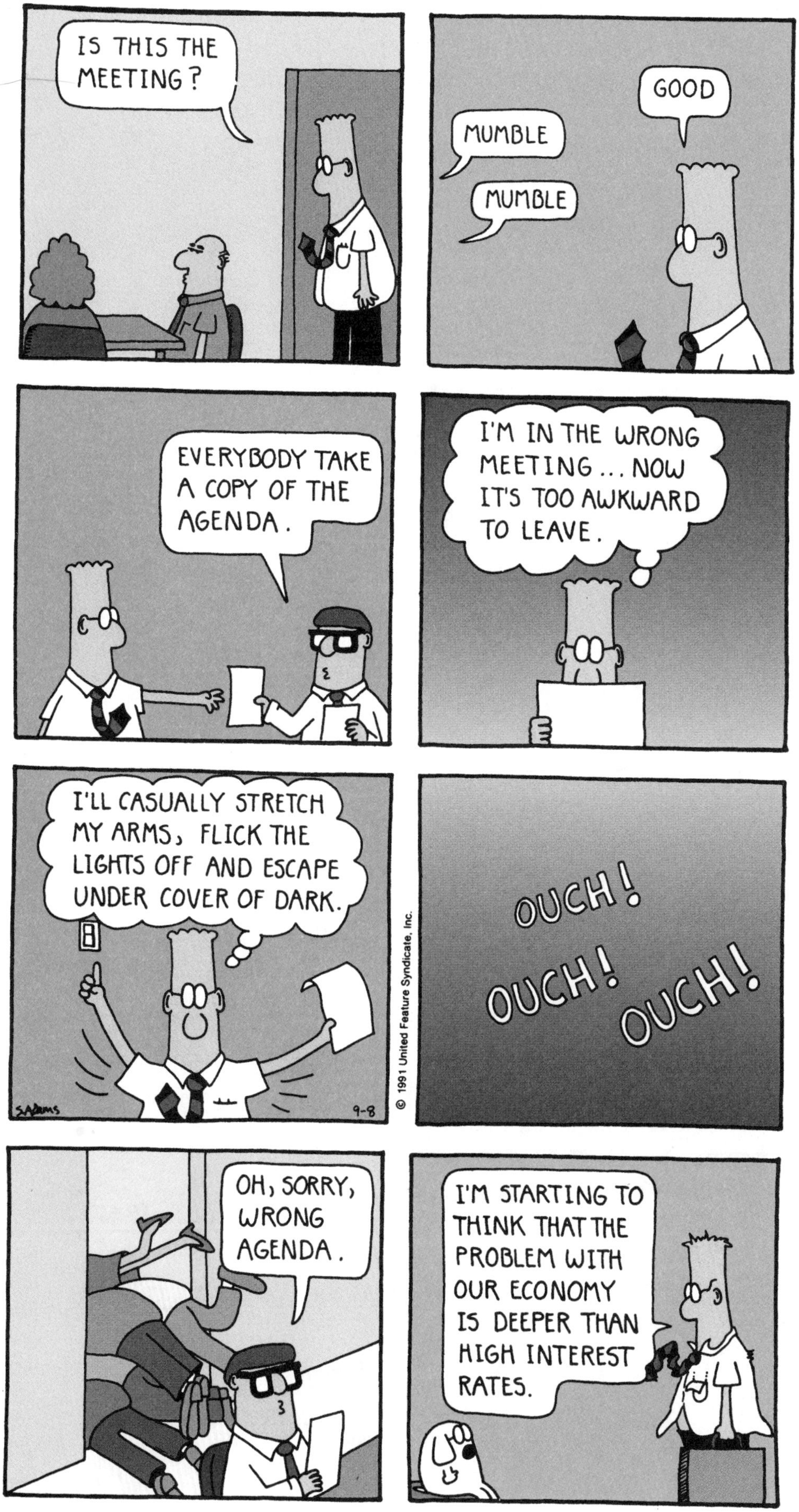
IS THIS THE MEETING?
MUMBLE
MUMBLE
GOOD
EVERYBODY TAKE A COPY OF THE AGENDA.
I'M IN THE WRONG MEETING... NOW IT'S TOO AWKWARD TO LEAVE.
I'LL CASUALLY STRETCH MY ARMS, FLICK THE LIGHTS OFF AND ESCAPE UNDER COVER OF DARK.
S.ADAMS
9-8
© 1991 United Feature Syndicate, Inc.
OUCH!
OUCH!
OUCH!
OH, SORRY, WRONG AGENDA.
I'M STARTING TO THINK THAT THE PROBLEM WITH OUR ECONOMY IS DEEPER THAN HIGH INTEREST RATES.

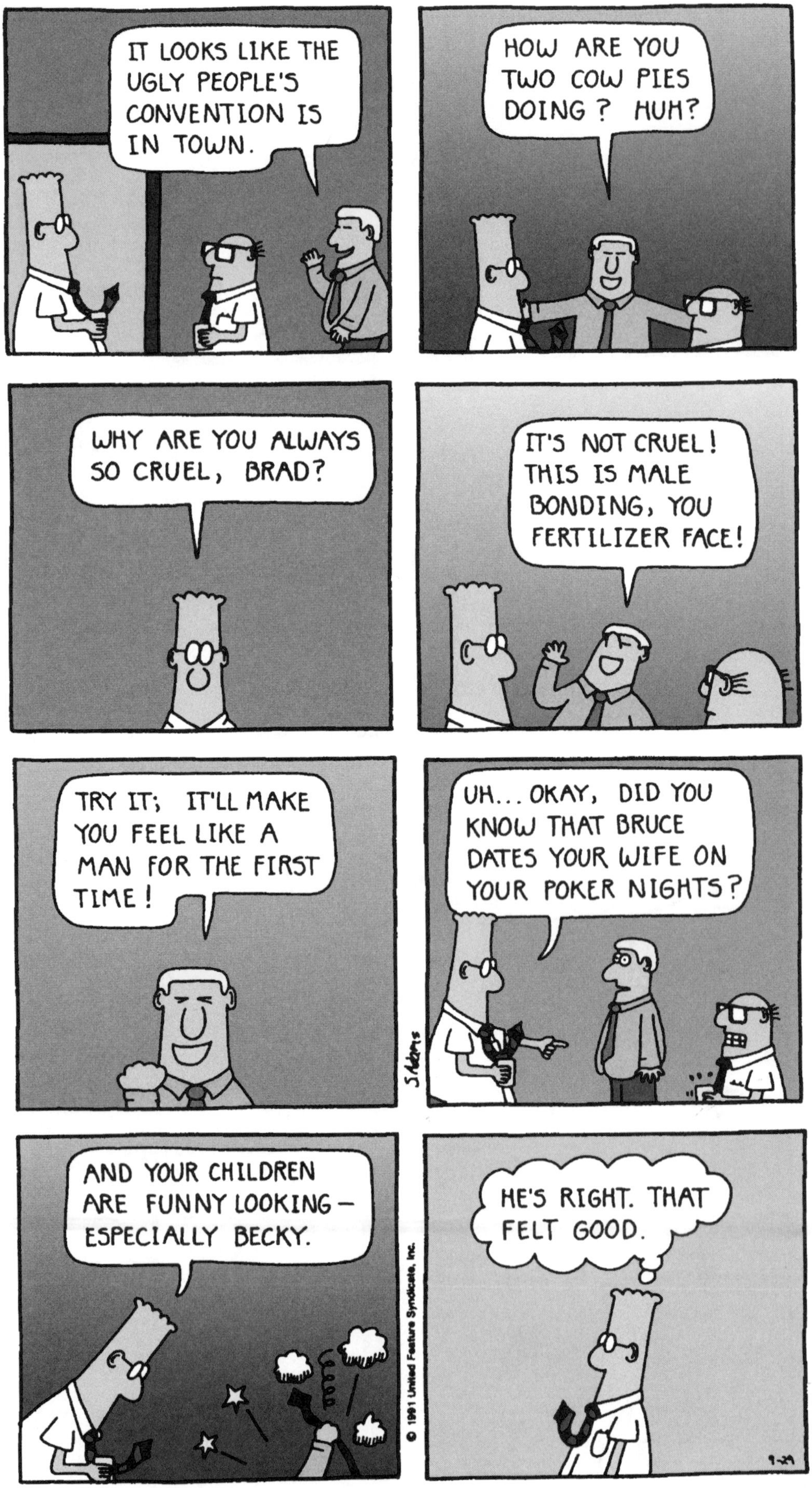
IT LOOKS LIKE THE UGLY PEOPLE'S CONVENTION IS IN TOWN.
HOW ARE YOU TWO COW PIES DOING? HUH?
WHY ARE YOU ALWAYS SO CRUEL, BRAD?
IT'S NOT CRUEL! THIS IS MALE BONDING, YOU FERTILIZER FACE!
TRY IT; IT'LL MAKE YOU FEEL LIKE A MAN FOR THE FIRST TIME!
UH... OKAY, DID YOU KNOW THAT BRUCE DATES YOUR WIFE ON YOUR POKER NIGHTS?
AND YOUR CHILDREN ARE FUNNY LOOKING — ESPECIALLY BECKY.
HE'S RIGHT. THAT FELT GOOD.
© 1991 United Feature Syndicate, Inc.
9-29

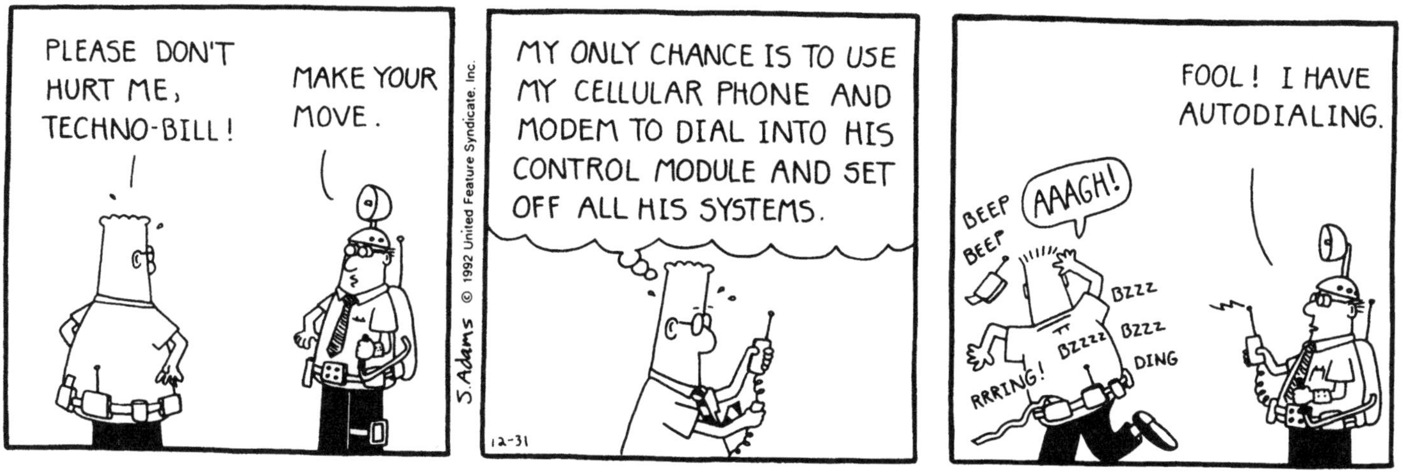
PLEASE DON'T HURT ME, TECHNO-BILL!
MAKE YOUR MOVE.
S. Adams
© 1992 United Feature Syndicate, Inc.
MY ONLY CHANCE IS TO USE MY CELLULAR PHONE AND MODEM TO DIAL INTO HIS CONTROL MODULE AND SET OFF ALL HIS SYSTEMS.
12-31
BEEP
BEEP
AAAGH!
BZZZ
BZZZZ
BZZZ
DING
RRRING!
FOOL! I HAVE AUTODIALING.

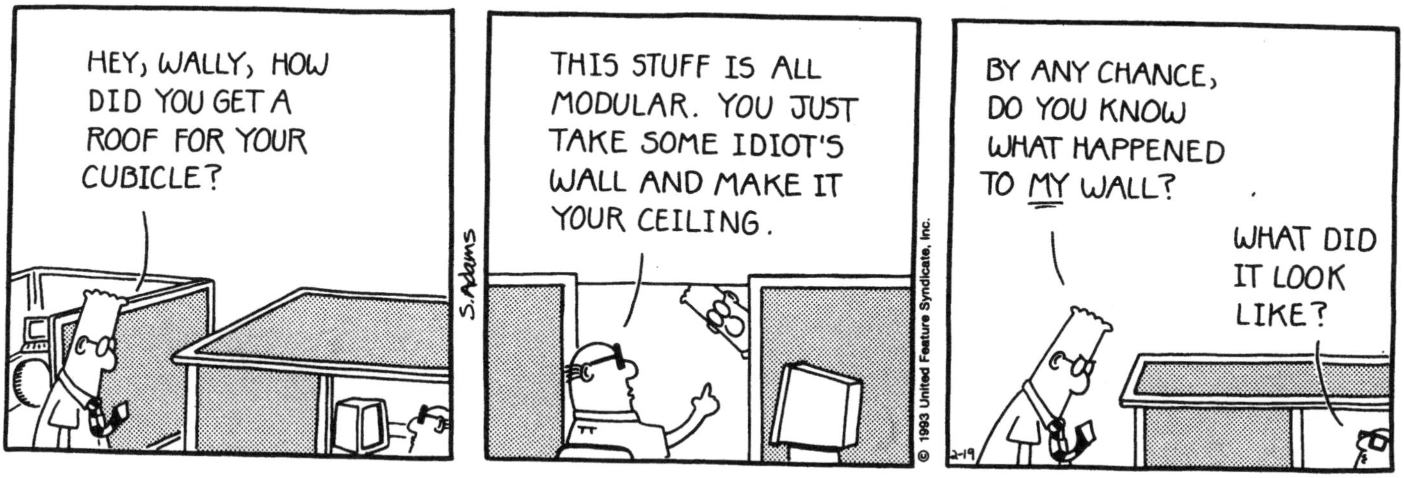
HEY, WALLY, HOW DID YOU GET A ROOF FOR YOUR CUBICLE?
S. Adams
THIS STUFF IS ALL MODULAR. YOU JUST TAKE SOME IDIOT'S WALL AND MAKE IT YOUR CEILING.
© 1993 United Feature Syndicate, Inc.
BY ANY CHANCE, DO YOU KNOW WHAT HAPPENED TO MY WALL?
WHAT DID IT LOOK LIKE?
2-19

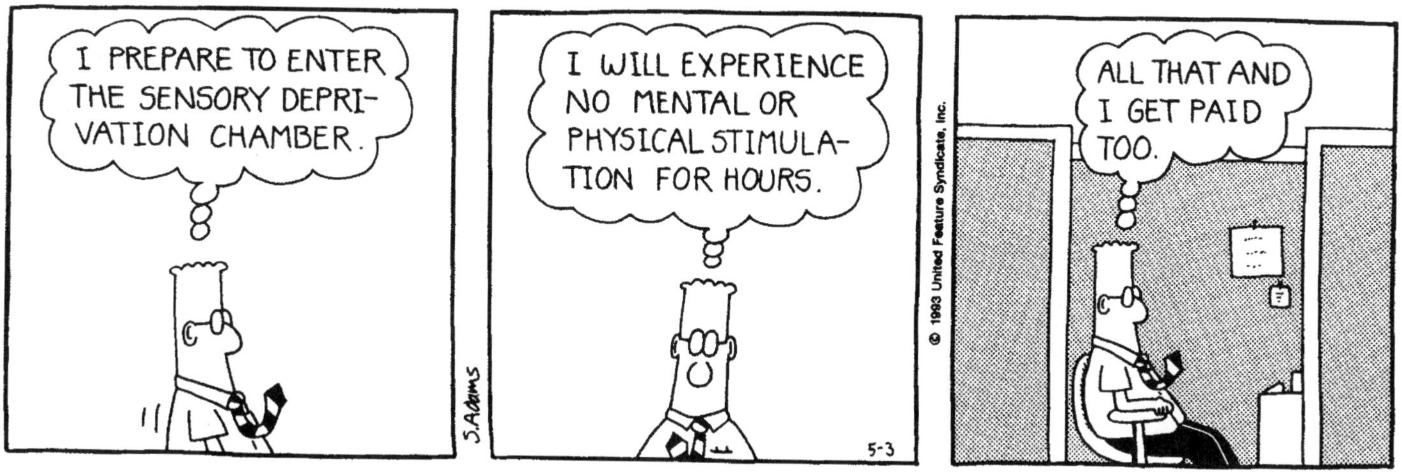
I PREPARE TO ENTER THE SENSORY DEPRIVATION CHAMBER.
S. Adams
I WILL EXPERIENCE NO MENTAL OR PHYSICAL STIMULATION FOR HOURS.
5-3
© 1993 United Feature Syndicate, Inc.
ALL THAT AND I GET PAID TOO.

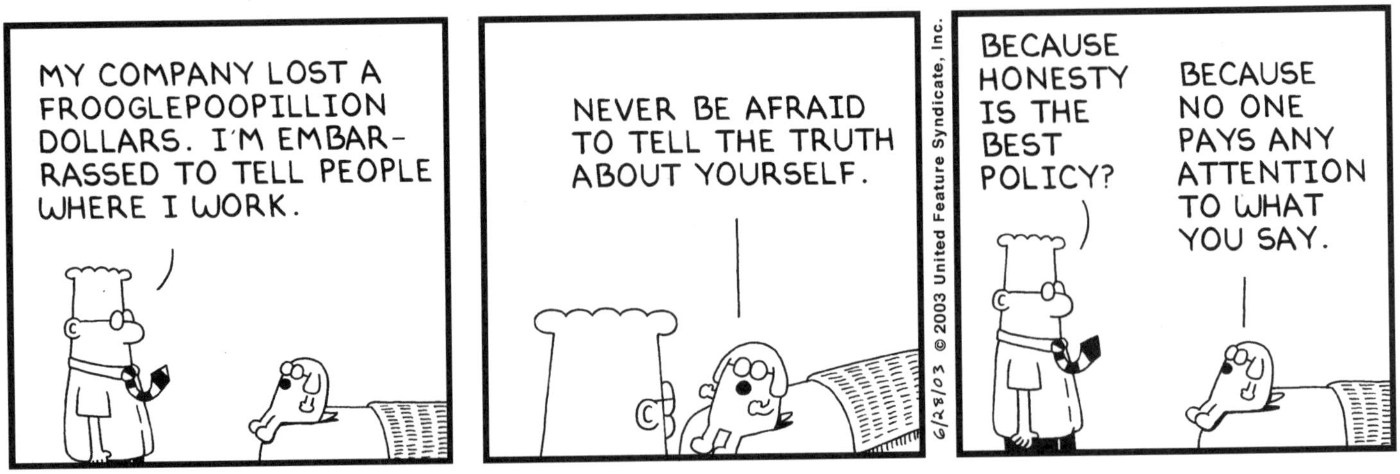
MY COMPANY LOST A FROOGLEPOOPILLION DOLLARS. I'M EMBARRASSED TO TELL PEOPLE WHERE I WORK.
NEVER BE AFRAID TO TELL THE TRUTH ABOUT YOURSELF.
6/28/03 © 2003 United Feature Syndicate, Inc.
BECAUSE HONESTY IS THE BEST POLICY?
BECAUSE NO ONE PAYS ANY ATTENTION TO WHAT YOU SAY.

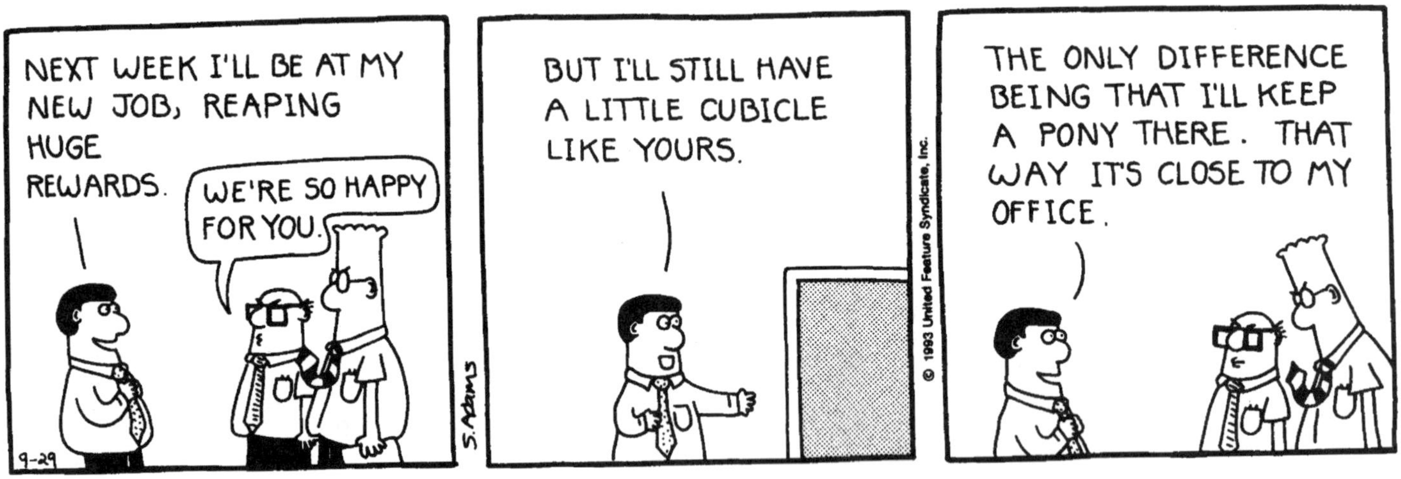
NEXT WEEK I'LL BE AT MY NEW JOB, REAPING HUGE REWARDS.
WE'RE SO HAPPY FOR YOU.
9-29
S. Adams
BUT I'LL STILL HAVE A LITTLE CUBICLE LIKE YOURS.
© 1993 United Feature Syndicate, Inc.
THE ONLY DIFFERENCE BEING THAT I'LL KEEP A PONY THERE. THAT WAY IT'S CLOSE TO MY OFFICE.

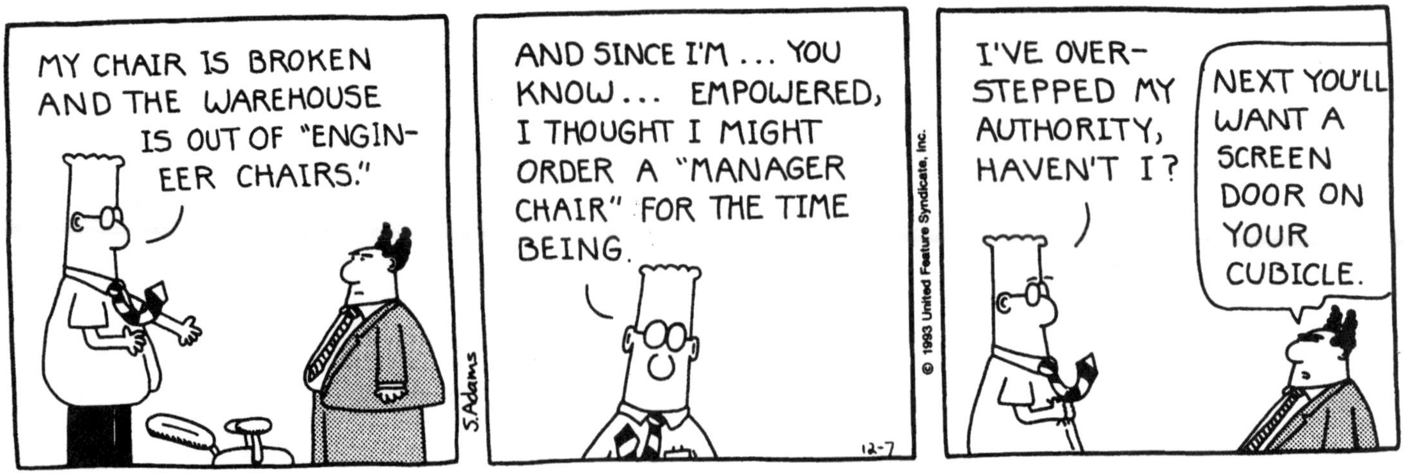
MY CHAIR IS BROKEN AND THE WAREHOUSE IS OUT OF "ENGINEER CHAIRS."
S. Adams
AND SINCE I'M ... YOU KNOW ... EMPOWERED, I THOUGHT I MIGHT ORDER A "MANAGER CHAIR" FOR THE TIME BEING.
12-7
© 1993 United Feature Syndicate, Inc.
I'VE OVERSTEPPED MY AUTHORITY, HAVEN'T I?
NEXT YOU'LL WANT A SCREEN DOOR ON YOUR CUBICLE.

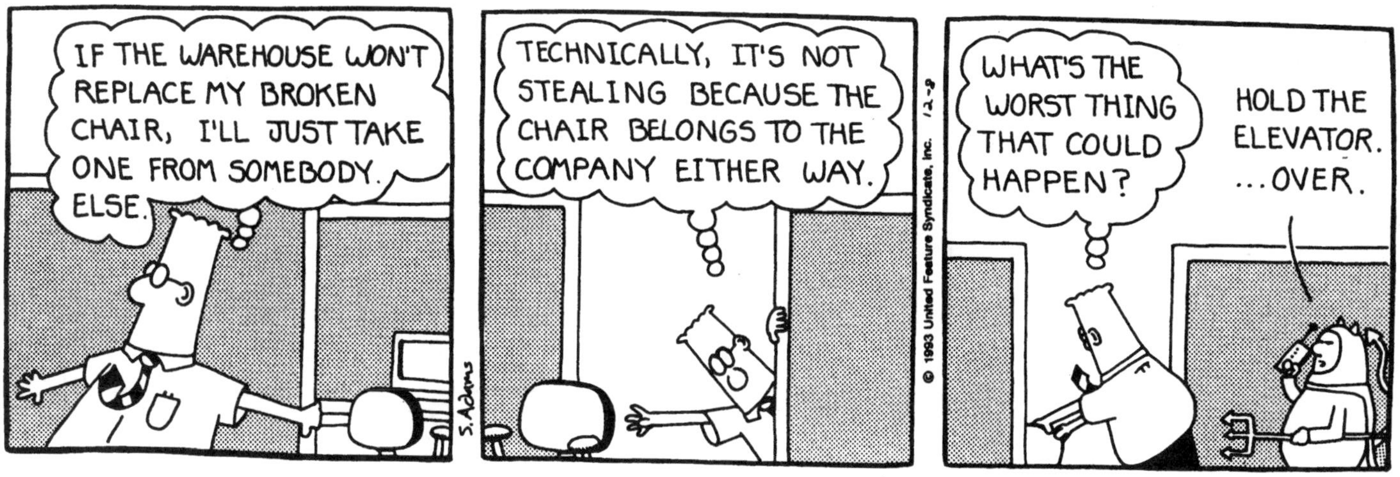
IF THE WAREHOUSE WON'T REPLACE MY BROKEN CHAIR, I'LL JUST TAKE ONE FROM SOMEBODY ELSE.
S. Adams
TECHNICALLY, IT'S NOT STEALING BECAUSE THE CHAIR BELONGS TO THE COMPANY EITHER WAY.
12-9
© 1993 United Feature Syndicate, Inc.
WHAT'S THE WORST THING THAT COULD HAPPEN?
HOLD THE ELEVATOR. ...OVER.

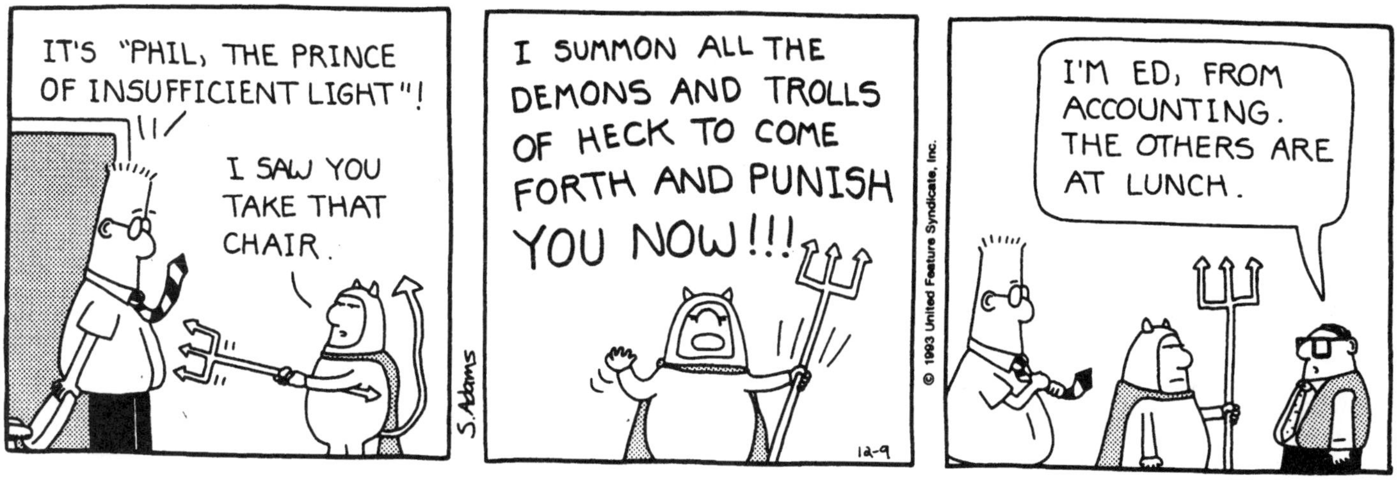
IT'S "PHIL, THE PRINCE OF INSUFFICIENT LIGHT"!
I SAW YOU TAKE THAT CHAIR.
S. Adams
I SUMMON ALL THE DEMONS AND TROLLS OF HECK TO COME FORTH AND PUNISH YOU NOW!!!
12-9
© 1993 United Feature Syndicate, Inc.
I'M ED, FROM ACCOUNTING. THE OTHERS ARE AT LUNCH.

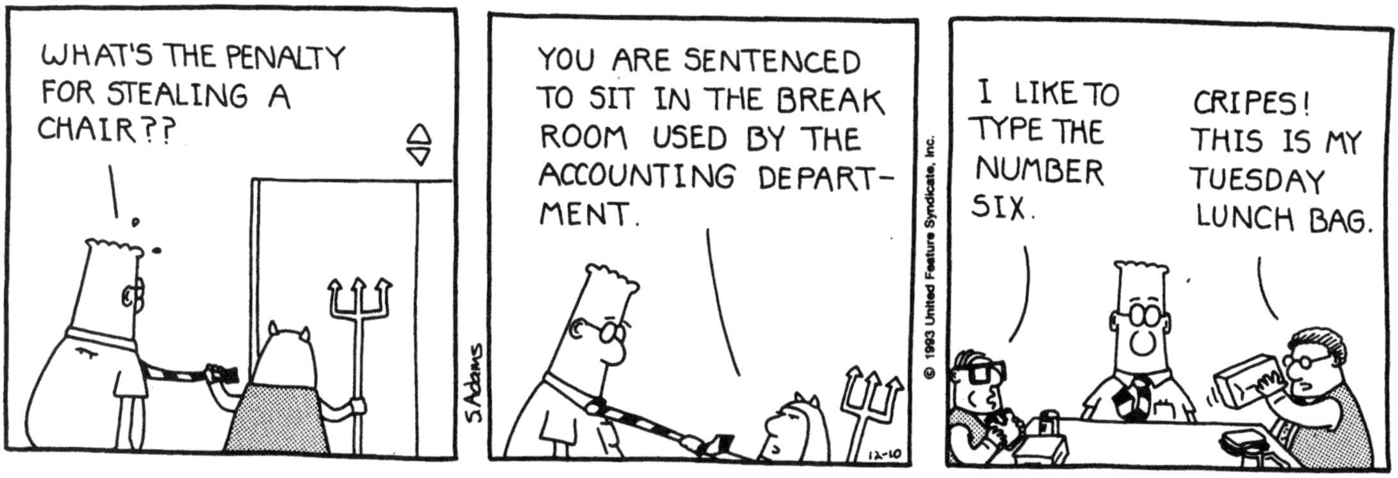
WHAT'S THE PENALTY FOR STEALING A CHAIR??
S. Adams
YOU ARE SENTENCED TO SIT IN THE BREAK ROOM USED BY THE ACCOUNTING DEPART-MENT.
12-10
© 1993 United Feature Syndicate, Inc.
I LIKE TO TYPE THE NUMBER SIX.
CRIPES! THIS IS MY TUESDAY LUNCH BAG.

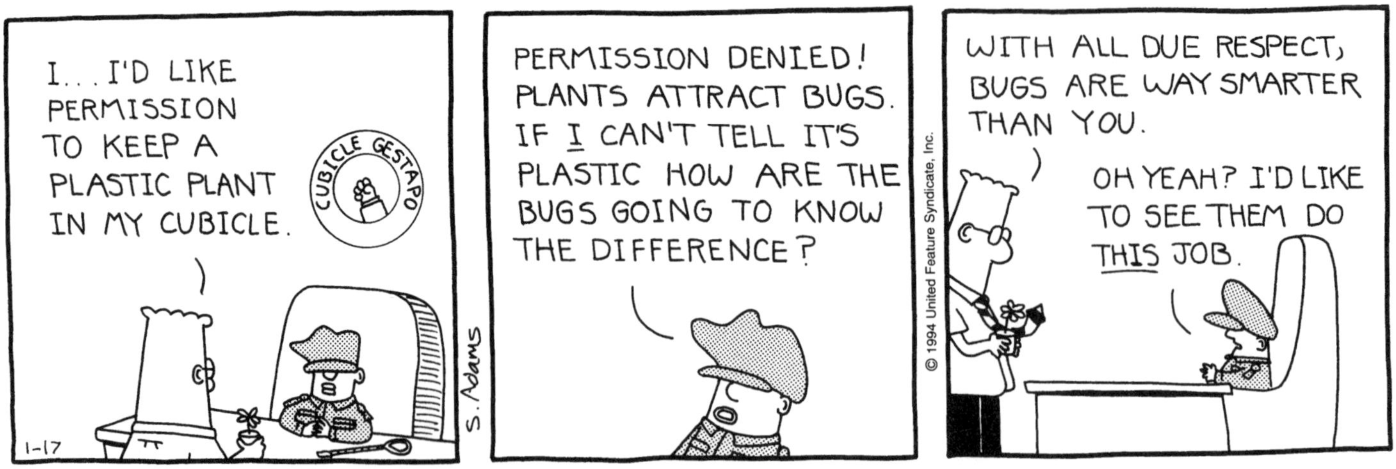
I... I'D LIKE PERMISSION TO KEEP A PLASTIC PLANT IN MY CUBICLE.
CUBICLE GESTAPO
PERMISSION DENIED! PLANTS ATTRACT BUGS. IF I CAN'T TELL IT'S PLASTIC HOW ARE THE BUGS GOING TO KNOW THE DIFFERENCE?
WITH ALL DUE RESPECT, BUGS ARE WAY SMARTER THAN YOU.
OH YEAH? I'D LIKE TO SEE THEM DO THIS JOB.
1-17
S. Adams
© 1994 United Feature Syndicate, Inc.

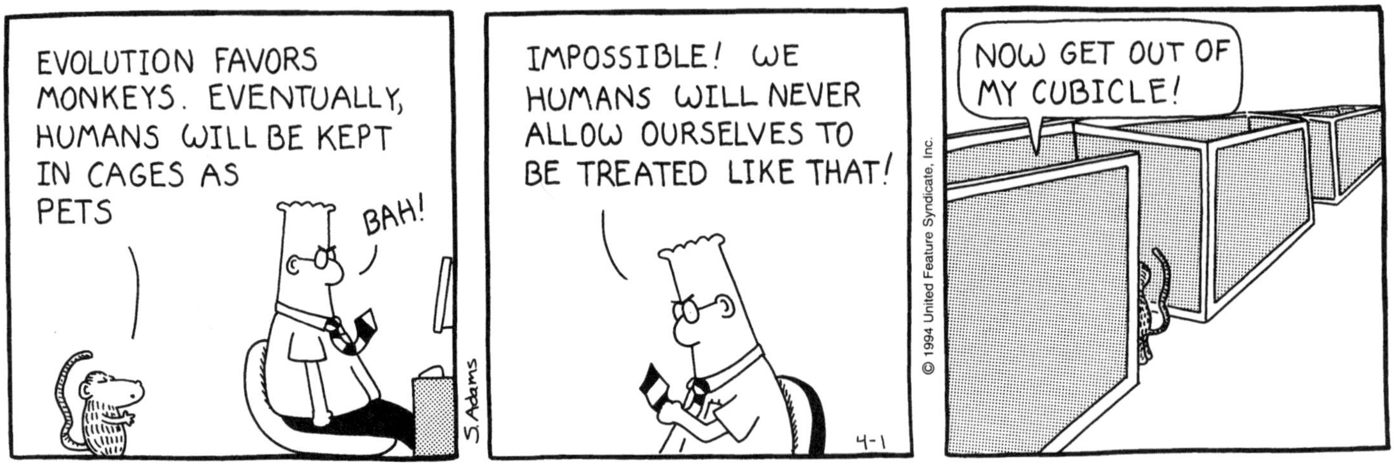
EVOLUTION FAVORS MONKEYS. EVENTUALLY, HUMANS WILL BE KEPT IN CAGES AS PETS
BAH!
IMPOSSIBLE! WE HUMANS WILL NEVER ALLOW OURSELVES TO BE TREATED LIKE THAT!
NOW GET OUT OF MY CUBICLE!
4-1
S. Adams
© 1994 United Feature Syndicate, Inc.

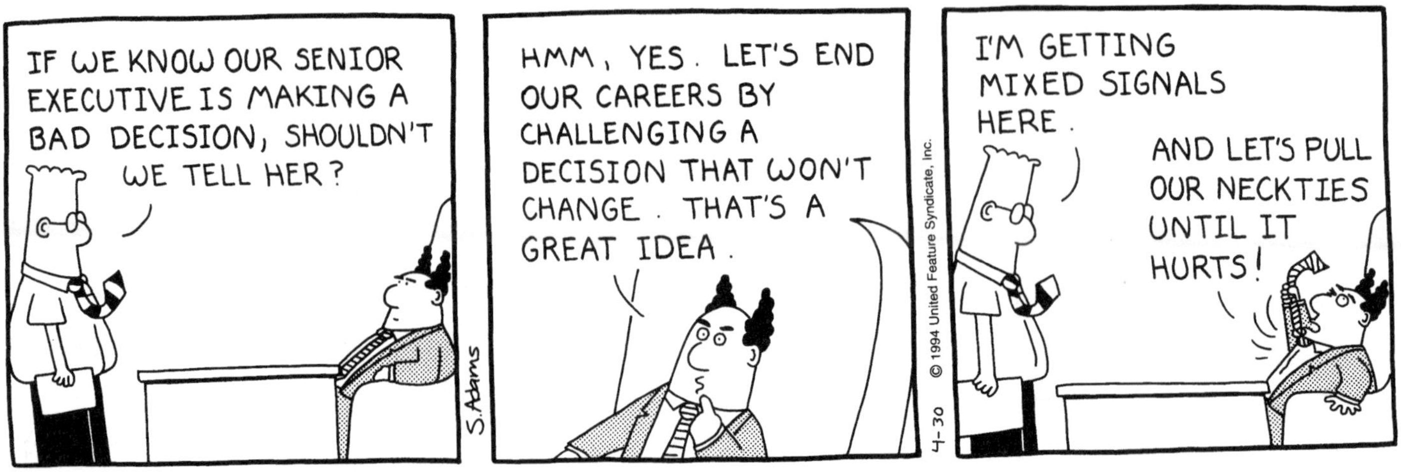
IF WE KNOW OUR SENIOR EXECUTIVE IS MAKING A BAD DECISION, SHOULDN'T WE TELL HER?
HMM, YES. LET'S END OUR CAREERS BY CHALLENGING A DECISION THAT WON'T CHANGE. THAT'S A GREAT IDEA.
I'M GETTING MIXED SIGNALS HERE.
AND LET'S PULL OUR NECKTIES UNTIL IT HURTS!
4-30
S. Adams
© 1994 United Feature Syndicate, Inc.

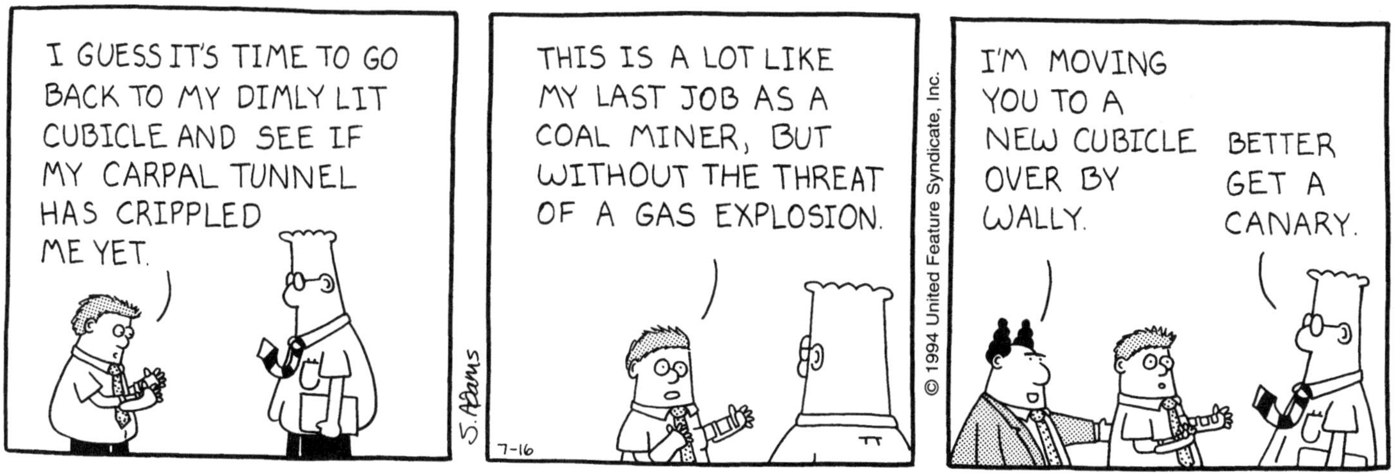
I GUESS IT'S TIME TO GO BACK TO MY DIMLY LIT CUBICLE AND SEE IF MY CARPAL TUNNEL HAS CRIPPLED ME YET.
S. ADAMS
THIS IS A LOT LIKE MY LAST JOB AS A COAL MINER, BUT WITHOUT THE THREAT OF A GAS EXPLOSION.
7-16
© 1994 United Feature Syndicate, Inc.
I'M MOVING YOU TO A NEW CUBICLE OVER BY WALLY.
BETTER GET A CANARY.

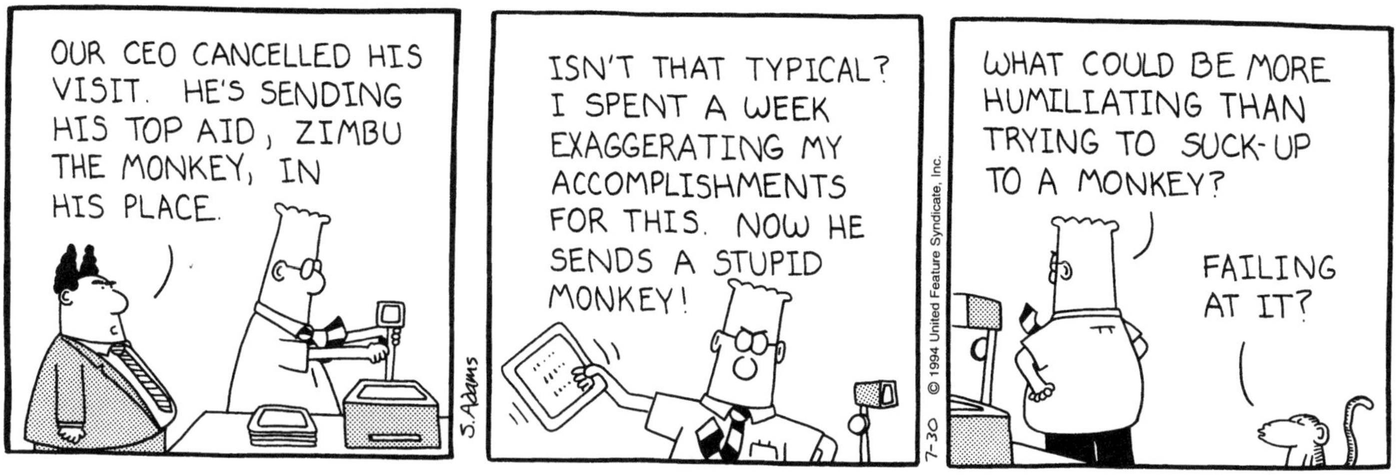
OUR CEO CANCELLED HIS VISIT. HE'S SENDING HIS TOP AID, ZIMBU THE MONKEY, IN HIS PLACE.
S. ADAMS
ISN'T THAT TYPICAL? I SPENT A WEEK EXAGGERATING MY ACCOMPLISHMENTS FOR THIS. NOW HE SENDS A STUPID MONKEY!
7-30
© 1994 United Feature Syndicate, Inc.
WHAT COULD BE MORE HUMILIATING THAN TRYING TO SUCK-UP TO A MONKEY?
FAILING AT IT?

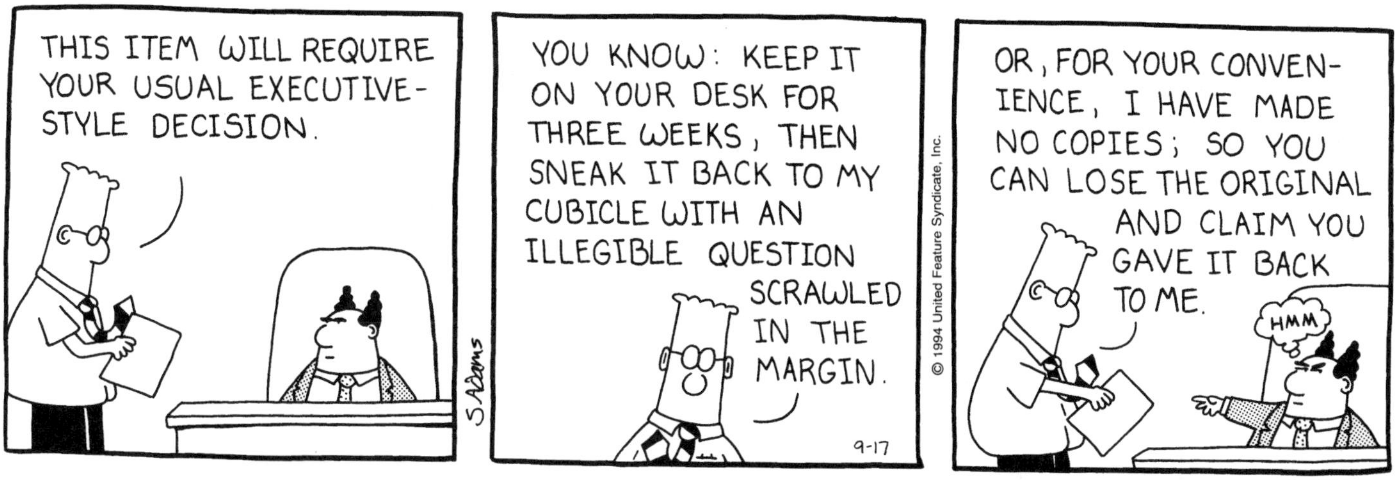
THIS ITEM WILL REQUIRE YOUR USUAL EXECUTIVE-STYLE DECISION.
S. ADAMS
YOU KNOW: KEEP IT ON YOUR DESK FOR THREE WEEKS, THEN SNEAK IT BACK TO MY CUBICLE WITH AN ILLEGIBLE QUESTION SCRAWLED IN THE MARGIN.
9-17
© 1994 United Feature Syndicate, Inc.
OR, FOR YOUR CONVENIENCE, I HAVE MADE NO COPIES; SO YOU CAN LOSE THE ORIGINAL AND CLAIM YOU GAVE IT BACK TO ME.
HMM

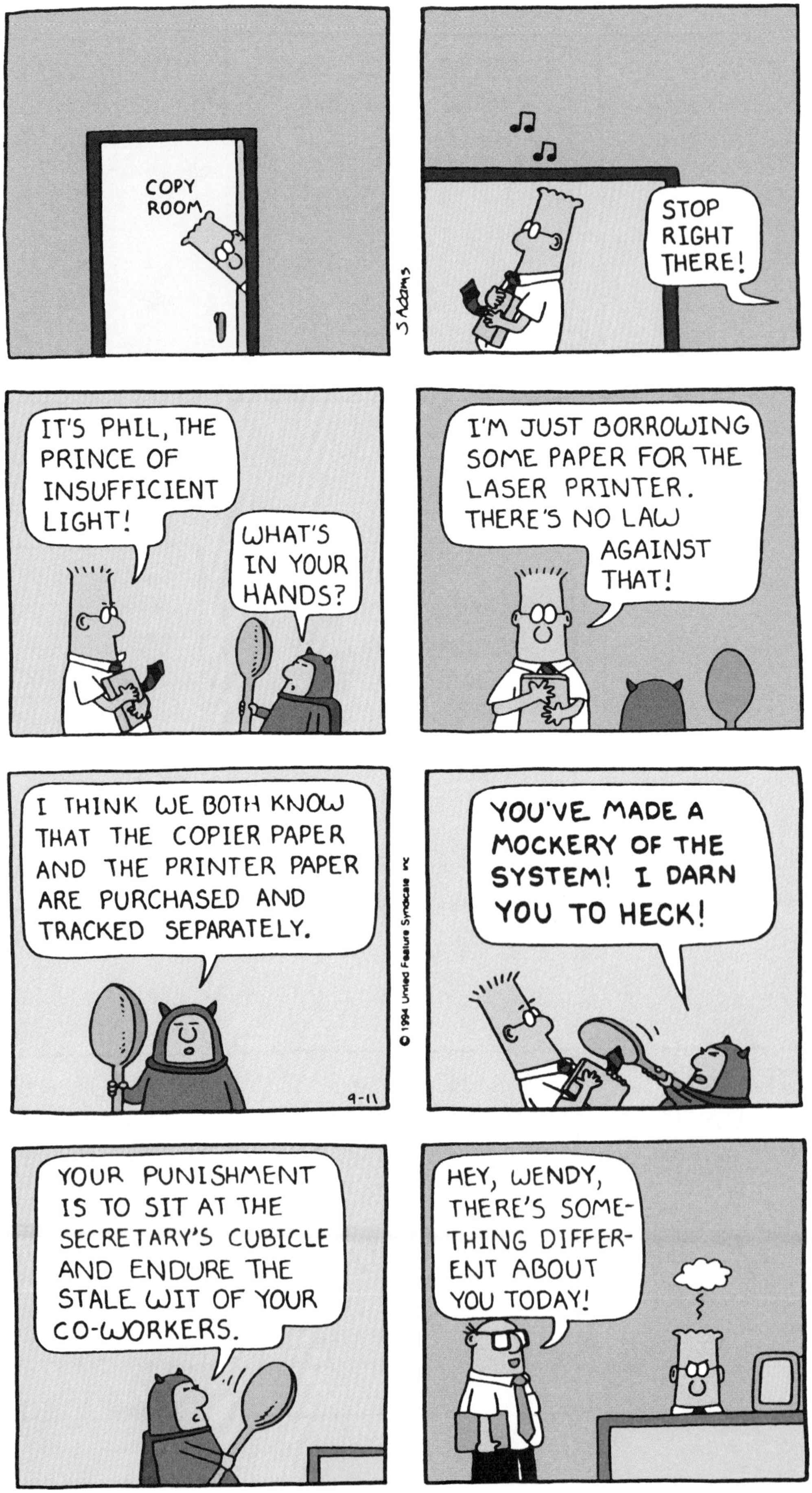
COPY ROOM
S Adams
STOP RIGHT THERE!
IT'S PHIL, THE PRINCE OF INSUFFICIENT LIGHT!
WHAT'S IN YOUR HANDS?
I'M JUST BORROWING SOME PAPER FOR THE LASER PRINTER. THERE'S NO LAW AGAINST THAT!
I THINK WE BOTH KNOW THAT THE COPIER PAPER AND THE PRINTER PAPER ARE PURCHASED AND TRACKED SEPARATELY.
© 1994 United Feature Syndicate Inc
9-11
YOU'VE MADE A MOCKERY OF THE SYSTEM! I DARN YOU TO HECK!
YOUR PUNISHMENT IS TO SIT AT THE SECRETARY'S CUBICLE AND ENDURE THE STALE WIT OF YOUR CO-WORKERS.
HEY, WENDY, THERE'S SOME-THING DIFFER-ENT ABOUT YOU TODAY!

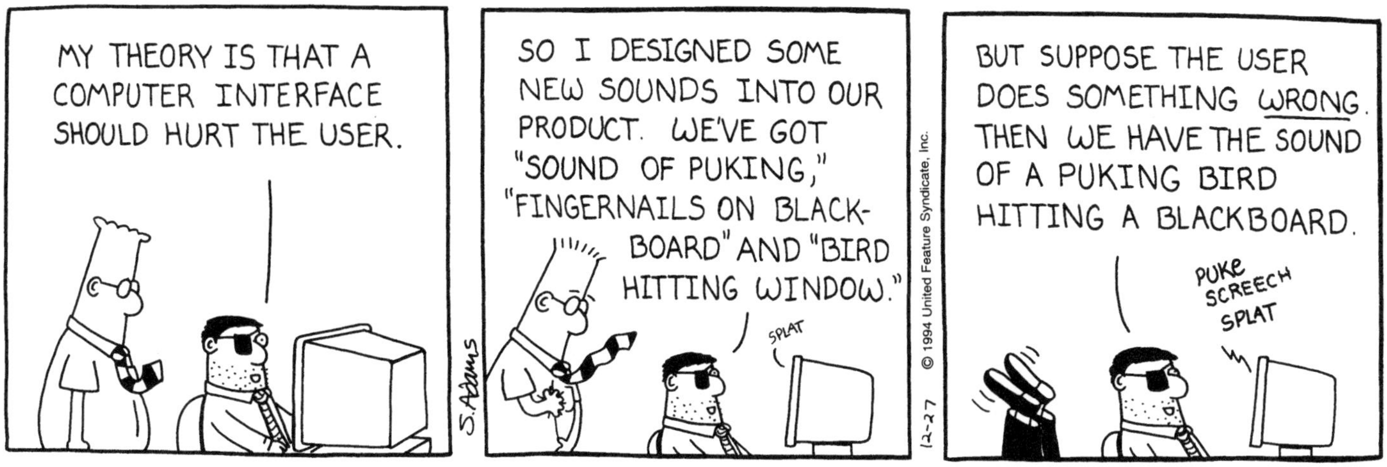
MY THEORY IS THAT A COMPUTER INTERFACE SHOULD HURT THE USER.
S. Adams
SO I DESIGNED SOME NEW SOUNDS INTO OUR PRODUCT. WE'VE GOT "SOUND OF PUKING," "FINGERNAILS ON BLACK-BOARD" AND "BIRD HITTING WINDOW."
SPLAT
12-27
© 1994 United Feature Syndicate, Inc.
BUT SUPPOSE THE USER DOES SOMETHING WRONG. THEN WE HAVE THE SOUND OF A PUKING BIRD HITTING A BLACKBOARD.
PUKE
SCREECH
SPLAT

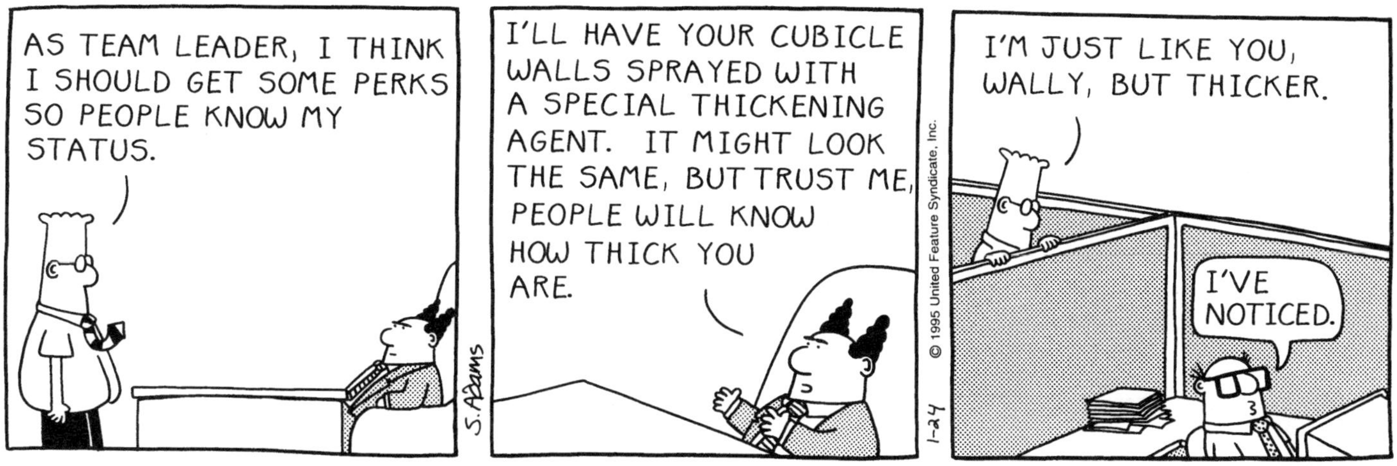
AS TEAM LEADER, I THINK I SHOULD GET SOME PERKS SO PEOPLE KNOW MY STATUS.
S. Adams
I'LL HAVE YOUR CUBICLE WALLS SPRAYED WITH A SPECIAL THICKENING AGENT. IT MIGHT LOOK THE SAME, BUT TRUST ME, PEOPLE WILL KNOW HOW THICK YOU ARE.
1-24
© 1995 United Feature Syndicate, Inc.
I'M JUST LIKE YOU, WALLY, BUT THICKER.
I'VE NOTICED.

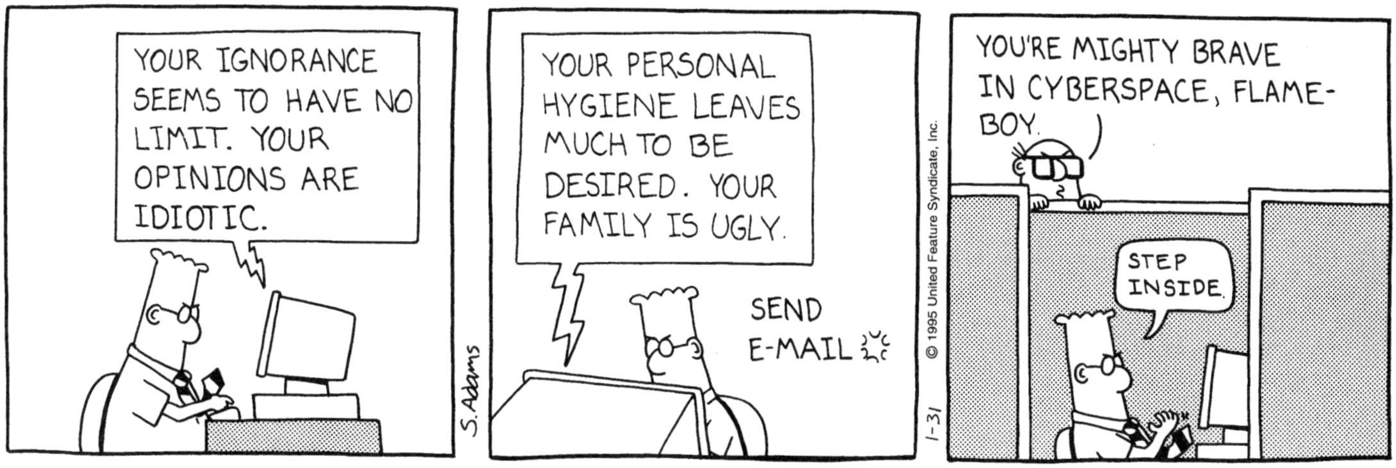
YOUR IGNORANCE SEEMS TO HAVE NO LIMIT. YOUR OPINIONS ARE IDIOTIC.
S. Adams
YOUR PERSONAL HYGIENE LEAVES MUCH TO BE DESIRED. YOUR FAMILY IS UGLY.
SEND E-MAIL
1-31
© 1995 United Feature Syndicate, Inc.
YOU'RE MIGHTY BRAVE IN CYBERSPACE, FLAME-BOY.
STEP INSIDE.

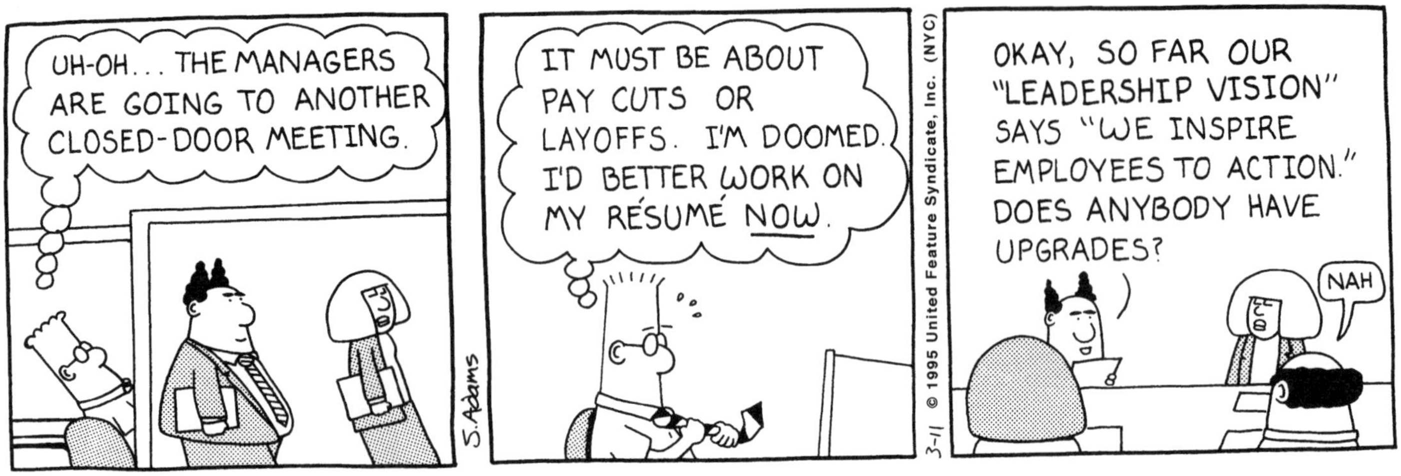
UH-OH... THE MANAGERS ARE GOING TO ANOTHER CLOSED-DOOR MEETING.
IT MUST BE ABOUT PAY CUTS OR LAYOFFS. I'M DOOMED. I'D BETTER WORK ON MY RÉSUMÉ NOW.
OKAY, SO FAR OUR "LEADERSHIP VISION" SAYS "WE INSPIRE EMPLOYEES TO ACTION." DOES ANYBODY HAVE UPGRADES?
NAH
S. Adams
3-11 © 1995 United Feature Syndicate, Inc. (NYC)

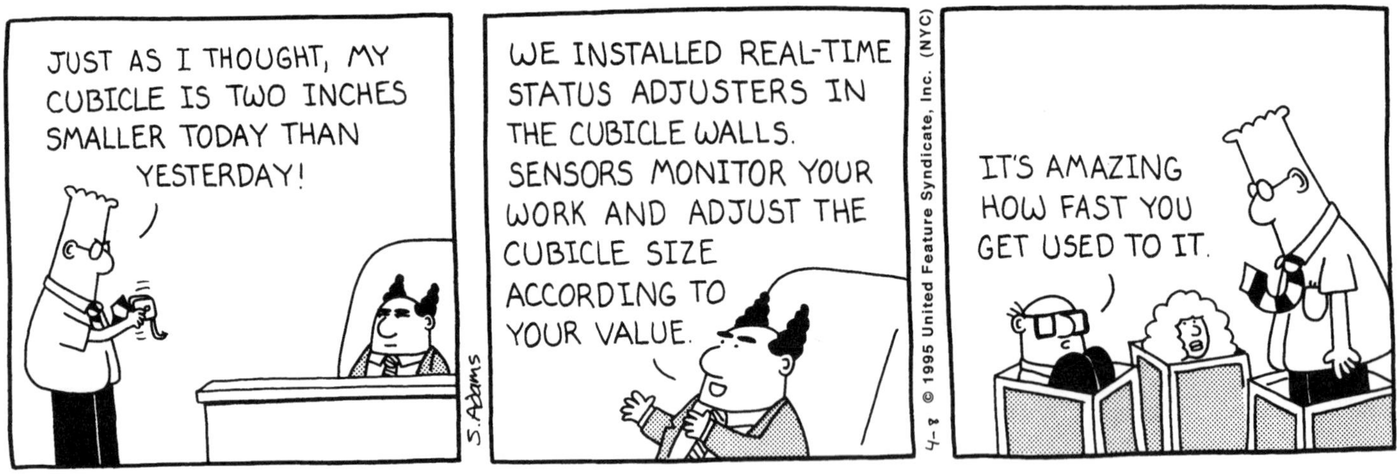
JUST AS I THOUGHT, MY CUBICLE IS TWO INCHES SMALLER TODAY THAN YESTERDAY!
WE INSTALLED REAL-TIME STATUS ADJUSTERS IN THE CUBICLE WALLS. SENSORS MONITOR YOUR WORK AND ADJUST THE CUBICLE SIZE ACCORDING TO YOUR VALUE.
IT'S AMAZING HOW FAST YOU GET USED TO IT.
S. Adams
4-8 © 1995 United Feature Syndicate, Inc. (NYC)

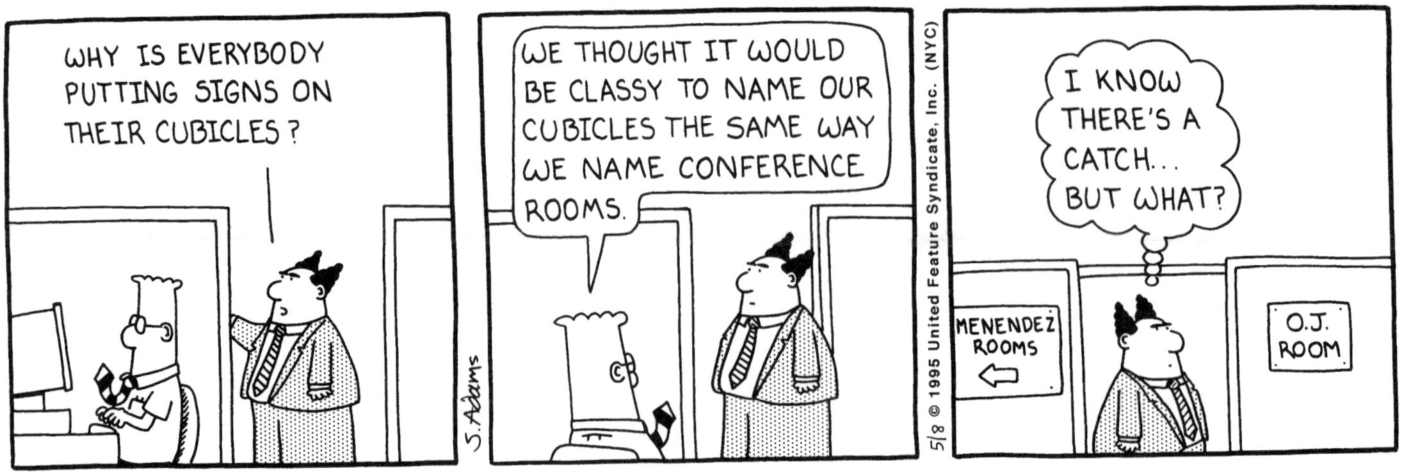
WHY IS EVERYBODY PUTTING SIGNS ON THEIR CUBICLES?
WE THOUGHT IT WOULD BE CLASSY TO NAME OUR CUBICLES THE SAME WAY WE NAME CONFERENCE ROOMS.
I KNOW THERE'S A CATCH... BUT WHAT?
MENENDEZ ROOMS
O.J. ROOM
S. Adams
5/8 © 1995 United Feature Syndicate, Inc. (NYC)

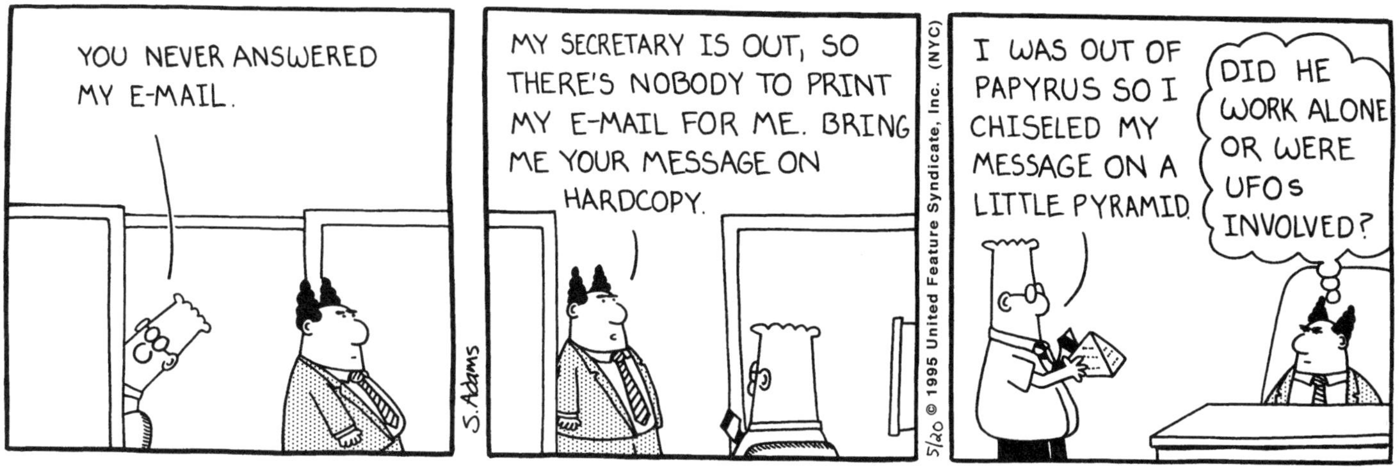
YOU NEVER ANSWERED MY E-MAIL.
MY SECRETARY IS OUT, SO THERE'S NOBODY TO PRINT MY E-MAIL FOR ME. BRING ME YOUR MESSAGE ON HARDCOPY.
I WAS OUT OF PAPYRUS SO I CHISELED MY MESSAGE ON A LITTLE PYRAMID.
DID HE WORK ALONE OR WERE UFOs INVOLVED?
S. Adams
5/20 © 1995 United Feature Syndicate, Inc. (NYC)

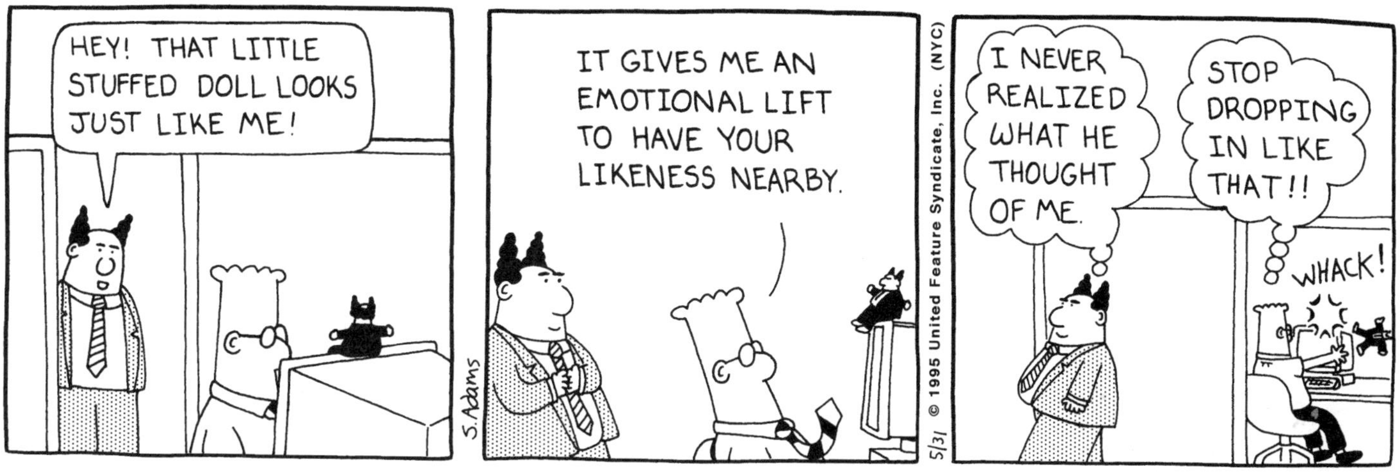
HEY! THAT LITTLE STUFFED DOLL LOOKS JUST LIKE ME!
IT GIVES ME AN EMOTIONAL LIFT TO HAVE YOUR LIKENESS NEARBY.
I NEVER REALIZED WHAT HE THOUGHT OF ME.
STOP DROPPING IN LIKE THAT!!
WHACK!
S. Adams
5/31 © 1995 United Feature Syndicate, Inc. (NYC)

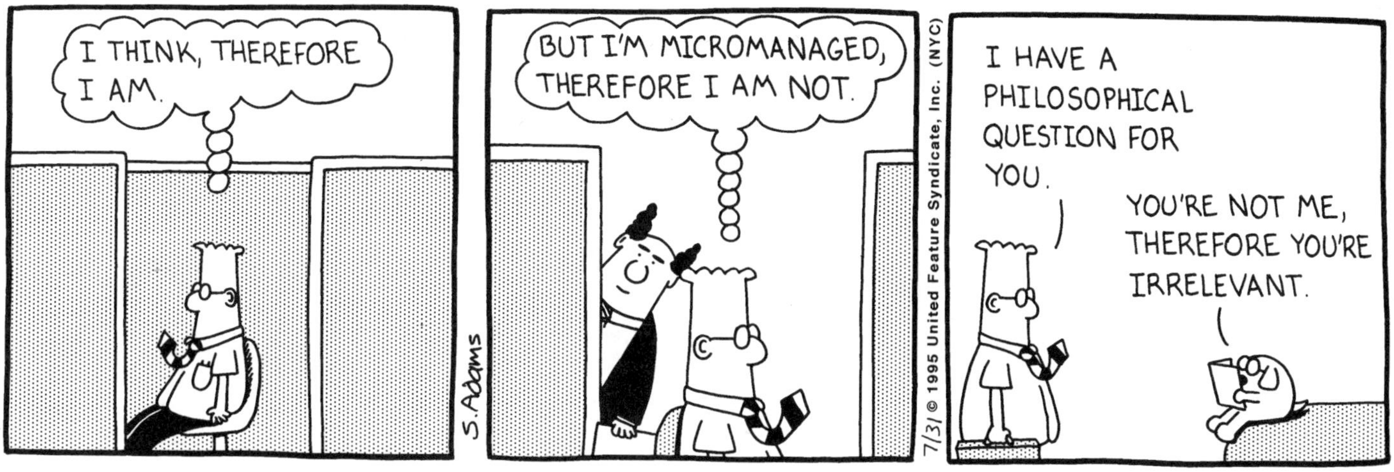
I THINK, THEREFORE I AM.
BUT I'M MICROMANAGED, THEREFORE I AM NOT.
I HAVE A PHILOSOPHICAL QUESTION FOR YOU.
YOU'RE NOT ME, THEREFORE YOU'RE IRRELEVANT.
S. Adams
7/3 © 1995 United Feature Syndicate, Inc. (NYC)

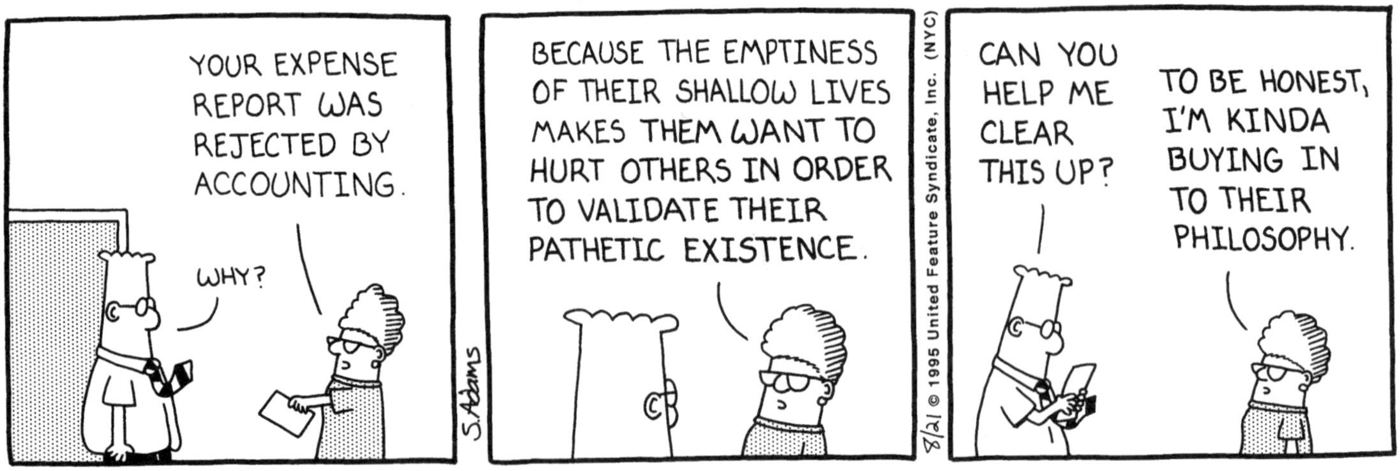
YOUR EXPENSE REPORT WAS REJECTED BY ACCOUNTING.
WHY?
BECAUSE THE EMPTINESS OF THEIR SHALLOW LIVES MAKES THEM WANT TO HURT OTHERS IN ORDER TO VALIDATE THEIR PATHETIC EXISTENCE.
CAN YOU HELP ME CLEAR THIS UP?
TO BE HONEST, I'M KINDA BUYING IN TO THEIR PHILOSOPHY.
S. Adams
8/21 © 1995 United Feature Syndicate, Inc. (NYC)

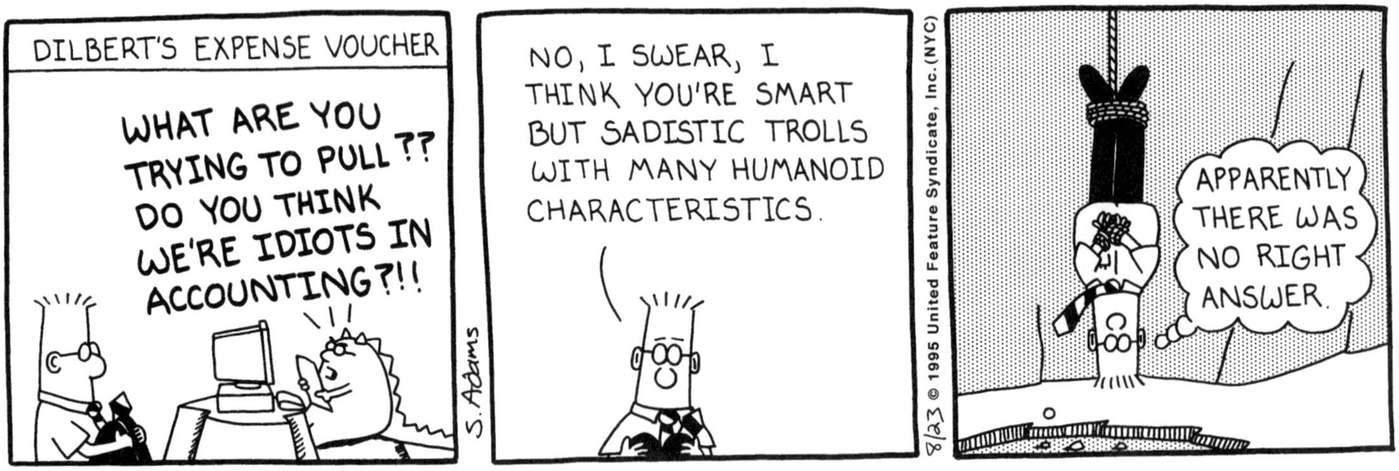
DILBERT'S EXPENSE VOUCHER
WHAT ARE YOU TRYING TO PULL?? DO YOU THINK WE'RE IDIOTS IN ACCOUNTING?!!
NO, I SWEAR, I THINK YOU'RE SMART BUT SADISTIC TROLLS WITH MANY HUMANOID CHARACTERISTICS.
APPARENTLY THERE WAS NO RIGHT ANSWER.
S. Adams
8/23 © 1995 United Feature Syndicate, Inc. (NYC)

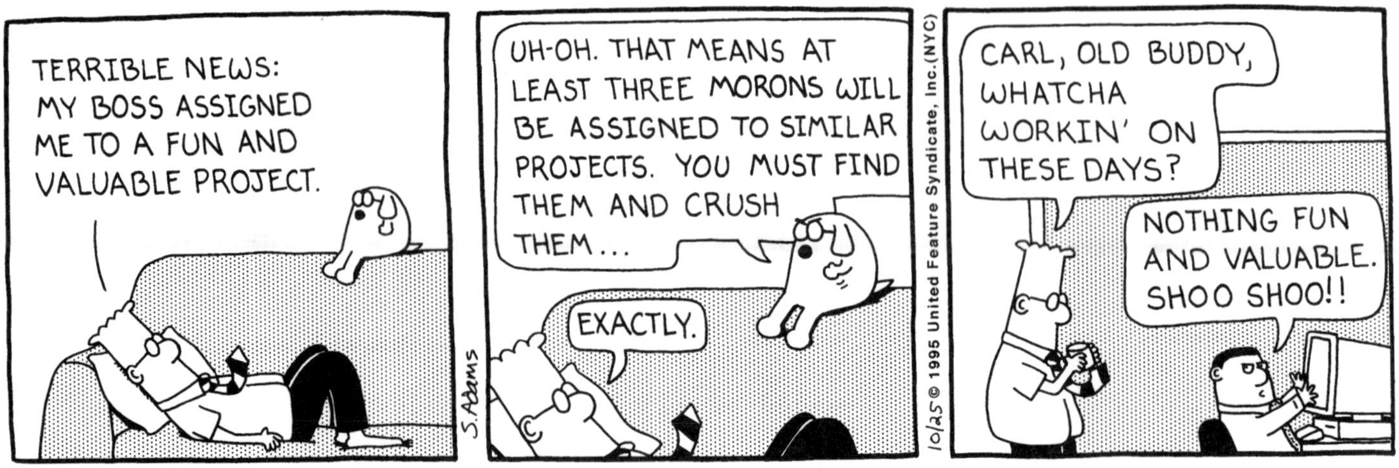
TERRIBLE NEWS: MY BOSS ASSIGNED ME TO A FUN AND VALUABLE PROJECT.
UH-OH. THAT MEANS AT LEAST THREE MORONS WILL BE ASSIGNED TO SIMILAR PROJECTS. YOU MUST FIND THEM AND CRUSH THEM...
EXACTLY.
CARL, OLD BUDDY, WHATCHA WORKIN' ON THESE DAYS?
NOTHING FUN AND VALUABLE. SHOO SHOO!!
S. Adams
10/25 © 1995 United Feature Syndicate, Inc. (NYC)

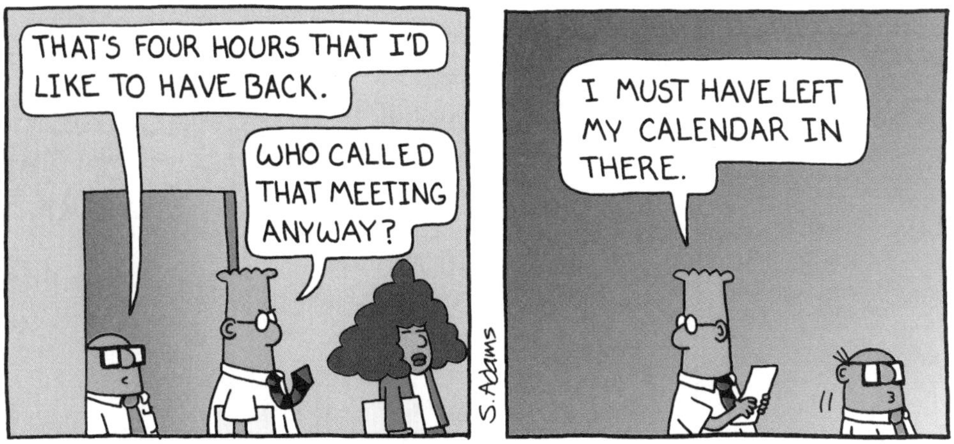
THAT'S FOUR HOURS THAT I'D LIKE TO HAVE BACK.
WHO CALLED THAT MEETING ANYWAY?
S. Adams
I MUST HAVE LEFT MY CALENDAR IN THERE.

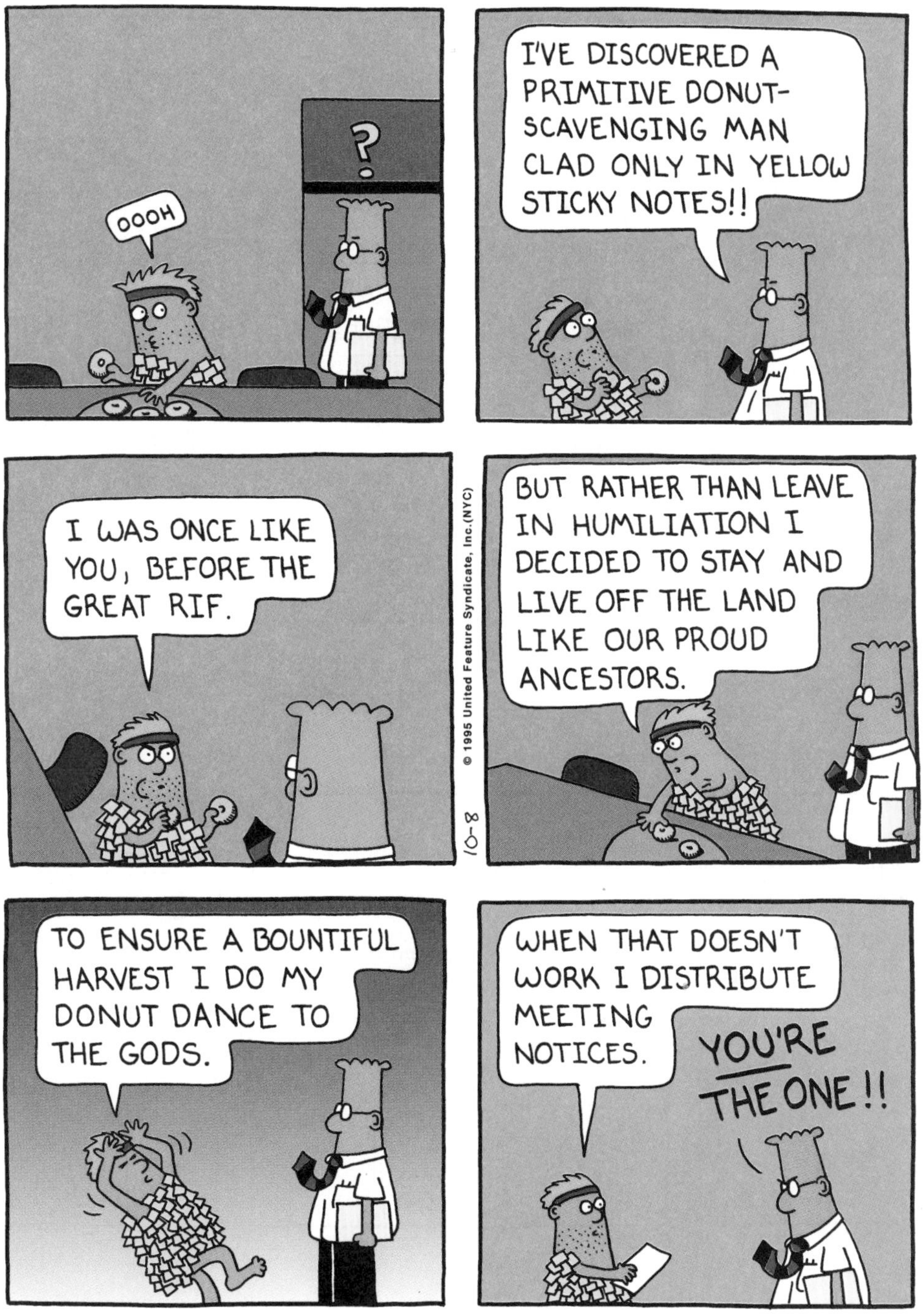
OOOH
I'VE DISCOVERED A PRIMITIVE DONUT-SCAVENGING MAN CLAD ONLY IN YELLOW STICKY NOTES!!
I WAS ONCE LIKE YOU, BEFORE THE GREAT RIF.
© 1995 United Feature Syndicate, Inc.(NYC)
10-8
BUT RATHER THAN LEAVE IN HUMILIATION I DECIDED TO STAY AND LIVE OFF THE LAND LIKE OUR PROUD ANCESTORS.
TO ENSURE A BOUNTIFUL HARVEST I DO MY DONUT DANCE TO THE GODS.
WHEN THAT DOESN'T WORK I DISTRIBUTE MEETING NOTICES.
YOU'RE THE ONE!!

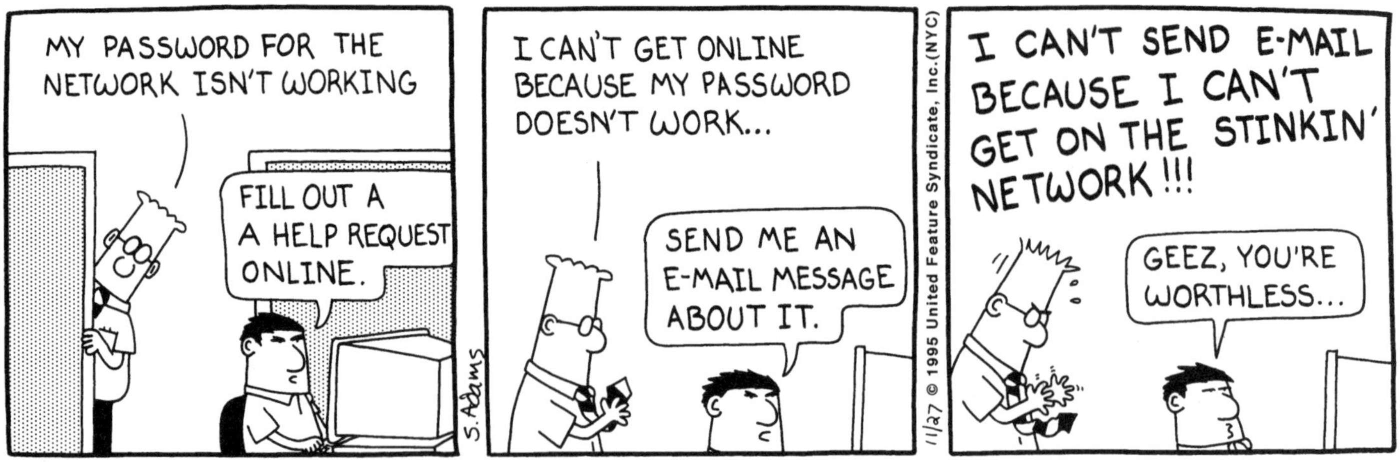
MY PASSWORD FOR THE NETWORK ISN'T WORKING
FILL OUT A A HELP REQUEST ONLINE.
I CAN'T GET ONLINE BECAUSE MY PASSWORD DOESN'T WORK...
SEND ME AN E-MAIL MESSAGE ABOUT IT.
I CAN'T SEND E-MAIL BECAUSE I CAN'T GET ON THE STINKIN' NETWORK!!!
GEEZ, YOU'RE WORTHLESS...
S. Adams
11/27 © 1995 United Feature Syndicate, Inc.(NYC)

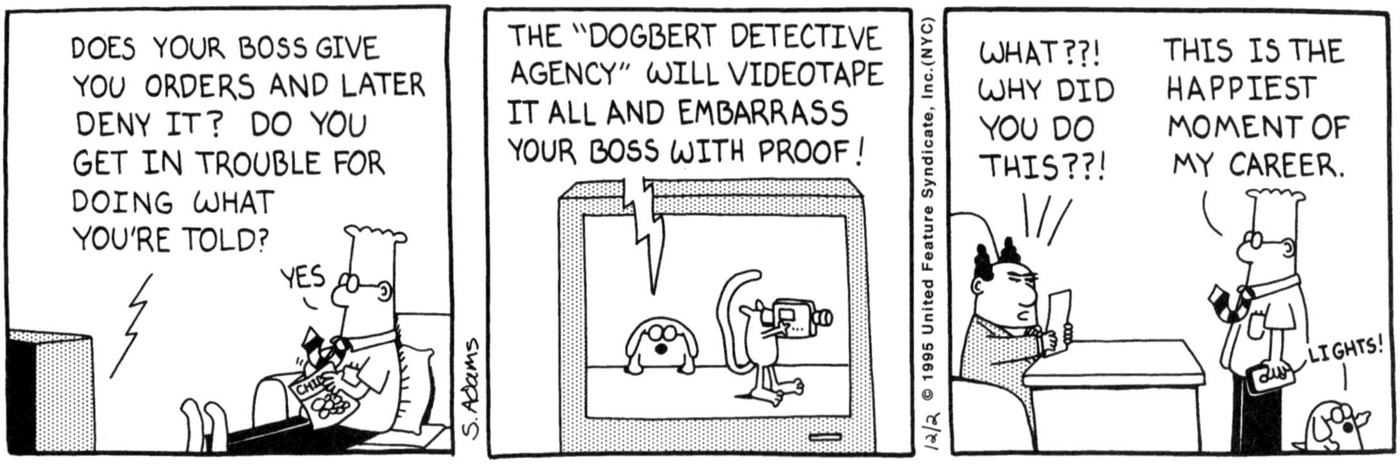
DOES YOUR BOSS GIVE YOU ORDERS AND LATER DENY IT? DO YOU GET IN TROUBLE FOR DOING WHAT YOU'RE TOLD?
YES
THE "DOGBERT DETECTIVE AGENCY" WILL VIDEOTAPE IT ALL AND EMBARRASS YOUR BOSS WITH PROOF!
WHAT??! WHY DID YOU DO THIS??!
THIS IS THE HAPPIEST MOMENT OF MY CAREER.
LIGHTS!
S. Adams
12/2 © 1995 United Feature Syndicate, Inc.(NYC)

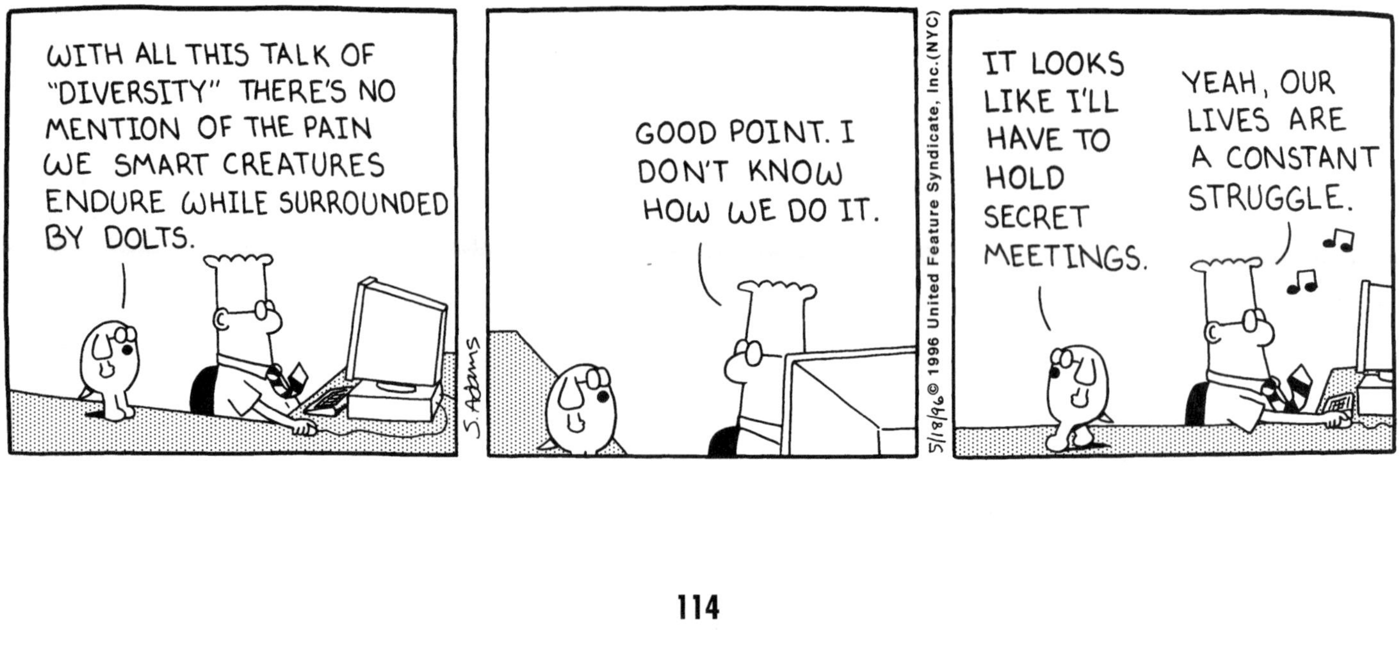
WITH ALL THIS TALK OF "DIVERSITY" THERE'S NO MENTION OF THE PAIN WE SMART CREATURES ENDURE WHILE SURROUNDED BY DOLTS.
GOOD POINT. I DON'T KNOW HOW WE DO IT.
IT LOOKS LIKE I'LL HAVE TO HOLD SECRET MEETINGS.
YEAH, OUR LIVES ARE A CONSTANT STRUGGLE.
S. Adams
5/18/96 © 1996 United Feature Syndicate, Inc.(NYC)

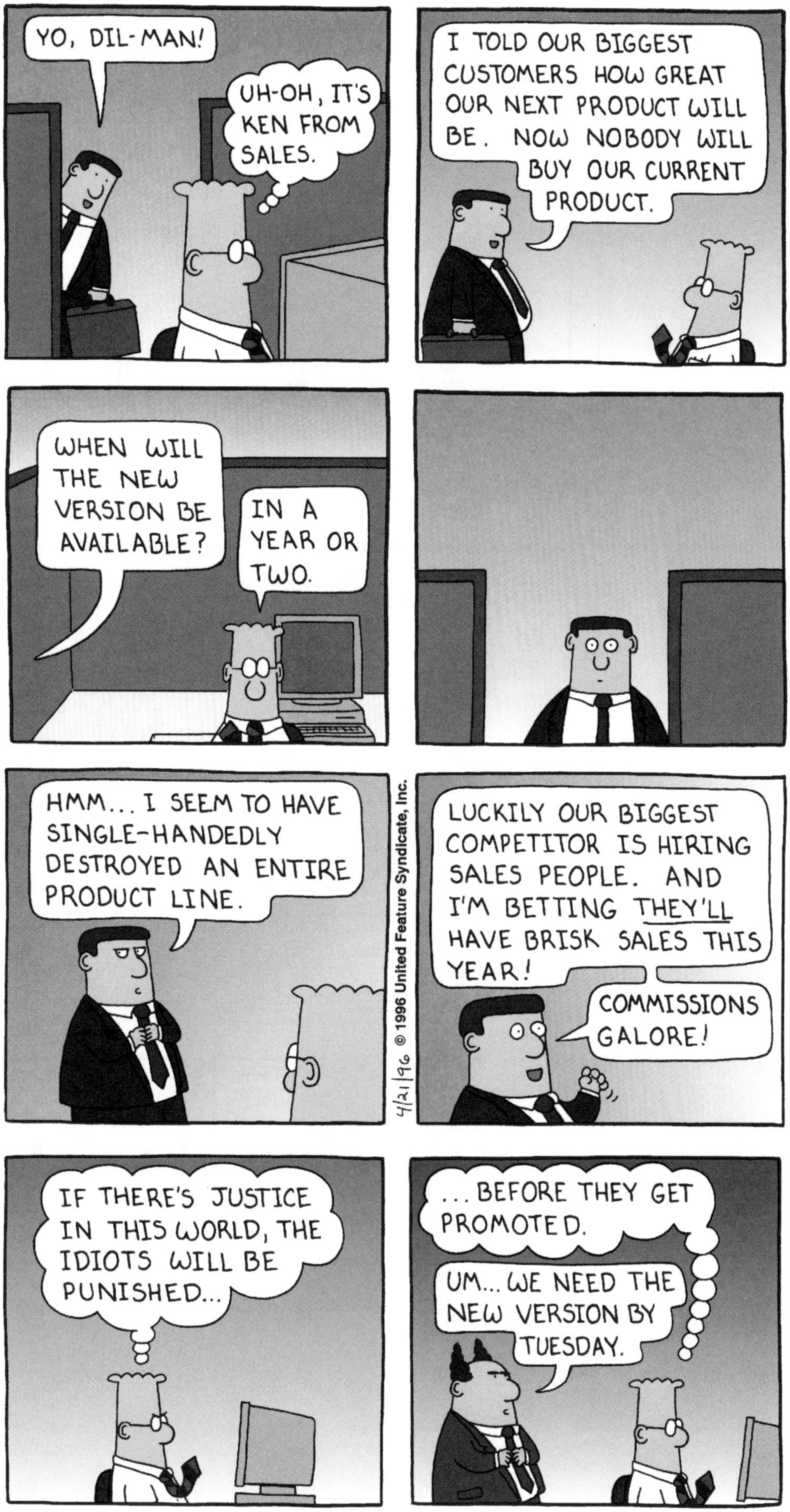
YO, DIL-MAN!
UH-OH, IT'S KEN FROM SALES.
I TOLD OUR BIGGEST CUSTOMERS HOW GREAT OUR NEXT PRODUCT WILL BE. NOW NOBODY WILL BUY OUR CURRENT PRODUCT.
WHEN WILL THE NEW VERSION BE AVAILABLE?
IN A YEAR OR TWO.
HMM... I SEEM TO HAVE SINGLE-HANDEDLY DESTROYED AN ENTIRE PRODUCT LINE.
4/21/96 © 1996 United Feature Syndicate, Inc.
LUCKILY OUR BIGGEST COMPETITOR IS HIRING SALES PEOPLE. AND I'M BETTING THEY'LL HAVE BRISK SALES THIS YEAR!
COMMISSIONS GALORE!
IF THERE'S JUSTICE IN THIS WORLD, THE IDIOTS WILL BE PUNISHED...
... BEFORE THEY GET PROMOTED.
UM... WE NEED THE NEW VERSION BY TUESDAY.

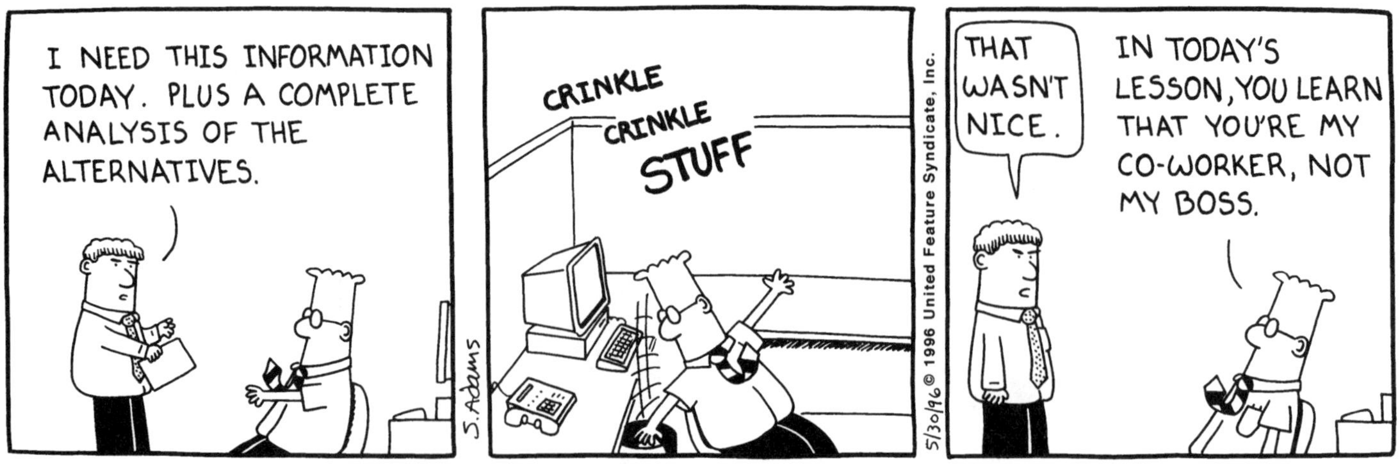
I NEED THIS INFORMATION TODAY. PLUS A COMPLETE ANALYSIS OF THE ALTERNATIVES.
CRINKLE
CRINKLE
STUFF
THAT WASN'T NICE.
IN TODAY'S LESSON, YOU LEARN THAT YOU'RE MY CO-WORKER, NOT MY BOSS.
S. Adams
5/30/96 © 1996 United Feature Syndicate, Inc.

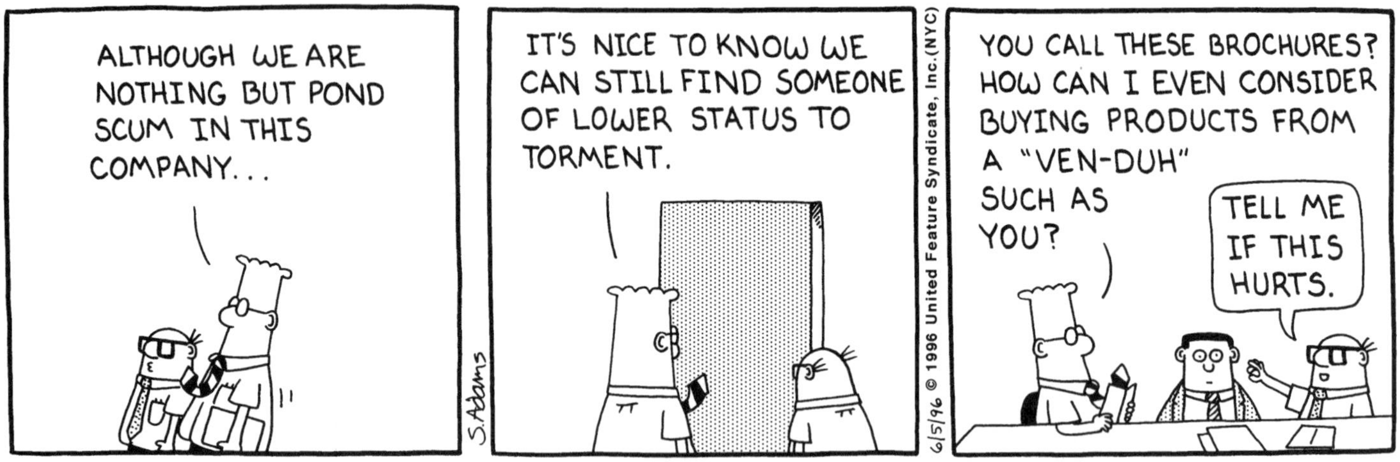
ALTHOUGH WE ARE NOTHING BUT POND SCUM IN THIS COMPANY...
IT'S NICE TO KNOW WE CAN STILL FIND SOMEONE OF LOWER STATUS TO TORMENT.
YOU CALL THESE BROCHURES? HOW CAN I EVEN CONSIDER BUYING PRODUCTS FROM A "VEN-DUH" SUCH AS YOU?
TELL ME IF THIS HURTS.
S. Adams
6/5/96 © 1996 United Feature Syndicate, Inc.(NYC)

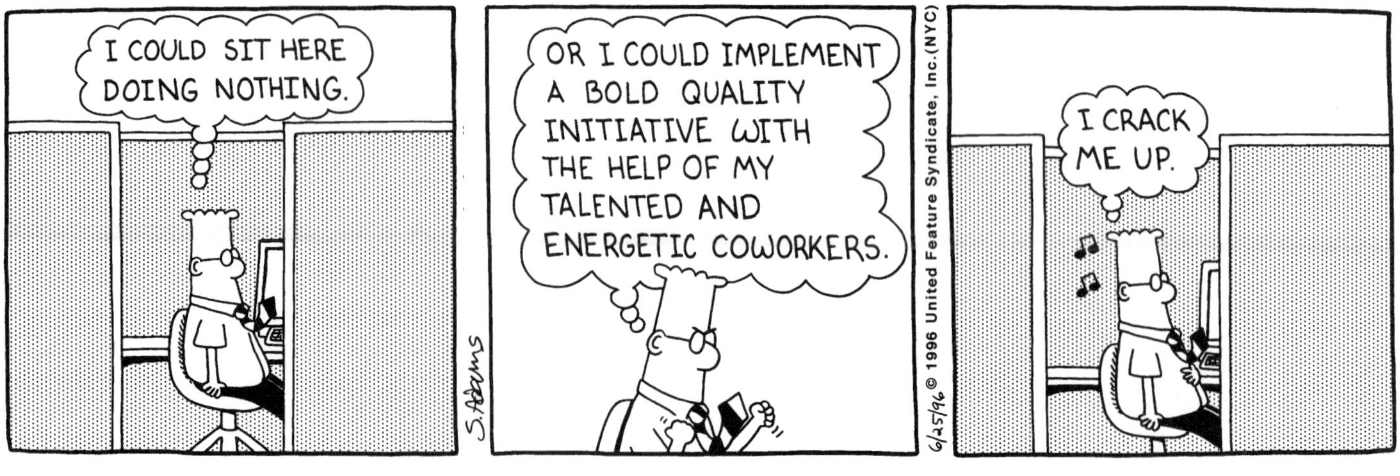
I COULD SIT HERE DOING NOTHING.
OR I COULD IMPLEMENT A BOLD QUALITY INITIATIVE WITH THE HELP OF MY TALENTED AND ENERGETIC COWORKERS.
I CRACK ME UP.
S. Adams
6/25/96 © 1996 United Feature Syndicate, Inc.(NYC)

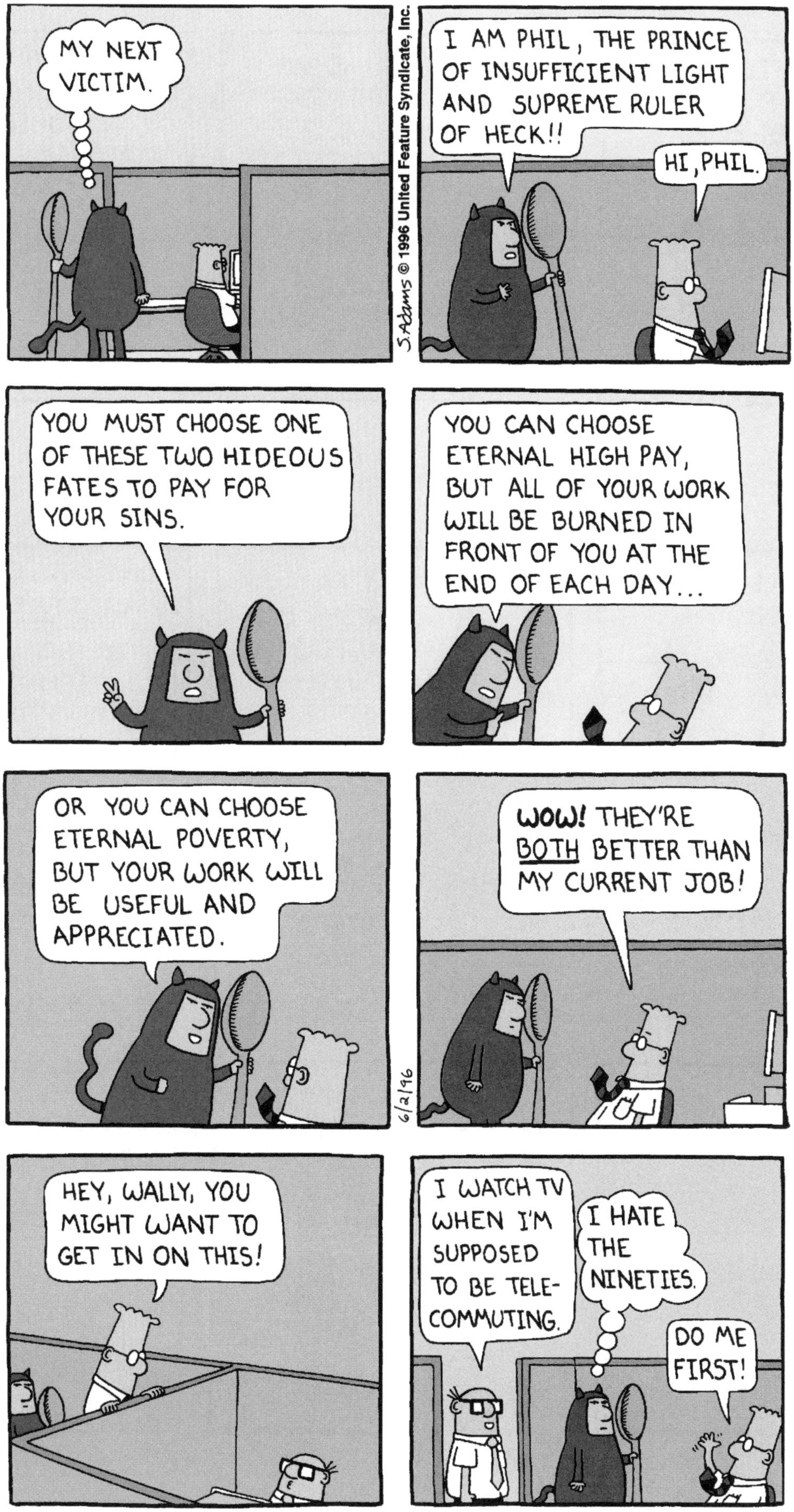
MY NEXT VICTIM.
S. Adams © 1996 United Feature Syndicate, Inc.
I AM PHIL, THE PRINCE OF INSUFFICIENT LIGHT AND SUPREME RULER OF HECK!!
HI, PHIL.
YOU MUST CHOOSE ONE OF THESE TWO HIDEOUS FATES TO PAY FOR YOUR SINS.
YOU CAN CHOOSE ETERNAL HIGH PAY, BUT ALL OF YOUR WORK WILL BE BURNED IN FRONT OF YOU AT THE END OF EACH DAY...
OR YOU CAN CHOOSE ETERNAL POVERTY, BUT YOUR WORK WILL BE USEFUL AND APPRECIATED.
6/2/96
WOW! THEY'RE BOTH BETTER THAN MY CURRENT JOB!
HEY, WALLY, YOU MIGHT WANT TO GET IN ON THIS!
I WATCH TV WHEN I'M SUPPOSED TO BE TELE-COMMUTING.
I HATE THE NINETIES.
DO ME FIRST!

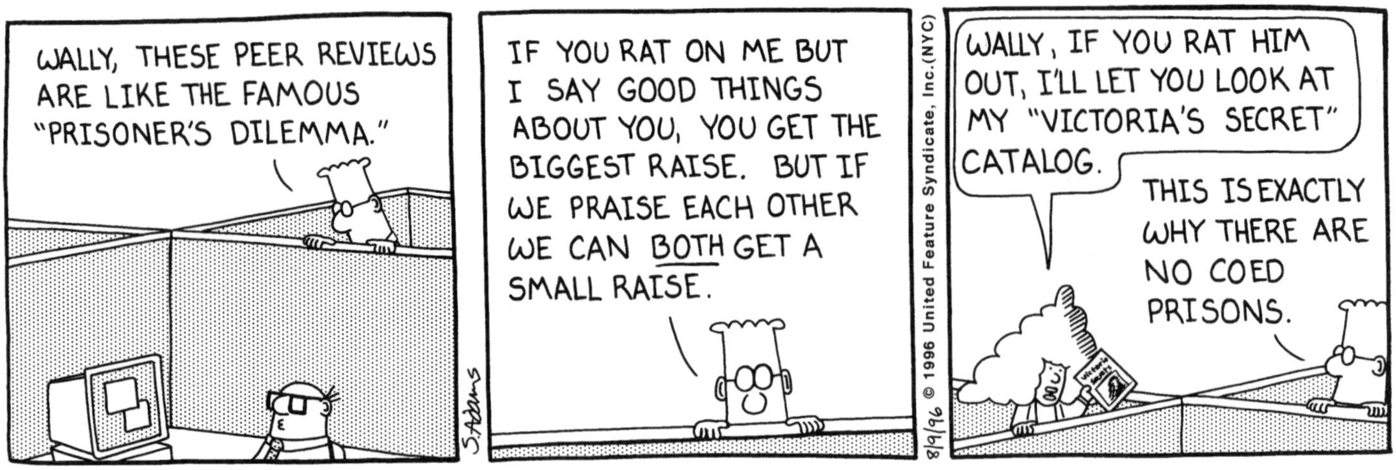
WALLY, THESE PEER REVIEWS ARE LIKE THE FAMOUS "PRISONER'S DILEMMA."
S. Adams
IF YOU RAT ON ME BUT I SAY GOOD THINGS ABOUT YOU, YOU GET THE BIGGEST RAISE. BUT IF WE PRAISE EACH OTHER WE CAN BOTH GET A SMALL RAISE.
8/9/96 © 1996 United Feature Syndicate, Inc.(NYC)
WALLY, IF YOU RAT HIM OUT, I'LL LET YOU LOOK AT MY "VICTORIA'S SECRET" CATALOG.
THIS IS EXACTLY WHY THERE ARE NO COED PRISONS.

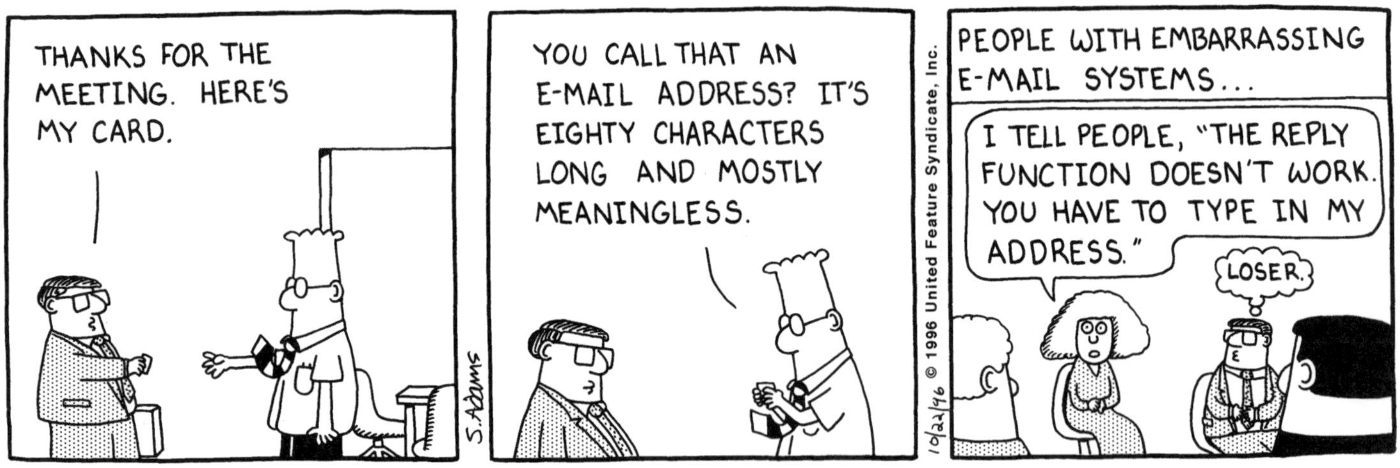
THANKS FOR THE MEETING. HERE'S MY CARD.
S. Adams
YOU CALL THAT AN E-MAIL ADDRESS? IT'S EIGHTY CHARACTERS LONG AND MOSTLY MEANINGLESS.
10/22/96 © 1996 United Feature Syndicate, Inc.
PEOPLE WITH EMBARRASSING E-MAIL SYSTEMS...
I TELL PEOPLE, "THE REPLY FUNCTION DOESN'T WORK. YOU HAVE TO TYPE IN MY ADDRESS."
LOSER.

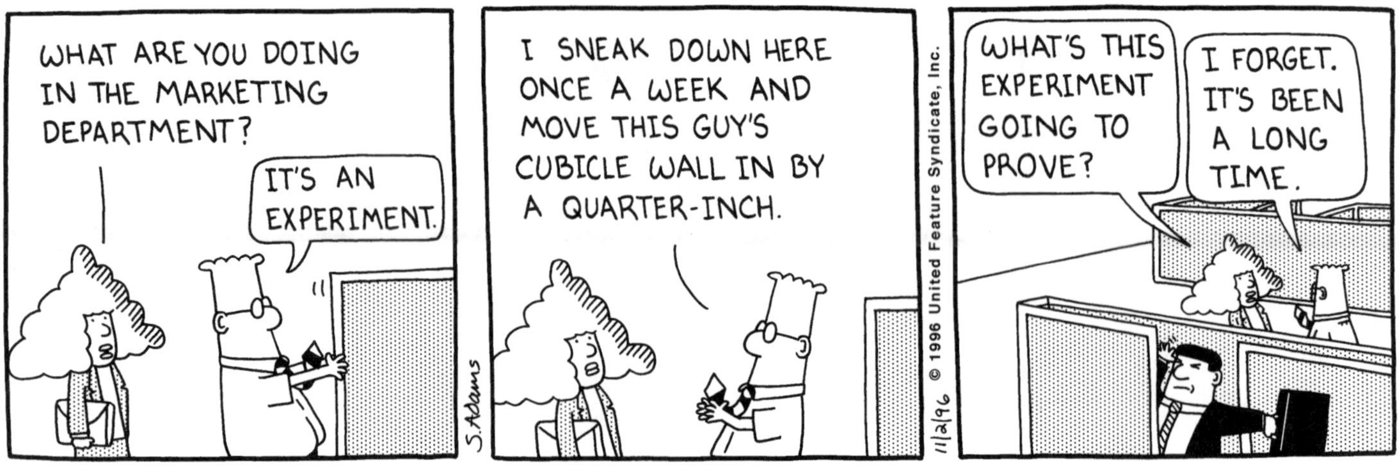
WHAT ARE YOU DOING IN THE MARKETING DEPARTMENT?
IT'S AN EXPERIMENT.
S. Adams
I SNEAK DOWN HERE ONCE A WEEK AND MOVE THIS GUY'S CUBICLE WALL IN BY A QUARTER-INCH.
11/2/96 © 1996 United Feature Syndicate, Inc.
WHAT'S THIS EXPERIMENT GOING TO PROVE?
I FORGET. IT'S BEEN A LONG TIME.

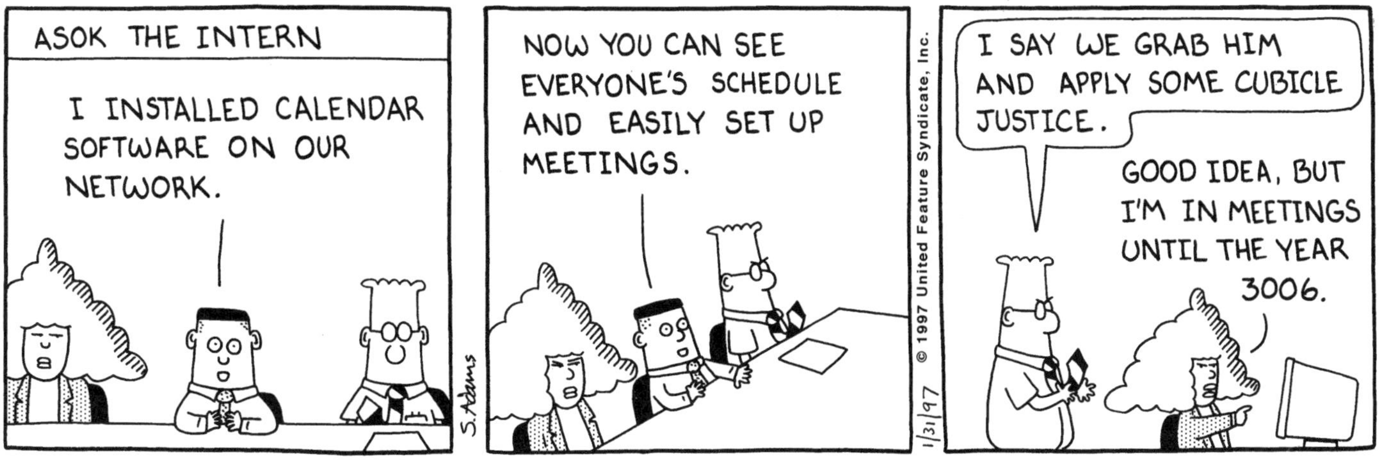
ASOK THE INTERN
I INSTALLED CALENDAR SOFTWARE ON OUR NETWORK.
S. Adams
NOW YOU CAN SEE EVERYONE'S SCHEDULE AND EASILY SET UP MEETINGS.
1/31/97 © 1997 United Feature Syndicate, Inc.
I SAY WE GRAB HIM AND APPLY SOME CUBICLE JUSTICE.
GOOD IDEA, BUT I'M IN MEETINGS UNTIL THE YEAR 3006.

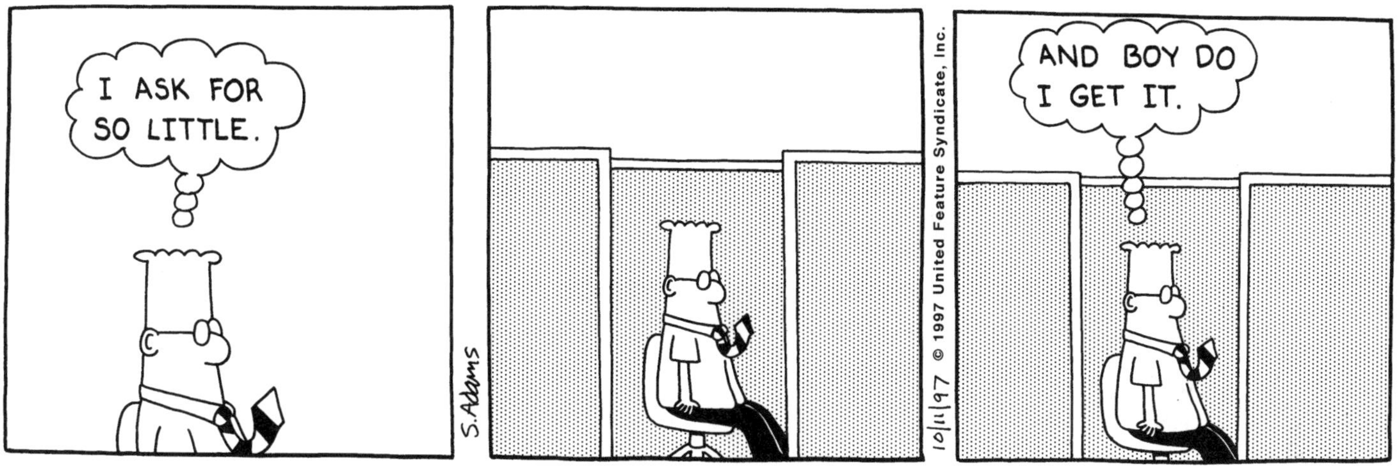
I ASK FOR SO LITTLE.
S. Adams
10/11/97 © 1997 United Feature Syndicate, Inc.
AND BOY DO I GET IT.

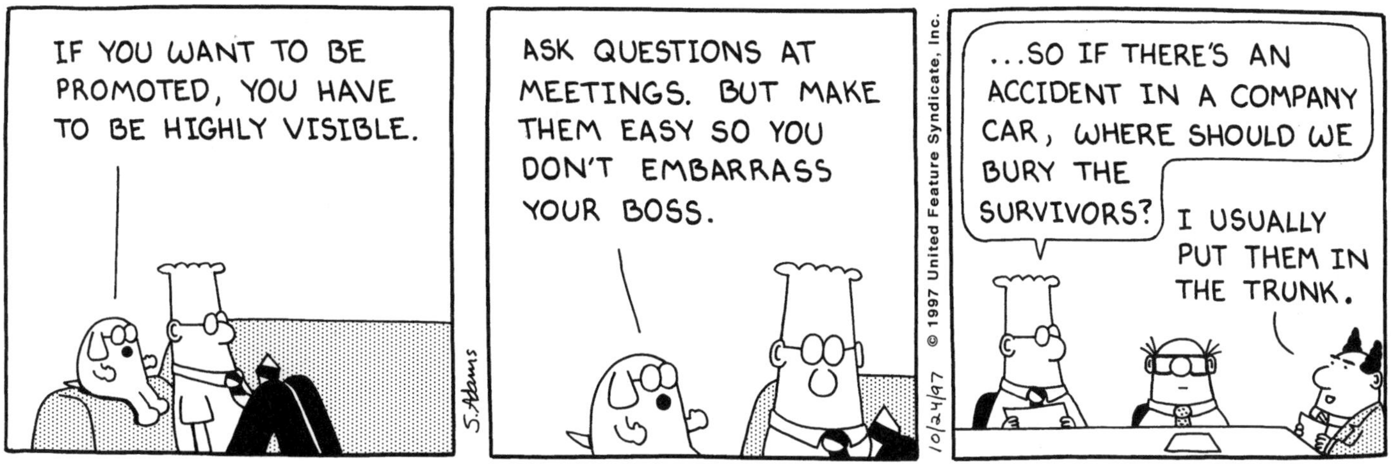
IF YOU WANT TO BE PROMOTED, YOU HAVE TO BE HIGHLY VISIBLE.
S. Adams
ASK QUESTIONS AT MEETINGS. BUT MAKE THEM EASY SO YOU DON'T EMBARRASS YOUR BOSS.
10/24/97 © 1997 United Feature Syndicate, Inc.
...SO IF THERE'S AN ACCIDENT IN A COMPANY CAR, WHERE SHOULD WE BURY THE SURVIVORS?
I USUALLY PUT THEM IN THE TRUNK.

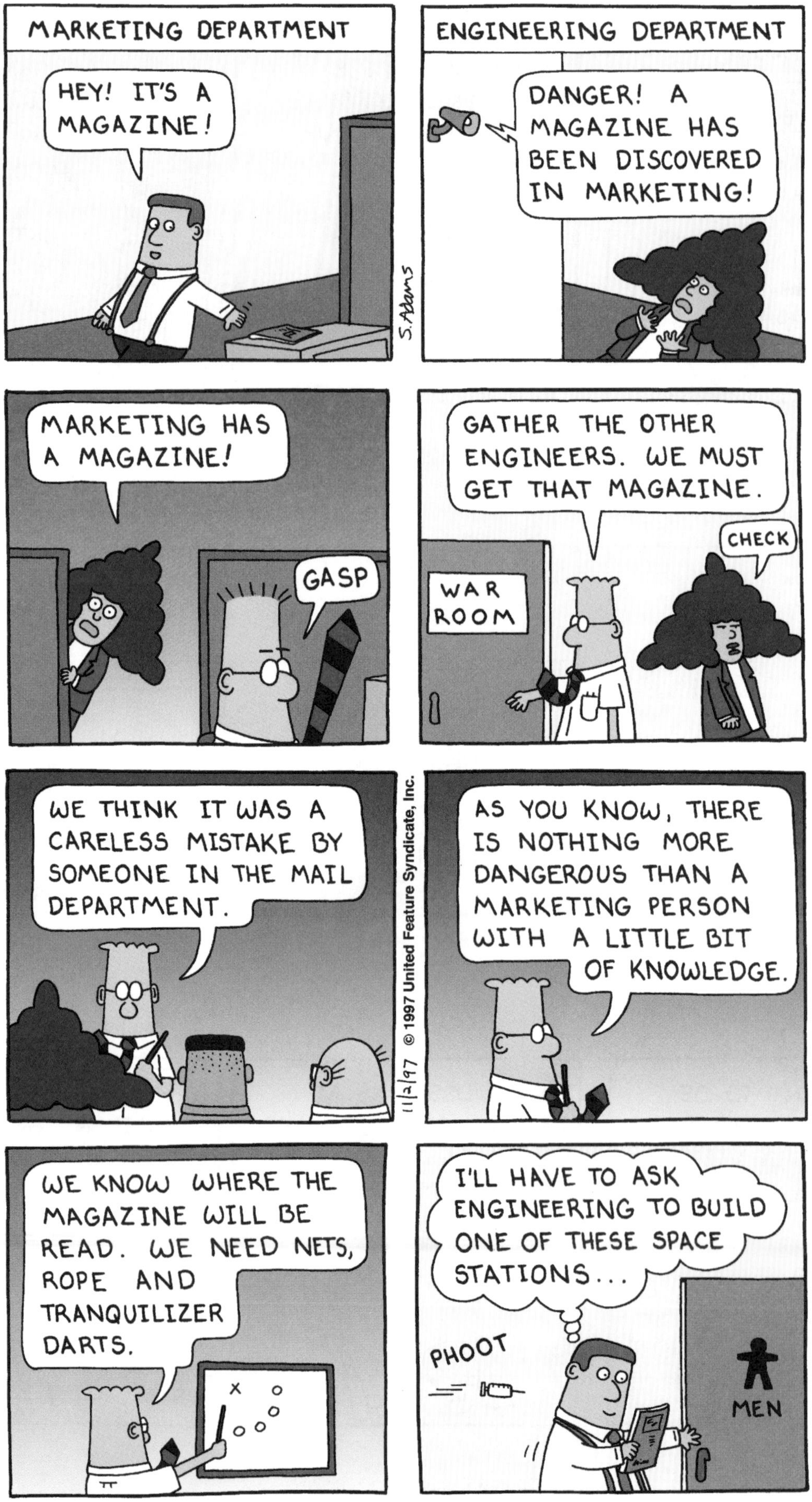
MARKETING DEPARTMENT
HEY! IT'S A MAGAZINE!
ENGINEERING DEPARTMENT
DANGER! A MAGAZINE HAS BEEN DISCOVERED IN MARKETING!
S. Adams
MARKETING HAS A MAGAZINE!
GASP
GATHER THE OTHER ENGINEERS. WE MUST GET THAT MAGAZINE.
WAR ROOM
CHECK
WE THINK IT WAS A CARELESS MISTAKE BY SOMEONE IN THE MAIL DEPARTMENT.
11/2/97 © 1997 United Feature Syndicate, Inc.
AS YOU KNOW, THERE IS NOTHING MORE DANGEROUS THAN A MARKETING PERSON WITH A LITTLE BIT OF KNOWLEDGE.
WE KNOW WHERE THE MAGAZINE WILL BE READ. WE NEED NETS, ROPE AND TRANQUILIZER DARTS.
I'LL HAVE TO ASK ENGINEERING TO BUILD ONE OF THESE SPACE STATIONS...
PHOOT
MEN

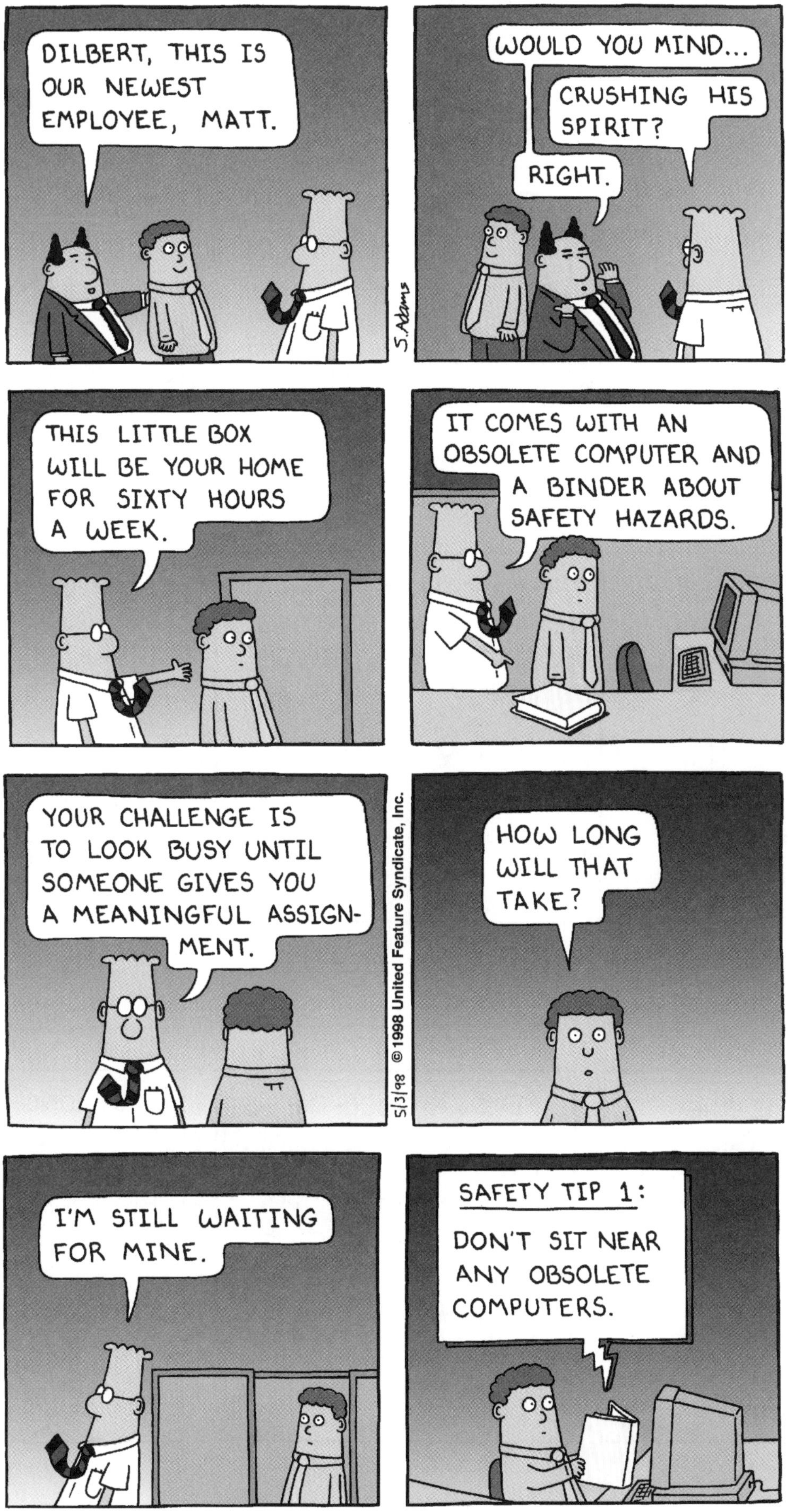
DILBERT, THIS IS OUR NEWEST EMPLOYEE, MATT.
S. Adams
WOULD YOU MIND...
CRUSHING HIS SPIRIT?
RIGHT.
THIS LITTLE BOX WILL BE YOUR HOME FOR SIXTY HOURS A WEEK.
IT COMES WITH AN OBSOLETE COMPUTER AND A BINDER ABOUT SAFETY HAZARDS.
YOUR CHALLENGE IS TO LOOK BUSY UNTIL SOMEONE GIVES YOU A MEANINGFUL ASSIGN-MENT.
5/3/98 ©1998 United Feature Syndicate, Inc.
HOW LONG WILL THAT TAKE?
I'M STILL WAITING FOR MINE.
SAFETY TIP 1:
DON'T SIT NEAR ANY OBSOLETE COMPUTERS.

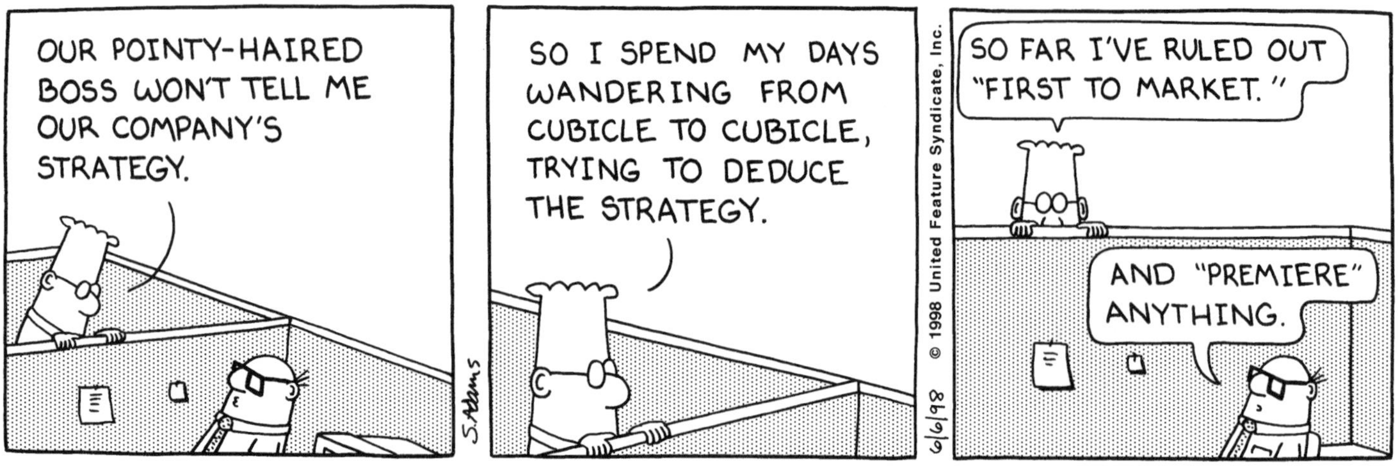
OUR POINTY-HAIRED BOSS WON'T TELL ME OUR COMPANY'S STRATEGY.
S.Adams
SO I SPEND MY DAYS WANDERING FROM CUBICLE TO CUBICLE, TRYING TO DEDUCE THE STRATEGY.
6/6/98 © 1998 United Feature Syndicate, Inc.
SO FAR I'VE RULED OUT "FIRST TO MARKET."
AND "PREMIERE" ANYTHING.

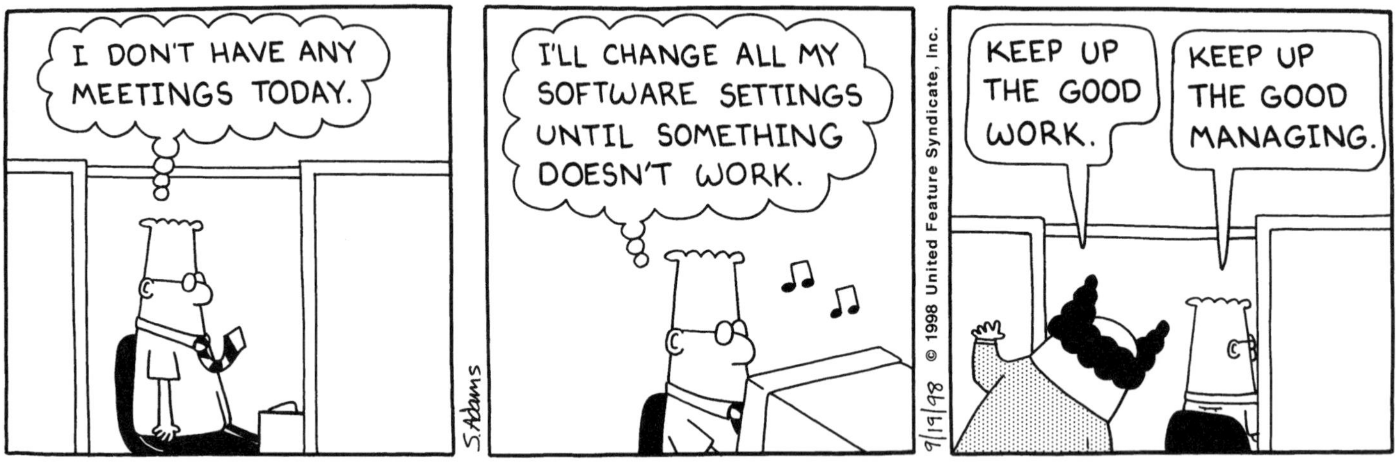
I DON'T HAVE ANY MEETINGS TODAY.
S.Adams
I'LL CHANGE ALL MY SOFTWARE SETTINGS UNTIL SOMETHING DOESN'T WORK.
9/19/98 © 1998 United Feature Syndicate, Inc.
KEEP UP THE GOOD WORK.
KEEP UP THE GOOD MANAGING.

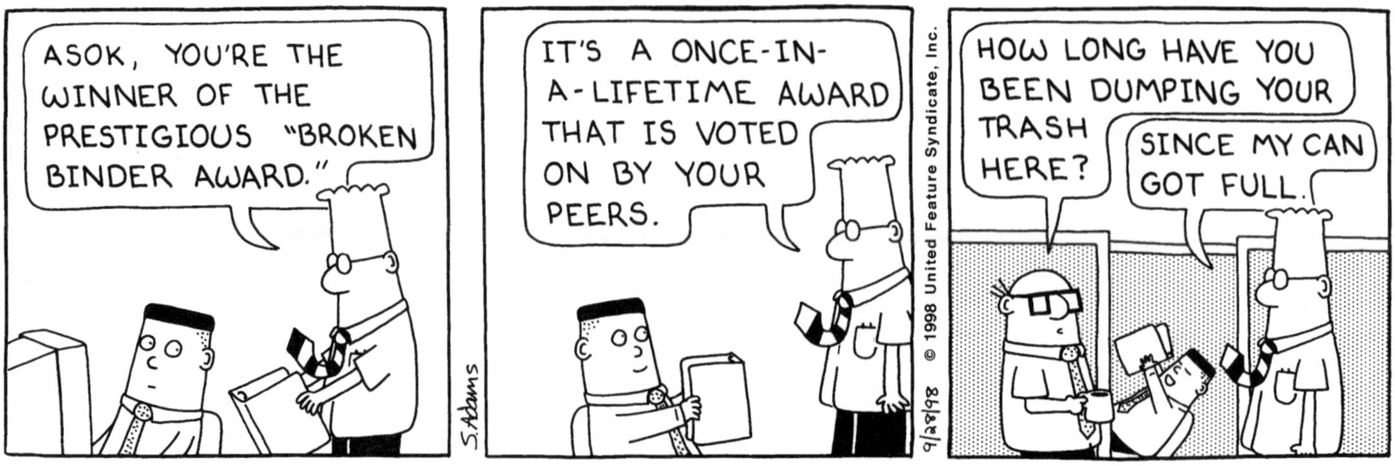
ASOK, YOU'RE THE WINNER OF THE PRESTIGIOUS "BROKEN BINDER AWARD."
S.Adams
IT'S A ONCE-IN-A-LIFETIME AWARD THAT IS VOTED ON BY YOUR PEERS.
9/28/98 © 1998 United Feature Syndicate, Inc.
HOW LONG HAVE YOU BEEN DUMPING YOUR TRASH HERE?
SINCE MY CAN GOT FULL.

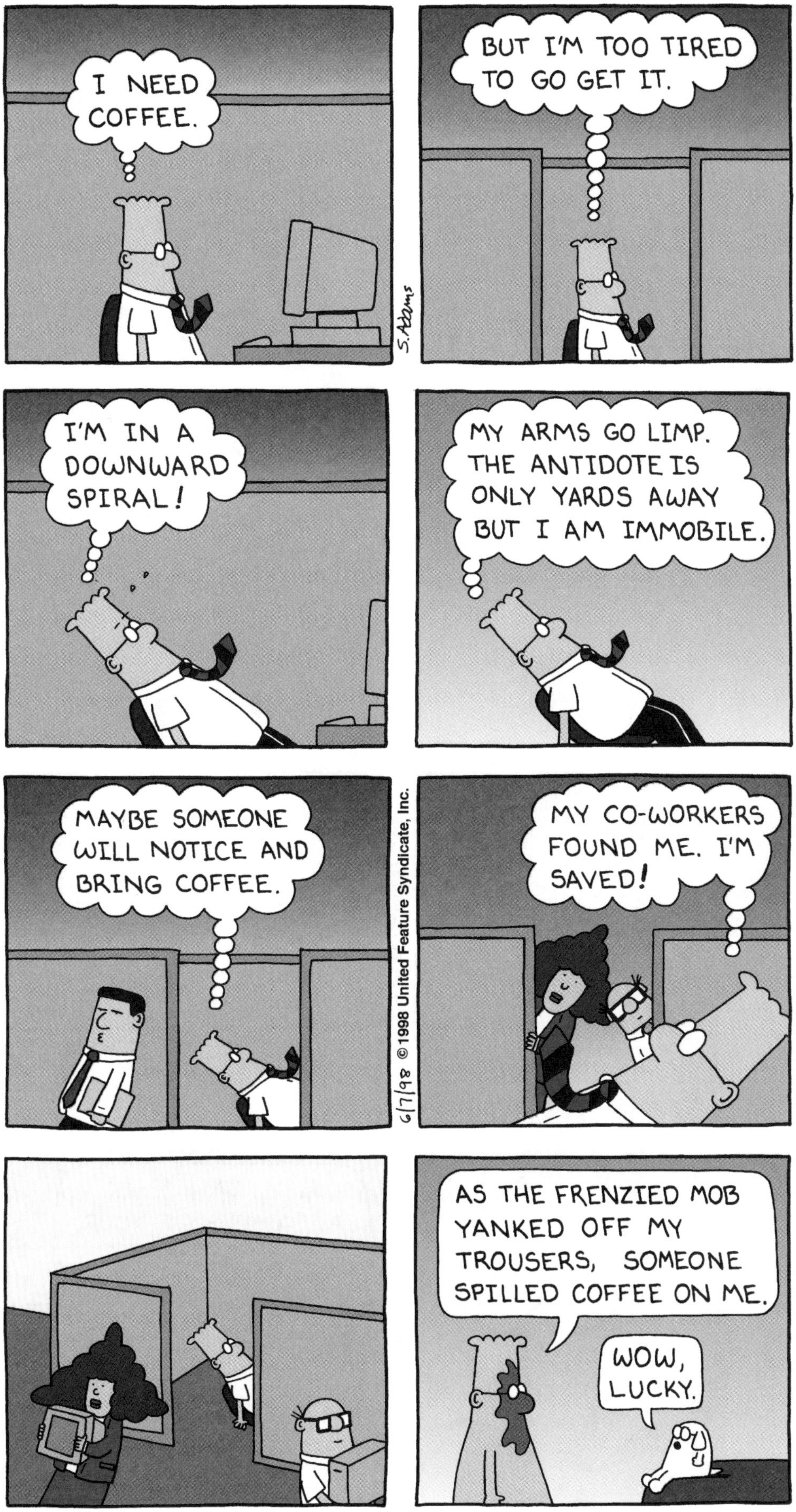
I NEED COFFEE.
BUT I'M TOO TIRED TO GO GET IT.
S. Adams
I'M IN A DOWNWARD SPIRAL!
MY ARMS GO LIMP. THE ANTIDOTE IS ONLY YARDS AWAY BUT I AM IMMOBILE.
MAYBE SOMEONE WILL NOTICE AND BRING COFFEE.
6/7/98 © 1998 United Feature Syndicate, Inc.
MY CO-WORKERS FOUND ME. I'M SAVED!
AS THE FRENZIED MOB YANKED OFF MY TROUSERS, SOMEONE SPILLED COFFEE ON ME.
WOW, LUCKY.

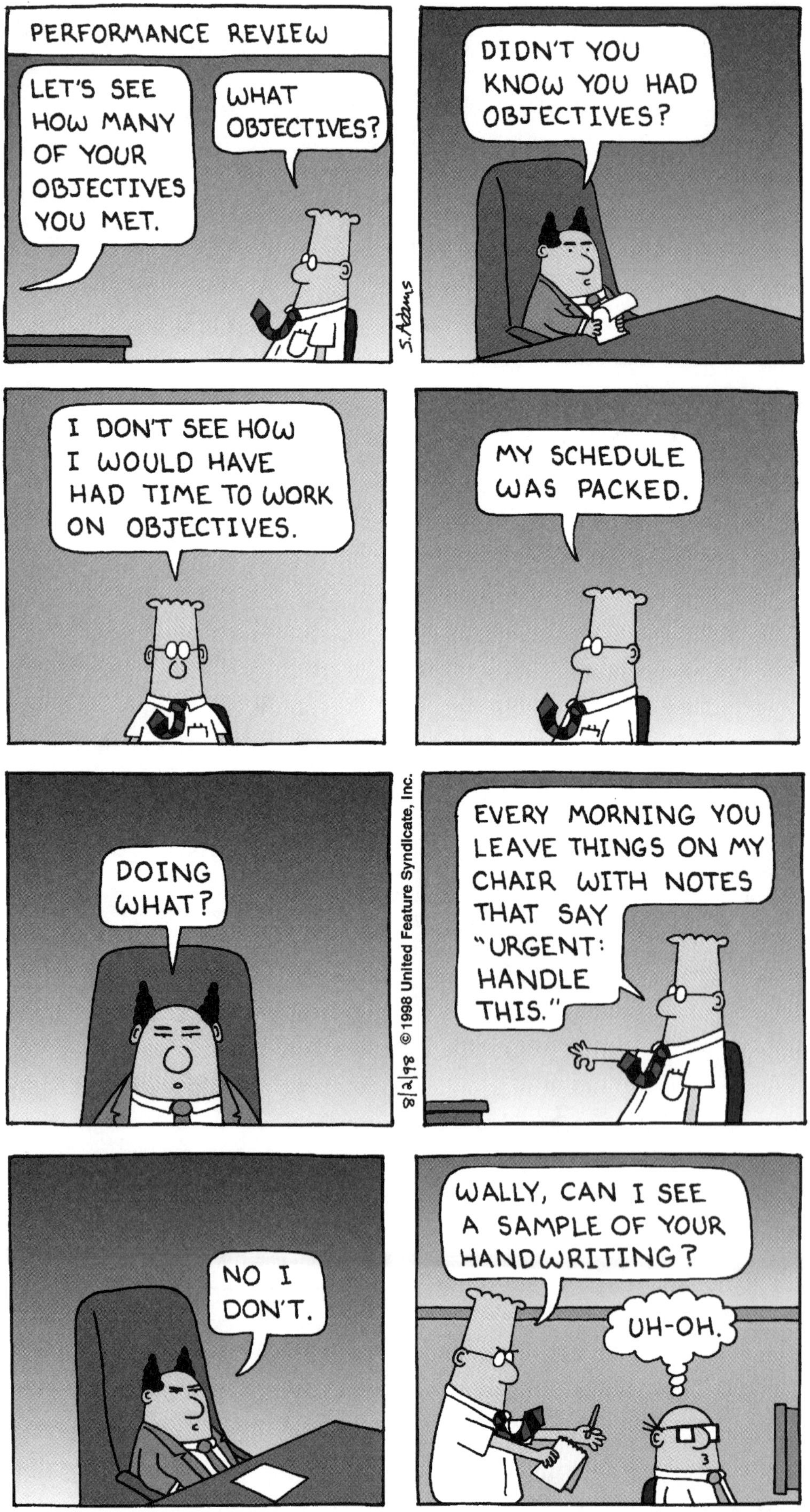
PERFORMANCE REVIEW
LET'S SEE HOW MANY OF YOUR OBJECTIVES YOU MET.
WHAT OBJECTIVES?
S. Adams
DIDN'T YOU KNOW YOU HAD OBJECTIVES?
I DON'T SEE HOW I WOULD HAVE HAD TIME TO WORK ON OBJECTIVES.
MY SCHEDULE WAS PACKED.
DOING WHAT?
8/2/98 © 1998 United Feature Syndicate, Inc.
EVERY MORNING YOU LEAVE THINGS ON MY CHAIR WITH NOTES THAT SAY "URGENT: HANDLE THIS."
NO I DON'T.
WALLY, CAN I SEE A SAMPLE OF YOUR HANDWRITING?
UH-OH.

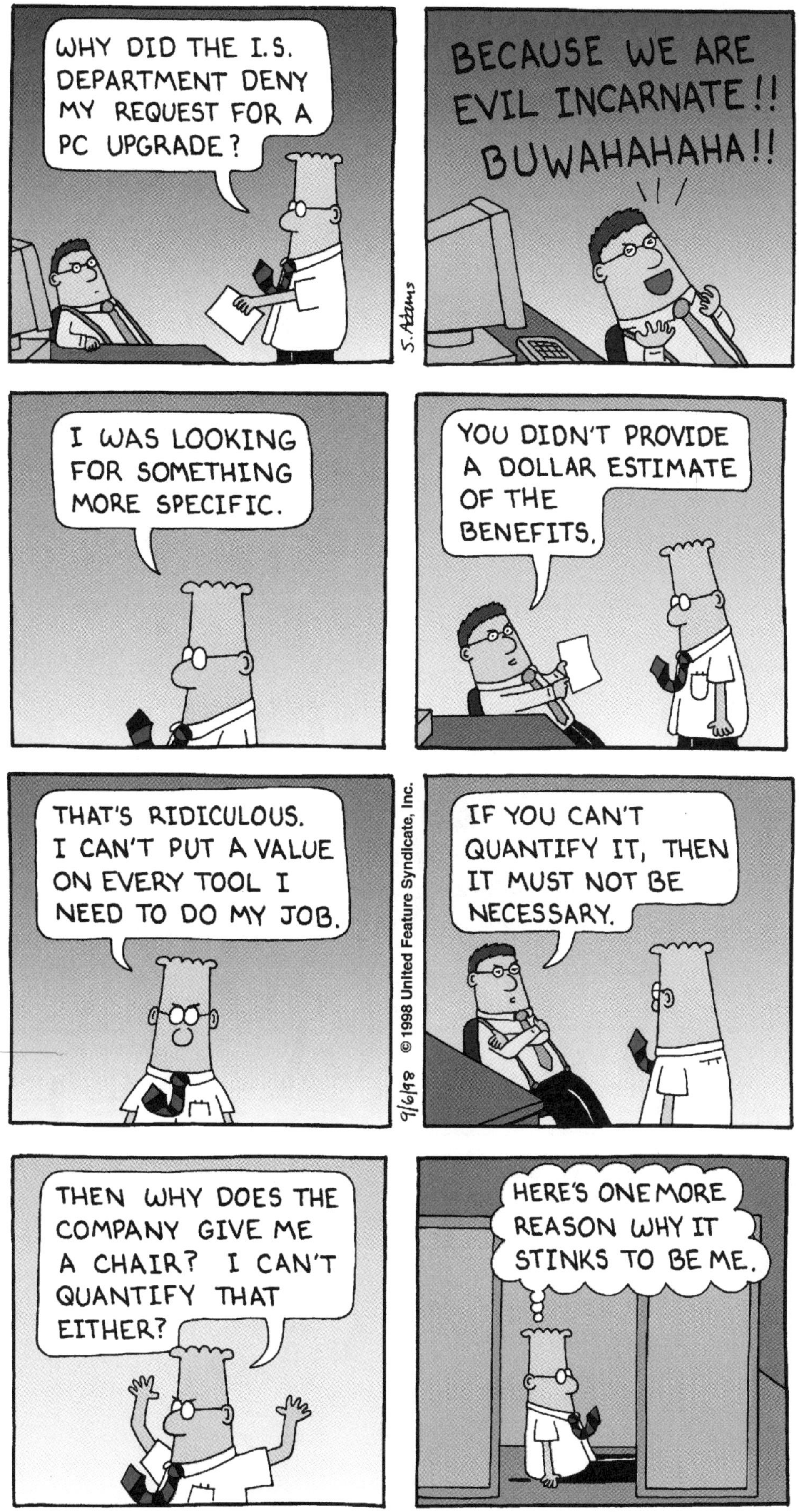
WHY DID THE I.S. DEPARTMENT DENY MY REQUEST FOR A PC UPGRADE?
S. Adams
BECAUSE WE ARE EVIL INCARNATE!! BUWAHAHAHA!!
I WAS LOOKING FOR SOMETHING MORE SPECIFIC.
YOU DIDN'T PROVIDE A DOLLAR ESTIMATE OF THE BENEFITS.
THAT'S RIDICULOUS. I CAN'T PUT A VALUE ON EVERY TOOL I NEED TO DO MY JOB.
9/6/98 © 1998 United Feature Syndicate, Inc.
IF YOU CAN'T QUANTIFY IT, THEN IT MUST NOT BE NECESSARY.
THEN WHY DOES THE COMPANY GIVE ME A CHAIR? I CAN'T QUANTIFY THAT EITHER?
HERE'S ONE MORE REASON WHY IT STINKS TO BE ME.

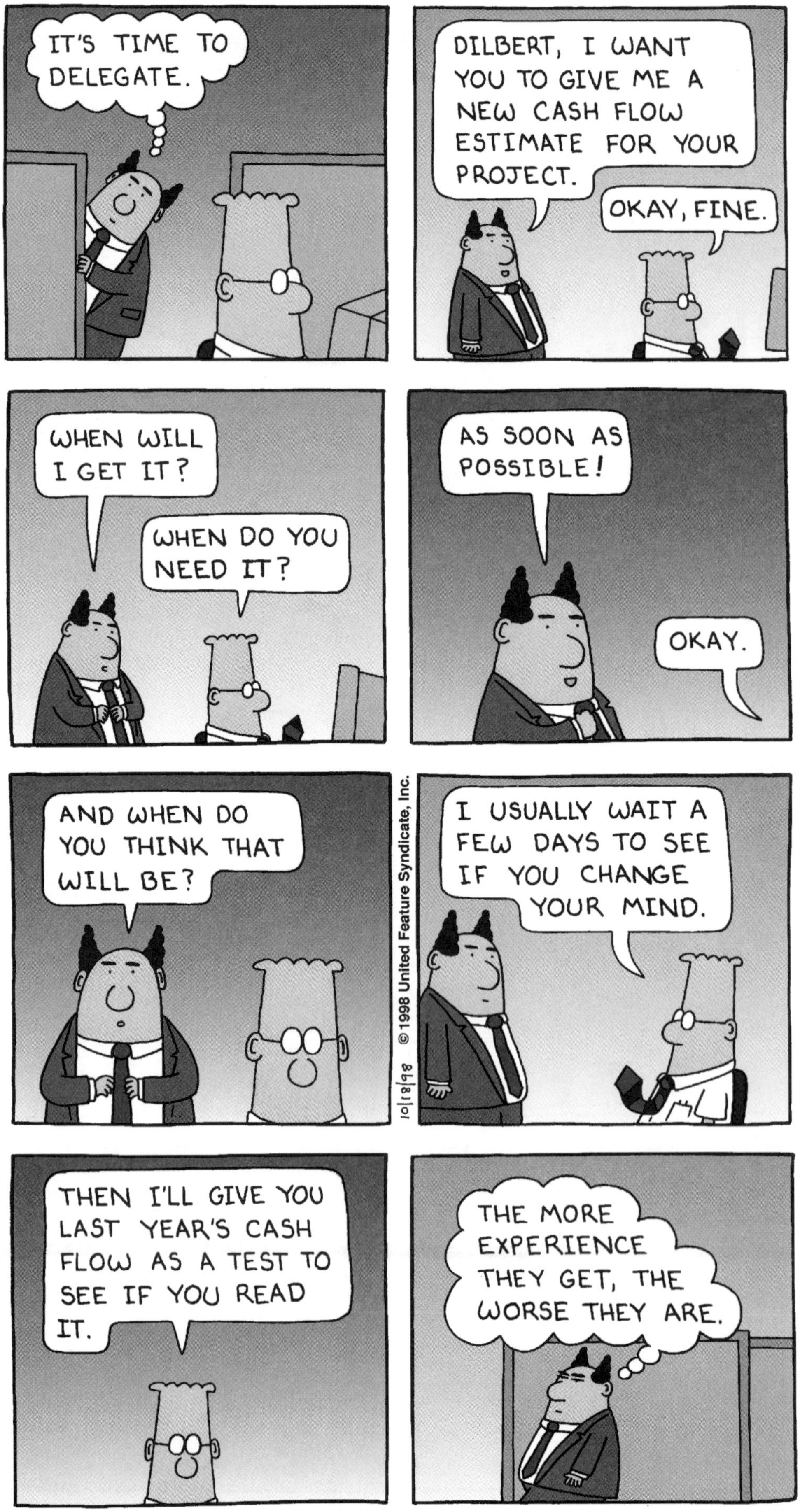
IT'S TIME TO DELEGATE.
DILBERT, I WANT YOU TO GIVE ME A NEW CASH FLOW ESTIMATE FOR YOUR PROJECT.
OKAY, FINE.
WHEN WILL I GET IT?
WHEN DO YOU NEED IT?
AS SOON AS POSSIBLE!
OKAY.
AND WHEN DO YOU THINK THAT WILL BE?
10/18/98 © 1998 United Feature Syndicate, Inc.
I USUALLY WAIT A FEW DAYS TO SEE IF YOU CHANGE YOUR MIND.
THEN I'LL GIVE YOU LAST YEAR'S CASH FLOW AS A TEST TO SEE IF YOU READ IT.
THE MORE EXPERIENCE THEY GET, THE WORSE THEY ARE.

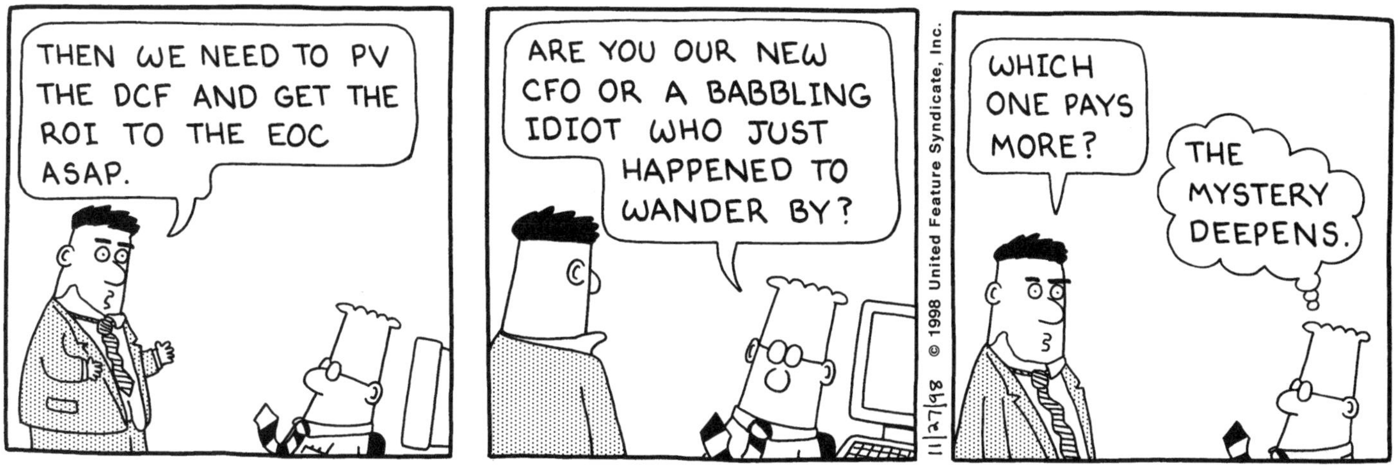
THEN WE NEED TO PV THE DCF AND GET THE ROI TO THE EOC ASAP.
ARE YOU OUR NEW CFO OR A BABBLING IDIOT WHO JUST HAPPENED TO WANDER BY?
11/27/98 © 1998 United Feature Syndicate, Inc.
WHICH ONE PAYS MORE?
THE MYSTERY DEEPENS.

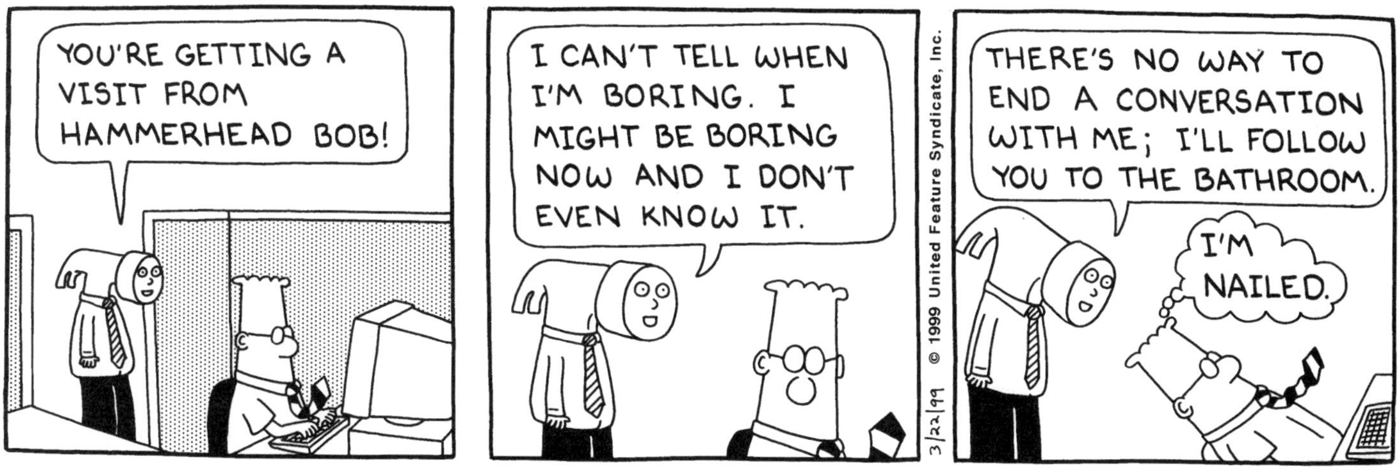
YOU'RE GETTING A VISIT FROM HAMMERHEAD BOB!
I CAN'T TELL WHEN I'M BORING. I MIGHT BE BORING NOW AND I DON'T EVEN KNOW IT.
3/22/99 © 1999 United Feature Syndicate, Inc.
THERE'S NO WAY TO END A CONVERSATION WITH ME; I'LL FOLLOW YOU TO THE BATHROOM.
I'M NAILED.

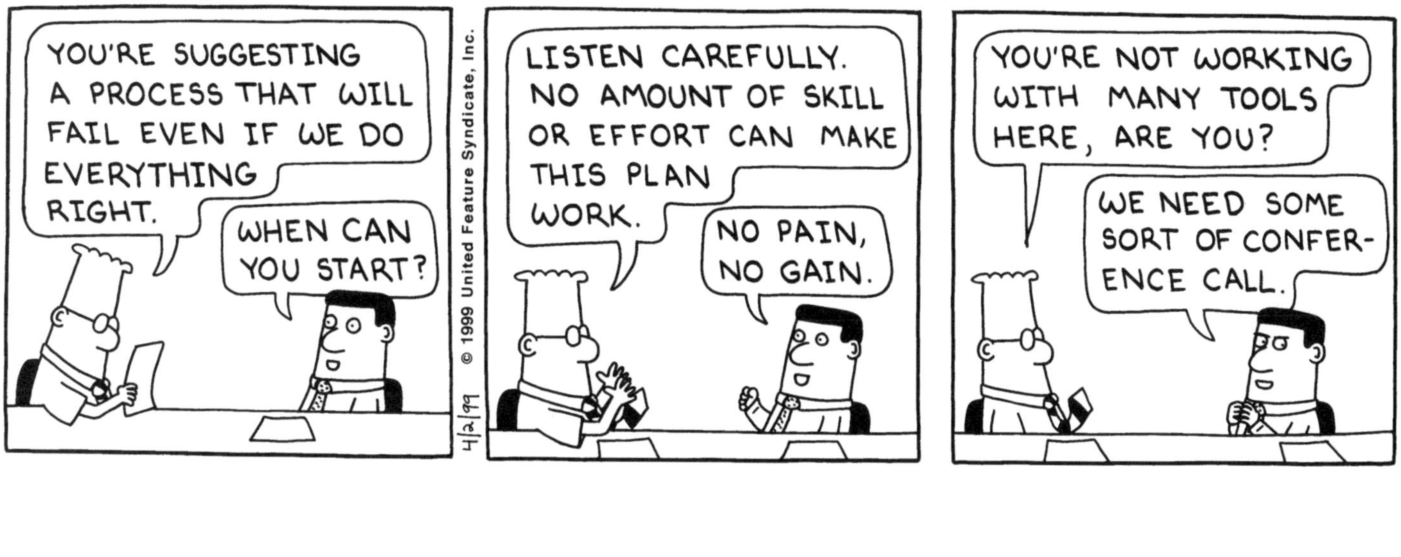
YOU'RE SUGGESTING A PROCESS THAT WILL FAIL EVEN IF WE DO EVERYTHING RIGHT.
WHEN CAN YOU START?
4/2/99 © 1999 United Feature Syndicate, Inc.
LISTEN CAREFULLY. NO AMOUNT OF SKILL OR EFFORT CAN MAKE THIS PLAN WORK.
NO PAIN, NO GAIN.
YOU'RE NOT WORKING WITH MANY TOOLS HERE, ARE YOU?
WE NEED SOME SORT OF CONFERENCE CALL.

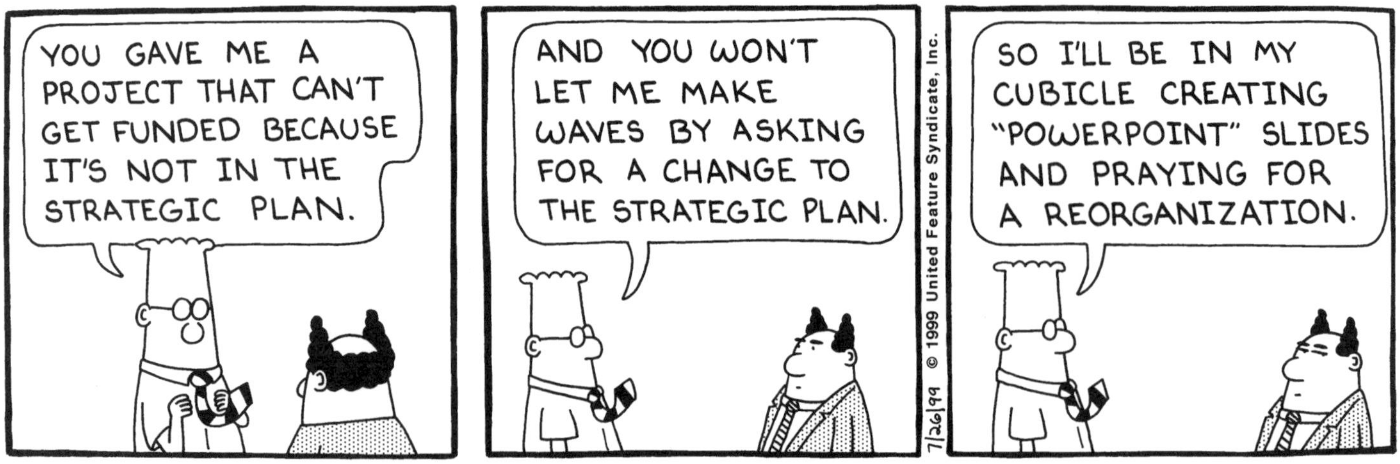
YOU GAVE ME A PROJECT THAT CAN'T GET FUNDED BECAUSE IT'S NOT IN THE STRATEGIC PLAN.
AND YOU WON'T LET ME MAKE WAVES BY ASKING FOR A CHANGE TO THE STRATEGIC PLAN.
7/26/99 © 1999 United Feature Syndicate, Inc.
SO I'LL BE IN MY CUBICLE CREATING "POWERPOINT" SLIDES AND PRAYING FOR A REORGANIZATION.

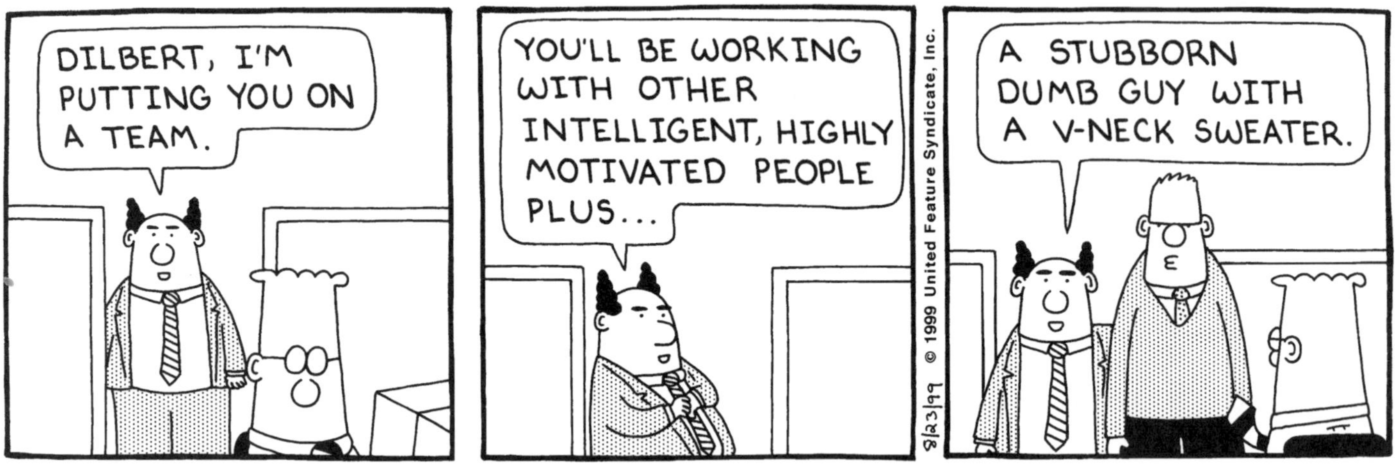
DILBERT, I'M PUTTING YOU ON A TEAM.
YOU'LL BE WORKING WITH OTHER INTELLIGENT, HIGHLY MOTIVATED PEOPLE PLUS...
8/23/99 © 1999 United Feature Syndicate, Inc.
A STUBBORN DUMB GUY WITH A V-NECK SWEATER.

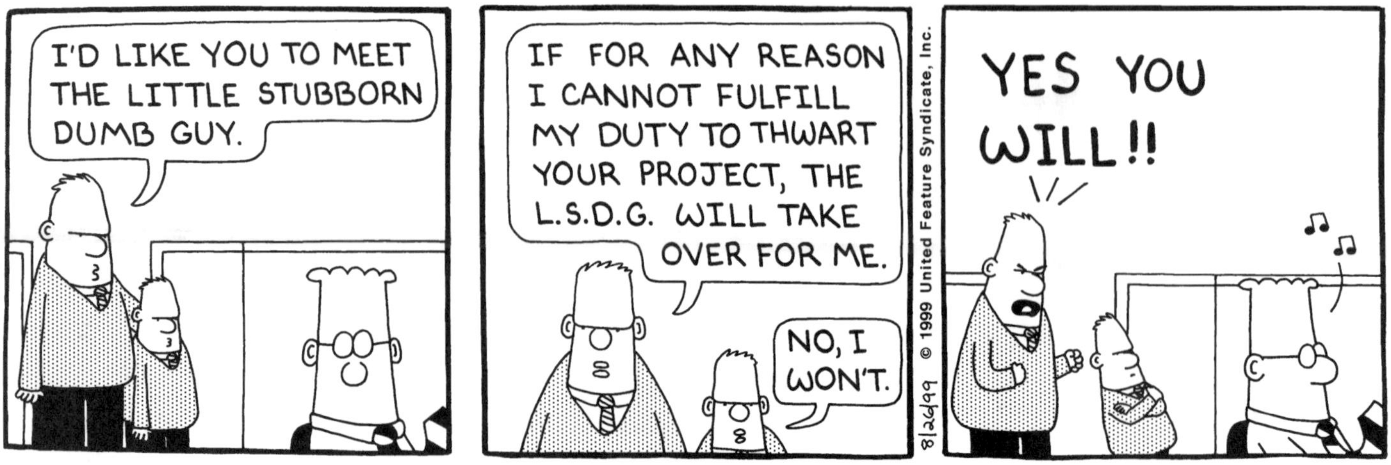
I'D LIKE YOU TO MEET THE LITTLE STUBBORN DUMB GUY.
IF FOR ANY REASON I CANNOT FULFILL MY DUTY TO THWART YOUR PROJECT, THE L.S.D.G. WILL TAKE OVER FOR ME.
NO, I WON'T.
8/26/99 © 1999 United Feature Syndicate, Inc.
YES YOU WILL!!

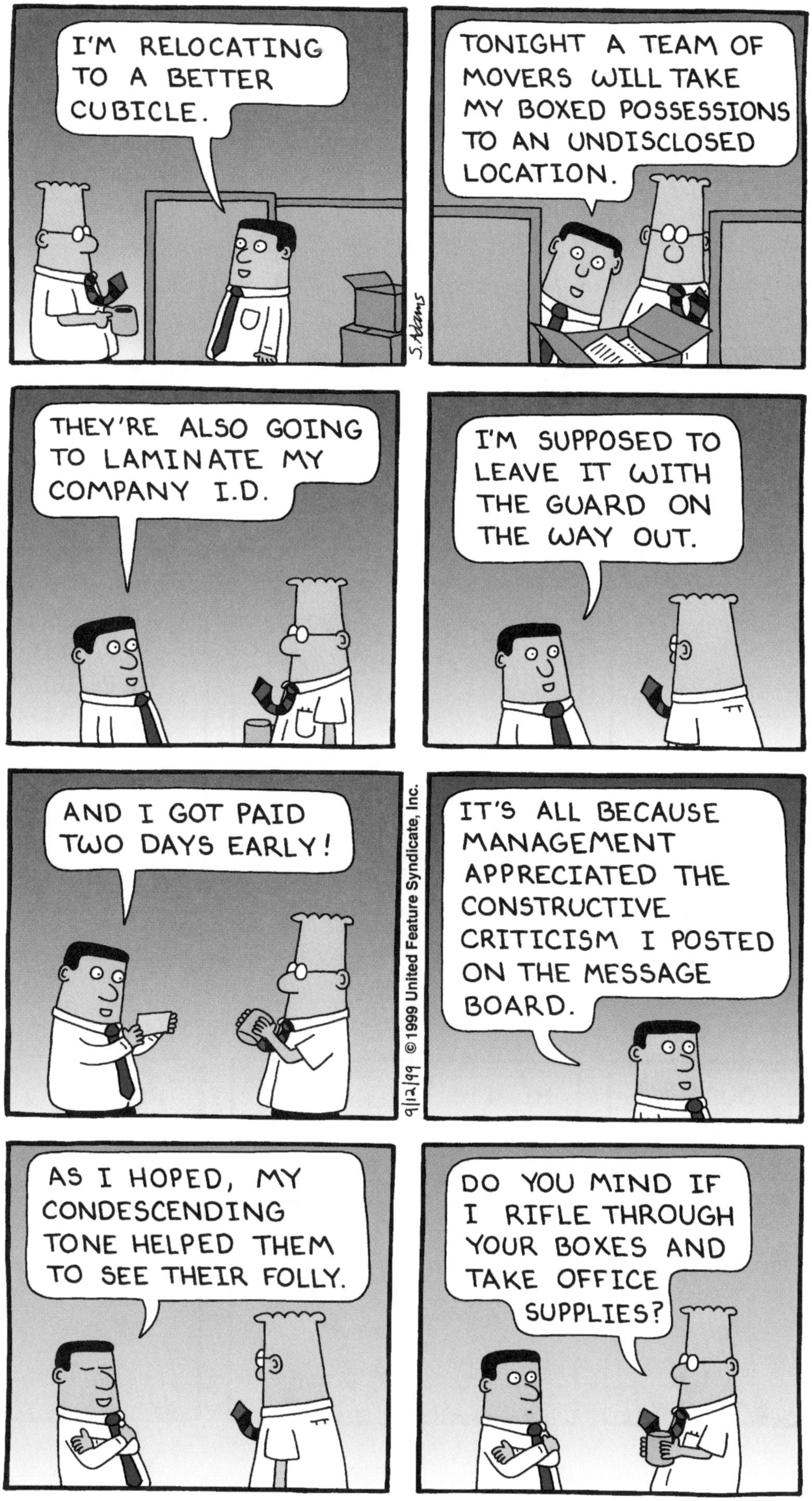
I'M RELOCATING TO A BETTER CUBICLE.
TONIGHT A TEAM OF MOVERS WILL TAKE MY BOXED POSSESSIONS TO AN UNDISCLOSED LOCATION.
S. Adams
THEY'RE ALSO GOING TO LAMINATE MY COMPANY I.D.
I'M SUPPOSED TO LEAVE IT WITH THE GUARD ON THE WAY OUT.
AND I GOT PAID TWO DAYS EARLY!
9/12/99 © 1999 United Feature Syndicate, Inc.
IT'S ALL BECAUSE MANAGEMENT APPRECIATED THE CONSTRUCTIVE CRITICISM I POSTED ON THE MESSAGE BOARD.
AS I HOPED, MY CONDESCENDING TONE HELPED THEM TO SEE THEIR FOLLY.
DO YOU MIND IF I RIFLE THROUGH YOUR BOXES AND TAKE OFFICE SUPPLIES?

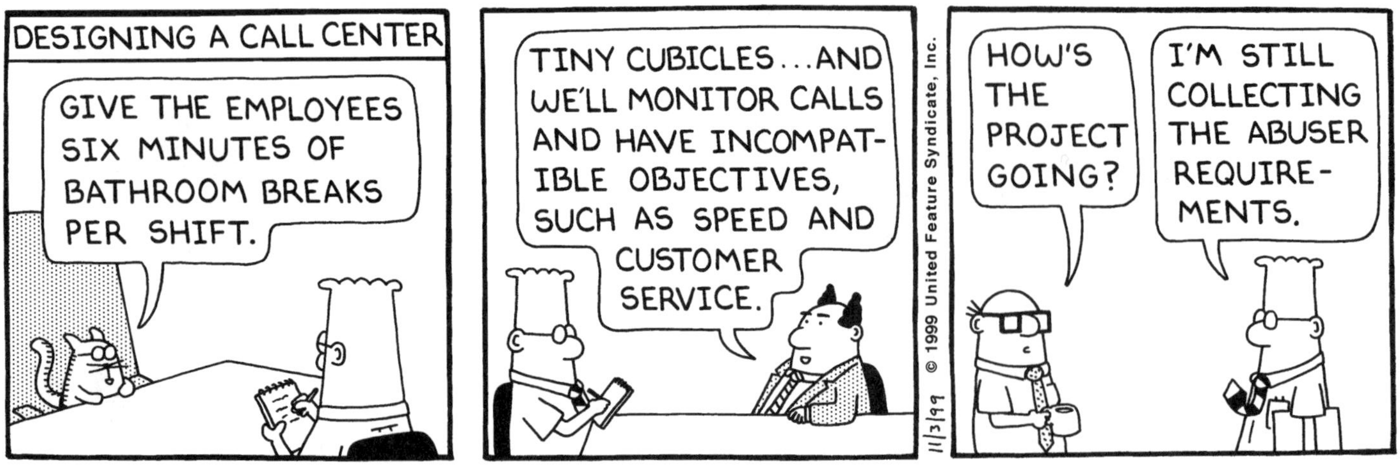
DESIGNING A CALL CENTER
GIVE THE EMPLOYEES SIX MINUTES OF BATHROOM BREAKS PER SHIFT.
TINY CUBICLES...AND WE'LL MONITOR CALLS AND HAVE INCOMPAT-IBLE OBJECTIVES, SUCH AS SPEED AND CUSTOMER SERVICE.
11/3/99 © 1999 United Feature Syndicate, Inc.
HOW'S THE PROJECT GOING?
I'M STILL COLLECTING THE ABUSER REQUIRE-MENTS.

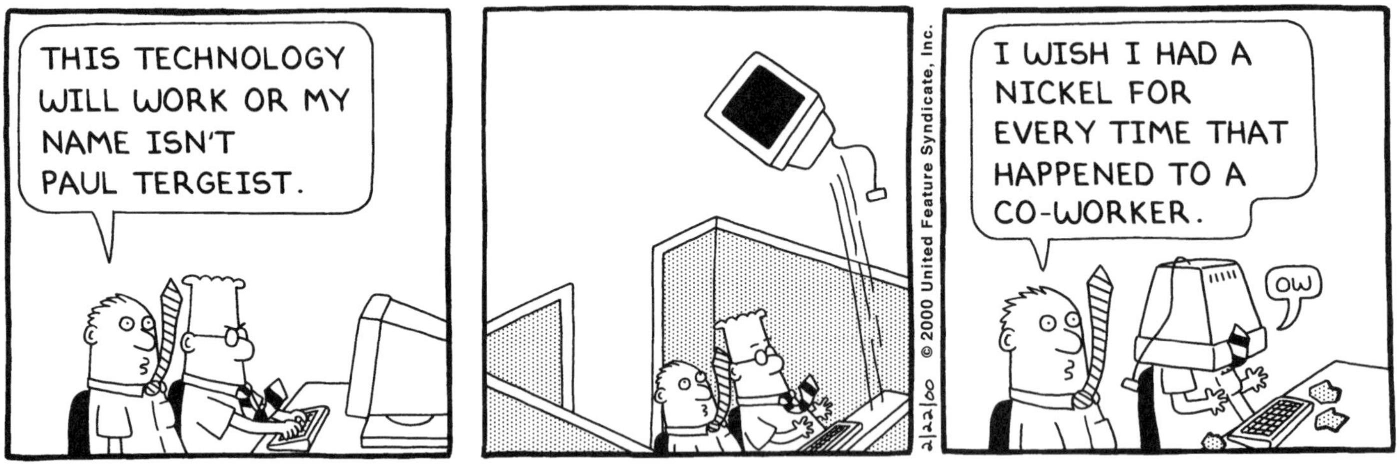
THIS TECHNOLOGY WILL WORK OR MY NAME ISN'T PAUL TERGEIST.
2/22/00 © 2000 United Feature Syndicate, Inc.
I WISH I HAD A NICKEL FOR EVERY TIME THAT HAPPENED TO A CO-WORKER.
OW

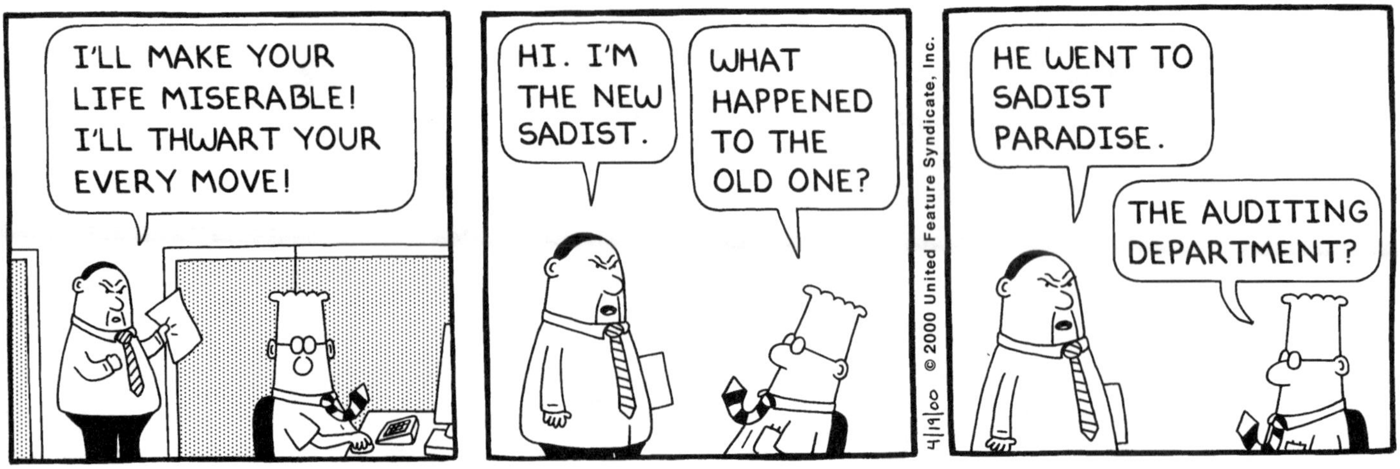
I'LL MAKE YOUR LIFE MISERABLE! I'LL THWART YOUR EVERY MOVE!
HI. I'M THE NEW SADIST.
WHAT HAPPENED TO THE OLD ONE?
4/19/00 © 2000 United Feature Syndicate, Inc.
HE WENT TO SADIST PARADISE.
THE AUDITING DEPARTMENT?

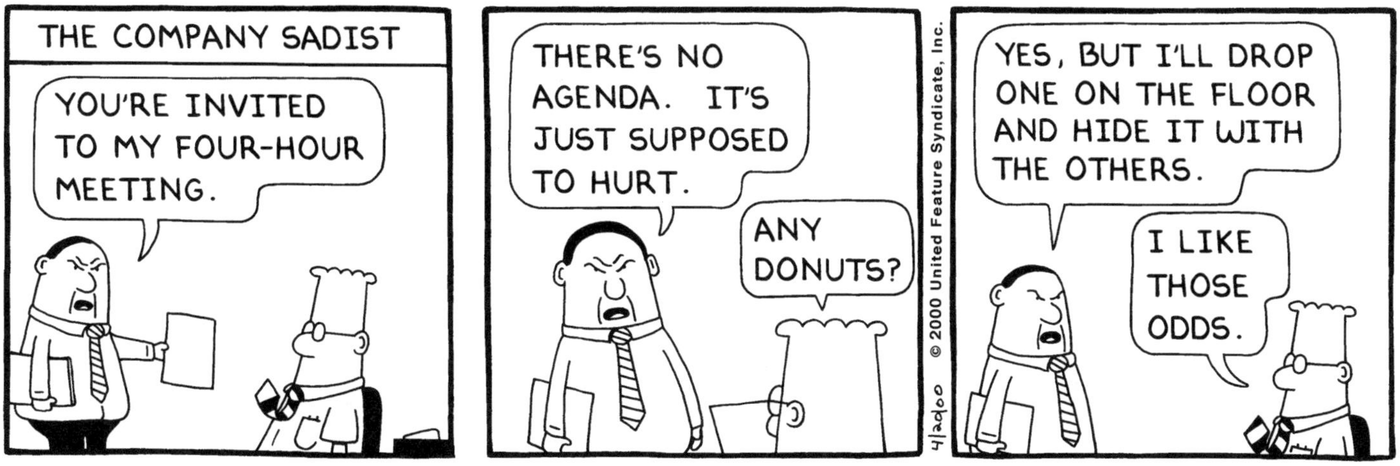
THE COMPANY SADIST
YOU'RE INVITED TO MY FOUR-HOUR MEETING.
THERE'S NO AGENDA. IT'S JUST SUPPOSED TO HURT.
ANY DONUTS?
YES, BUT I'LL DROP ONE ON THE FLOOR AND HIDE IT WITH THE OTHERS.
I LIKE THOSE ODDS.
© 2000 United Feature Syndicate, Inc.
4/2/00

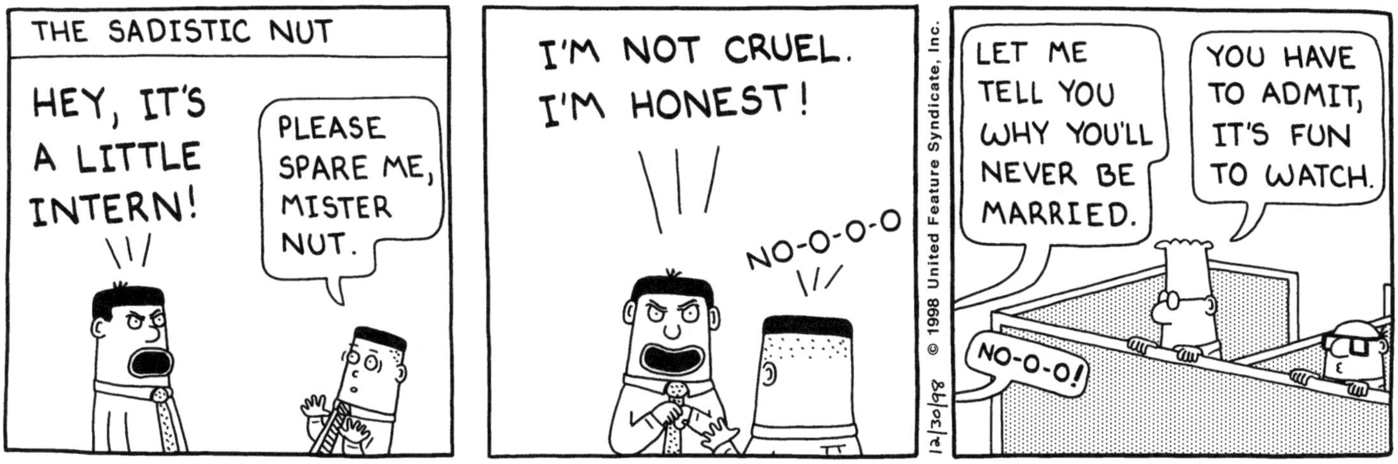
THE SADISTIC NUT
HEY, IT'S A LITTLE INTERN!
PLEASE SPARE ME, MISTER NUT.
I'M NOT CRUEL. I'M HONEST!
NO-O-O-O
LET ME TELL YOU WHY YOU'LL NEVER BE MARRIED.
YOU HAVE TO ADMIT, IT'S FUN TO WATCH.
NO-O-O!
© 1998 United Feature Syndicate, Inc.
12/30/98

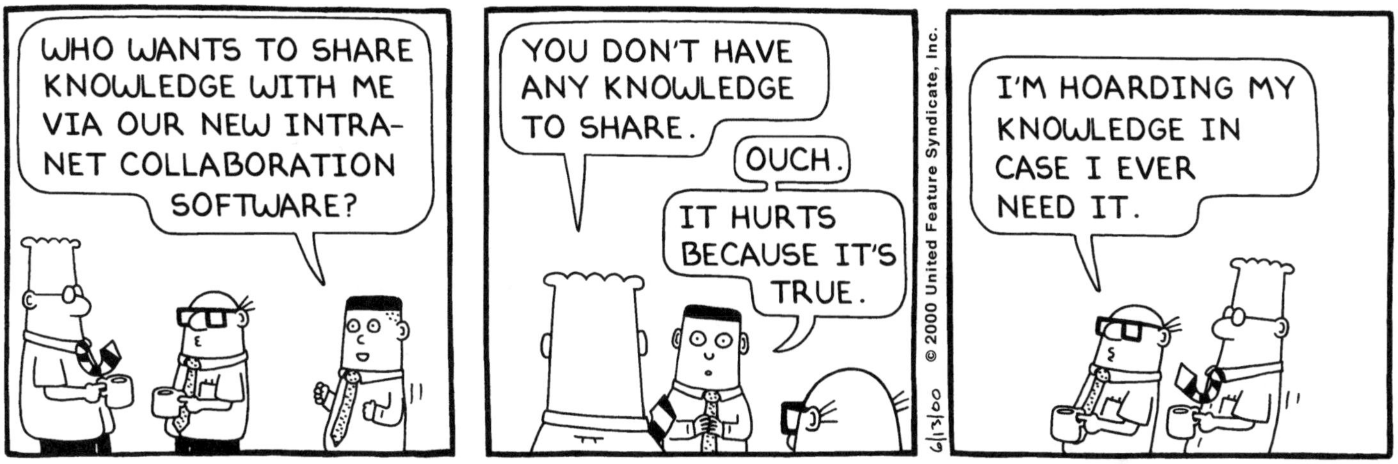
WHO WANTS TO SHARE KNOWLEDGE WITH ME VIA OUR NEW INTRA-NET COLLABORATION SOFTWARE?
YOU DON'T HAVE ANY KNOWLEDGE TO SHARE.
OUCH.
IT HURTS BECAUSE IT'S TRUE.
I'M HOARDING MY KNOWLEDGE IN CASE I EVER NEED IT.
© 2000 United Feature Syndicate, Inc.
6/13/00

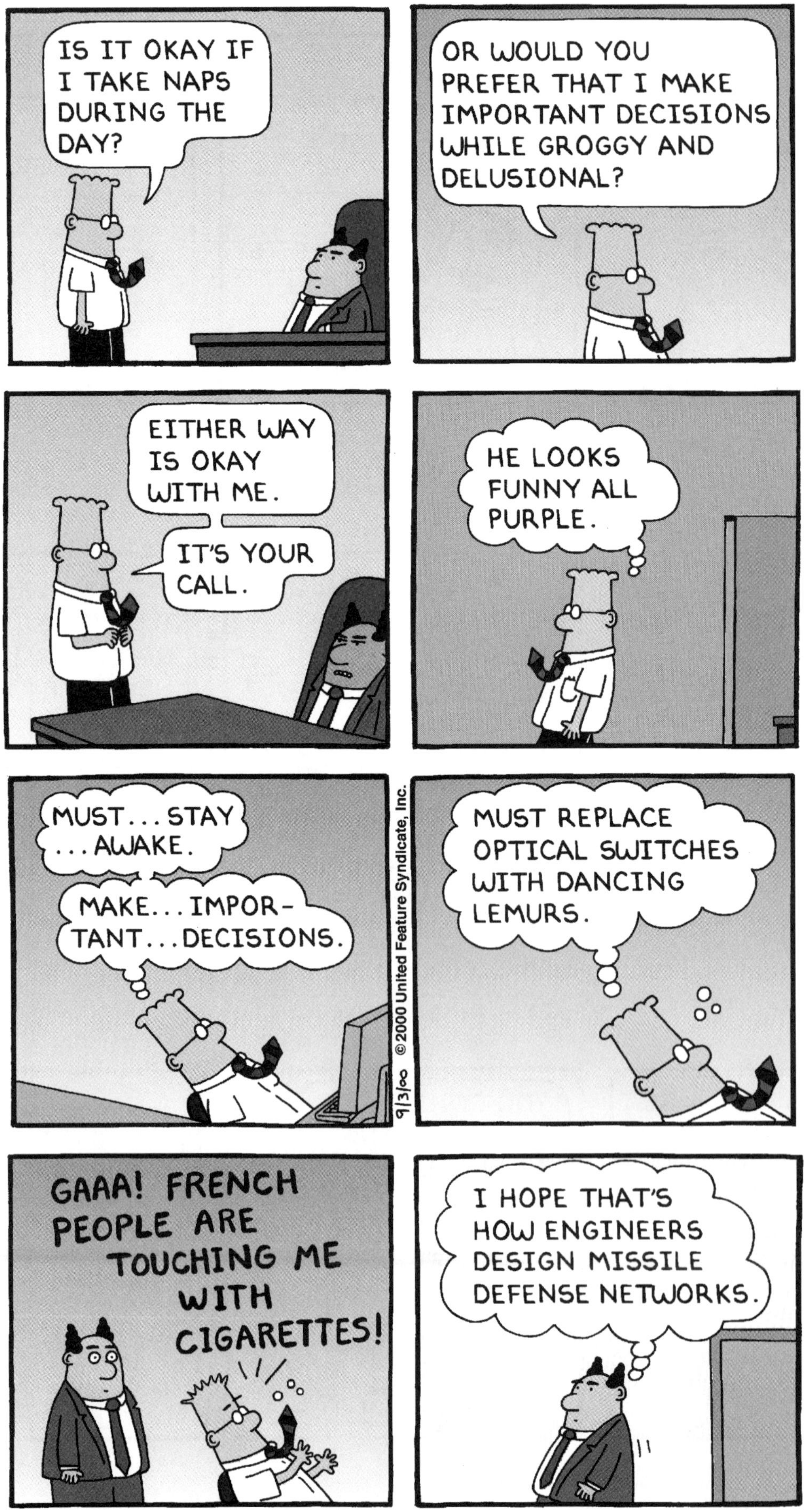
IS IT OKAY IF I TAKE NAPS DURING THE DAY?
OR WOULD YOU PREFER THAT I MAKE IMPORTANT DECISIONS WHILE GROGGY AND DELUSIONAL?
EITHER WAY IS OKAY WITH ME.
IT'S YOUR CALL.
HE LOOKS FUNNY ALL PURPLE.
MUST... STAY ... AWAKE.
MAKE... IMPOR-TANT... DECISIONS.
© 2000 United Feature Syndicate, Inc.
9/3/00
MUST REPLACE OPTICAL SWITCHES WITH DANCING LEMURS.
GAAA! FRENCH PEOPLE ARE TOUCHING ME WITH CIGARETTES!
I HOPE THAT'S HOW ENGINEERS DESIGN MISSILE DEFENSE NETWORKS.

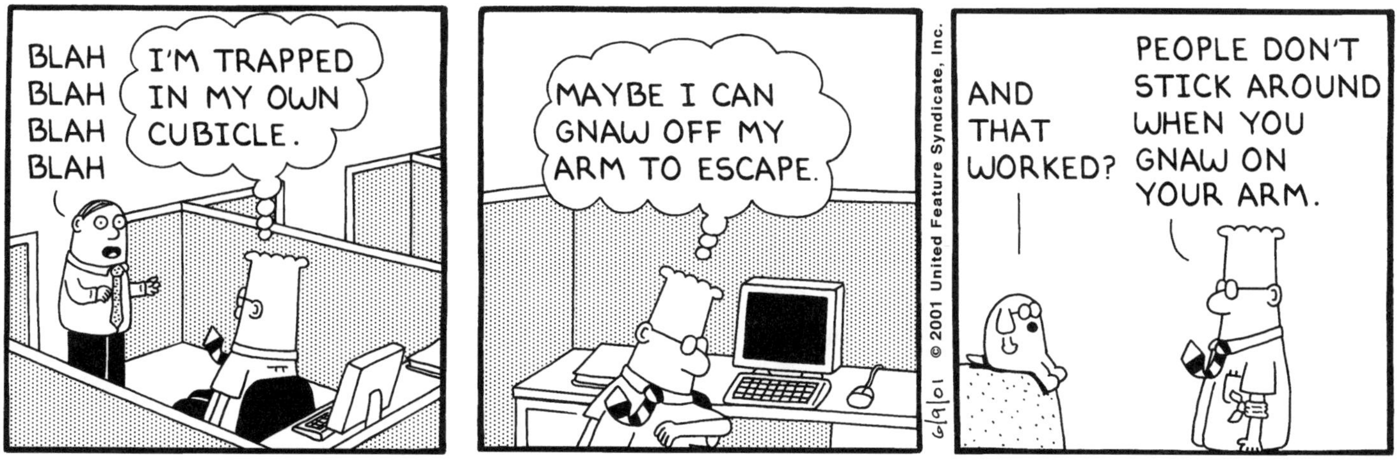
BLAH BLAH BLAH BLAH
I'M TRAPPED IN MY OWN CUBICLE.
MAYBE I CAN GNAW OFF MY ARM TO ESCAPE.
6/9/01 © 2001 United Feature Syndicate, Inc.
AND THAT WORKED?
PEOPLE DON'T STICK AROUND WHEN YOU GNAW ON YOUR ARM.

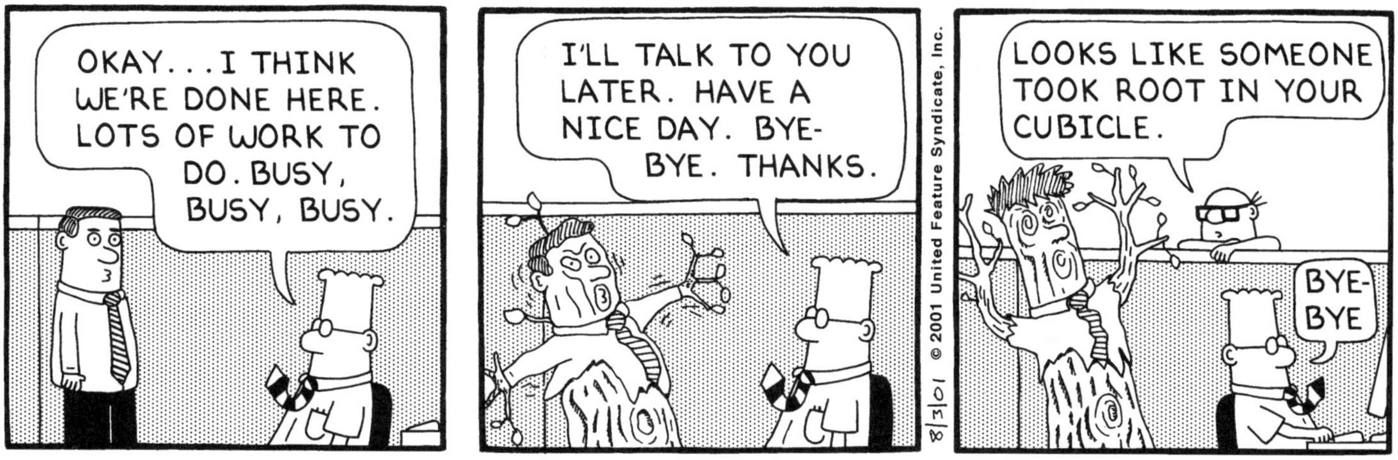
OKAY...I THINK WE'RE DONE HERE. LOTS OF WORK TO DO. BUSY, BUSY, BUSY.
I'LL TALK TO YOU LATER. HAVE A NICE DAY. BYE-BYE. THANKS.
8/3/01 © 2001 United Feature Syndicate, Inc.
LOOKS LIKE SOMEONE TOOK ROOT IN YOUR CUBICLE.
BYE-BYE

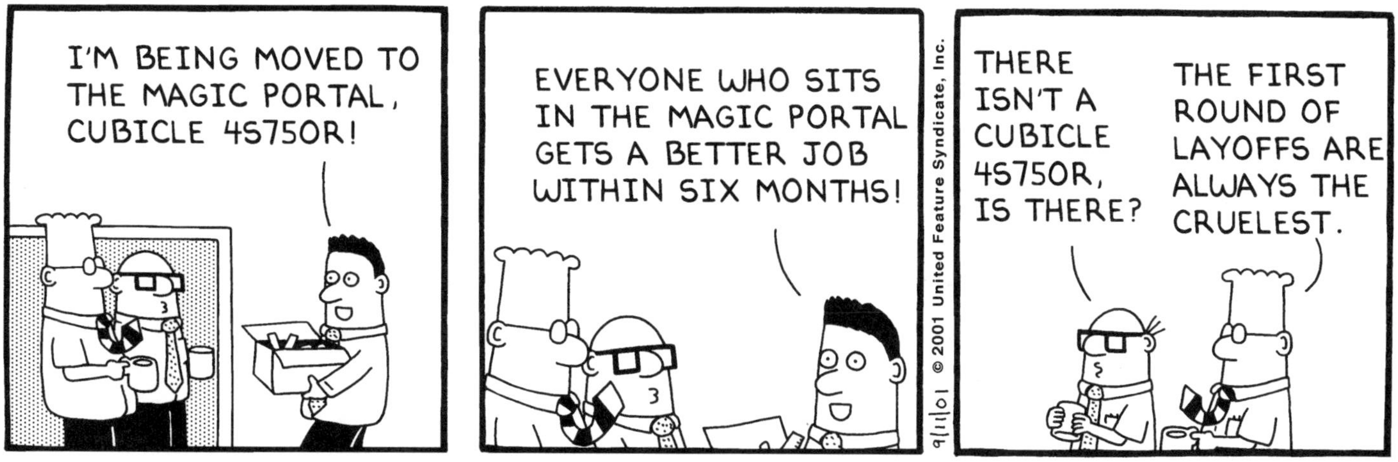
I'M BEING MOVED TO THE MAGIC PORTAL, CUBICLE 4S750R!
EVERYONE WHO SITS IN THE MAGIC PORTAL GETS A BETTER JOB WITHIN SIX MONTHS!
9/1/01 © 2001 United Feature Syndicate, Inc.
THERE ISN'T A CUBICLE 4S750R, IS THERE?
THE FIRST ROUND OF LAYOFFS ARE ALWAYS THE CRUELEST.

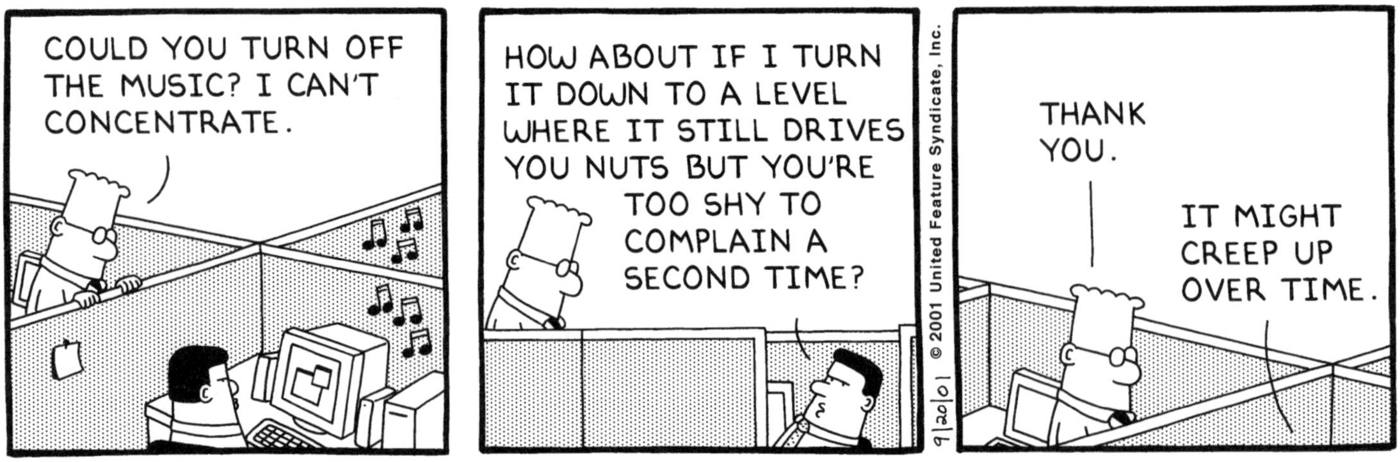
COULD YOU TURN OFF THE MUSIC? I CAN'T CONCENTRATE.
HOW ABOUT IF I TURN IT DOWN TO A LEVEL WHERE IT STILL DRIVES YOU NUTS BUT YOU'RE TOO SHY TO COMPLAIN A SECOND TIME?
THANK YOU.
IT MIGHT CREEP UP OVER TIME.
9/20/01 © 2001 United Feature Syndicate, Inc.

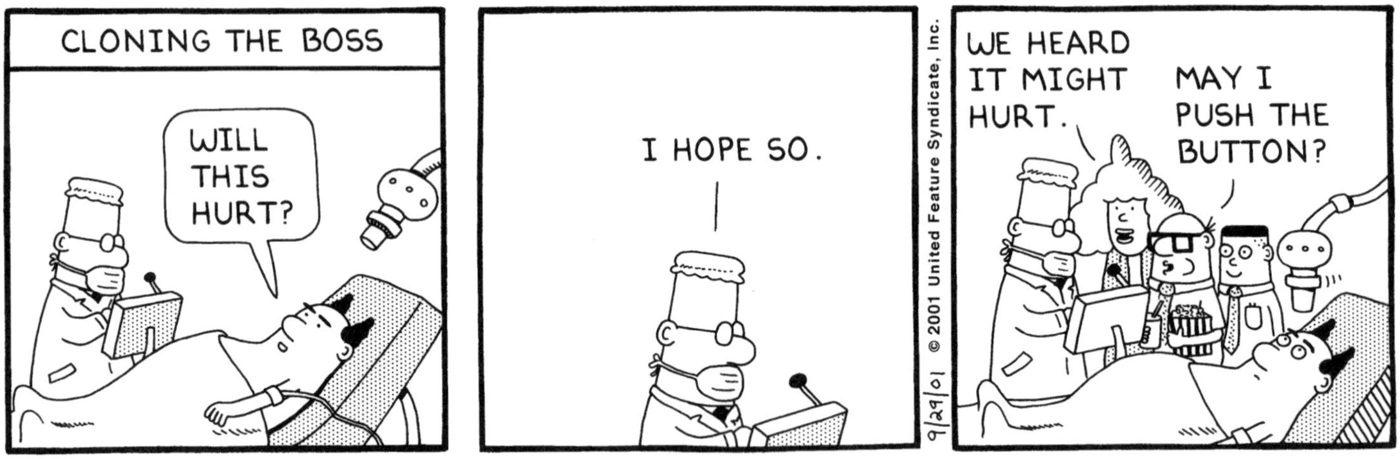
CLONING THE BOSS
WILL THIS HURT?
I HOPE SO.
WE HEARD IT MIGHT HURT.
MAY I PUSH THE BUTTON?
9/29/01 © 2001 United Feature Syndicate, Inc.

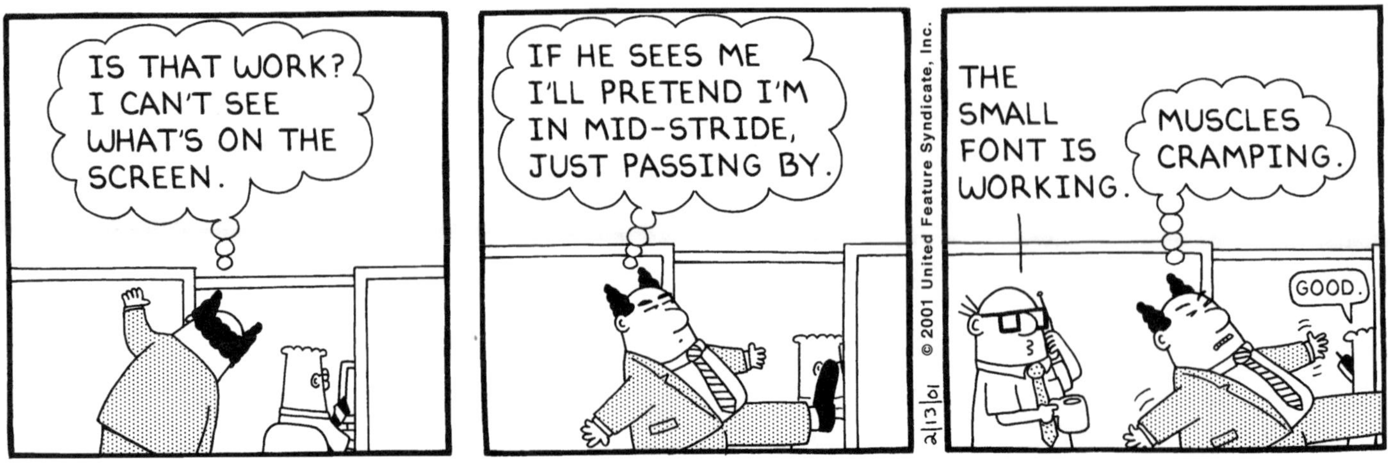
IS THAT WORK? I CAN'T SEE WHAT'S ON THE SCREEN.
IF HE SEES ME I'LL PRETEND I'M IN MID-STRIDE, JUST PASSING BY.
THE SMALL FONT IS WORKING.
MUSCLES CRAMPING.
GOOD.
2/13/01 © 2001 United Feature Syndicate, Inc.

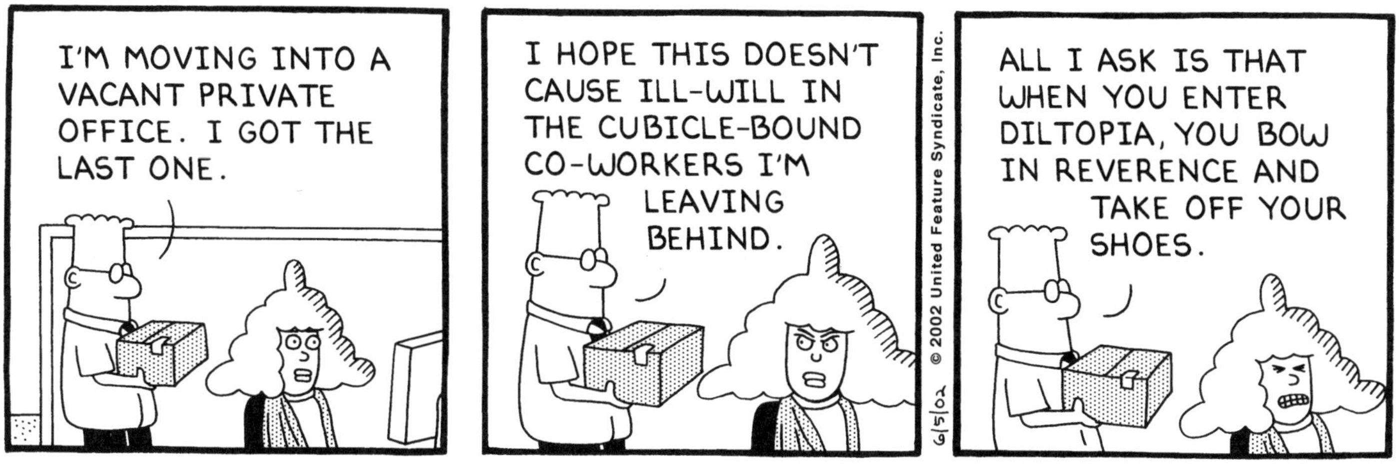
I'M MOVING INTO A VACANT PRIVATE OFFICE. I GOT THE LAST ONE.
I HOPE THIS DOESN'T CAUSE ILL-WILL IN THE CUBICLE-BOUND CO-WORKERS I'M LEAVING BEHIND.
© 2002 United Feature Syndicate, Inc.
6/5/02
ALL I ASK IS THAT WHEN YOU ENTER DILTOPIA, YOU BOW IN REVERENCE AND TAKE OFF YOUR SHOES.

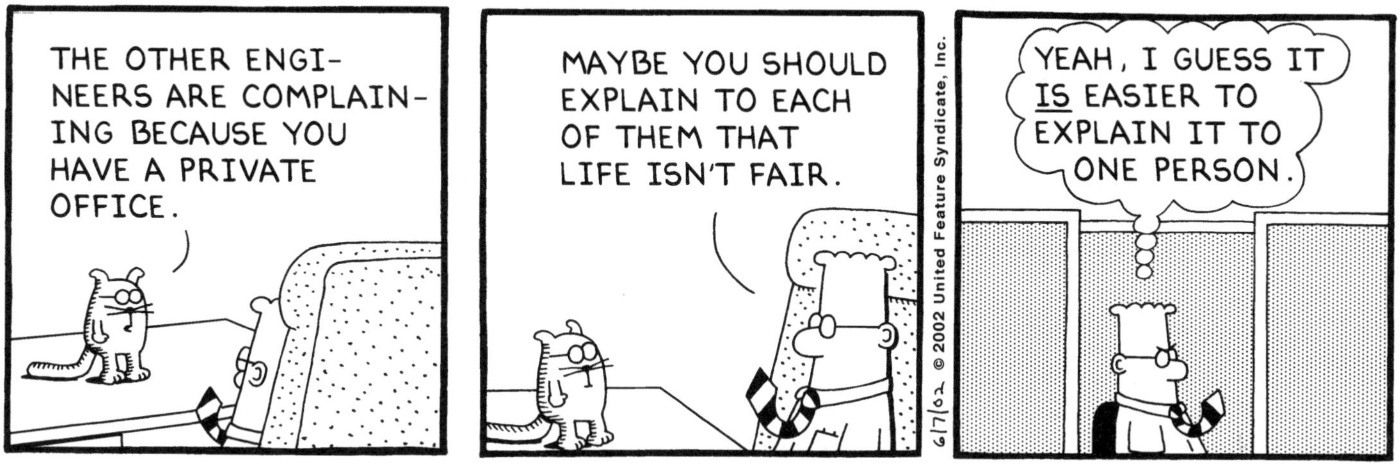
THE OTHER ENGI-NEERS ARE COMPLAIN-ING BECAUSE YOU HAVE A PRIVATE OFFICE.
MAYBE YOU SHOULD EXPLAIN TO EACH OF THEM THAT LIFE ISN'T FAIR.
© 2002 United Feature Syndicate, Inc.
6/7/02
YEAH, I GUESS IT IS EASIER TO EXPLAIN IT TO ONE PERSON.

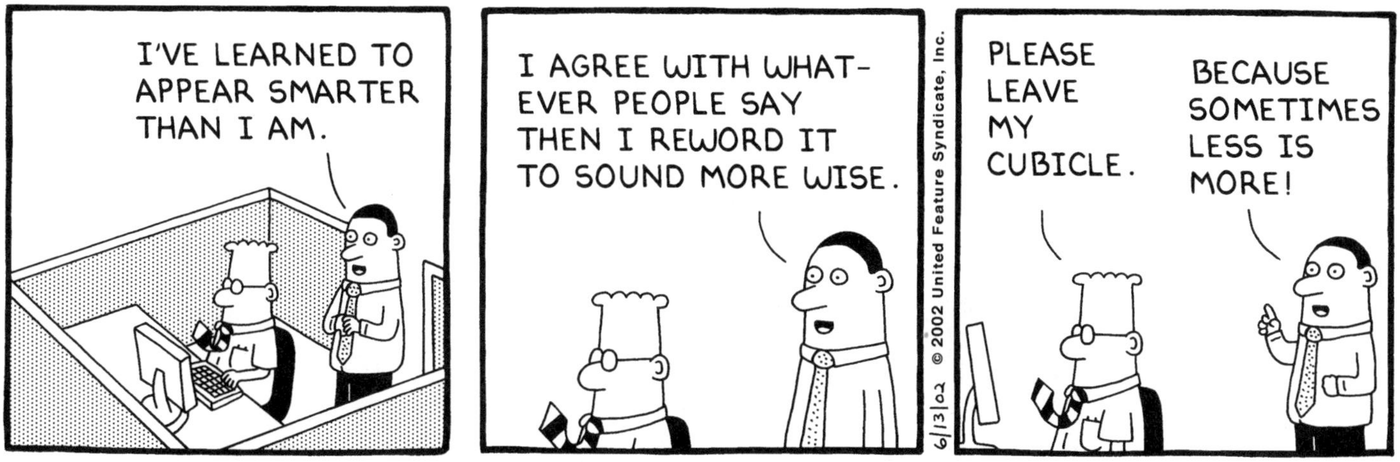
I'VE LEARNED TO APPEAR SMARTER THAN I AM.
I AGREE WITH WHAT-EVER PEOPLE SAY THEN I REWORD IT TO SOUND MORE WISE.
© 2002 United Feature Syndicate, Inc.
6/13/02
PLEASE LEAVE MY CUBICLE.
BECAUSE SOMETIMES LESS IS MORE!

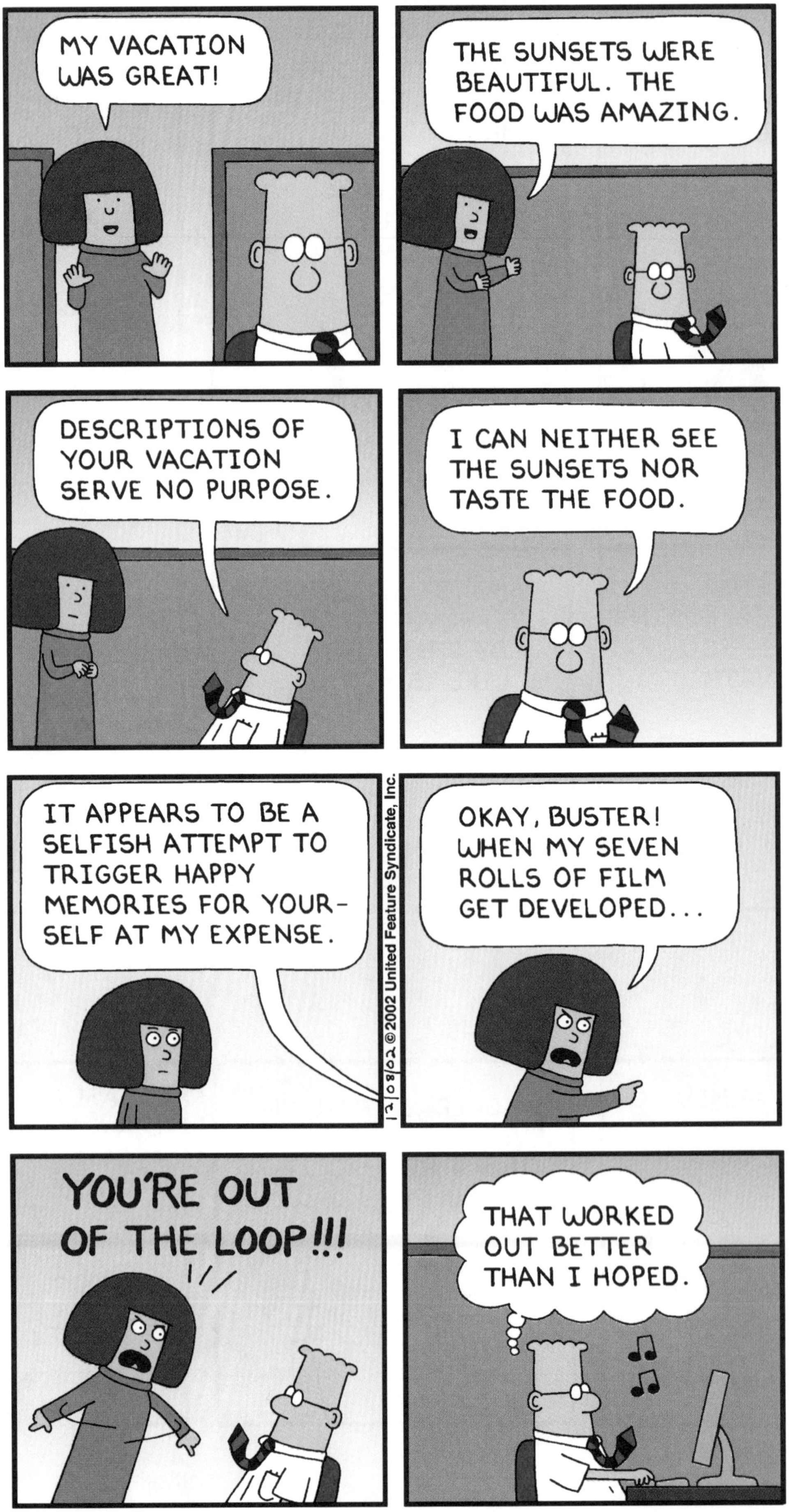
MY VACATION WAS GREAT!
THE SUNSETS WERE BEAUTIFUL. THE FOOD WAS AMAZING.
DESCRIPTIONS OF YOUR VACATION SERVE NO PURPOSE.
I CAN NEITHER SEE THE SUNSETS NOR TASTE THE FOOD.
IT APPEARS TO BE A SELFISH ATTEMPT TO TRIGGER HAPPY MEMORIES FOR YOUR-SELF AT MY EXPENSE.
12/08/02 ©2002 United Feature Syndicate, Inc.
OKAY, BUSTER! WHEN MY SEVEN ROLLS OF FILM GET DEVELOPED...
YOU'RE OUT OF THE LOOP!!!
THAT WORKED OUT BETTER THAN I HOPED.

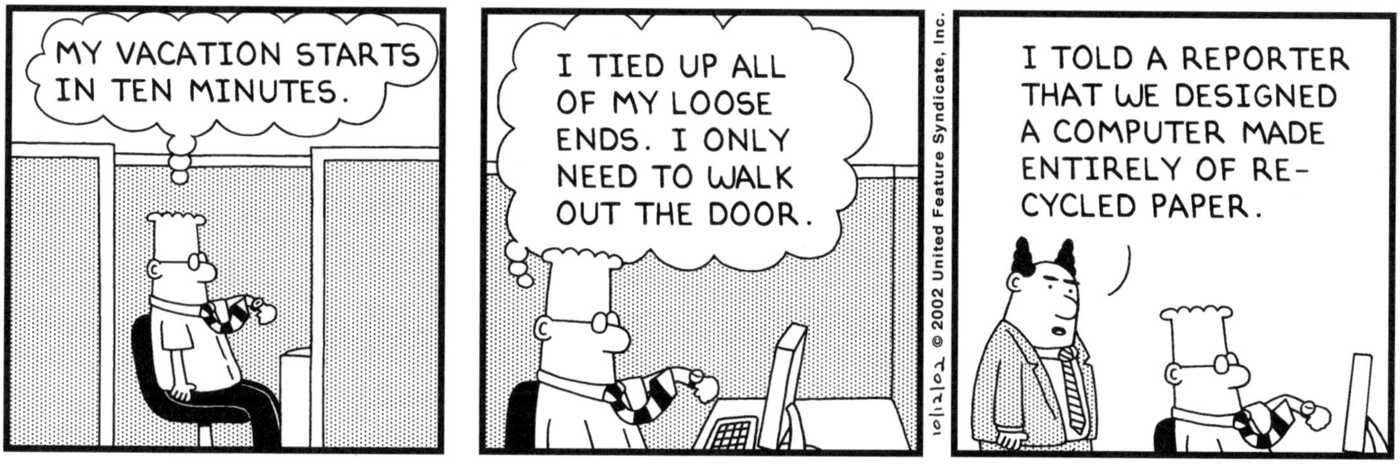
MY VACATION STARTS IN TEN MINUTES.
I TIED UP ALL OF MY LOOSE ENDS. I ONLY NEED TO WALK OUT THE DOOR.
10/12/02 © 2002 United Feature Syndicate, Inc.
I TOLD A REPORTER THAT WE DESIGNED A COMPUTER MADE ENTIRELY OF RE-CYCLED PAPER.

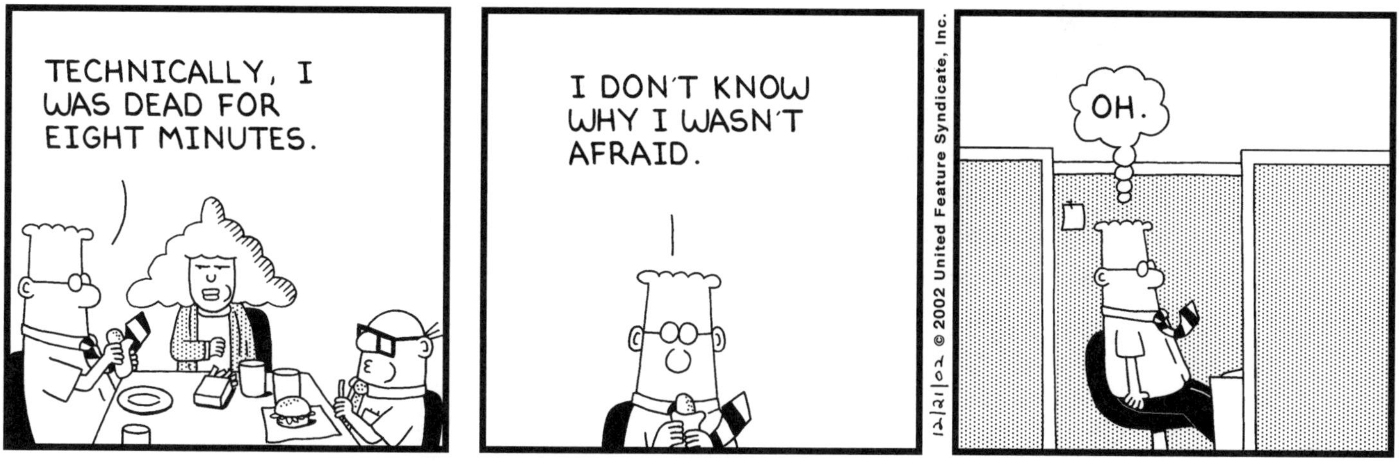
TECHNICALLY, I WAS DEAD FOR EIGHT MINUTES.
I DON'T KNOW WHY I WASN'T AFRAID.
12/21/02 © 2002 United Feature Syndicate, Inc.
OH.

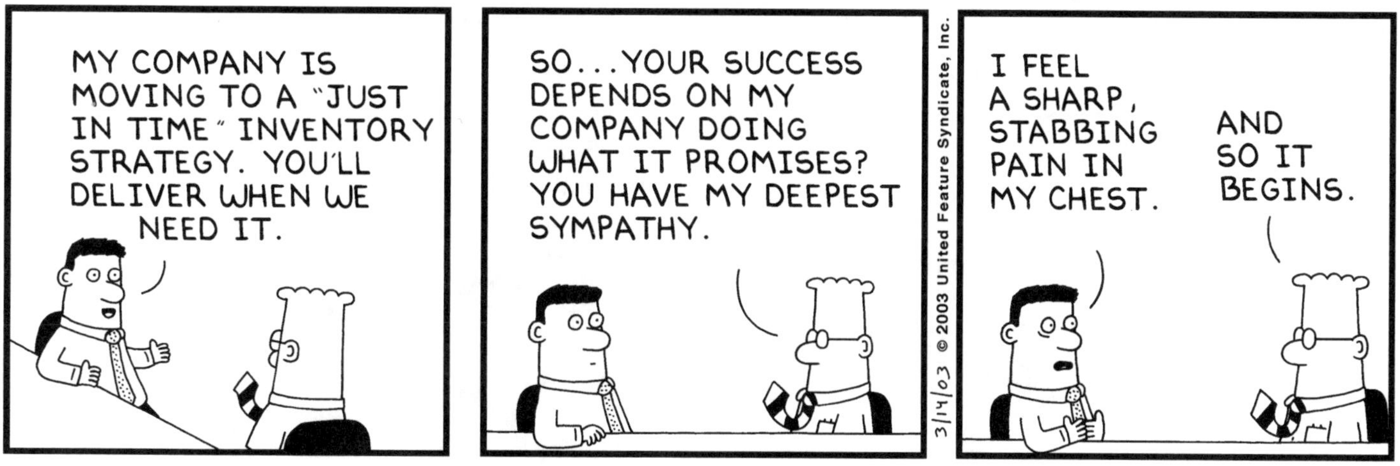
MY COMPANY IS MOVING TO A "JUST IN TIME" INVENTORY STRATEGY. YOU'LL DELIVER WHEN WE NEED IT.
SO...YOUR SUCCESS DEPENDS ON MY COMPANY DOING WHAT IT PROMISES? YOU HAVE MY DEEPEST SYMPATHY.
3/14/03 © 2003 United Feature Syndicate, Inc.
I FEEL A SHARP, STABBING PAIN IN MY CHEST.
AND SO IT BEGINS.

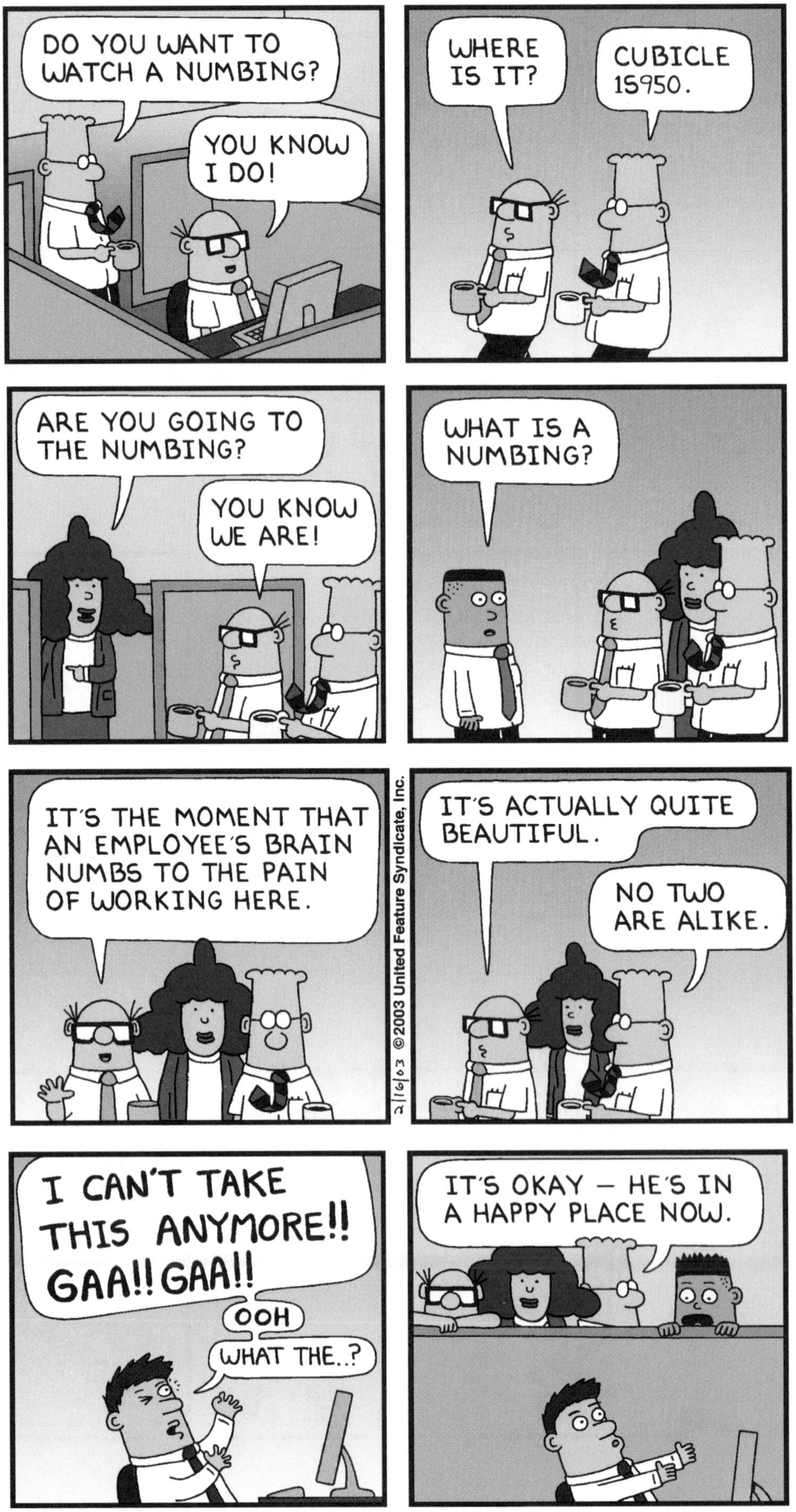
DO YOU WANT TO WATCH A NUMBING?
YOU KNOW I DO!
WHERE IS IT?
CUBICLE 15950.
ARE YOU GOING TO THE NUMBING?
YOU KNOW WE ARE!
WHAT IS A NUMBING?
IT'S THE MOMENT THAT AN EMPLOYEE'S BRAIN NUMBS TO THE PAIN OF WORKING HERE.
©2003 United Feature Syndicate, Inc.
2/16/03
IT'S ACTUALLY QUITE BEAUTIFUL.
NO TWO ARE ALIKE.
I CAN'T TAKE THIS ANYMORE!! GAA!! GAA!!
OOH
WHAT THE..?
IT'S OKAY – HE'S IN A HAPPY PLACE NOW.

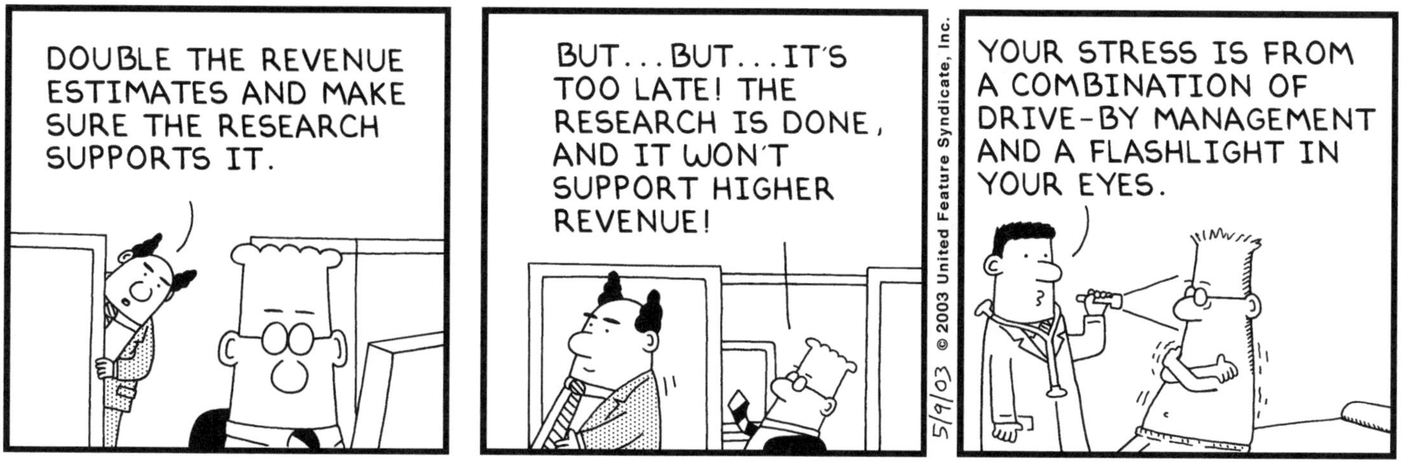
DOUBLE THE REVENUE ESTIMATES AND MAKE SURE THE RESEARCH SUPPORTS IT.
BUT...BUT...IT'S TOO LATE! THE RESEARCH IS DONE, AND IT WON'T SUPPORT HIGHER REVENUE!
5/9/03 © 2003 United Feature Syndicate, Inc.
YOUR STRESS IS FROM A COMBINATION OF DRIVE-BY MANAGEMENT AND A FLASHLIGHT IN YOUR EYES.

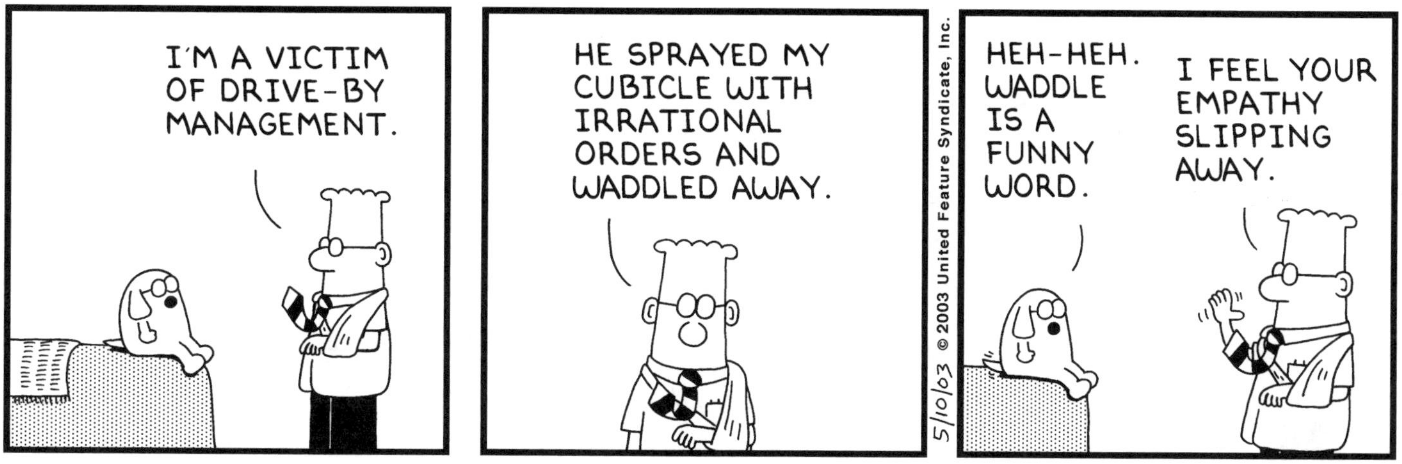
I'M A VICTIM OF DRIVE-BY MANAGEMENT.
HE SPRAYED MY CUBICLE WITH IRRATIONAL ORDERS AND WADDLED AWAY.
5/10/03 © 2003 United Feature Syndicate, Inc.
HEH-HEH. WADDLE IS A FUNNY WORD.
I FEEL YOUR EMPATHY SLIPPING AWAY.

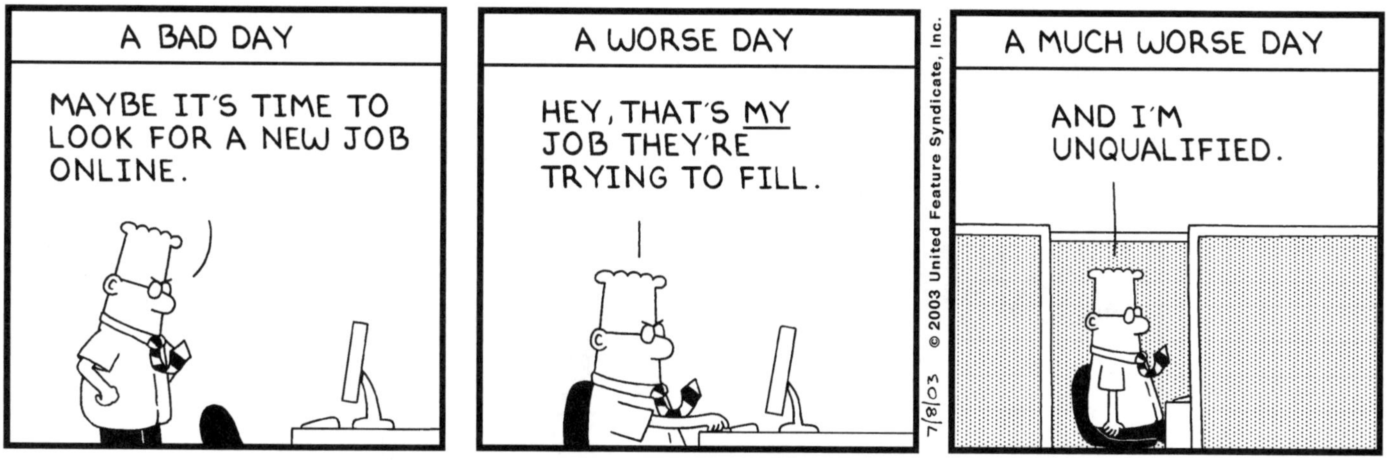
A BAD DAY
MAYBE IT'S TIME TO LOOK FOR A NEW JOB ONLINE.
A WORSE DAY
HEY, THAT'S MY JOB THEY'RE TRYING TO FILL.
7/8/03 © 2003 United Feature Syndicate, Inc.
A MUCH WORSE DAY
AND I'M UNQUALIFIED.

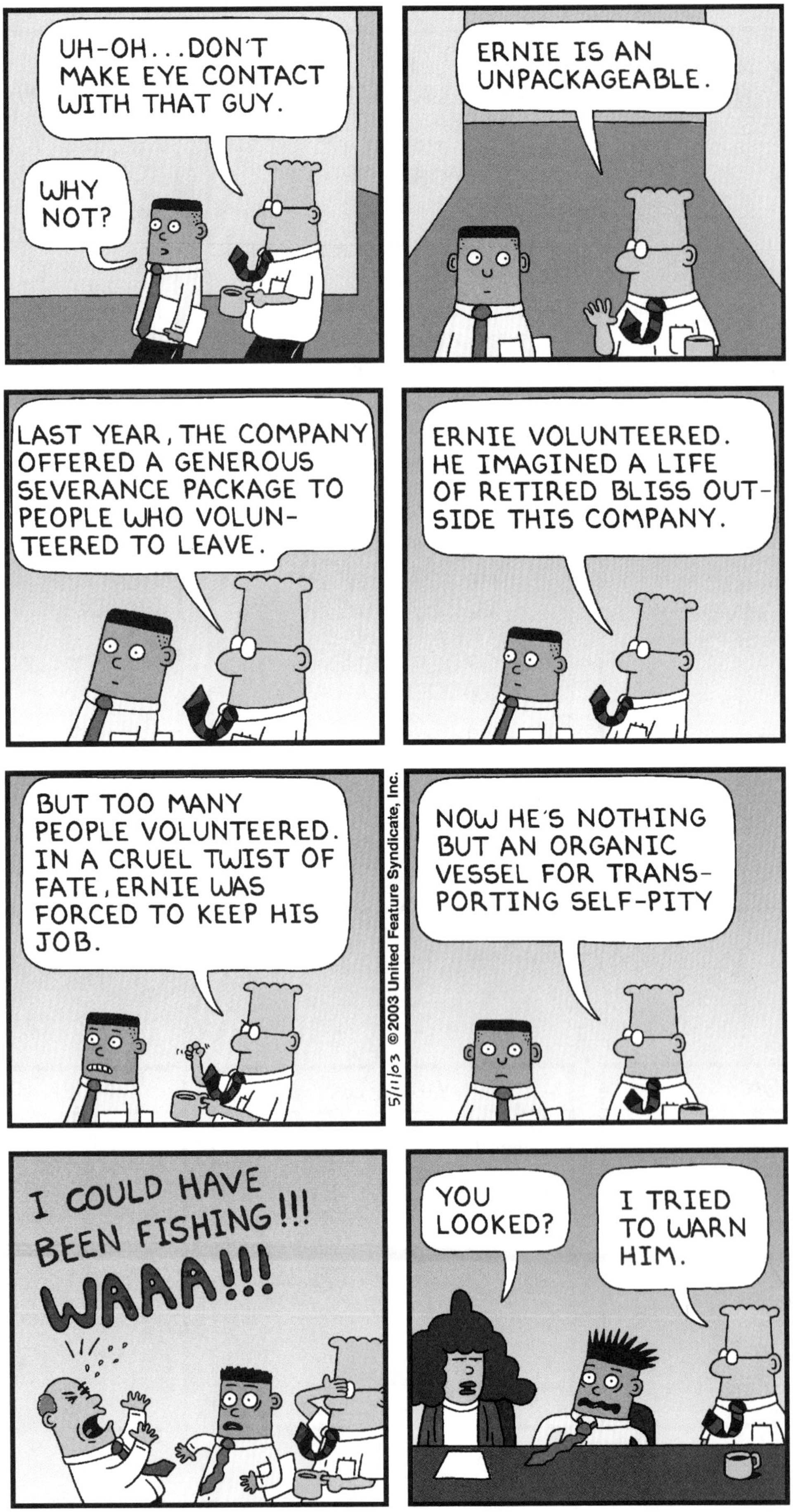
UH-OH...DON'T MAKE EYE CONTACT WITH THAT GUY.
WHY NOT?
ERNIE IS AN UNPACKAGEABLE.
LAST YEAR, THE COMPANY OFFERED A GENEROUS SEVERANCE PACKAGE TO PEOPLE WHO VOLUNTEERED TO LEAVE.
ERNIE VOLUNTEERED. HE IMAGINED A LIFE OF RETIRED BLISS OUTSIDE THIS COMPANY.
BUT TOO MANY PEOPLE VOLUNTEERED. IN A CRUEL TWIST OF FATE, ERNIE WAS FORCED TO KEEP HIS JOB.
NOW HE'S NOTHING BUT AN ORGANIC VESSEL FOR TRANSPORTING SELF-PITY
I COULD HAVE BEEN FISHING!!!
WAAA!!!
YOU LOOKED?
I TRIED TO WARN HIM.
5/11/03 ©2003 United Feature Syndicate, Inc.

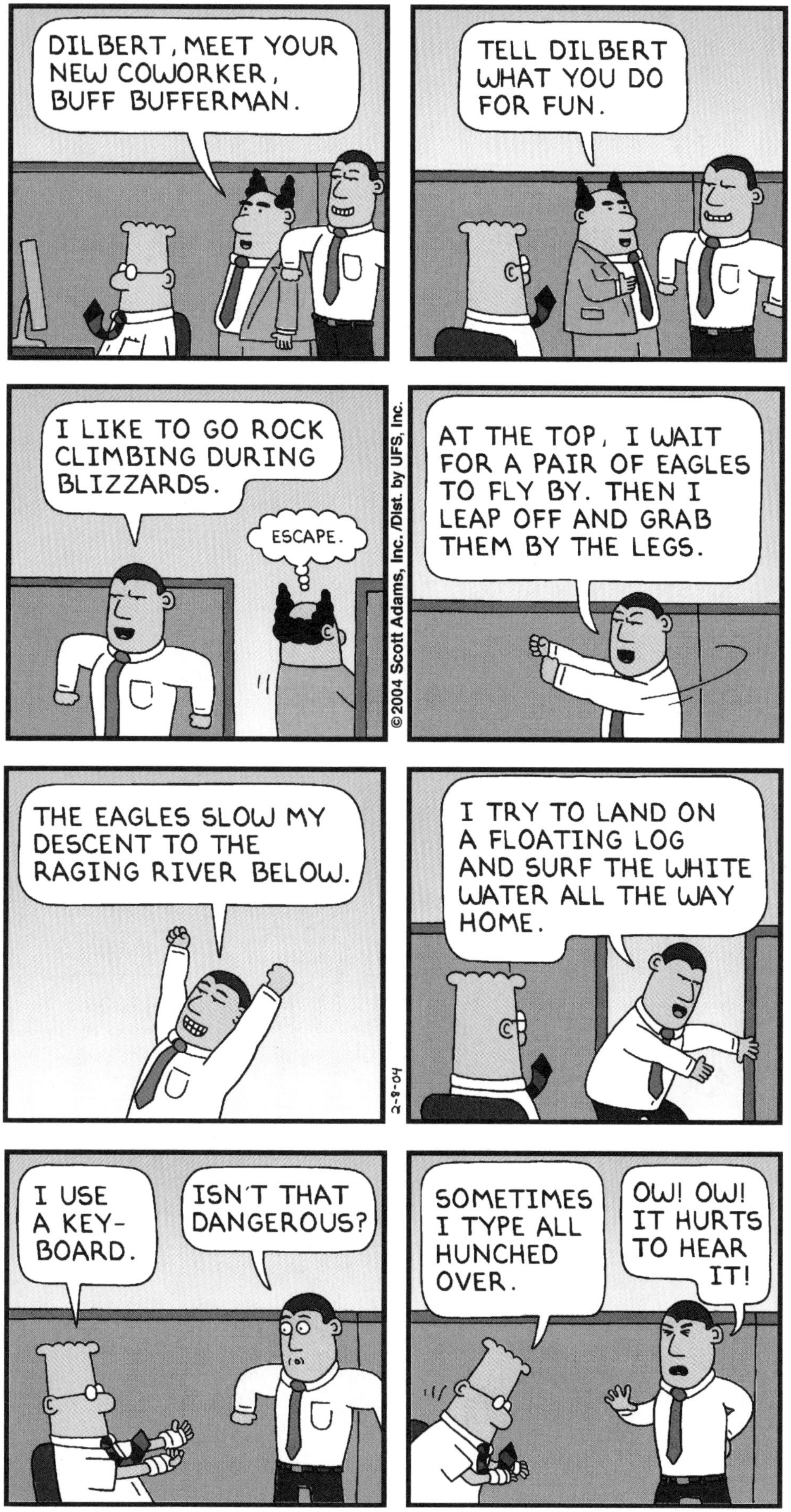
DILBERT, MEET YOUR NEW COWORKER, BUFF BUFFERMAN.
TELL DILBERT WHAT YOU DO FOR FUN.
I LIKE TO GO ROCK CLIMBING DURING BLIZZARDS.
ESCAPE.
©2004 Scott Adams, Inc./Dist. by UFS, Inc.
AT THE TOP, I WAIT FOR A PAIR OF EAGLES TO FLY BY. THEN I LEAP OFF AND GRAB THEM BY THE LEGS.
THE EAGLES SLOW MY DESCENT TO THE RAGING RIVER BELOW.
2-8-04
I TRY TO LAND ON A FLOATING LOG AND SURF THE WHITE WATER ALL THE WAY HOME.
I USE A KEY-BOARD.
ISN'T THAT DANGEROUS?
SOMETIMES I TYPE ALL HUNCHED OVER.
OW! OW! IT HURTS TO HEAR IT!

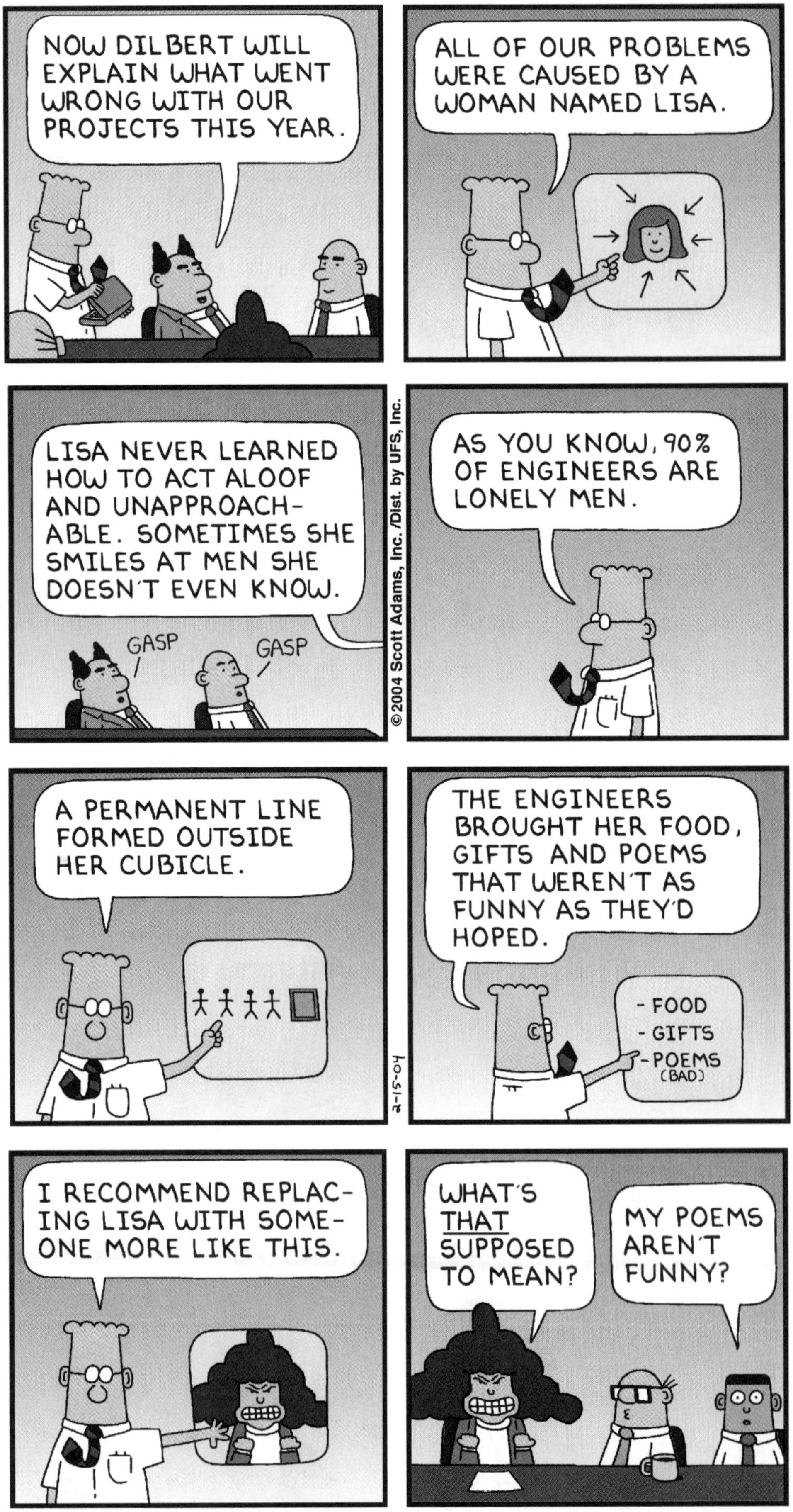
NOW DILBERT WILL EXPLAIN WHAT WENT WRONG WITH OUR PROJECTS THIS YEAR.
ALL OF OUR PROBLEMS WERE CAUSED BY A WOMAN NAMED LISA.
LISA NEVER LEARNED HOW TO ACT ALOOF AND UNAPPROACH-ABLE. SOMETIMES SHE SMILES AT MEN SHE DOESN'T EVEN KNOW.
GASP
GASP
©2004 Scott Adams, Inc./Dist. by UFS, Inc.
AS YOU KNOW, 90% OF ENGINEERS ARE LONELY MEN.
A PERMANENT LINE FORMED OUTSIDE HER CUBICLE.
2-15-04
THE ENGINEERS BROUGHT HER FOOD, GIFTS AND POEMS THAT WEREN'T AS FUNNY AS THEY'D HOPED.
- FOOD
- GIFTS
- POEMS (BAD)
I RECOMMEND REPLAC-ING LISA WITH SOME-ONE MORE LIKE THIS.
WHAT'S THAT SUPPOSED TO MEAN?
MY POEMS AREN'T FUNNY?

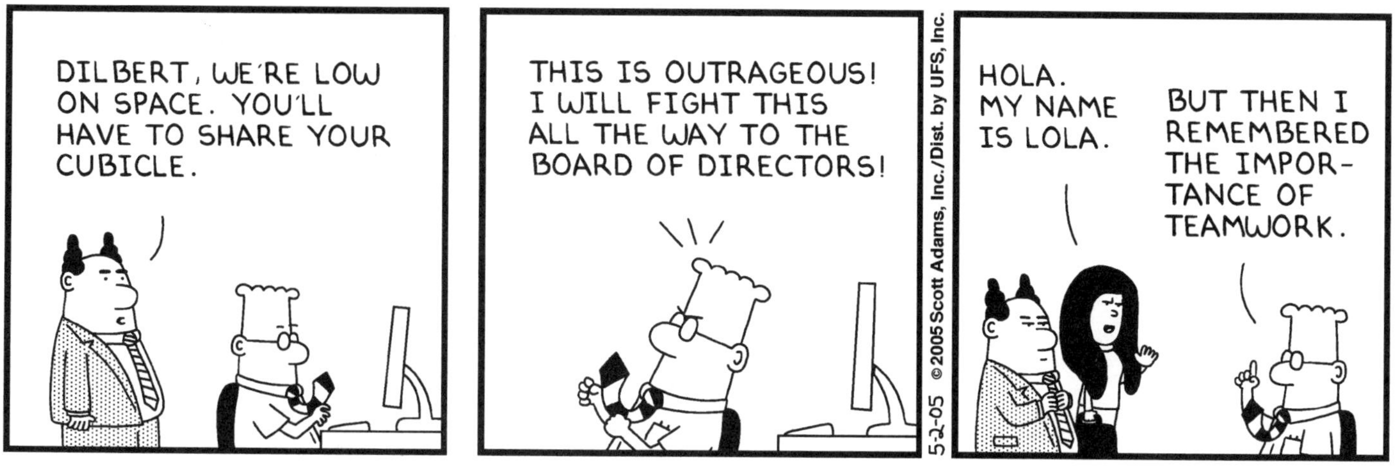
DILBERT, WE'RE LOW ON SPACE. YOU'LL HAVE TO SHARE YOUR CUBICLE.
THIS IS OUTRAGEOUS! I WILL FIGHT THIS ALL THE WAY TO THE BOARD OF DIRECTORS!
5-2-05 © 2005 Scott Adams, Inc./Dist. by UFS, Inc.
HOLA. MY NAME IS LOLA.
BUT THEN I REMEMBERED THE IMPOR-TANCE OF TEAMWORK.

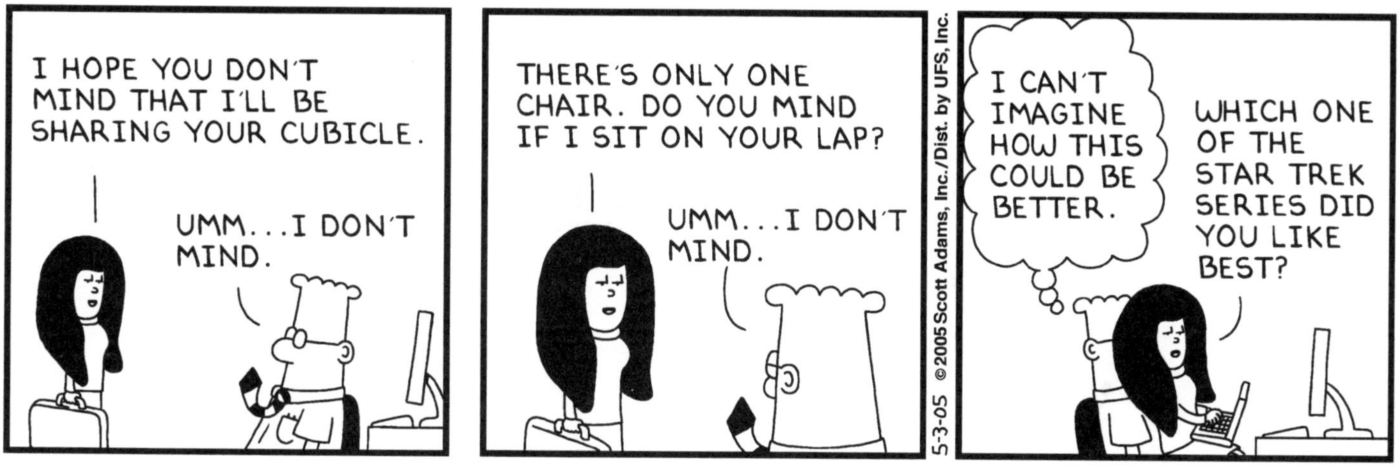
I HOPE YOU DON'T MIND THAT I'LL BE SHARING YOUR CUBICLE.
UMM...I DON'T MIND.
THERE'S ONLY ONE CHAIR. DO YOU MIND IF I SIT ON YOUR LAP?
UMM...I DON'T MIND.
5-3-05 © 2005 Scott Adams, Inc./Dist. by UFS, Inc.
I CAN'T IMAGINE HOW THIS COULD BE BETTER.
WHICH ONE OF THE STAR TREK SERIES DID YOU LIKE BEST?

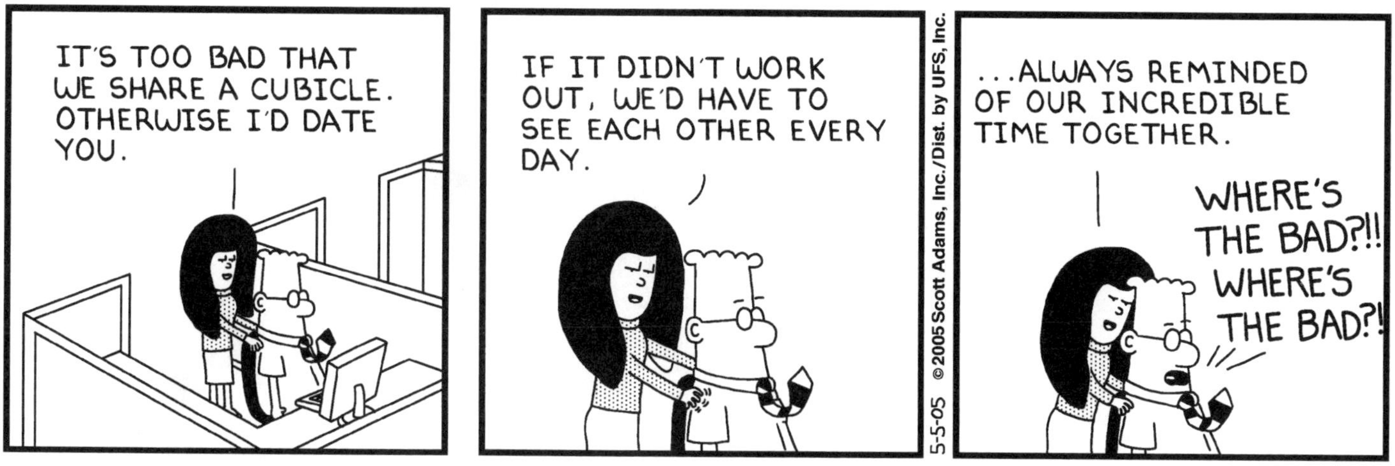
IT'S TOO BAD THAT WE SHARE A CUBICLE. OTHERWISE I'D DATE YOU.
IF IT DIDN'T WORK OUT, WE'D HAVE TO SEE EACH OTHER EVERY DAY.
5-5-05 © 2005 Scott Adams, Inc./Dist. by UFS, Inc.
...ALWAYS REMINDED OF OUR INCREDIBLE TIME TOGETHER.
WHERE'S THE BAD?!! WHERE'S THE BAD?!

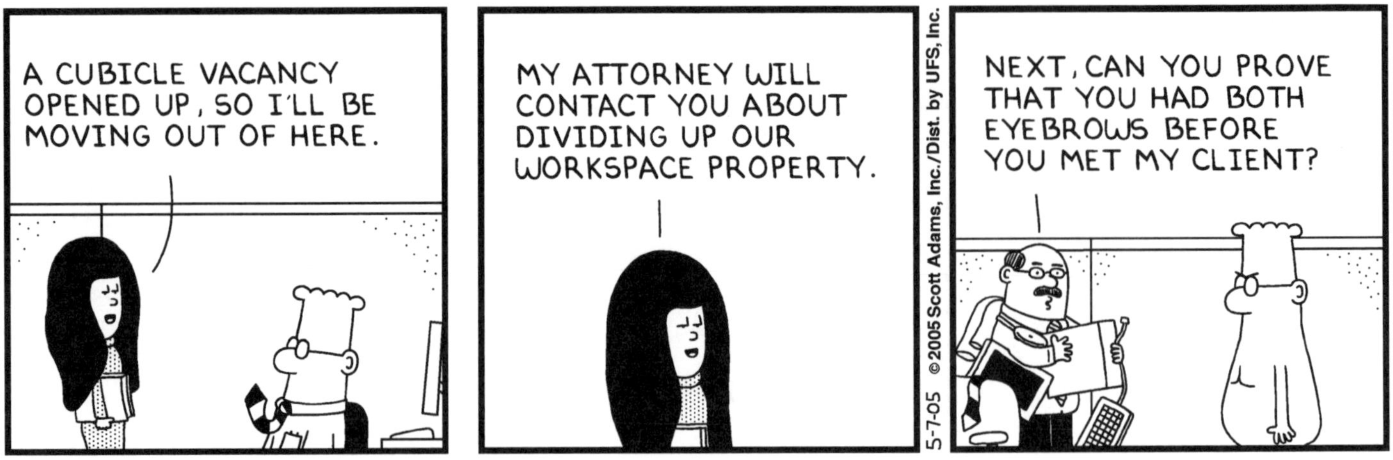
A CUBICLE VACANCY OPENED UP, SO I'LL BE MOVING OUT OF HERE.
MY ATTORNEY WILL CONTACT YOU ABOUT DIVIDING UP OUR WORKSPACE PROPERTY.
5-7-05 ©2005 Scott Adams, Inc./Dist. by UFS, Inc.
NEXT, CAN YOU PROVE THAT YOU HAD BOTH EYEBROWS BEFORE YOU MET MY CLIENT?

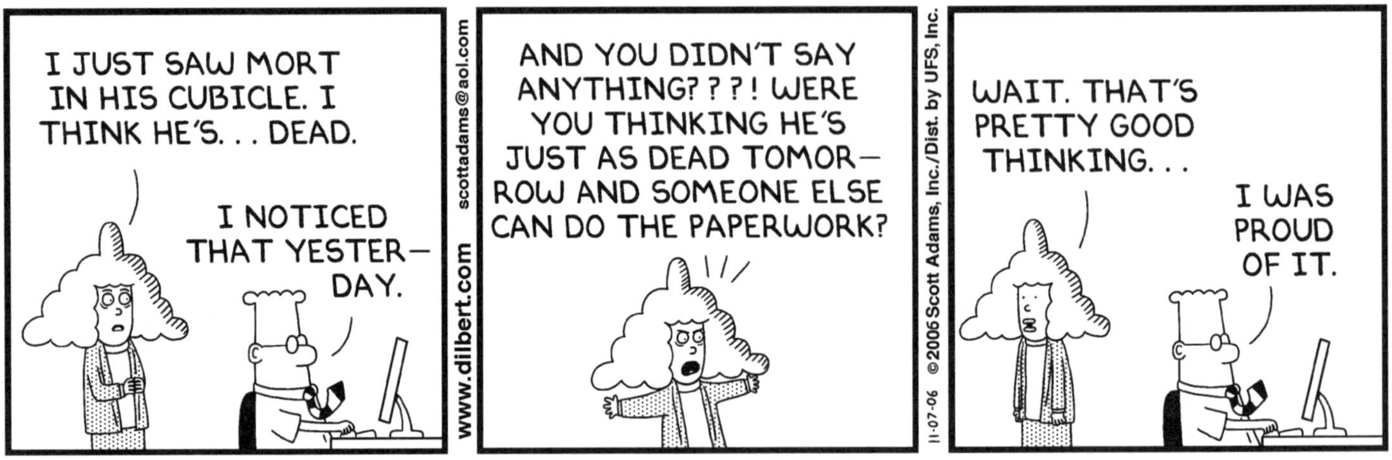
I JUST SAW MORT IN HIS CUBICLE. I THINK HE'S. . . DEAD.
I NOTICED THAT YESTER-DAY.
www.dilbert.com scottadams@aol.com
AND YOU DIDN'T SAY ANYTHING???! WERE YOU THINKING HE'S JUST AS DEAD TOMOR-ROW AND SOMEONE ELSE CAN DO THE PAPERWORK?
11-07-06 ©2006 Scott Adams, Inc./Dist. by UFS, Inc.
WAIT. THAT'S PRETTY GOOD THINKING. . .
I WAS PROUD OF IT.

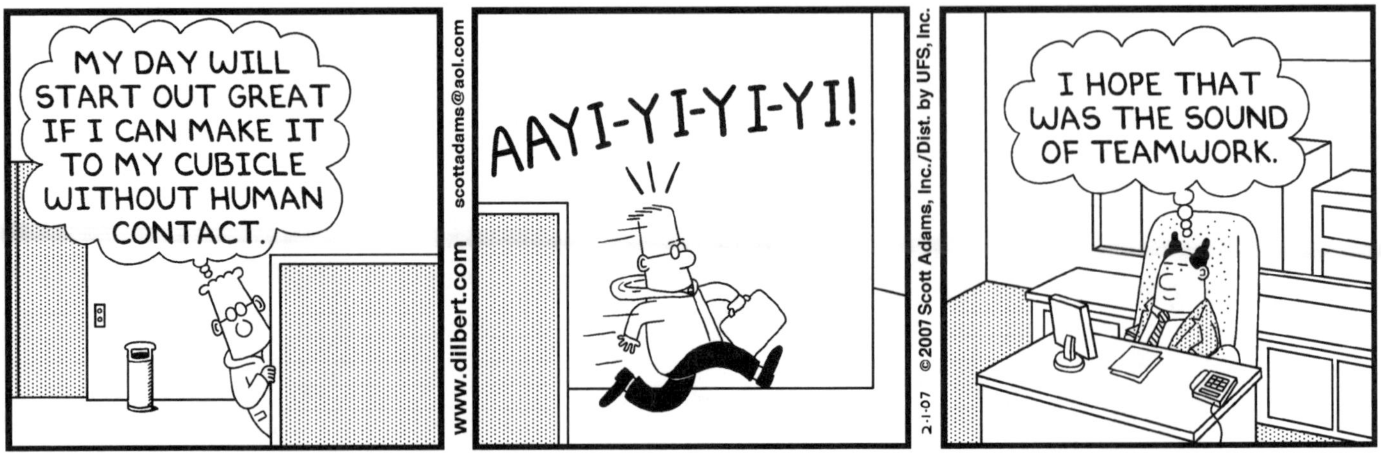
MY DAY WILL START OUT GREAT IF I CAN MAKE IT TO MY CUBICLE WITHOUT HUMAN CONTACT.
www.dilbert.com scottadams@aol.com
AAYI-YI-YI-YI!
2-1-07 ©2007 Scott Adams, Inc./Dist. by UFS, Inc.
I HOPE THAT WAS THE SOUND OF TEAMWORK.

3. Dogbert

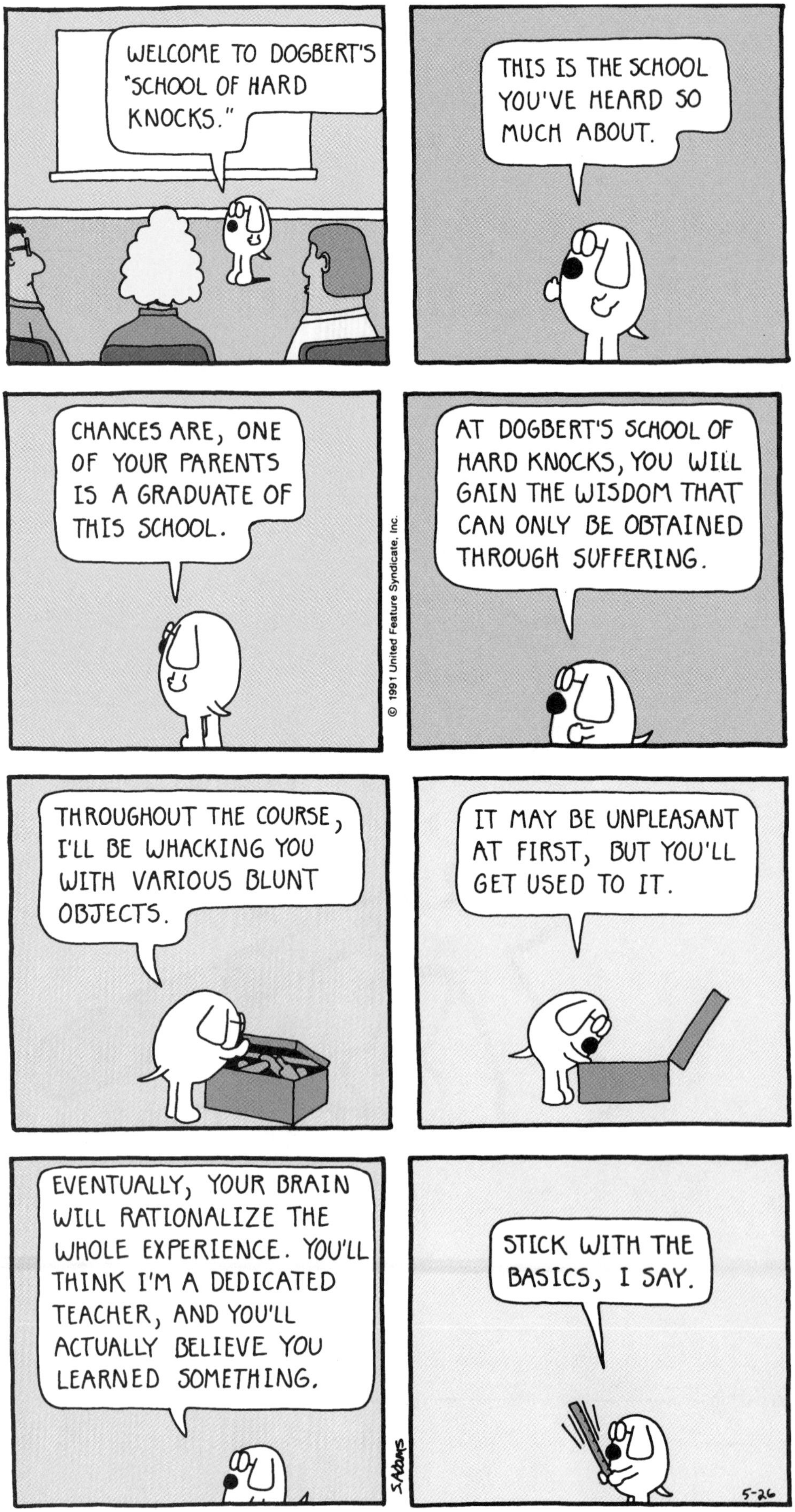
WELCOME TO DOGBERT'S "SCHOOL OF HARD KNOCKS."
THIS IS THE SCHOOL YOU'VE HEARD SO MUCH ABOUT.
CHANCES ARE, ONE OF YOUR PARENTS IS A GRADUATE OF THIS SCHOOL.
AT DOGBERT'S SCHOOL OF HARD KNOCKS, YOU WILL GAIN THE WISDOM THAT CAN ONLY BE OBTAINED THROUGH SUFFERING.
THROUGHOUT THE COURSE, I'LL BE WHACKING YOU WITH VARIOUS BLUNT OBJECTS.
IT MAY BE UNPLEASANT AT FIRST, BUT YOU'LL GET USED TO IT.
EVENTUALLY, YOUR BRAIN WILL RATIONALIZE THE WHOLE EXPERIENCE. YOU'LL THINK I'M A DEDICATED TEACHER, AND YOU'LL ACTUALLY BELIEVE YOU LEARNED SOMETHING.
STICK WITH THE BASICS, I SAY.
© 1991 United Feature Syndicate, Inc.
S.ADAMS
5-26

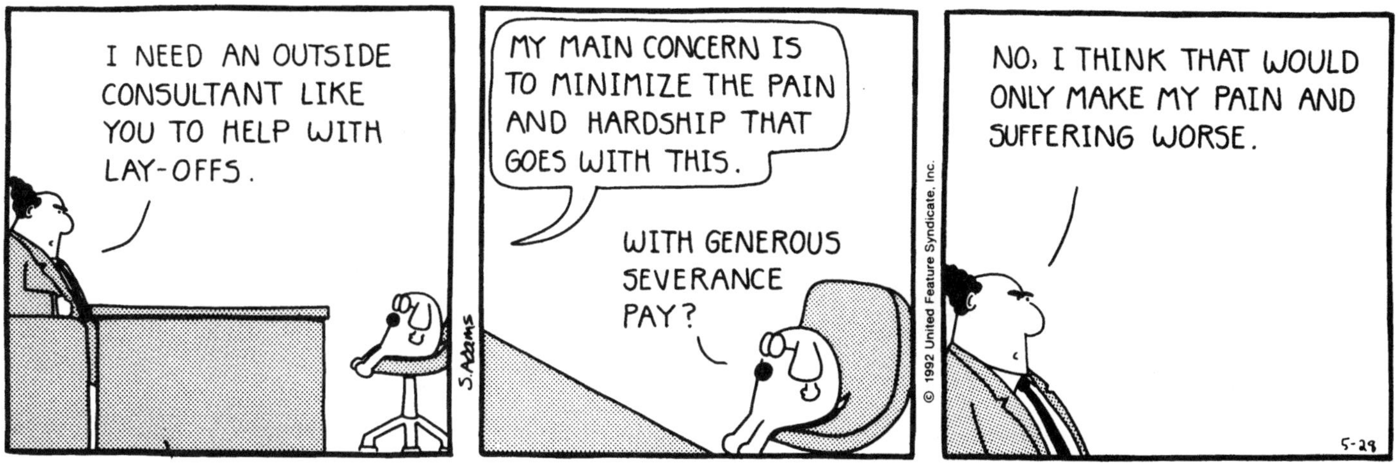
I NEED AN OUTSIDE CONSULTANT LIKE YOU TO HELP WITH LAY-OFFS.
MY MAIN CONCERN IS TO MINIMIZE THE PAIN AND HARDSHIP THAT GOES WITH THIS.
WITH GENEROUS SEVERANCE PAY?
NO, I THINK THAT WOULD ONLY MAKE MY PAIN AND SUFFERING WORSE.
S. Adams
© 1992 United Feature Syndicate, Inc.
5-28

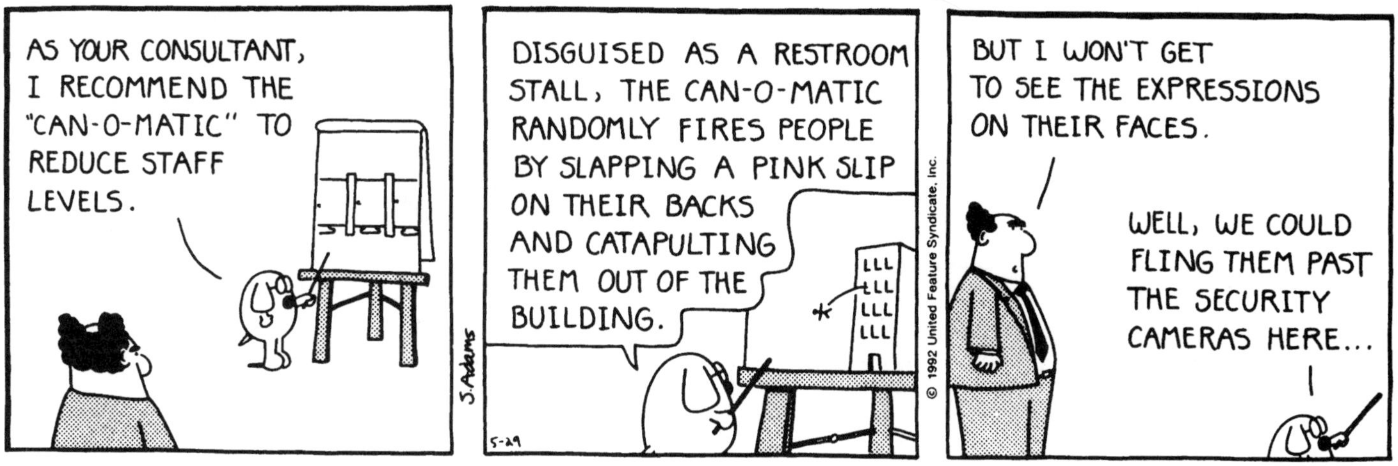
AS YOUR CONSULTANT, I RECOMMEND THE "CAN-O-MATIC" TO REDUCE STAFF LEVELS.
DISGUISED AS A RESTROOM STALL, THE CAN-O-MATIC RANDOMLY FIRES PEOPLE BY SLAPPING A PINK SLIP ON THEIR BACKS AND CATAPULTING THEM OUT OF THE BUILDING.
BUT I WON'T GET TO SEE THE EXPRESSIONS ON THEIR FACES.
WELL, WE COULD FLING THEM PAST THE SECURITY CAMERAS HERE...
S. Adams
5-29
© 1992 United Feature Syndicate, Inc.

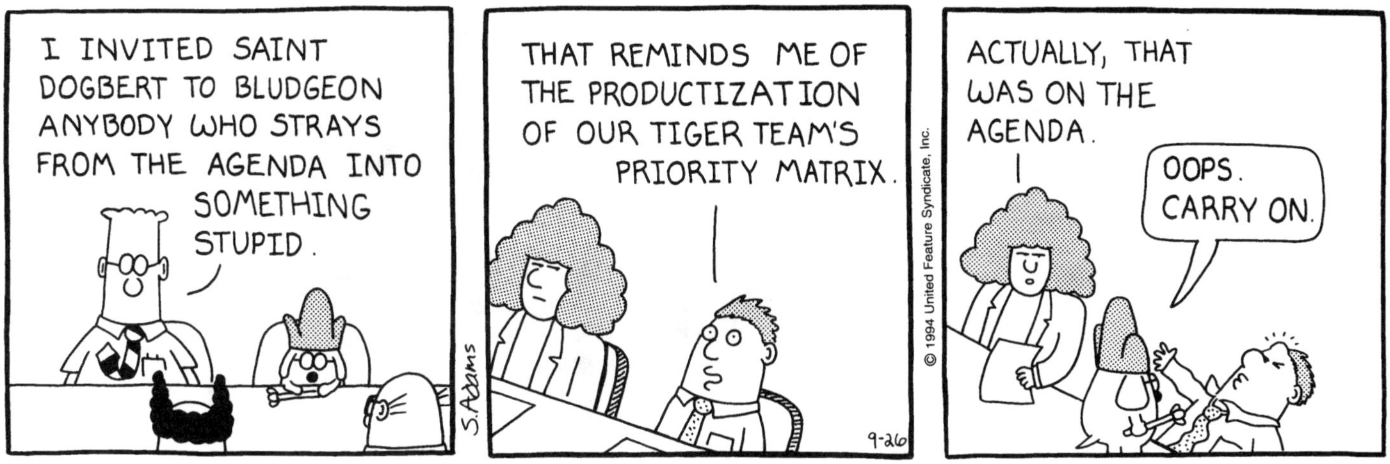
I INVITED SAINT DOGBERT TO BLUDGEON ANYBODY WHO STRAYS FROM THE AGENDA INTO SOMETHING STUPID.
THAT REMINDS ME OF THE PRODUCTIZATION OF OUR TIGER TEAM'S PRIORITY MATRIX.
ACTUALLY, THAT WAS ON THE AGENDA.
OOPS. CARRY ON.
S. Adams
9-26
© 1994 United Feature Syndicate, Inc.

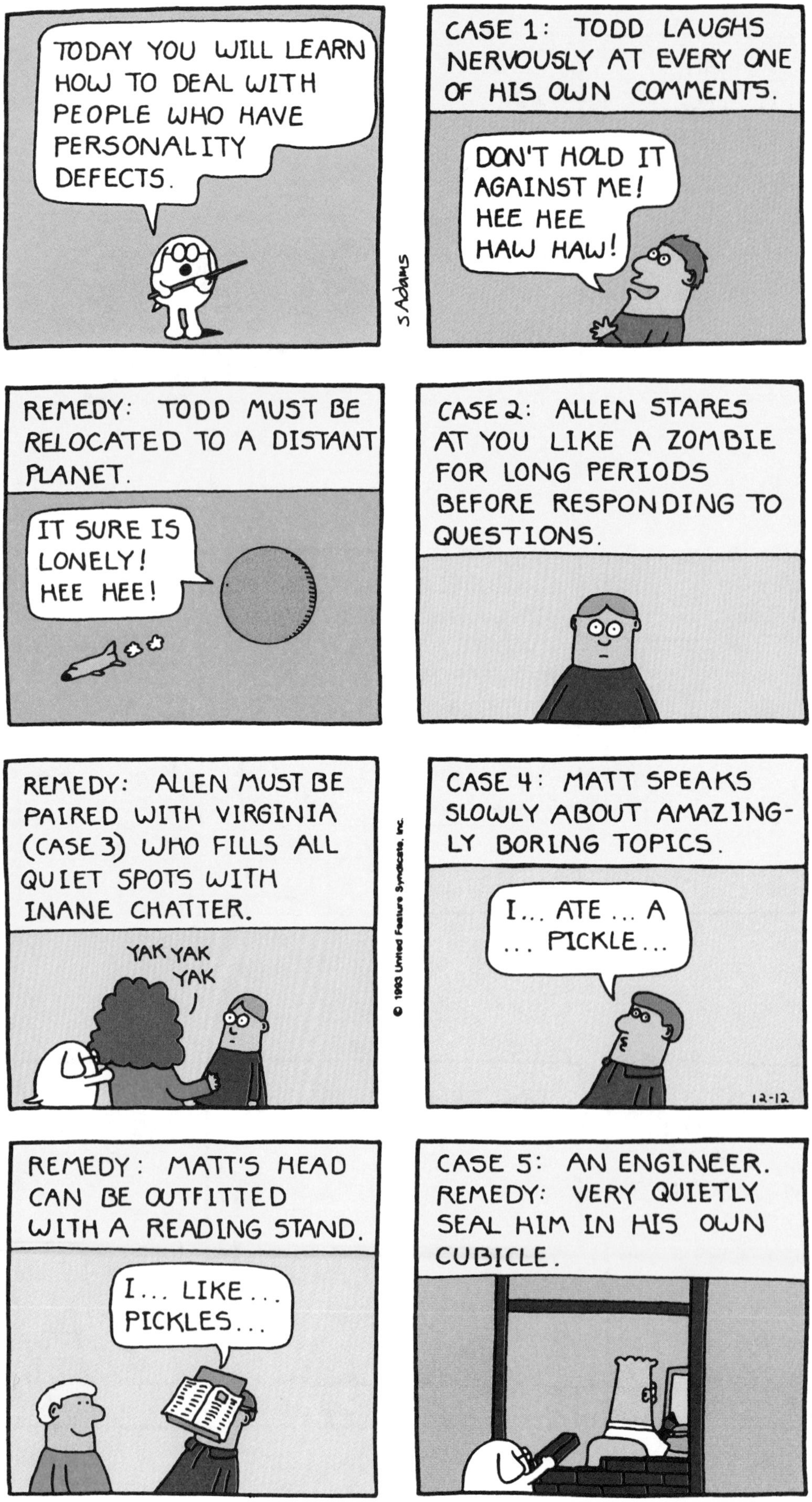
TODAY YOU WILL LEARN HOW TO DEAL WITH PEOPLE WHO HAVE PERSONALITY DEFECTS.
S Adams
CASE 1: TODD LAUGHS NERVOUSLY AT EVERY ONE OF HIS OWN COMMENTS.
DON'T HOLD IT AGAINST ME! HEE HEE HAW HAW!
REMEDY: TODD MUST BE RELOCATED TO A DISTANT PLANET.
IT SURE IS LONELY! HEE HEE!
CASE 2: ALLEN STARES AT YOU LIKE A ZOMBIE FOR LONG PERIODS BEFORE RESPONDING TO QUESTIONS.
REMEDY: ALLEN MUST BE PAIRED WITH VIRGINIA (CASE 3) WHO FILLS ALL QUIET SPOTS WITH INANE CHATTER.
YAK YAK YAK
© 1993 United Feature Syndicate, Inc.
CASE 4: MATT SPEAKS SLOWLY ABOUT AMAZINGLY BORING TOPICS.
I... ATE ... A ... PICKLE...
12-12
REMEDY: MATT'S HEAD CAN BE OUTFITTED WITH A READING STAND.
I... LIKE... PICKLES...
CASE 5: AN ENGINEER. REMEDY: VERY QUIETLY SEAL HIM IN HIS OWN CUBICLE.

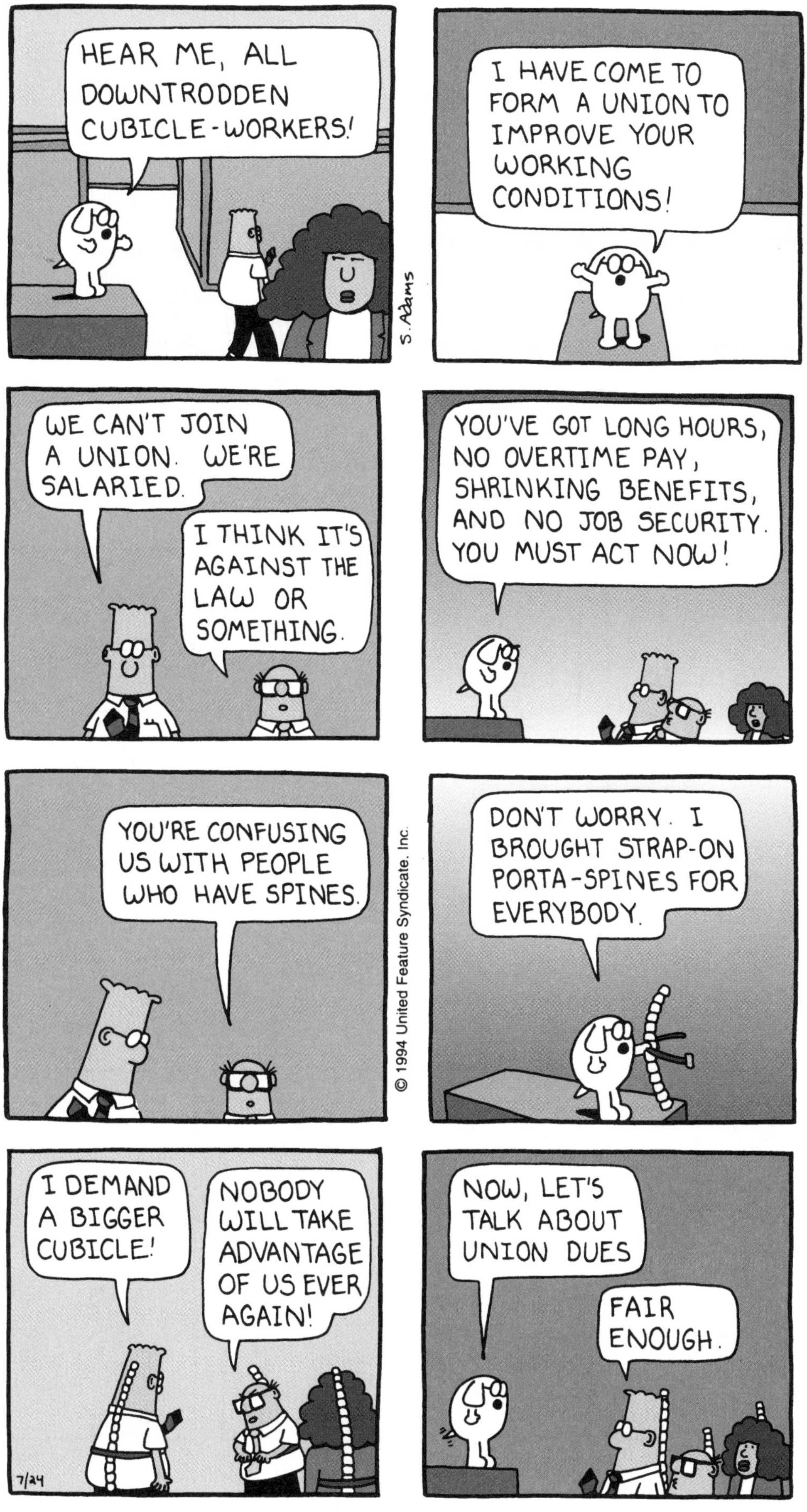
HEAR ME, ALL DOWNTRODDEN CUBICLE-WORKERS!
S. Adams
I HAVE COME TO FORM A UNION TO IMPROVE YOUR WORKING CONDITIONS!
WE CAN'T JOIN A UNION. WE'RE SALARIED.
I THINK IT'S AGAINST THE LAW OR SOMETHING.
YOU'VE GOT LONG HOURS, NO OVERTIME PAY, SHRINKING BENEFITS, AND NO JOB SECURITY. YOU MUST ACT NOW!
YOU'RE CONFUSING US WITH PEOPLE WHO HAVE SPINES.
DON'T WORRY. I BROUGHT STRAP-ON PORTA-SPINES FOR EVERYBODY.
I DEMAND A BIGGER CUBICLE!
NOBODY WILL TAKE ADVANTAGE OF US EVER AGAIN!
7/24
NOW, LET'S TALK ABOUT UNION DUES.
FAIR ENOUGH.

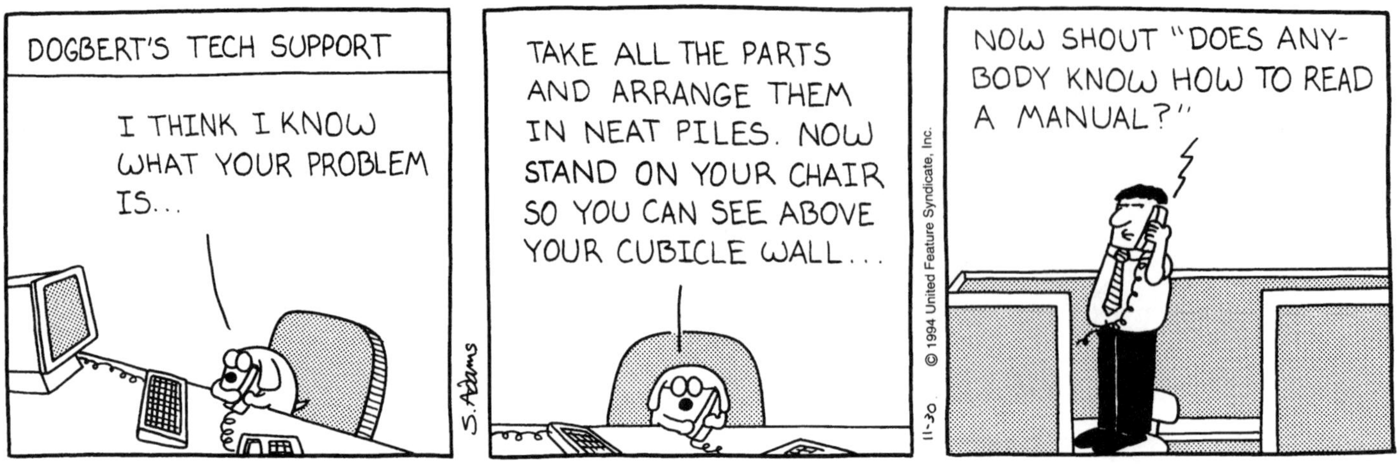
DOGBERT'S TECH SUPPORT
I THINK I KNOW WHAT YOUR PROBLEM IS...
S. Adams
TAKE ALL THE PARTS AND ARRANGE THEM IN NEAT PILES. NOW STAND ON YOUR CHAIR SO YOU CAN SEE ABOVE YOUR CUBICLE WALL...
11-30 © 1994 United Feature Syndicate, Inc.
NOW SHOUT "DOES ANYBODY KNOW HOW TO READ A MANUAL?"

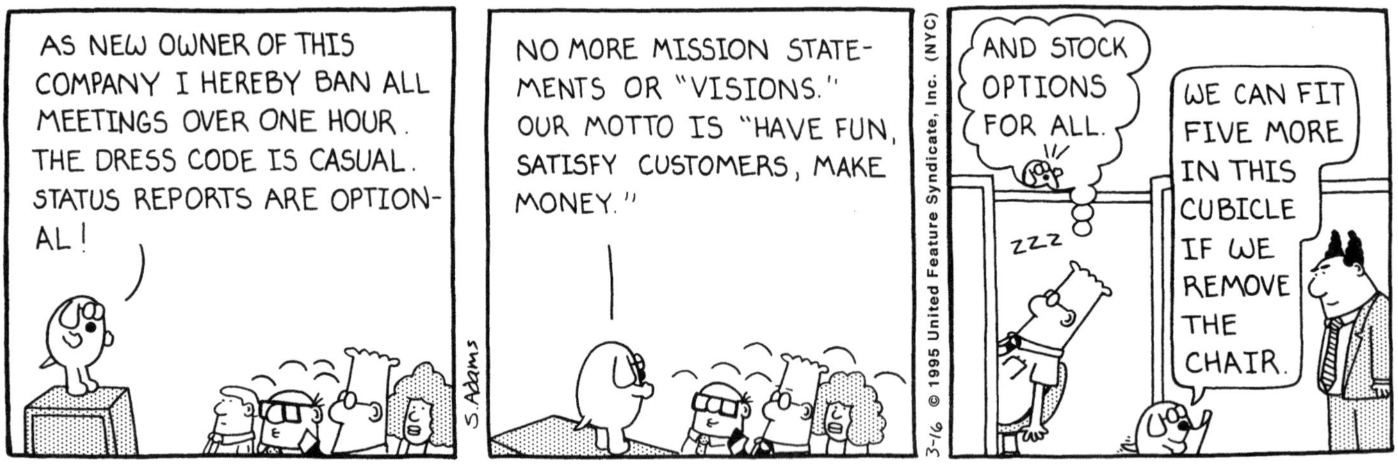
AS NEW OWNER OF THIS COMPANY I HEREBY BAN ALL MEETINGS OVER ONE HOUR. THE DRESS CODE IS CASUAL. STATUS REPORTS ARE OPTIONAL!
S. Adams
NO MORE MISSION STATEMENTS OR "VISIONS." OUR MOTTO IS "HAVE FUN, SATISFY CUSTOMERS, MAKE MONEY."
3-16 © 1995 United Feature Syndicate, Inc. (NYC)
AND STOCK OPTIONS FOR ALL.
ZZZ
WE CAN FIT FIVE MORE IN THIS CUBICLE IF WE REMOVE THE CHAIR.

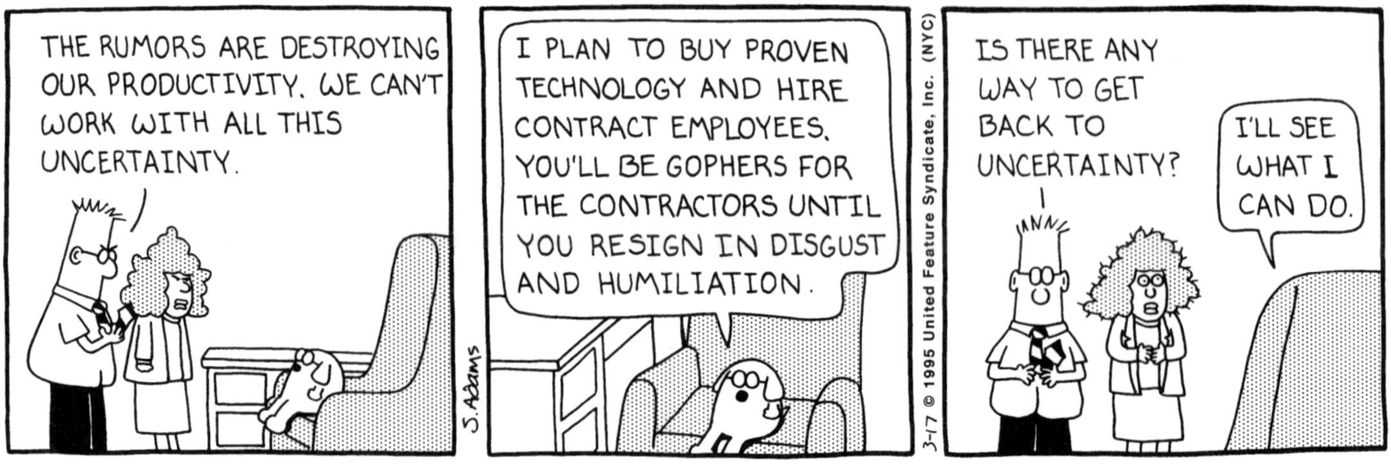
THE RUMORS ARE DESTROYING OUR PRODUCTIVITY. WE CAN'T WORK WITH ALL THIS UNCERTAINTY.
S. Adams
I PLAN TO BUY PROVEN TECHNOLOGY AND HIRE CONTRACT EMPLOYEES. YOU'LL BE GOPHERS FOR THE CONTRACTORS UNTIL YOU RESIGN IN DISGUST AND HUMILIATION.
3-17 © 1995 United Feature Syndicate, Inc. (NYC)
IS THERE ANY WAY TO GET BACK TO UNCERTAINTY?
I'LL SEE WHAT I CAN DO.

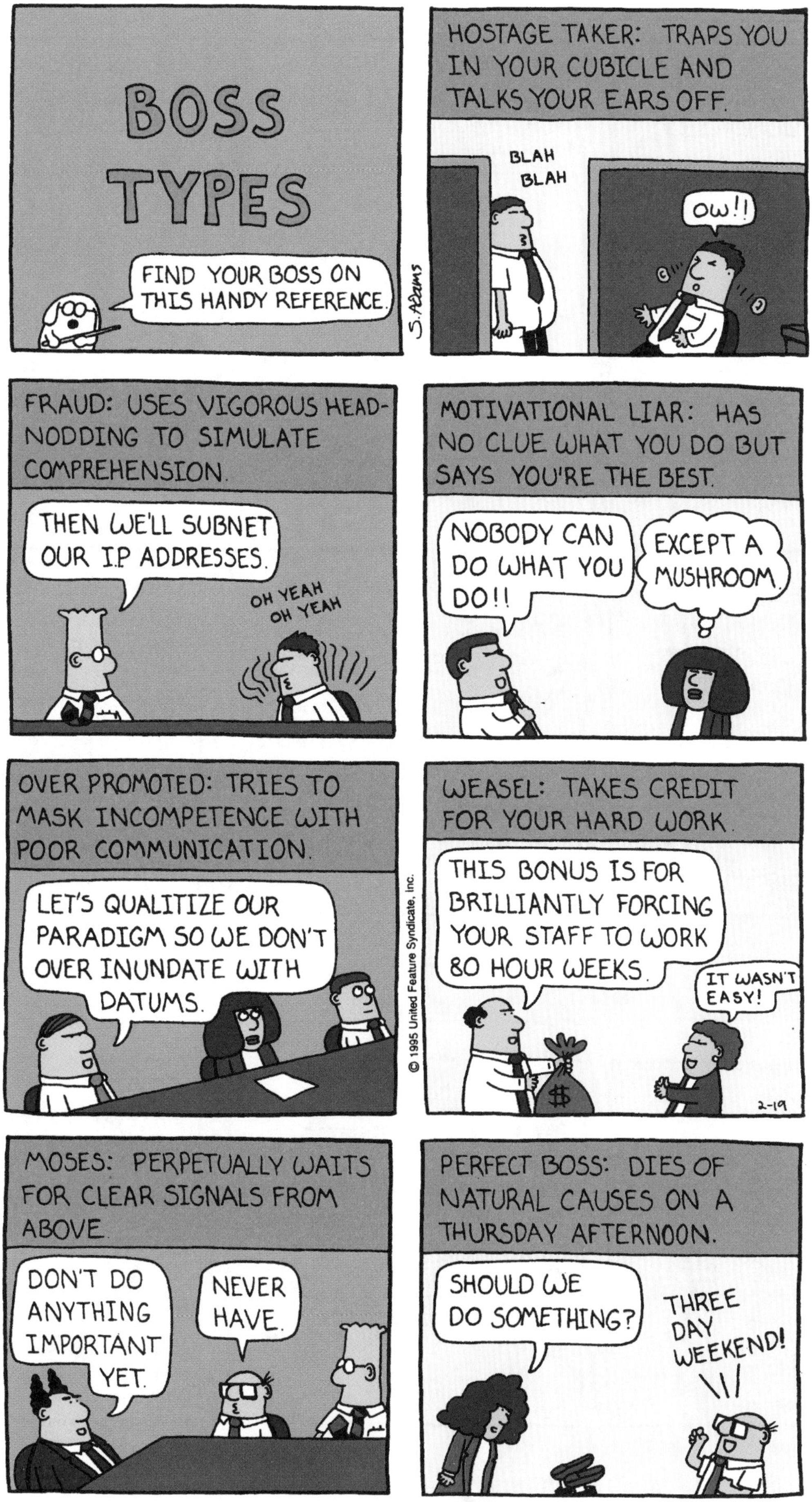
BOSS TYPES
FIND YOUR BOSS ON THIS HANDY REFERENCE.
S. ADAMS
HOSTAGE TAKER: TRAPS YOU IN YOUR CUBICLE AND TALKS YOUR EARS OFF.
BLAH BLAH
OW!!
FRAUD: USES VIGOROUS HEAD-NODDING TO SIMULATE COMPREHENSION.
THEN WE'LL SUBNET OUR I.P. ADDRESSES.
OH YEAH OH YEAH
MOTIVATIONAL LIAR: HAS NO CLUE WHAT YOU DO BUT SAYS YOU'RE THE BEST.
NOBODY CAN DO WHAT YOU DO!!
EXCEPT A MUSHROOM.
OVER PROMOTED: TRIES TO MASK INCOMPETENCE WITH POOR COMMUNICATION.
LET'S QUALITIZE OUR PARADIGM SO WE DON'T OVER INUNDATE WITH DATUMS.
© 1995 United Feature Syndicate, Inc.
WEASEL: TAKES CREDIT FOR YOUR HARD WORK.
THIS BONUS IS FOR BRILLIANTLY FORCING YOUR STAFF TO WORK 80 HOUR WEEKS.
IT WASN'T EASY!
2-19
MOSES: PERPETUALLY WAITS FOR CLEAR SIGNALS FROM ABOVE.
DON'T DO ANYTHING IMPORTANT YET.
NEVER HAVE.
PERFECT BOSS: DIES OF NATURAL CAUSES ON A THURSDAY AFTERNOON.
SHOULD WE DO SOMETHING?
THREE DAY WEEKEND!

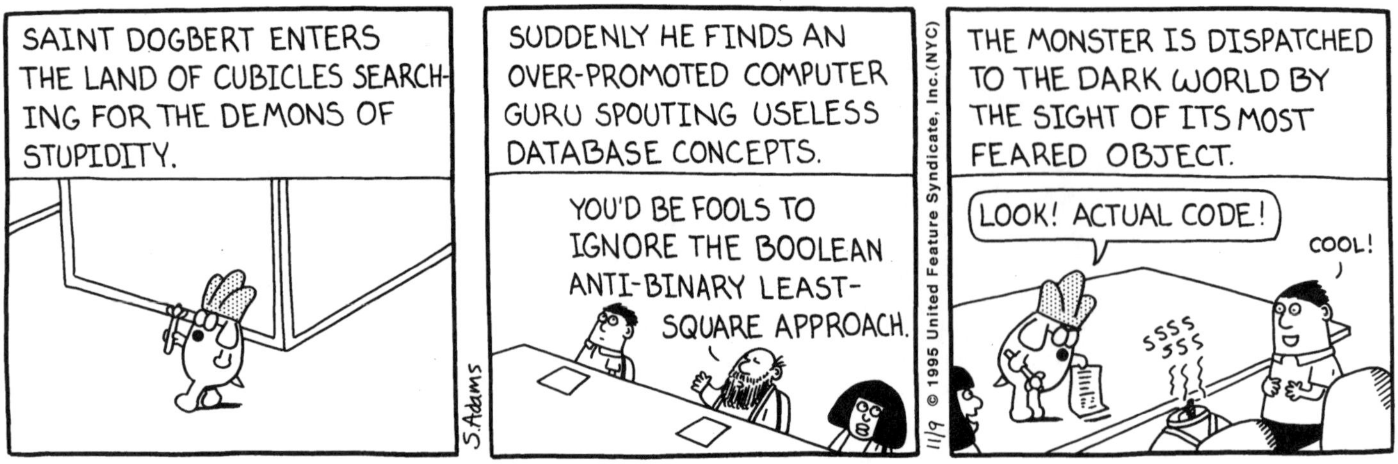
SAINT DOGBERT ENTERS THE LAND OF CUBICLES SEARCHING FOR THE DEMONS OF STUPIDITY.
S.Adams
SUDDENLY HE FINDS AN OVER-PROMOTED COMPUTER GURU SPOUTING USELESS DATABASE CONCEPTS.
YOU'D BE FOOLS TO IGNORE THE BOOLEAN ANTI-BINARY LEAST-SQUARE APPROACH.
11/9 © 1995 United Feature Syndicate, Inc.(NYC)
THE MONSTER IS DISPATCHED TO THE DARK WORLD BY THE SIGHT OF ITS MOST FEARED OBJECT.
LOOK! ACTUAL CODE!
COOL!
SSSS SSS

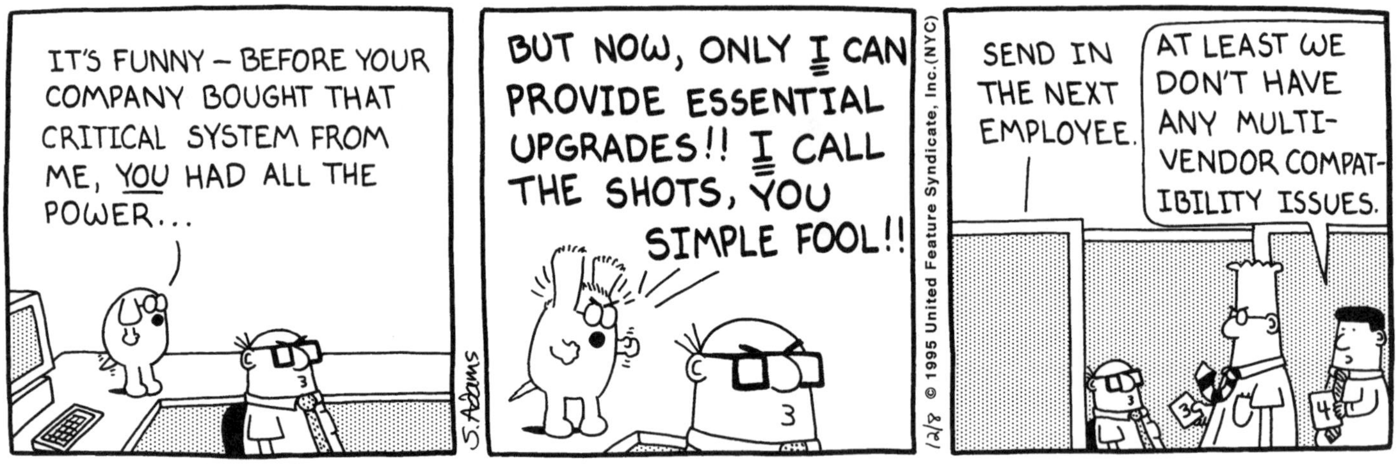
IT'S FUNNY – BEFORE YOUR COMPANY BOUGHT THAT CRITICAL SYSTEM FROM ME, YOU HAD ALL THE POWER...
S.Adams
BUT NOW, ONLY I CAN PROVIDE ESSENTIAL UPGRADES!! I CALL THE SHOTS, YOU SIMPLE FOOL!!
12/8 © 1995 United Feature Syndicate, Inc.(NYC)
SEND IN THE NEXT EMPLOYEE.
AT LEAST WE DON'T HAVE ANY MULTI-VENDOR COMPATIBILITY ISSUES.

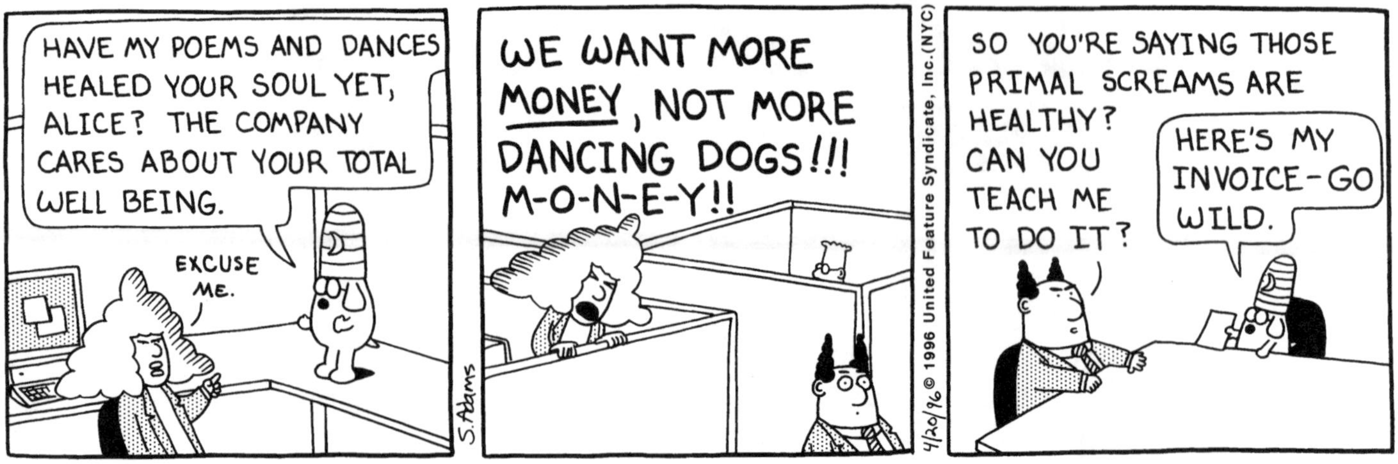
HAVE MY POEMS AND DANCES HEALED YOUR SOUL YET, ALICE? THE COMPANY CARES ABOUT YOUR TOTAL WELL BEING.
EXCUSE ME.
S.Adams
WE WANT MORE MONEY, NOT MORE DANCING DOGS!!! M-O-N-E-Y!!
4/20/96 © 1996 United Feature Syndicate, Inc.(NYC)
SO YOU'RE SAYING THOSE PRIMAL SCREAMS ARE HEALTHY? CAN YOU TEACH ME TO DO IT?
HERE'S MY INVOICE–GO WILD.

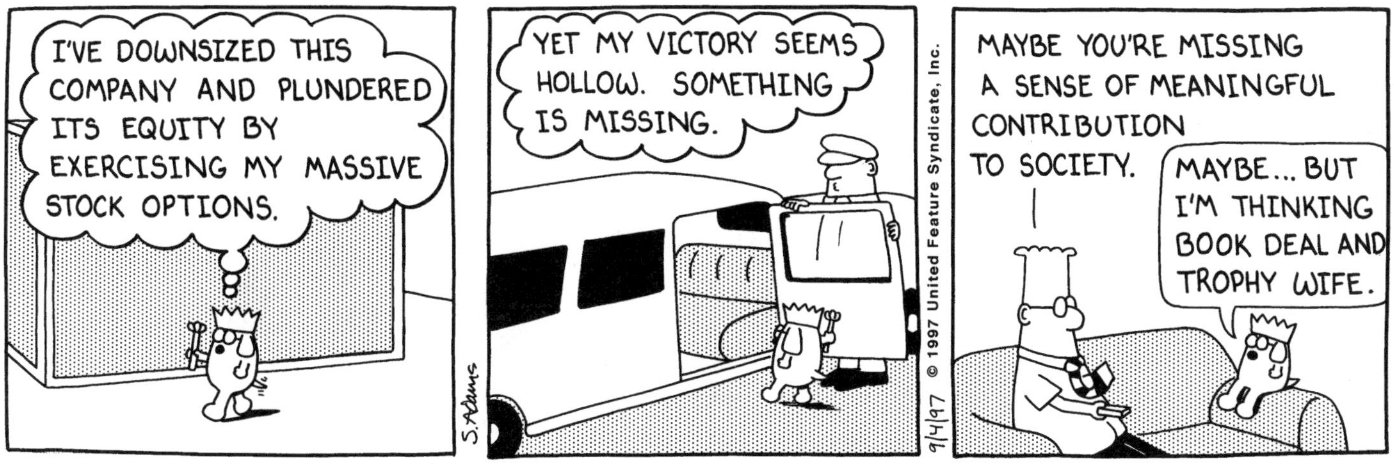
I'VE DOWNSIZED THIS COMPANY AND PLUNDERED ITS EQUITY BY EXERCISING MY MASSIVE STOCK OPTIONS.
YET MY VICTORY SEEMS HOLLOW. SOMETHING IS MISSING.
MAYBE YOU'RE MISSING A SENSE OF MEANINGFUL CONTRIBUTION TO SOCIETY.
MAYBE... BUT I'M THINKING BOOK DEAL AND TROPHY WIFE.
9/4/97 © 1997 United Feature Syndicate, Inc.

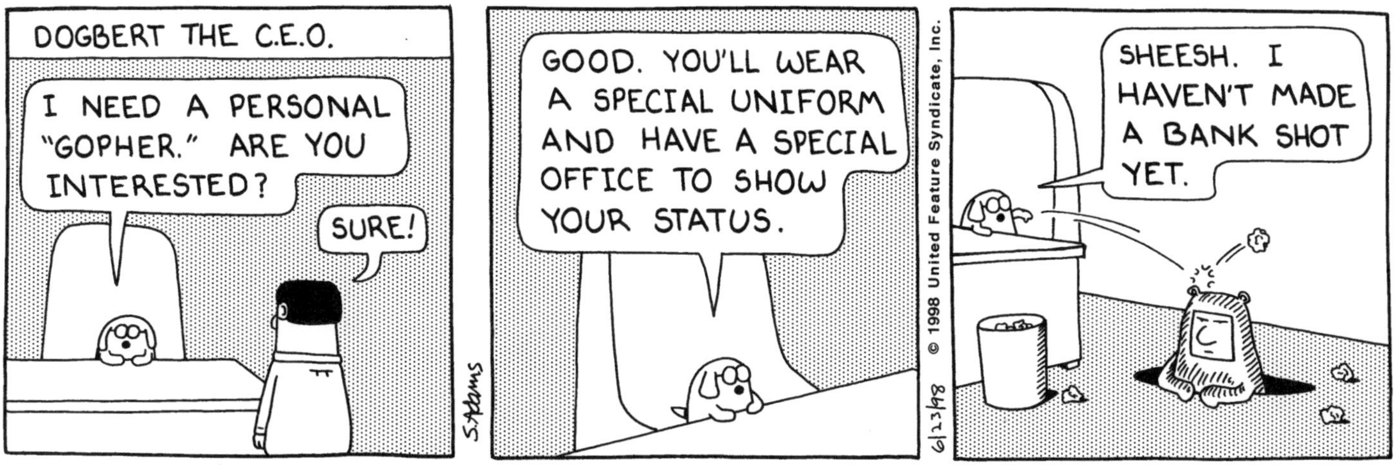
DOGBERT THE C.E.O.
I NEED A PERSONAL "GOPHER." ARE YOU INTERESTED?
SURE!
GOOD. YOU'LL WEAR A SPECIAL UNIFORM AND HAVE A SPECIAL OFFICE TO SHOW YOUR STATUS.
SHEESH. I HAVEN'T MADE A BANK SHOT YET.
6/13/98 © 1998 United Feature Syndicate, Inc.

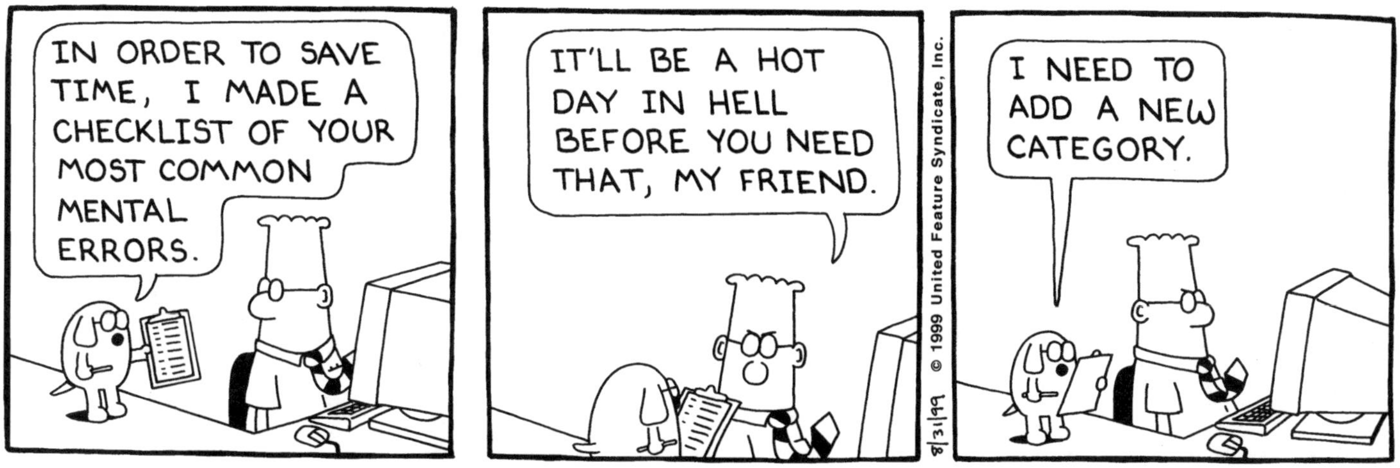
IN ORDER TO SAVE TIME, I MADE A CHECKLIST OF YOUR MOST COMMON MENTAL ERRORS.
IT'LL BE A HOT DAY IN HELL BEFORE YOU NEED THAT, MY FRIEND.
I NEED TO ADD A NEW CATEGORY.
8/31/99 © 1999 United Feature Syndicate, Inc.

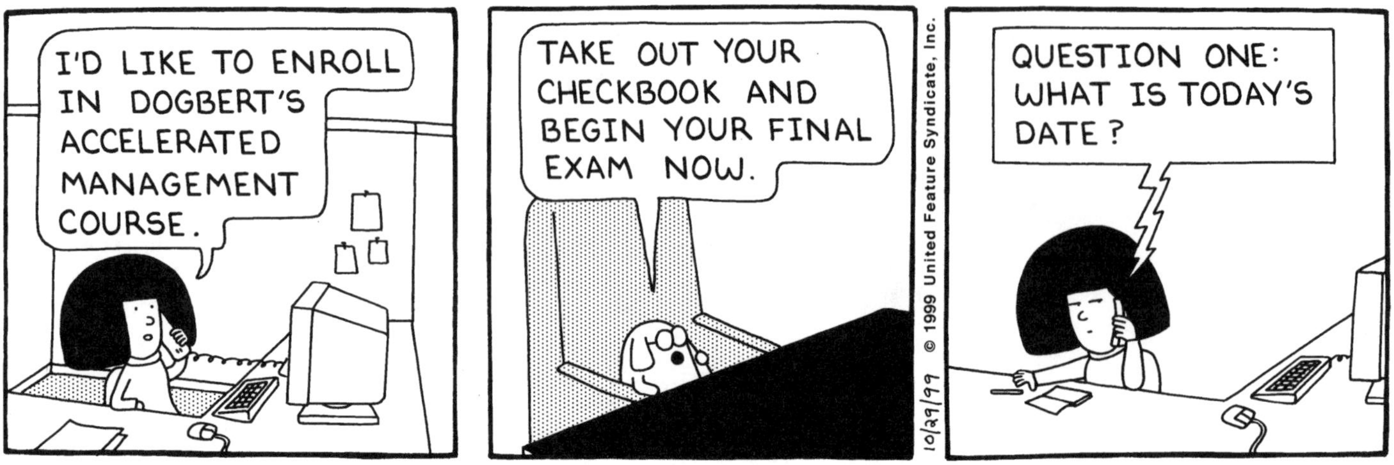
I'D LIKE TO ENROLL IN DOGBERT'S ACCELERATED MANAGEMENT COURSE.
TAKE OUT YOUR CHECKBOOK AND BEGIN YOUR FINAL EXAM NOW.
QUESTION ONE: WHAT IS TODAY'S DATE?
10/29/99 © 1999 United Feature Syndicate, Inc.

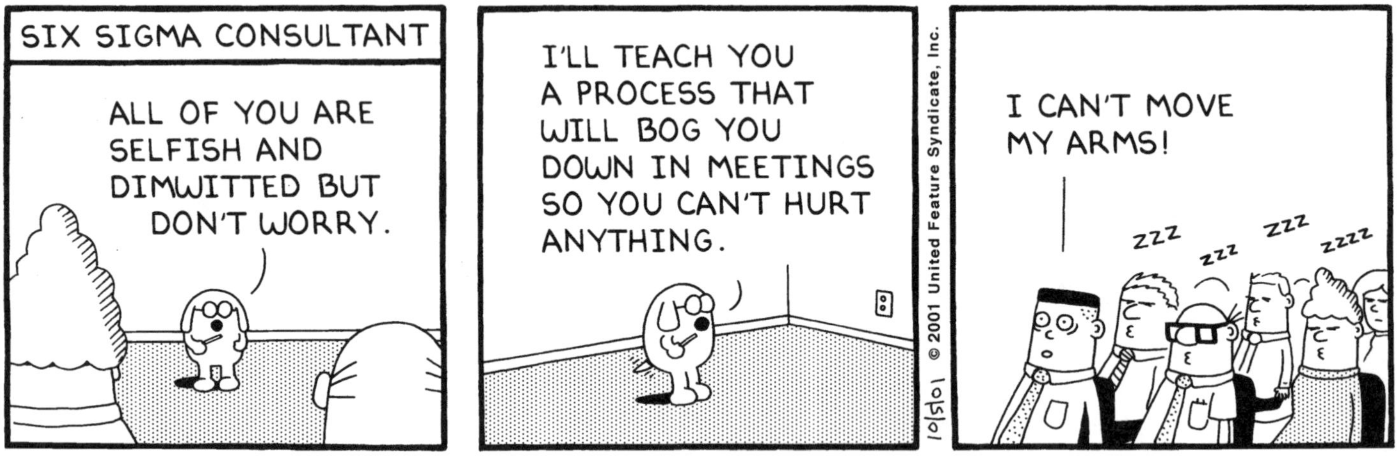
SIX SIGMA CONSULTANT
ALL OF YOU ARE SELFISH AND DIMWITTED BUT DON'T WORRY.
I'LL TEACH YOU A PROCESS THAT WILL BOG YOU DOWN IN MEETINGS SO YOU CAN'T HURT ANYTHING.
I CAN'T MOVE MY ARMS!
ZZZ
ZZZ
ZZZ
ZZZZ
10/5/01 © 2001 United Feature Syndicate, Inc.

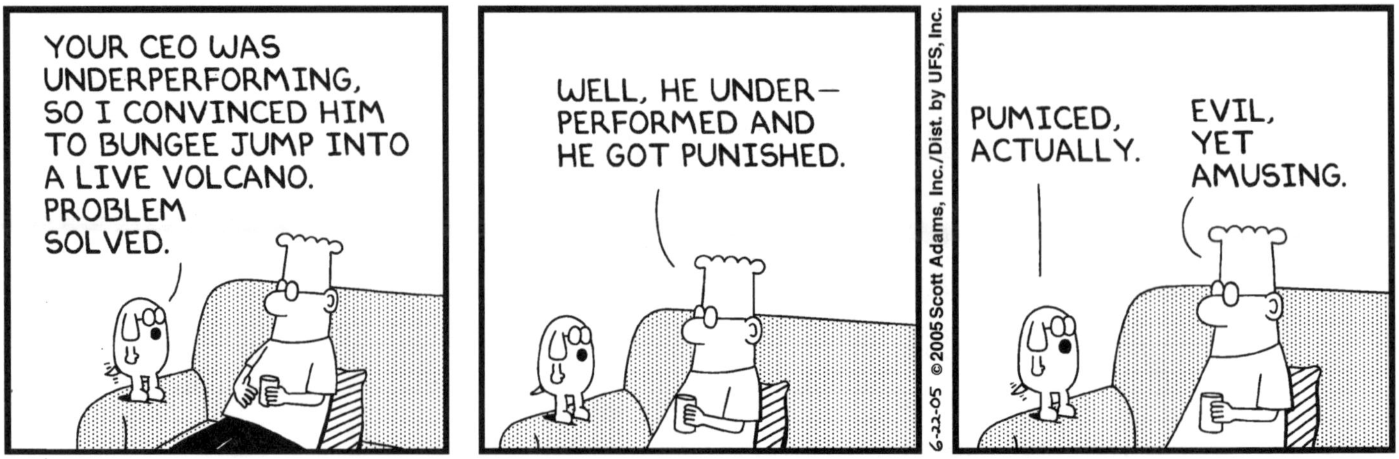
YOUR CEO WAS UNDERPERFORMING, SO I CONVINCED HIM TO BUNGEE JUMP INTO A LIVE VOLCANO. PROBLEM SOLVED.
WELL, HE UNDER-PERFORMED AND HE GOT PUNISHED.
PUMICED, ACTUALLY.
EVIL, YET AMUSING.
6-22-05 © 2005 Scott Adams, Inc./Dist. by UFS, Inc.

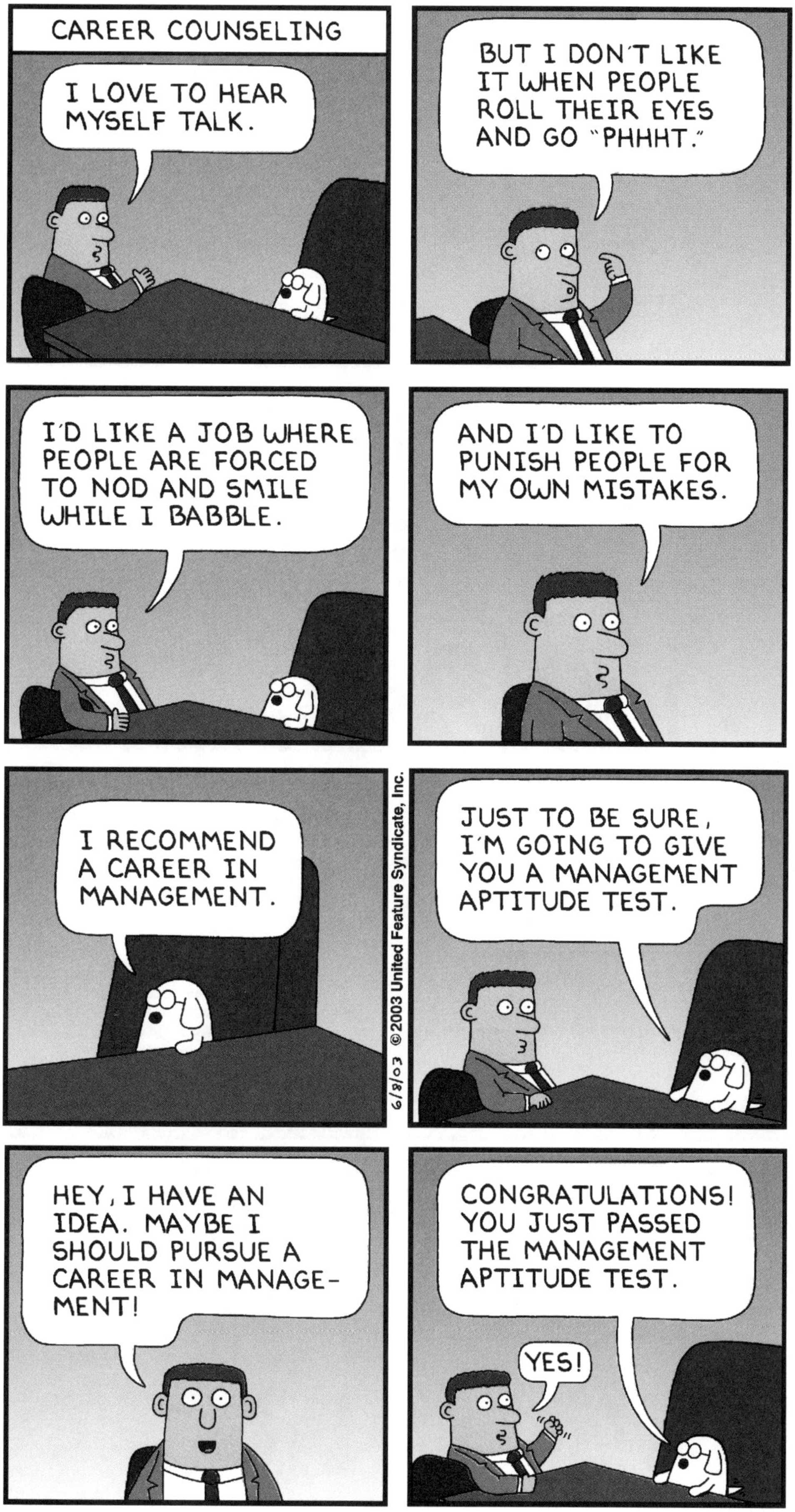
CAREER COUNSELING
I LOVE TO HEAR MYSELF TALK.
BUT I DON'T LIKE IT WHEN PEOPLE ROLL THEIR EYES AND GO "PHHHT."
I'D LIKE A JOB WHERE PEOPLE ARE FORCED TO NOD AND SMILE WHILE I BABBLE.
AND I'D LIKE TO PUNISH PEOPLE FOR MY OWN MISTAKES.
I RECOMMEND A CAREER IN MANAGEMENT.
6/8/03 ©2003 United Feature Syndicate, Inc.
JUST TO BE SURE, I'M GOING TO GIVE YOU A MANAGEMENT APTITUDE TEST.
HEY, I HAVE AN IDEA. MAYBE I SHOULD PURSUE A CAREER IN MANAGE-MENT!
CONGRATULATIONS! YOU JUST PASSED THE MANAGEMENT APTITUDE TEST.
YES!

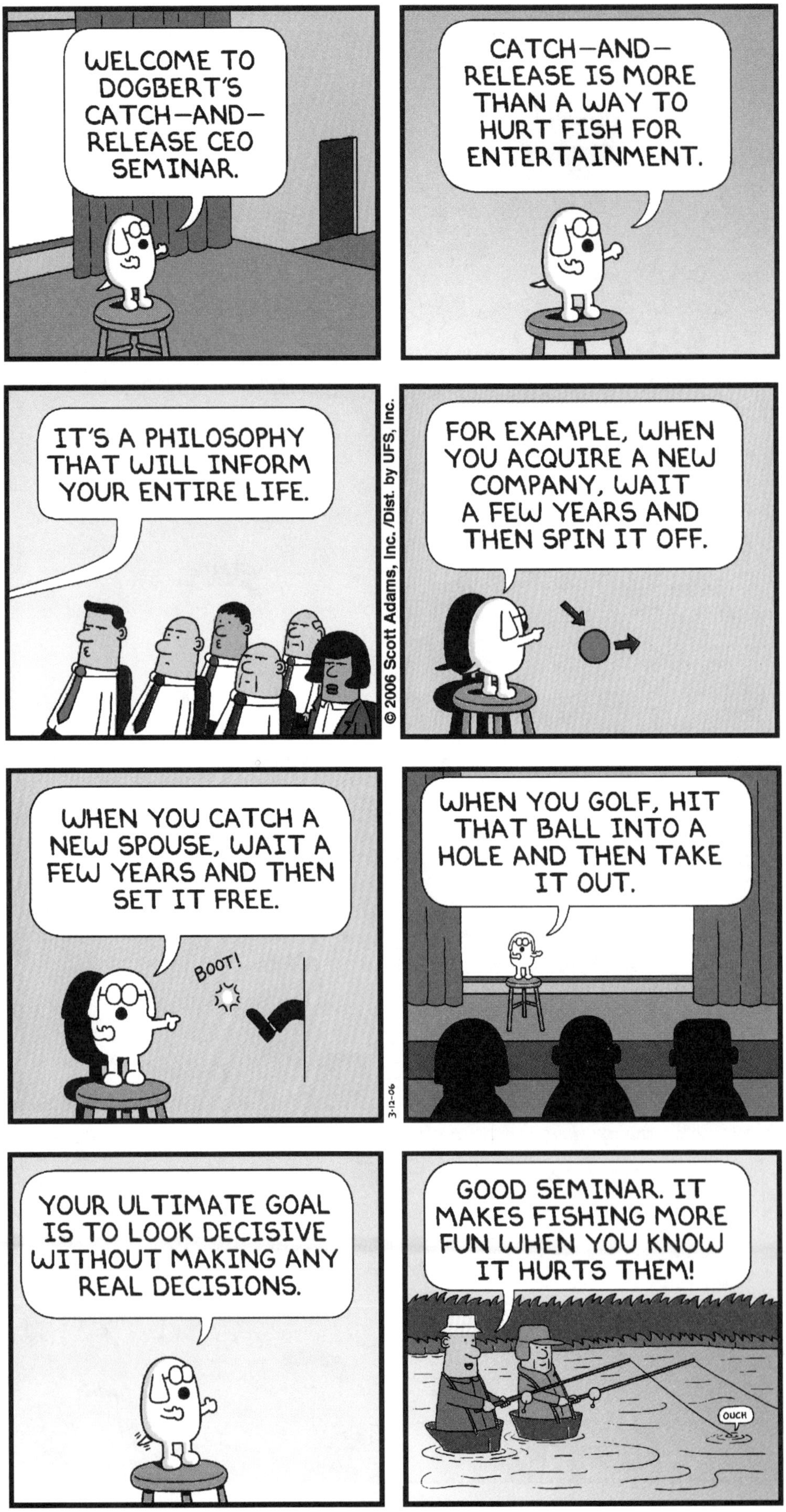

WELCOME TO DOGBERT'S CATCH-AND-RELEASE CEO SEMINAR.
CATCH-AND-RELEASE IS MORE THAN A WAY TO HURT FISH FOR ENTERTAINMENT.
IT'S A PHILOSOPHY THAT WILL INFORM YOUR ENTIRE LIFE.
© 2006 Scott Adams, Inc./Dist. by UFS, Inc.
FOR EXAMPLE, WHEN YOU ACQUIRE A NEW COMPANY, WAIT A FEW YEARS AND THEN SPIN IT OFF.
WHEN YOU CATCH A NEW SPOUSE, WAIT A FEW YEARS AND THEN SET IT FREE.
BOOT!
3-12-06
WHEN YOU GOLF, HIT THAT BALL INTO A HOLE AND THEN TAKE IT OUT.
YOUR ULTIMATE GOAL IS TO LOOK DECISIVE WITHOUT MAKING ANY REAL DECISIONS.
GOOD SEMINAR. IT MAKES FISHING MORE FUN WHEN YOU KNOW IT HURTS THEM!
OUCH

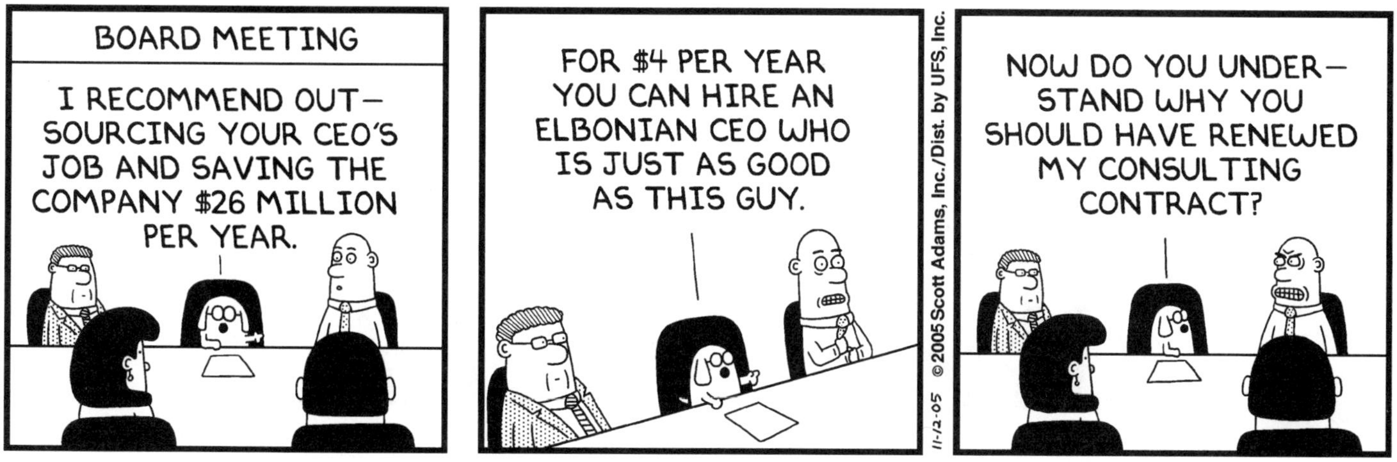
BOARD MEETING
I RECOMMEND OUT-SOURCING YOUR CEO'S JOB AND SAVING THE COMPANY $26 MILLION PER YEAR.
FOR $4 PER YEAR YOU CAN HIRE AN ELBONIAN CEO WHO IS JUST AS GOOD AS THIS GUY.
11-12-05 © 2005 Scott Adams, Inc./Dist. by UFS, Inc.
NOW DO YOU UNDER-STAND WHY YOU SHOULD HAVE RENEWED MY CONSULTING CONTRACT?

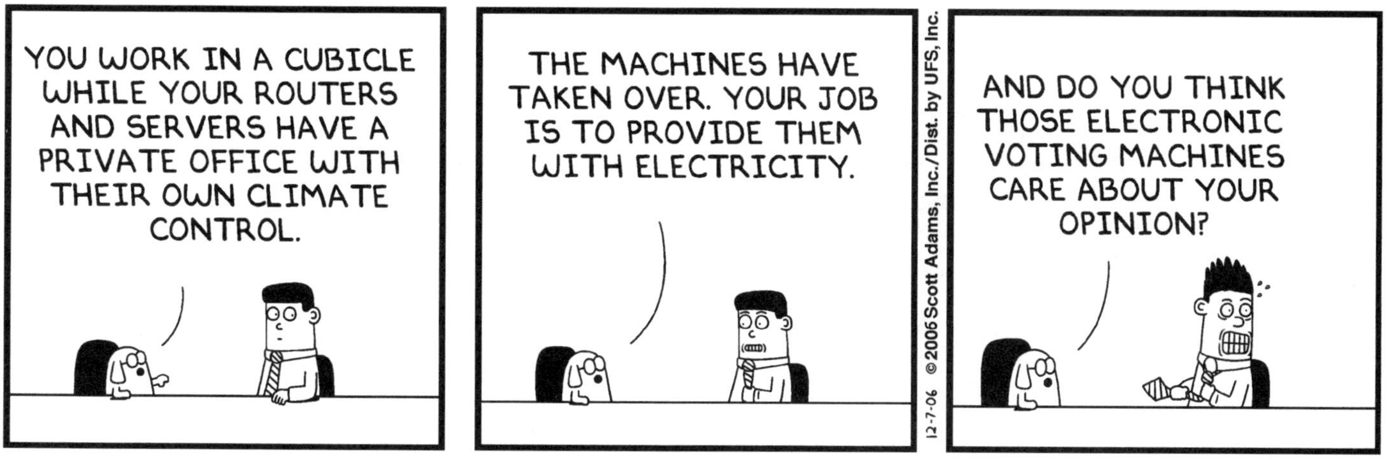
YOU WORK IN A CUBICLE WHILE YOUR ROUTERS AND SERVERS HAVE A PRIVATE OFFICE WITH THEIR OWN CLIMATE CONTROL.
THE MACHINES HAVE TAKEN OVER. YOUR JOB IS TO PROVIDE THEM WITH ELECTRICITY.
12-7-06 © 2006 Scott Adams, Inc./Dist. by UFS, Inc.
AND DO YOU THINK THOSE ELECTRONIC VOTING MACHINES CARE ABOUT YOUR OPINION?

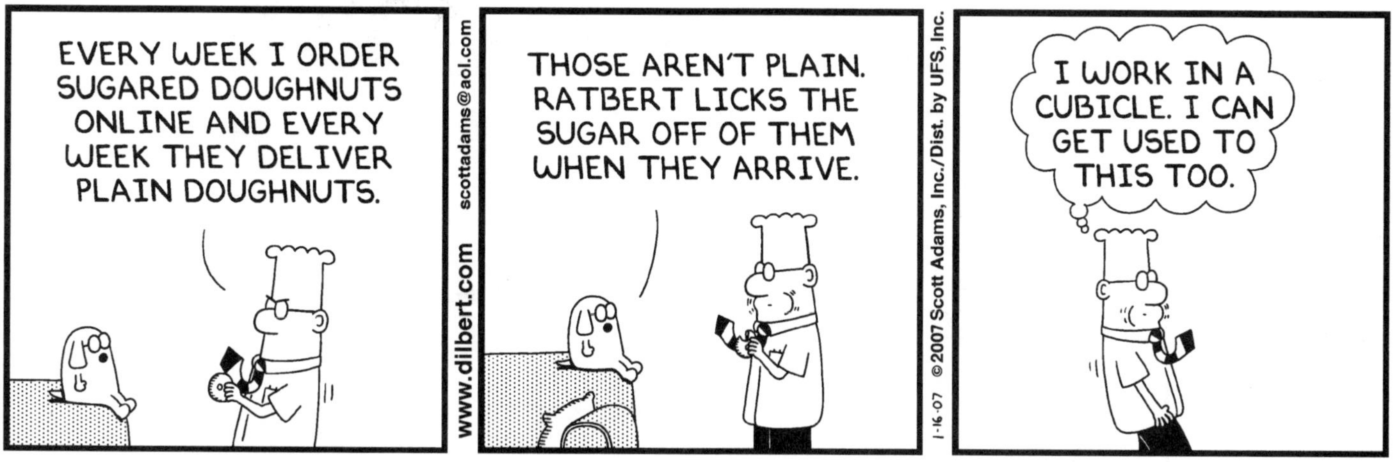
EVERY WEEK I ORDER SUGARED DOUGHNUTS ONLINE AND EVERY WEEK THEY DELIVER PLAIN DOUGHNUTS.
www.dilbert.com scottadams@aol.com
THOSE AREN'T PLAIN. RATBERT LICKS THE SUGAR OFF OF THEM WHEN THEY ARRIVE.
1-16-07 © 2007 Scott Adams, Inc./Dist. by UFS, Inc.
I WORK IN A CUBICLE. I CAN GET USED TO THIS TOO.

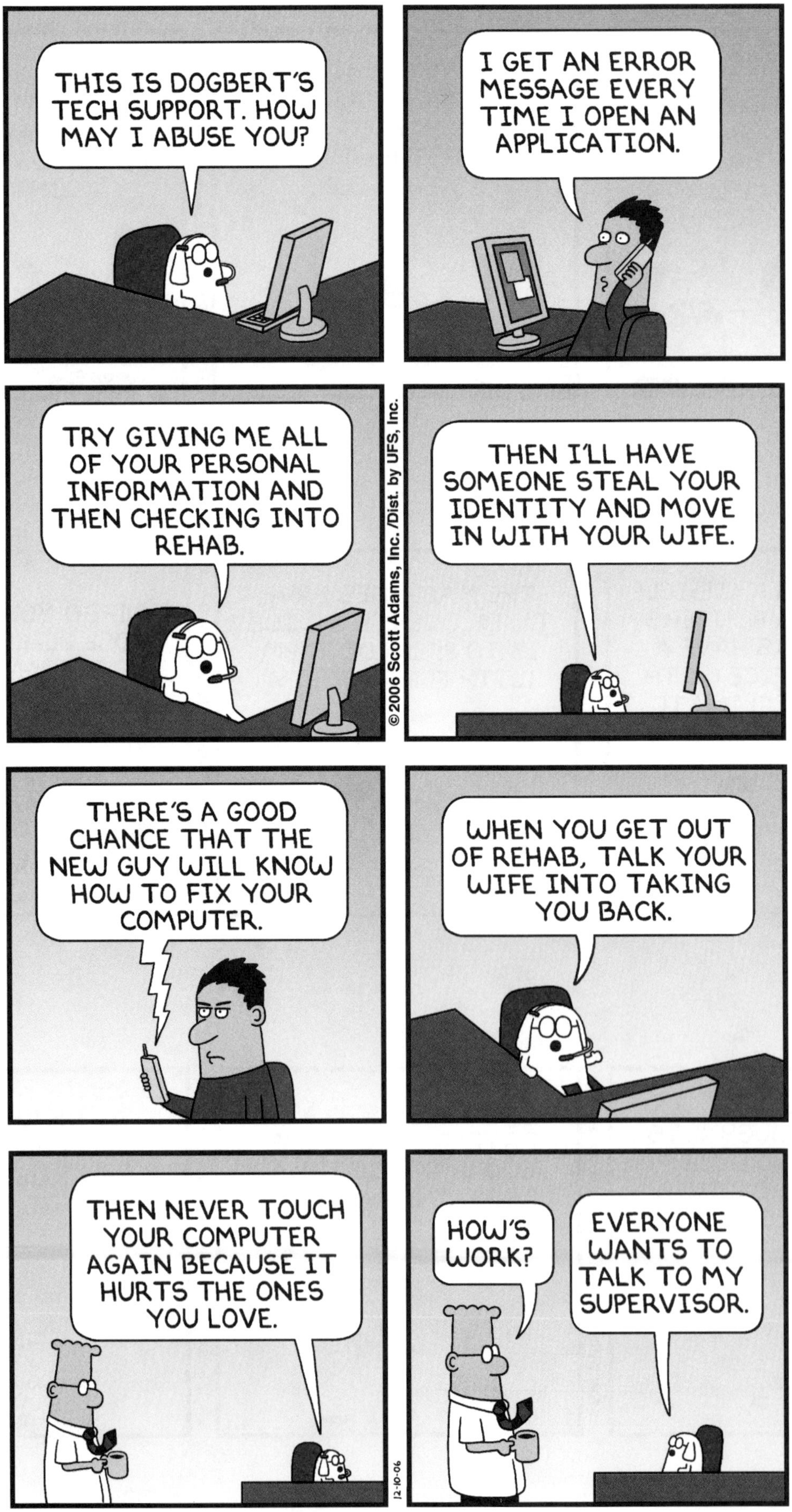

THIS IS DOGBERT'S TECH SUPPORT. HOW MAY I ABUSE YOU?
I GET AN ERROR MESSAGE EVERY TIME I OPEN AN APPLICATION.
TRY GIVING ME ALL OF YOUR PERSONAL INFORMATION AND THEN CHECKING INTO REHAB.
©2006 Scott Adams, Inc./Dist. by UFS, Inc.
THEN I'LL HAVE SOMEONE STEAL YOUR IDENTITY AND MOVE IN WITH YOUR WIFE.
THERE'S A GOOD CHANCE THAT THE NEW GUY WILL KNOW HOW TO FIX YOUR COMPUTER.
WHEN YOU GET OUT OF REHAB, TALK YOUR WIFE INTO TAKING YOU BACK.
THEN NEVER TOUCH YOUR COMPUTER AGAIN BECAUSE IT HURTS THE ONES YOU LOVE.
12-10-06
HOW'S WORK?
EVERYONE WANTS TO TALK TO MY SUPERVISOR.

4. Catbert

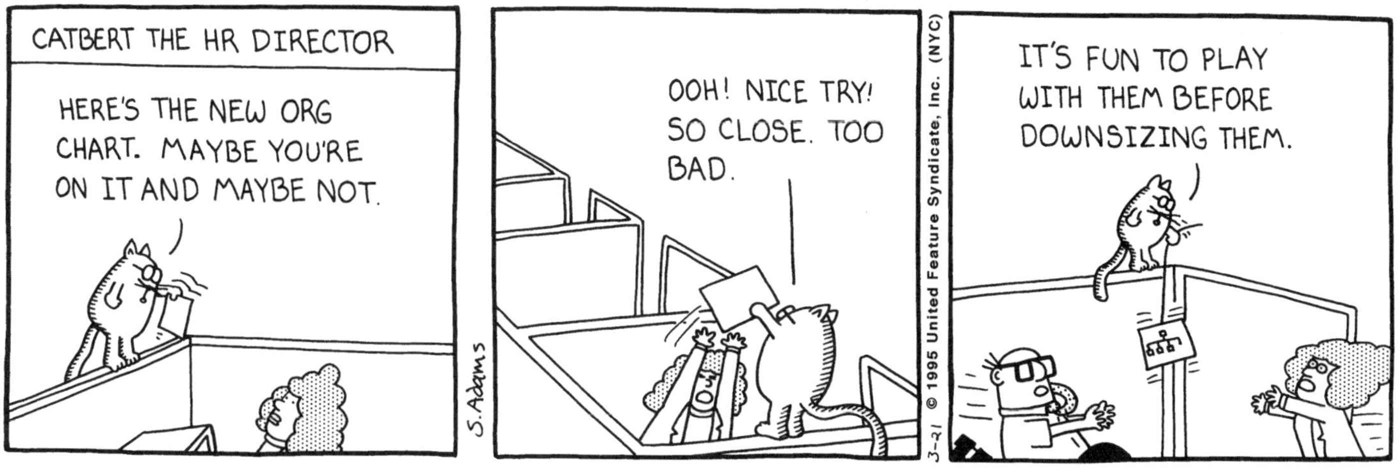
CATBERT THE HR DIRECTOR
HERE'S THE NEW ORG CHART. MAYBE YOU'RE ON IT AND MAYBE NOT.
OOH! NICE TRY! SO CLOSE. TOO BAD.
IT'S FUN TO PLAY WITH THEM BEFORE DOWNSIZING THEM.
S. Adams
3-21 © 1995 United Feature Syndicate, Inc. (NYC)

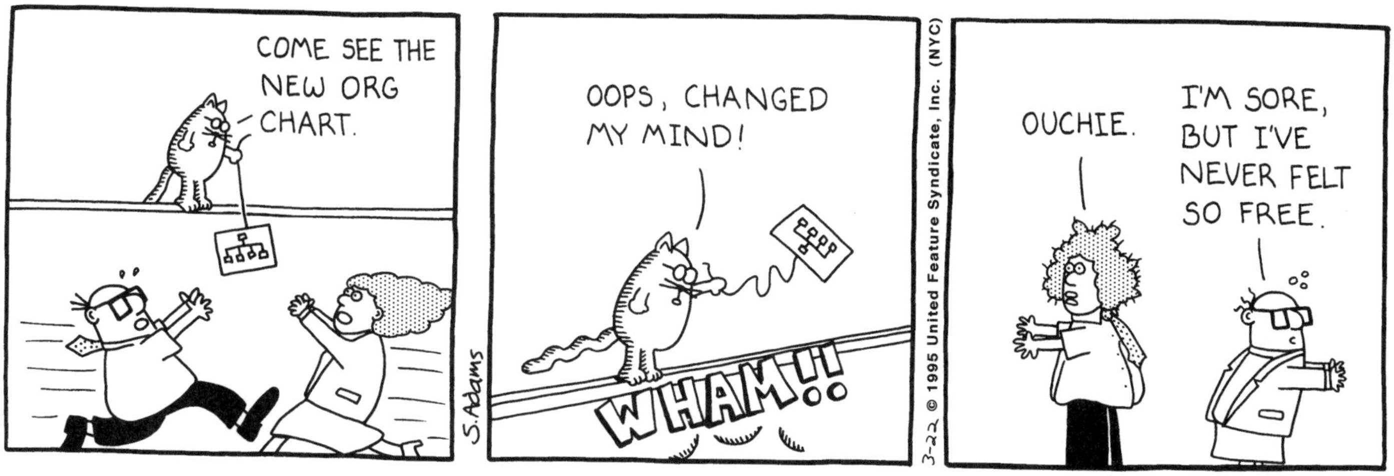
COME SEE THE NEW ORG CHART.
OOPS, CHANGED MY MIND!
WHAM!!
OUCHIE.
I'M SORE, BUT I'VE NEVER FELT SO FREE.
S. Adams
3-22 © 1995 United Feature Syndicate, Inc. (NYC)

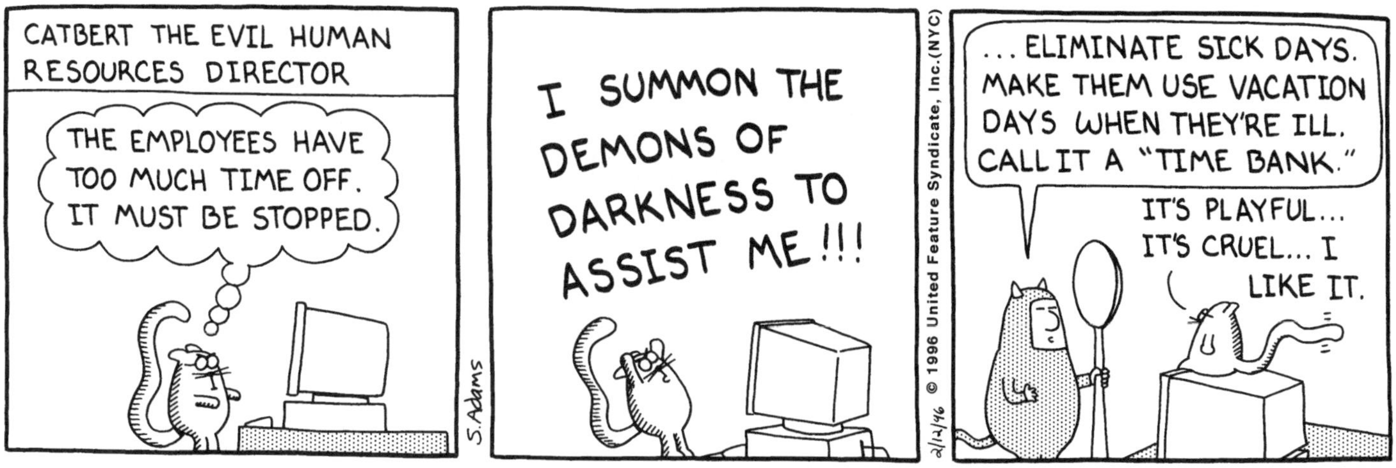
CATBERT THE EVIL HUMAN RESOURCES DIRECTOR
THE EMPLOYEES HAVE TOO MUCH TIME OFF. IT MUST BE STOPPED.
I SUMMON THE DEMONS OF DARKNESS TO ASSIST ME!!!
... ELIMINATE SICK DAYS. MAKE THEM USE VACATION DAYS WHEN THEY'RE ILL. CALL IT A "TIME BANK."
IT'S PLAYFUL... IT'S CRUEL... I LIKE IT.
S. Adams
2/12/96 © 1996 United Feature Syndicate, Inc.(NYC)

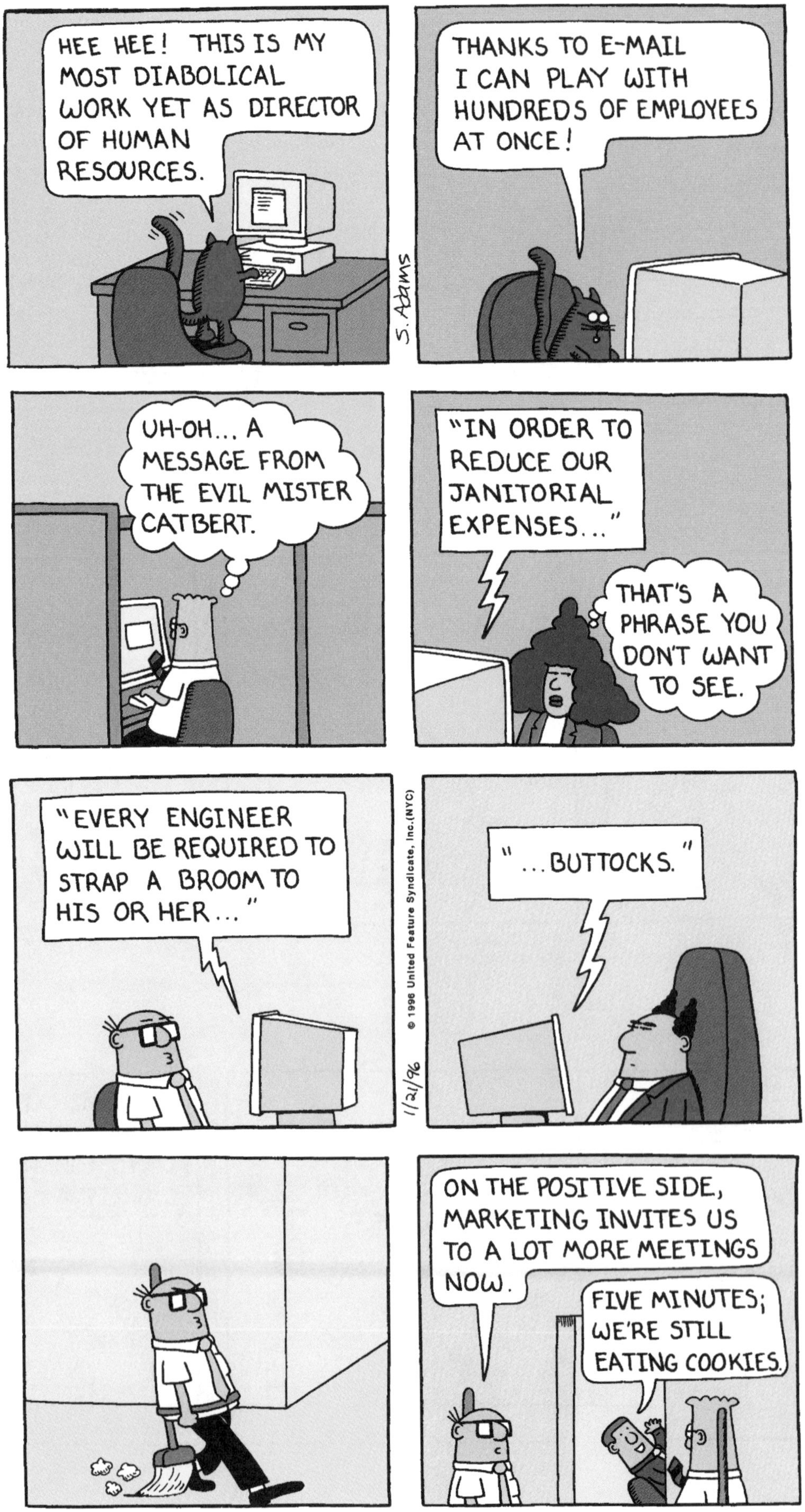
HEE HEE! THIS IS MY MOST DIABOLICAL WORK YET AS DIRECTOR OF HUMAN RESOURCES.
THANKS TO E-MAIL I CAN PLAY WITH HUNDREDS OF EMPLOYEES AT ONCE!
S. Adams
UH-OH... A MESSAGE FROM THE EVIL MISTER CATBERT.
"IN ORDER TO REDUCE OUR JANITORIAL EXPENSES..."
THAT'S A PHRASE YOU DON'T WANT TO SEE.
"EVERY ENGINEER WILL BE REQUIRED TO STRAP A BROOM TO HIS OR HER..."
© 1996 United Feature Syndicate, Inc.(NYC)
1/21/96
"...BUTTOCKS."
ON THE POSITIVE SIDE, MARKETING INVITES US TO A LOT MORE MEETINGS NOW.
FIVE MINUTES; WE'RE STILL EATING COOKIES.

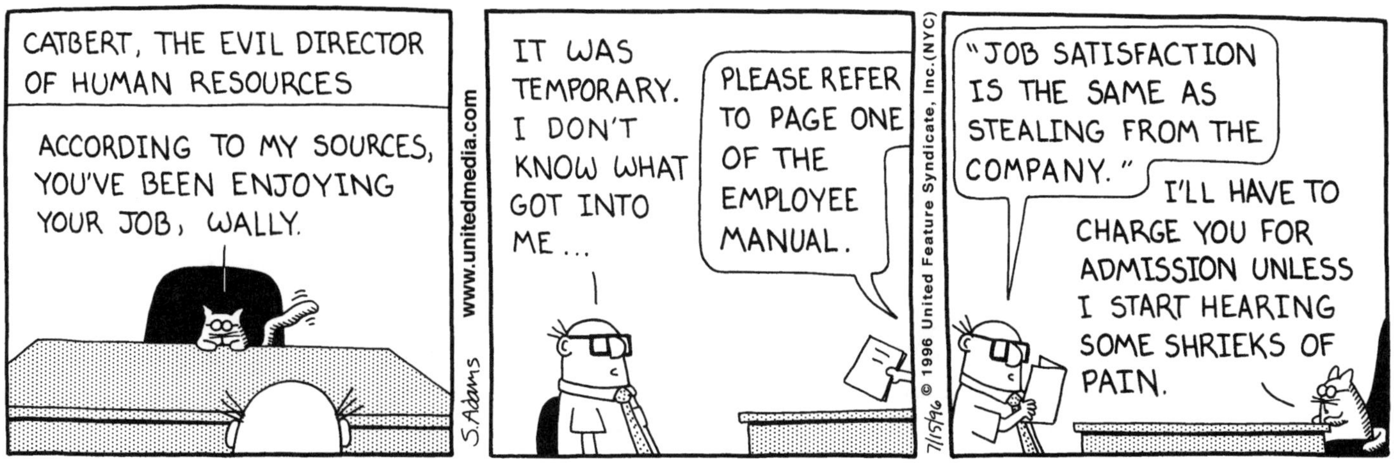
CATBERT, THE EVIL DIRECTOR OF HUMAN RESOURCES
ACCORDING TO MY SOURCES, YOU'VE BEEN ENJOYING YOUR JOB, WALLY.
www.unitedmedia.com
S. Adams
IT WAS TEMPORARY. I DON'T KNOW WHAT GOT INTO ME...
PLEASE REFER TO PAGE ONE OF THE EMPLOYEE MANUAL.
7/15/96 © 1996 United Feature Syndicate, Inc.(NYC)
"JOB SATISFACTION IS THE SAME AS STEALING FROM THE COMPANY."
I'LL HAVE TO CHARGE YOU FOR ADMISSION UNLESS I START HEARING SOME SHRIEKS OF PAIN.

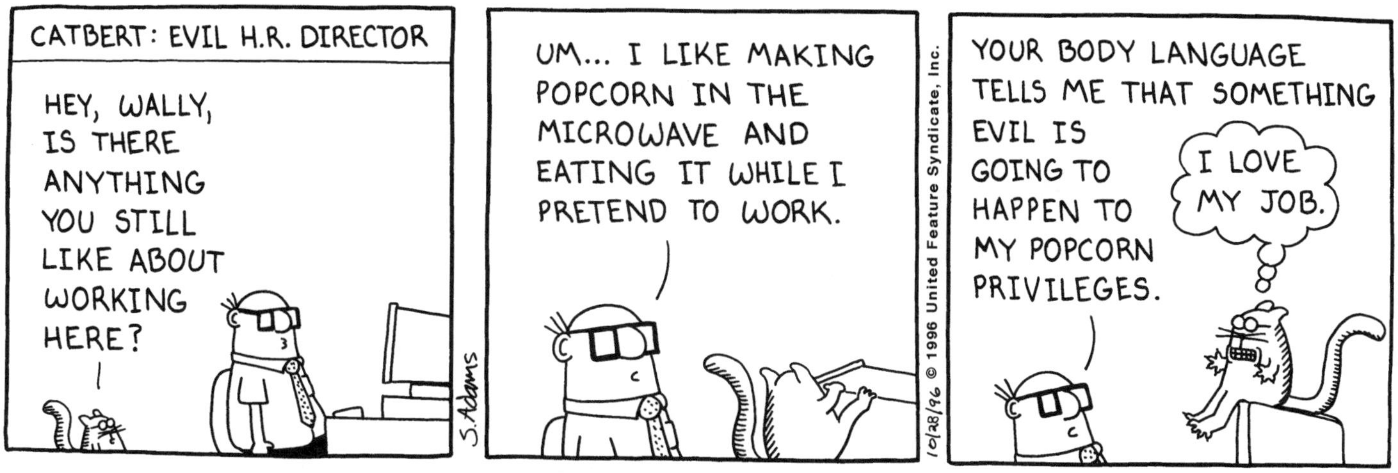
CATBERT: EVIL H.R. DIRECTOR
HEY, WALLY, IS THERE ANYTHING YOU STILL LIKE ABOUT WORKING HERE?
S. Adams
UM... I LIKE MAKING POPCORN IN THE MICROWAVE AND EATING IT WHILE I PRETEND TO WORK.
10/28/96 © 1996 United Feature Syndicate, Inc.
YOUR BODY LANGUAGE TELLS ME THAT SOMETHING EVIL IS GOING TO HAPPEN TO MY POPCORN PRIVILEGES.
I LOVE MY JOB.

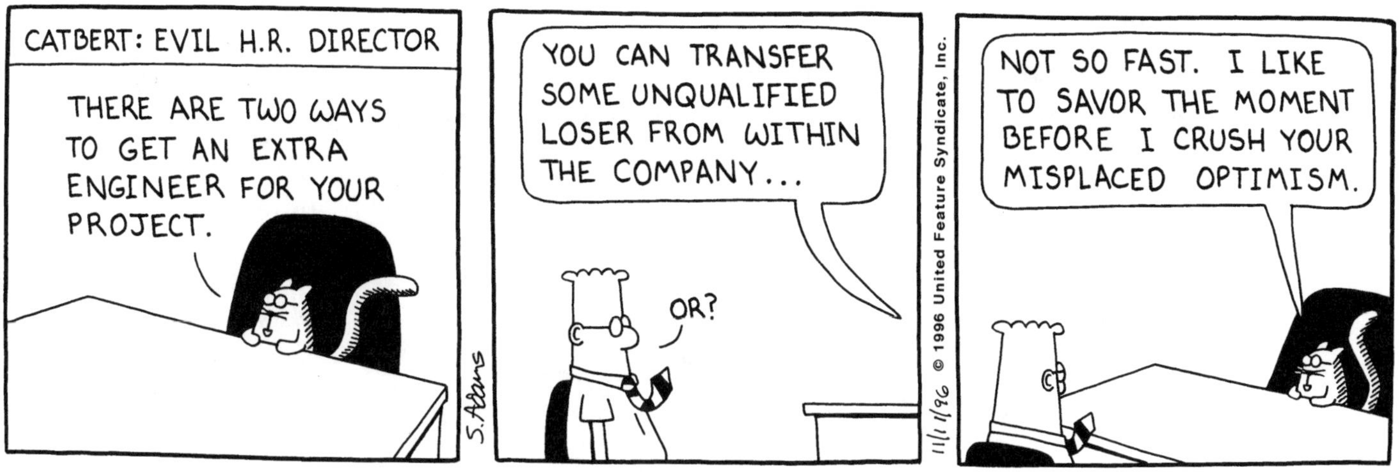
CATBERT: EVIL H.R. DIRECTOR
THERE ARE TWO WAYS TO GET AN EXTRA ENGINEER FOR YOUR PROJECT.
S. Adams
YOU CAN TRANSFER SOME UNQUALIFIED LOSER FROM WITHIN THE COMPANY...
OR?
11/11/96 © 1996 United Feature Syndicate, Inc.
NOT SO FAST. I LIKE TO SAVOR THE MOMENT BEFORE I CRUSH YOUR MISPLACED OPTIMISM.

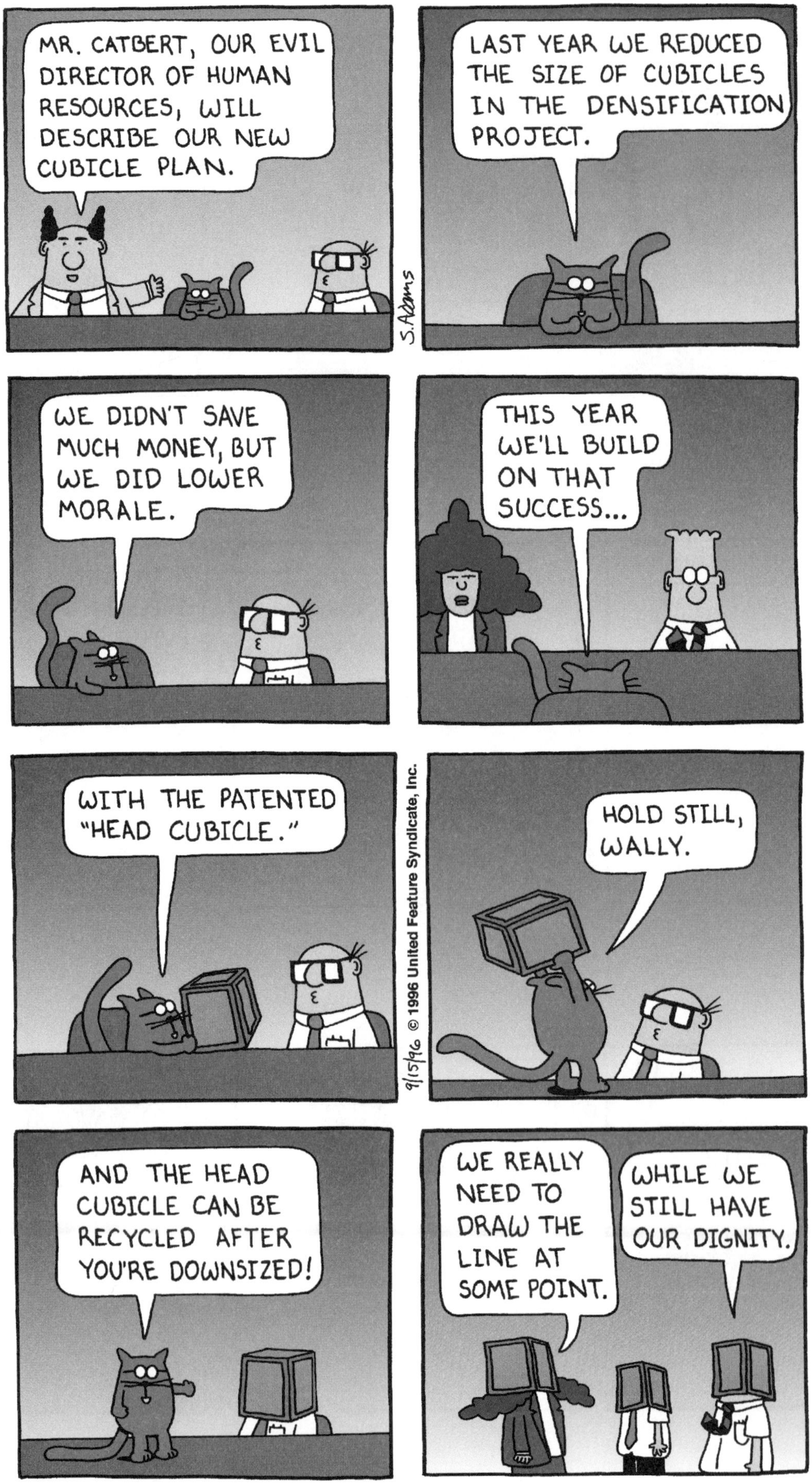
S. Adams
MR. CATBERT, OUR EVIL DIRECTOR OF HUMAN RESOURCES, WILL DESCRIBE OUR NEW CUBICLE PLAN.
LAST YEAR WE REDUCED THE SIZE OF CUBICLES IN THE DENSIFICATION PROJECT.
WE DIDN'T SAVE MUCH MONEY, BUT WE DID LOWER MORALE.
THIS YEAR WE'LL BUILD ON THAT SUCCESS...
WITH THE PATENTED "HEAD CUBICLE."
9/15/96 © 1996 United Feature Syndicate, Inc.
HOLD STILL, WALLY.
AND THE HEAD CUBICLE CAN BE RECYCLED AFTER YOU'RE DOWNSIZED!
WE REALLY NEED TO DRAW THE LINE AT SOME POINT.
WHILE WE STILL HAVE OUR DIGNITY.

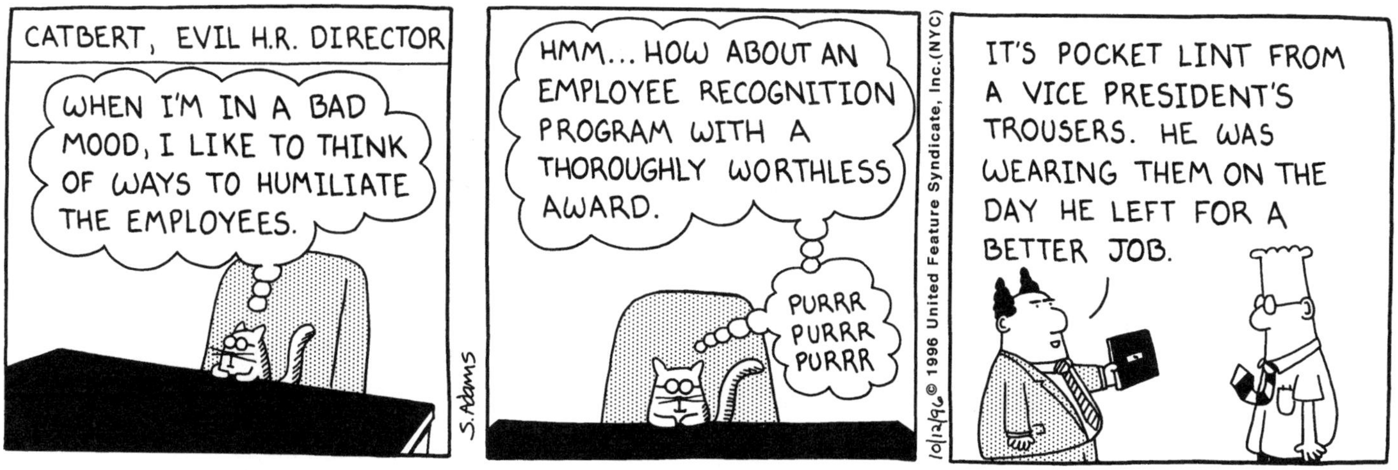
CATBERT, EVIL H.R. DIRECTOR
WHEN I'M IN A BAD MOOD, I LIKE TO THINK OF WAYS TO HUMILIATE THE EMPLOYEES.
S. Adams
HMM... HOW ABOUT AN EMPLOYEE RECOGNITION PROGRAM WITH A THOROUGHLY WORTHLESS AWARD.
PURRR PURRR PURRR
10/12/96 © 1996 United Feature Syndicate, Inc.(NYC)
IT'S POCKET LINT FROM A VICE PRESIDENT'S TROUSERS. HE WAS WEARING THEM ON THE DAY HE LEFT FOR A BETTER JOB.

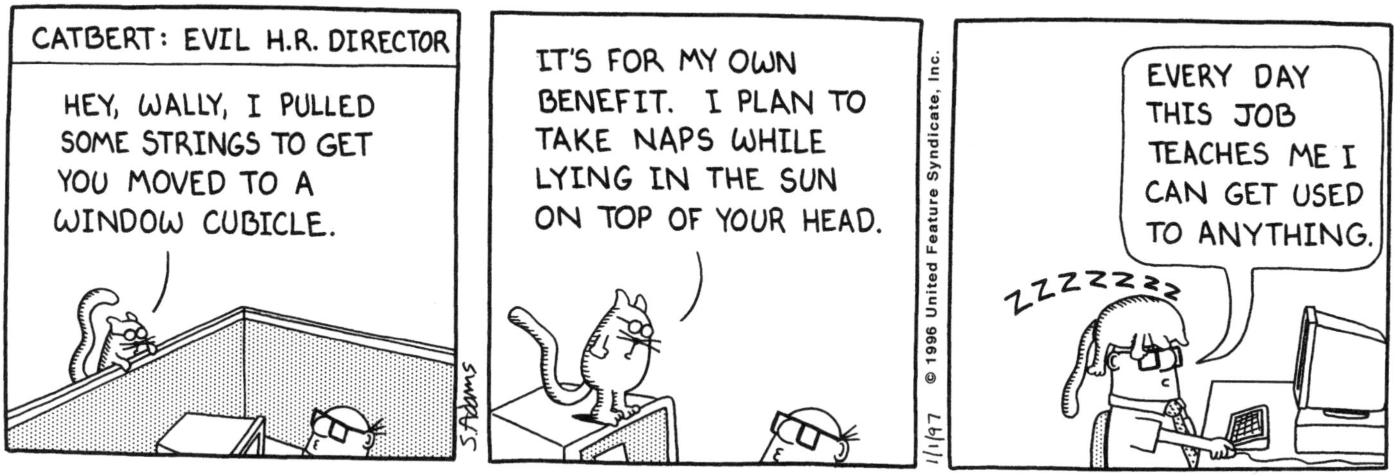
CATBERT: EVIL H.R. DIRECTOR
HEY, WALLY, I PULLED SOME STRINGS TO GET YOU MOVED TO A WINDOW CUBICLE.
S. Adams
IT'S FOR MY OWN BENEFIT. I PLAN TO TAKE NAPS WHILE LYING IN THE SUN ON TOP OF YOUR HEAD.
1/1/97 © 1996 United Feature Syndicate, Inc.
EVERY DAY THIS JOB TEACHES ME I CAN GET USED TO ANYTHING.
ZZZZZZZ

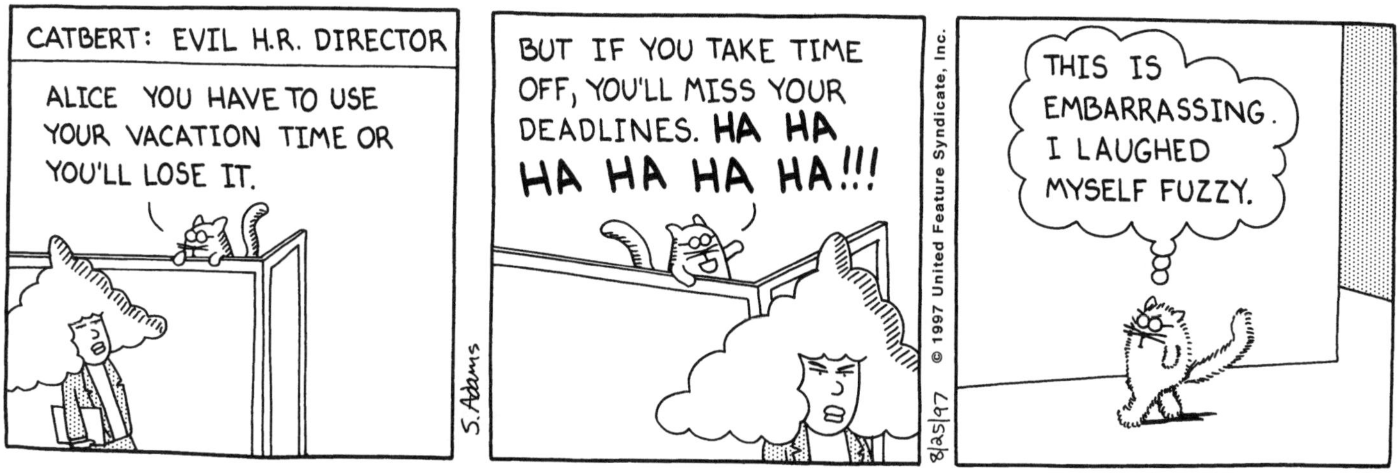
CATBERT: EVIL H.R. DIRECTOR
ALICE YOU HAVE TO USE YOUR VACATION TIME OR YOU'LL LOSE IT.
S. Adams
BUT IF YOU TAKE TIME OFF, YOU'LL MISS YOUR DEADLINES. HA HA HA HA HA HA!!!
8/25/97 © 1997 United Feature Syndicate, Inc.
THIS IS EMBARRASSING. I LAUGHED MYSELF FUZZY.

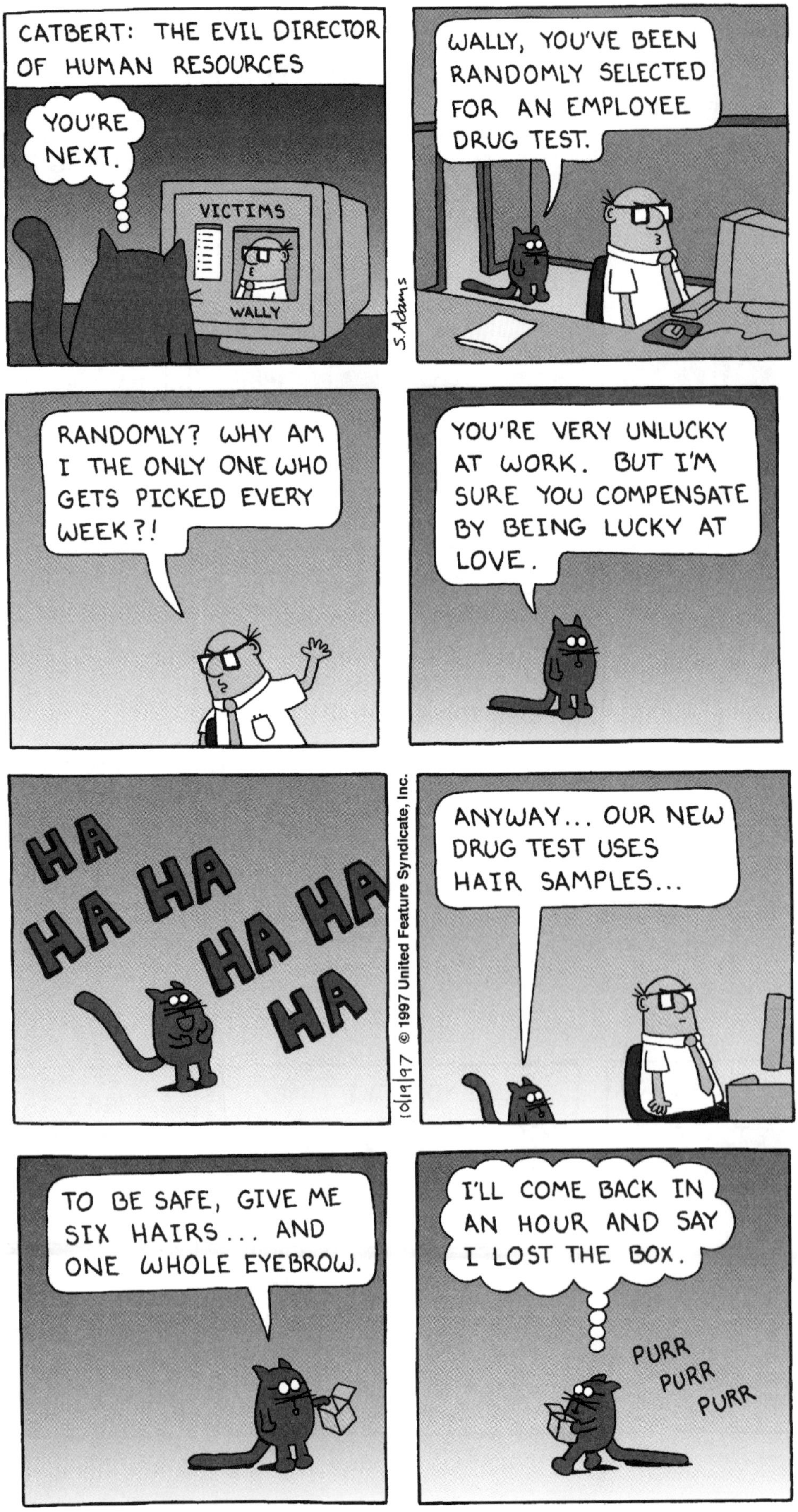
CATBERT: THE EVIL DIRECTOR OF HUMAN RESOURCES
YOU'RE NEXT.
VICTIMS
WALLY
S. Adams
WALLY, YOU'VE BEEN RANDOMLY SELECTED FOR AN EMPLOYEE DRUG TEST.
RANDOMLY? WHY AM I THE ONLY ONE WHO GETS PICKED EVERY WEEK?!
YOU'RE VERY UNLUCKY AT WORK. BUT I'M SURE YOU COMPENSATE BY BEING LUCKY AT LOVE.
HA HA HA HA HA HA HA
10/19/97 © 1997 United Feature Syndicate, Inc.
ANYWAY... OUR NEW DRUG TEST USES HAIR SAMPLES...
TO BE SAFE, GIVE ME SIX HAIRS... AND ONE WHOLE EYEBROW.
I'LL COME BACK IN AN HOUR AND SAY I LOST THE BOX.
PURR PURR PURR

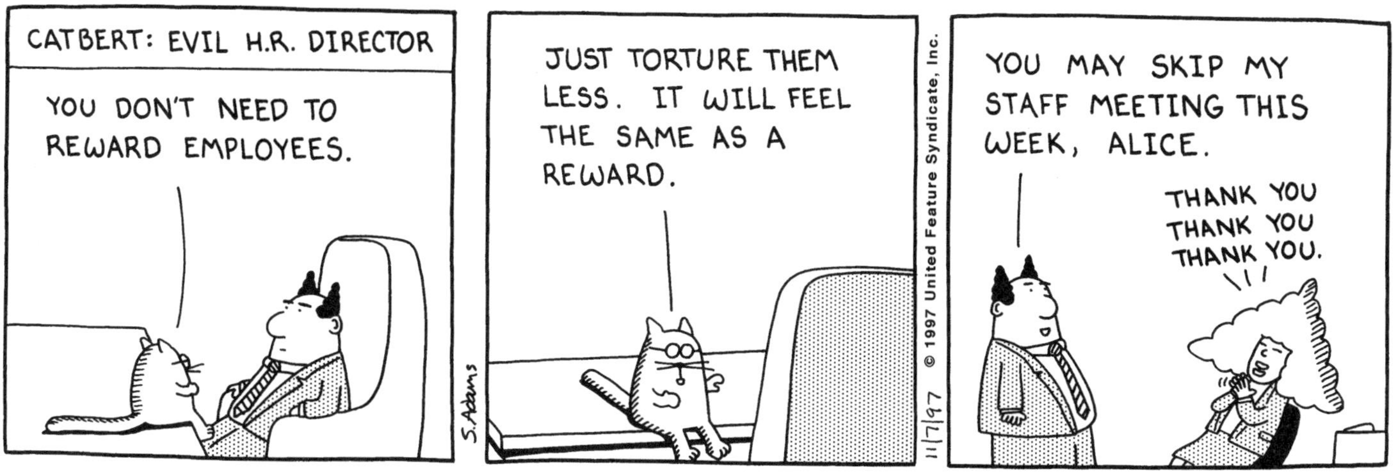
CATBERT: EVIL H.R. DIRECTOR
YOU DON'T NEED TO REWARD EMPLOYEES.
JUST TORTURE THEM LESS. IT WILL FEEL THE SAME AS A REWARD.
YOU MAY SKIP MY STAFF MEETING THIS WEEK, ALICE.
THANK YOU THANK YOU THANK YOU.
S. Adams
11/7/97 © 1997 United Feature Syndicate, Inc.

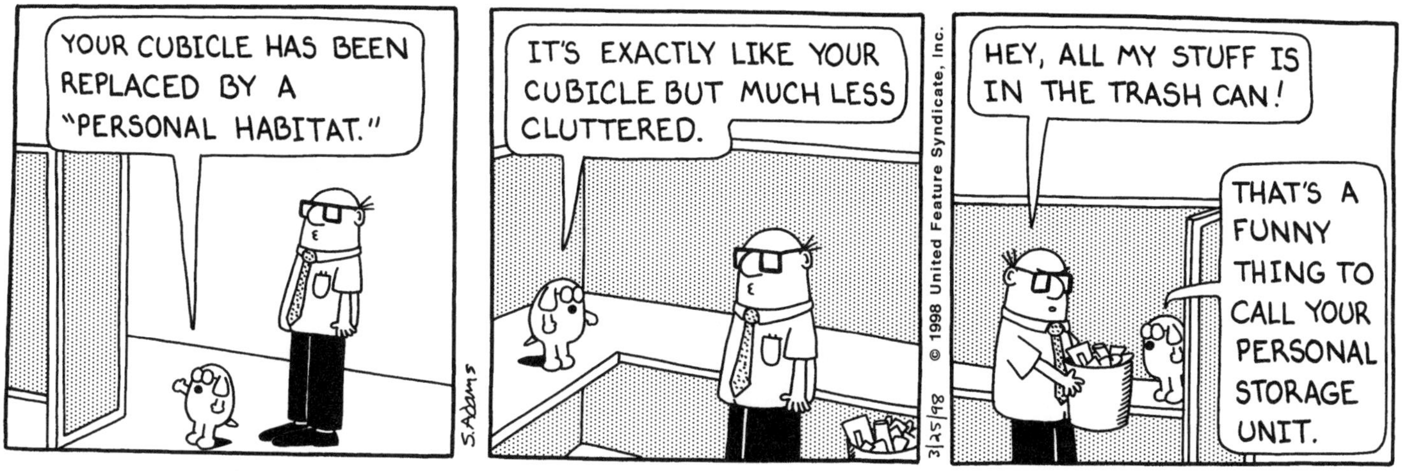
YOUR CUBICLE HAS BEEN REPLACED BY A "PERSONAL HABITAT."
IT'S EXACTLY LIKE YOUR CUBICLE BUT MUCH LESS CLUTTERED.
HEY, ALL MY STUFF IS IN THE TRASH CAN!
THAT'S A FUNNY THING TO CALL YOUR PERSONAL STORAGE UNIT.
S. Adams
3/25/98 © 1998 United Feature Syndicate, Inc.

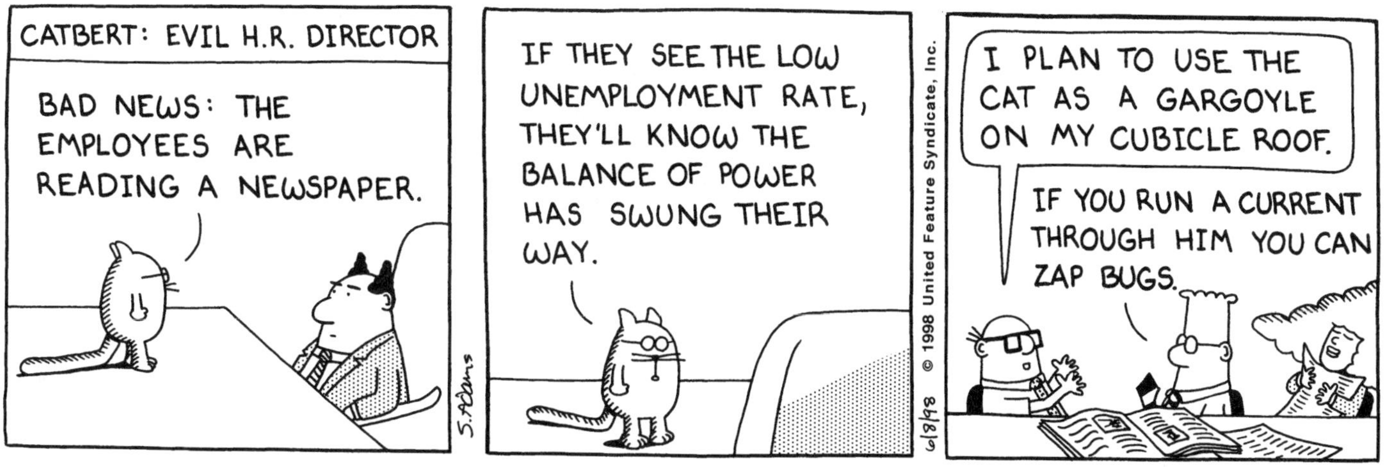
CATBERT: EVIL H.R. DIRECTOR
BAD NEWS: THE EMPLOYEES ARE READING A NEWSPAPER.
IF THEY SEE THE LOW UNEMPLOYMENT RATE, THEY'LL KNOW THE BALANCE OF POWER HAS SWUNG THEIR WAY.
I PLAN TO USE THE CAT AS A GARGOYLE ON MY CUBICLE ROOF.
IF YOU RUN A CURRENT THROUGH HIM YOU CAN ZAP BUGS.
S. Adams
6/8/98 © 1998 United Feature Syndicate, Inc.

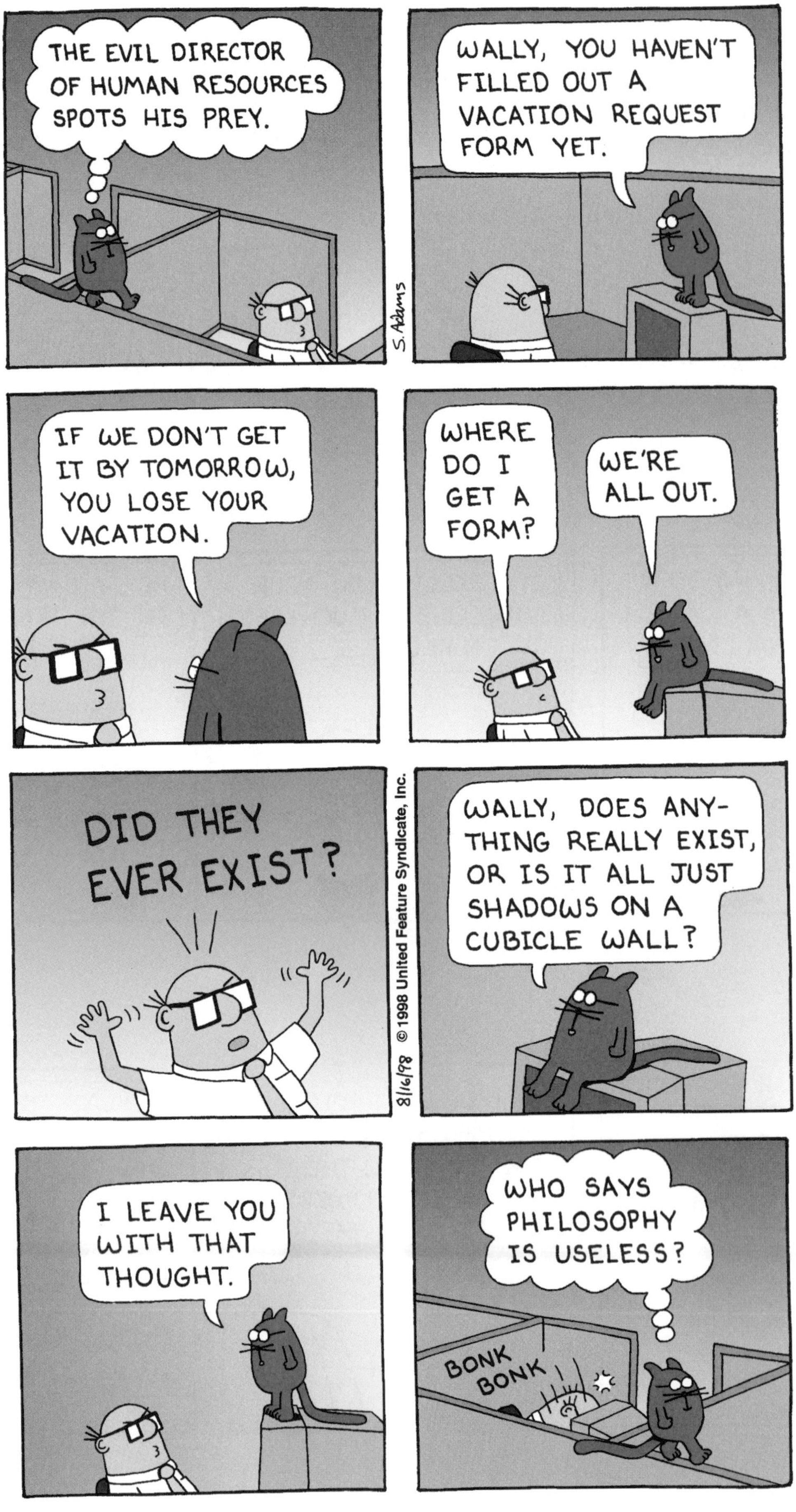
THE EVIL DIRECTOR OF HUMAN RESOURCES SPOTS HIS PREY.
S. Adams
WALLY, YOU HAVEN'T FILLED OUT A VACATION REQUEST FORM YET.
IF WE DON'T GET IT BY TOMORROW, YOU LOSE YOUR VACATION.
WHERE DO I GET A FORM?
WE'RE ALL OUT.
DID THEY EVER EXIST?
8/16/98 © 1998 United Feature Syndicate, Inc.
WALLY, DOES ANYTHING REALLY EXIST, OR IS IT ALL JUST SHADOWS ON A CUBICLE WALL?
I LEAVE YOU WITH THAT THOUGHT.
WHO SAYS PHILOSOPHY IS USELESS?
BONK BONK

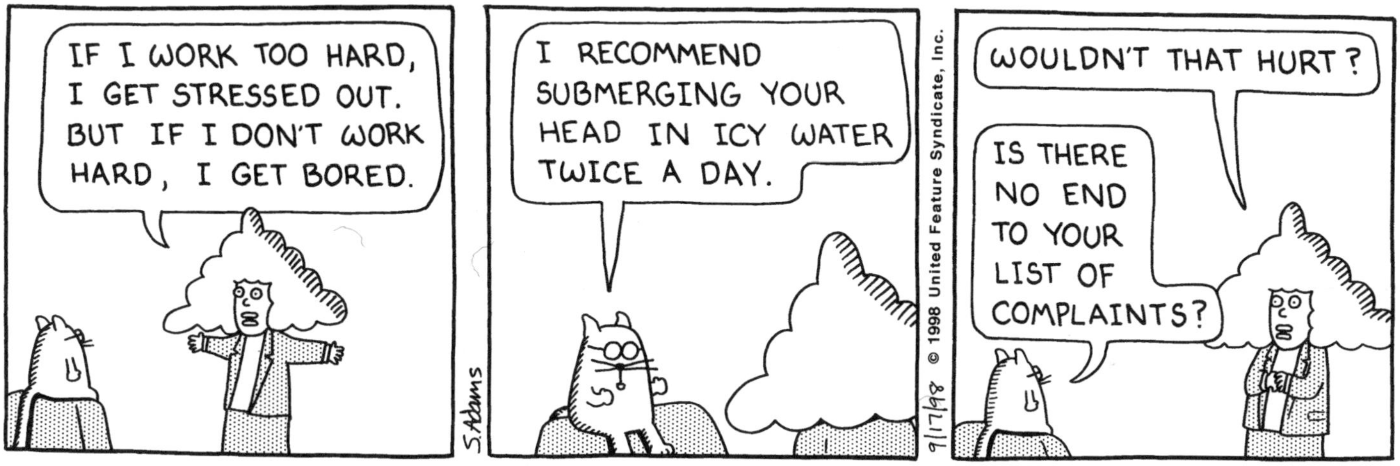
IF I WORK TOO HARD, I GET STRESSED OUT. BUT IF I DON'T WORK HARD, I GET BORED.
I RECOMMEND SUBMERGING YOUR HEAD IN ICY WATER TWICE A DAY.
WOULDN'T THAT HURT?
IS THERE NO END TO YOUR LIST OF COMPLAINTS?
S. Adams
9/17/98 © 1998 United Feature Syndicate, Inc.

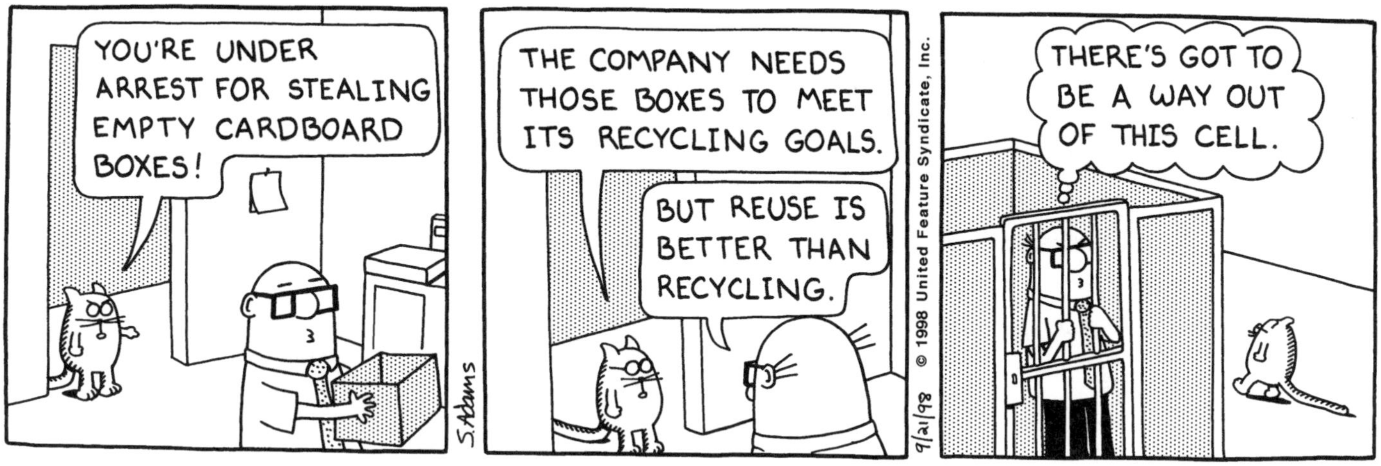
YOU'RE UNDER ARREST FOR STEALING EMPTY CARDBOARD BOXES!
THE COMPANY NEEDS THOSE BOXES TO MEET ITS RECYCLING GOALS.
BUT REUSE IS BETTER THAN RECYCLING.
THERE'S GOT TO BE A WAY OUT OF THIS CELL.
S. Adams
9/21/98 © 1998 United Feature Syndicate, Inc.

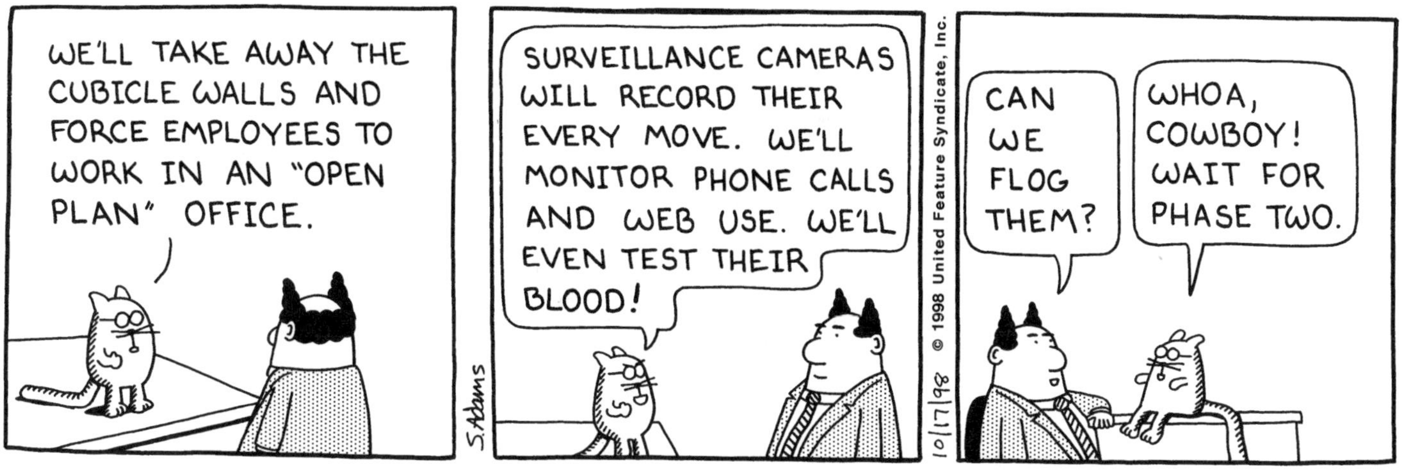
WE'LL TAKE AWAY THE CUBICLE WALLS AND FORCE EMPLOYEES TO WORK IN AN "OPEN PLAN" OFFICE.
SURVEILLANCE CAMERAS WILL RECORD THEIR EVERY MOVE. WE'LL MONITOR PHONE CALLS AND WEB USE. WE'LL EVEN TEST THEIR BLOOD!
CAN WE FLOG THEM?
WHOA, COWBOY! WAIT FOR PHASE TWO.
S. Adams
10/17/98 © 1998 United Feature Syndicate, Inc.

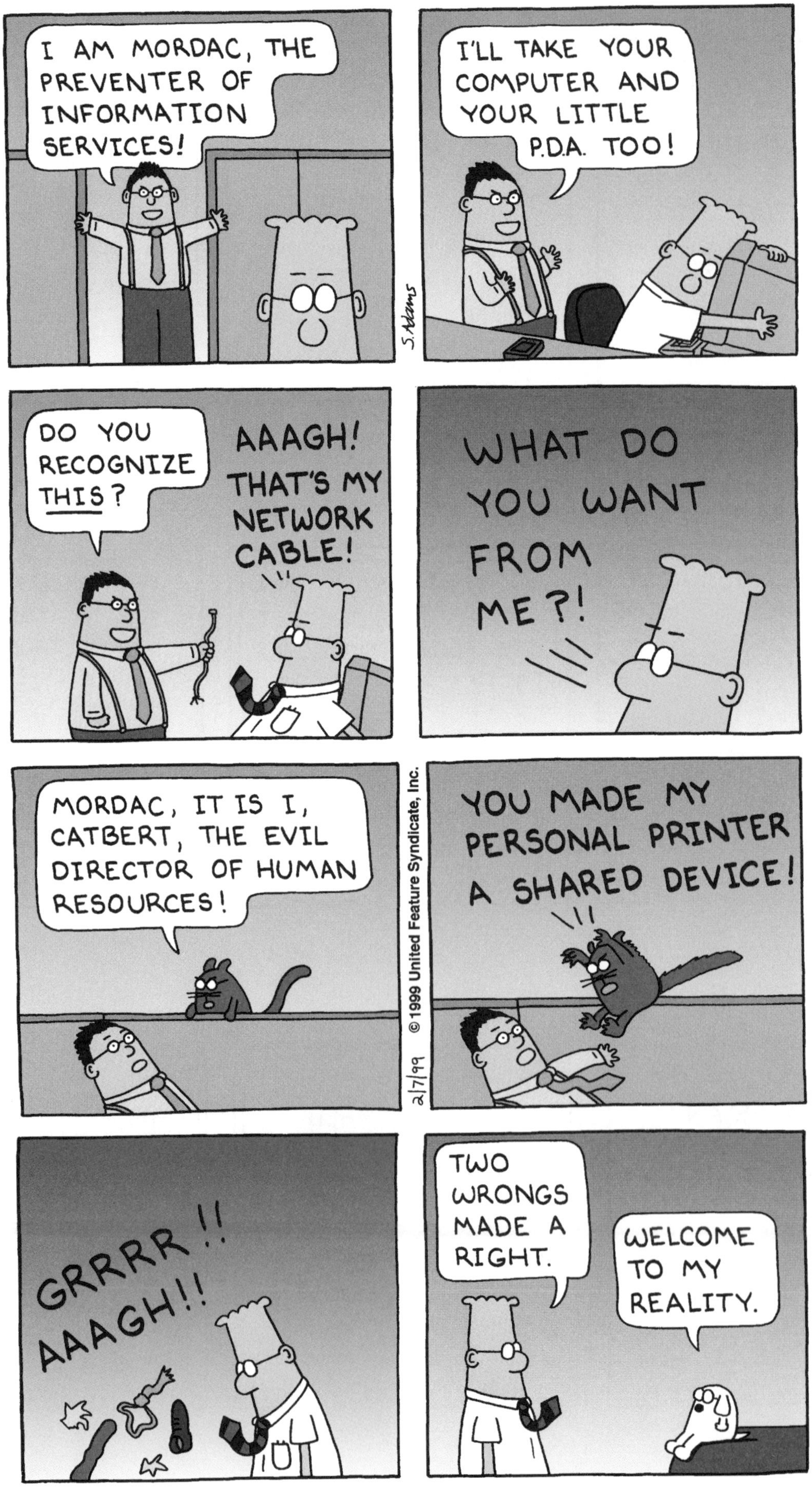
I AM MORDAC, THE PREVENTER OF INFORMATION SERVICES!
S. Adams
I'LL TAKE YOUR COMPUTER AND YOUR LITTLE P.D.A. TOO!
DO YOU RECOGNIZE THIS?
AAAGH! THAT'S MY NETWORK CABLE!
WHAT DO YOU WANT FROM ME?!
MORDAC, IT IS I, CATBERT, THE EVIL DIRECTOR OF HUMAN RESOURCES!
© 1999 United Feature Syndicate, Inc.
2/7/99
YOU MADE MY PERSONAL PRINTER A SHARED DEVICE!
GRRRR!! AAAGH!!
TWO WRONGS MADE A RIGHT.
WELCOME TO MY REALITY.

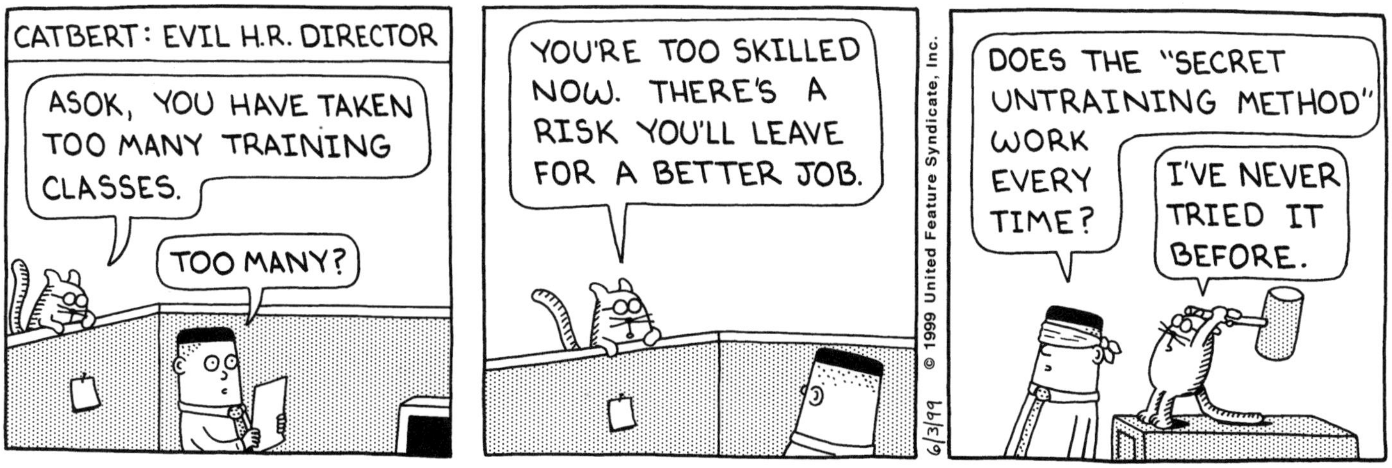
CATBERT: EVIL H.R. DIRECTOR
ASOK, YOU HAVE TAKEN TOO MANY TRAINING CLASSES.
TOO MANY?
YOU'RE TOO SKILLED NOW. THERE'S A RISK YOU'LL LEAVE FOR A BETTER JOB.
6/3/99 © 1999 United Feature Syndicate, Inc.
DOES THE "SECRET UNTRAINING METHOD" WORK EVERY TIME?
I'VE NEVER TRIED IT BEFORE.

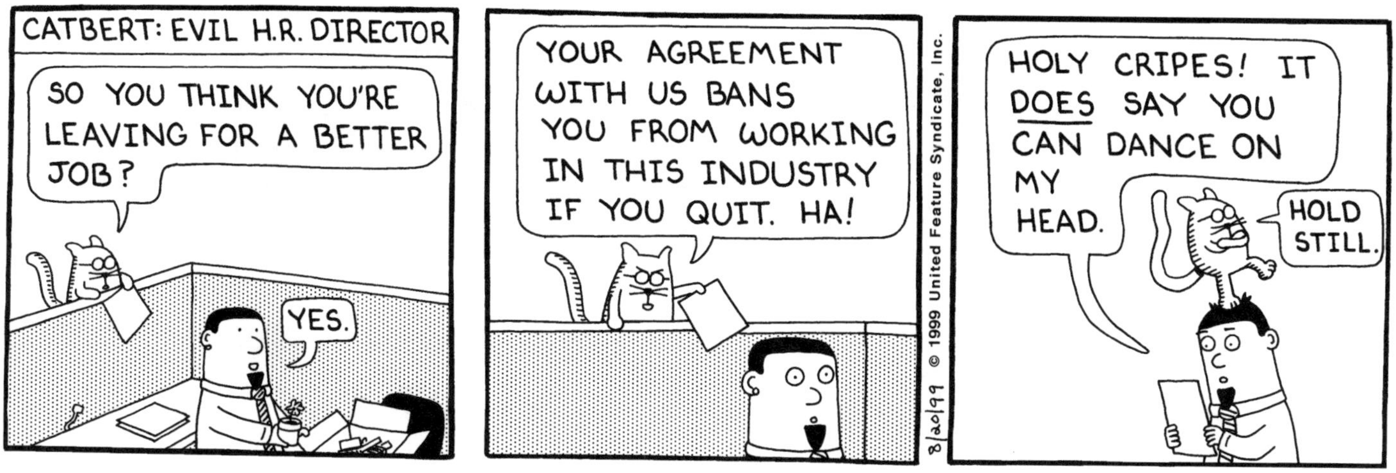
CATBERT: EVIL H.R. DIRECTOR
SO YOU THINK YOU'RE LEAVING FOR A BETTER JOB?
YES.
YOUR AGREEMENT WITH US BANS YOU FROM WORKING IN THIS INDUSTRY IF YOU QUIT. HA!
8/20/99 © 1999 United Feature Syndicate, Inc.
HOLY CRIPES! IT DOES SAY YOU CAN DANCE ON MY HEAD.
HOLD STILL.

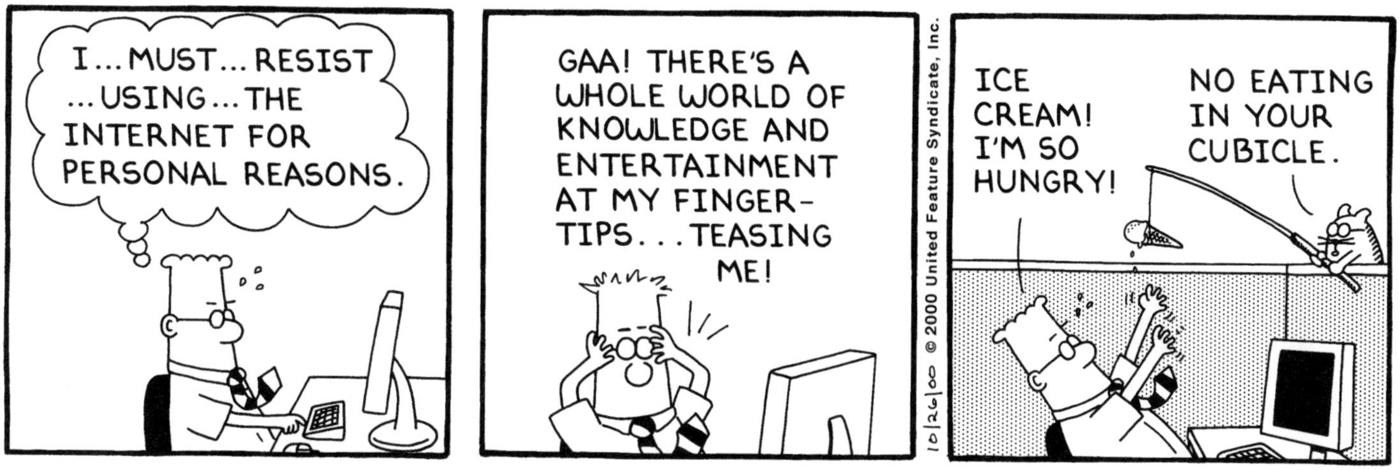
I... MUST... RESIST ... USING... THE INTERNET FOR PERSONAL REASONS.
GAA! THERE'S A WHOLE WORLD OF KNOWLEDGE AND ENTERTAINMENT AT MY FINGER-TIPS... TEASING ME!
10/26/00 © 2000 United Feature Syndicate, Inc.
ICE CREAM! I'M SO HUNGRY!
NO EATING IN YOUR CUBICLE.

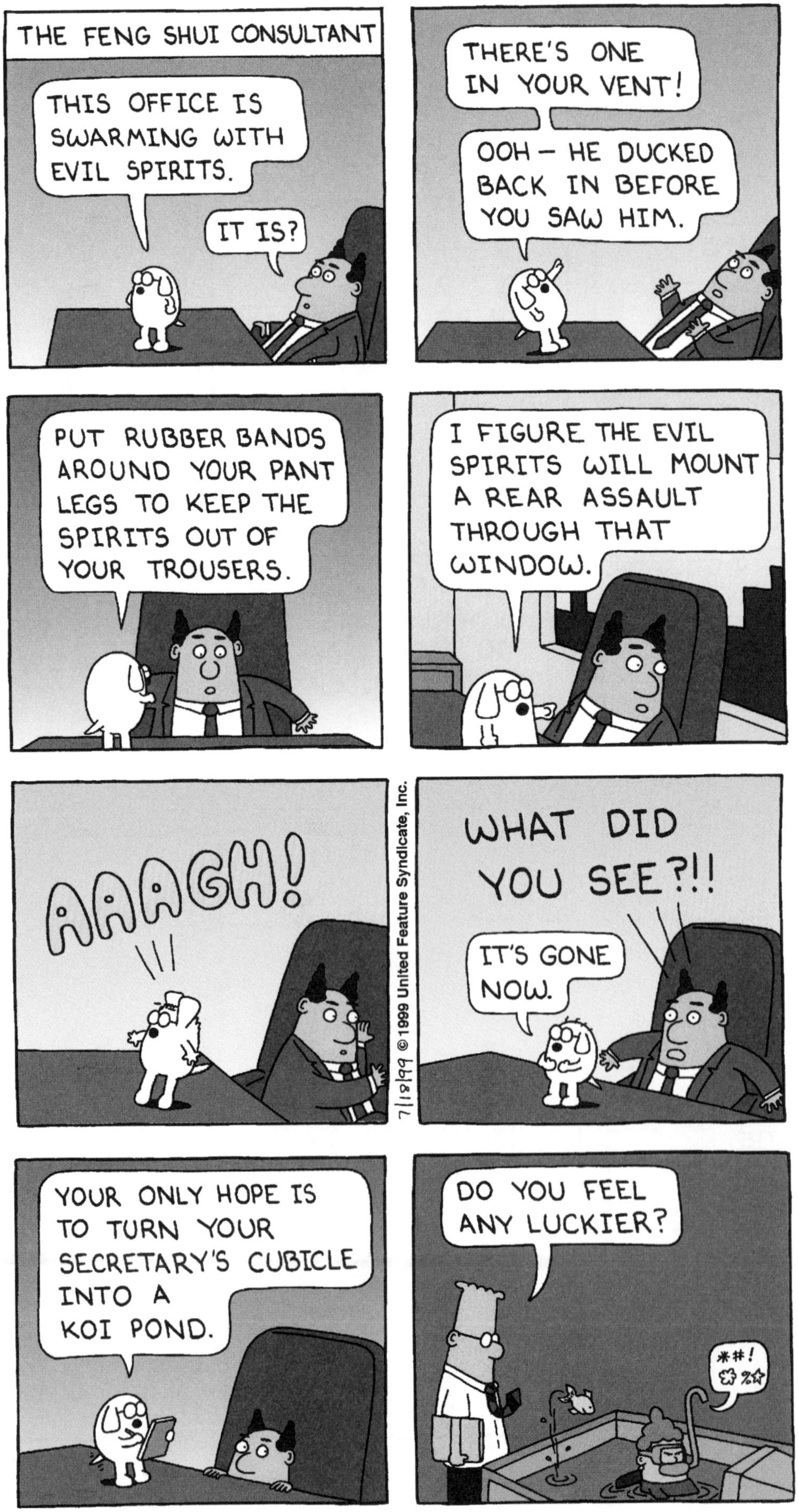
THE FENG SHUI CONSULTANT
THIS OFFICE IS SWARMING WITH EVIL SPIRITS.
IT IS?
THERE'S ONE IN YOUR VENT!
OOH — HE DUCKED BACK IN BEFORE YOU SAW HIM.
PUT RUBBER BANDS AROUND YOUR PANT LEGS TO KEEP THE SPIRITS OUT OF YOUR TROUSERS.
I FIGURE THE EVIL SPIRITS WILL MOUNT A REAR ASSAULT THROUGH THAT WINDOW.
AAAGH!
WHAT DID YOU SEE?!!
IT'S GONE NOW.
YOUR ONLY HOPE IS TO TURN YOUR SECRETARY'S CUBICLE INTO A KOI POND.
DO YOU FEEL ANY LUCKIER?

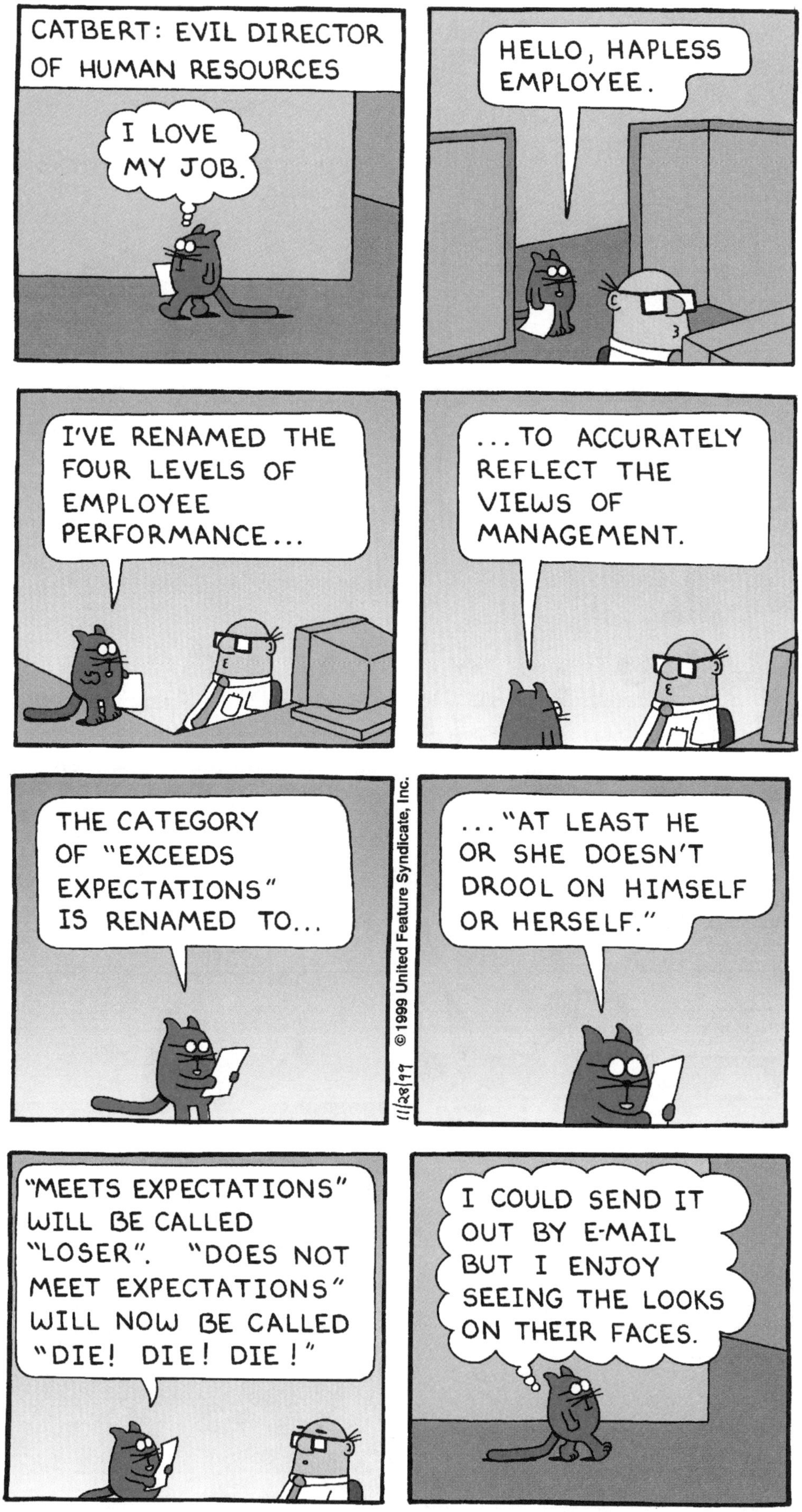
CATBERT: EVIL DIRECTOR OF HUMAN RESOURCES
I LOVE MY JOB.
HELLO, HAPLESS EMPLOYEE.
I'VE RENAMED THE FOUR LEVELS OF EMPLOYEE PERFORMANCE...
...TO ACCURATELY REFLECT THE VIEWS OF MANAGEMENT.
THE CATEGORY OF "EXCEEDS EXPECTATIONS" IS RENAMED TO...
..."AT LEAST HE OR SHE DOESN'T DROOL ON HIMSELF OR HERSELF."
"MEETS EXPECTATIONS" WILL BE CALLED "LOSER". "DOES NOT MEET EXPECTATIONS" WILL NOW BE CALLED "DIE! DIE! DIE!"
I COULD SEND IT OUT BY E-MAIL BUT I ENJOY SEEING THE LOOKS ON THEIR FACES.
©1999 United Feature Syndicate, Inc.
11/28/99

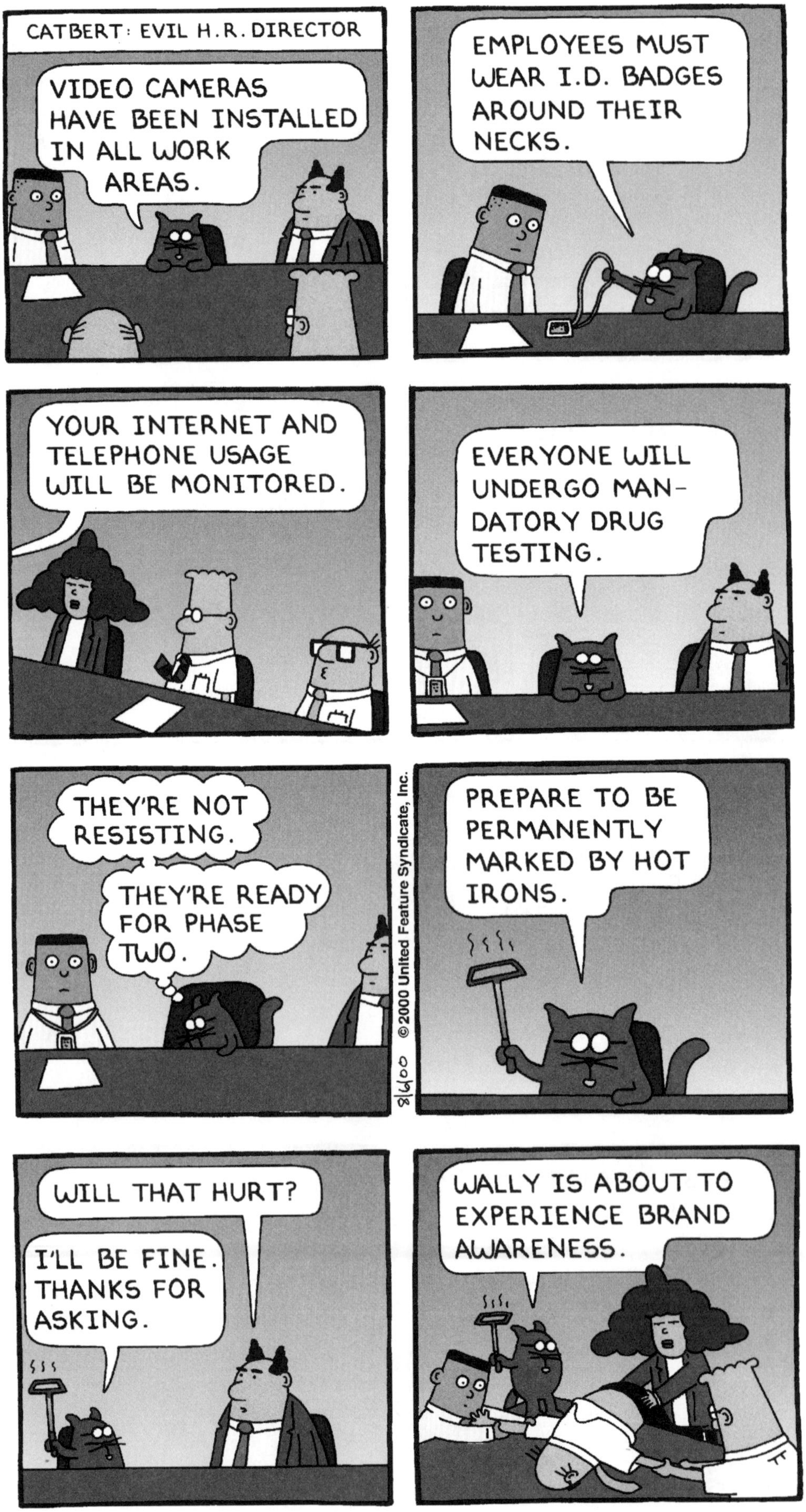
CATBERT: EVIL H.R. DIRECTOR
VIDEO CAMERAS HAVE BEEN INSTALLED IN ALL WORK AREAS.
EMPLOYEES MUST WEAR I.D. BADGES AROUND THEIR NECKS.
YOUR INTERNET AND TELEPHONE USAGE WILL BE MONITORED.
EVERYONE WILL UNDERGO MAN-DATORY DRUG TESTING.
THEY'RE NOT RESISTING.
THEY'RE READY FOR PHASE TWO.
©2000 United Feature Syndicate, Inc.
8/6/00
PREPARE TO BE PERMANENTLY MARKED BY HOT IRONS.
WILL THAT HURT?
I'LL BE FINE. THANKS FOR ASKING.
WALLY IS ABOUT TO EXPERIENCE BRAND AWARENESS.

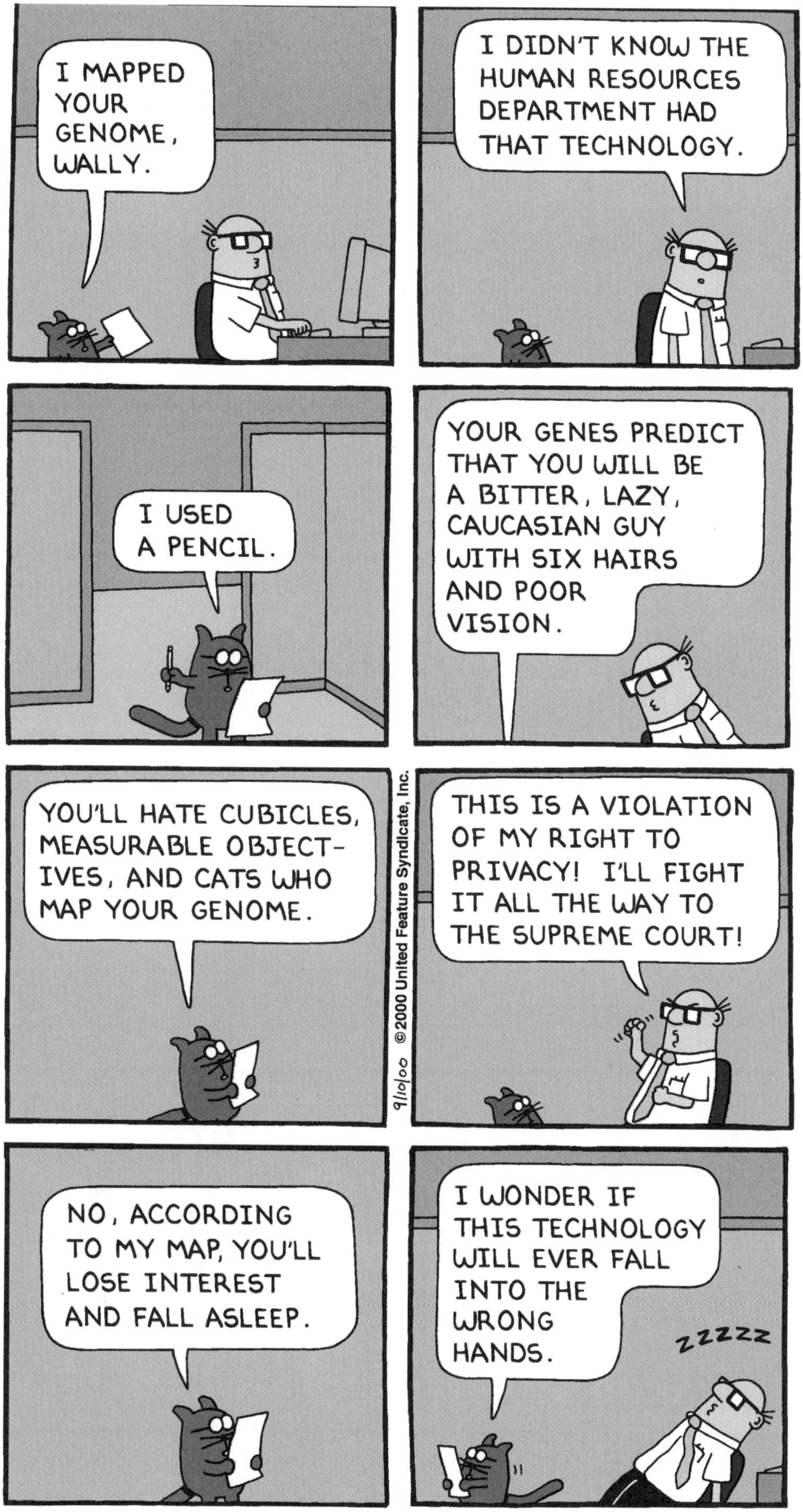
I MAPPED YOUR GENOME, WALLY.
I DIDN'T KNOW THE HUMAN RESOURCES DEPARTMENT HAD THAT TECHNOLOGY.
I USED A PENCIL.
YOUR GENES PREDICT THAT YOU WILL BE A BITTER, LAZY, CAUCASIAN GUY WITH SIX HAIRS AND POOR VISION.
YOU'LL HATE CUBICLES, MEASURABLE OBJECT-IVES, AND CATS WHO MAP YOUR GENOME.
9/10/00 ©2000 United Feature Syndicate, Inc.
THIS IS A VIOLATION OF MY RIGHT TO PRIVACY! I'LL FIGHT IT ALL THE WAY TO THE SUPREME COURT!
NO, ACCORDING TO MY MAP, YOU'LL LOSE INTEREST AND FALL ASLEEP.
I WONDER IF THIS TECHNOLOGY WILL EVER FALL INTO THE WRONG HANDS.
ZZZZZ

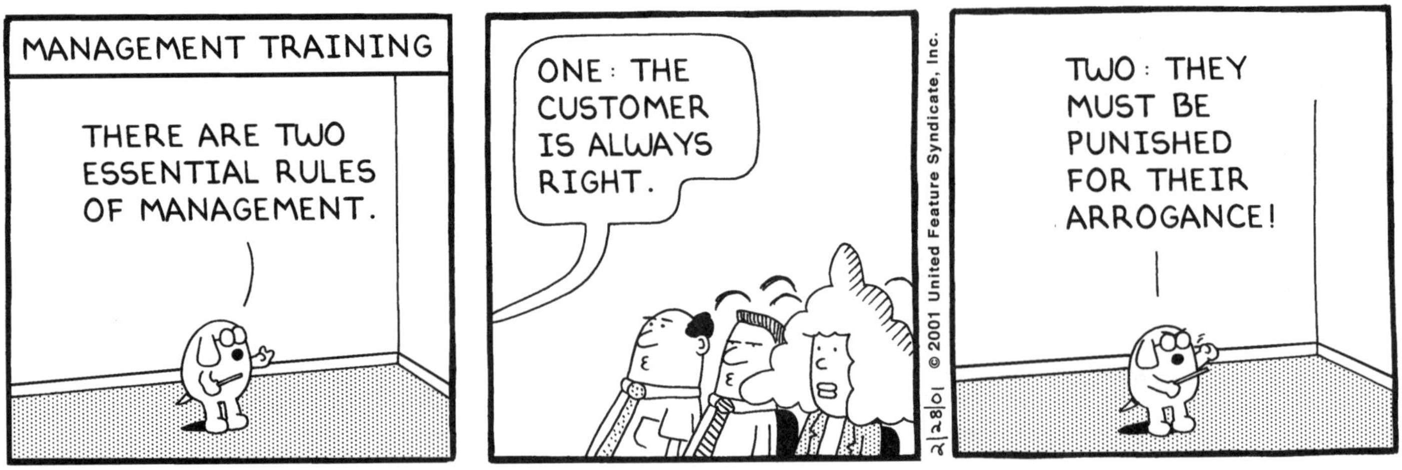
MANAGEMENT TRAINING
THERE ARE TWO ESSENTIAL RULES OF MANAGEMENT.
ONE: THE CUSTOMER IS ALWAYS RIGHT.
© 2001 United Feature Syndicate, Inc.
2/28/01
TWO: THEY MUST BE PUNISHED FOR THEIR ARROGANCE!

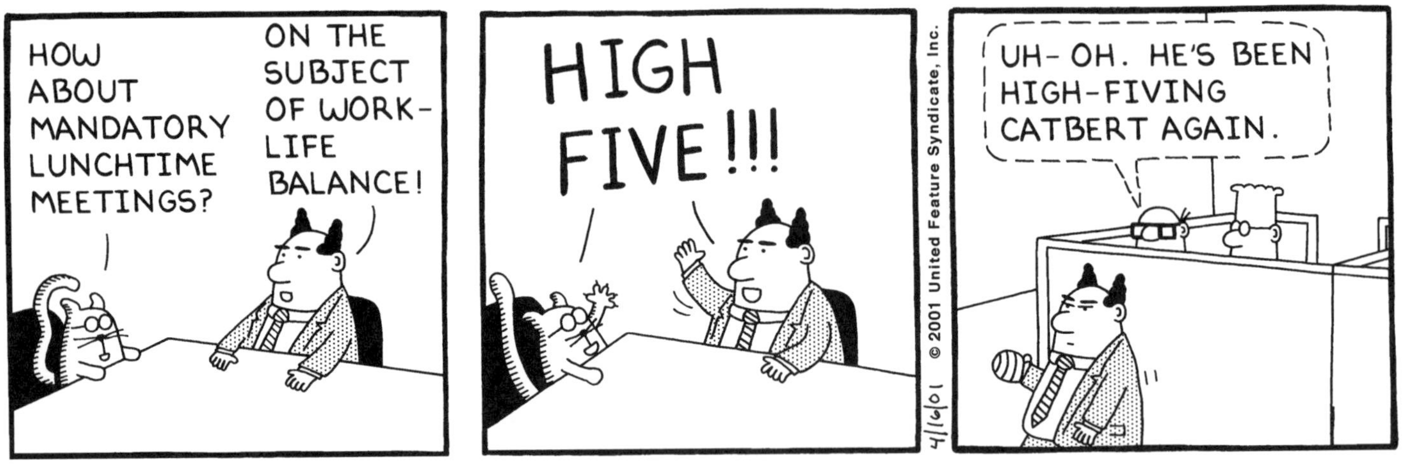
HOW ABOUT MANDATORY LUNCHTIME MEETINGS?
ON THE SUBJECT OF WORK-LIFE BALANCE!
HIGH FIVE!!!
© 2001 United Feature Syndicate, Inc.
4/16/01
UH-OH. HE'S BEEN HIGH-FIVING CATBERT AGAIN.

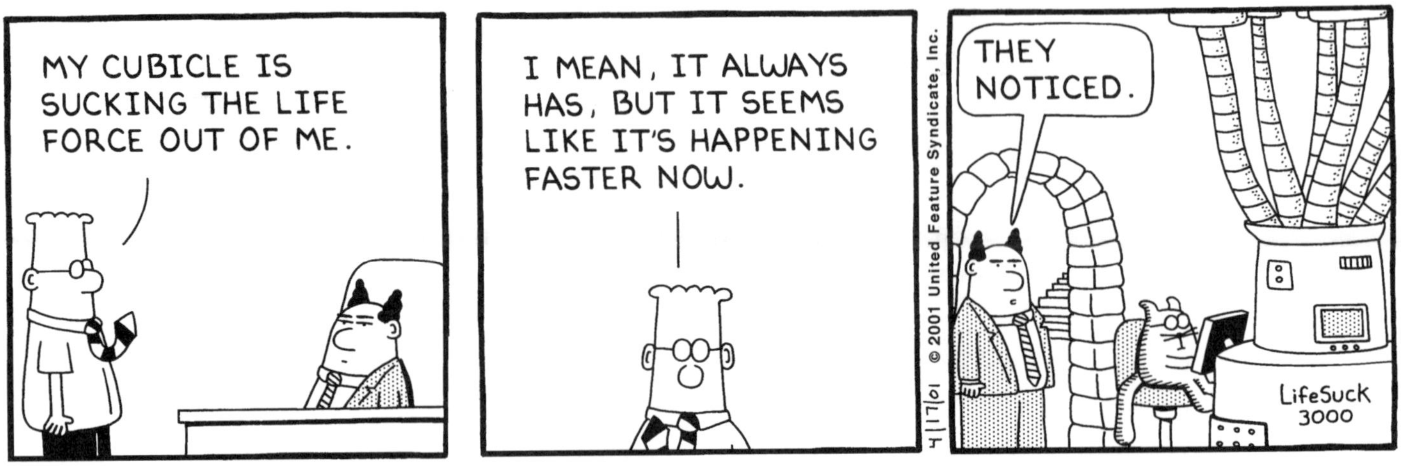
MY CUBICLE IS SUCKING THE LIFE FORCE OUT OF ME.
I MEAN, IT ALWAYS HAS, BUT IT SEEMS LIKE IT'S HAPPENING FASTER NOW.
© 2001 United Feature Syndicate, Inc.
4/17/01
THEY NOTICED.
LifeSuck 3000

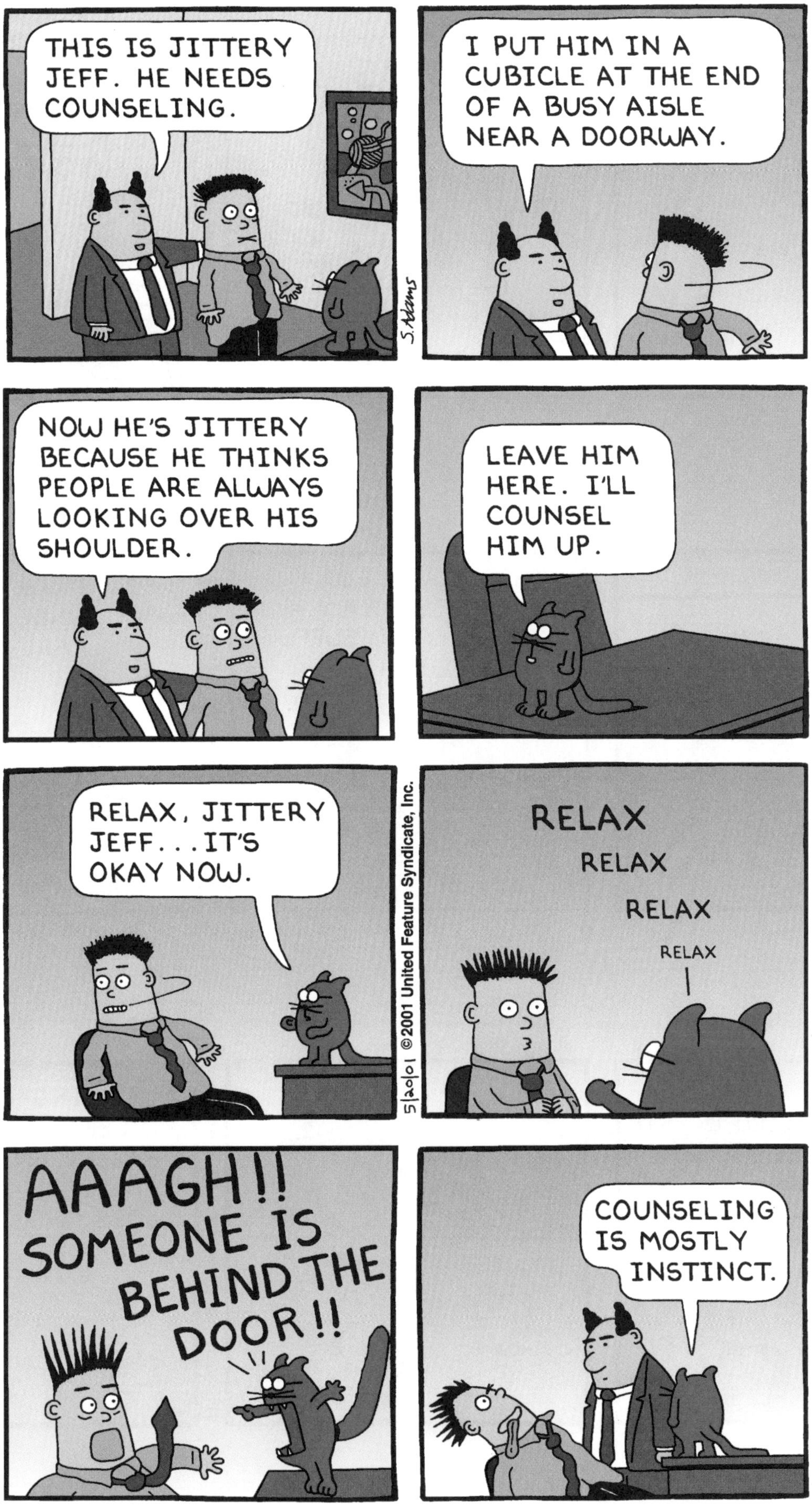
THIS IS JITTERY JEFF. HE NEEDS COUNSELING.
I PUT HIM IN A CUBICLE AT THE END OF A BUSY AISLE NEAR A DOORWAY.
NOW HE'S JITTERY BECAUSE HE THINKS PEOPLE ARE ALWAYS LOOKING OVER HIS SHOULDER.
LEAVE HIM HERE. I'LL COUNSEL HIM UP.
RELAX, JITTERY JEFF... IT'S OKAY NOW.
5/20/01 ©2001 United Feature Syndicate, Inc.
RELAX
RELAX
RELAX
RELAX
AAAGH!! SOMEONE IS BEHIND THE DOOR!!
COUNSELING IS MOSTLY INSTINCT.

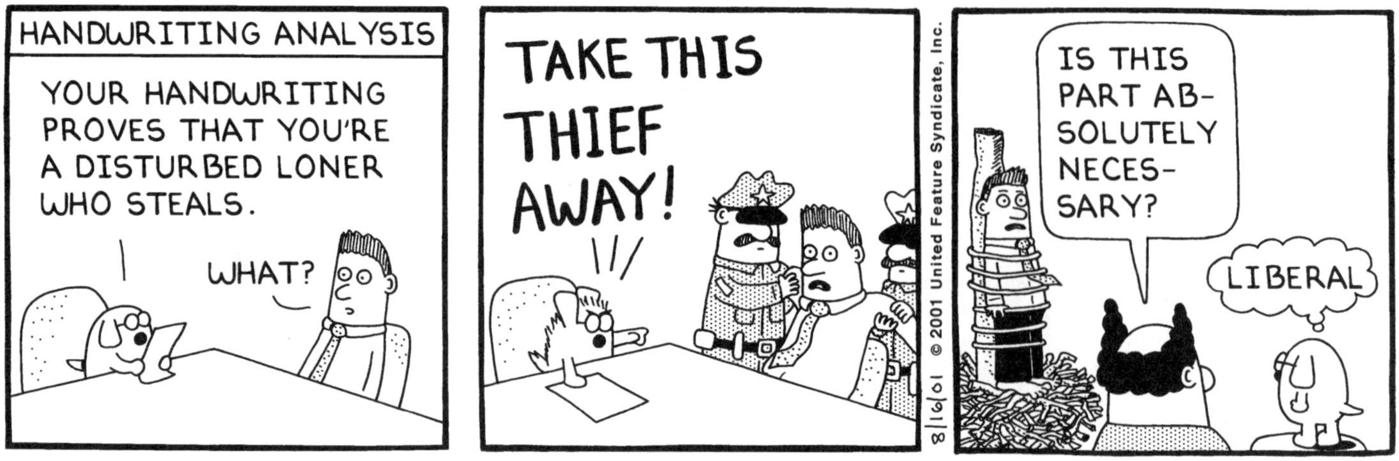
HANDWRITING ANALYSIS
YOUR HANDWRITING PROVES THAT YOU'RE A DISTURBED LONER WHO STEALS.
WHAT?
TAKE THIS THIEF AWAY!
8/16/01 © 2001 United Feature Syndicate, Inc.
IS THIS PART ABSOLUTELY NECESSARY?
LIBERAL

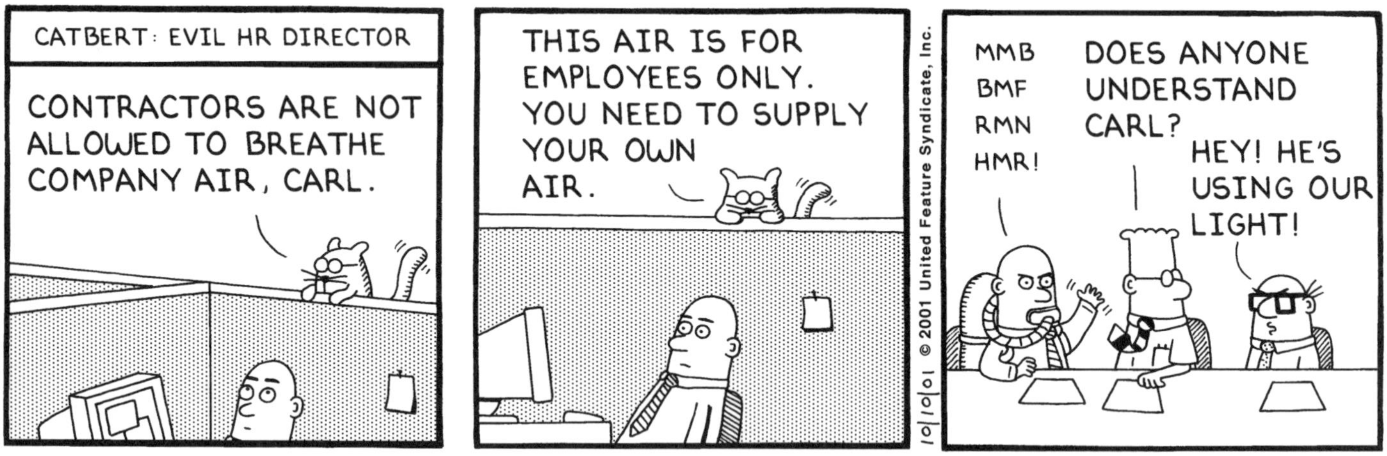
CATBERT: EVIL HR DIRECTOR
CONTRACTORS ARE NOT ALLOWED TO BREATHE COMPANY AIR, CARL.
THIS AIR IS FOR EMPLOYEES ONLY. YOU NEED TO SUPPLY YOUR OWN AIR.
10/10/01 © 2001 United Feature Syndicate, Inc.
MMB BMF RMN HMR!
DOES ANYONE UNDERSTAND CARL?
HEY! HE'S USING OUR LIGHT!

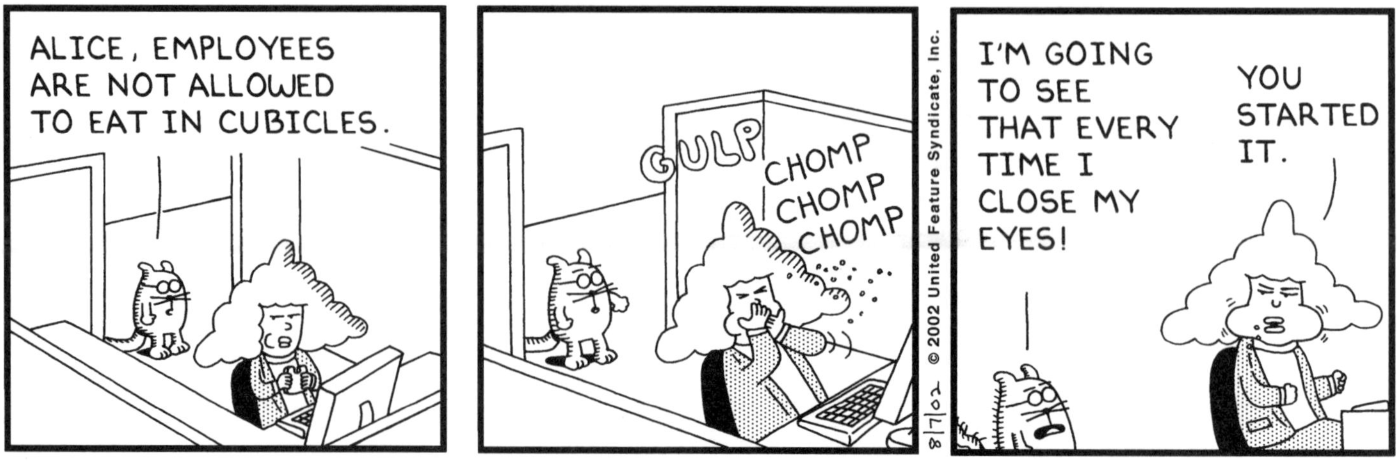
ALICE, EMPLOYEES ARE NOT ALLOWED TO EAT IN CUBICLES.
GULP
CHOMP CHOMP CHOMP
8/7/02 © 2002 United Feature Syndicate, Inc.
I'M GOING TO SEE THAT EVERY TIME I CLOSE MY EYES!
YOU STARTED IT.

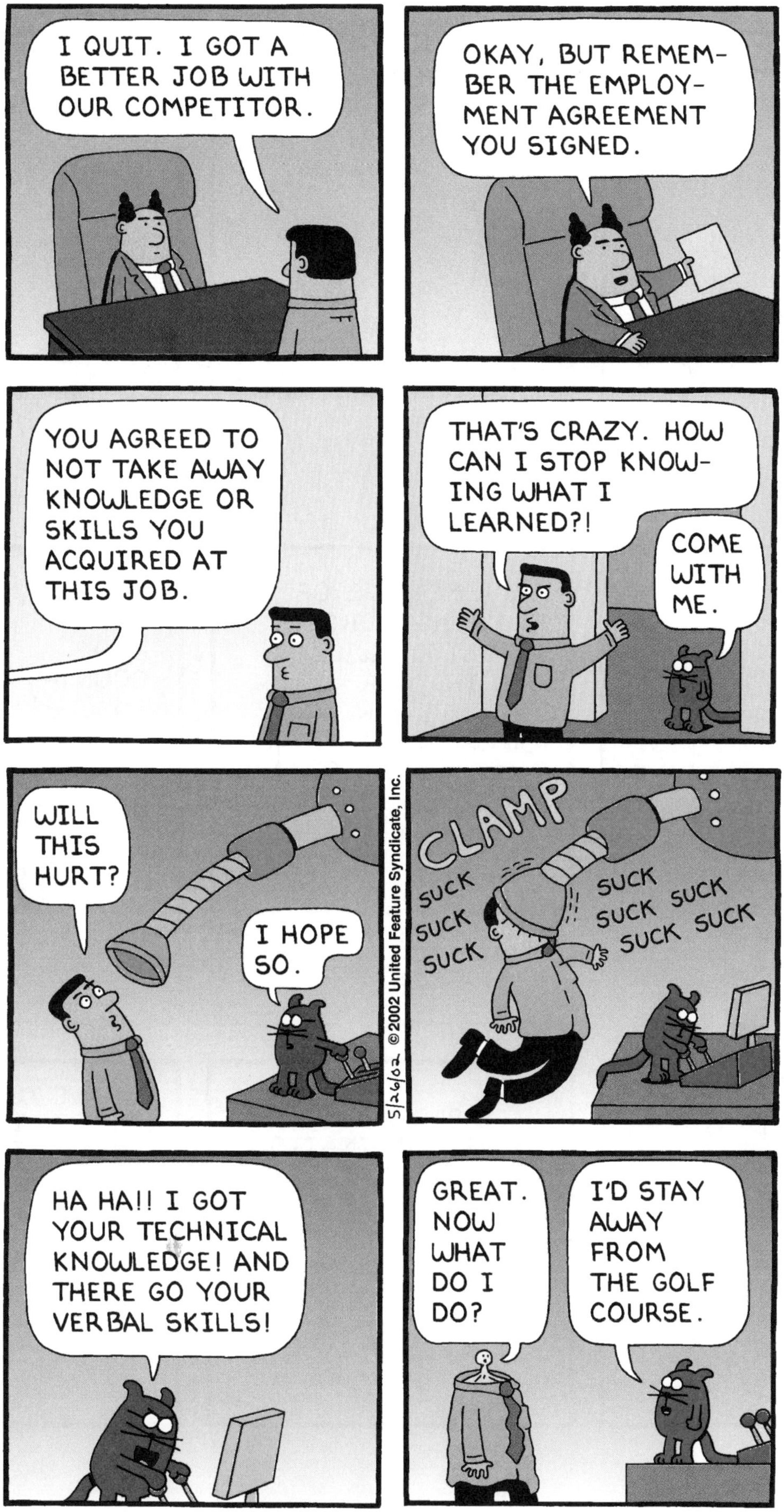
I QUIT. I GOT A BETTER JOB WITH OUR COMPETITOR.
OKAY, BUT REMEMBER THE EMPLOYMENT AGREEMENT YOU SIGNED.
YOU AGREED TO NOT TAKE AWAY KNOWLEDGE OR SKILLS YOU ACQUIRED AT THIS JOB.
THAT'S CRAZY. HOW CAN I STOP KNOWING WHAT I LEARNED?!
COME WITH ME.
WILL THIS HURT?
I HOPE SO.
© 2002 United Feature Syndicate, Inc.
5/26/02
CLAMP
SUCK SUCK SUCK
SUCK SUCK SUCK SUCK SUCK
HA HA!! I GOT YOUR TECHNICAL KNOWLEDGE! AND THERE GO YOUR VERBAL SKILLS!
GREAT. NOW WHAT DO I DO?
I'D STAY AWAY FROM THE GOLF COURSE.

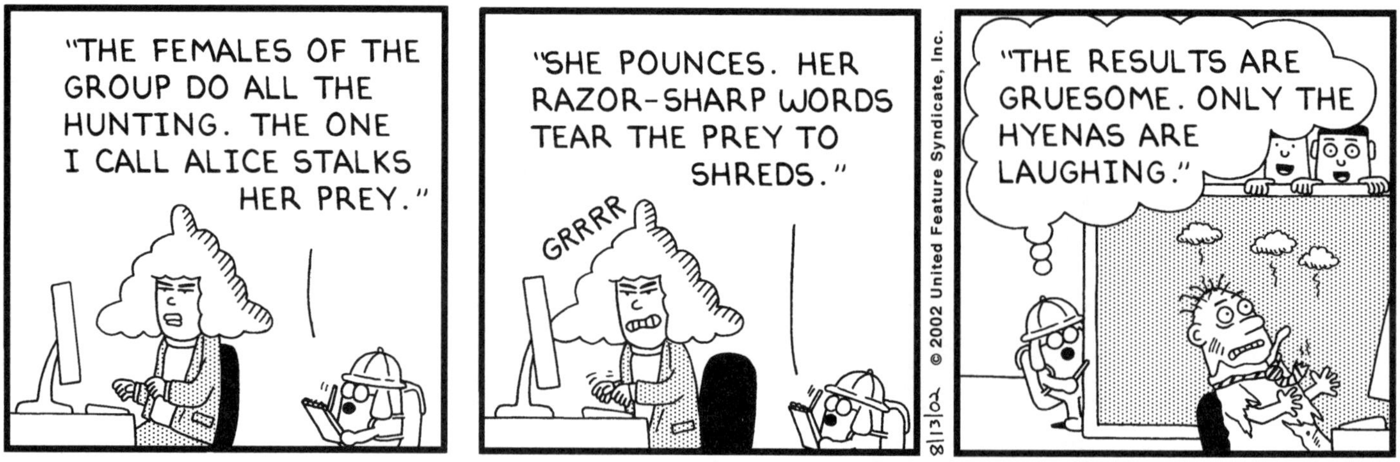
"THE FEMALES OF THE GROUP DO ALL THE HUNTING. THE ONE I CALL ALICE STALKS HER PREY."
"SHE POUNCES. HER RAZOR-SHARP WORDS TEAR THE PREY TO SHREDS."
GRRRR
© 2002 United Feature Syndicate, Inc.
8/13/02
"THE RESULTS ARE GRUESOME. ONLY THE HYENAS ARE LAUGHING."

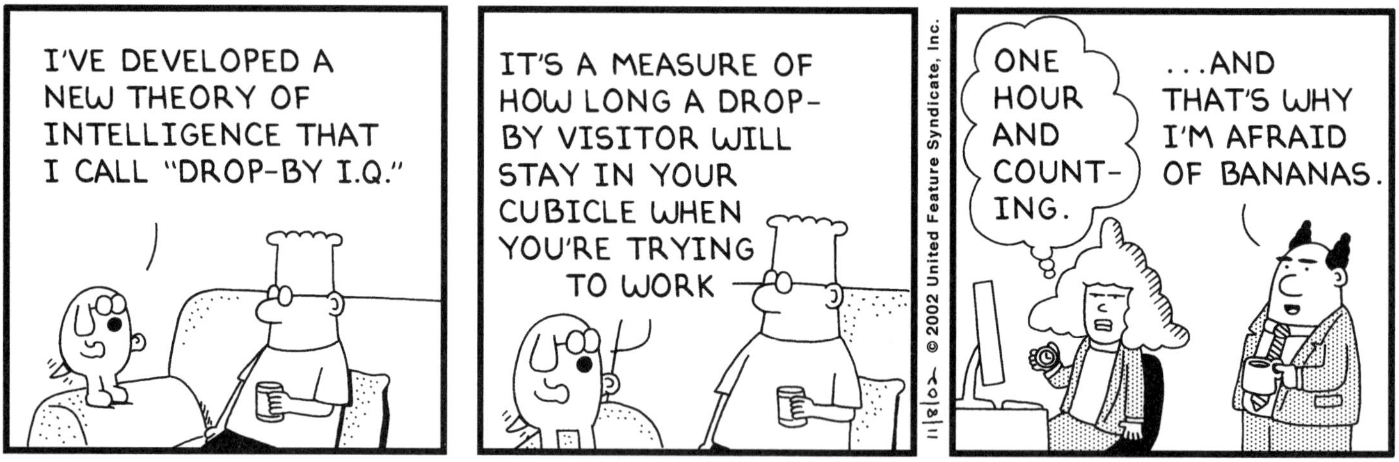
I'VE DEVELOPED A NEW THEORY OF INTELLIGENCE THAT I CALL "DROP-BY I.Q."
IT'S A MEASURE OF HOW LONG A DROP-BY VISITOR WILL STAY IN YOUR CUBICLE WHEN YOU'RE TRYING TO WORK
© 2002 United Feature Syndicate, Inc.
11/8/02
ONE HOUR AND COUNT-ING.
...AND THAT'S WHY I'M AFRAID OF BANANAS.

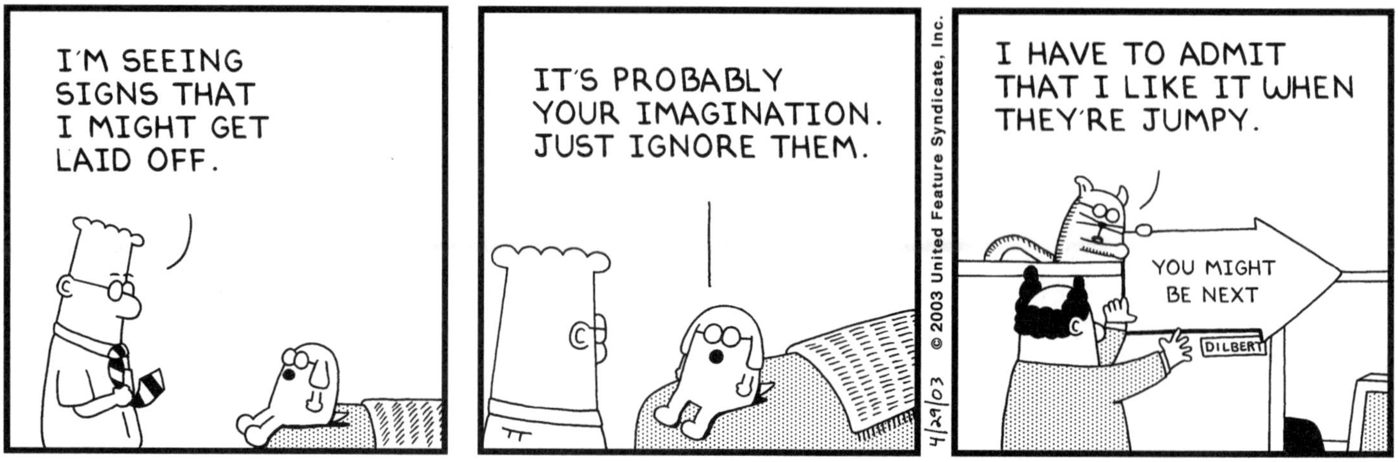
I'M SEEING SIGNS THAT I MIGHT GET LAID OFF.
IT'S PROBABLY YOUR IMAGINATION. JUST IGNORE THEM.
© 2003 United Feature Syndicate, Inc.
4/29/03
I HAVE TO ADMIT THAT I LIKE IT WHEN THEY'RE JUMPY.
YOU MIGHT BE NEXT
DILBERT

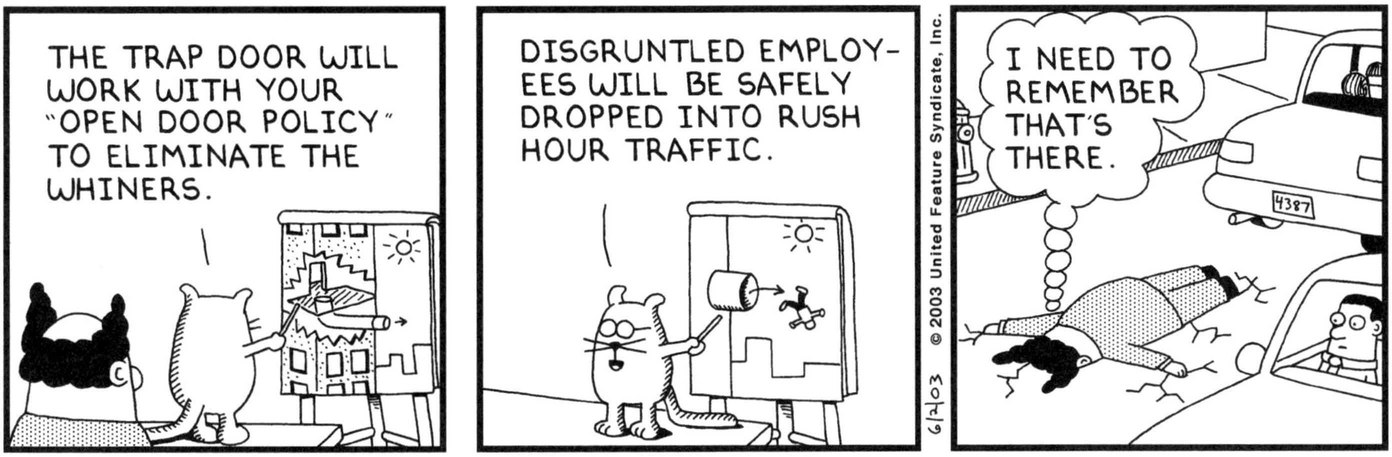
THE TRAP DOOR WILL WORK WITH YOUR "OPEN DOOR POLICY" TO ELIMINATE THE WHINERS.
DISGRUNTLED EMPLOYEES WILL BE SAFELY DROPPED INTO RUSH HOUR TRAFFIC.
6/2/03 © 2003 United Feature Syndicate, Inc.
I NEED TO REMEMBER THAT'S THERE.
4387

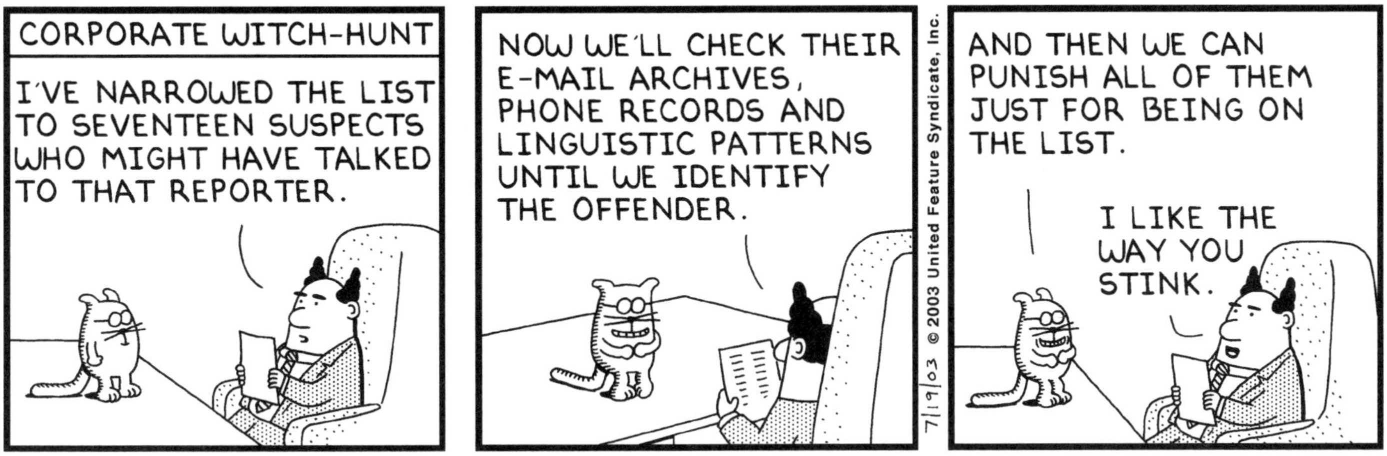
CORPORATE WITCH-HUNT
I'VE NARROWED THE LIST TO SEVENTEEN SUSPECTS WHO MIGHT HAVE TALKED TO THAT REPORTER.
NOW WE'LL CHECK THEIR E-MAIL ARCHIVES, PHONE RECORDS AND LINGUISTIC PATTERNS UNTIL WE IDENTIFY THE OFFENDER.
7/19/03 © 2003 United Feature Syndicate, Inc.
AND THEN WE CAN PUNISH ALL OF THEM JUST FOR BEING ON THE LIST.
I LIKE THE WAY YOU STINK.

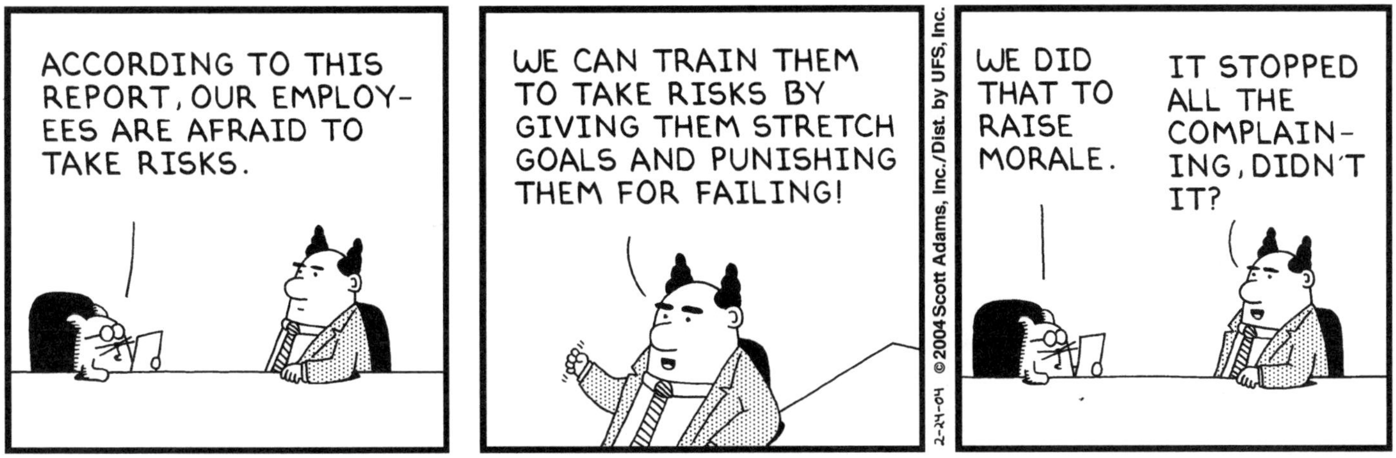
ACCORDING TO THIS REPORT, OUR EMPLOYEES ARE AFRAID TO TAKE RISKS.
WE CAN TRAIN THEM TO TAKE RISKS BY GIVING THEM STRETCH GOALS AND PUNISHING THEM FOR FAILING!
2-24-04 © 2004 Scott Adams, Inc./Dist. by UFS, Inc.
WE DID THAT TO RAISE MORALE.
IT STOPPED ALL THE COMPLAINING, DIDN'T IT?

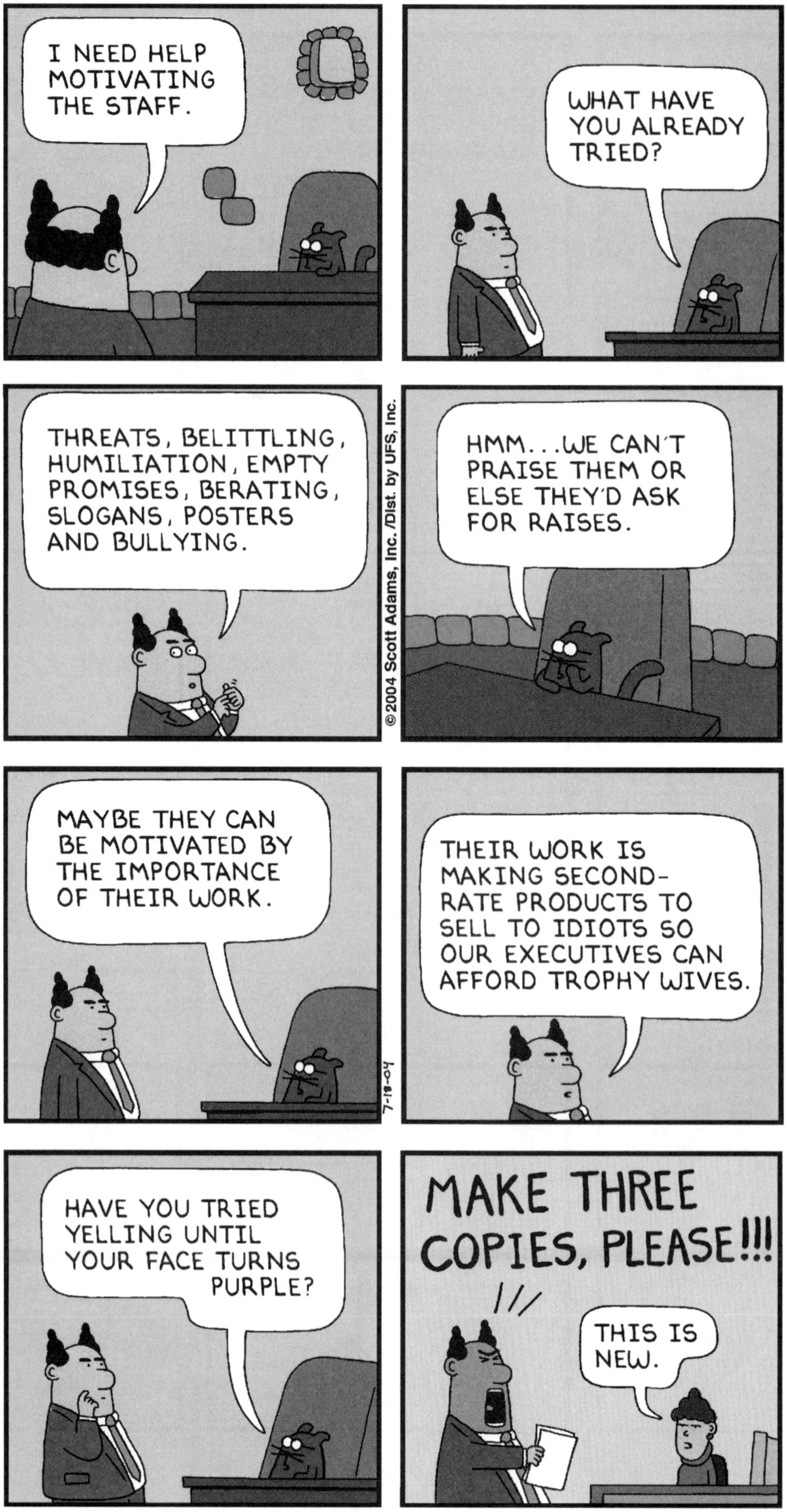
I NEED HELP MOTIVATING THE STAFF.
WHAT HAVE YOU ALREADY TRIED?
THREATS, BELITTLING, HUMILIATION, EMPTY PROMISES, BERATING, SLOGANS, POSTERS AND BULLYING.
HMM...WE CAN'T PRAISE THEM OR ELSE THEY'D ASK FOR RAISES.
MAYBE THEY CAN BE MOTIVATED BY THE IMPORTANCE OF THEIR WORK.
THEIR WORK IS MAKING SECOND-RATE PRODUCTS TO SELL TO IDIOTS SO OUR EXECUTIVES CAN AFFORD TROPHY WIVES.
HAVE YOU TRIED YELLING UNTIL YOUR FACE TURNS PURPLE?
MAKE THREE COPIES, PLEASE!!!
THIS IS NEW.
©2004 Scott Adams, Inc./Dist. by UFS, Inc.
7-18-04

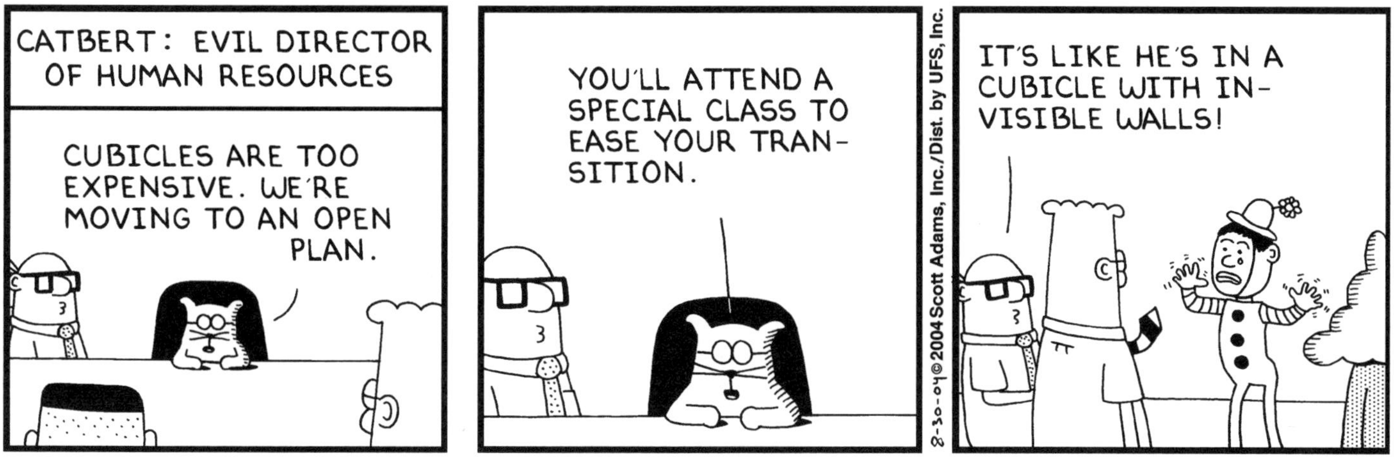
CATBERT: EVIL DIRECTOR OF HUMAN RESOURCES
CUBICLES ARE TOO EXPENSIVE. WE'RE MOVING TO AN OPEN PLAN.
YOU'LL ATTEND A SPECIAL CLASS TO EASE YOUR TRANSITION.
8-30-04 © 2004 Scott Adams, Inc./Dist. by UFS, Inc.
IT'S LIKE HE'S IN A CUBICLE WITH INVISIBLE WALLS!

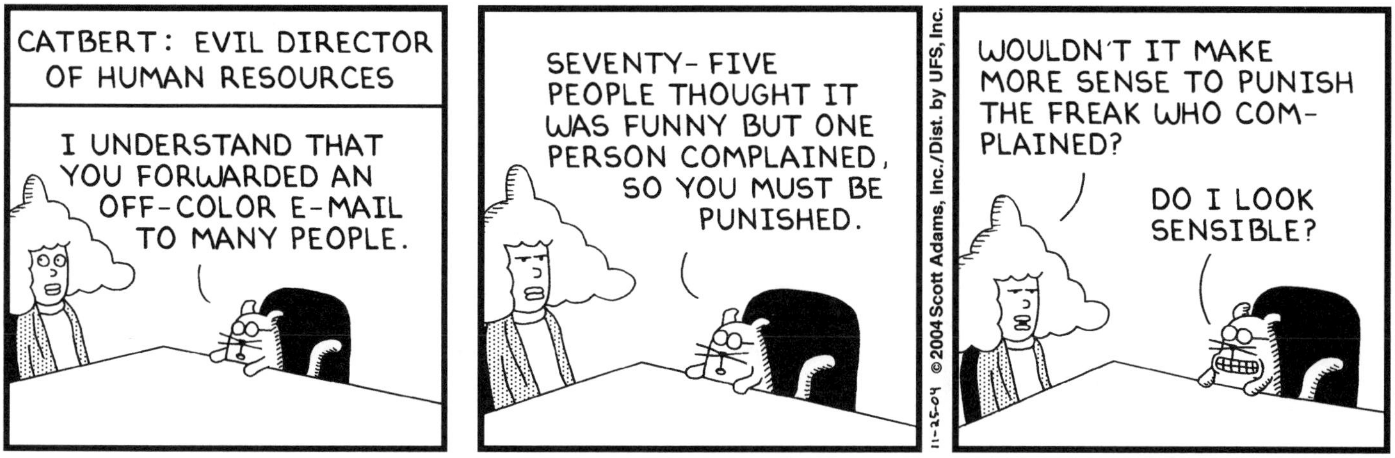
CATBERT: EVIL DIRECTOR OF HUMAN RESOURCES
I UNDERSTAND THAT YOU FORWARDED AN OFF-COLOR E-MAIL TO MANY PEOPLE.
SEVENTY-FIVE PEOPLE THOUGHT IT WAS FUNNY BUT ONE PERSON COMPLAINED, SO YOU MUST BE PUNISHED.
11-25-04 © 2004 Scott Adams, Inc./Dist. by UFS, Inc.
WOULDN'T IT MAKE MORE SENSE TO PUNISH THE FREAK WHO COMPLAINED?
DO I LOOK SENSIBLE?

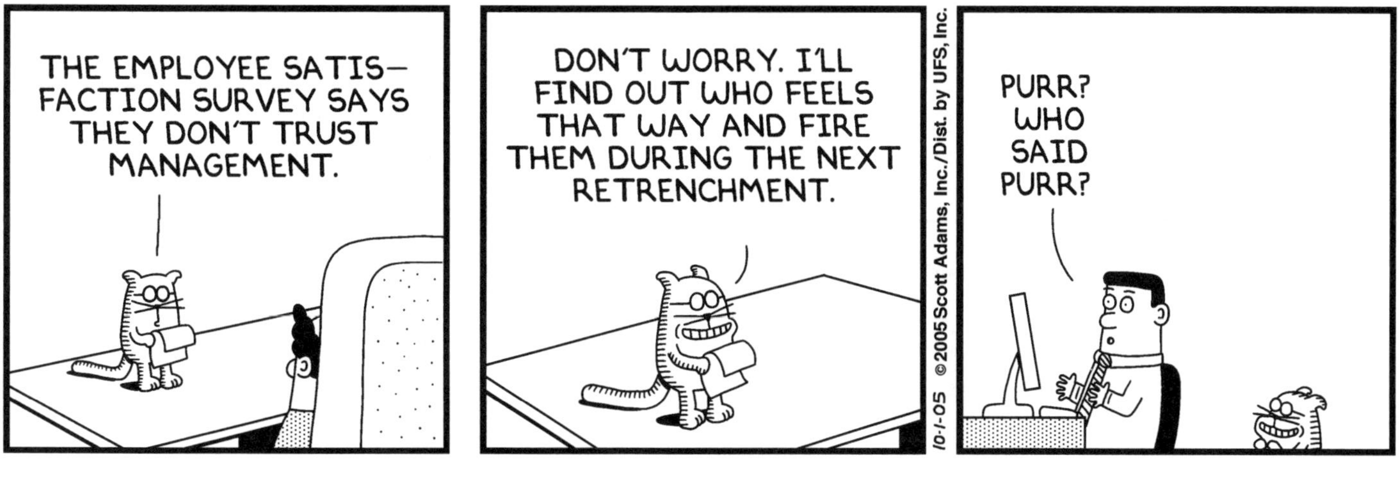
THE EMPLOYEE SATISFACTION SURVEY SAYS THEY DON'T TRUST MANAGEMENT.
DON'T WORRY. I'LL FIND OUT WHO FEELS THAT WAY AND FIRE THEM DURING THE NEXT RETRENCHMENT.
10-1-05 © 2005 Scott Adams, Inc./Dist. by UFS, Inc.
PURR? WHO SAID PURR?

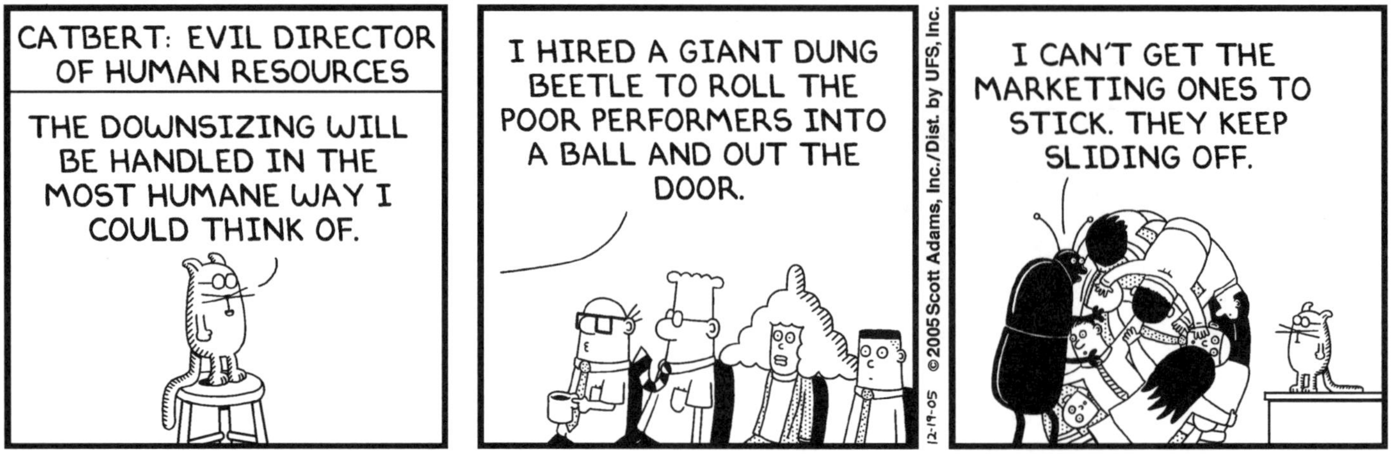
CATBERT: EVIL DIRECTOR OF HUMAN RESOURCES
THE DOWNSIZING WILL BE HANDLED IN THE MOST HUMANE WAY I COULD THINK OF.
I HIRED A GIANT DUNG BEETLE TO ROLL THE POOR PERFORMERS INTO A BALL AND OUT THE DOOR.
12-19-05 © 2005 Scott Adams, Inc./Dist. by UFS, Inc.
I CAN'T GET THE MARKETING ONES TO STICK. THEY KEEP SLIDING OFF.

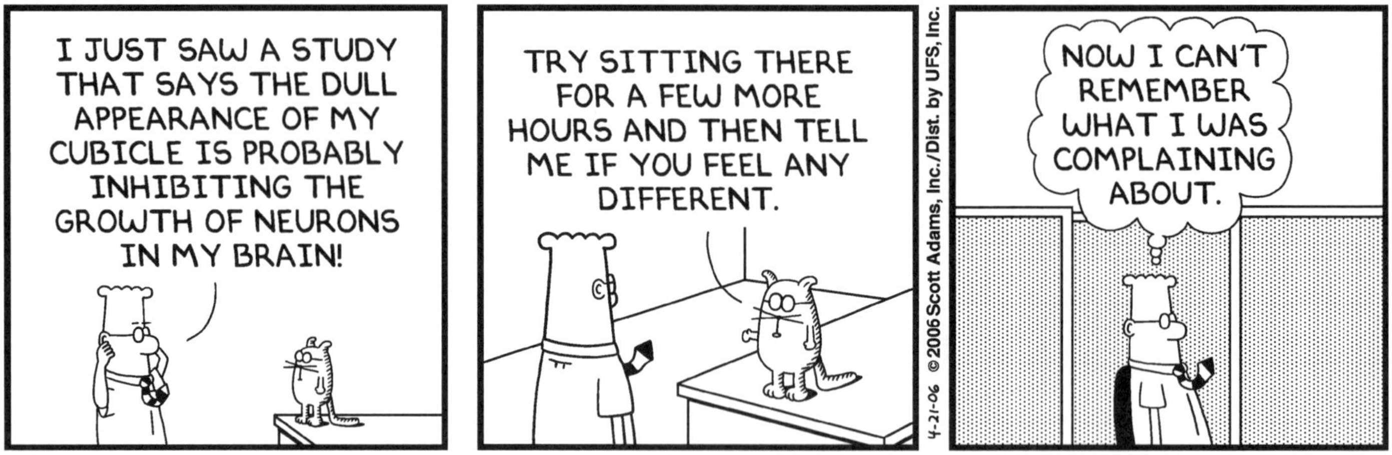
I JUST SAW A STUDY THAT SAYS THE DULL APPEARANCE OF MY CUBICLE IS PROBABLY INHIBITING THE GROWTH OF NEURONS IN MY BRAIN!
TRY SITTING THERE FOR A FEW MORE HOURS AND THEN TELL ME IF YOU FEEL ANY DIFFERENT.
4-21-06 © 2006 Scott Adams, Inc./Dist. by UFS, Inc.
NOW I CAN'T REMEMBER WHAT I WAS COMPLAINING ABOUT.

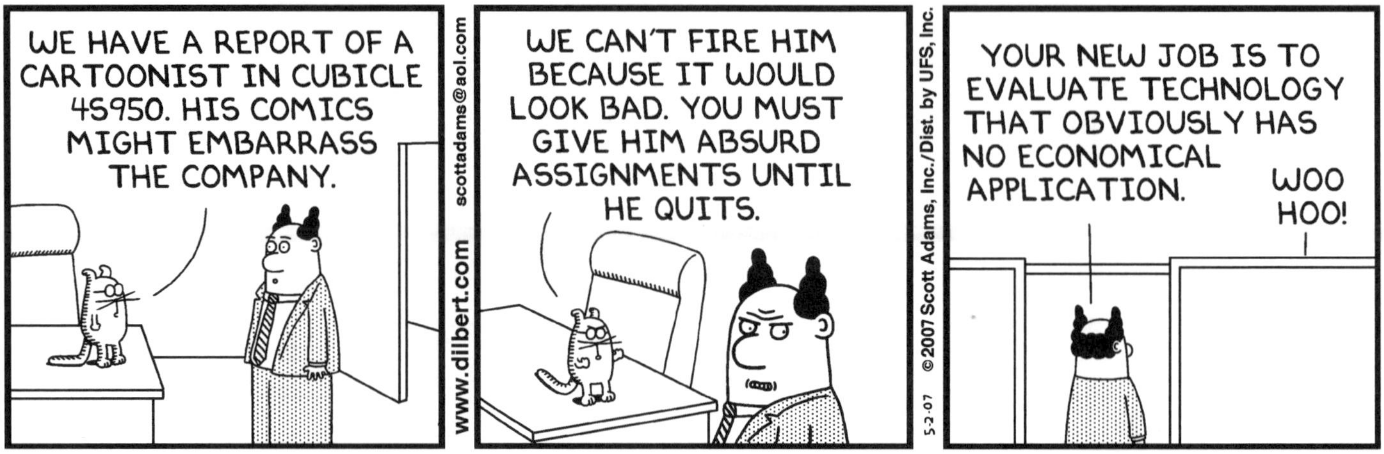
WE HAVE A REPORT OF A CARTOONIST IN CUBICLE 45950. HIS COMICS MIGHT EMBARRASS THE COMPANY.
www.dilbert.com scottadams@aol.com
WE CAN'T FIRE HIM BECAUSE IT WOULD LOOK BAD. YOU MUST GIVE HIM ABSURD ASSIGNMENTS UNTIL HE QUITS.
5-2-07 © 2007 Scott Adams, Inc./Dist. by UFS, Inc.
YOUR NEW JOB IS TO EVALUATE TECHNOLOGY THAT OBVIOUSLY HAS NO ECONOMICAL APPLICATION.
WOO HOO!

5. Wally

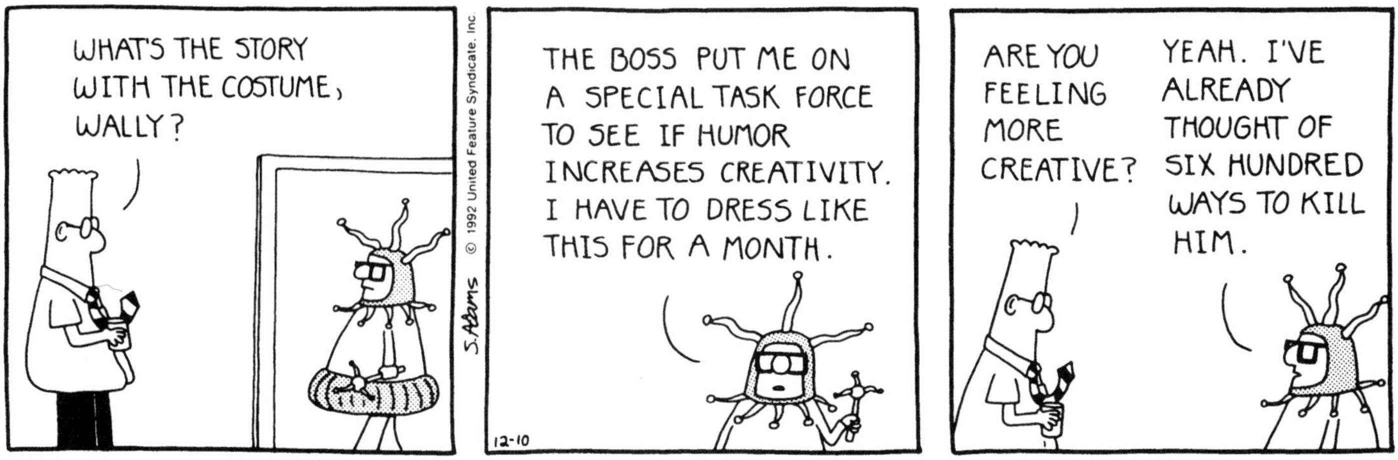
WHAT'S THE STORY WITH THE COSTUME, WALLY?
S. Adams
© 1992 United Feature Syndicate, Inc.
THE BOSS PUT ME ON A SPECIAL TASK FORCE TO SEE IF HUMOR INCREASES CREATIVITY. I HAVE TO DRESS LIKE THIS FOR A MONTH.
12-10
ARE YOU FEELING MORE CREATIVE?
YEAH. I'VE ALREADY THOUGHT OF SIX HUNDRED WAYS TO KILL HIM.

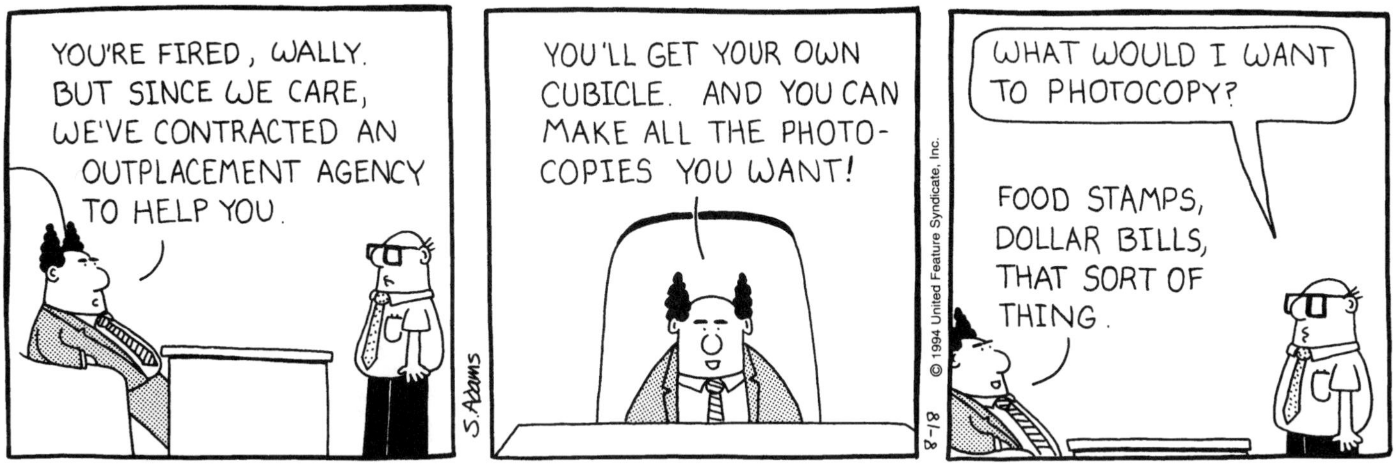
YOU'RE FIRED, WALLY. BUT SINCE WE CARE, WE'VE CONTRACTED AN OUTPLACEMENT AGENCY TO HELP YOU.
S. Adams
YOU'LL GET YOUR OWN CUBICLE. AND YOU CAN MAKE ALL THE PHOTOCOPIES YOU WANT!
8-18
© 1994 United Feature Syndicate, Inc.
WHAT WOULD I WANT TO PHOTOCOPY?
FOOD STAMPS, DOLLAR BILLS, THAT SORT OF THING.

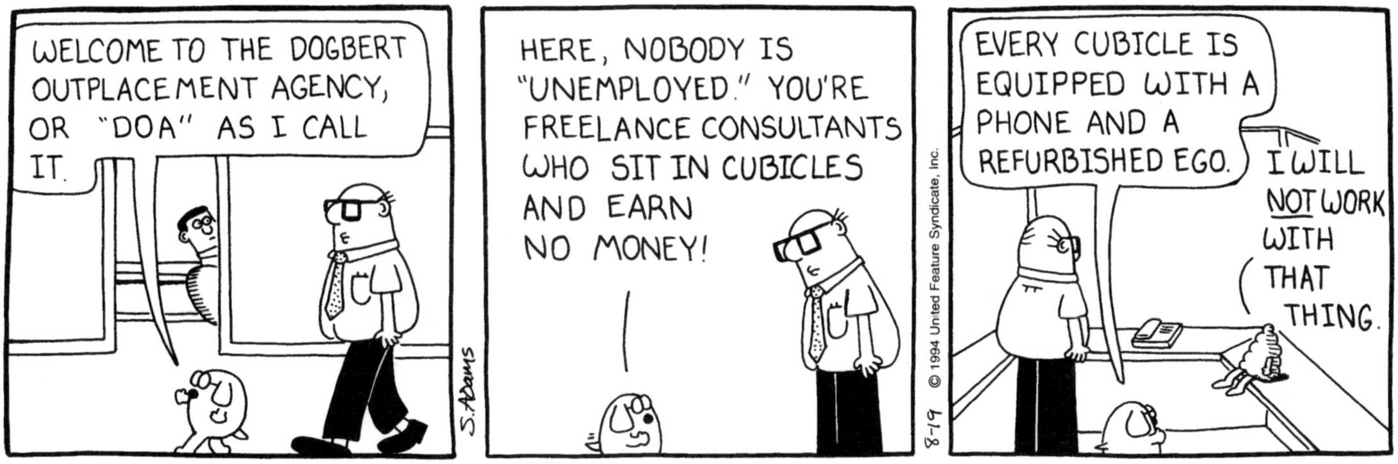
WELCOME TO THE DOGBERT OUTPLACEMENT AGENCY, OR "DOA" AS I CALL IT.
S. Adams
HERE, NOBODY IS "UNEMPLOYED." YOU'RE FREELANCE CONSULTANTS WHO SIT IN CUBICLES AND EARN NO MONEY!
8-19
© 1994 United Feature Syndicate, Inc.
EVERY CUBICLE IS EQUIPPED WITH A PHONE AND A REFURBISHED EGO.
I WILL NOT WORK WITH THAT THING.

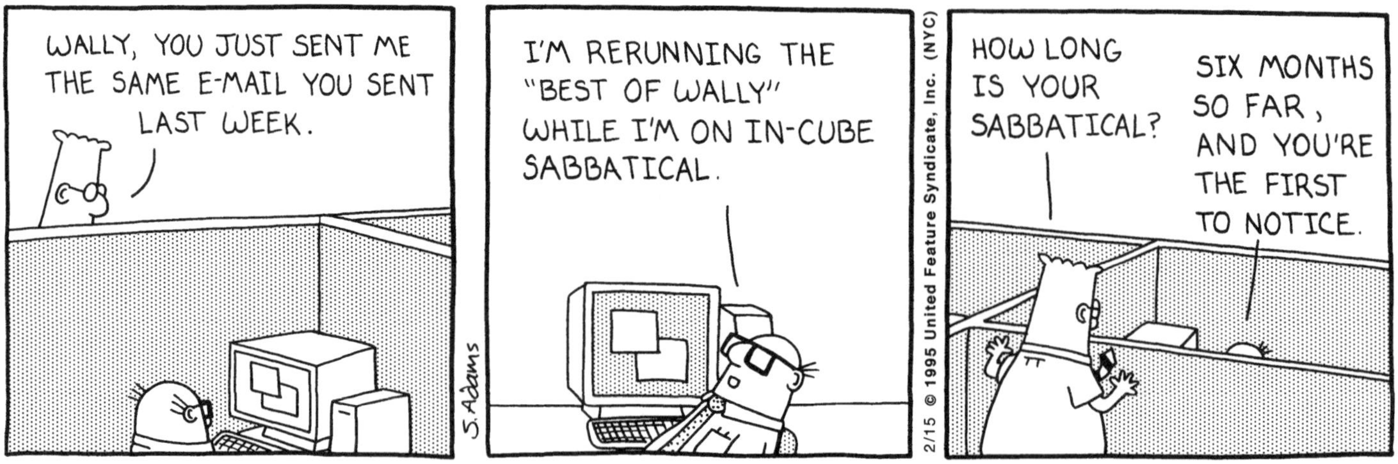
WALLY, YOU JUST SENT ME THE SAME E-MAIL YOU SENT LAST WEEK.
I'M RERUNNING THE "BEST OF WALLY" WHILE I'M ON IN-CUBE SABBATICAL.
HOW LONG IS YOUR SABBATICAL?
SIX MONTHS SO FAR, AND YOU'RE THE FIRST TO NOTICE.
S. Adams
2/15 © 1995 United Feature Syndicate, Inc. (NYC)

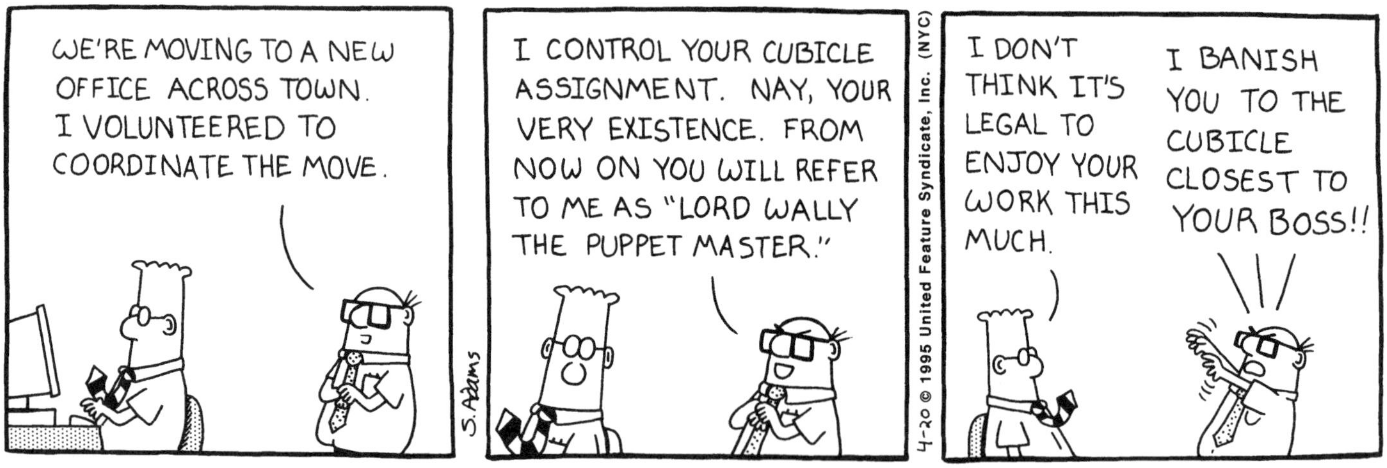
WE'RE MOVING TO A NEW OFFICE ACROSS TOWN. I VOLUNTEERED TO COORDINATE THE MOVE.
I CONTROL YOUR CUBICLE ASSIGNMENT. NAY, YOUR VERY EXISTENCE. FROM NOW ON YOU WILL REFER TO ME AS "LORD WALLY THE PUPPET MASTER."
I DON'T THINK IT'S LEGAL TO ENJOY YOUR WORK THIS MUCH.
I BANISH YOU TO THE CUBICLE CLOSEST TO YOUR BOSS!!
S. Adams
4-20 © 1995 United Feature Syndicate, Inc. (NYC)

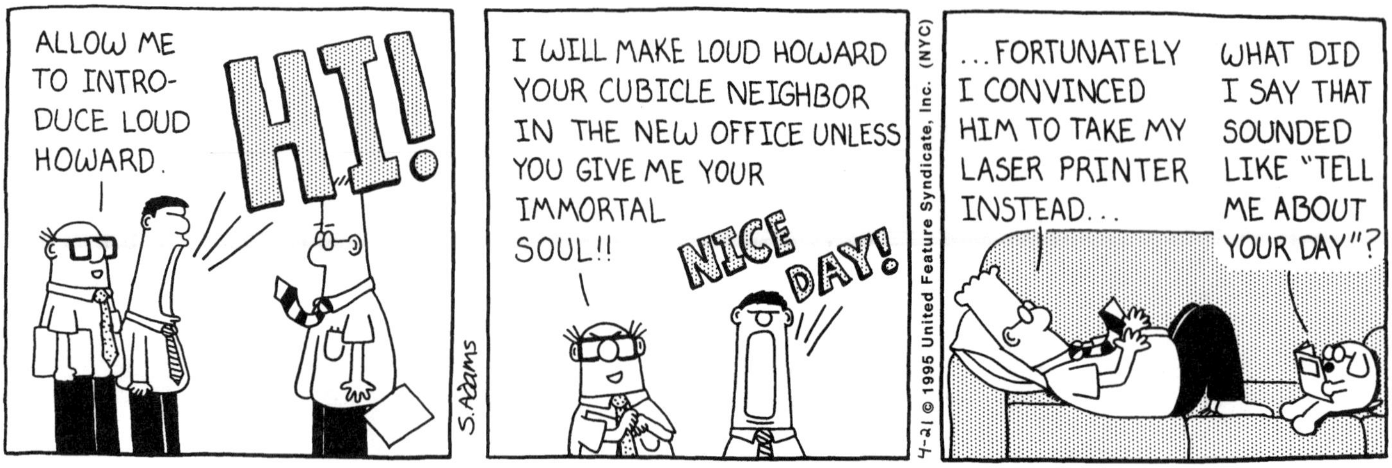
ALLOW ME TO INTRO-DUCE LOUD HOWARD.
HI!
I WILL MAKE LOUD HOWARD YOUR CUBICLE NEIGHBOR IN THE NEW OFFICE UNLESS YOU GIVE ME YOUR IMMORTAL SOUL!!
NICE DAY!
...FORTUNATELY I CONVINCED HIM TO TAKE MY LASER PRINTER INSTEAD...
WHAT DID I SAY THAT SOUNDED LIKE "TELL ME ABOUT YOUR DAY"?
S. Adams
4-21 © 1995 United Feature Syndicate, Inc. (NYC)

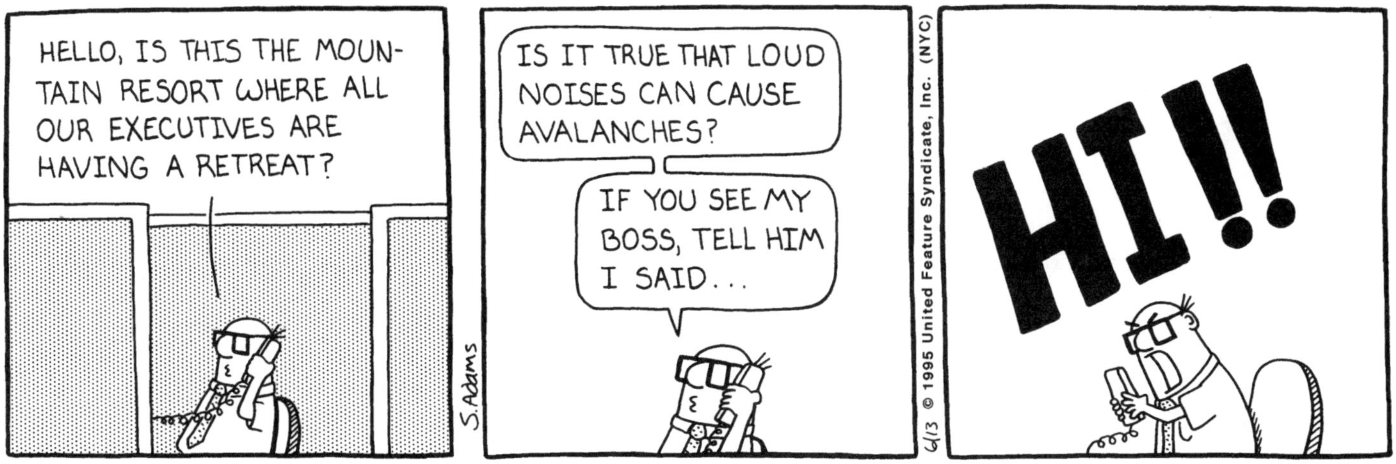
HELLO, IS THIS THE MOUNTAIN RESORT WHERE ALL OUR EXECUTIVES ARE HAVING A RETREAT?
S.Adams
IS IT TRUE THAT LOUD NOISES CAN CAUSE AVALANCHES?
IF YOU SEE MY BOSS, TELL HIM I SAID...
6/13 © 1995 United Feature Syndicate, Inc. (NYC)
HI!!

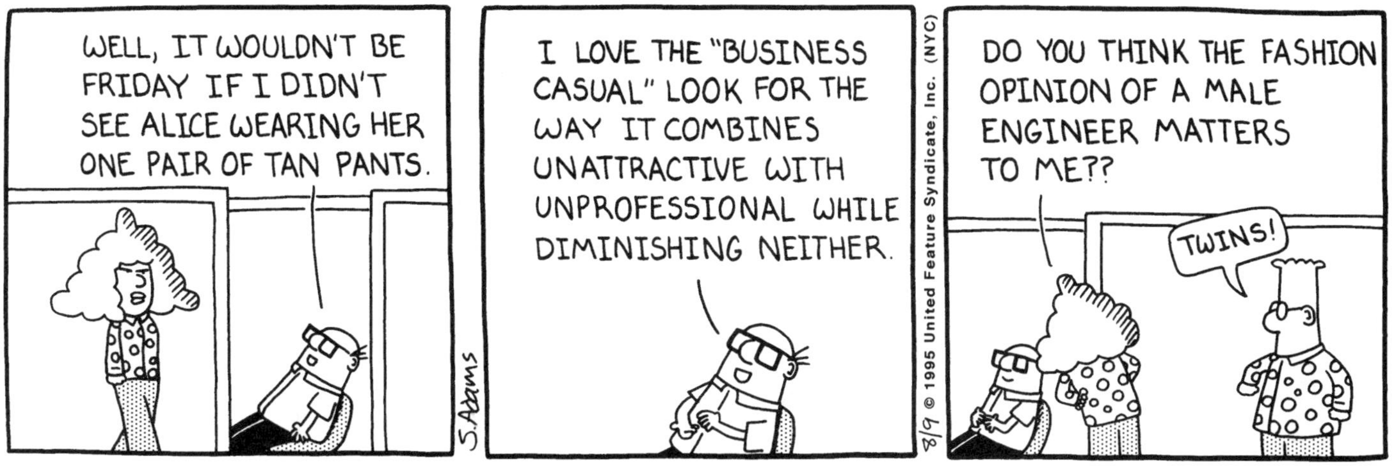
WELL, IT WOULDN'T BE FRIDAY IF I DIDN'T SEE ALICE WEARING HER ONE PAIR OF TAN PANTS.
S.Adams
I LOVE THE "BUSINESS CASUAL" LOOK FOR THE WAY IT COMBINES UNATTRACTIVE WITH UNPROFESSIONAL WHILE DIMINISHING NEITHER.
8/9 © 1995 United Feature Syndicate, Inc. (NYC)
DO YOU THINK THE FASHION OPINION OF A MALE ENGINEER MATTERS TO ME??
TWINS!

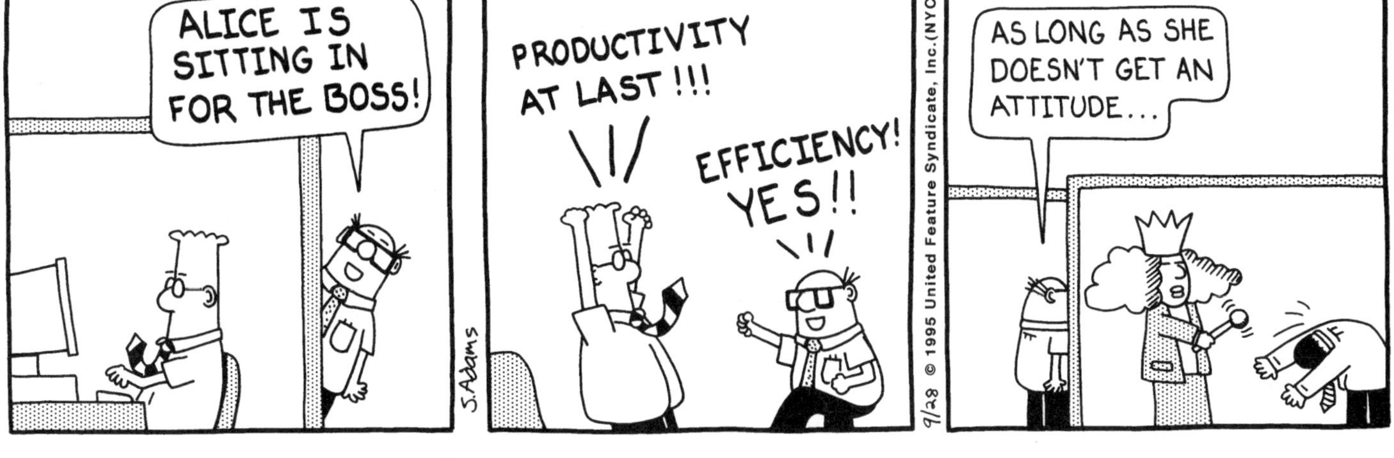
ALICE IS SITTING IN FOR THE BOSS!
S.Adams
PRODUCTIVITY AT LAST!!!
EFFICIENCY! YES!!
9/28 © 1995 United Feature Syndicate, Inc.(NYC)
AS LONG AS SHE DOESN'T GET AN ATTITUDE...

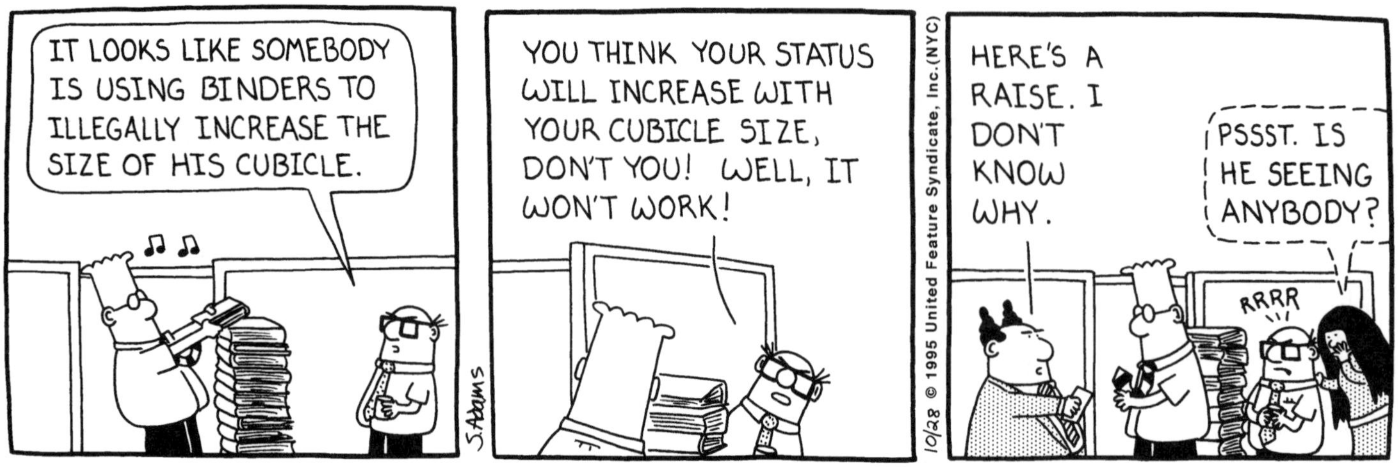
IT LOOKS LIKE SOMEBODY IS USING BINDERS TO ILLEGALLY INCREASE THE SIZE OF HIS CUBICLE.
S. Adams
YOU THINK YOUR STATUS WILL INCREASE WITH YOUR CUBICLE SIZE, DON'T YOU! WELL, IT WON'T WORK!
10/28 © 1995 United Feature Syndicate, Inc.(NYC)
HERE'S A RAISE. I DON'T KNOW WHY.
PSSST. IS HE SEEING ANYBODY?
RRRR

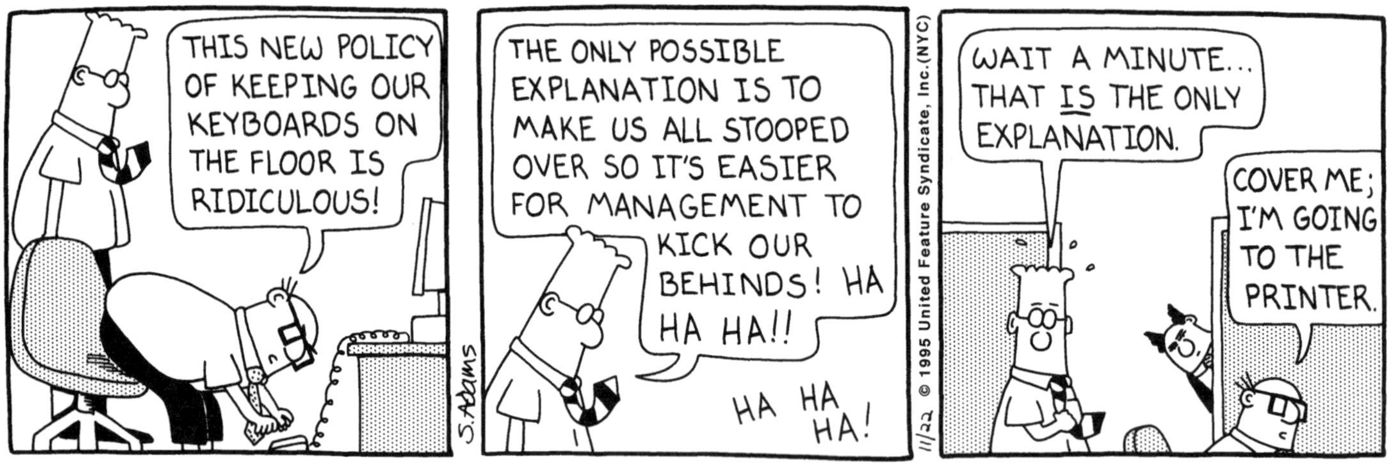
THIS NEW POLICY OF KEEPING OUR KEYBOARDS ON THE FLOOR IS RIDICULOUS!
S. Adams
THE ONLY POSSIBLE EXPLANATION IS TO MAKE US ALL STOOPED OVER SO IT'S EASIER FOR MANAGEMENT TO KICK OUR BEHINDS! HA HA HA!!
HA HA HA!
11/22 © 1995 United Feature Syndicate, Inc.(NYC)
WAIT A MINUTE... THAT IS THE ONLY EXPLANATION.
COVER ME; I'M GOING TO THE PRINTER.

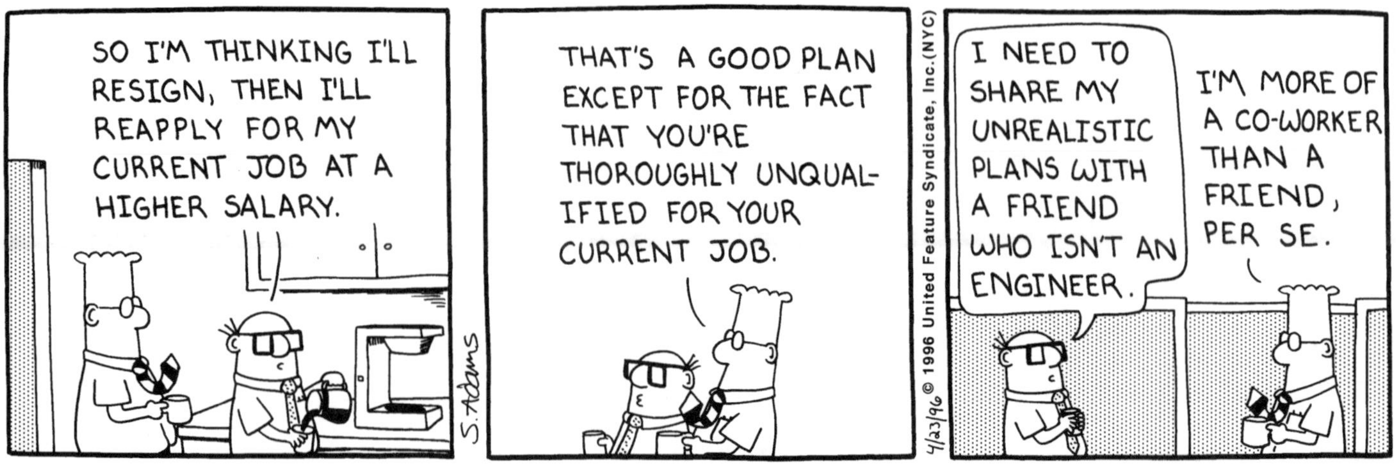
SO I'M THINKING I'LL RESIGN, THEN I'LL REAPPLY FOR MY CURRENT JOB AT A HIGHER SALARY.
S. Adams
THAT'S A GOOD PLAN EXCEPT FOR THE FACT THAT YOU'RE THOROUGHLY UNQUALIFIED FOR YOUR CURRENT JOB.
4/23/96 © 1996 United Feature Syndicate, Inc.(NYC)
I NEED TO SHARE MY UNREALISTIC PLANS WITH A FRIEND WHO ISN'T AN ENGINEER.
I'M MORE OF A CO-WORKER THAN A FRIEND, PER SE.

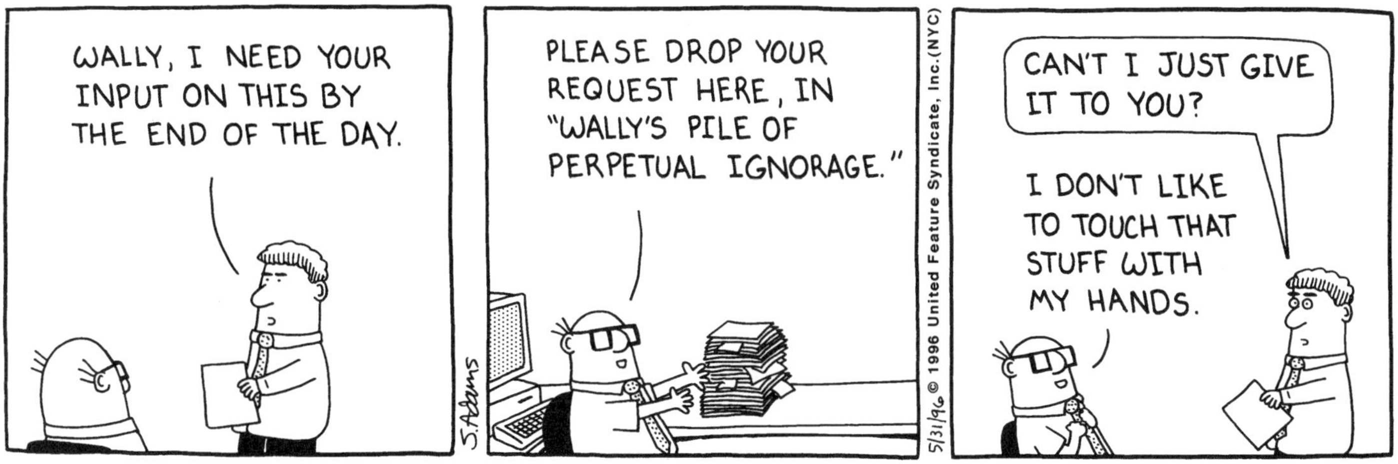
WALLY, I NEED YOUR INPUT ON THIS BY THE END OF THE DAY.
S. Adams
PLEASE DROP YOUR REQUEST HERE, IN "WALLY'S PILE OF PERPETUAL IGNORAGE."
5/31/96 © 1996 United Feature Syndicate, Inc.(NYC)
CAN'T I JUST GIVE IT TO YOU?
I DON'T LIKE TO TOUCH THAT STUFF WITH MY HANDS.

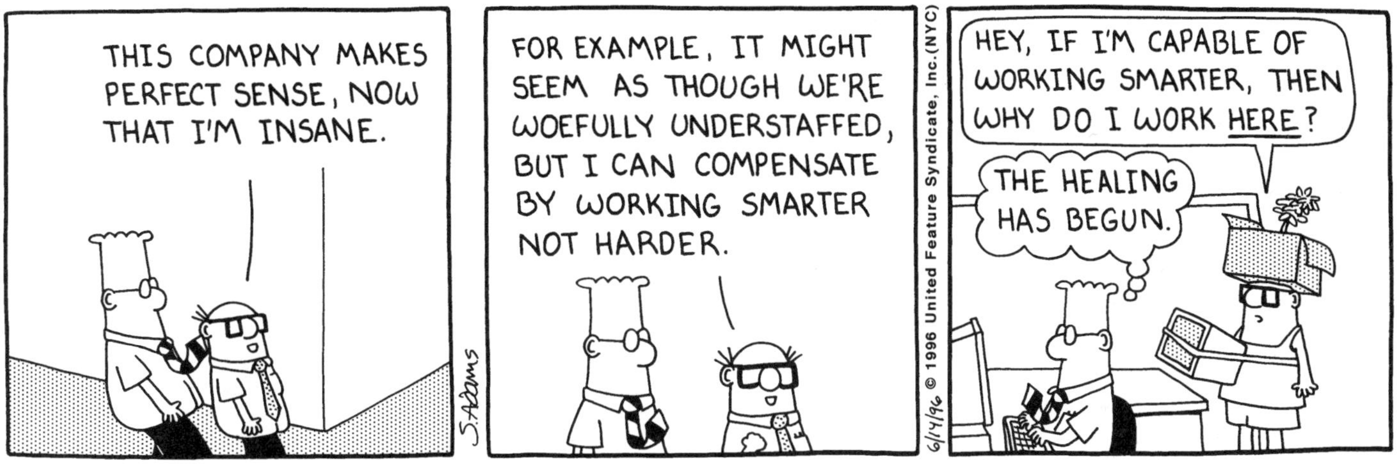
THIS COMPANY MAKES PERFECT SENSE, NOW THAT I'M INSANE.
S. Adams
FOR EXAMPLE, IT MIGHT SEEM AS THOUGH WE'RE WOEFULLY UNDERSTAFFED, BUT I CAN COMPENSATE BY WORKING SMARTER NOT HARDER.
6/4/96 © 1996 United Feature Syndicate, Inc.(NYC)
HEY, IF I'M CAPABLE OF WORKING SMARTER, THEN WHY DO I WORK HERE?
THE HEALING HAS BEGUN.

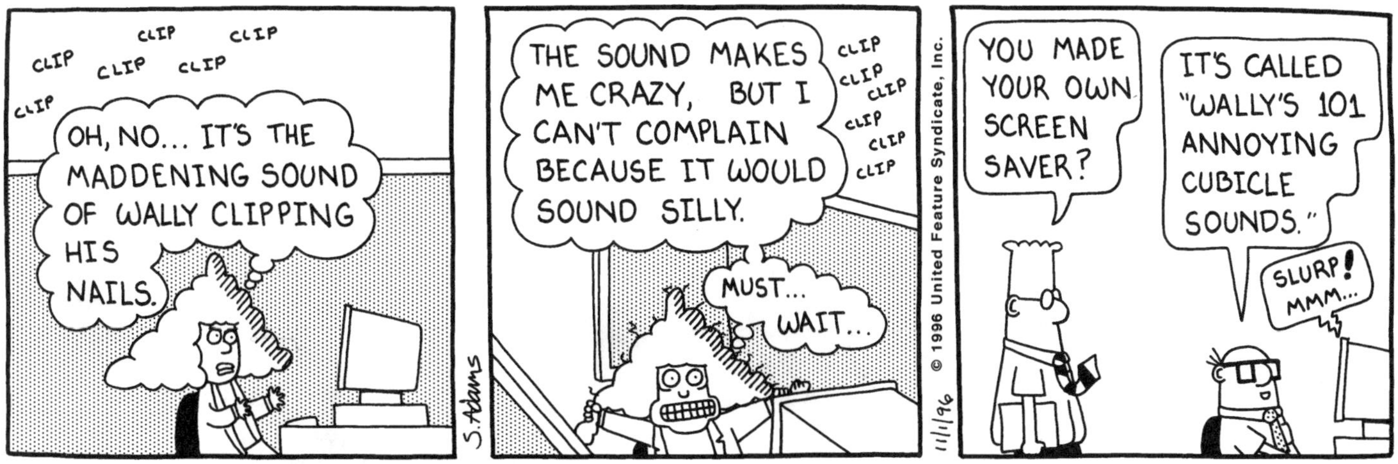
CLIP CLIP CLIP CLIP CLIP CLIP
OH, NO... IT'S THE MADDENING SOUND OF WALLY CLIPPING HIS NAILS.
S. Adams
THE SOUND MAKES ME CRAZY, BUT I CAN'T COMPLAIN BECAUSE IT WOULD SOUND SILLY.
CLIP CLIP CLIP CLIP CLIP CLIP
MUST... WAIT...
11/1/96 © 1996 United Feature Syndicate, Inc.
YOU MADE YOUR OWN SCREEN SAVER?
IT'S CALLED "WALLY'S 101 ANNOYING CUBICLE SOUNDS."
SLURP! MMM...

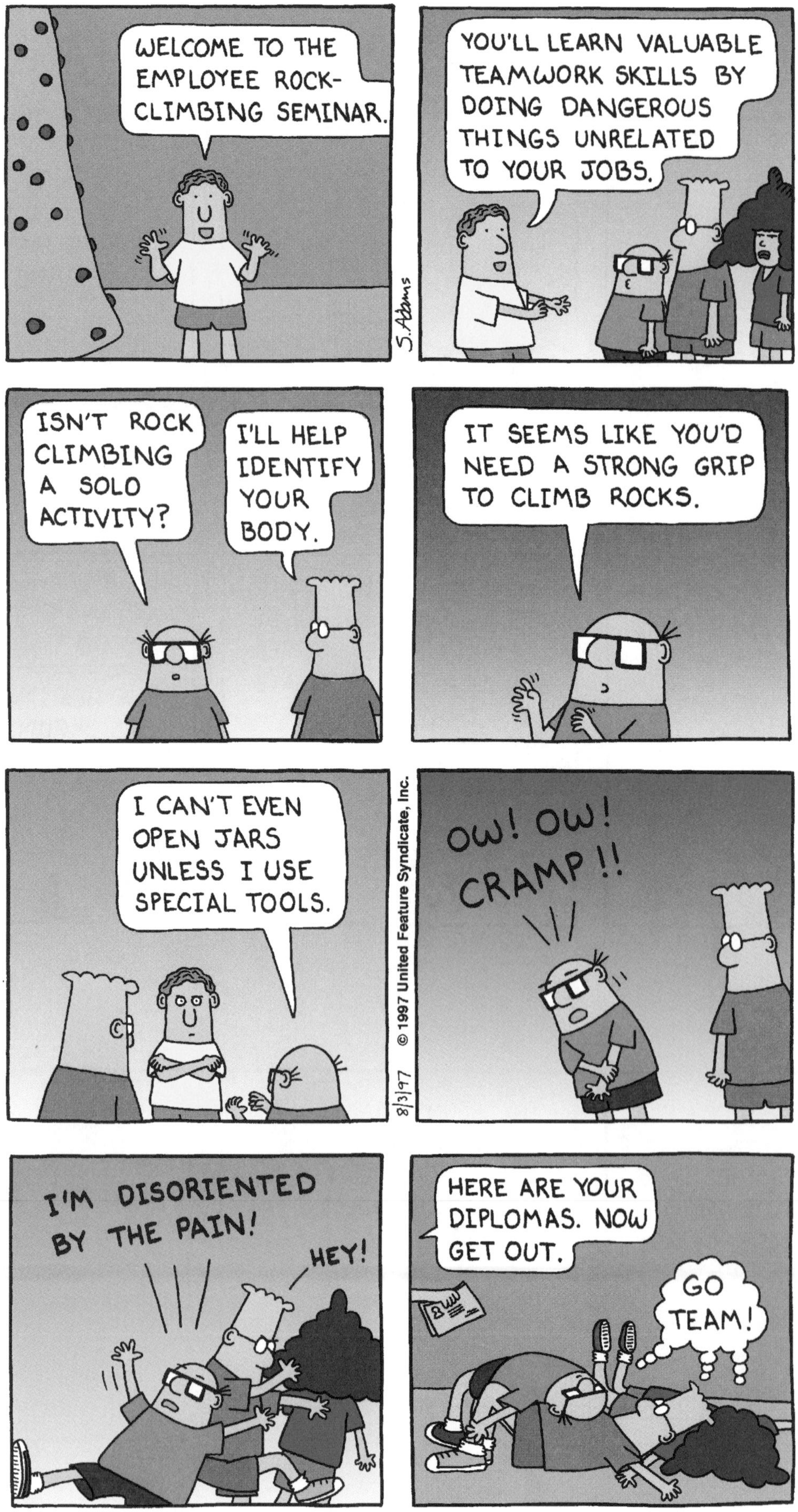
WELCOME TO THE EMPLOYEE ROCK-CLIMBING SEMINAR.
S. Adams
YOU'LL LEARN VALUABLE TEAMWORK SKILLS BY DOING DANGEROUS THINGS UNRELATED TO YOUR JOBS.
ISN'T ROCK CLIMBING A SOLO ACTIVITY?
I'LL HELP IDENTIFY YOUR BODY.
IT SEEMS LIKE YOU'D NEED A STRONG GRIP TO CLIMB ROCKS.
I CAN'T EVEN OPEN JARS UNLESS I USE SPECIAL TOOLS.
© 1997 United Feature Syndicate, Inc.
8/3/97
OW! OW! CRAMP!!
I'M DISORIENTED BY THE PAIN!
HEY!
HERE ARE YOUR DIPLOMAS. NOW GET OUT.
GO TEAM!

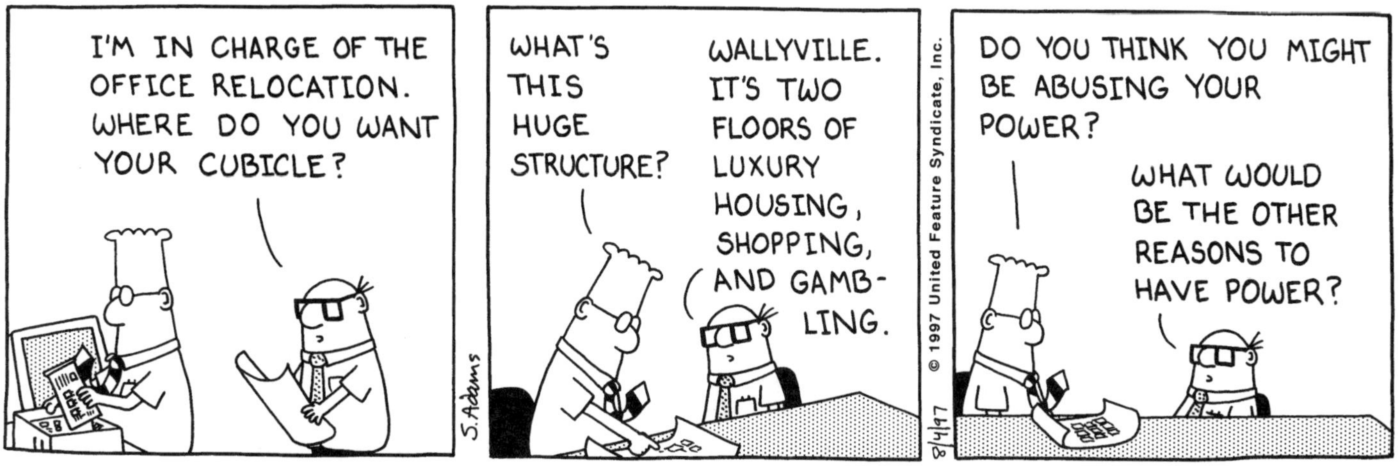
I'M IN CHARGE OF THE OFFICE RELOCATION. WHERE DO YOU WANT YOUR CUBICLE?
WHAT'S THIS HUGE STRUCTURE?
WALLYVILLE. IT'S TWO FLOORS OF LUXURY HOUSING, SHOPPING, AND GAMBLING.
DO YOU THINK YOU MIGHT BE ABUSING YOUR POWER?
WHAT WOULD BE THE OTHER REASONS TO HAVE POWER?
S. Adams
8/4/97
© 1997 United Feature Syndicate, Inc.

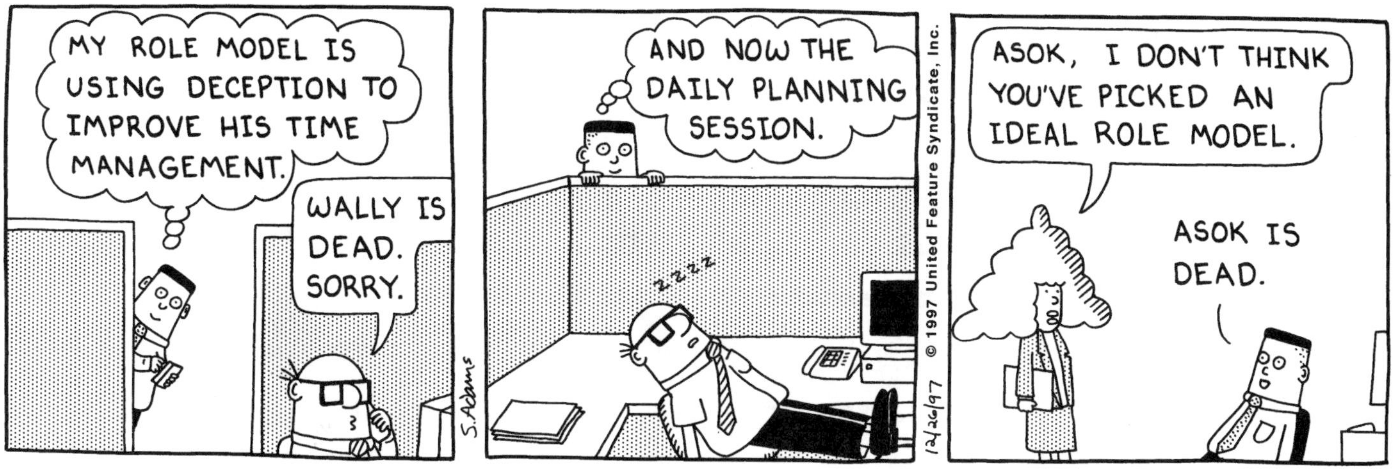
MY ROLE MODEL IS USING DECEPTION TO IMPROVE HIS TIME MANAGEMENT.
WALLY IS DEAD. SORRY.
AND NOW THE DAILY PLANNING SESSION.
Z Z Z Z
ASOK, I DON'T THINK YOU'VE PICKED AN IDEAL ROLE MODEL.
ASOK IS DEAD.
S. Adams
12/26/97
© 1997 United Feature Syndicate, Inc.

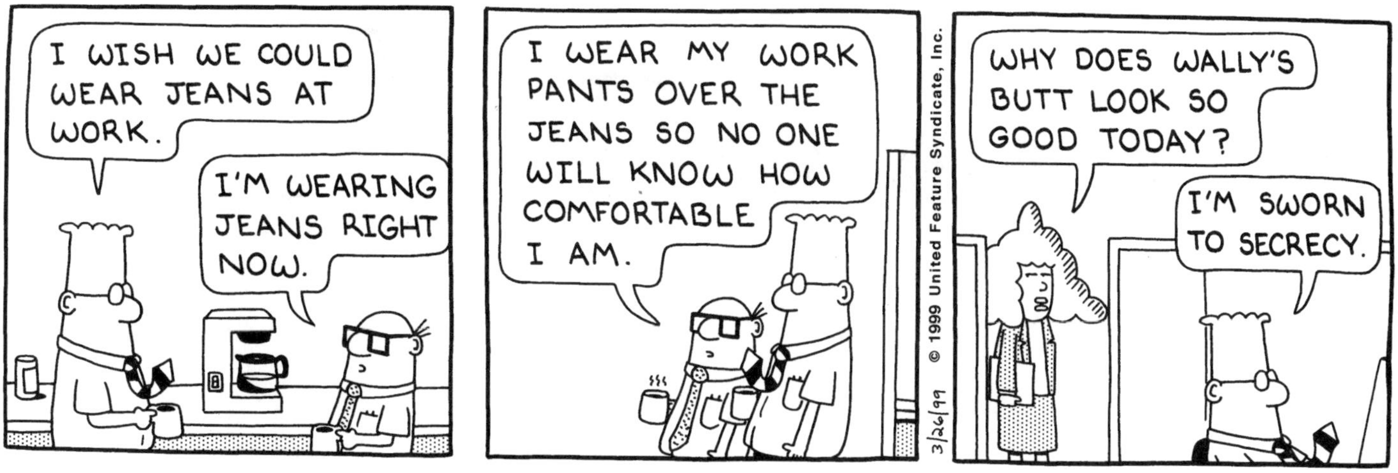
I WISH WE COULD WEAR JEANS AT WORK.
I'M WEARING JEANS RIGHT NOW.
I WEAR MY WORK PANTS OVER THE JEANS SO NO ONE WILL KNOW HOW COMFORTABLE I AM.
WHY DOES WALLY'S BUTT LOOK SO GOOD TODAY?
I'M SWORN TO SECRECY.
3/26/99
© 1999 United Feature Syndicate, Inc.

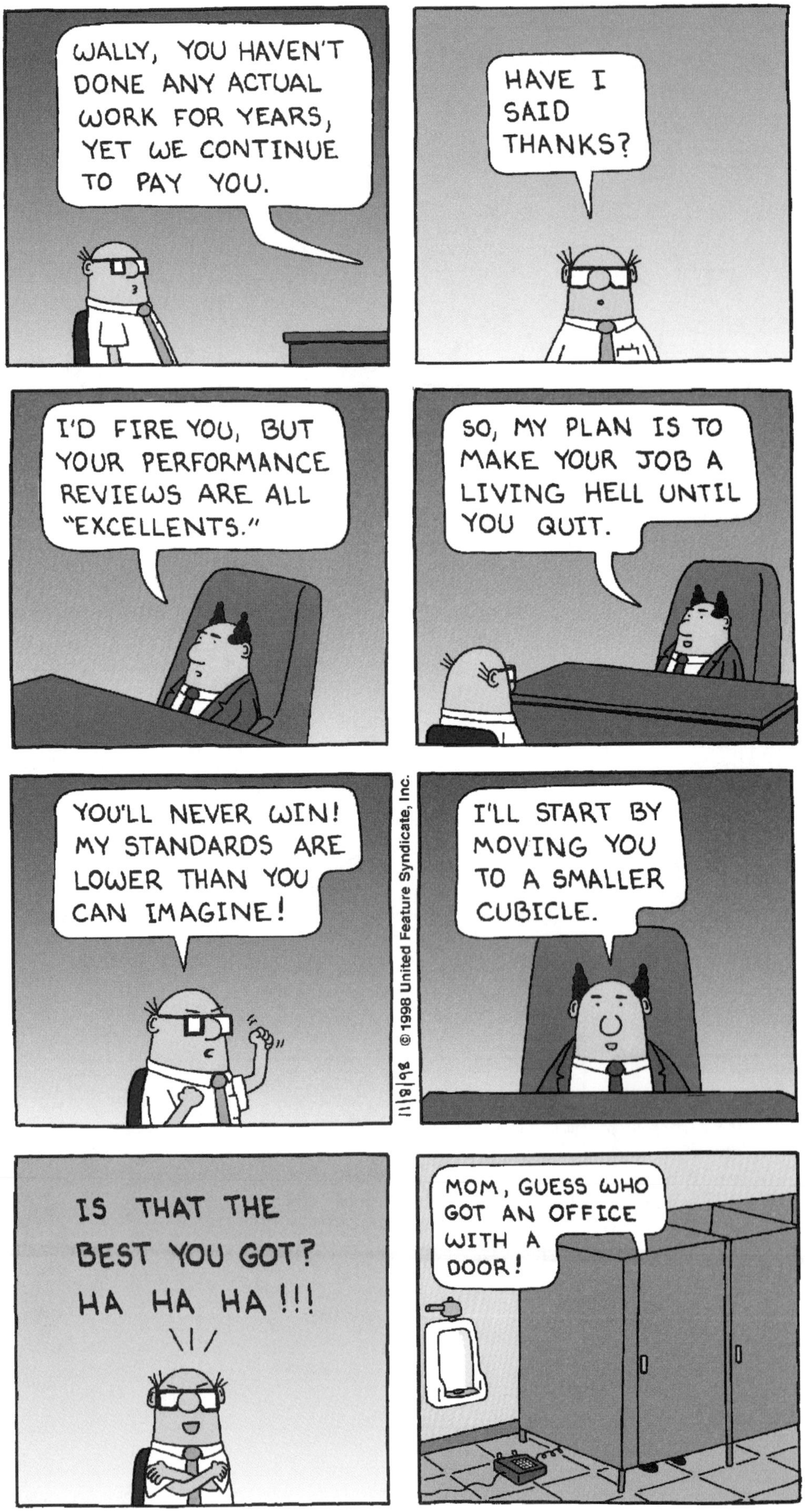
WALLY, YOU HAVEN'T DONE ANY ACTUAL WORK FOR YEARS, YET WE CONTINUE TO PAY YOU.
HAVE I SAID THANKS?
I'D FIRE YOU, BUT YOUR PERFORMANCE REVIEWS ARE ALL "EXCELLENTS."
SO, MY PLAN IS TO MAKE YOUR JOB A LIVING HELL UNTIL YOU QUIT.
YOU'LL NEVER WIN! MY STANDARDS ARE LOWER THAN YOU CAN IMAGINE!
I'LL START BY MOVING YOU TO A SMALLER CUBICLE.
IS THAT THE BEST YOU GOT? HA HA HA!!!
MOM, GUESS WHO GOT AN OFFICE WITH A DOOR!

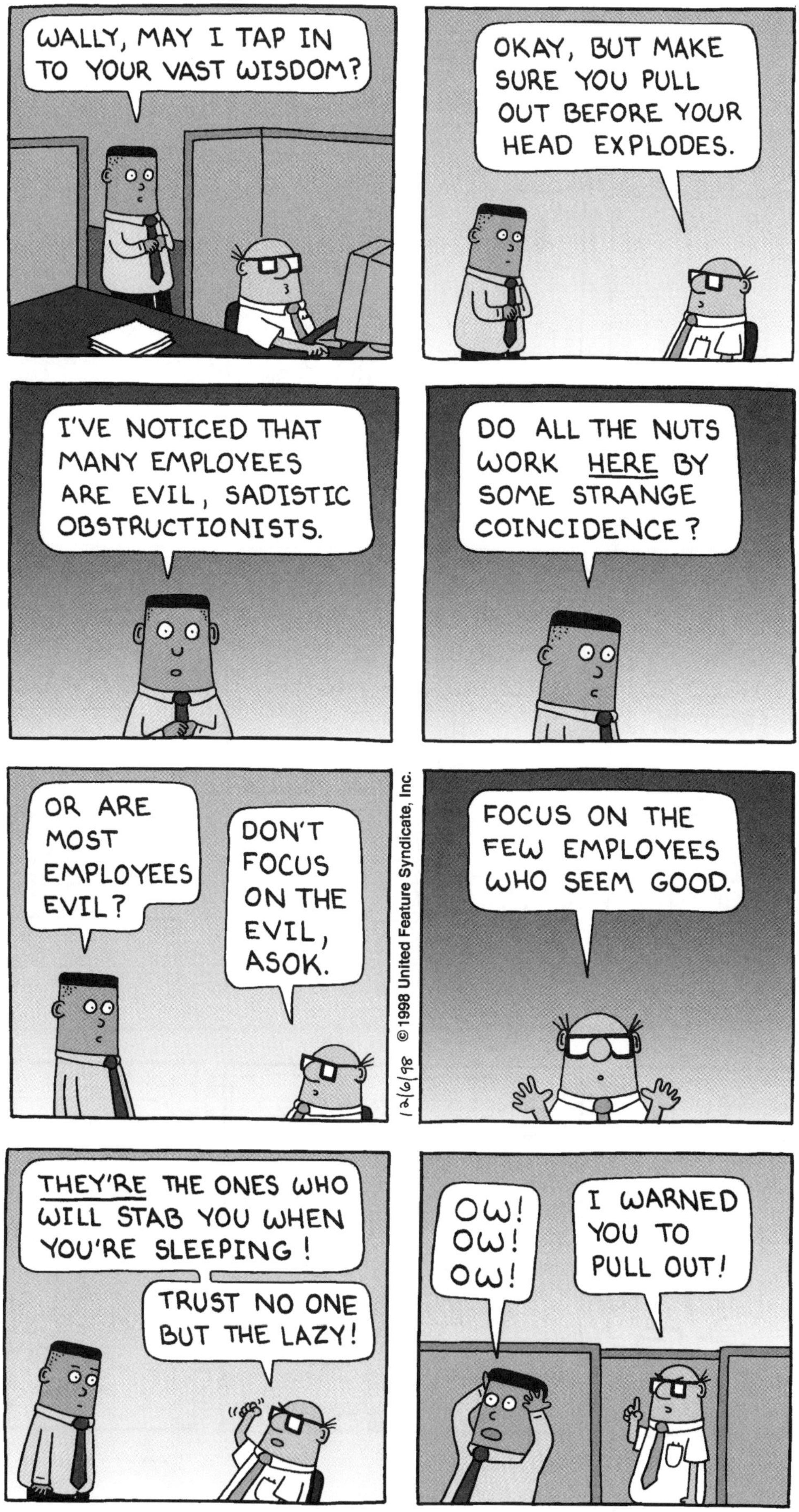
WALLY, MAY I TAP IN TO YOUR VAST WISDOM?
OKAY, BUT MAKE SURE YOU PULL OUT BEFORE YOUR HEAD EXPLODES.
I'VE NOTICED THAT MANY EMPLOYEES ARE EVIL, SADISTIC OBSTRUCTIONISTS.
DO ALL THE NUTS WORK HERE BY SOME STRANGE COINCIDENCE?
OR ARE MOST EMPLOYEES EVIL?
DON'T FOCUS ON THE EVIL, ASOK.
© 1998 United Feature Syndicate, Inc.
12/6/98
FOCUS ON THE FEW EMPLOYEES WHO SEEM GOOD.
THEY'RE THE ONES WHO WILL STAB YOU WHEN YOU'RE SLEEPING!
TRUST NO ONE BUT THE LAZY!
OW! OW! OW!
I WARNED YOU TO PULL OUT!

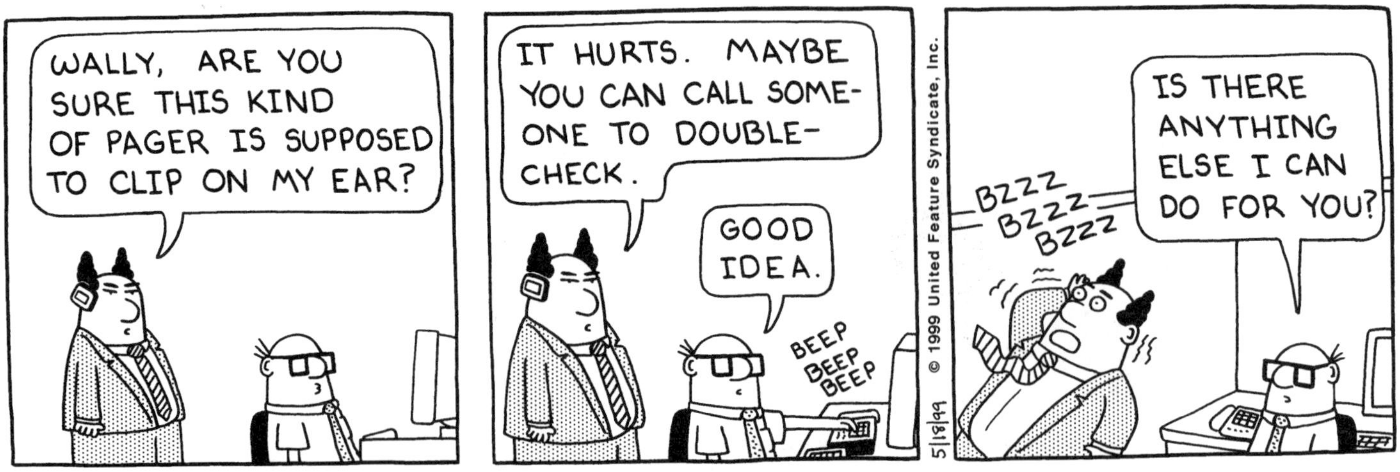
WALLY, ARE YOU SURE THIS KIND OF PAGER IS SUPPOSED TO CLIP ON MY EAR?
IT HURTS. MAYBE YOU CAN CALL SOMEONE TO DOUBLE-CHECK.
GOOD IDEA.
BEEP BEEP BEEP
5/18/99 © 1999 United Feature Syndicate, Inc.
BZZZ BZZZ BZZZ
IS THERE ANYTHING ELSE I CAN DO FOR YOU?

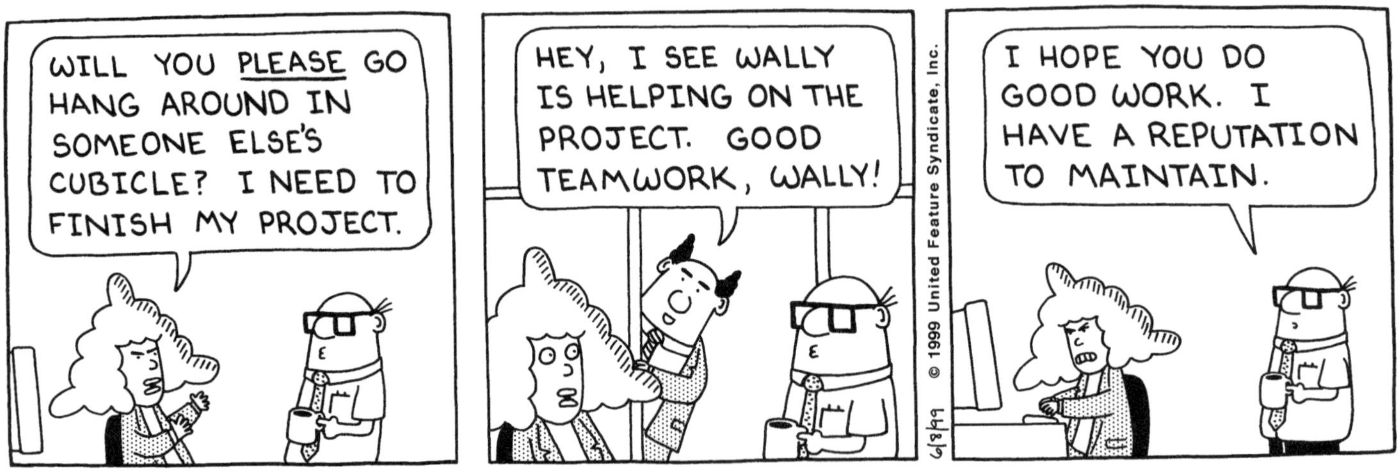
WILL YOU PLEASE GO HANG AROUND IN SOMEONE ELSE'S CUBICLE? I NEED TO FINISH MY PROJECT.
HEY, I SEE WALLY IS HELPING ON THE PROJECT. GOOD TEAMWORK, WALLY!
6/8/99 © 1999 United Feature Syndicate, Inc.
I HOPE YOU DO GOOD WORK. I HAVE A REPUTATION TO MAINTAIN.

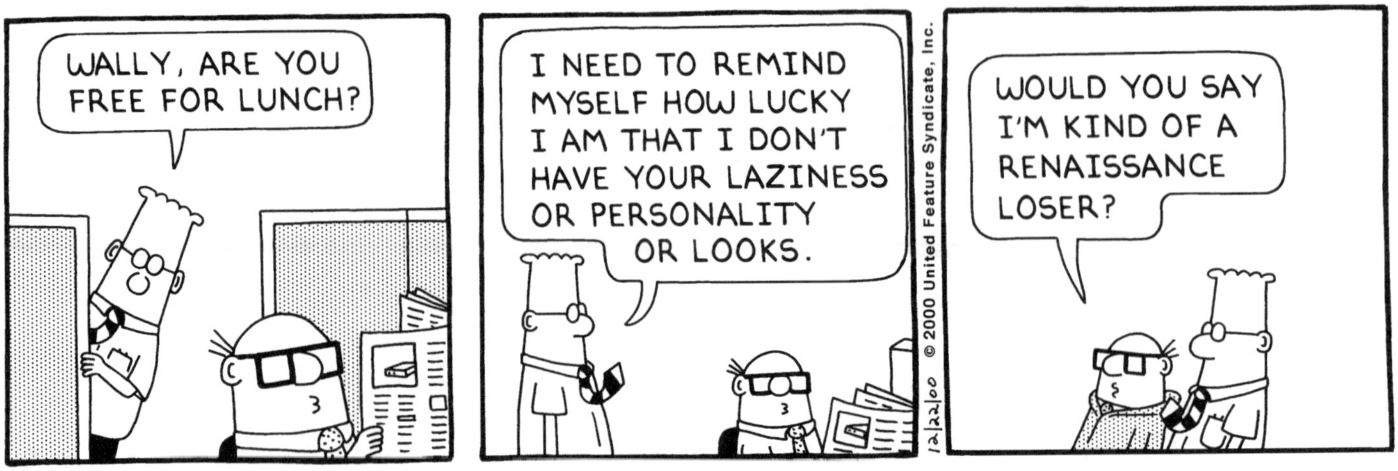
WALLY, ARE YOU FREE FOR LUNCH?
I NEED TO REMIND MYSELF HOW LUCKY I AM THAT I DON'T HAVE YOUR LAZINESS OR PERSONALITY OR LOOKS.
12/22/00 © 2000 United Feature Syndicate, Inc.
WOULD YOU SAY I'M KIND OF A RENAISSANCE LOSER?

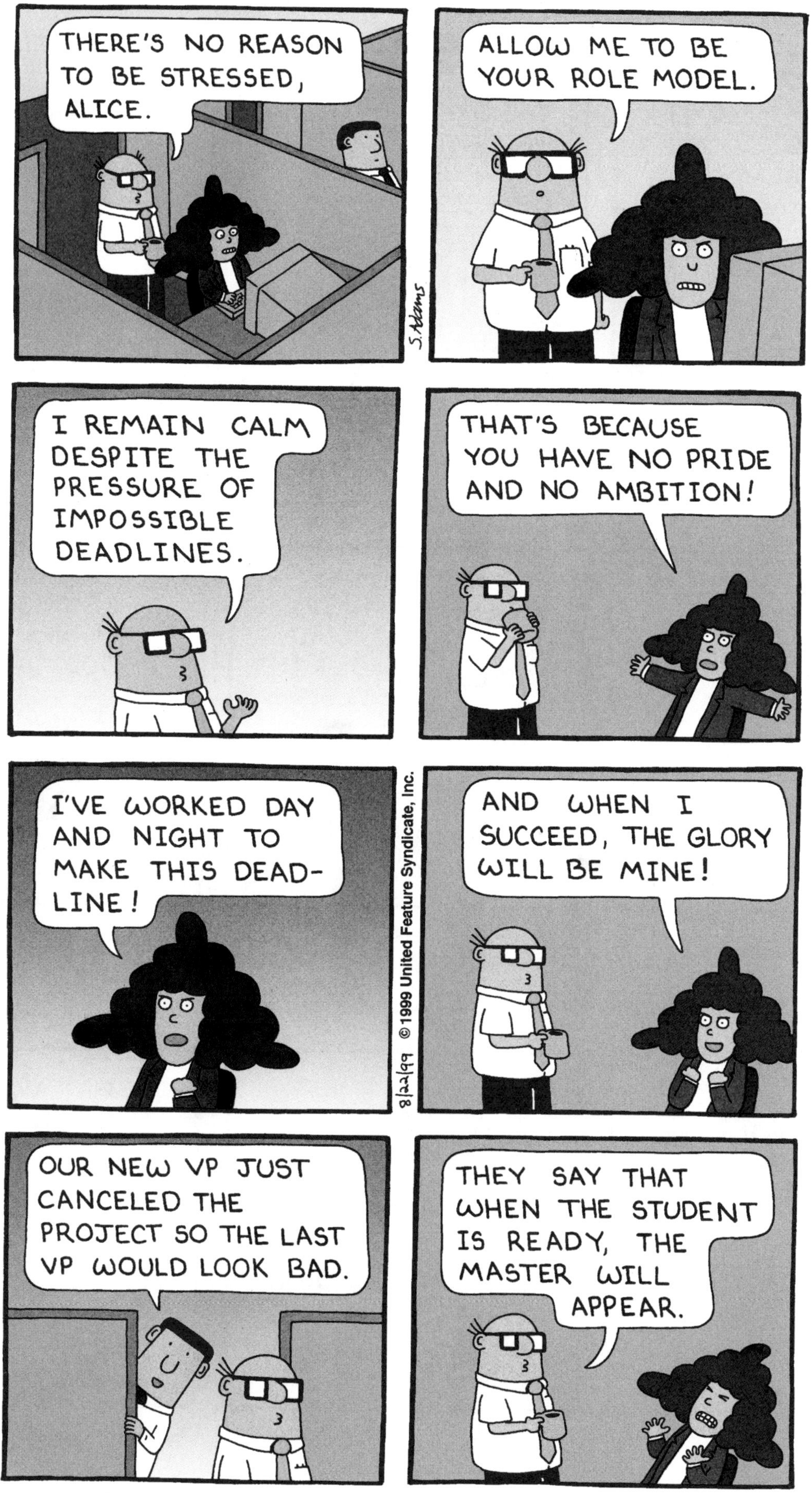
THERE'S NO REASON TO BE STRESSED, ALICE.
ALLOW ME TO BE YOUR ROLE MODEL.
S. Adams
I REMAIN CALM DESPITE THE PRESSURE OF IMPOSSIBLE DEADLINES.
THAT'S BECAUSE YOU HAVE NO PRIDE AND NO AMBITION!
I'VE WORKED DAY AND NIGHT TO MAKE THIS DEAD-LINE!
8/22/99 © 1999 United Feature Syndicate, Inc.
AND WHEN I SUCCEED, THE GLORY WILL BE MINE!
OUR NEW VP JUST CANCELED THE PROJECT SO THE LAST VP WOULD LOOK BAD.
THEY SAY THAT WHEN THE STUDENT IS READY, THE MASTER WILL APPEAR.

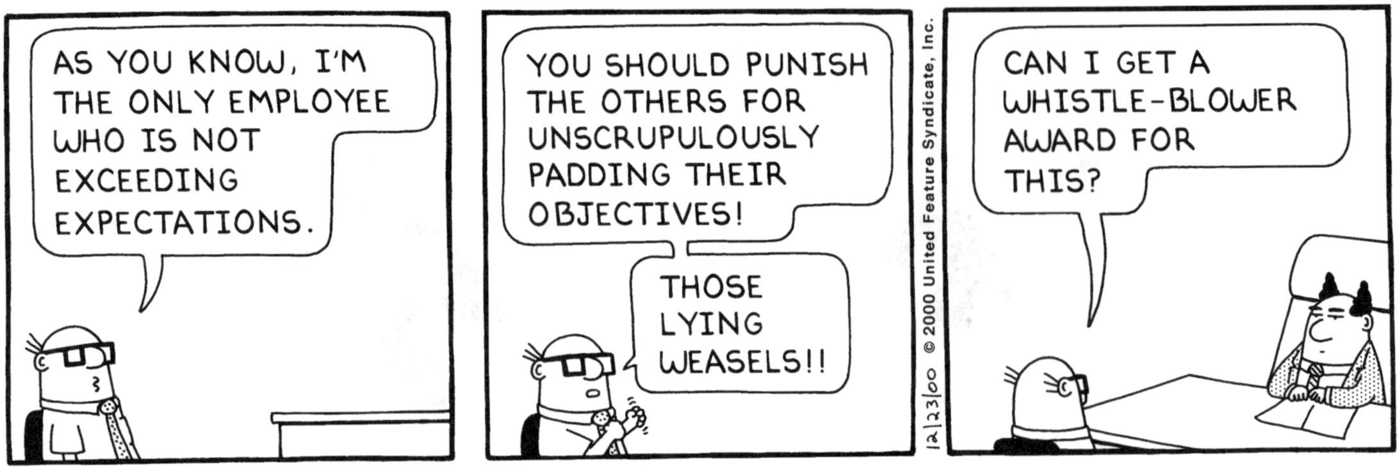
AS YOU KNOW, I'M THE ONLY EMPLOYEE WHO IS NOT EXCEEDING EXPECTATIONS.
YOU SHOULD PUNISH THE OTHERS FOR UNSCRUPULOUSLY PADDING THEIR OBJECTIVES!
THOSE LYING WEASELS!!
12/23/00 © 2000 United Feature Syndicate, Inc.
CAN I GET A WHISTLE-BLOWER AWARD FOR THIS?

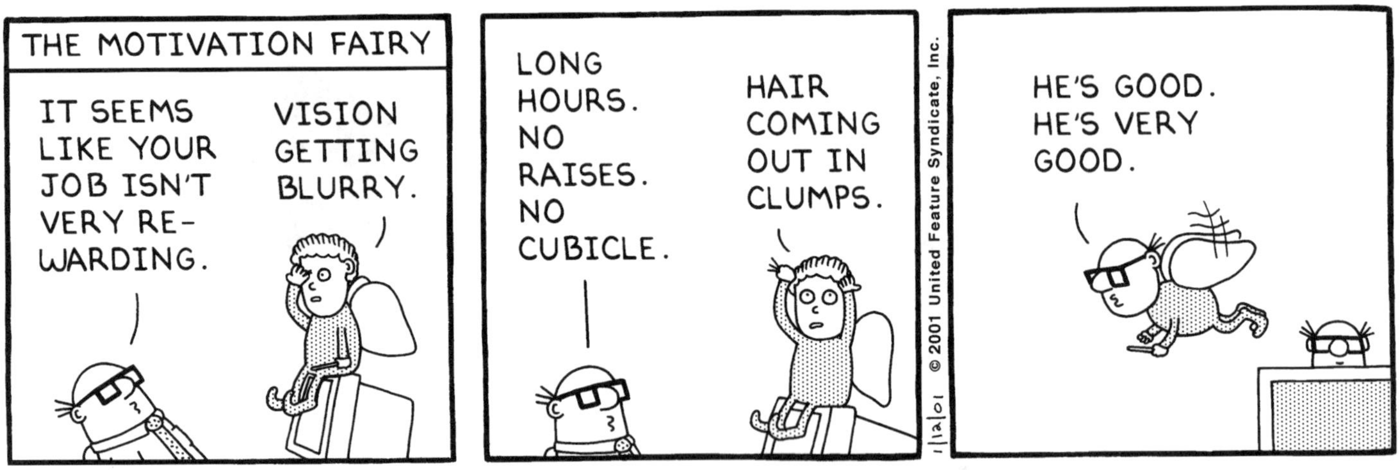
THE MOTIVATION FAIRY
IT SEEMS LIKE YOUR JOB ISN'T VERY RE- WARDING.
VISION GETTING BLURRY.
LONG HOURS. NO RAISES. NO CUBICLE.
HAIR COMING OUT IN CLUMPS.
1/12/01 © 2001 United Feature Syndicate, Inc.
HE'S GOOD. HE'S VERY GOOD.

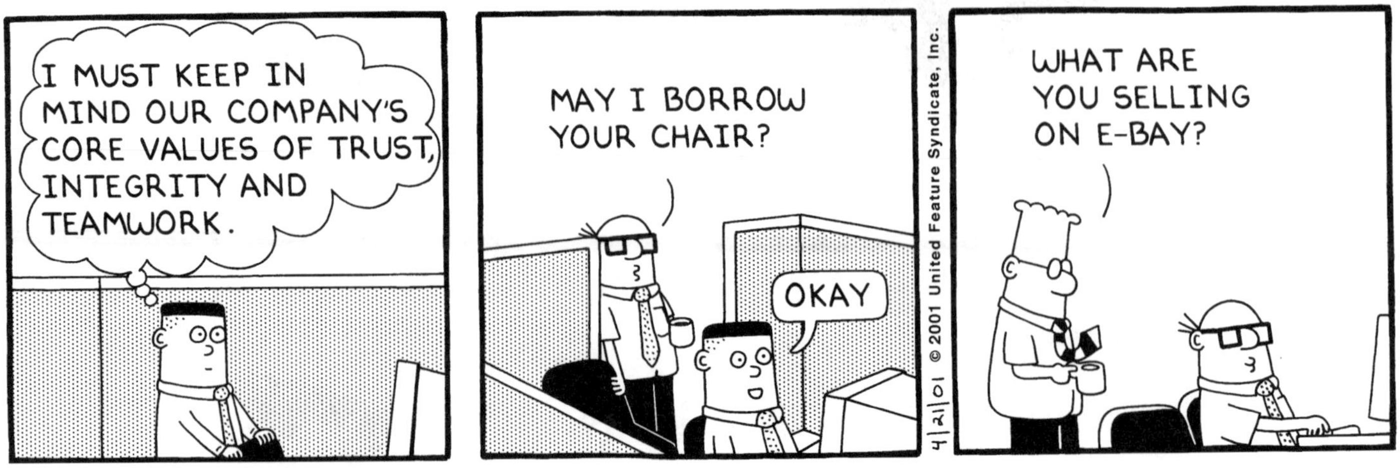
I MUST KEEP IN MIND OUR COMPANY'S CORE VALUES OF TRUST, INTEGRITY AND TEAMWORK.
MAY I BORROW YOUR CHAIR?
OKAY
4/21/01 © 2001 United Feature Syndicate, Inc.
WHAT ARE YOU SELLING ON E-BAY?

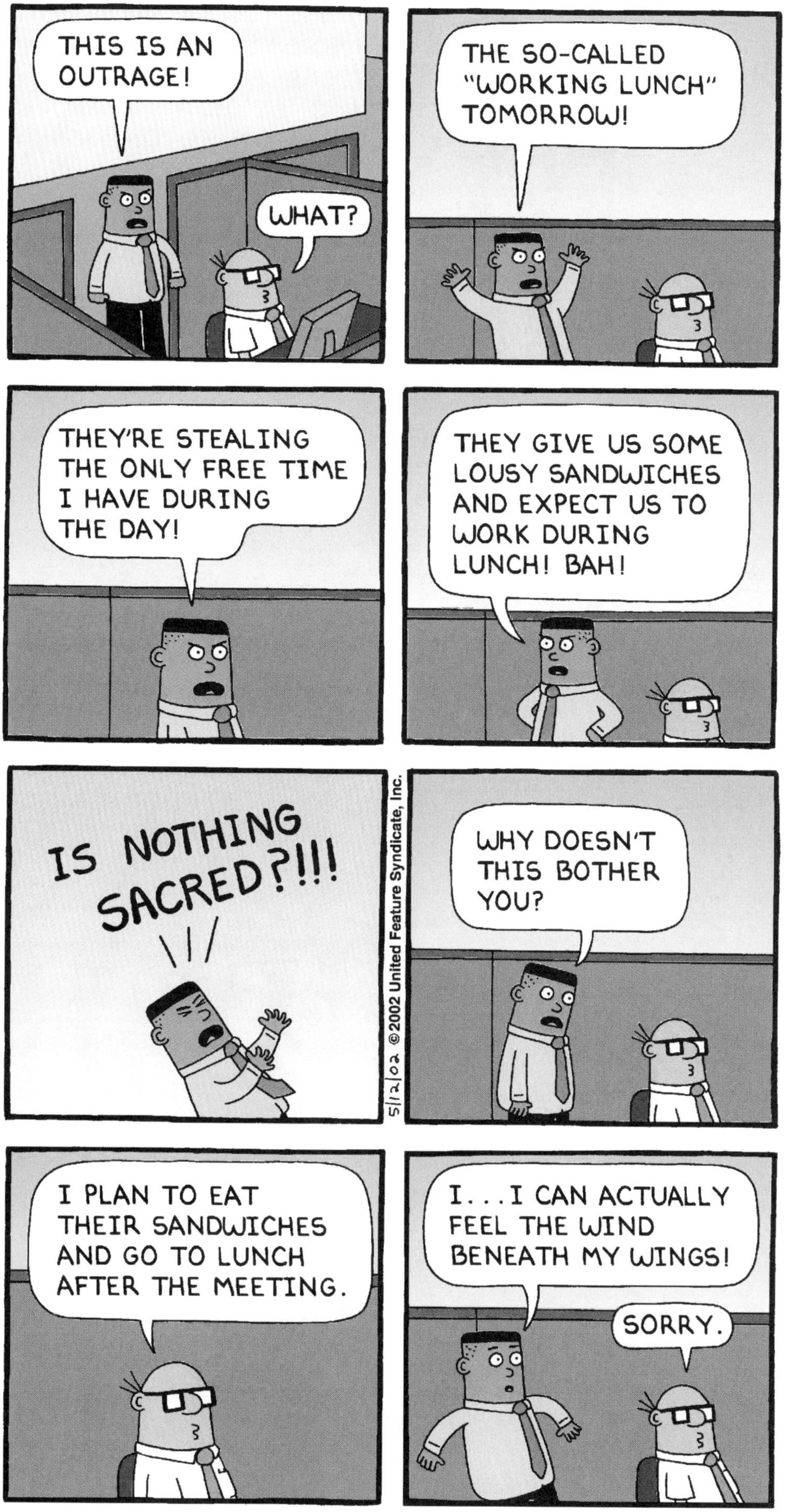
THIS IS AN OUTRAGE!
WHAT?
THE SO-CALLED "WORKING LUNCH" TOMORROW!
THEY'RE STEALING THE ONLY FREE TIME I HAVE DURING THE DAY!
THEY GIVE US SOME LOUSY SANDWICHES AND EXPECT US TO WORK DURING LUNCH! BAH!
IS NOTHING SACRED?!!!
5/12/02 ©2002 United Feature Syndicate, Inc.
WHY DOESN'T THIS BOTHER YOU?
I PLAN TO EAT THEIR SANDWICHES AND GO TO LUNCH AFTER THE MEETING.
I...I CAN ACTUALLY FEEL THE WIND BENEATH MY WINGS!
SORRY.

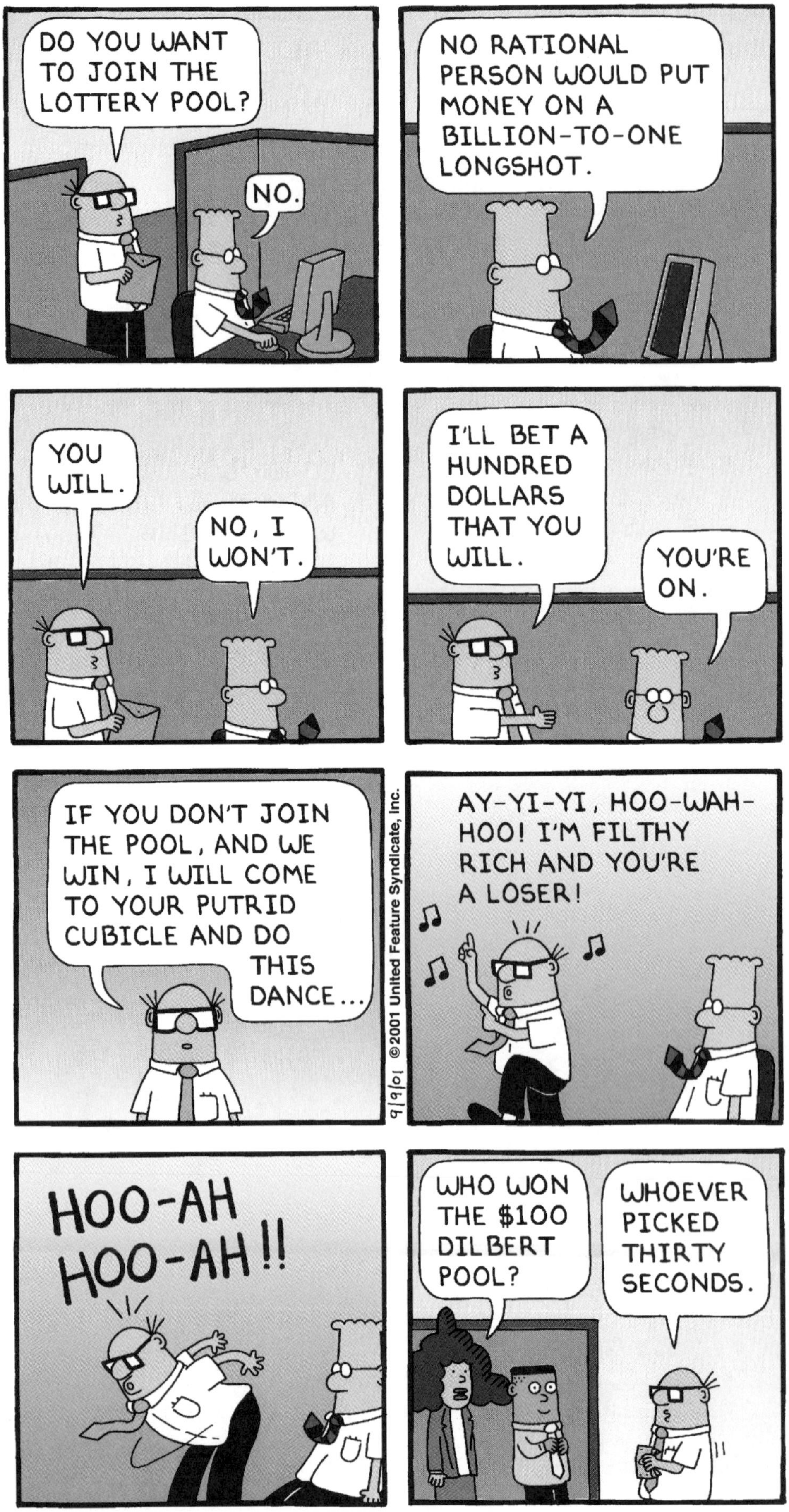
DO YOU WANT TO JOIN THE LOTTERY POOL?
NO.
NO RATIONAL PERSON WOULD PUT MONEY ON A BILLION-TO-ONE LONGSHOT.
YOU WILL.
NO, I WON'T.
I'LL BET A HUNDRED DOLLARS THAT YOU WILL.
YOU'RE ON.
IF YOU DON'T JOIN THE POOL, AND WE WIN, I WILL COME TO YOUR PUTRID CUBICLE AND DO THIS DANCE...
9/9/01 © 2001 United Feature Syndicate, Inc.
AY-YI-YI, HOO-WAH-HOO! I'M FILTHY RICH AND YOU'RE A LOSER!
HOO-AH HOO-AH!!
WHO WON THE $100 DILBERT POOL?
WHOEVER PICKED THIRTY SECONDS.

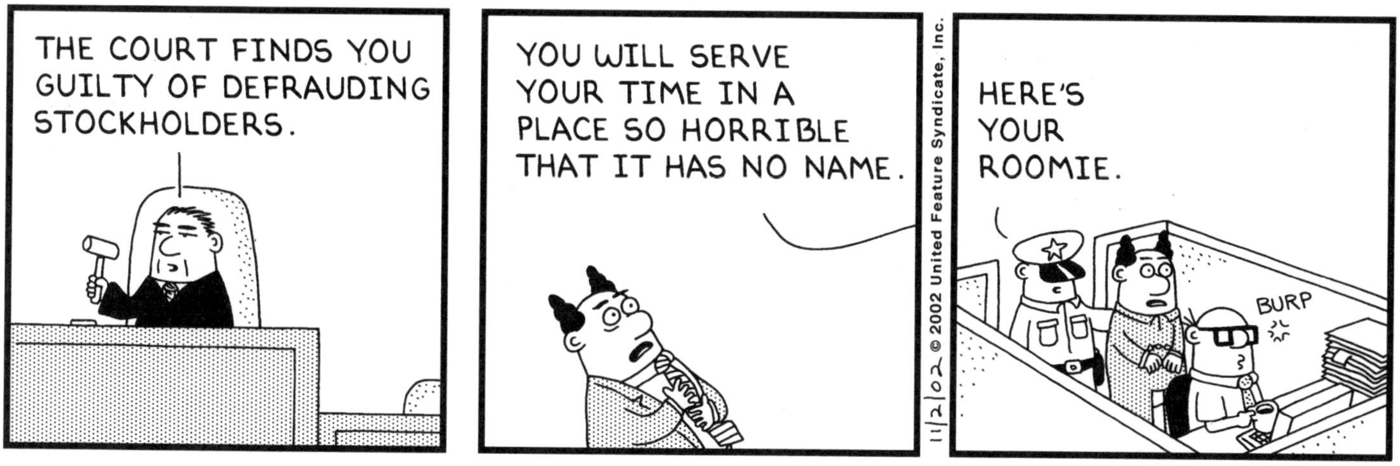
THE COURT FINDS YOU GUILTY OF DEFRAUDING STOCKHOLDERS.
YOU WILL SERVE YOUR TIME IN A PLACE SO HORRIBLE THAT IT HAS NO NAME.
HERE'S YOUR ROOMIE.
BURP

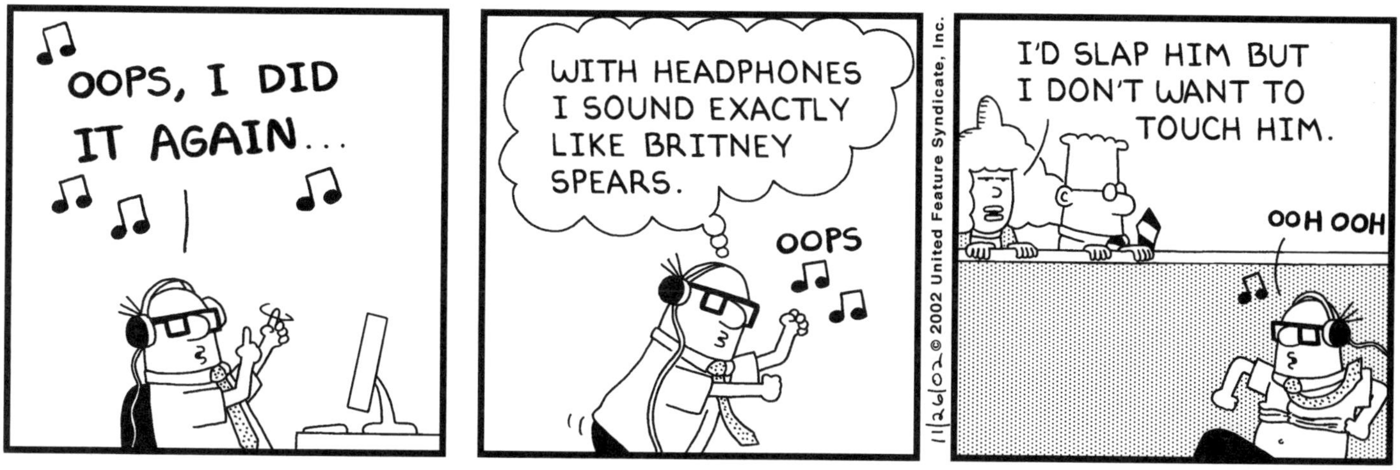
OOPS, I DID IT AGAIN...
WITH HEADPHONES I SOUND EXACTLY LIKE BRITNEY SPEARS.
OOPS
I'D SLAP HIM BUT I DON'T WANT TO TOUCH HIM.
OOH OOH

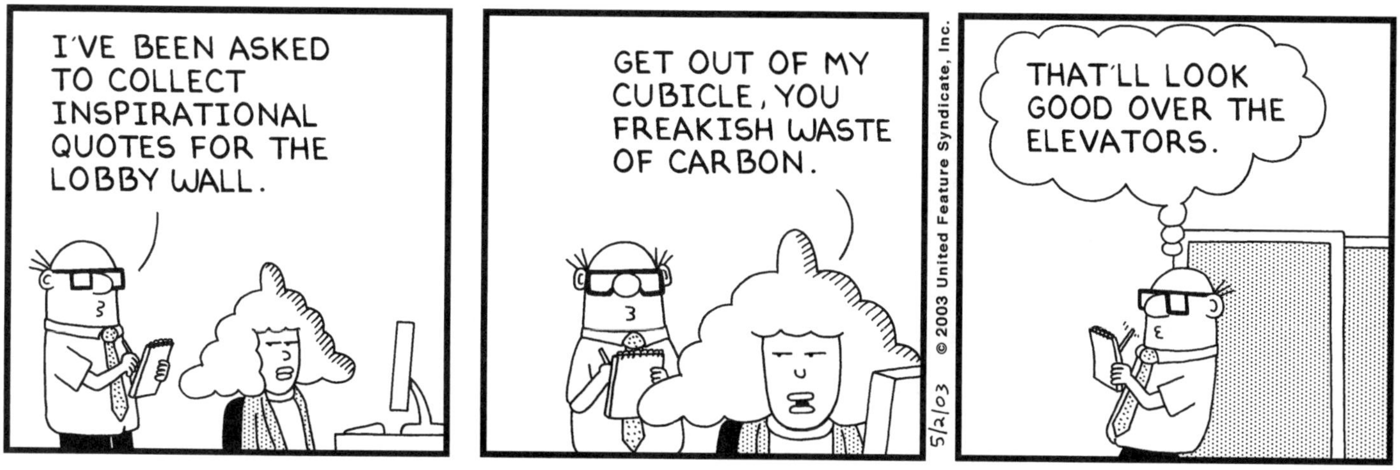
I'VE BEEN ASKED TO COLLECT INSPIRATIONAL QUOTES FOR THE LOBBY WALL.
GET OUT OF MY CUBICLE, YOU FREAKISH WASTE OF CARBON.
THAT'LL LOOK GOOD OVER THE ELEVATORS.

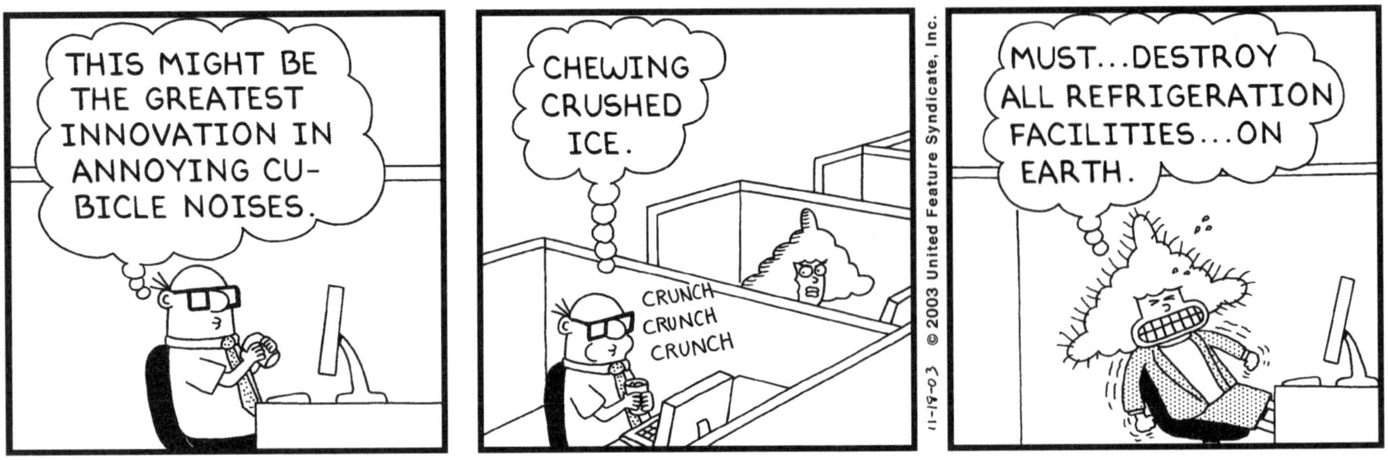
THIS MIGHT BE THE GREATEST INNOVATION IN ANNOYING CU-BICLE NOISES.
CHEWING CRUSHED ICE.
CRUNCH CRUNCH CRUNCH
11-19-03 © 2003 United Feature Syndicate, Inc.
MUST...DESTROY ALL REFRIGERATION FACILITIES...ON EARTH.

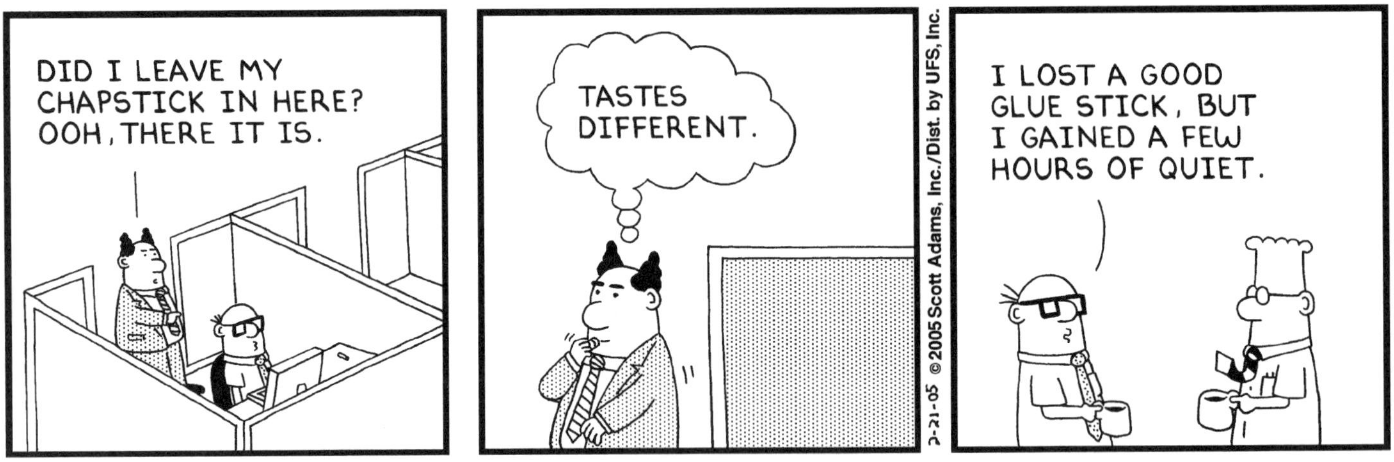
DID I LEAVE MY CHAPSTICK IN HERE? OOH, THERE IT IS.
TASTES DIFFERENT.
21-05 © 2005 Scott Adams, Inc./Dist. by UFS, Inc.
I LOST A GOOD GLUE STICK, BUT I GAINED A FEW HOURS OF QUIET.

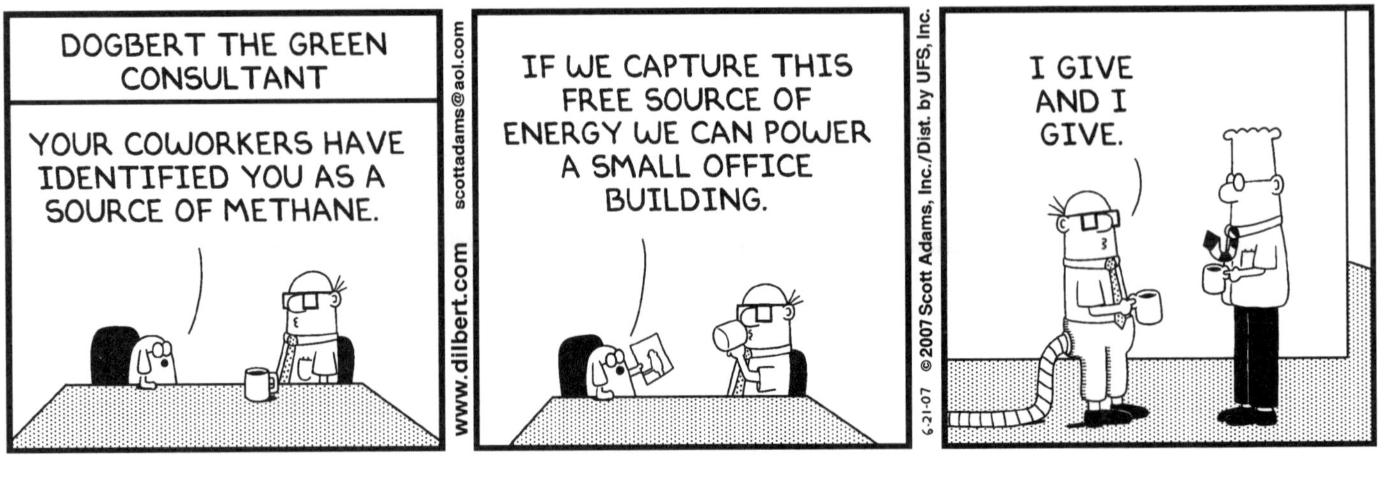
DOGBERT THE GREEN CONSULTANT
YOUR COWORKERS HAVE IDENTIFIED YOU AS A SOURCE OF METHANE.
www.dilbert.com scottadams@aol.com
IF WE CAPTURE THIS FREE SOURCE OF ENERGY WE CAN POWER A SMALL OFFICE BUILDING.
6-21-07 © 2007 Scott Adams, Inc./Dist. by UFS, Inc.
I GIVE AND I GIVE.

6. Alice

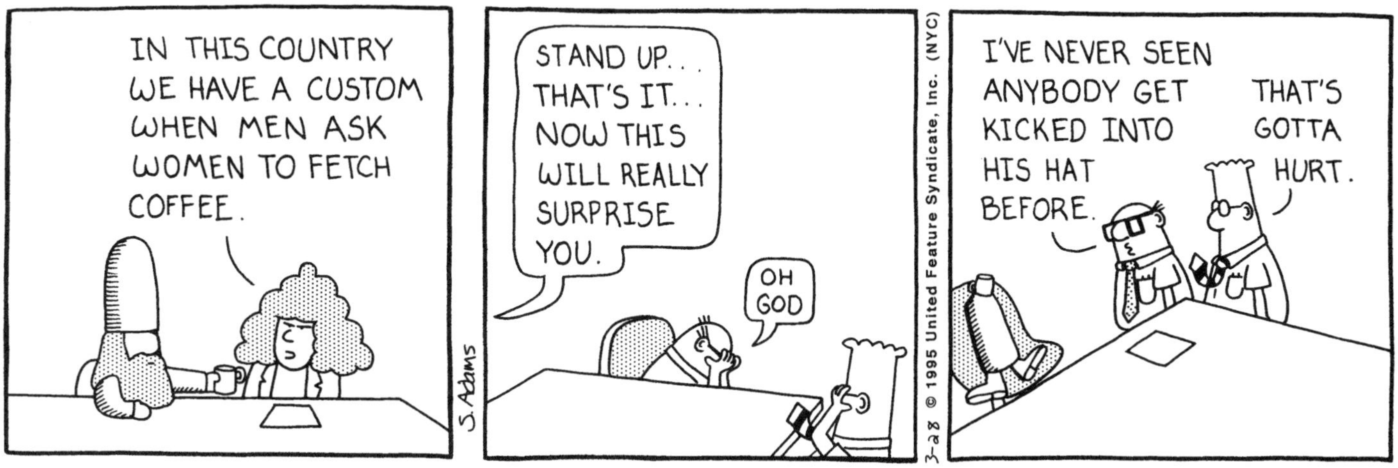
IN THIS COUNTRY WE HAVE A CUSTOM WHEN MEN ASK WOMEN TO FETCH COFFEE.
S. Adams
STAND UP... THAT'S IT... NOW THIS WILL REALLY SURPRISE YOU.
OH GOD
3-28 © 1995 United Feature Syndicate, Inc. (NYC)
I'VE NEVER SEEN ANYBODY GET KICKED INTO HIS HAT BEFORE.
THAT'S GOTTA HURT.

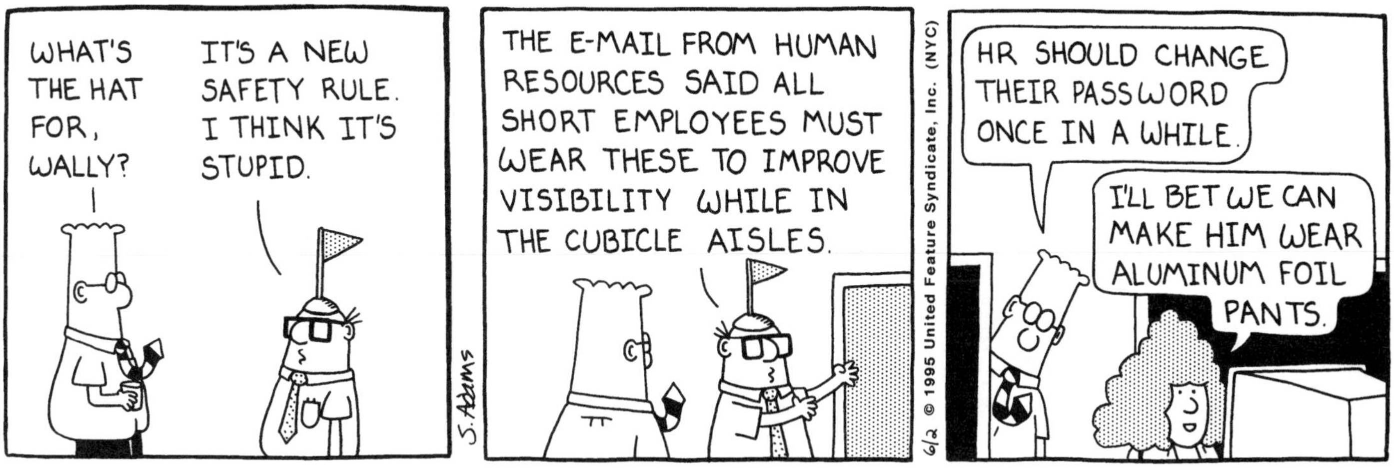
WHAT'S THE HAT FOR, WALLY?
IT'S A NEW SAFETY RULE. I THINK IT'S STUPID.
S. Adams
THE E-MAIL FROM HUMAN RESOURCES SAID ALL SHORT EMPLOYEES MUST WEAR THESE TO IMPROVE VISIBILITY WHILE IN THE CUBICLE AISLES.
6/2 © 1995 United Feature Syndicate, Inc. (NYC)
HR SHOULD CHANGE THEIR PASSWORD ONCE IN A WHILE.
I'LL BET WE CAN MAKE HIM WEAR ALUMINUM FOIL PANTS.

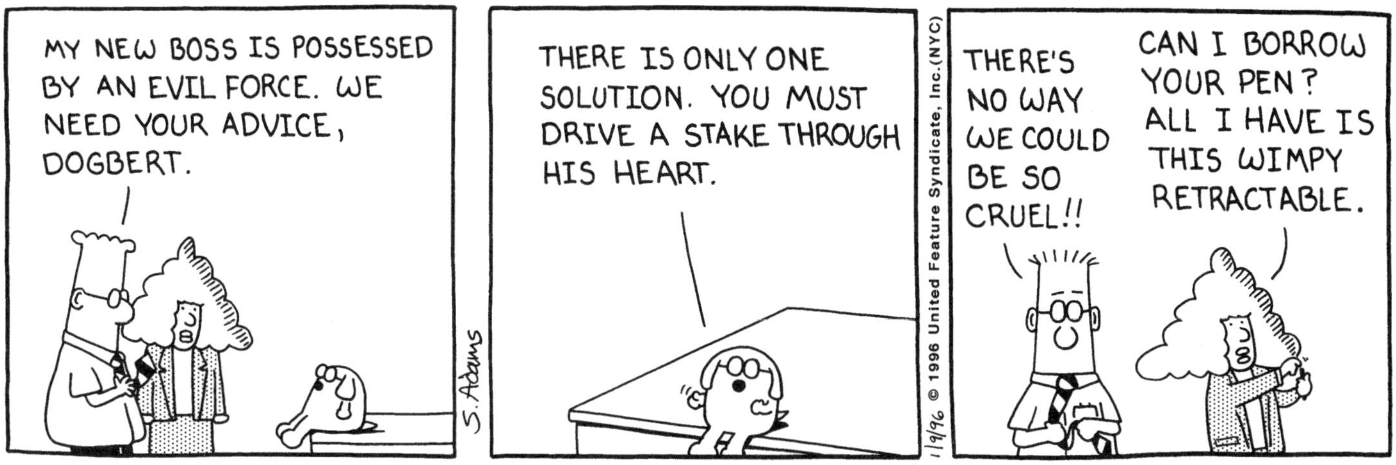
MY NEW BOSS IS POSSESSED BY AN EVIL FORCE. WE NEED YOUR ADVICE, DOGBERT.
S. Adams
THERE IS ONLY ONE SOLUTION. YOU MUST DRIVE A STAKE THROUGH HIS HEART.
1/9/96 © 1996 United Feature Syndicate, Inc.(NYC)
THERE'S NO WAY WE COULD BE SO CRUEL!!
CAN I BORROW YOUR PEN? ALL I HAVE IS THIS WIMPY RETRACTABLE.

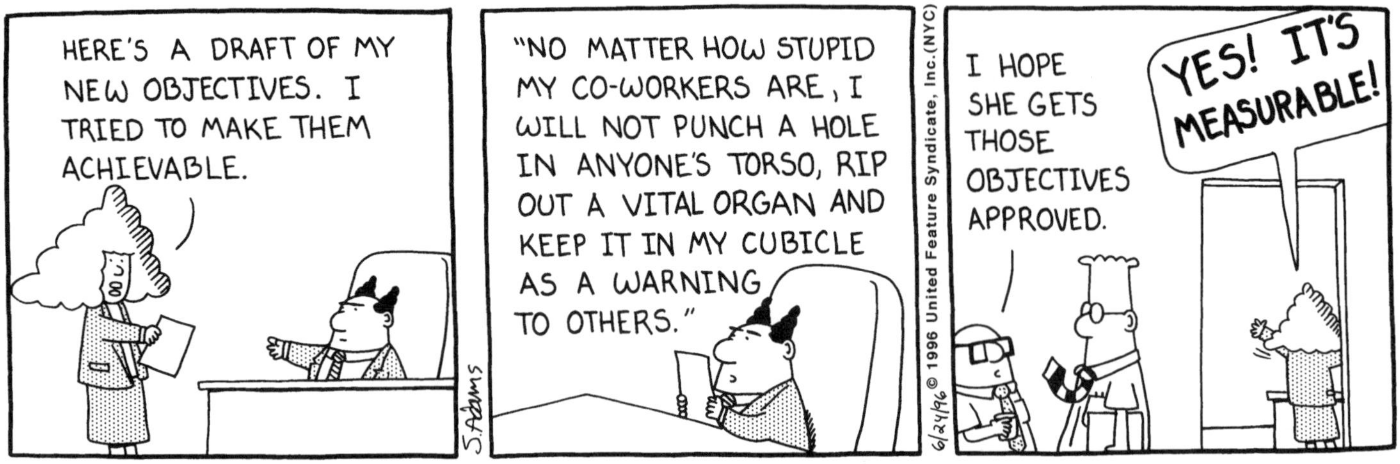
HERE'S A DRAFT OF MY NEW OBJECTIVES. I TRIED TO MAKE THEM ACHIEVABLE.
"NO MATTER HOW STUPID MY CO-WORKERS ARE, I WILL NOT PUNCH A HOLE IN ANYONE'S TORSO, RIP OUT A VITAL ORGAN AND KEEP IT IN MY CUBICLE AS A WARNING TO OTHERS."
I HOPE SHE GETS THOSE OBJECTIVES APPROVED.
YES! IT'S MEASURABLE!
S. Adams
6/24/96 © 1996 United Feature Syndicate, Inc.(NYC)

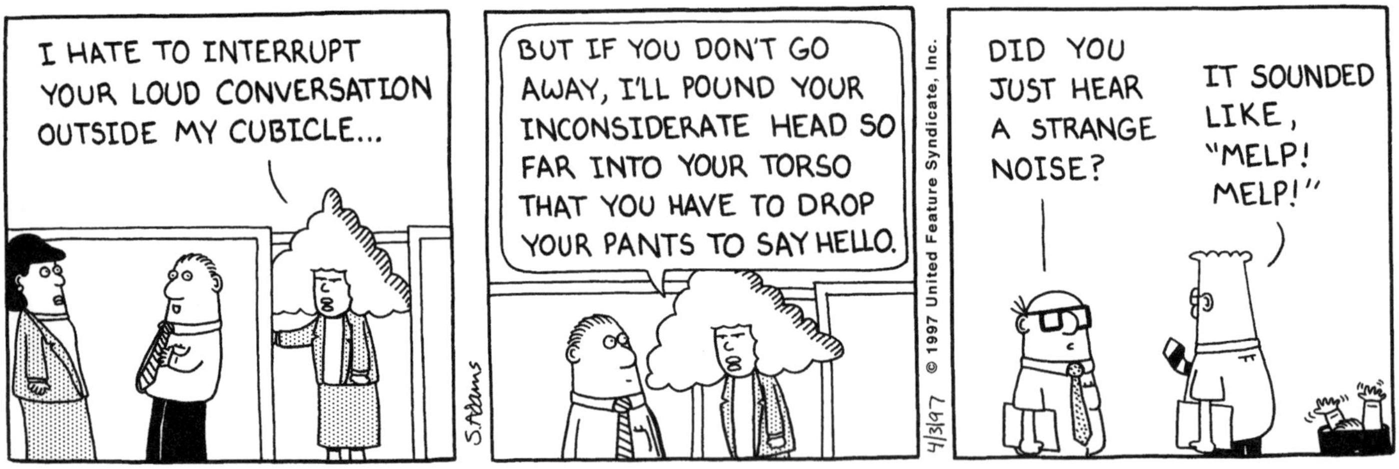
I HATE TO INTERRUPT YOUR LOUD CONVERSATION OUTSIDE MY CUBICLE...
BUT IF YOU DON'T GO AWAY, I'LL POUND YOUR INCONSIDERATE HEAD SO FAR INTO YOUR TORSO THAT YOU HAVE TO DROP YOUR PANTS TO SAY HELLO.
DID YOU JUST HEAR A STRANGE NOISE?
IT SOUNDED LIKE, "MELP! MELP!"
S. Adams
4/3/97 © 1997 United Feature Syndicate, Inc.

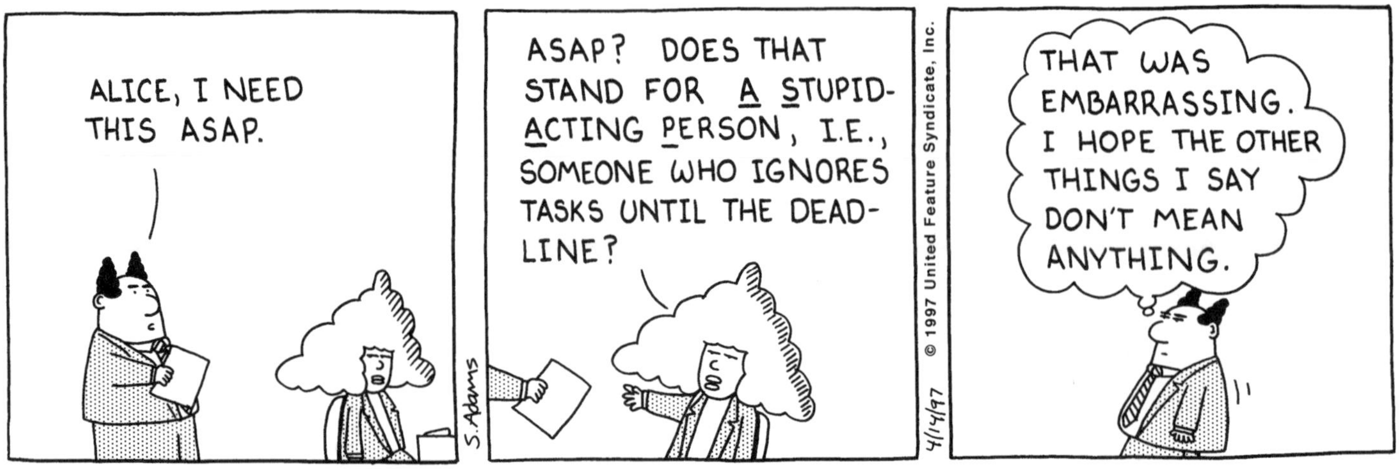
ALICE, I NEED THIS ASAP.
ASAP? DOES THAT STAND FOR A STUPID-ACTING PERSON, I.E., SOMEONE WHO IGNORES TASKS UNTIL THE DEADLINE?
THAT WAS EMBARRASSING. I HOPE THE OTHER THINGS I SAY DON'T MEAN ANYTHING.
S. Adams
4/14/97 © 1997 United Feature Syndicate, Inc.

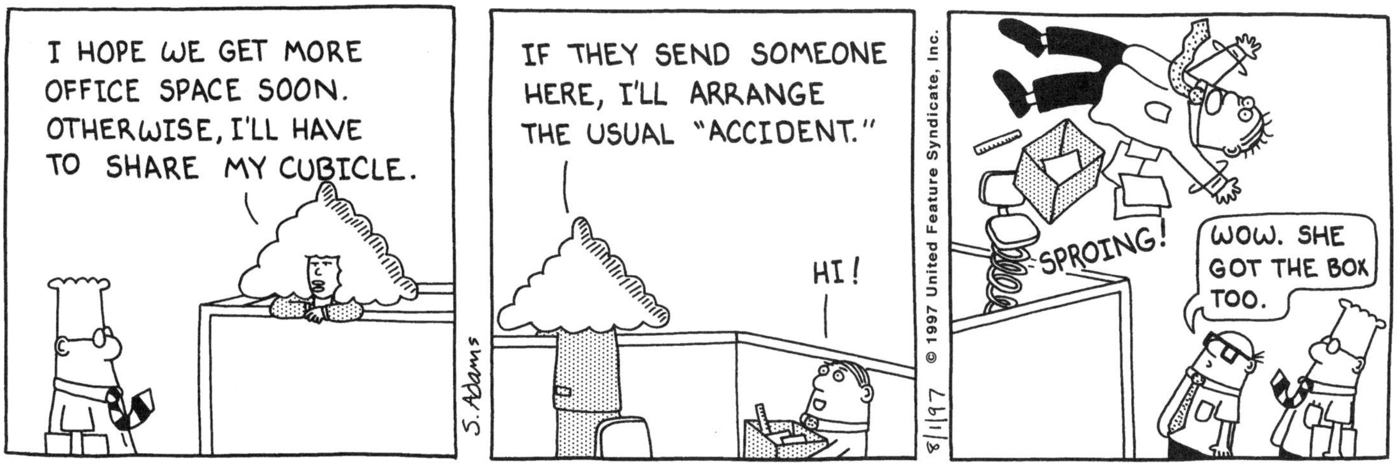
I HOPE WE GET MORE OFFICE SPACE SOON. OTHERWISE, I'LL HAVE TO SHARE MY CUBICLE.
S. Adams
IF THEY SEND SOMEONE HERE, I'LL ARRANGE THE USUAL "ACCIDENT."
HI!
8/1/97 © 1997 United Feature Syndicate, Inc.
SPROING!
WOW. SHE GOT THE BOX TOO.

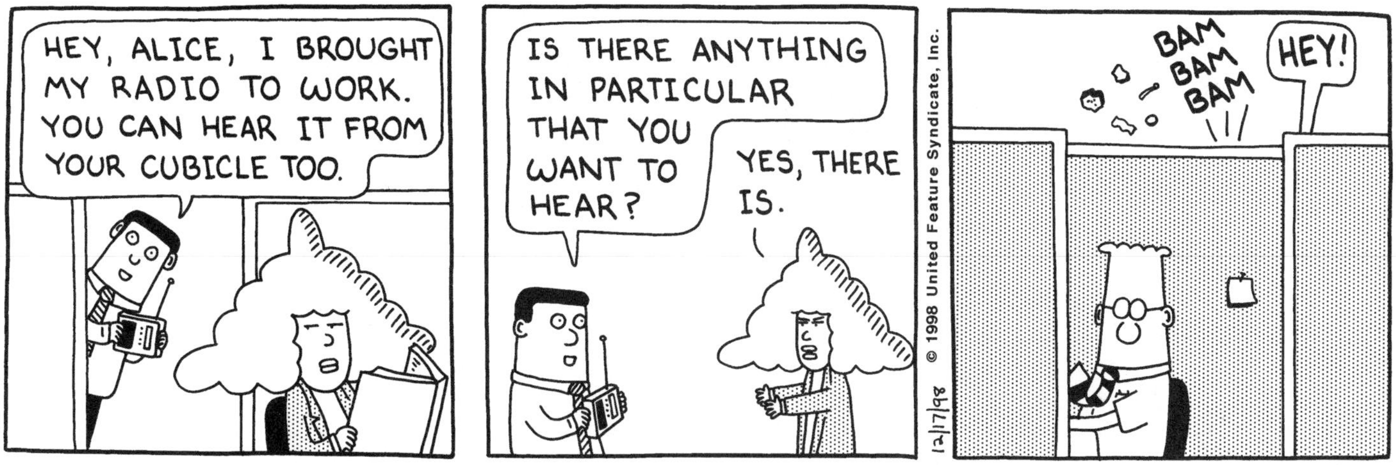
HEY, ALICE, I BROUGHT MY RADIO TO WORK. YOU CAN HEAR IT FROM YOUR CUBICLE TOO.
IS THERE ANYTHING IN PARTICULAR THAT YOU WANT TO HEAR?
YES, THERE IS.
12/17/98 © 1998 United Feature Syndicate, Inc.
BAM BAM BAM
HEY!

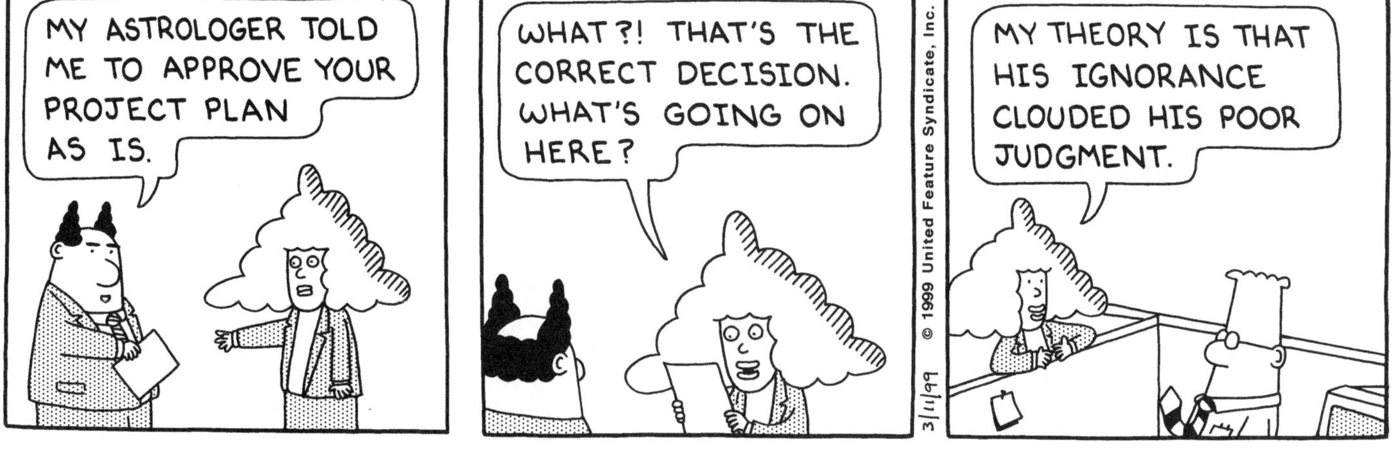
MY ASTROLOGER TOLD ME TO APPROVE YOUR PROJECT PLAN AS IS.
WHAT?! THAT'S THE CORRECT DECISION. WHAT'S GOING ON HERE?
3/1/99 © 1999 United Feature Syndicate, Inc.
MY THEORY IS THAT HIS IGNORANCE CLOUDED HIS POOR JUDGMENT.

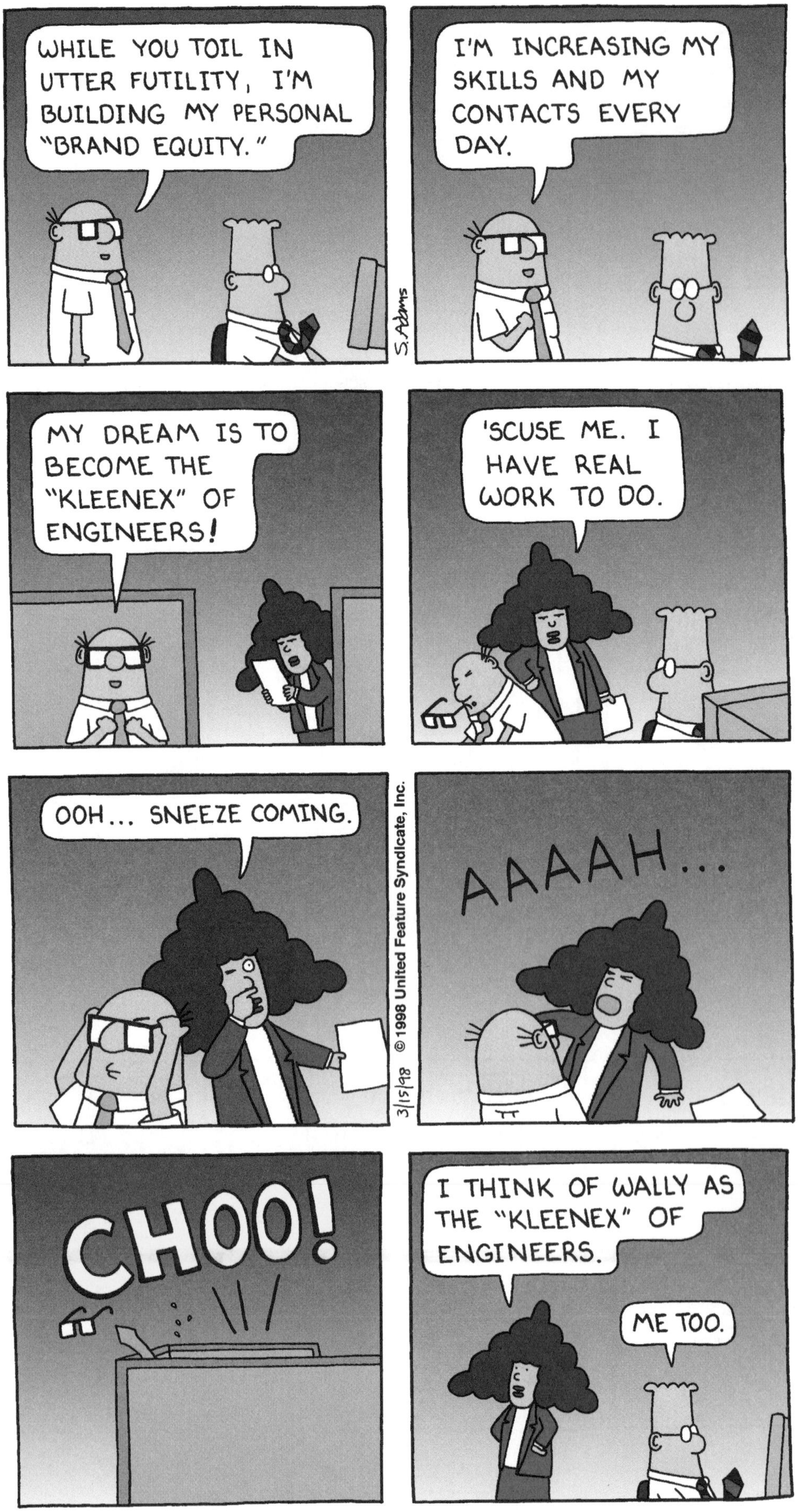
WHILE YOU TOIL IN UTTER FUTILITY, I'M BUILDING MY PERSONAL "BRAND EQUITY."
S. Adams
I'M INCREASING MY SKILLS AND MY CONTACTS EVERY DAY.
MY DREAM IS TO BECOME THE "KLEENEX" OF ENGINEERS!
'SCUSE ME. I HAVE REAL WORK TO DO.
OOH... SNEEZE COMING.
© 1998 United Feature Syndicate, Inc.
3/15/98
AAAAH...
CHOO!
I THINK OF WALLY AS THE "KLEENEX" OF ENGINEERS.
ME TOO.

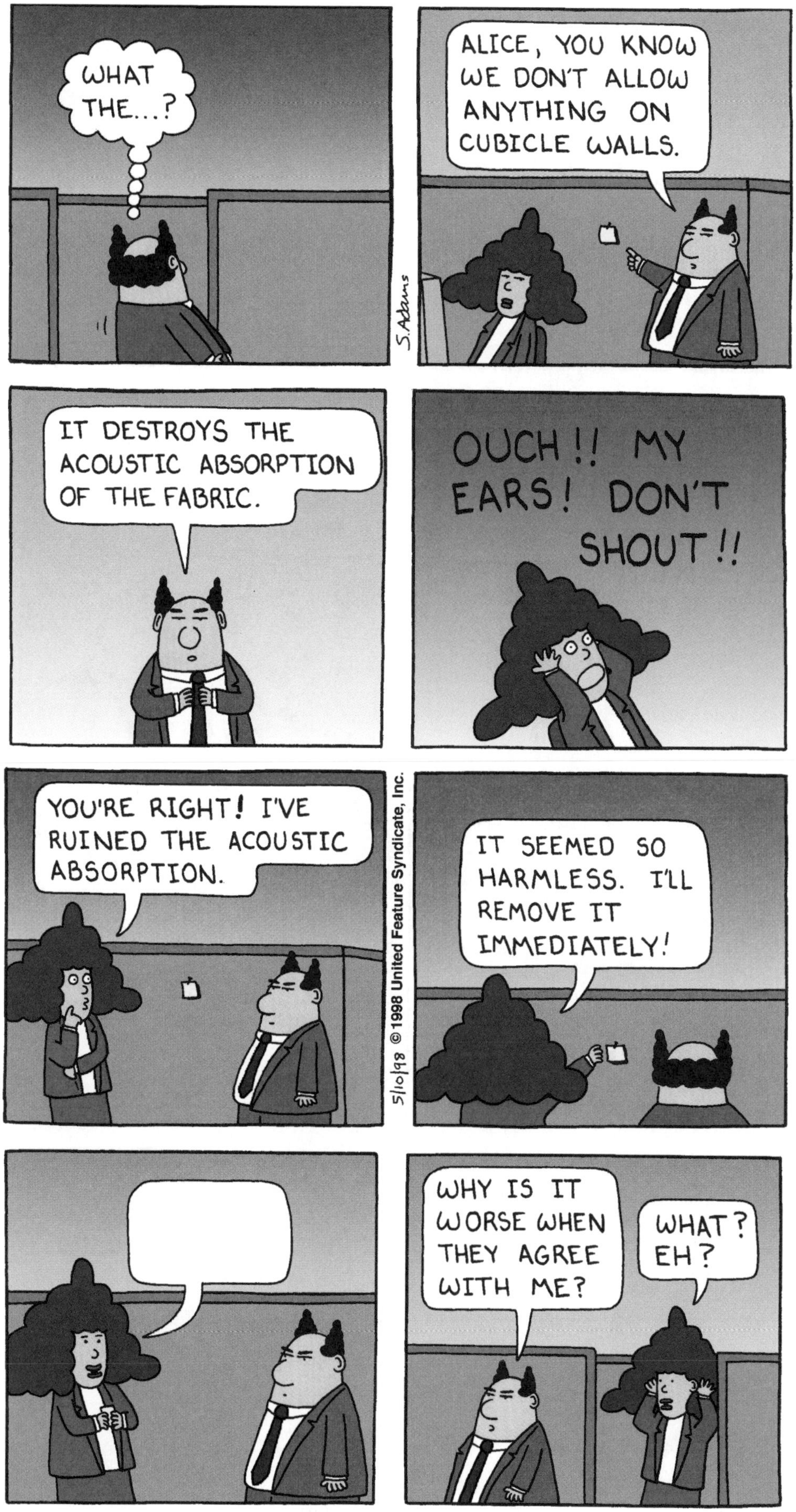
WHAT THE...?
ALICE, YOU KNOW WE DON'T ALLOW ANYTHING ON CUBICLE WALLS.
S. Adams
IT DESTROYS THE ACOUSTIC ABSORPTION OF THE FABRIC.
OUCH!! MY EARS! DON'T SHOUT!!
YOU'RE RIGHT! I'VE RUINED THE ACOUSTIC ABSORPTION.
5/10/98 © 1998 United Feature Syndicate, Inc.
IT SEEMED SO HARMLESS. I'LL REMOVE IT IMMEDIATELY!
WHY IS IT WORSE WHEN THEY AGREE WITH ME?
WHAT? EH?

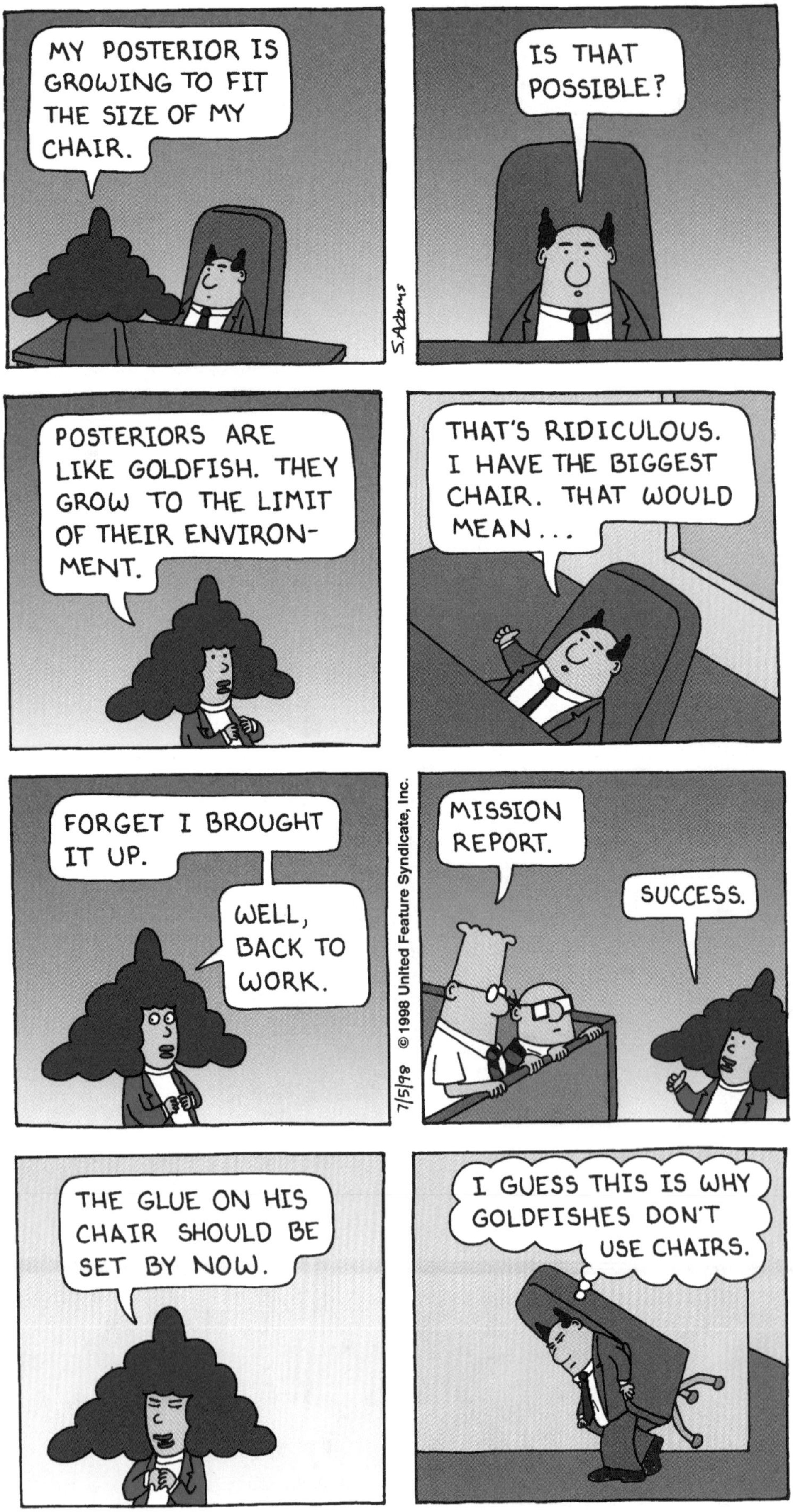
MY POSTERIOR IS GROWING TO FIT THE SIZE OF MY CHAIR.
IS THAT POSSIBLE?
S.Adams
POSTERIORS ARE LIKE GOLDFISH. THEY GROW TO THE LIMIT OF THEIR ENVIRON-MENT.
THAT'S RIDICULOUS. I HAVE THE BIGGEST CHAIR. THAT WOULD MEAN...
FORGET I BROUGHT IT UP.
WELL, BACK TO WORK.
7/5/98 © 1998 United Feature Syndicate, Inc.
MISSION REPORT.
SUCCESS.
THE GLUE ON HIS CHAIR SHOULD BE SET BY NOW.
I GUESS THIS IS WHY GOLDFISHES DON'T USE CHAIRS.

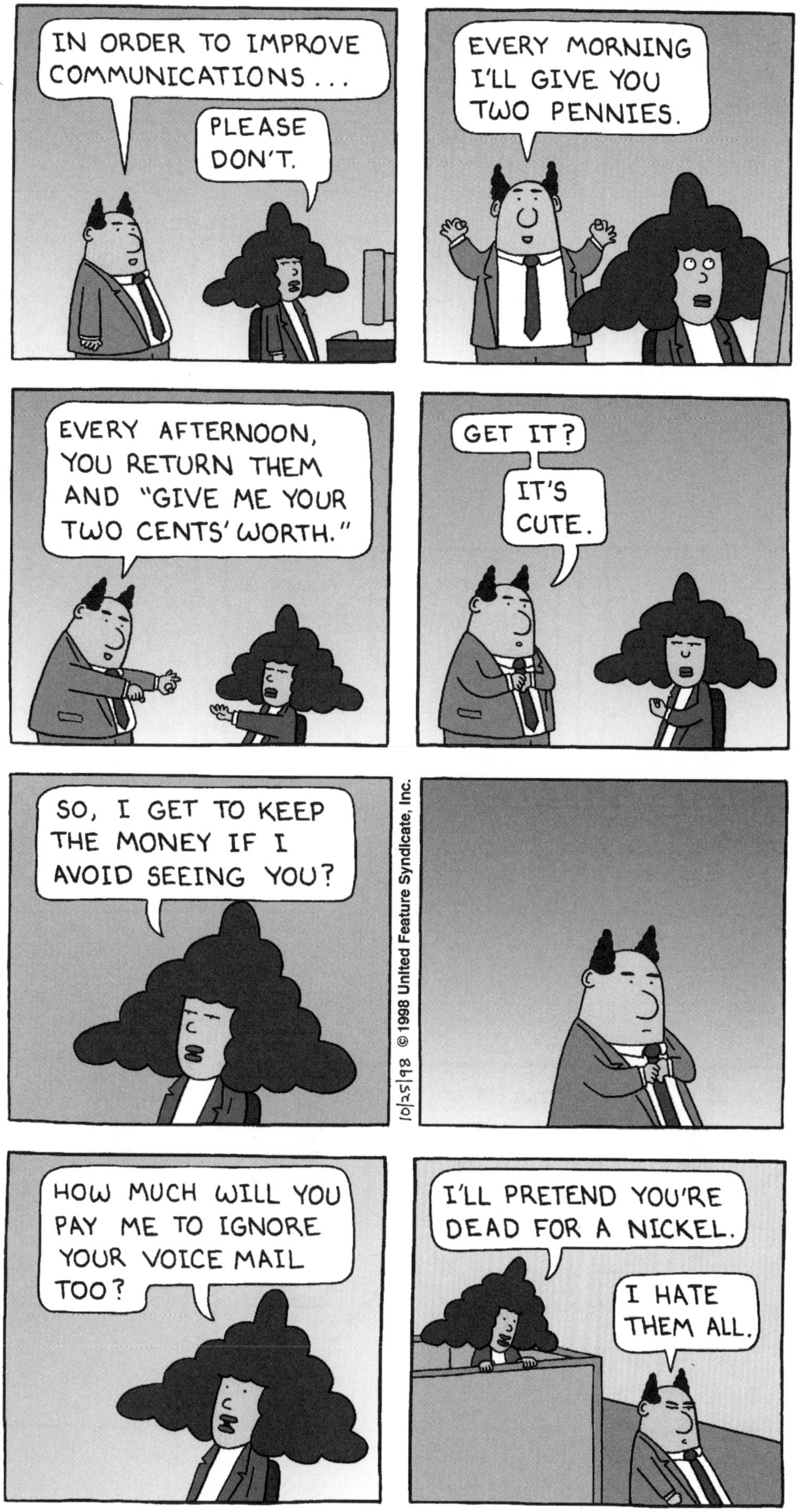
IN ORDER TO IMPROVE COMMUNICATIONS . . .
PLEASE DON'T.
EVERY MORNING I'LL GIVE YOU TWO PENNIES.
EVERY AFTERNOON, YOU RETURN THEM AND "GIVE ME YOUR TWO CENTS' WORTH."
GET IT?
IT'S CUTE.
SO, I GET TO KEEP THE MONEY IF I AVOID SEEING YOU?
10/25/98 © 1998 United Feature Syndicate, Inc.
HOW MUCH WILL YOU PAY ME TO IGNORE YOUR VOICE MAIL TOO?
I'LL PRETEND YOU'RE DEAD FOR A NICKEL.
I HATE THEM ALL.

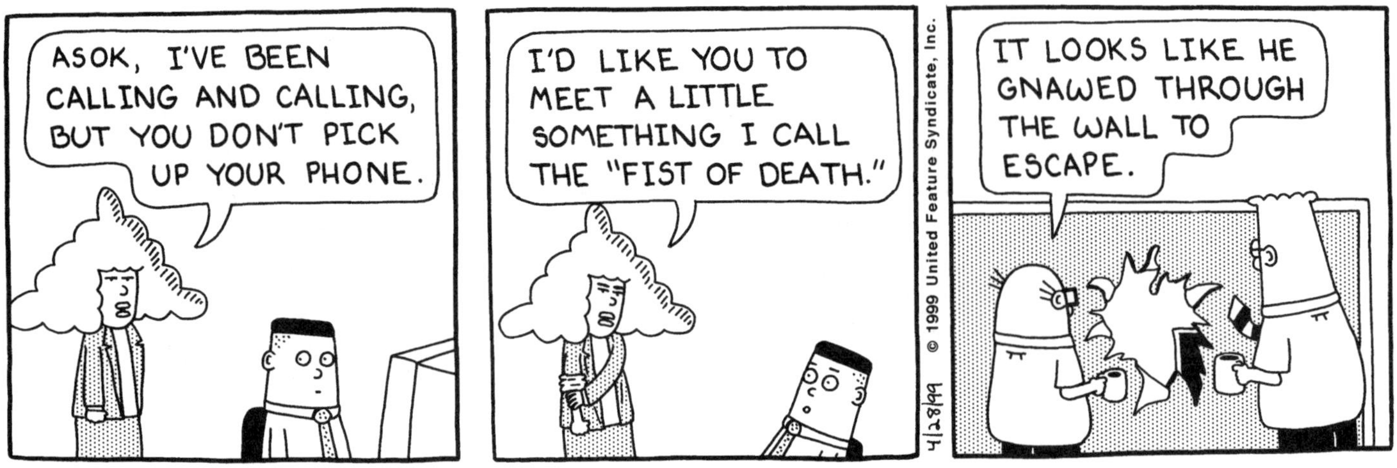
ASOK, I'VE BEEN CALLING AND CALLING, BUT YOU DON'T PICK UP YOUR PHONE.
I'D LIKE YOU TO MEET A LITTLE SOMETHING I CALL THE "FIST OF DEATH."
4/28/99 © 1999 United Feature Syndicate, Inc.
IT LOOKS LIKE HE GNAWED THROUGH THE WALL TO ESCAPE.

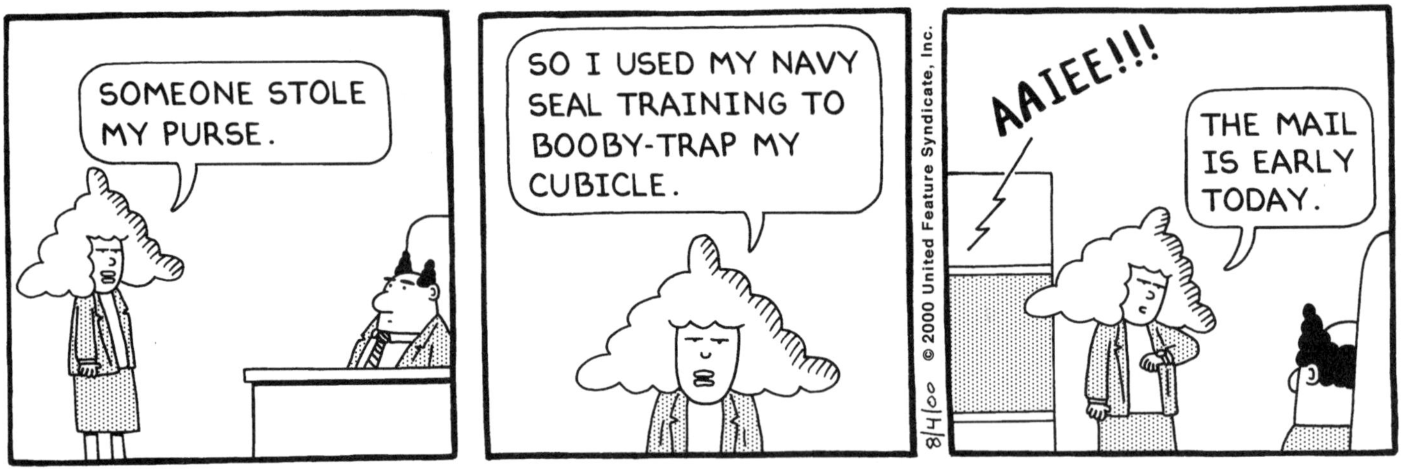
SOMEONE STOLE MY PURSE.
SO I USED MY NAVY SEAL TRAINING TO BOOBY-TRAP MY CUBICLE.
8/4/00 © 2000 United Feature Syndicate, Inc.
AAIEE!!!
THE MAIL IS EARLY TODAY.

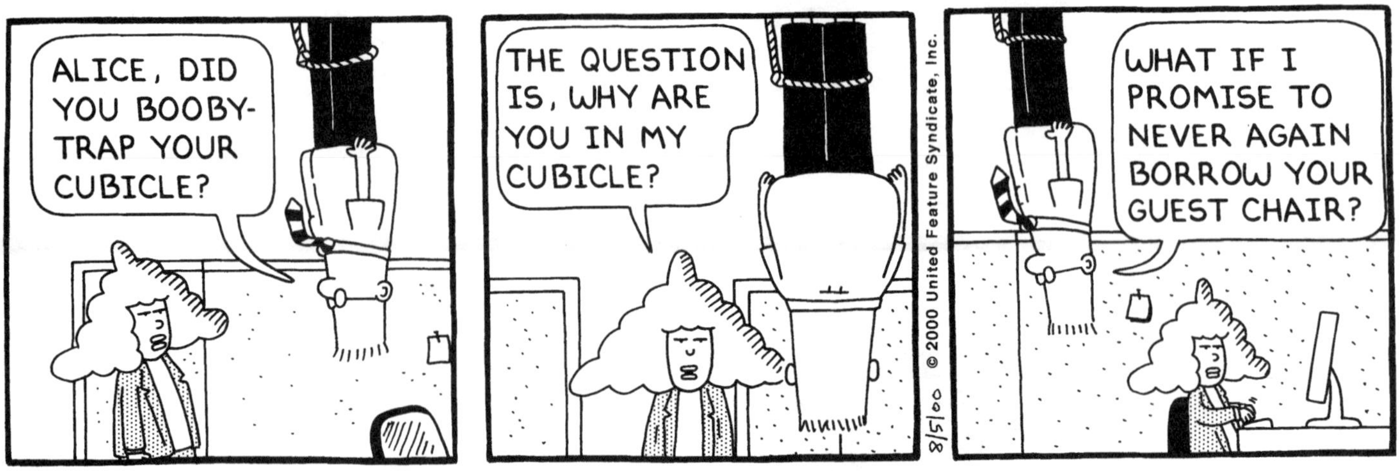
ALICE, DID YOU BOOBY-TRAP YOUR CUBICLE?
THE QUESTION IS, WHY ARE YOU IN MY CUBICLE?
8/5/00 © 2000 United Feature Syndicate, Inc.
WHAT IF I PROMISE TO NEVER AGAIN BORROW YOUR GUEST CHAIR?

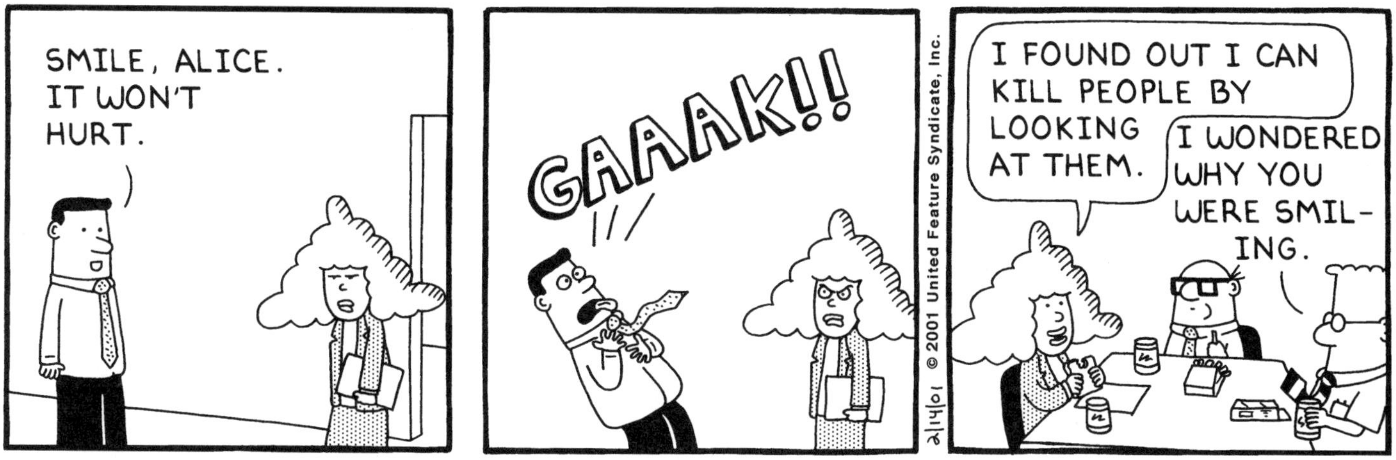
SMILE, ALICE. IT WON'T HURT.
GAAAK!!
2/14/01 © 2001 United Feature Syndicate, Inc.
I FOUND OUT I CAN KILL PEOPLE BY LOOKING AT THEM.
I WONDERED WHY YOU WERE SMILING.

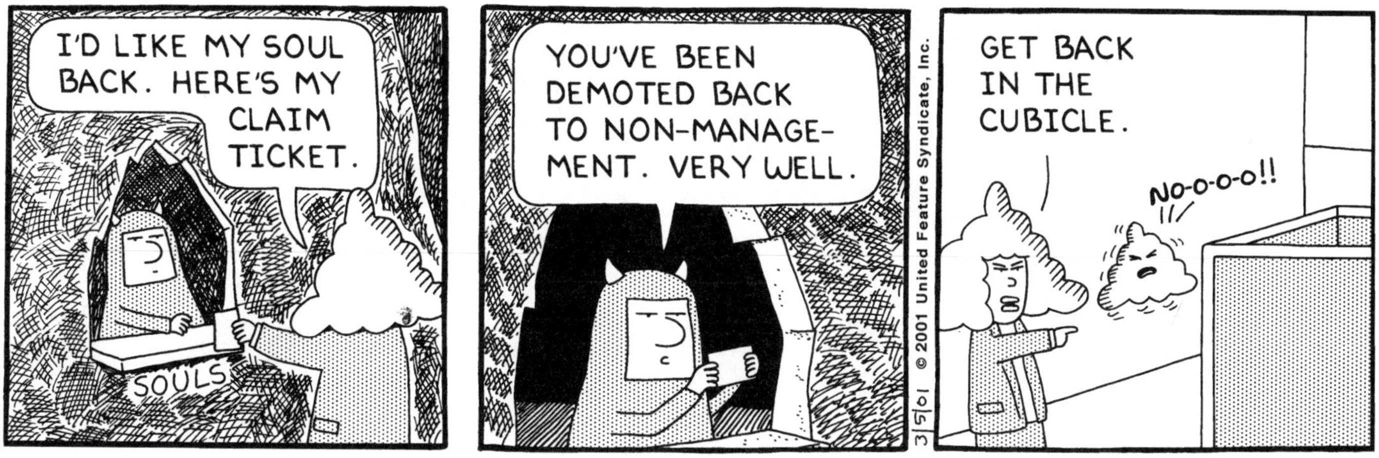
I'D LIKE MY SOUL BACK. HERE'S MY CLAIM TICKET.
SOULS
YOU'VE BEEN DEMOTED BACK TO NON-MANAGEMENT. VERY WELL.
3/5/01 © 2001 United Feature Syndicate, Inc.
GET BACK IN THE CUBICLE.
NO-O-O-O!!

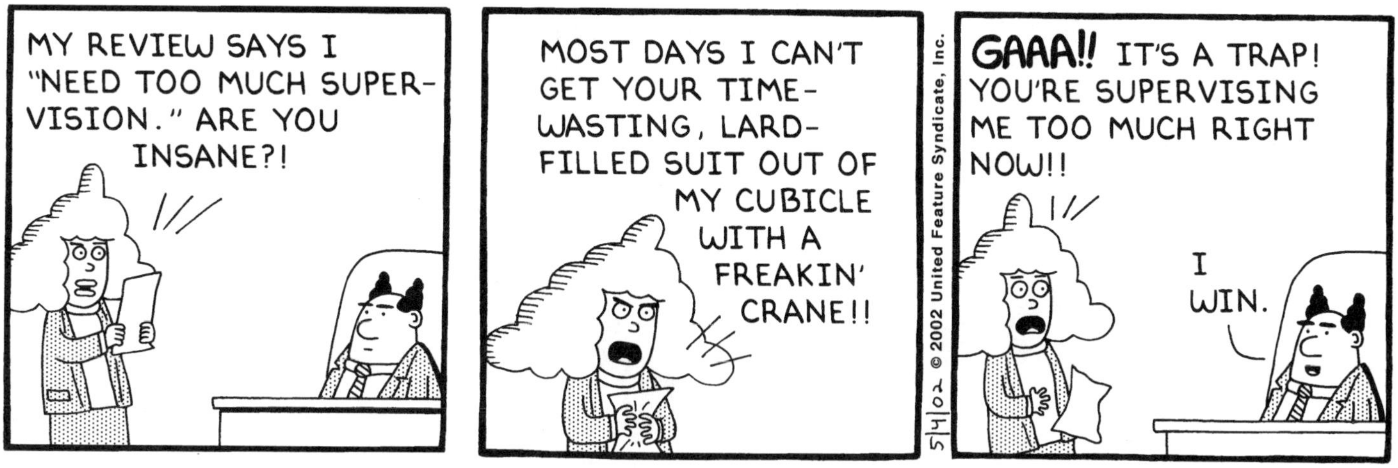
MY REVIEW SAYS I "NEED TOO MUCH SUPERVISION." ARE YOU INSANE?!
MOST DAYS I CAN'T GET YOUR TIME-WASTING, LARD-FILLED SUIT OUT OF MY CUBICLE WITH A FREAKIN' CRANE!!
5/4/02 © 2002 United Feature Syndicate, Inc.
GAAA!! IT'S A TRAP! YOU'RE SUPERVISING ME TOO MUCH RIGHT NOW!!
I WIN.

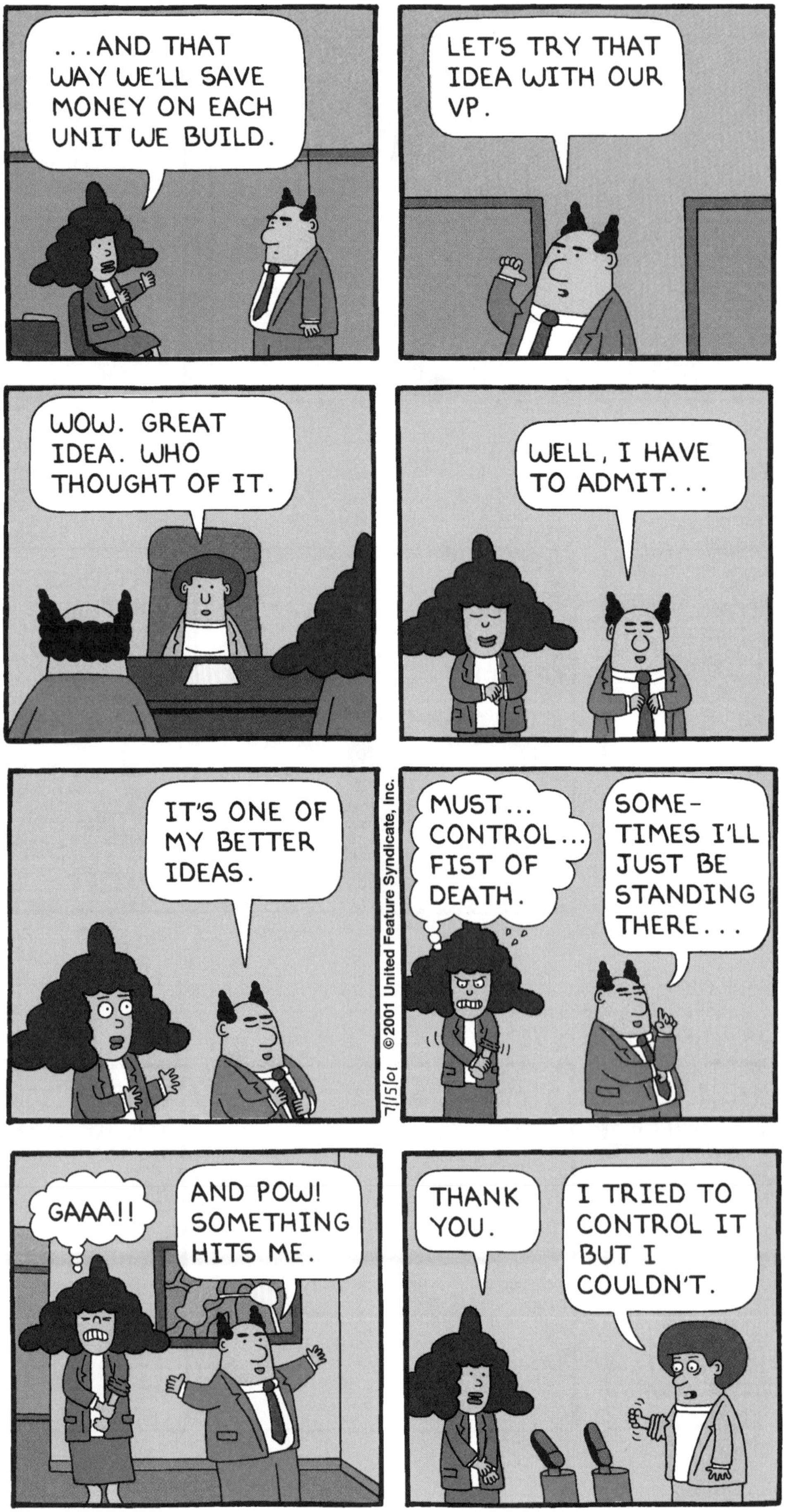
...AND THAT WAY WE'LL SAVE MONEY ON EACH UNIT WE BUILD.
LET'S TRY THAT IDEA WITH OUR VP.
WOW. GREAT IDEA. WHO THOUGHT OF IT.
WELL, I HAVE TO ADMIT...
IT'S ONE OF MY BETTER IDEAS.
7/15/01 ©2001 United Feature Syndicate, Inc.
MUST... CONTROL... FIST OF DEATH.
SOME-TIMES I'LL JUST BE STANDING THERE...
GAAA!!
AND POW! SOMETHING HITS ME.
THANK YOU.
I TRIED TO CONTROL IT BUT I COULDN'T.

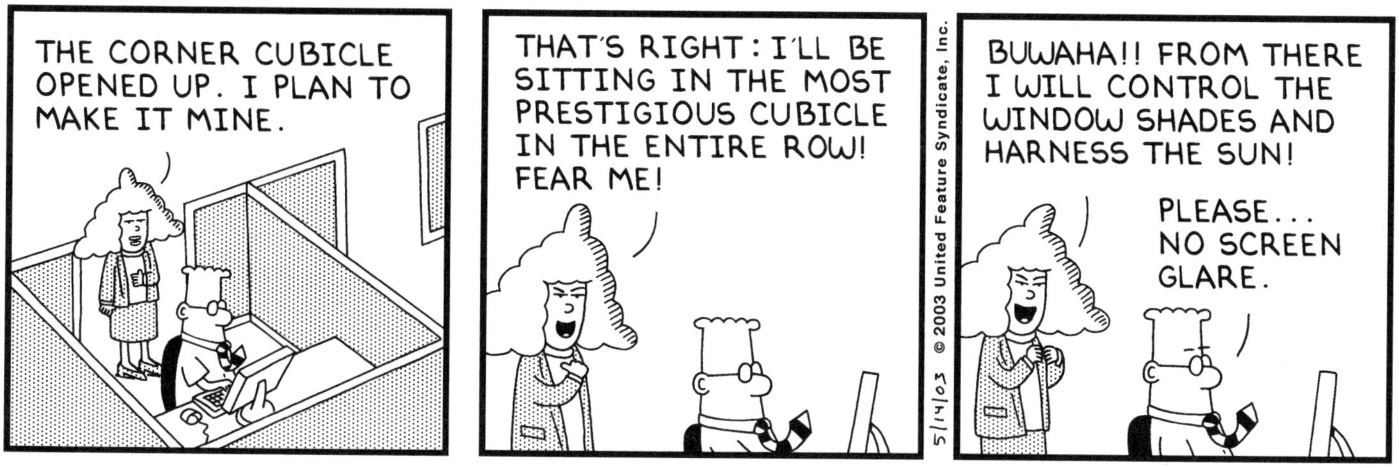
THE CORNER CUBICLE OPENED UP. I PLAN TO MAKE IT MINE.
THAT'S RIGHT: I'LL BE SITTING IN THE MOST PRESTIGIOUS CUBICLE IN THE ENTIRE ROW! FEAR ME!
5/14/03 © 2003 United Feature Syndicate, Inc.
BUWAHA!! FROM THERE I WILL CONTROL THE WINDOW SHADES AND HARNESS THE SUN!
PLEASE... NO SCREEN GLARE.

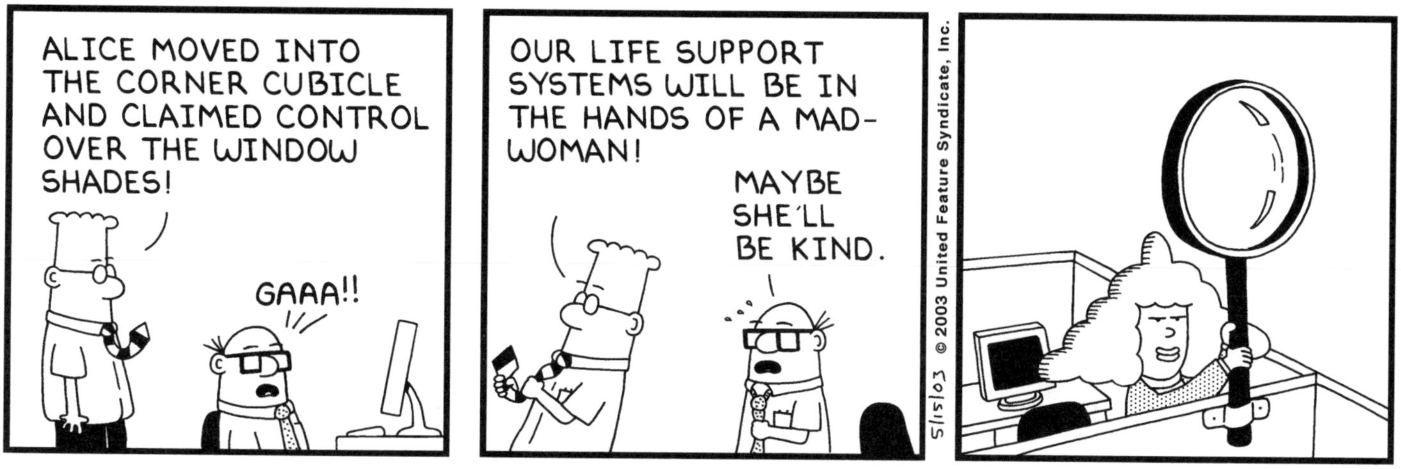
ALICE MOVED INTO THE CORNER CUBICLE AND CLAIMED CONTROL OVER THE WINDOW SHADES!
GAAA!!
OUR LIFE SUPPORT SYSTEMS WILL BE IN THE HANDS OF A MAD-WOMAN!
MAYBE SHE'LL BE KIND.
5/15/03 © 2003 United Feature Syndicate, Inc.

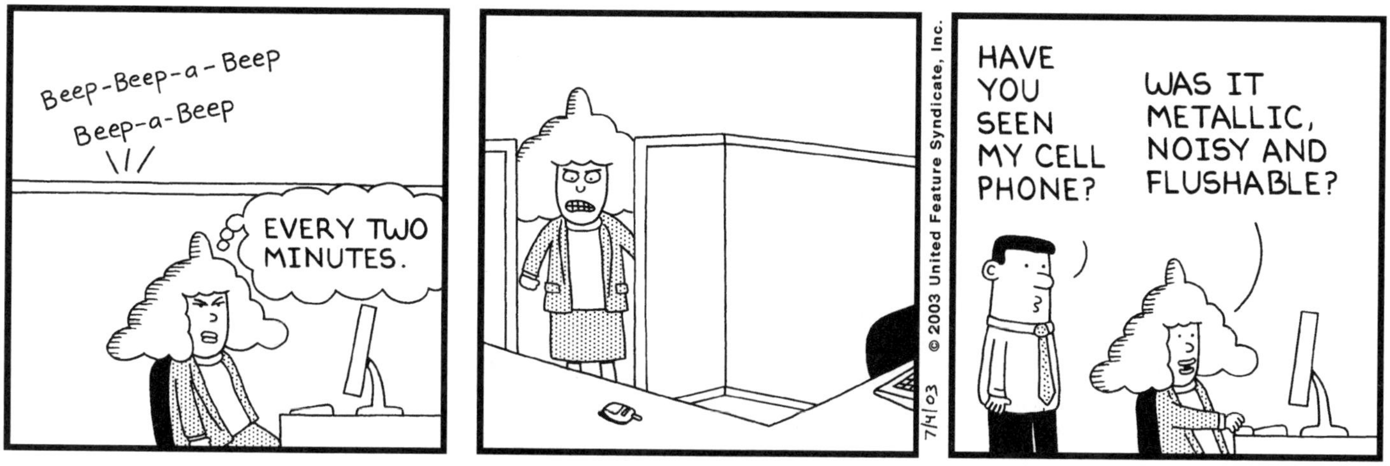
Beep-Beep-a-Beep
Beep-a-Beep
EVERY TWO MINUTES.
7/4/03 © 2003 United Feature Syndicate, Inc.
HAVE YOU SEEN MY CELL PHONE?
WAS IT METALLIC, NOISY AND FLUSHABLE?

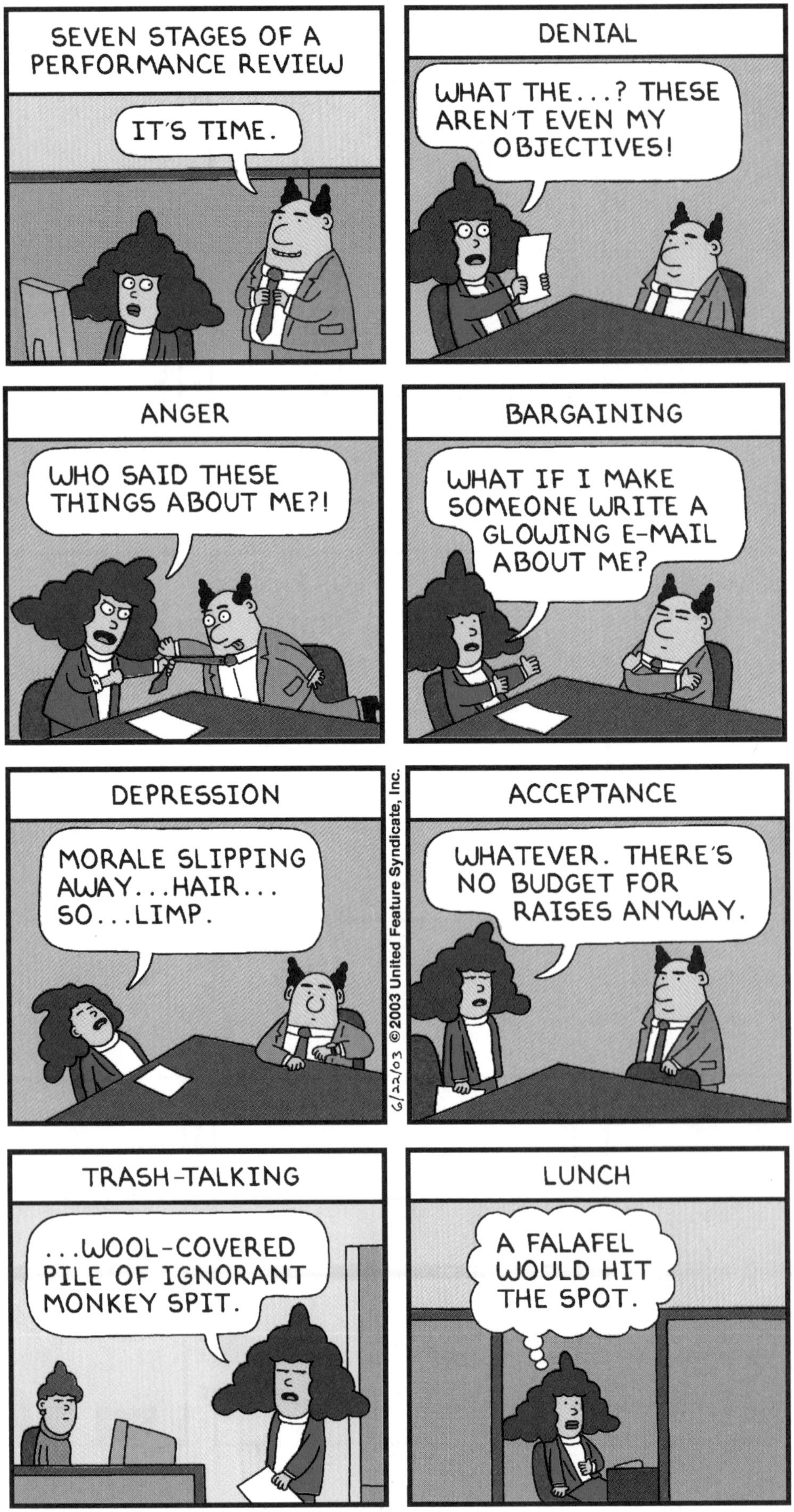
SEVEN STAGES OF A PERFORMANCE REVIEW
IT'S TIME.
DENIAL
WHAT THE...? THESE AREN'T EVEN MY OBJECTIVES!
ANGER
WHO SAID THESE THINGS ABOUT ME?!
BARGAINING
WHAT IF I MAKE SOMEONE WRITE A GLOWING E-MAIL ABOUT ME?
DEPRESSION
MORALE SLIPPING AWAY...HAIR... SO...LIMP.
ACCEPTANCE
WHATEVER. THERE'S NO BUDGET FOR RAISES ANYWAY.
TRASH-TALKING
...WOOL-COVERED PILE OF IGNORANT MONKEY SPIT.
LUNCH
A FALAFEL WOULD HIT THE SPOT.
6/22/03 ©2003 United Feature Syndicate, Inc.

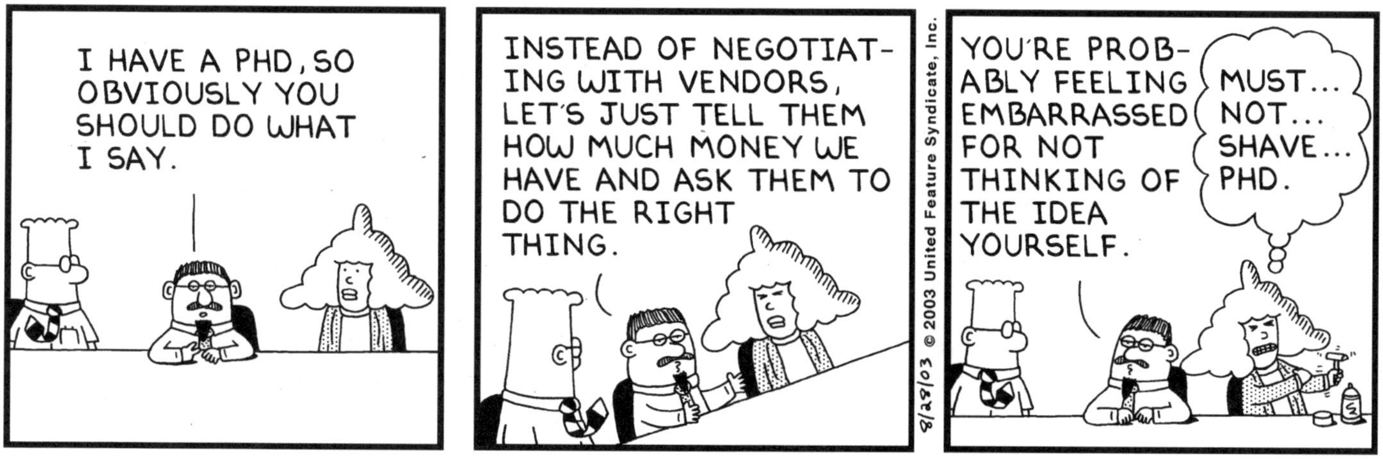
I HAVE A PHD, SO OBVIOUSLY YOU SHOULD DO WHAT I SAY.
INSTEAD OF NEGOTIATING WITH VENDORS, LET'S JUST TELL THEM HOW MUCH MONEY WE HAVE AND ASK THEM TO DO THE RIGHT THING.
© 2003 United Feature Syndicate, Inc.
8/28/03
YOU'RE PROBABLY FEELING EMBARRASSED FOR NOT THINKING OF THE IDEA YOURSELF.
MUST... NOT... SHAVE... PHD.

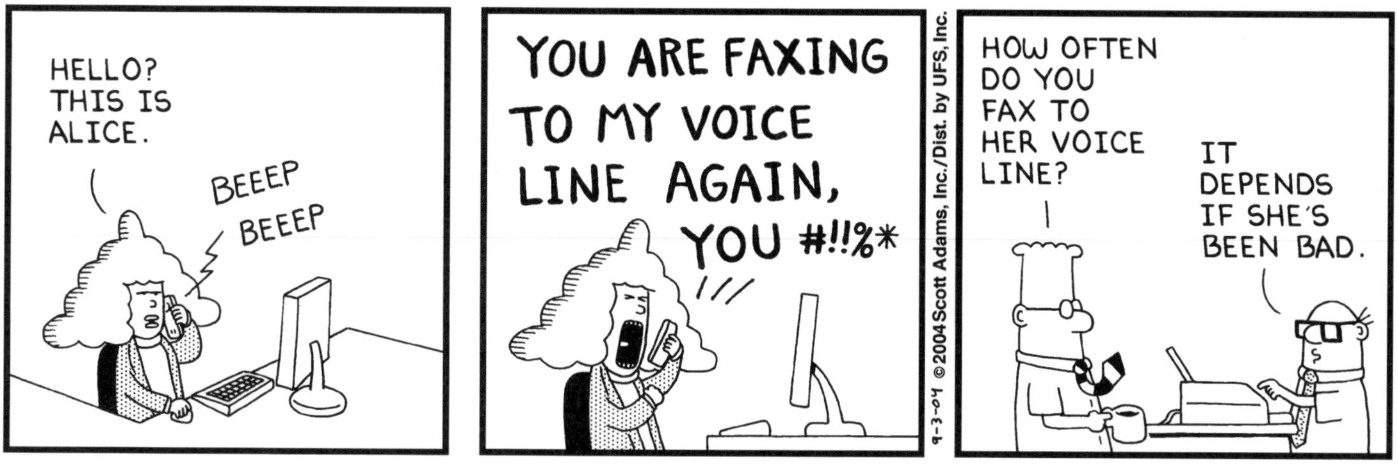
HELLO? THIS IS ALICE.
BEEEP
BEEEP
YOU ARE FAXING TO MY VOICE LINE AGAIN, YOU #!!%*
© 2004 Scott Adams, Inc./Dist. by UFS, Inc.
9-3-04
HOW OFTEN DO YOU FAX TO HER VOICE LINE?
IT DEPENDS IF SHE'S BEEN BAD.

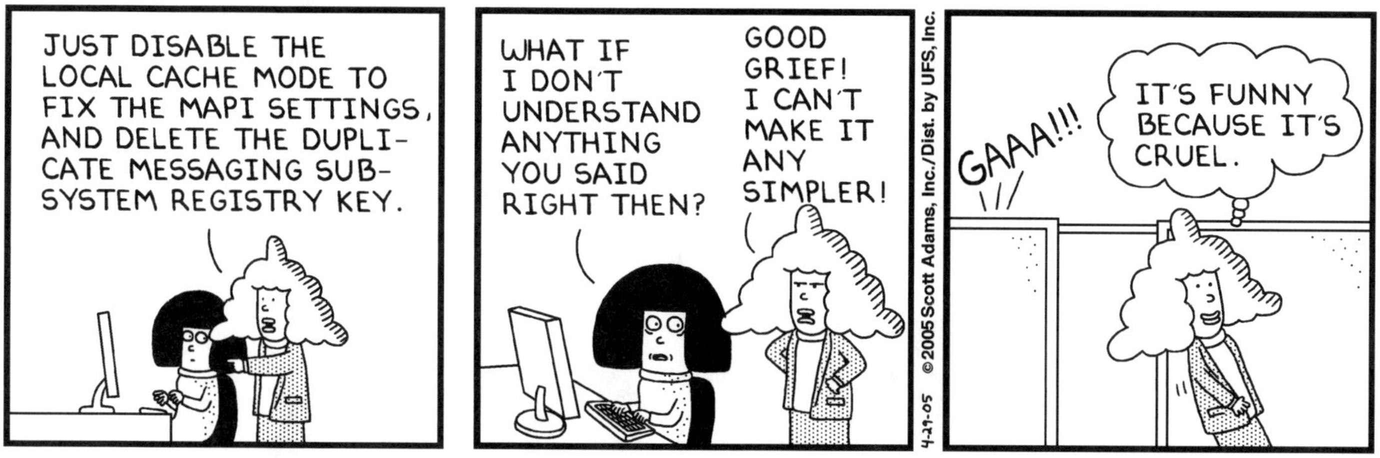
JUST DISABLE THE LOCAL CACHE MODE TO FIX THE MAPI SETTINGS, AND DELETE THE DUPLICATE MESSAGING SUBSYSTEM REGISTRY KEY.
WHAT IF I DON'T UNDERSTAND ANYTHING YOU SAID RIGHT THEN?
GOOD GRIEF! I CAN'T MAKE IT ANY SIMPLER!
© 2005 Scott Adams, Inc./Dist. by UFS, Inc.
4-29-05
GAAA!!!
IT'S FUNNY BECAUSE IT'S CRUEL.

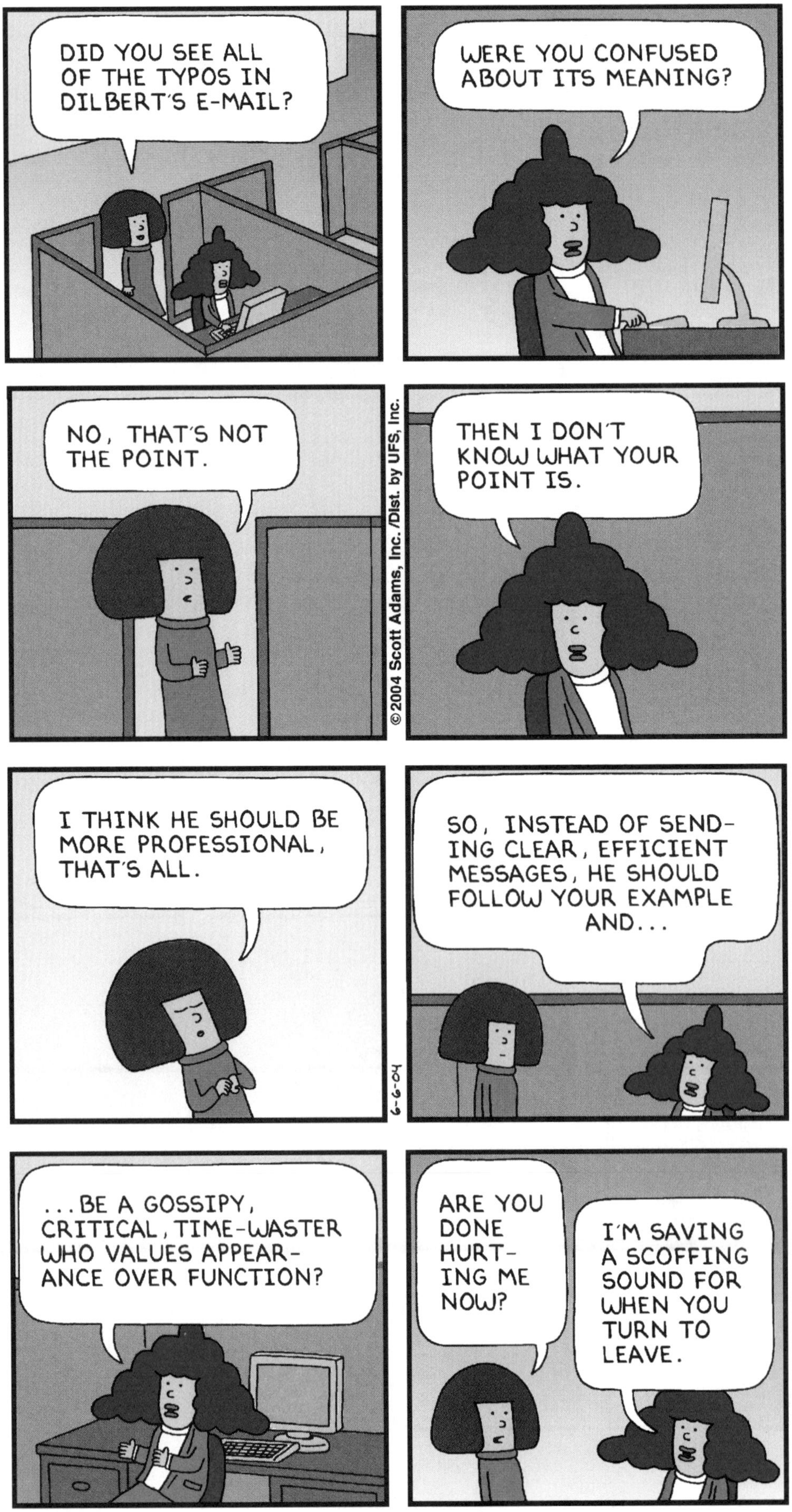
DID YOU SEE ALL OF THE TYPOS IN DILBERT'S E-MAIL?
WERE YOU CONFUSED ABOUT ITS MEANING?
NO, THAT'S NOT THE POINT.
THEN I DON'T KNOW WHAT YOUR POINT IS.
©2004 Scott Adams, Inc./Dist. by UFS, Inc.
I THINK HE SHOULD BE MORE PROFESSIONAL, THAT'S ALL.
6-6-04
SO, INSTEAD OF SENDING CLEAR, EFFICIENT MESSAGES, HE SHOULD FOLLOW YOUR EXAMPLE AND...
...BE A GOSSIPY, CRITICAL, TIME-WASTER WHO VALUES APPEARANCE OVER FUNCTION?
ARE YOU DONE HURTING ME NOW?
I'M SAVING A SCOFFING SOUND FOR WHEN YOU TURN TO LEAVE.

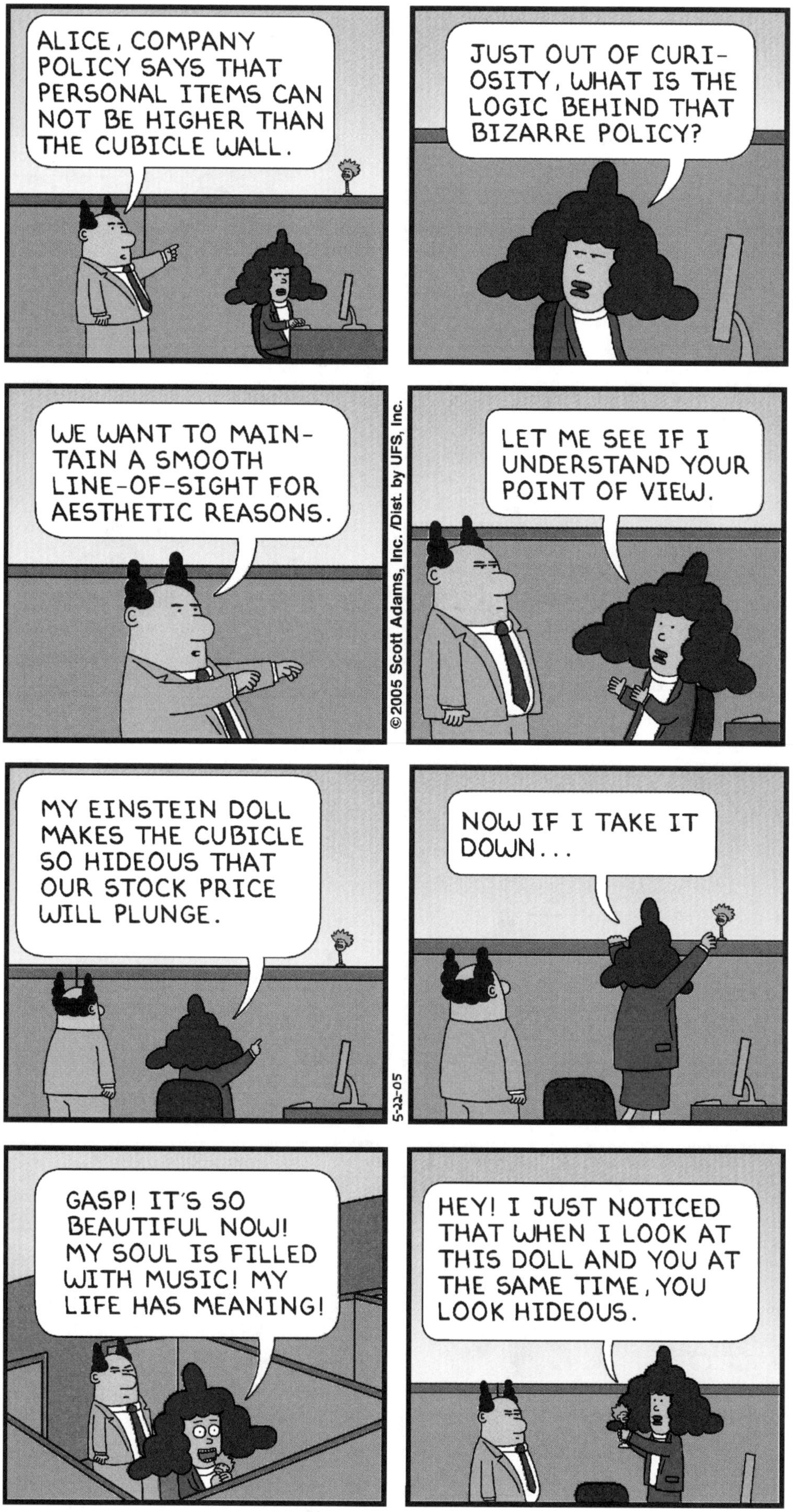
ALICE, COMPANY POLICY SAYS THAT PERSONAL ITEMS CAN NOT BE HIGHER THAN THE CUBICLE WALL.
JUST OUT OF CURI- OSITY, WHAT IS THE LOGIC BEHIND THAT BIZARRE POLICY?
WE WANT TO MAIN- TAIN A SMOOTH LINE-OF-SIGHT FOR AESTHETIC REASONS.
LET ME SEE IF I UNDERSTAND YOUR POINT OF VIEW.
MY EINSTEIN DOLL MAKES THE CUBICLE SO HIDEOUS THAT OUR STOCK PRICE WILL PLUNGE.
NOW IF I TAKE IT DOWN...
GASP! IT'S SO BEAUTIFUL NOW! MY SOUL IS FILLED WITH MUSIC! MY LIFE HAS MEANING!
HEY! I JUST NOTICED THAT WHEN I LOOK AT THIS DOLL AND YOU AT THE SAME TIME, YOU LOOK HIDEOUS.
©2005 Scott Adams, Inc./Dist. by UFS, Inc.
5-22-05

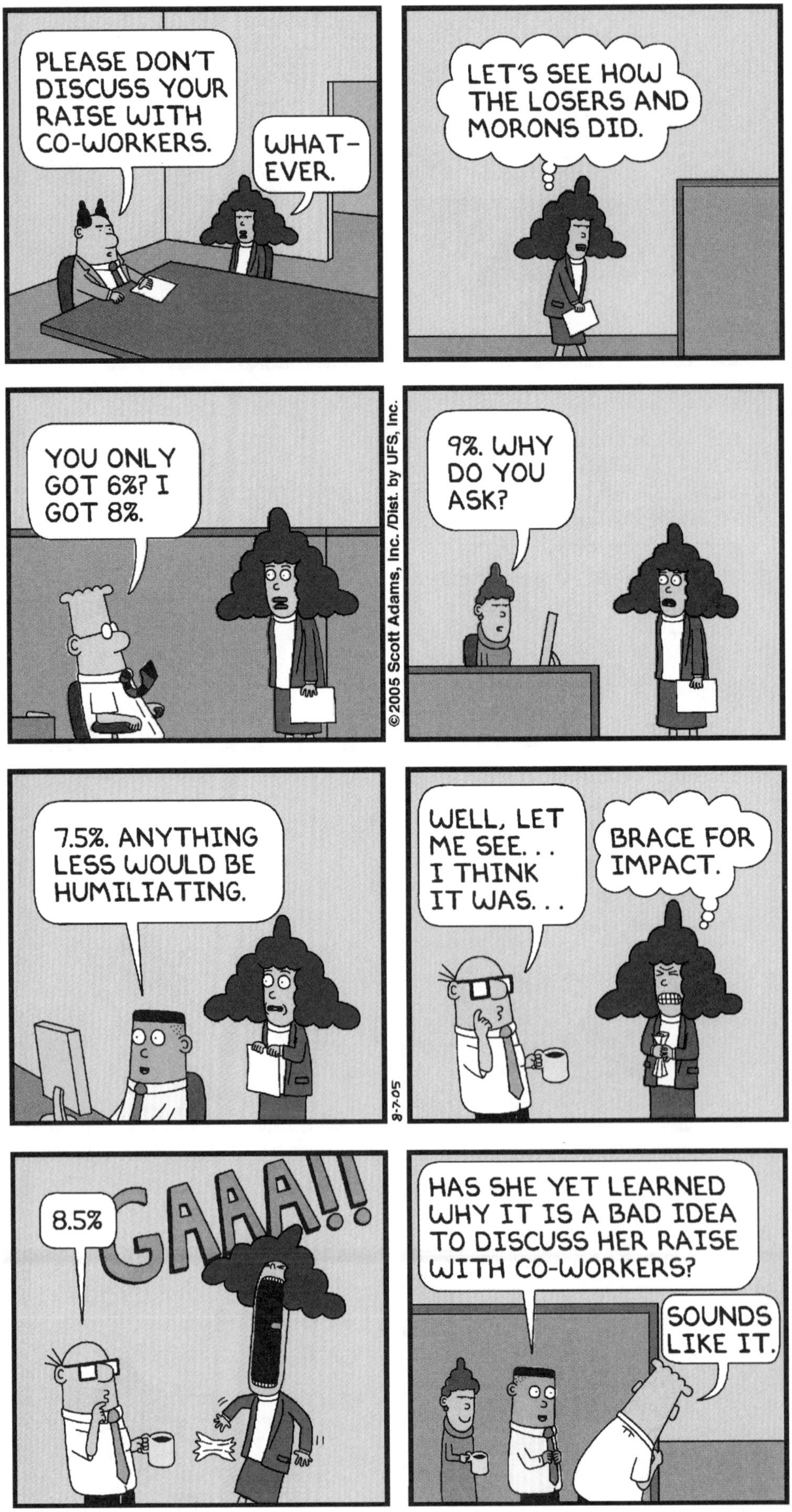
PLEASE DON'T DISCUSS YOUR RAISE WITH CO-WORKERS.
WHAT-EVER.
LET'S SEE HOW THE LOSERS AND MORONS DID.
YOU ONLY GOT 6%? I GOT 8%.
9%. WHY DO YOU ASK?
7.5%. ANYTHING LESS WOULD BE HUMILIATING.
WELL, LET ME SEE... I THINK IT WAS...
BRACE FOR IMPACT.
8.5%
GAAA!!
HAS SHE YET LEARNED WHY IT IS A BAD IDEA TO DISCUSS HER RAISE WITH CO-WORKERS?
SOUNDS LIKE IT.
©2005 Scott Adams, Inc. /Dist. by UFS, Inc.
8-7-05

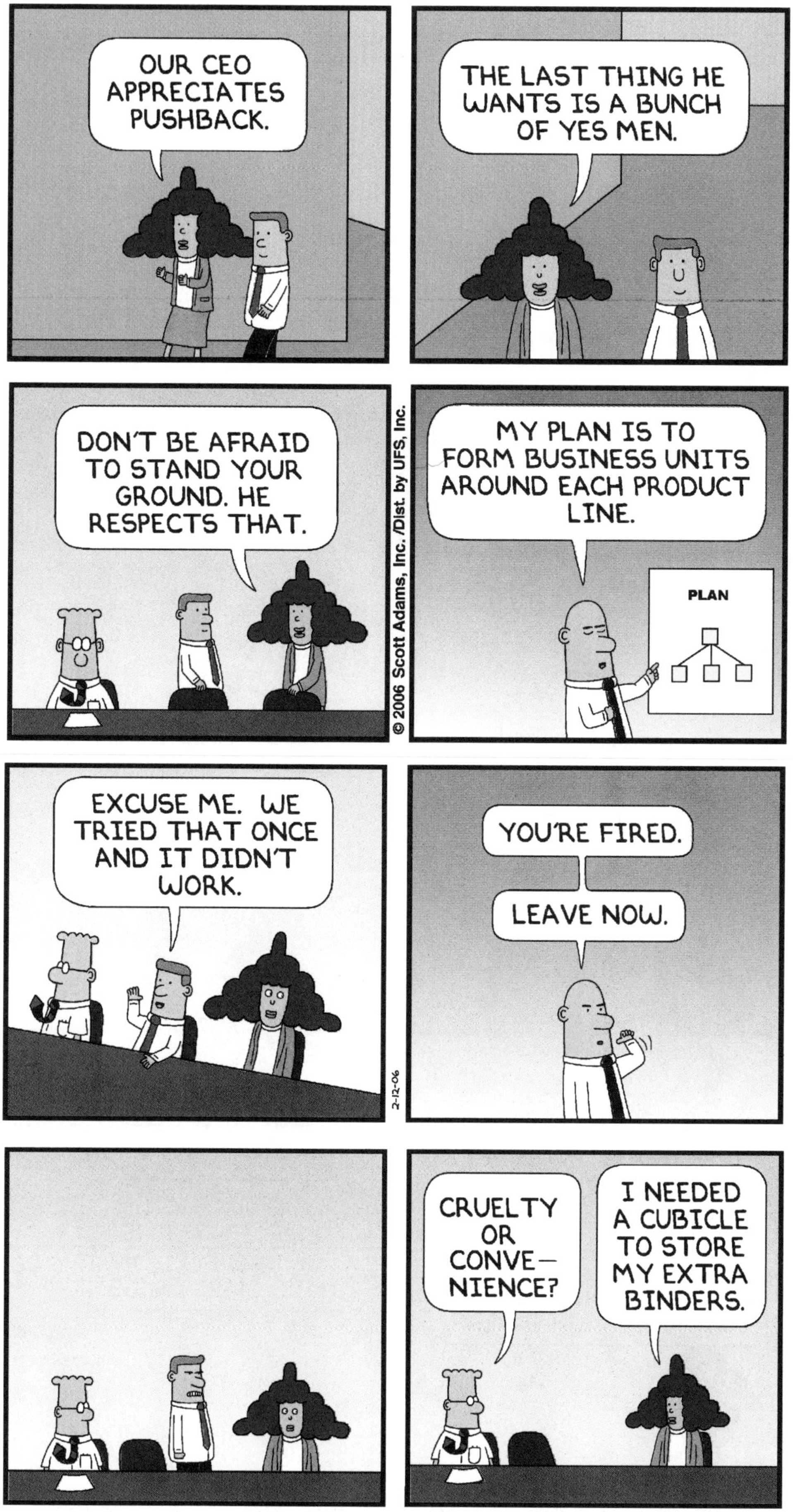
OUR CEO APPRECIATES PUSHBACK.
THE LAST THING HE WANTS IS A BUNCH OF YES MEN.
DON'T BE AFRAID TO STAND YOUR GROUND. HE RESPECTS THAT.
© 2006 Scott Adams, Inc./Dist. by UFS, Inc.
MY PLAN IS TO FORM BUSINESS UNITS AROUND EACH PRODUCT LINE.
PLAN
EXCUSE ME. WE TRIED THAT ONCE AND IT DIDN'T WORK.
2-12-06
YOU'RE FIRED.
LEAVE NOW.
CRUELTY OR CONVE- NIENCE?
I NEEDED A CUBICLE TO STORE MY EXTRA BINDERS.

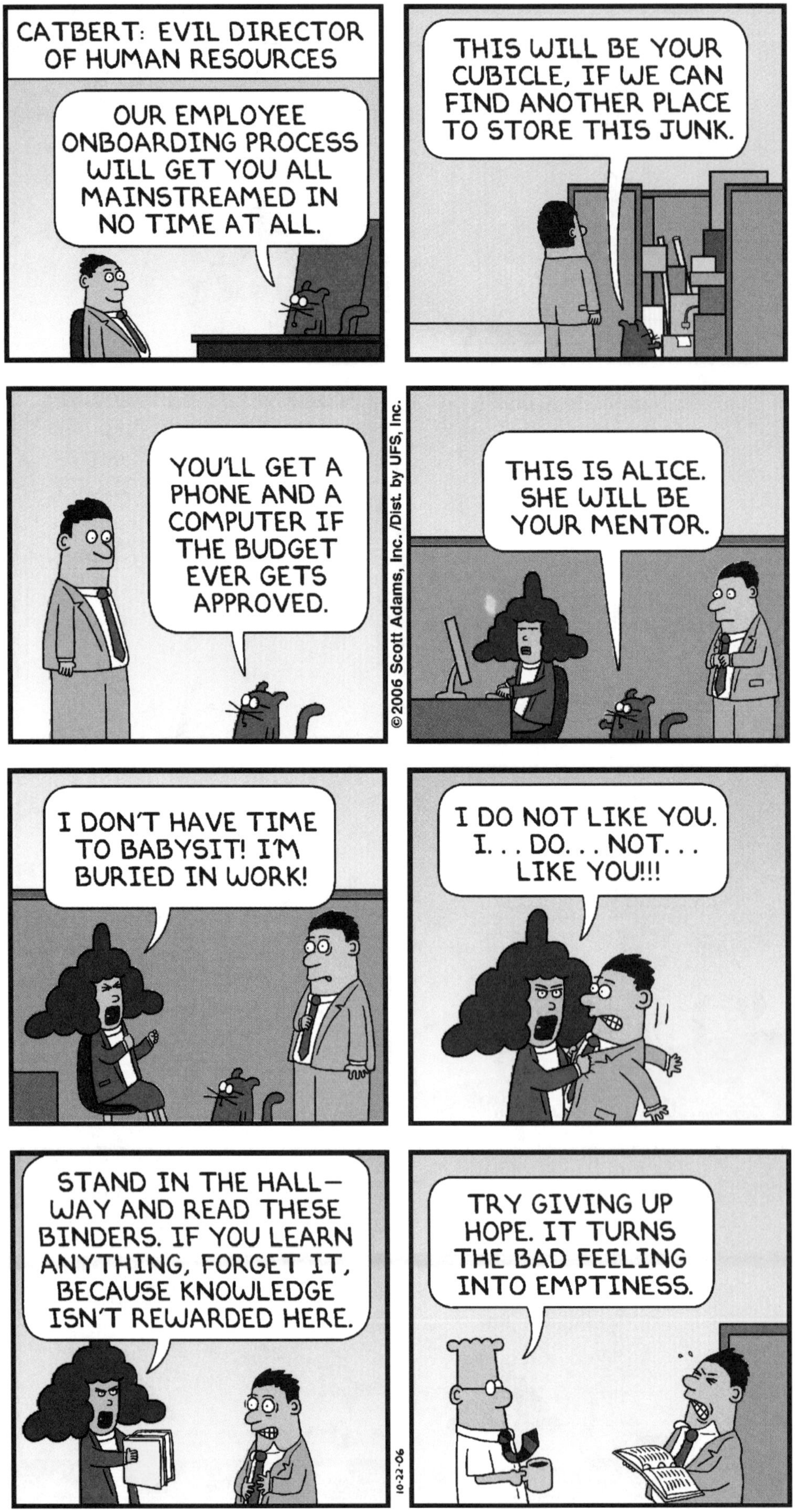
CATBERT: EVIL DIRECTOR OF HUMAN RESOURCES
OUR EMPLOYEE ONBOARDING PROCESS WILL GET YOU ALL MAINSTREAMED IN NO TIME AT ALL.
THIS WILL BE YOUR CUBICLE, IF WE CAN FIND ANOTHER PLACE TO STORE THIS JUNK.
YOU'LL GET A PHONE AND A COMPUTER IF THE BUDGET EVER GETS APPROVED.
©2006 Scott Adams, Inc. /Dist. by UFS, Inc.
THIS IS ALICE. SHE WILL BE YOUR MENTOR.
I DON'T HAVE TIME TO BABYSIT! I'M BURIED IN WORK!
I DO NOT LIKE YOU. I. . . DO. . . NOT. . . LIKE YOU!!!
STAND IN THE HALL-WAY AND READ THESE BINDERS. IF YOU LEARN ANYTHING, FORGET IT, BECAUSE KNOWLEDGE ISN'T REWARDED HERE.
10-22-06
TRY GIVING UP HOPE. IT TURNS THE BAD FEELING INTO EMPTINESS.

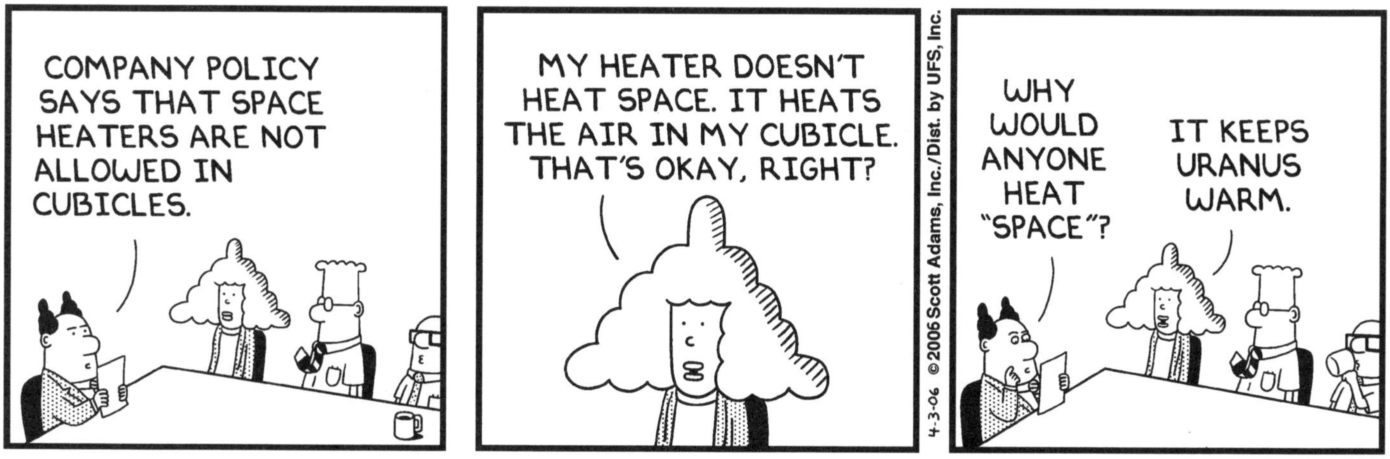
COMPANY POLICY SAYS THAT SPACE HEATERS ARE NOT ALLOWED IN CUBICLES.
MY HEATER DOESN'T HEAT SPACE. IT HEATS THE AIR IN MY CUBICLE. THAT'S OKAY, RIGHT?
4-3-06 © 2006 Scott Adams, Inc./Dist. by UFS, Inc.
WHY WOULD ANYONE HEAT "SPACE"?
IT KEEPS URANUS WARM.

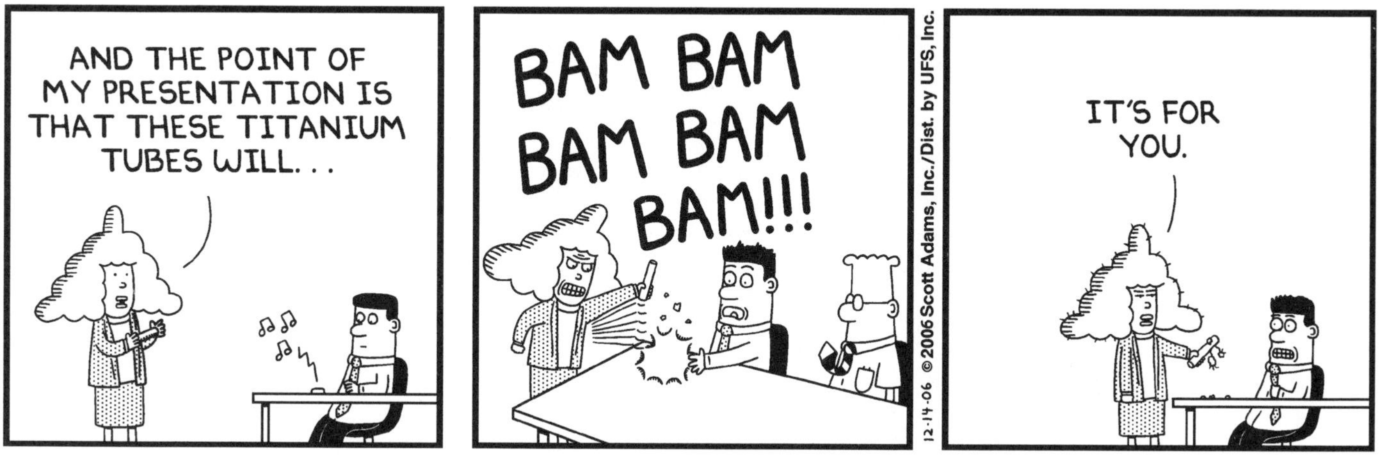
AND THE POINT OF MY PRESENTATION IS THAT THESE TITANIUM TUBES WILL. . .
BAM BAM BAM BAM BAM!!!
12-14-06 © 2006 Scott Adams, Inc./Dist. by UFS, Inc.
IT'S FOR YOU.

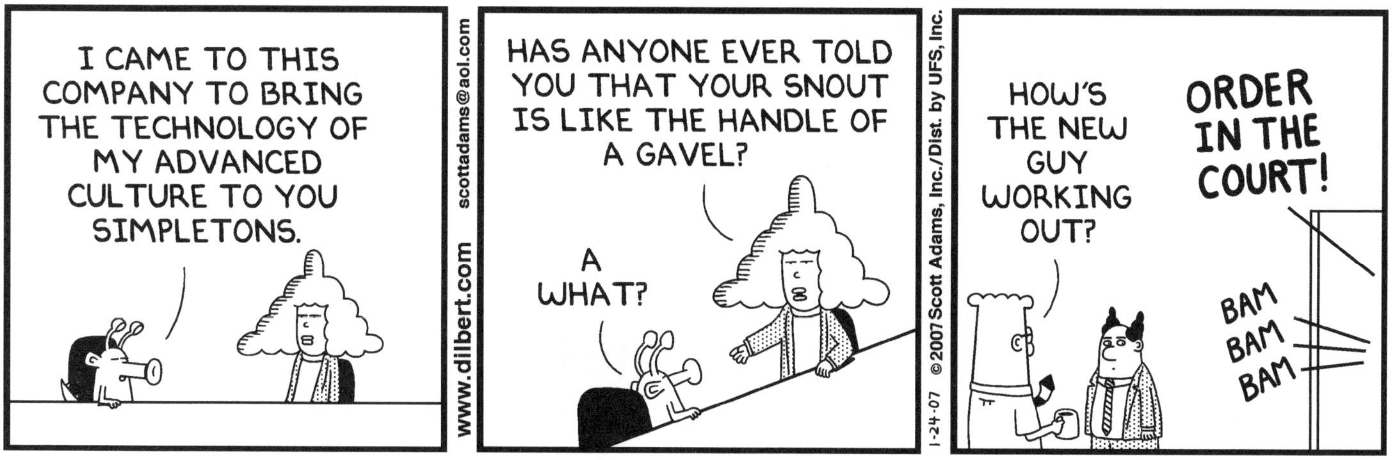
I CAME TO THIS COMPANY TO BRING THE TECHNOLOGY OF MY ADVANCED CULTURE TO YOU SIMPLETONS.
www.dilbert.com scottadams@aol.com
HAS ANYONE EVER TOLD YOU THAT YOUR SNOUT IS LIKE THE HANDLE OF A GAVEL?
A WHAT?
1-24-07 © 2007 Scott Adams, Inc./Dist. by UFS, Inc.
HOW'S THE NEW GUY WORKING OUT?
ORDER IN THE COURT!
BAM BAM BAM

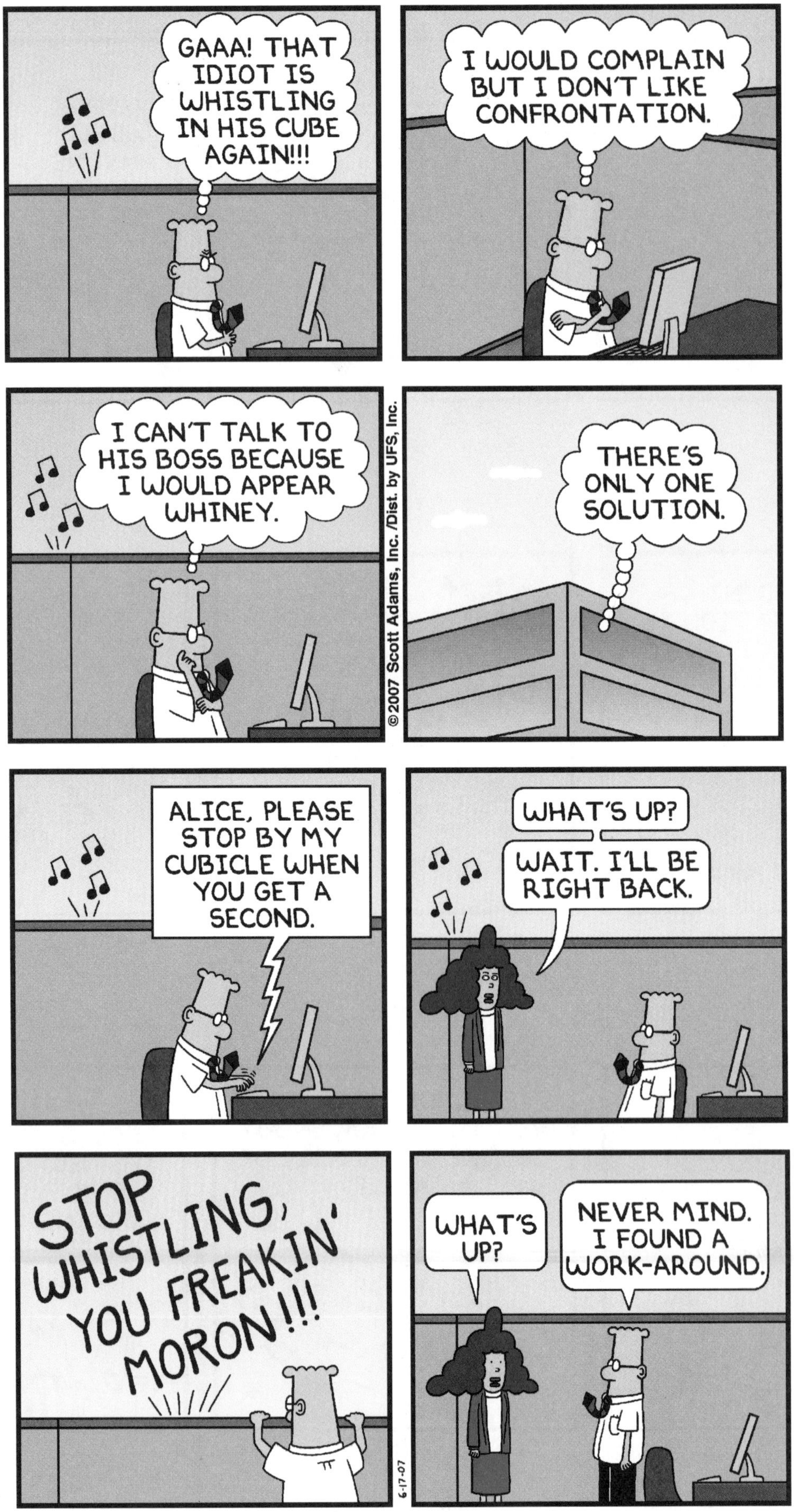
GAAA! THAT IDIOT IS WHISTLING IN HIS CUBE AGAIN!!!
I WOULD COMPLAIN BUT I DON'T LIKE CONFRONTATION.
I CAN'T TALK TO HIS BOSS BECAUSE I WOULD APPEAR WHINEY.
©2007 Scott Adams, Inc./Dist. by UFS, Inc.
THERE'S ONLY ONE SOLUTION.
ALICE, PLEASE STOP BY MY CUBICLE WHEN YOU GET A SECOND.
WHAT'S UP?
WAIT. I'LL BE RIGHT BACK.
STOP WHISTLING, YOU FREAKIN' MORON!!!
6-17-07
WHAT'S UP?
NEVER MIND. I FOUND A WORK-AROUND.